The Palgrave Handbook of Youth Mobility and Educational Migration

David Cairns
Editor

The Palgrave Handbook of Youth Mobility and Educational Migration

2nd ed. 2022

Editor
David Cairns
ISCTE – Instituto Universitário de Lisboa (ISCTE-IUL)
Centro de Investigação e Estudos de Sociologia
Lisbon, Portugal

ISBN 978-3-030-99446-4   ISBN 978-3-030-99447-1 (eBook)
https://doi.org/10.1007/978-3-030-99447-1

© The Editor(s) (if applicable) and The Author(s), under exclusive licence to Springer Nature Switzerland AG 2021, 2022
This work is subject to copyright. All rights are solely and exclusively licensed by the Publisher, whether the whole or part of the material is concerned, specifically the rights of translation, reprinting, reuse of illustrations, recitation, broadcasting, reproduction on microfilms or in any other physical way, and transmission or information storage and retrieval, electronic adaptation, computer software, or by similar or dissimilar methodology now known or hereafter developed.
The use of general descriptive names, registered names, trademarks, service marks, etc. in this publication does not imply, even in the absence of a specific statement, that such names are exempt from the relevant protective laws and regulations and therefore free for general use.
The publisher, the authors and the editors are safe to assume that the advice and information in this book are believed to be true and accurate at the date of publication. Neither the publisher nor the authors or the editors give a warranty, expressed or implied, with respect to the material contained herein or for any errors or omissions that may have been made. The publisher remains neutral with regard to jurisdictional claims in published maps and institutional affiliations.

Cover illustration: Westend61

This Palgrave Macmillan imprint is published by the registered company Springer Nature Switzerland AG.
The registered company address is: Gewerbestrasse 11, 6330 Cham, Switzerland

Acknowledgements

The editor would like to thank everyone who has contributed to this book, especially colleagues at ISCTE-IUL, including Thais França, Daniel Malet Calvo and Mara Clemente, and my fellow mobility researchers who assisted with the evaluation of the various chapters, especially Leonardo Azevedo, Valentina Cuzzocrea and Ewa Krzaklewska. I would also like to acknowledge the support of everyone at Palgrave Macmillan, including Sharla Plant and Poppy Hull. That much of the editing work was undertaken during the Covid-19 pandemic also needs to be acknowledged, and it is to the enormous credit of everyone associated with this book that they were able to complete their work with the minimum amount of complaints or disruption.

Contents

1 **Introduction: The Intermittency of Youth Migration** 1
David Cairns and Mara Clemente

Part I

2 **Introducing Youth Mobility and Migration** 13
David Cairns, Valentina Cuzzocrea, and Ewa Krzaklewska

3 **Mobility Becoming Migration: Understanding Youth Spatiality in the Twenty-First Century** 17
David Cairns

4 **Migration Decision-Making, Mobility Capital and Reflexive Learning** 25
David Cairns

5 **Inherited Dreams of 'the West': Eastern European Students' Paths to Denmark** 35
Mette Ginnerskov-Dahlberg

6 **Unpacking the Mobility Capacities and Imperatives of the 'Global Generation'** 47
Paula Pustulka and Dominika Winogrodzka

7 **Why Student Mobility Does Not Automatically Lead to Better Understanding: Reflections on the Concept of Intercultural Learning** 63
Thor-André Skrefsrud

Part II

8 **Free Movement in Education** 77
David Cairns and Leonardo Francisco de Azevedo

9	Youth Educational Mobility: The Start of Intellectual Migration ... 83
	Lucia Lo, Yixi Lu, Wei Li, Yining Tan, and Zheng Lu

10 Understanding Educational Migration from Greece to the UK
    in Times of Crisis.. 97
    Vasiliki Toumanidou

11 Transnational Mobility, Education and Social Positioning between
    Brazil and Germany.. 107
    Javier A. Carnicer and Sara Fürstenau

12 Refugees' Access to Higher Education in Italy: An Opportunity
    Lost for the 'Lost Generation'............................... 119
    Marcela Gola Boutros, Dulce Pimentel, and Alina Esteves

13 After Mobility: The Long-Term Impact of Study Abroad on
    Professional Teacher Behaviour............................. 131
    Grada Okken and Robert Coelen

14 Dispositives of Internationalization in Brazilian Science:
    The Unified Postgraduate Examination in Physics 143
    Nicolás José Isola

15 'I had to move somewhere:' Leaving Finland to Study in Sweden .. 155
    Blanka Henriksson

Part III

16 Institutionalized Mobility Inside and Outside Erasmus 171
    David Cairns and Thais França

17 Erasmus at 30: Institutional Mobility at Higher Education in
    Perspective.. 177
    Alexandra Ribeiro

18 Learning in Transition: Erasmus+ as an Opportunity for
    Internationalization 187
    Sahizer Samuk, Birte Nienaber, Emilia Kmiotek-Meier, Volha
    Vysotskaya, Jan Skrobanek, Tuba Ardic, Irina Pavlova, Daniela
    Elena Marinescu, and Laura Muresan

19 Mobility and Participation: The Intertwined Movement of Youth
    and Ideas 199
    Airi-Alina Allaste and Raili Nugin

20 The Super-Mobile Student: Global Educational Trajectories
    in Erasmus Mundus 213
    Karolina Czerska-Shaw and Ewa Krzaklewska

21 Educational Mobility of South African Youth: Insights from Erasmus
    Mundus Action 2.. 225
    Samia Chasi

22 Intra-regional Academic Mobility in Central Asia: The OSCE
    Academy in Bishkek, Kyrgyzstan 237
    Hélène Syed Zwick

23 South–South Student Mobility: International Students from
    Portuguese-Speaking Africa in Brazil......................... 249
    Thais França and Beatriz Padilla

24 Mobile and Immobile Students' Characteristics and Programme
    Choices.. 261
    Eva Maria Vögtle

25 Identity Challenges and Pedagogical Consequences:
    International Students in Higher Education Pathway Programmes
    in Australia.. 275
    Louise Kaktiņš

Part IV

26 Working towards Mobility...................................... 291
    David Cairns

27 Beyond Skills: Facets of Mobility in Romania's Vocational Education
    and Training 297
    Maria-Carmen Pantea

28 Using Cross-border Mobility in Vocational Education and Training
    in the Greater Region SaarLorLux............................ 311
    Birte Nienaber, H. Peter Dörrenbächer, Ines Funk, Isabelle Pigeron-
    Piroth, Rachid Belkacem, Malte Helfer, Claudia Polzin-Haumann,
    and Christina Reissner

29 Vocational Learning Abroad: The Case of German VET Mobility .. 323
    Tabea Schlimbach, Karen Hemming, and Valentina Cuzzocrea

30 Youth as Temporary Workers Abroad: The Experiences of Australia,
    Canada and New Zealand 337
    Peter G. Ghazarian

31 International Work Placements: Developing Intercultural Skills? .. 347
    Sophie Cranston, Emma Bates, and Helena Pimlott-Wilson

32 Abroad Forever? Embedding Spatial Mobility in Academic Work
    Trajectories in Italy.. 359
    Davide Filippi, Sebastiano Benasso, and Luca Guzzetti

33 Italian Youth and the Experience of Highly Qualified Migration
    to the United Kingdom 373
    Monica Santoro

Part V

34 Mobility at the Margins 385
    David Cairns, Daniel Malet Calvo, and Mara Clemente

35 Mobility Choices in Post-Soviet States: How the EU Attracts
    Youth in Its Shared Neighbourhood with Russia 393
    Marine Sargsyan

36 From Forced Migration to Mobility: Dreaming of Home
    Within 'Rooted Mobilities'................................ 403
    Sahizer Samuk, Derya Acuner, and Yesim Tonga Uriarte

37 'I was not prepared to go to Spain': Work Mobility of Young
    People at the Margins in Portugal 415
    Mara Clemente

38 Crossing the Line: Current and Future Challenges in Youth
    Mobility 429
    Jeanine B. van Halteren

39 Youth Mobility, Mental Health and Risky Behaviours 441
    Giovanni Aresi, Elena Marta, and Simon C. Moore

40 Rethinking the Value(s) of Short-Term Youth Mobility:
    Neoliberal Ideals and Counterhegemonic Possibilities 455
    Emrullah Yasin Çiftçi and A. Cendel Karaman

41 A Wonderful But Uncertain Time: Youth Transitions of Erasmus
    Students and Lisbon's Housing Crisis 467
    Daniel Malet Calvo

42 Conclusion: Youth Migration in the Age of Pandemic Immobility .. 479
    David Cairns, Thais França, Daniel Malet Calvo, and Leonardo
    Francisco de Azevedo

Index 491

Notes on Contributors

Derya Acuner is based in Italy, at IMT School of Advanced Studies Lucca, having graduated from the Business Administration department of Ankara University in 2010. Since 2013 she has worked with civil society organizations in the fields of collective memory and women's rights.

Airi-Alina Allaste Professor of Sociology at Tallinn University, Estonia, focuses her research, publications and teaching on youth-related topics, qualitative methods and the analyses of meanings that people attribute to their lives. She has been the coordinator of many projects on youth cultures, lifestyles, participation and motilities and edited seven books/special issues on these topics. She is also vice-president of the international research committee of the Sociology of Youth, ISA, and member of numerous other networks, including RAY.

Tuba Ardic is a PhD candidate at University of Bergen and she has been teaching and studying at HVL Sogndal Campus since 2014. Her research interests include youth mobility in Europe, migration and forced migration, refugee studies, frame analysis, belonging and identity. She worked for three years at the Horizon 2020 MOVE project, conducting fieldwork in Norway.

Giovanni Aresi is a Postdoctoral Research Fellow and Adjunct Professor of Social and Community Health Psychology at Università Cattolica del Sacro Cuore, Italy. He is also a researcher at the CERISVICO centre for research in Community Development and Organisational Coexistence at the same university, and an honorary research fellow at Cardiff University. His research focuses on the determinants of health behaviours and positive youth development, with a primary emphasis on cross-cultural differences and youth mobility.

Leonardo Francisco de Azevedo PhD student in Social Sciences at Federal University of Juiz de Fora, Brazil. His research interests include the internationalization of higher education, skilled migration, brain drain and brain circulation.

Emma Bates is a Postgraduate Researcher at Loughborough University, UK. Her work centres on exploring young women's experiences of higher education and work—drawing out the significance of race, gender and age in their experience of youth transitions.

Rachid Belkacem is a Lecturer in Economics and Management at University of Lorraine, working on labour markets in international and cross-border comparatives perspectives and economic and social development in cross-border context.

Sebastiano Benasso is Research Fellow and Adjunct Professor in Sociology at the University of Genoa. His main research interests are the biographical transitions of young adults, life course de-standardization, youth cultures and lifestyles.

David Cairns Principal Researcher at the Centre for Research and Studies in Sociology, ISCTE-University Institute of Lisbon, works mainly in the fields of youth, mobility, education, employment and participation. He has participated in two large-scale European Commission-funded studies and is currently working on a project entitled *Circulation of Science*, looking at the governance of scientific careers. He has over 100 publications to date, including seven books and numerous articles in international peer-reviewed journals.

Javier A. Carnicer is postdoctoral researcher and lecturer of Intercultural Education at the University of Hamburg, Germany. His work explores the implications of migration and social inequality for educational institutions and educational theory. His current research focuses on transnational social networks, migration and educational mobility between Brazil and Europe.

Samia Chasi serves as Strategic Advisor to the International Education Association of South Africa (IEASA). She is a practitioner-scholar with more than 20 years of experience in higher education internationalisation via positions in international offices of German and South African universities, an agency of the European Commission as well as representations of the DAAD, Nuffic and the British Council in South Africa.

Emrullah Yasin Çiftçi Research Assistant at Middle East Technical University, is working on a PhD centred on neoliberal common sense, international student mobility and language teacher education. His research interests include language teacher education, critical interculturality, political economy in language education, critical discourse studies and qualitative inquiry.

Mara Clemente is an Integrated Researcher based at the Centre for Research and Studies in Sociology, ISCTE-University Institute of Lisbon, Portugal, and also an Associate Researcher of the Emigration Observatory (OEm) of the same institute. Her research interests are focused on migration and gender issues, and qualitative research methods, with her fields of expertise covering human trafficking, refugees, sex work and sex tourism.

Robert Coelen is a Professor at NHL Stenden University of Applied Sciences and Director of the Centre for Internationalisation of Education (CIE) at the Campus Fryslân of the University of Groningen. He is a visiting professor at Tongji University and East China Normal University in Shanghai. He co-supervises a group of PhD students from around the world at the CIE who are working on projects related to internationalization of education. He gained his academic degrees (B.Sc. (Hons), M.Sc., PhD, and Grad Cert. Ed.) from universities in Australia and was a natural science academic before turning to education as his field of research. For the last 15 years he has reviewed manuscripts for various journals in the field of education, including the *Journal of Studies in International Education*, *Journal of Applied Research in Higher Education*, and *Studies in Higher Education*. His latest book (co-edited) was entitled *Internationalization and Employability*.

Sophie Cranston Lecturer in Geography at Loughborough University, with an empirical focus on British migration, her research looks at skilled forms of international mobility, focusing on the relationships between categorizations, experiences and the migration industries. Her recent work investigates youth mobilities, investigating tensions within discussions of global identities.

Valentina Cuzzocrea is Associate Professor at the University of Cagliari, a member of the Pool of European Youth Researchers (PEYR) and past coordinator of the European Sociological Association Research Network 'Youth & Generation.' She has published internationally in various journals, working at the intersection between youth studies and mobility studies.

Karolina Czerska-Shaw holds a PhD in Sociology and is assistant professor at the Institute of European Studies, Jagiellonian University in Krakow. Her research interests include migration and integration policies and practices, civic education and citizenship testing schemes, as well as issues of belonging in transnational social spaces and international student mobility. She has served as an academic coordinator for various international degree programmes for over 12 years, working closely with international students through teaching, support services and mentoring.

H. Peter Dörrenbächer Professor of Human Geography at Saarland University, Saarbrücken, with previous positions and teaching activities at the University of Trier, Institut d'Études Politiques de Paris (Sciences Po Paris), Technical University of Munich and Goethe University Frankfurt. He is also a member of the Steering Board of the Centre for Border Studies of the UniGR (University of the Greater Region), Director of the tri-national Master Programme Border Studies and Member of the Advisory Committee for Urban Development of the City of Saarbrücken. His research interests include Economic Geography and Border Studies with a particular focus on regional structural change, the institutionalization of cross-border regions, cross-border labour mobility and vocational training.

Alina Esteves has PhD and Master's degrees in Human Geography (Universidade de Lisboa, Portugal). Currently, she is Assistant Professor of Human Geography at the Institute of Geography and Spatial Planning (IGOT), Universidade de Lisboa, and a researcher at the Unit MIGRARE—Migration, Spaces and Societies at the Centre for Geographical Studies (CEG-IGOT). She works in migration studies, with a particular focus on the portability of welfare rights across borders, feedback mechanisms and integration at the local level.

Davide Filippi is Research Fellow at the University of Genoa, working on the project, 'De-bordering activities and citizenship from below of asylum seekers in Italy. Policies, practices, people.' His main research interests are in the transformation of the neoliberal academy and the mobility of young adults in Europe.

Thais França is an Integrated Researcher at the Centre for Research and Studies in Sociology of ISCTE-University Institute of Lisbon and visiting assistant professor of the Master in Labour Sciences and Industrial Relations. Her research interests focus on migration, mobilities, gender, social inequalities and post-colonial studies, including a project on scientific and gender equality during the Covid-19 pandemic.

Ines Funk is a Scientific Assistant at the Department of Geography at Saarland University. She studied Cultural Studies at Saarland University and completed her PhD in Geography in 2015. Her research interests are in Border Studies, especially cross-border labour and training markets, as well as Health Geography. She is also a member of the UniGR Centre for Border Studies.

Sara Fürstenau is Professor of Intercultural Education at the University of Hamburg. Her research areas include multilingualism and language education, school and curriculum development in the migration society, as well as transnational migration and education.

Peter G. Ghazarian is an Assistant Professor in Leadership Studies at Ashland University and a Guest Professor of Education at Keimyung University. He has worked in leadership studies and international education in the United States, United Kingdom, Germany and Korea, and has a broad range of research interests related to social and economic changes rooted in globalization.

Mette Ginnerskov-Dahlberg Researcher at Uppsala University, is an anthropologist by training and holds a PhD degree in European Studies from Aarhus University. Her work focuses on student flows from Eastern to Western Europe, and the relationship between educational mobility and long-term migration. Specializing in ethnography with a longitudinal methodology, she is particularly interested in the lived experience of migration, the link between geographical and social mobility, and the labour market integration of student migrants.

Marcela Gola Boutros holds a Master's degree in Migration, Inter-Ethnicity and Transnationalism from the Universidade Nova de Lisboa, Portugal, with her research focused on asylum seekers' and refugees' access to higher education in Italy. She is currently based in the UK, primarily focused on economic migration, transnational corporations and issues relating to families of settled persons.

Luca Guzzetti is a sociologist, teaching Sociology of Communication at the University of Genoa. His main research interests include science, technology, media and politics.

Malte Helfer is a Geographer and Senior Researcher at the Department of Geography and Spatial Planning at the University of Luxembourg. His research interests are geographic information systems and interactive mapping, cultural/industrial tourism, cultural/industrial heritage and the Greater Region SaarLorLux.

Karen Hemming has worked as Senior Researcher at the German Youth Institute (DJI) in the Youth transitions department since 2015, having studied for her diploma and PhD at the Universities of Leipzig and Hamburg respectively. She works with an interdisciplinary perspective including sociology, educational sciences and psychology on topics related to children and youth.

Blanka Henriksson is Assistant Professor of Cultural Analysis at Åbo Akademi University in Finland. She holds a PhD, and a title of docent, in folklore studies and her research has mainly focused on identity processes, minority, and performative borders, but she has also studied childlore, gendered traditions, memory practices, and memorial culture.

Nicolás José Isola is an Executive Coach, having formerly been a Postdoctoral Fellow of São Paulo Research Foundation, Campinas State University, Brazil.

Louise Kaktins teaches academic communication at the Department of Linguistics, Macquarie University. She has wide-ranging academic interests and extensive experience in developing courses related to effective professional communication, academic literacy and professional ethics. Her main research area concerns academic identities of international students in pathway programmes and the pedagogical implications

A. Cendel Karaman is Associate Professor at the Department of Foreign Language Education, at University of Wisconsin-Madison and Vice Dean of the Faculty of Education at Middle East Technical University. He is the author of several articles in the field of teacher education with a focus on systems thinking, intercultural education, field experiences, identity, curriculum and professional development.

Emilia Kmiotek-Meier has been a Postdoctoral Researcher at the University of Cologne since May 2019, where she coordinates the project 'Successful at the labour market,' on focusing higher education graduates' competencies. She obtained her PhD from the University of Luxembourg in 2019, her thesis focusing on credit and degree student mobility from Luxembourg.

Ewa Krzaklewska is Assistant Professor at the Institute of Sociology of the Jagiellonian University in Krakow, Poland. Her research interests relate to youth sociology, including transitions to adulthood, youth mobility, youth work and policy, as well as gender equality and family studies. She has been studying youth mobility for several years, starting with the 2005 Erasmus Student Network survey on Erasmus students' experiences.

Wei Li is a Professor at the Asian Pacific American Studies/School of Social Transformation and Associate Director at School of Geographical Sciences and Urban Planning in Arizona State University. Her foci of research are immigration and integration, and transnational connections, focusing on the Pacific Rim. She is the author, [co-]editor or translator of seven scholarly books, three journal thematic issues, and has 147 other academic publications.

Lucia Lo is Professor Emerita and former head of Geography at York University, Canada. Her research focuses on the role of immigrants in economic development and urban transformation. Trained as an economic geographer in the spatial science tradition at McMaster University and the University of Toronto, she brought innovative perspectives to examining immigrant integration and settlement issues. Her latest book publication is entitled *Social Infrastructure and Vulnerability in the Suburbs*, and her current research is on intellectual migration.

Yixi Lu is Associate Professor of Sociology at the Research Institute of Social Development in Southwestern University of Finance and Economics in China, having received her PhD from the Department of Sociology at the University of Saskatchewan in Canada. Her research areas include international migration and integration, immigration policy, education, Chinese diaspora and China studies, and social dimensions of health and healthcare experiences. She is presently conducting research on the returnees and foreigners in China.

Zheng Lu is Associate Professor at the School of Economics, Sichuan University, China. He holds a PhD in economics from Sichuan University, China and BA in management from Southwest University, China. His research covers topics in the fields of regional economics, rural economic development and human capital mobility. He has published articles in various journals.

Daniel Malet Calvo Associated Researcher at the Centre for Research and Studies in Sociology of the University Institute of Lisbon (ISCTE-IUL), is conducting research on international higher education students and their role in urban change. He holds a PhD in Social Anthropology from University of Barcelona, where he also has graduated with a BA in Social and Cultural Anthropology, and a BA in History.

Daniela Elena Marinescu is Associate Professor at the Department of Economic Informatics and Cybernetics—The Bucharest University of Economic Studies. Her research focuses on micro and macroeconomic modelling, especially Industrial Organization, Agency Theory, Labour Economics, Health Economics and Educational Economics.

Elena Marta is Full Professor of Social and Community Psychology at Università Cattolica del Sacro Cuore, Italy. She is also director of the CERISVICO centre for research in Community Development and Organisational Coexistence at the same university. Her main research interests are in young adults' healthy behaviours, volunteerism, mentoring programmes and community development.

Simon C. Moore is Professor of Public Health Research at Cardiff University. He holds an honours degree in sociology and psychology and a PhD in the area of experimental psychology. He leads several large projects, mostly in the area of alcohol, alcohol-related harm and substance use. Through this work he aims to bring a multidisciplinary perspective that identifies pathways to misuse and opportunities to reduce harm. He is also co-director of the Cardiff Crime and Security University Research Institute.

Laura Muresan is Professor of English at the Bucharest University of Economic Studies, where she coordinates an English-medium Academic Development Master's course. She has coordinated European projects on Quality Assurance in language education and participated as long-term expert in the Horizon 2020 MOVE project. Her research interests include internationalization processes in Higher Education, as well as pedagogical interventions for improving students' and scholars' academic literacies and language competences for successfully engaging in international academic and professional exchanges.

Birte Nienaber is a Political Geographer in migration, border studies and European regional development. She studied Geography, Political Science and Ethnology at the Universities of Münster (Germany) and Rouen (France) and worked at the Leibniz-Institute of Regional Geography in Leipzig (Germany), Saarland University, Saarbrücken (Germany) and since 2013, has been an Associate Professor at the University of Luxembourg. Her main research focus is on youth mobility and migration, integration, asylum, border studies, inside and into Europe.

Raili Nugin is a Researcher at Tallinn University. Her main fields of research are in rural identities and mobilities, the transition-to-adulthood, generations, cultural heritage and rural communities. She has published a monograph on the generation born in the 1970s in Estonia and her work has been published in several edited volumes as well as journals on these topics.

Grada Okken is a practitioner-researcher in the field of international and intercultural education. As a PhD candidate at the Centre for Internationalisation of Education and University of Groningen, she is exploring the long-term outcomes of Study Abroad on teacher behaviour and intercultural teaching competence in specific. As a practitioner, she works as a Lecturer at NHL Stenden University of Applied Sciences in The Netherlands.

Beatriz Padilla has PhD and Master's degrees in Sociology (University of Illinois, Urbana-Champaign), Master's in Public Affairs (University of Texas, Austin, United States), and a BA in Political Sciences and Public Administration (National University of Cuyo, Argentina). Currently, she is Assistant Professor at University of South Florida and an Associated Researcher at Instituto Universitario de Lisboa (ISCTE-IUL). Her main lines of research are in migration, diversity, gender, health, inequalities and public policies.

Maria-Carmen Pantea is Associate Professor at Babeș-Bolyai University, Romania. Her research focuses on youth studies, particularly the relationship between young people and work in its various forms, including graduates' over-qualification, entrepreneurship and vocational education and training. She is the author of *Precarity and Vocational Education and Training. Craftsmanship and Employability in Romania* (Palgrave, 2019) and a member of the Pool of European

Youth Researchers of the EU-CoE Youth Partnership and an editorial board member of the European Training Foundation.

Irina Pavlova has an MSc degree in European Affairs from the University of Lund, Sweden. She has an interdisciplinary background from political and social sciences. Since 2016, she has worked as a lecturer in Sociology at the Western Norway University of Applied Sciences (HVL). Her main research interests are internationalization in higher education, employability, regional development in rural areas, youth and mobility.

Isabelle Pigeron-Piroth is a Research Specialist at the University of Luxembourg. Her main research fields are employment and mobilities in cross-border contexts. Her work engages with cross-border labour markets and their impacts and challenges in cross-border development inside the Greater Region Saar-Lor-Lux. She is also interested in the comparison with other cross-border spaces.

Dulce Pimentel is Assistant Professor of Human Geography at the Department of Geography and Regional Planning, NOVA FCSH, and researcher at the Interdisciplinary Centre of Social Sciences (CICS.NOVA), Universidade Nova de Lisboa. Her research includes work on geodemography and migrations, and she is currently the coordinator for the Master Studies in Migration, Inter-Ethnicity and Transnationalism programme (Universidade Nova de Lisboa).

Helena Pimlott-Wilson is Reader in Geography at Loughborough University, UK. Her research focuses on the shifting importance of education and employment in the reproduction of classed power. Recent work investigates the aspirations of young people from socio-economically diverse areas in the UK, international mobility of students for higher education and work placements, and the alternative and supplementary education industries.

Claudia Polzin-Haumann is chair of Romance Linguistics at the Department of Romance Languages and Literatures at Saarland University, with special emphasis on French and Spanish. She is a member of the UniGR-Center for Border Studies and several research groups and has contributed to numerous research projects in the field of applied linguistics. She is co-director of the Institut für Sprachen und Mehrsprachigkeit and currently holds the position of Vice-President for European and International Relations at Saarland University.

Paula Pustulka is Assistant Professor at SWPS University of Social Sciences and Humanities in Warsaw. At SWPS, she is the Director of the Youth Research Center and Principal Investigator for the GEMTRA project on transitions to motherhood across three generations of Polish women. She has extensively published on Polish migrant families settled in Europe, with a strong focus on family practices and parenting, as well as particular experiences of men, women and children in mobility projects.

Christina Reissner is a Senior Researcher and teaches at the Department of Romance Languages at Saarland University, where she heads the department of

Early Foreign Language Learning (French) and of the Virtual Center of European Intercomprehension. Her research focuses on (Applied) Romance linguistics, pluri−/multilingualism, language policies, (multi)language learning and teaching, and border studies.

Alexandra Ribeiro graduated with Bachelor's and Master's degrees in Political Science from the University of Minho, Portugal. Her work has focused on the study of citizens' political behavior, social movements, the impact of collective action, self-management and various attempts at making new forms of democracy.

Sahizer Samuk completed her Bachelor's degree in Political Science at Bogazici University in 2006 and has worked as a reporter in documentary making in Africa and the Middle East and studied at Koç University and the IMT School for Advanced Studies Lucca. More recently, she has been a postdoc at the University of Luxembourg, working on the MOVE Project, which focused on youth mobility within the EU. She is currently working as a post-doctoral researcher at UBIQUAL, Department of Sociology, University of Pisa, Italy.

Monica Santoro is Associate Professor at the University of Milan, where she teaches Sociology of Family. Her research topics include youth conditions, family and demographic transformations and family relationships.

Marine Sargsyan PhD candidate in European and International Affairs at Roma Tre University, Department of Political Science, has extensive work experience in the youth field, as founder and through the activities of the Initiative Group Alpbach Armenia youth NGO based in Armenia. Her academic work includes a book, *Student and Graduate Mobility in Armenia* (Palgrave Macmillan, 2019), and research at the Davis Center for Russia and Eurasian Studies at Harvard University, and the European Institute at Columbia University.

Tabea Schlimbach is Senior Researcher at the Youth Transitions research unit of the German Youth Institute (DJI). Her main research areas are school-to-work transitions and migration, with a strong focus on youth at risk of unemployment. She is specialized in qualitative research and has been involved in numerous projects, including national longitudinal studies, evaluations of government programs as well as collaborative European initiatives such as the Horizon 2020-funded research project MOVE on European youth mobility (2015–2018).

Thor-André Skrefsrud is Professor of Education at the Faculty of Education of Inland Norway University of Applied Sciences. His research interests include multicultural education, intercultural learning and educational philosophy.

Jan Skrobanek is Professor of Sociology at the Department of Social Sciences, Western Norway University of Applied Sciences. His research interests include ethnic identity, discrimination and ethnicization, agency, mobility and/or employment as well as developments of transition patterns of vulnerable youth in a global perspective. He is also interested in methods of quantitative social research, cross-national comparative research and evaluation designs for intervention programmes.

Hélène Syed Zwick is a French researcher and teaching economist, with over 10 years of international experience. She has lived and worked in three different continents (Europe, Africa and Asia). Presently, she is Executive Director of ESLSCA Research Center and Associate Professor in Economics at ESLSCA University, Egypt. She is also an international consultant, having worked with the ILO, World Bank and the IOM. Her research interests include international student mobility, forced migration economics and labour economics.

Yining Tan is a PhD candidate in Geography at Arizona State University. Her research focuses on skilled migration between China and the United States. Combining qualitative interviews with GIScience, she is studying the mobility of skilled migrants in relation to the intersection of race, gender and citizenship.

Vasiliki Toumanidou is a doctoral researcher and teaching assistant at the School of Sociology and Social Policy at the University of Leeds. Her PhD research project has examined student migration from Greece to the UK in times of economic recession. Prior to starting her PhD, she studied at Aristotle University of Thessaloniki and Brunel University in London, and worked as a primary school teacher in Greece. Her research interests relate to youth transitions, life course studies, student migration/mobility, socio-economic and educational inequalities, higher education and education policy.

Yesim Tonga Uriarte is an assistant professor at the Analysis and Management of Cultural Heritage department at IMT Lucca. She obtained her PhD from the same department and holds an MA degree in Arts and Heritage: Policy, Management and Education (Maastricht University) and a bachelor's degree in Economics (Bogazici University). Her main research interests cover temporary organizing in cultural and creative industries, relations between temporality and institutional maintenance, project-based cultural organizations and evaluation of cultural policies and cultural projects.

Jeanine B. van Halteren is a PhD candidate in Educational Science at Oslo Metropolitan University (OsloMet), with a MPhil in Multicultural and International Education from Oslo University College (HiO) and MA in Career Counselling from University of South-Eastern Norway (USN). Her research interests include social and educational inequalities, affect and the ethical dimension, embodied learning and relational aesthetics. Currently she studies safeguarding of the intangible cultural heritage in apprenticeships in small and rare crafts, at the intersection of tradition and innovation.

Eva Maria Vögtle completed her PhD in 2013 at the Department of Politics and Public Administration at the University of Konstanz, conducting research on national conditions of transnational policy convergence in the realm of the Bologna Process. At present, she is Postdoctoral Research Associate at the German Centre for Higher Education Research and Science Studies (DZHW). Since 2020, her research has focused on types of university admission regimes and academic freedom measures in a European comparative perspective as well international student mobility.

Volha Vysotskaya is a Postdoctorate Researcher at the Department of Geography and Spatial Planning at the University of Luxembourg. She previously studied Social Sciences in the field of Social Change, Population Dynamics, and the Life Course at the Bremen International Graduate School of social Sciences (BIGSSS), Germany, specializing in youth transition, life course, mobility and migration.

Dominika Winogrodzka is a PhD student at the Interdisciplinary Doctoral School of SWPS University of Social Sciences and Humanities in Warsaw, preparing a dissertation on the impact of international mobility on the socio-professional sequences of young people from middle-towns in Poland. At SWPS University, she is also a member of the Youth Research Center and Mobility Research Group, with her research interests concentrating on youth mobility and youth work, social research methods and data visualization.

List of Figures

Fig. 24.1　Students' mobility experience (No data for Switzerland (CH)). Share of all students (in %). (Data source: Eurostudent VI) 263

Fig. 24.2　Differences in enrolment abroad by gender. Share of students who have been enrolled abroad (in %). (Data source: Eurostudent VI) 264

Fig. 24.3　Enrolment abroad by type of higher education institution. Share of students who have been enrolled abroad (in %). (Data source: Eurostudent VI) 266

Fig. 24.4　Temporary enrolment abroad by educational background (The binary aggregation of higher education background applied in Eurostudent into 'without higher education background' and 'with higher education background' may obscure the fact that in the different countries, qualifications at the same ISCED level may be regarded to be higher education in one country and vocational training in another. For example, German Master crafts(wo)men vocational qualifications are at ISCED level 6 (professional) in the qualification framework, i.e. equivalent to the level of higher education. However, these types of degrees are not typically regarded to be part of the higher education system in Germany. Austrian Master crafts(wo)men qualifications, in contrast, are at ISCED level 5 (and are nationally not regarded to be higher education either)). Share of students (in %). (Data source: Eurostudent VI) 267

Fig. 24.5　Organisational framework for enrolment abroad. Share of students who have been enrolled abroad (in %). (Data source: Eurostudent VI) 268

Fig. 24.6 Primary source of funding used for enrolment abroad (No data for Germany (DE). No data for item 'Regular study grants/loans from home country' for Albania, France, Croatia, Italy, Serbia. No data for item 'Special study grant/loan from home country for going abroad' for Austria, Switzerland, the Czech Republic, Malta, Romania, Turkey. No data for item 'Study grants/loans from host country' for Switzerland, Ireland. No data for item 'other' for Italy, Malta, Slovakia). Share of students who have been enrolled abroad (in %). (Data source: Eurostudent VI)............ 269

Chapter 1
Introduction: The Intermittency of Youth Migration

David Cairns and Mara Clemente

This book presents different perspectives on youth migration, focusing upon research from a wide range of geographical contexts. While diverse, what theoretically unites the assembled chapters is the idea that migration as practised by young people has fragmented into disparate episodes. Rather than becoming migrants in the classical sense of following a path with a clear beginning, middle and end, young people tend to move intermittently, in an often circular manner and for different, frequently overlapping reasons such as education, work and training. They may not even see themselves as migrants—especially in the very early stages of a spatial trajectory—but when we take into account the accumulation of mobility experiences being consumed, starting with what may be relatively short duration stays abroad, we come to see that they *are* actually practising migration, albeit in a manner different to established ideas that centre on the idea of settlement. Another way of looking at this situation would be to see moves abroad during the youth phase as precursors to longer duration stays later in life. What happens at a young age hence comes to matter a great deal to professional development, as this can be the time of life when the knowledge and skills required to become a migrant are generated, along with an awareness of how to make effective decisions about where and when to go.[1]

Having stated this position, a more straightforward way of introducing this book would be to say that different chapters have been collated with a view to representing some of the most prominent topics in the youth mobility research field. There is however a desire to show the connections, literal and imaginative, that exist between seemingly unrelated experiences. As noted above, this includes the idea of youth

---

D. Cairns (✉) • M. Clemente
ISCTE – Instituto Universitário de Lisboa (ISCTE-IUL), Centro de Investigação e Estudos de Sociologia, Lisbon, Portugal
e-mail: david.cairns@iscte-iul.pt

mobility as informing later life migration, heightening its significance. This is not the only connection made in this book. We also seek to bring forms of youth mobility that have been placed at the margins of society into the centre of the research field, and discuss mobility in terms of its contribution to migration. Not accepting young people categorized as 'migrants' in media and policy discourse as consumers of mainstream mobility values denies the fact that these individuals have 'normal' aspirations to engage in internationalized forms of work and learning. Furthermore, excluding those who engage in student exchanges, work placements or training exercises from migration frameworks contributes to their social and economic marginalization in host societies, potentially denying them access to vital support structures.

The aspiration to make a better life for oneself via mobility is also transversal, shared by young people in the centre-ground and at the margins of society; those rich in social and economic capital, who wish to consolidate or multiply their wealth, and others moving without resources or support in an attempt to escape hardship. How these young people are perceived may however differ. The former are seen as good consumers and net contributors to society, while the latter may be marked as vulnerable and made into a social problem due to their dependence on public largess. Mobility can be further problematized in political and public discourse when it takes place outside the regular channels of circulation between sending, transit and receiving countries, to the point of being defined, in some cases, as a product of criminal behaviour. This helps explain why, instead of being seen as mobile youth, 'the poor' come to be described as 'involuntary' or 'forced' migrants, perhaps even 'victims of trafficking.'

There is clearly a great deal of room for exploration of the full spectrum of youth mobility, taking into account the contradictions of mobility and migration, as well as a need to challenge many taken-for-granted assumptions. No one, for instance, thinks of international students and trainees as 'victims of trafficking' even though they may have been divested of thousands of euros or dollars and compelled to work for minimal wages in order to make ends meet. Problematized categories of mobility do however seem to be the exclusive preserve of 'poor people' who migrate in what might be seen as an irregular manner. The categories mobilized in politics and the media, and sometimes by the protagonists themselves, are an integral part of the problematization of young people's migration, particularly where there is a failure to take into account the complexity of their motivations and ambitions, and the challenges they face in managing their incipient migration trajectories.

One of these challenges is simply attaining coherence in regard to one's own mobility. Internationalized experiences of education, training and work are not generally linear but characterized by continuous fragmentation and a need for improvisation. There is also a need to recognize the exploitation mechanisms that are built into migration systems, often disguised as 'opportunities' but laden with hidden costs, and barriers in relation to bureaucracy, even in countries that—in theory— have open borders.[2] Policies can also strengthen marginality through controversial intervention practices such as detention and encouraging young people to make 'voluntary' returns once they are no longer deemed contributors to the host society.

At a more quotidian level, that much youth mobility policy, and youth policy per se, is aimed at supporting agencies and institutions rather than directly engaging with an inclusive range of young people means that support is usually lacking, creating a dichotomy between official discourses that endorse the value of youth circulation to societies and the reality of young people having to shoulder the costs of embodying internationalization.

These initial remarks bring to light some of the most basic concerns in regard to the intermittent state of youth migration, wherein episodic mobility is nested within an individualized migration trajectory, dependent upon one's own resources. This is a starting point that recognizes the agency of young people, something that can be easily denuded for those whose mobility has been either problematized, monetarized or used as some kind of political plaything. In reality, we are left with a situation wherein millions of young people construct their migration trajectories in a ramshackle manner, including many individuals in vulnerable positions, moving abroad without a safety net or the guarantee of any kind of profit despite the promise of individualized success.

Mobility Imperatives and Motivations

One reason for this book being issued at this time relates to the growing popularity of various forms of youth mobility. The impression created by a decade or more of serious scholarship on this topic is that young people from across the world feel compelled to circulate, to seek out new or at least different ways of learning, training and working, combined with some form of personal development, with a view to pursing individualized success. The take-up of mobility nevertheless remains patchy.[3] In a number of countries, especially in the more prosperous regions of the European Union (EU), youth mobility is popular to the point of becoming a relatively mundane part of education and training. Elsewhere, it remains more elusive and thus continues to possess a certain cachet. There are also young people who, while very small in numbers, engage in forms of mobility that attract a huge degree of media and political attention, perhaps due to the exceptionality of their experiences, a recent example being the arrival of young refugees in 2015. However, in the case of minority and majority youth populations, we can see mobility as an individual response to social and economic conditions in present place of residence, whether this is a lack of appropriate opportunities, prevalent inequalities or threats to personal well-being, all of which can contribute to the generation of a very strong mobility imperative.[4]

Noting the existence of societal conditions, whether the structure of local labour markets and the distribution of educational opportunities or various forms of discrimination and marginalization, provides one means of understanding migration decision-making, but throughout this book we will seek to move beyond describing self-evident contextual factors, acknowledging the importance of individual motivations in the practice of mobility. It is certainly the case that many young people move abroad out of desperation and frustration, and hope, rather than carefully calculated cost-benefit analysis. For this reason, we cannot ignore the need for prosperity and security. But we also need to accept other motivations, such as the strong associations travel has with leisure. There is a danger that this could create the impression that being mobile while young is a less than serious preoccupation, lacking gravitas. However, while the promise of a good time may be used as an enticement, it is unlikely to be the principal reason for embarking on what may be mentally and physically arduous journeys. An important corrective function of this book is hence to take young people's mobility seriously and not dismiss it as holidaymaking, especially as there is a great deal of effort involved on their part.

In regard to our own motivations for preparing this book, the authors come from a wide range of professional backgrounds, but mostly within the social sciences, and are for the most part aware of how young people wish to improve their personal and professional circumstances, and perhaps escape personal hardship and societal difficulties, through engaging in mobility. Geographically, contributions have been sought from the traditional centres of youth mobility research, Europe and the Anglophone world, and other regions, including the Global South. A globalized phenomenon absolutely needs to take a global approach in order to acknowledge the diversity and the commonalities in the practice of internationalized learning in particular. We are nevertheless subject to the vagaries of authorial preferences in regard to the topics covered in this book. While the balance between Global North and Global South may appear somewhat skewed towards the former, this is a reflection of the greater popularity of youth mobility research, especially in Europe, rather than a desired outcome. Within Europe, there is also a strong focus on short-term educational exchanges (including via Erasmus), again reflecting the current state of the youth mobility research field, and perhaps explaining why the title of this book denotes an educational focus. For these reasons, no spurious claims of representativity will be made in regard to coverage of the youth mobility research field, with the emphasis more upon depth rather than breadth. Despite our shortcomings, we nevertheless wish to share knowledge and insights of what we have observed firsthand, and perhaps bring to light some frustrations with the manner in which youth mobility is conceptualized, especially the uncomfortable manner in which young 'migrants' are viewed as a threat to society, with other 'mobiles' seen as vital contributors to a nation's wealth and well-being.

Finally, we also have to admit at this stage that we may be documenting practices that, while not necessarily at an end, have for the most part entered a period of hiatus. It is impossible to ignore the fact that the *Palgrave Handbook of Youth Mobility and Educational Migration* was prepared at a time of profound social and political upheaval across the world, with the Covid-19 pandemic placing geographical mobility under strain in ways we could not ever have imagined. Entire societies have been locked down, strangers defined as people to be feared and travel something to be endured rather than enjoyed. While the work presented in this book was prepared before the pandemic, there were already signs of strain within mobility systems, especially in relation to overheated institutionalized mobility platforms and underprepared free circulation that generated vulnerabilities, something that may now have exacerbated during the pandemic.[5] We are hence looking at mobility and migration at a time when certain practices started to become dysfunctional in regard to their detrimental impact on individuals and societies.

The Structure of This Book

The book is organized into 41 chapters, including this brief contextual introduction and a concluding discussion, which looks to reappraise the content of the chapters in the light of the Covid-19 pandemic. In assembling these chapters, an attempt has been made to cover what we see as the most prominent aspects of the youth mobility research field and bring to light relatively undocumented experiences, sidestepping some topics that are already extensively covered in existing literature.[6] Therefore, while we acknowledge the importance of developments such as the Erasmus programme in Europe, we do not focus exclusively on mobility within this framework, extending the scope of the book to the Global South and self-motivated forms of circulation.

The basic structure also reflects the current state of the youth mobility research field. Three main strands are quite apparent in regard to existing studies: work that relates to young people's mobility in tertiary-level education, moving abroad for training purposes and seeking employment abroad, albeit with certain topics falling between these dividing lines.[7] Studies of mobility within education and work, and to a lesser extent training, also oscillate between exchanges undertaken via institutional structures, such as Erasmus, and free movers who organize and pay for their own mobility. That a significant amount of research has been conducted on both modalities explains why we have a demarcation between the two in this book, although experiences often overlap, with free movers also engaging in institutional mobility and vice versa. What is left to consider are the more marginal aspects of youth mobility, exceptional experiences that do not fall inside any neat category.

In sum, we have a diverse range of mobility to cover. In doing so, we hope to strike a balance between documenting the successes and failings of these modalities, moving beyond simplistic and stereotypical ideas, for example that student exchanges are predominantly the preserve of the middle classes in rich Western countries and that young people from disadvantaged backgrounds feature more prominently in accounts of negative migration experience, especially individuals who have travelled to the Global North from the Global South. Theoretical exploration is also presented alongside empirical evidence, the latter using mostly original qualitative material. What we are left with are five basic areas within which chapters have been grouped as follows.

Introducing Youth Mobility and Migration

Chapters 3–7 provide a space for theoretical-based discussion, introducing the idea that young people's mobility is characterized by fluidity and precarity, with migration broken down into episodic commodity forms. As a result of this fragmentation, becoming and remaining geographical mobile requires a great deal of thought, effort and resources. This perspective hence recognizes the contributions young people make to their own mobility; rather than being passive or casual, undertaken without thought or planning, spatial choices are premeditated, with the consequences of these decisions essentially privatized in monetary and emotional terms.

This view, of youth migration as concatenated mobility, is viewed as a politically acceptable means of 'allowing' young people to circulate with a relatively high degree of freedom, reflecting a neoliberal orthodoxy designed to benefit institutions rather than individuals. However, much of this mobility takes place without an effective safety net, helping explain why events such as the 2020 pandemic have had a profound impact on mobile young people. They were among the people made vulnerable by societal lockdowns, the abrupt closure of national frontiers and the shifting of education, work and training onto online platforms, with the prospect of incipient migration trajectories being curtailed or at least interrupted for a substantial period of time. We therefore have to acknowledge that the opening-up of borders and democratizing access to certain forms of mobility came at the price of introducing risk and precarity into youth migration, the effects of which may take years to manifest.

Free Movement in Education

Chapters 9–14 take an in-depth look at free movement in tertiary education. As discussed above, there is recognition that young people make their own mobility, to a certain extent, using their own agency, and that along with the economic costs, the responsibility for coping with the challenges of living abroad are privatized for 'free' movers. While operating within prevailing structures of opportunities for learning, training and working, with marked contrasts between the Global North and Global South, circulating young people are generally left to themselves to make decisions and make sense of their own migration trajectory, working out how to secure a passage from one mobility phase to the next.

Also explored in these chapters is the internationalization of tertiary education, something that is dependent upon a high degree of cooperation between universities situated in different country, and intercultural conviviality among and between students and staff, despite the fact that these parties are simultaneously in competition with one another for limited resources and sought after opportunities. At a more quotidian level, social class and cultural inheritances (including language fluency) also come into play in defining mobility choices, with some young people occupying a more favourable starting position than others. The impact made by teaching professionals can also be significant, particularly where they offer encouragement and practical support. In looking at educational free movers, we can hence learn more about where migration starts, and sometimes where it stops, taking into additional consideration the roles played by public and policy discourses that define 'migration.'

Institutionalized Mobility Inside and Outside Erasmus

Chapters 16–24 look at institutional mobility, including exchanges made through platforms such as Erasmus. In the past, it has been argued that student mobility, whether undertaken for a semester or a longer period of time, is a form of migration in itself.[8] However, in keeping with the emphasis in this book on youth migration as accumulative, student exchange visits are interpreted more as preliminary steps in a larger migration project, albeit taking more regularized forms compared to the examples of free movement discussed in Chaps. 9–14 of the book. Completing an educational or training course abroad also brings with it accreditation and, in the case of moving abroad for the duration of a degree programme, an actual diploma, implying a certain standardization and predictability of outcomes. In other words, the outcomes of institutional mobility are more quantifiable and visible than free movement, making these 'products' marketable and replicable.

This idea, that spending a fixed period of time abroad through a platform such as Erasmus, with measurable results, may help explain the popularity of the programme and many others like it, especially among policymakers who wish to invest in programmes with guaranteed returns. Despite this apparent success, the socio-demographic and geo-demographic inclusivity of student mobility platforms has always been in question, challenging the idea of the programme as an unqualified success story for European society (Cairns 2017). Ironically, in programmes that are explicitly international, it can be failures to take into account differences at national and regional levels that undermine aspirations towards equality of access, since not everyone is starting with the same advantages and disadvantages. Following a 'one size fits all' approach to participation in student mobility programmes will always lead to partial or superficial success, especially in contexts where learners are travelling without prior experience of internationalized learning to places unable or unwilling to accommodate large incoming student populations.

Working Towards Mobility

Having stressed the importance of mobility in training and employment for young people, we must also acknowledge the limited quality of research in these areas. While this book has tried to address this oversight, the relatively low number of contributions received means that training and work have been collapsed into Chaps. 26–32 of the book to ensure that some kind of coverage can be attained, focusing on the idea that training and working with a mobility dimension plays an important role in the transition from education to work. Also evident is that, as with student mobility, much of this movement takes place within institutional structures and in internationalized groups, taking advantage of the dynamics such environments offer for intercultural exchange and collaboration, as well as the expertise of specialist training providers. But, mirroring developments in tertiary education, there is also strong emphasis on ingraining neoliberal values into trainees and young workers, most obviously in a focus upon entrepreneurial dynamics.

In more practical terms, we can see that much of this mobility is aimed at relatively young age groups (i.e. 16- to-18-year-olds), and has involved small groups of young people taking relatively short stays abroad, measured in weeks and months rather than years. Arguably the most valuable research on this topic relates to mobility in Vocational Education and Training (VET), which does feature prominently in these chapters of the book. Significantly, while not always awarded the respect given to student movers, those who engage in mobility at this level wish to enhance not only their skills and abilities but also transform their personal outlook on the world, which they hope will become more cosmopolitan. What we can infer from the evidence is that their geographical movement is not just utilitarian, but also feeds into ontological narratives about making life a mobile project. However, mobility for work and training, when not well managed, can become more symbolic than substantial, another line on a CV rather than a viable means of securing stable employment.

Mobility at the Margins

Finally, we come to Chaps. 34–40 that consider experiences of young people's mobility that feature heavily in policy and media discourse, making these issues hard to ignore despite the fact that publicized accounts rarely reflect young migrants' actual experiences. This is first and foremost the case in 'human trafficking,' historically characterized by unsubstantiated claims and spurious statistics, not to mention ineffective interventions and the allocation of high levels of public funding. There is an uncomfortable tension between what passes for political and public debate on this issue, manifest in these individuals being converted into subjects amenable to exploitation for the political and economic capital they can generate for governments and agencies, the most obvious recent example in Europe being young people who moved to the EU during the 2015 refugee crisis, also acknowledging more long-standing concerns regarding the trafficking of youth.

In evaluating this position, it is necessary to investigate further the experiences of young people who have experienced mobility episodes that have had an obvious negative impact on their personal well-being, and to do so in their own terms, using in-depth evidence that documents actual experiences rather than passively consuming what may be heavily biased media narratives and political discourse. Using problematized forms of mobility as a means to attract attention and money can in turn be problematic for society, such as in the case of spurious links being made between the Covid-19 pandemic and trafficking at a time when governments around the world should be concentrating their resources on public health and the new economic crisis.

Less well publicized is the marginality generated by what are thought of as relatively benign forms of youth circulation. Acknowledging the inherent precarity of young people's migratory behaviour is a key concern throughout this book, and developing this theme beyond the theoretical perspectives of Chaps. 3–7, we consider the contribution precarious migration makes to physical and mental frailty. Another marginalized theme within youth mobility research concerns the negative impact of intensified levels of student circulation on urban environments. This is particularly evident in cities that lack the infrastructure to host expanded number of exchangees, something that can be detrimental to international students and local residents alike.

Some Brief Notes About Editing This Book

Putting together this book has involved a great deal of editorial decision-making. While authors have been given the liberty to express themselves as they deem necessary in their chapters, we have tried to treat our research subjects with respect and avoid attaching prejudices and value judgements in our assessments of their mobility. While editorial interventions have largely been restricted to the reorganizing the structure of chapters, reducing verbiage, correcting spelling and grammar, uncritical terminology that has pejorative or racist associations has been avoided (e.g., terms such as 'immigrant' and 'ex-patriot,' as well as dichotomies between 'voluntary' and 'involuntary' migrants). Attempts have also been made to avoid making inappropriate regional comparisons, such as can be the case with perspectives privileging the alleged 'civilization' of the Global North to the detriment of people from the Global South. The use of secondary statistics is also largely avoided, since such figures are always out-of-date at the time of publication and generally accessible online.

Notes

1. See Cairns (2021a, b) in this book for a continuation of this discussion.
2. This topic, of 'opportunities' laden with hidden costs, was discussed extensively in Cairns et al. (2017) in the context of intra-European circulation among the highly qualified, including students, interns and scientists.

3. Various statistics exist in regard to estimating the prevalence of various forms of youth mobility, the most popular being the UNESCO *Global Flow of Tertiary-Level Students* database. Little, if any, comprehensive data seems to exist regarding the mobility of trainees and young workers.
4. This idea of 'reflexive imperative' has been explored extensively by the editor in various works (see, e.g., Cairns et al. 2017), and is linked to the sociological idea of a 'reflexive imperative' within life planning (see Archer 2012).
5. In the conclusion of this book, we discuss some results from research conducted with international students during the pandemic (see Cairns et al. 2021).
6. Most obviously, this includes studies of 'credit mobility' exchanges among undergraduates via Erasmus and other institutional platforms (see, e.g., Brooks and Waters 2011; Feyen and Krzaklewska 2013; Van Mol 2014; Cairns et al. 2018).
7. Examples of harder-to-classify mobility include work placements (Deakin 2014) and international internships (Cuzzocrea and Cairns 2020).
8. See, for instance, studies by Findlay (2011) and Raghuram (2013).

References

Archer, M. S. (2012). *The reflexive imperative in late modernity*. Cambridge: Cambridge University Press.
Brooks, R., & Waters, J. (2011). *Student mobilities, migration and the internationalization of higher education*. London: Palgrave Macmillan.
Cairns, D. (2017). The Erasmus undergraduate exchange programme: A highly qualified success story? *Children's Geographies, 15*(6), 728–740.
Cairns, D. (2021a). Mobility becoming migration: Understanding youth spatiality in the twenty-first century. In D. Cairns (Ed.), *The Palgrave handbook of youth mobility and educational migration*. Basingstoke: Palgrave Macmillan.
Cairns, D. (2021b). Migration decision-making, mobility capital and reflexive learning. In D. Cairns (Ed.), *The Palgrave handbook of youth mobility and educational migration*. Basingstoke: Palgrave Macmillan.
Cairns, D., Cuzzocrea, V., Briggs, D. and Veloso, L. 2017. *The Consequences of Mobility: Reflexivity, Social Inequality and the Reproduction of Precariousness in Highly Qualified Migration*. Basingstoke: Palgrave Macmillan.
Cairns, D., Krzaklewska, E., Cuzzocrea, V., & Allaste, A.-A. (2018). *Mobility, education and employability in the European Union: Inside Erasmus*. Basingstoke: Palgrave Macmillan.
Cairns, D., França, T., Malet Calvo, D., & Azevedo, L. (2021). Conclusion: Youth migration in the age of pandemic immobility. In D. Cairns (Ed.), *The Palgrave handbook of youth mobility and educational migration*. Basingstoke: Palgrave Macmillan.
Cuzzocrea, V., & Cairns, D. (2020). Mobile moratorium? The case of young people undertaking international internships. *Mobilities, 16*(3), 416–430.
Deakin, H. (2014). The drivers to Erasmus work placement mobility for UK students. *Children's Geographies, 12*(1), 25–39.
Feyen, B., & Krzaklewska, E. (Eds.). (2013). *The ERASMUS phenomenon—Symbol of a new European generation*. Frankfurt: Peter Lang.
Findlay, A. M. (2011). An assessment of supply and demand-size theorizations of international student mobility. *International Migration, 49*(2), 162–190.
Raghuram, P. (2013). Theorising the spaces of student migration. *Population, Space and Place, 19*, 138–154.
Van Mol, C. (2014). *Intra-European student mobility in international higher education circuits*. Basingstoke: Palgrave Macmillan.

Part I

Chapter 2
Introducing Youth Mobility and Migration

David Cairns, Valentina Cuzzocrea, and Ewa Krzaklewska

This chapter focuses on theoretical issues of relevance to the study of youth mobility. The aim is to introduce some of the conceptual tools researchers have developed to help explain young people's spatial movement, especially in education, work and training contexts. We reappraise the relationship between mobility and migration, seeing them as nested rather than distinct practices. The chapters also discuss how mobility is imaginatively integrated into life planning, with moving abroad while young initiating a migration trajectory. This work is, we hope, an appropriate starting point for this book in establishing a starting point for mobility and arguing that what happens in the youth phase has lasting value.

In regard to including mobility within the broader framework of migration, the idea is that what that takes place while young can become part of a greater continuum. Using the evidence contained in this book, we are hence able to conceptually re-appraise 'migration,' focusing on how it actually happens rather than how it has been traditionally conceptualized by many academics in the field of Migration Studies. This idea also views a migration trajectory as fluid and fragmented. Rather than moving definitively from one place to another and staying there, young people prevaricate and circulate. That this process is incremental means mobility and immobility co-exist within this trajectory, rather than the former supplanting the latter. Our understanding of migration thus goes from being definitive and solid to a

---

D. Cairns (✉)
ISCTE – Instituto Universitário de Lisboa (ISCTE-IUL), Centro de Investigação e Estudos de Sociologia, Lisbon, Portugal
e-mail: david.cairns@iscte-iul.pt

V. Cuzzocrea
University of Cagliari, Cagliari, Italy

E. Krzaklewska
Jagiellonian University, Krakow, Poland

© The Author(s), under exclusive license to Springer Nature Switzerland AG 2022
D. Cairns (ed.), *The Palgrave Handbook of Youth Mobility and Educational Migration*, https://doi.org/10.1007/978-3-030-99447-1_2

point where intangibility and unpredictability can create a migrant unselfconsciously, to the point of being taken for granted by many young people.[1]

Equally self-evident is the importance of decision-making. When a migration trajectory is broken down into a series of hard-to-connect phases, working out what to do next becomes a fundamental concern, especially when these mobility episodes come at a high economic and emotional cost, imbued with risk, precarity and unpredictable outcomes. Putting this decision-making process into more sociological terms, constructing migration out of mobility relies on the exercise of reflexivity, and by the idea that what young people are required to do is inherit, accumulate and invest mobility capital.[2] That this form of capital is a fragile, perishable and quite hard-to-obtain commodity explains why the mobility decision—or the series of mobility decisions that need to be made—acquires such importance in contemporary migration.[3]

From the point of view of young people, this approach enables us to recognize their agency in making mobility choices and the roles played by family members, friends, educators, trainers and employers in constructing a migration trajectory. Young people make decisions using their own resources and intuition allied to the knowledge and information available to them, however imperfect. Their choices can also be grounded in an extra-economic logic, moving beyond a simple desire to accumulate immediate wealth, recognizing the aspiration to become part of a globalized culture or to follow lifestyles that revolve around international conviviality.

These themes are represented throughout this book. Mette Ginnerskov-Dahlberg continues the discussion of mobility decision-making in Chap. 5, looking at the role of family relationships, especially the role of parents in encouraging migration among their children. This helps us understand how and why mobility happens, using evidence from Denmark as a means of illustrating inter-generationally transmitted mobility predispositions among students from post-communist societies, a process that is largely imaginative considering that these parents have had little or no actual mobility experience. 'History' therefore matters to how people relate to in the present day, with parents providing an impetus for their children to pursue opportunities to which they themselves had limited access during the era of state socialism. This perspective also helps explain why the creation of a mobility favouring habitus needs to be recognized as a process taking place across a sustained period of time; in this case, traversing the decades between generations.[4]

To further help us appreciate how mobility happens, various heuristic ideas have been developed, encapsulating some of the key aspects of decision-making. In Chap. 6, Paula Pustulka and Dominika Winogrodzka acknowledge two conceptual building blocks of contemporary migration: mobility capacity and mobility imperative, focusing on the Polish context. These ideas enable us to look beyond the obvious economic motivations, linking structural conditions with personal agency. Although moving far beyond the traditional 'push and pull' theories about the origins of mobility, this perspective does not contradict the idea that much migration is economically driven. However, it is acknowledged that there is no way to become an economic migrant without being in possession of the requisite knowledge and skills: to follow a mobility imperative you need to have a mobility capacity. Furthermore, particularly within Europe, there is much mobility taking place that is quite obviously not driven by financial imperatives but rather other motivations, such as the desire to acquire cosmopolitan dispositions.[5] Some people may actually enjoy exploration and engaging in the 'fun' dimension of the youth phase of life.[6] We therefore acknowledge that mobility can be about seeking out a particular lifestyle as well as pursuing a career. Imagining that a better life, or at least a different life, awaits one abroad thus constitutes an alternate or additional mobility imperative, albeit with desires constrained by the relatively high costs of circulation.[7]

Other conceptual materials include the relevance of interculturality, with Thor-André Skrefsrud looking at the difficulty of generating this faculty via student mobility in Chap. 7. The idea of an internationalized learning hub is certainly seductive for learners and educators; places in which students from across the world learn from each other. Out of their social bonds, established through spending a fixed period of time within an international group, a supranational learning space can be established, characterized as experimental and dynamic, but at the same time, intense and fragile, socially inclusive (of other international students) and exclusive (omitting the presence of local cultures). Therefore, having cited issues such as historical and familial legacies, and recognized mobility imperatives and capacities, it is also appropriate to acknowledge the significance of peer relationships in the formation of migration trajectories, with positive and negative consequences.[8]

Interculturality is not only a highly evocative and emblematic way of 'being together' at a formative point of the life course but also of (geo)political importance. It has value for states and transnational entities such as the EU, as well as education and training institutions, who rely upon internationalization in order to brand themselves with cosmopolitanism. Tertiary education in particular comes to be imagined as a chic product, this being an effective way to justify its elevated cost to students. A premium product however can only sustain its cachet when comparatively rare (i.e. it *must* be socially exclusive), explaining why youth mobility is always likely to remain a niche product, lacking the potential to contribute to social inclusion. For societies on the other hand, the presence of young, and not so young, migrants might be less valued. As Skrefsrud points out, international migrants do not necessarily enhance the cosmopolitan outlooks of people in the host community. Quite the opposite. Their presence may be a source of alienation, inviting increased scepticism towards human globalization and hostility towards incomers, who come to be seen as different from what is perceived as 'normal' because of their interculturality. We therefore need to take account of the perverse effects of mobility and acknowledge that raising levels of youth circulation does not necessarily lead to freer and more equal societies.

Notes

1. The idea that migration consists of nested mobility episodes that start in the youth phase of the life course is explored further in Chap. 3 of this book (Cairns 2021a).
2. Mobility decision-making is elaborated upon in Chap. 4 (Cairns 2021b), building on perspectives developed in our previous work (see, e.g. Cairns et al. 2017).

3. This is also an issue that is widely recognized in youth mobility policies, most visibly in the EU supported Erasmus+ programme, which has emphasised the importance of 'learning mobility,' not only in the sense of learning about mobility opportunities but also how to take advantage of them.
4. For an earlier discussion of the relationship between youth mobility predispositions and habitus, see Cairns et al. (2013).
5. This is in fact a long-standing theme in youth mobility research. See, for instance, King and Ruiz-Gelices (2003) or Skrbis et al. (2014).
6. For a more in-depth account of having 'fun' during mobility, see Krzaklewska (2019).
7. This idea points towards looking at mobility decisions as being oriented around choosing 'a life' rather than just subscribing to a lifestyle (Cairns 2014: 28).
8. These intercultural environments have been conceptualized as learning 'bubble' environments by Cuzzocrea et al. (2021).

References

Cairns, D. (2014). *Youth transitions, international student mobility and spatial reflexivity: Being mobile?* Basingstoke: Palgrave Macmillan.

Cairns, D. (2021a). Mobility becoming migration: Understanding youth spatiality in the twenty-first century. In D. Cairns (Ed.), *The Palgrave handbook of youth mobility and educational migration*. Basingstoke: Palgrave Macmillan.

Cairns, D. (2021b). Migration decision-making, mobility capital and reflexive learning. In D. Cairns (Ed.), *The Palgrave handbook of youth mobility and educational migration*. Basingstoke: Palgrave Macmillan.

Cairns, D., Growiec, K., & Smyth, J. (2013). Leaving Northern Ireland: The youth mobility field, habitus and recession among undergraduates in Belfast. *British Journal of Sociology of Education, 34*(4), 544–562.

Cairns, D., Cuzzocrea, V., Briggs, D., & Veloso, L. (2017). *The consequences of mobility: Reflexivity, social inequality and the reproduction of precariousness in highly qualified migration*. Basingstoke: Palgrave Macmillan.

Cuzzocrea, V., Krzaklewska, E., & Cairns, D. (2021). 'There is no me, there is only us': The Erasmus bubble as a transient form of transnational collectivity. In V. Cuzzocrea, B. Gook, & B. Schiermer (Eds.), *Forms of collective engagements in youth transition: A global perspective*. Brill: Leiden.

King, R., & Ruiz-Gelices, E. (2003). International student migration and the European 'year abroad:' Effects on European identity and subsequent migration behaviour. *International Journal of Population Geography, 9*(3), 229–252.

Krzaklewska, E. (2019). Youth, mobility and generations – the meanings and impact of migration and mobility experiences on transitions to adulthood. *Studia Migracyjne – Przegląd Polonijny, 1*(171), 41–59.

Skrbis, Z., Woodward, I., & Bean, C. (2014). Seeds of cosmopolitan future? Young people and their aspirations for future mobility. *Journal of Youth Studies, 17*(5), 614–625.

Chapter 3
Mobility Becoming Migration: Understanding Youth Spatiality in the Twenty-First Century

David Cairns

The aim of this chapter, and the next, is to provide readers with an expanded introduction of sorts, engaging with prominent theoretical themes in the study of youth spatiality. Of particular interest is appreciating the relationship between our two main terms of reference, migration and mobility, the former having a certain gravitas, the latter a more youthful and carefree aura. This chapter will however show that the distinction between these two modalities is artificial and detrimental to our appreciation of youth spatiality, with mobility and migration being linked both literally and imaginatively. While the intention is certainly not to reinvent the entire youth mobility research field, we can provide some ideas for a conceptual rethink, starting with acknowledgement of the importance of integrating mobility with migration, and vice versa, moving towards outlining a youth mobility paradigm capable of accommodating a diverse range of perspectives. This includes drawing upon evidence from the Global North and Global South, and both long-duration and fixed-term forms of exchange.

At a theoretical level, a union of sorts is hence proposed, uniting the different mobility practices that take place within an individual biography, starting in the youth phase. In the past, specific exercises of mobility have tended to be presented by researchers as discreet exercises; for example student exchanges, international internship and work placements. However, looking at mobility episodes in isolation tends to underestimate their significance. These exercises may have value at the time of their undertaking, in acquiring new skills or credentials, but it is only when this formative mobility is conjoined with later in life mobility episodes that the importance of what has gone before is revealed, the antecedents enabling the subsequent sojourns to happen, thus establishing a spatial continuum. What is being learnt in the present may therefore have a bearing upon the future, creating a

D. Cairns (✉)
ISCTE – Instituto Universitário de Lisboa (ISCTE-IUL), Centro de Investigação e Estudos de Sociologia, Lisbon, Portugal
e-mail: david.cairns@iscte-iul.pt

© The Author(s), under exclusive license to Springer Nature Switzerland AG 2022
D. Cairns (ed.), *The Palgrave Handbook of Youth Mobility and Educational Migration*, https://doi.org/10.1007/978-3-030-99447-1_3

long-duration, if intermittent, migration trajectory out of what may have appeared to be unrelated, even ephemeral experiences. The idea then is that an accumulation of short-duration or circulatory mobility episodes now becomes migration and that young people learn how to be migrants through being mobile.

Mobility Becoming Migration

What then does this mean for mobile young people? The impression created by reading the chapters of this book is that a change took place in the practice of migration at some time in the early twenty-first century, due perhaps to the proliferation of opportunities for undertaking mobility while young and the relative openness of national borders at this time. That specific mobility practices were presented as being discrete from one another obscured the connections that existed between these episodes, and downplayed the fact that it was generally up to individual young people to put together these disparate pieces as part of a 'do-it-yourself' approach, rather than external institutions and agencies who only focused on the mobility that happened under their auspices.[1]

There are many examples in this book of mobility becoming migration. As an illustration, we can consider the chapter of Sahizer Samuk and colleagues. Using interview material from Romania, Norway and Luxembourg, taken from a recently completed European Commission-funded study, they illustrate how student mobility acts as an 'eye-opener' for new experiences, broadening awareness of a wide range of future possibilities, with the value of the experience emerging not immediately but rather many years later. In regard to how this happens, the antecedent mobility contributes to the development of new competences and teaches young people how to overcome the difficulties that invariably arise after moving abroad. The basic idea then is that 'mobility produces mobility' (Samuk et al. 2021), and participating in one programme can lead to joining another; in the case of this chapter, an important nuance is the revelation that it is often the same people who participate in different schemes operating under the Erasmus+ umbrella, which supports mobility at different points in a career trajectory, across a wide range of locations.

Elsewhere in the world, mobility practices may be more isolated from one another, disconnected from a unifying narrative. Thais França and Beatriz Padilla (2021) look at the experiences of students travelling from Portuguese-speaking African countries to Brazil, as part of a mobility programme operated by the University for International Integration of the Afro-Brazilian Lusophony (UNILAB). Their analysis highlights the importance of new mobility trajectories for learners in the Global South, but also acknowledges some of the difficulties students have in the host institution and community due to a lack of social integration, something that may limit the impact emergent forms of mobility have on the likelihood of making subsequent moves abroad. What may happen is that they remain mobile students rather than become future migrants, making the exchange experience a one-off adventure rather than a preliminary stage in a settlement process (see also Prazeres

2013). Therefore, not everyone can learn how to be a migrant through being mobile at the same pace or in the same manner, with possible disadvantages present due to spatial location and/or socio-demographic background.[2]

A New Youth Migration Paradigm: The Spatial Consumer

The impression emerging from these initial reflections on the work contained in this book is that a new and much more inclusive migration paradigm is required for theorizing a fuller range of spatial practices among youth. This paradigm needs to integrate existing knowledge, especially about classic forms of migration, such as economic and political motivated circulation, and be capable of accommodating recent developments such as the expansion of student mobility systems, the emergence of spatialized training programmes and the imperative many young people face in regard to seeking employment opportunities abroad. We also need to accept that certain individuals become mobile out of a striving to become part of what they imagine is a cosmopolitan elite and that they may need to be able to cope with a high level of precariousness. And fundamentally, this new model should reject binary categorizations between 'mobility' and 'migration,' instead emphasising the connections and evident fluidity of youth spatiality.

So how then might we build this new paradigm? As a starting point, there is much that can be retained from traditional views on migration since people continue to move between countries for quite obvious reasons; for, example to escape from economic hardship or political unrest in one's present place of residence. We might want to acknowledge regional differences in mobility norms and values, and that many want to move away from poverty and towards prosperity, whether this is movement from the Global South to the Global North or within these regions. And we can also consider what have become mainstream forms of youth mobility, especially for students, but not without glossing over the negative aspects of these experiences alongside celebrating the alleged wonderfulness of internationalization.

Another valuable observation concerns the interpolation of leisure and notions of self-actualization, especially into work and training abroad. In this book, being able to think of the experience as an extended holiday and an opportunity for self-improvement is cited as an inspiration for undertaking vocational mobility by Pantea (2021), and in temporary work migration to Australia, Canada and New Zealand by Ghazarian (2021). Further obfuscation of hidden costs may take place through disguising a migration pathway as some kind of a 'rite of passage' (see also Ho et al. 2014; Yoon 2014). Such moves are seen, by some, as a challenge to prove oneself and, for others, as a chance to build understanding and new connections with people in new places. In both cases, mobility is seen as an opportunity for personal growth (Clarke 2005). This helps explain why the contemporary migrant comes to be seen as a spatial consumer: making reflexive choices based on what fits their personality and professional needs and desires. Equally significant is the fact that mobile subjects subject themselves to a form of self-discipline, or reflexive entrepreneurialism, responding to a mobility imperative associated with the neoliberal governance of education, training systems and labour markets (see Filippi et al. 2021).

It is important to state that this means of conceptualizing migration is very much in its incipient stages, being difficult to attain and harder to sustain. One reason, as outlined by Syed Zwick (2021) in her chapter is the challenge involved in investing mobility capital. She details the frustration felt by many graduates from Central Asia who find their plans for moving to 'the West' thwarted by various barriers and limitations, most prominently, the lack of access to foreign job markets. There are however signs of pragmatism among spatial consumers. For example, work with Thai students has revealed that they may temporarily work abroad in Australia as a means to explore life in the country before moving there permanently (Wattanacharoensil and Talawanich 2018). In looking for illustrations of other new ways of practicing migration, the chapter of Vasiliki Toumanidou (2021), focusing on Greek postgraduate students' migration from Greece to the United Kingdom, shows how their decision-making has been influenced by multiple factors, mostly as an intended first step in a broader migration project.[3] This chapter also draws parallels between these students' decision-making processes and the idea of 'liquid migration' (Engbersen and Snel 2013), a perspective that harks back to ideas in Anglophone sociology associated with the work of Zygmunt Bauman.

Putting the 'new migrant' who operates within this framework into economic terms, he or she is an idealized neoliberal subject, the spatial self-entrepreneur. Self-financing, self-motivating but perhaps also somewhat self-centred. Borrowing a few ideas from Emrullah Yasin Çiftçi and A. Cendel Karaman (2021) in Chap. 39, we can see this person as a kind of 'homo mobilicus,' in not just meeting the current but anticipating the future demands of the neoliberal labour market. Not only flexible about what they do, but where they do it. Durations. Destinations. Social and family relationships. All reframed by the search for elusive foundations and depth, and a wish to move beyond the touristic surfaces of over-familiar environments.

The Success of Mobility and Migration

Why then does youth mobility, in all its forms, concern us as social scientists? While there are no reliable and comprehensive statistics available, it is safe to assume that the global mobile youth population encompasses millions of individuals. In explaining this popularity, it is hard to ignore an association with individualized success, whether in material forms or less tangible aspects of personal development. The idea of moving abroad as a means to accumulate wealth is certainly familiar, with more implicit forms of success expressed through ideas such as cosmopolitanism and interculturality, as well as the positive connotations mobility acquires through its association with leisure. Spatial mobility thereby comes to be thought of as a relatively pleasurable means of fostering personal and professional growth, becoming tied to social mobility and, at a greater stretch, the idea becoming a hyper-mobile global citizen (Czerska-Shaw and Krzaklewska 2021).[4]

Despite its eminent desirability, the growing popularity of youth mobility has not necessarily been benign for societies. On the contrary, certain forms of spatiality have been conceptualized in terms of their potential to create social distinctions between those on the move and their stay-at-home counterparts, benefitting the former at the expense of the latter, generating not levelling social inequalities.[5] In the past, a mobility interregnum was used as a kind of moratorium phase for the children of the bourgeoisie, travelling abroad for a substantial period of time between secondary and tertiary education, or as a postgraduate intermission, sometimes described rather literally as a 'gap year' (Simpson 2004; Vogt 2018; see also Henriksson 2021). While no doubt interesting for the participants, such practices could be detrimental to social cohesion and have served to define the mobile citizen as a divisive and disruptive individual with a feeling of superiority generated at the expense of the members of host communities and peers left at home. In other words, youth mobility as an elitist practice (see also Heath 2007; Bagnoli 2009; King 2011).

Mobility today is, we hope, not always an exclusive practice but the association with individualized and exceptional success remains strong, something that in itself can become a cause for concern when expectations are unrealistic or influenced by misleading information. In fact, rather than become members of a global migratory elite, geographically mobile young people may end up integrating themselves deeper into an internationalized precariat, a theme already extensively explored in youth transitions literature.[6] Many of the contributions to this book will therefore revisit the relationship mobility has with success and failure, in a broader range of contexts, covering the Global South as well as the Global North.

Conclusion: Mobility Becoming Migration and Migration Becoming Mobility

Since young people seem to have been practising migration differently in the twenty-first century, at least compared to how we imagined migration to happen in the past, it is logical that we might want to update our understanding. This explains why there is an imperative to create a paradigm that simultaneously integrates mobility and migration, with these two modalities seen as intrinsically linked, the former constructed out of fragments of the latter. Young people, especially those in education, work and training, seem to be the pioneers in this respect. For them, mobility is familiar, especially in such short duration episodic formats, and it may be the more solid and long-form types of migration that provide novelty. It is however noticeable that young people themselves find it difficult to articulate the meaning of their actions. As Pustulka and Winogrodzka note in their chapter, even where they do not move abroad for strictly economic reasons, the manner in which they explain their mobility and how their stories are narrated by external parties is tied to the 'old language' that somewhat disparages the idea of becoming a migrant (2021).

It can also be difficult for young people to escape the old migration categories, especially for those moving between the Global North and Global South through irregular channels. This extends to the ability to move out of problematized migration categories and into 'softer' mobility modes. In this book, Marcela Boutros and colleagues look at the reception and integration of refugees in the Italian higher education system. Their account underlines the importance of tertiary education as a means to 'escape' the refugee category, through developing valuable skills and aptitudes (Boutros et al. 2021). Drawing on in-depth ethnographic research, Mara Clemente meanwhile looks at how socio-economic and educational background continues to affect young people's experiences, equating certain mobility practices with human trafficking, including exploration of forced labour. What emerges from her analysis is the view that categories such as 'voluntary' migrant and 'trafficked' migrant rely on over-simplistic assumptions, and are binary and static understandings of how mobility works, with an evident dichotomy reflecting legal and public discourses rather than migrants' voices (Clemente 2021). Discourses of migration and mobility may therefore hide forms of coercion that have become deeply embedded in policymaking.

The present does not efface the past in our theorization, with the simultaneous existence of old and new forms and representations of migration recognized in the same paradigm. We can now see young people's migration as characterized by temporality, flexibility, fluidity and open-endedness, and perhaps a sense of placelessness and social disembeddedness (see also Castells 1996). This also helps explain why they may feel a pronounced sense of transience during mobility (Cranston 2016), since the journey never feels as if it has been completed. 'Migration' is always a work-in-progress, neither easy nor cost free. The downside of being a peripatetic self-entrepreneur is not only the separation from family and friends that inevitably ensues from spending time living in another country but also the financial cost of undertaking successive mobility phases, with balancing these costs and benefits an unavoidable aspect of youth spatiality in the twenty-first century.

Notes

1. While the term 'learning mobility' is frequently used by policymakers and civic society agencies, especially at European level, its significance is usually misunderstood. Learning mobility is not just about moving the learning environment to another country and promoting intercultural encounters but also about acquiring practical skills and gathering knowledge about how to migrate.
2. The limitations of the idea that mobility is divorced from migration can be described in terms of liminality (see, e.g., Butcher 2011; Cranston 2016); being perpetually stationed at a threshold position to a society without fully entering. In this sense, over-definition as 'mobility' leads to being stuck in a kind of stand-by position in society, lacking the benefits of a 'migrant' designation and the prospect of permanent settlement. Therefore,

'mobility' becomes inherently unstable, and perhaps unsustainable, due to the high cost of maintaining a holding position.
3. Their specific intention is to enhance employability and career prospects through social and cultural capital accumulation, a perspective that is similar to what takes place in many undergraduate exchanges (see Cairns et al. 2018).
4. We might see this idea, or ideal, as the youth equivalent to the idea of becoming a mythical 'Eurostar.' See Favell (2008).
5. This can be regarded as another long-standing theme in youth mobility research. See especially Murphy-Lejeune (2002).
6. For example, in a book entitled, *The Consequences of Mobility*, to which two authors to this collection contributed (David Cairns and Valentina Cuzzocrea), we argued that the expectation of individualized success helped drive highly qualified young Europeans abroad, but often resulted in disrupting rather than enhancing an educational or career trajectory due to a failure to take into account the unpredictability of outcomes (Cairns et al. 2017).

References

Bagnoli, A. (2009). On an 'introspective journey': Identities and travel in young people's lives. *European Societies, 11*(3), 325–345.
Boutros, M., Pimentel, D., & Esteve, A. (2021). Refugees' access to higher education in Italy: An opportunity lost for the 'lost generation. In D. Cairns (Ed.), *The Palgrave handbook of youth mobility and educational migration*. Basingstoke: Palgrave Macmillan.
Butcher, M. (2011). *Managing cultural change: Reclaiming synchronicity in a mobile world*. UK: Ashgate.
Cairns, D., Cuzzocrea, V., Briggs, D., & Veloso, L. (2017). *The consequences of mobility: Reflexivity, social inequality and the reproduction of precariousness in highly qualified migration*. Basingstoke: Palgrave Macmillan.
Cairns, D., Krzaklewska, E., Cuzzocrea, V., & Allaste, A.-A. (2018). *Mobility, education and employability in the European Union: Inside Erasmus*. Basingstoke: Palgrave Macmillan.
Castells, M. (1996). *The rise of the network society*. Oxford: Blackwell.
Çiftçi, E. Y., & Karaman, A. C. (2021). Rethinking the value(s) of short-term youth mobility: Neoliberal ideals and counterhegemonic possibilities. In D. Cairns (Ed.), *The Palgrave handbook of youth mobility and educational migration*. Basingstoke: Palgrave Macmillan.
Clarke, N. (2005). Detailing transnational lives of the middle: British working holidaymakers in Australia. *Journal of Ethnic and Migration Studies, 31*(2), 307–322.
Clemente, M. (2021). 'I was not prepared to go to Spain': Work mobility of young people at the margins in Portugal. In D. Cairns (Ed.), *The Palgrave handbook of youth mobility and educational migration*. Basingstoke: Palgrave Macmillan.
Cranston, S. (2016). Producing migrant encounter: Learning to be a British expatriate in Singapore through the global mobility industry. *Environment and Planning D: Society and Space, 34*(4), 655–671.
Czerska-Shaw, K., & Krzaklewska, E. (2021). The super-mobile student: Global educational trajectories in Erasmus Mundus. In D. Cairns (Ed.), *The Palgrave handbook of youth mobility and educational migration*. Basingstoke: Palgrave Macmillan.
Engbersen, G., & Snel, E. (2013). Liquid migration: Dynamic and fluid patterns of post-accession migration. In B. Glorius, I. Grabowska-Lusinska, & A. Rindoks (Eds.), *Mobility in transition: Migration patterns after EU enlargement* (pp. 21–40). Amsterdam: Amsterdam University Press.

Favell, A. (2008). *Eurostars and Eurocities: Free movement and mobility in an integrating Europe*. Oxford: Blackwell.

Filippi, D., Benasso, S., & Guzzetti, L. (2021). Abroad forever? Embedding spatial mobility in academic work trajectories in Italy. In D. Cairns (Ed.), *The Palgrave handbook of youth mobility and educational migration*. Basingstoke: Palgrave Macmillan.

França, T., & Padilla, B. (2021). South-South student mobility: International students from Portuguese-speaking Africa in Brazil. In D. Cairns (Ed.), *The Palgrave handbook of youth mobility and educational migration*. Basingstoke: Palgrave Macmillan.

Ghazarian, P. (2021). Youth as temporary workers abroad: The experiences of Australia, Canada and New Zealand. In D. Cairns (Ed.), *The Palgrave handbook of youth mobility and educational migration*. Basingstoke: Palgrave Macmillan.

Heath, S. (2007). Widening the gap: Pre-university gap years and the 'economy of experience'. *British Journal of Sociology of Education, 28*(1), 89–103.

Henriksson, B. (2021). 'I had to move somewhere': Leaving Finland to study in Sweden. In D. Cairns (Ed.), *The Palgrave handbook of youth mobility and educational migration*. Basingstoke: Palgrave Macmillan.

Ho, C.-I., Lin, P.-Y., & Huang, S.-C. (2014). Exploring Taiwanese working holiday-makers' motivations: An analysis of means-end hierarchies. *Journal of Hospitality and Tourism Research, 38*(4), 463–486.

King, A. (2011). Minding the gap? Young people's accounts of taking a gap year as a form of identity work in higher education. *Journal of Youth Studies, 14*(3), 341–357.

Murphy-Lejeune, E. (2002). *Student mobility and narrative in Europe. The new strangers*. London: Routledge.

Pantea, M. (2021). Beyond skills: Facets of mobility in Romania's vocational education and training. In D. Cairns (Ed.), *The Palgrave handbook of youth mobility and educational migration*. Basingstoke: Palgrave Macmillan.

Prazeres, L. (2013). International and intra-national student mobility: Trends, motivations and identity. *Geography Compass, 7*(11), 804–820.

Pustulka, P., & Winogrodzka, D. (2021). Unpacking the mobility capacities and imperatives of the 'global generation'. In D. Cairns (Ed.), *The Palgrave handbook of youth mobility and educational migration*. Basingstoke: Palgrave Macmillan.

Samuk, S., Nienaber, B., Kmiotek-Meier, E., Vysotskaya, V., Skrobanek, J., Ardic, T., Pavlova, I., Marinescu, D. E., & Muresan, L. (2021). Learning in transition: Erasmus+ as an opportunity for internationalization. In D. Cairns (Ed.), *The Palgrave handbook of youth mobility and educational migration*. Basingstoke: Palgrave Macmillan.

Simpson, K. (2004). 'Doing development': The gap year, volunteer-tourists and a popular practice of development. *Journal of International Development, 16*(5), 681–692.

Toumanidou, V. (2021). Understanding educational migration from Greece to the UK in times of crisis. In D. Cairns (Ed.), *The Palgrave handbook of youth mobility and educational migration*. Basingstoke: Palgrave Macmillan.

Vogt, C. (2018). The timing of a time out: The gap year in life course context. *Journal of Education and Work, 31*(1), 47–58.

Wattanacharoensil, W., & Talawanich, S. (2018). An insight into the motivation of Thai working and holiday makers (WHMs). In C. Khoo-Lattimore & E. C. L. Yang (Eds.), *Asian youth travelers* (pp. 15–37). Singapore: Springer.

Yoon, K. (2014). The racialised mobility of transnational working holidays. *Identities: Global Studies in Culture and Power, 21*(5), 586–603.

Zwick, S. (2021). Intra-regional academic mobility in Central Asia: The OSCE Academy in Bishkek, Kyrgyzstan. In D. Cairns (Ed.), *The Palgrave handbook of youth mobility and educational migration*. Basingstoke: Palgrave Macmillan.

Chapter 4
Migration Decision-Making, Mobility Capital and Reflexive Learning

David Cairns

In the previous chapter, the idea was introduced that migration can be constructed out of an accumulation of miscellaneous mobility experiences. Through this means, young people can become migrants in a relatively tacit and unconscious manner, encapsulating a sense of flux and inherent precarity. In this chapter, we continue exploration of this theme, looking at the specific issues of migration decision-making and the means through which different mobility phases become connected, interpolating into the discussion the concept of 'mobility capital.' The connections between different mobility episodes are important to consider, as is the means through which one decision affects the next, making migration a concatenation of what may have otherwise been seen as separate experiences (see Samuk et al. 2021). This will be explained as a reflexive learning process, requiring young people to use their own agency and the ability to learn how to be mobile from family members, peers, educators, trainers and employers.

In some respects, this chapter represents a continuation of existing debates about the formation of a migration trajectory. It is hypothesized that during the first two decades of the twenty-first century, with an increase in proliferation of youth mobility, a change occurred in regard to the generality of a 'do-it-yourself' approach to migration, certainly within the European context but also in other global regions. This would potentially increase the relevance of these ideas, but also perhaps show-up some uncomfortable 'Western' biases in the constitution of existing theoretical paradigms within the youth mobility research field, making us aware of our own limitations as mobility researchers schooled in certain spatially orthodox ways of thinking.

D. Cairns (✉)
ISCTE – Instituto Universitário de Lisboa (ISCTE-IUL), Centro de Investigação e Estudos de Sociologia, Lisbon, Portugal
e-mail: david.cairns@iscte-iul.pt

© The Author(s), under exclusive license to Springer Nature Switzerland AG 2022
D. Cairns (ed.), *The Palgrave Handbook of Youth Mobility and Educational Migration*, https://doi.org/10.1007/978-3-030-99447-1_4

The Migration Decision

Decision-making is a universal concern among people seeking to be mobile. While it is not impossible that decisions will be impulsive, a large degree of premeditation is more likely considering the need to plan and make provision for departures and arrivals, not to mention the accumulation of sufficient levels of social and economic capital prior to this point.[1] It is also probable that this decision will be multifaceted, taking into account the fact that mobility has diversified into various forms, traversing education, training and work, in addition to the leisure sphere. Therefore, deciding to undertake a student exchange may acquire more gravitas due to the fact that it can be a prerequisite phase for other, perhaps longer-duration stays abroad, as a part of a work placement or employment.

Another aspect of mobility in the twenty-first century is that migration can be relatively unselfconscious, to the point of feeling almost accidental or unexpected (see Cairns 2021). This is not the same as saying that migration is unplanned. On the contrary, as noted earlier, a great deal of thought and effort may have taken place. Rather, it is the attainment of a semblance of permanence within a framework branded as 'mobility' and assumed to be transient that comes as a surprise. Therefore, the migration decisions of young people actually start as mobility decisions. This is a feature that is very much implied rather than openly acknowledged, at least in institutional forms of exchange (see Chap. 15 of this book), but the incremental nature of migration trajectories is nevertheless vital to appreciate as this reveals the personal challenge entailed in the process of repeatedly having to decide what to do next.

Mobility Capital

The concept of 'mobility capital' is of major significance to our understanding of youth migration decision-making, providing a means of explaining the value of working, studying and training abroad. In perspectives derived from Bourdieu's conceptualization of various capitals (see, e.g., Bourdieu 1986), mobility is recognized as a valuable resource, akin to cultural capital. In simple terms, this category quantifies the ability to, for example, attain a high level of fluency in foreign languages and access jobs in international labour markets. In practice, this form of capital can include knowledge inherited from parents and what is accumulated during a stay abroad, such as information about specific destinations or guidance regarding how to live in a particular society, as well as the actual 'profit' gained during these stays, whether in terms of financial returns or less tangibly in the form of acquiring a mobility capacity. As possessing this capacity increases the scope of one's life chances, this form of capital is something individuals will try to accumulate and multiply, with its rarity giving it a certain cachet.[2]

This cachet, and the desire to accumulate, and perhaps monopolize, mobility capital helps explain why social closure has been identified as a potential problem, creating exclusion and reproducing socio-demographic and economic inequalities, especially where young people are utilizing mobility capital inherited from their families (Murphy-Lejeune 2002, 52). However, while deploying mobility capital is associated with the accumulation of human capital by authors including Murphy-Lejeune, using existing stocks to 'finance' mobility episodes does not necessarily lead to positive outcomes. This issue is discussed in a previous publication on the intra-European circulation of the highly qualified, which illustrates how the costs of becoming and remaining mobile always seem to outweigh the financial returns, making the 'migration by mobility' process a means for resource subtraction rather than multiplication (see Cairns et al. 2017). Mobility capital may therefore be lost rather than gained through engaging in a piecemeal approach to migration.

Outside Europe, this situation may be different. In a previous article, the means through which mobility capital was generated and later deployed after returning home was illustrated in the context of Chinese students moving to Norway for post-graduate education (see Hu and Cairns 2017). That new skills and qualifications were being acquired was an important part of the study-abroad experience, forming additional components of mobility capital, but these were not the only acquisitions. What was being learned was effectively a different way to live, taking on new values and predispositions. One example was recognizing environmentalism as a valuable form of civic engagement, demonstrating a willingness to engage in recycling was not only seen as conscientious but also a way of integrating into a society such as Norway where environmental considerations are prominent. More pragmatically, enhancing foreign language skills and gaining an understanding of European working culture was deployed on return to China, effectively using a specific aspect of mobility capital to support career development.

The accumulation of mobility capital can obviously contribute to the construction of a mobility capacity (see Pustulka and Winogrodzka 2021), a potentially durable predisposition that can last throughout the rest of a lifetime. This helps explain why accumulating mobility can lead to migrancy, not just adding up the time spent abroad but consolidating what takes place while living in other societies. In practice, this can involve earning the financial resources to fund subsequent mobility exercises and a change in perspective; the expansion of awareness of how other people live in different places, ultimately feeling that one is part of a global culture of circulation in people, ideas and capital.

Arriving at Migration

The preceding discussion implies that the basic question of why young people move between countries can be related to the mobilization and the pursuit of a specific form of capital, but even recognizing this property we are left with many unresolved issues. Principally, there is the issue of why some people move abroad while others prefer to stay closer to home, especially where there is an equivalence of socio-economic circumstances. In some cases, there may be a strong imperative to leave, grounded in difficult economic or political circumstances, as well as any number of personal factors, but this does not mean that everyone departs. One possibility illustrated in this book is the inheriting of migration dispositions, with the desire to move abroad learnt from friends, parents or other role models who are exceptionally rich in mobility capital (Dahlberg 2021). Through this means, their capital can be accessed through intergenerational transmission or exchange between siblings and peers, often prior to the first point of departure on a trajectory.

Looking more specifically at the spatial lives of young people, other assumptions surrounding mobility decision-making will be familiar to many readers, some of which are discussed in Chap. 9 of this book by Lucia Lo and her colleagues (2021), using a framework they term 'intellectual migration.' Student migrants in particular are seen as mobilized by an intense competition for places, and advantaged by an often greater inheritance of social and economic resources, presumably compared to their less well-educated peers (see also Fong 2011; Leung 2013). Their mobility is however constrained by the restrictions and fixities of time, space, boundaries, communities of origin and the legal ability to enter certain destination countries, as well as their personal identities and experiences (Li and Lo 2012; Teferra 2005; Vertovec 2001).

Other migration prerequisites are more obvious. Young people are thought to have more disposable income and free time than other age groups, at least those from comfortable middle-class backgrounds, meaning that they can travel more often and for longer durations. At this stage in their lives, it is also assumed that they have a preoccupation with enhancing their career profiles through CV-enhancing stays at prestigious international learning hubs. Maybe they are also seeking hedonistic adventure away from the staid confines of their home country or an escape from degraded education systems and labour market instability. They might want to move away from their families and friends or wish to be reunited with those from whom they are separated by distance. All these assumptions, relating to different 'drivers' of outward mobility may contain some truth, but by this measure, stating what we already know is always going to be an inadequate explanation in explaining how young people arrive at mobility, in not recognizing the complexity or the diversity of the decisions being made.

Mobility in Pieces

Part of the complexity of twenty-first-century migration relates to the idea of a migration trajectory being comprised of fragments of mobility as introduced in the previous chapter (Cairns 2021). Rather than face a definitive choice at only one point in time, individuals need to make interlocking decisions over a sustained period, a process that may involve a great deal of circulation between different locations, and stays at home and abroad. While it may still happen in some cases, the idea of migration as a one-off event, with a very clear beginning and end, needs to be challenged and replaced by recognition of migration as being in constant state of flux. We also need to acknowledge the difficulty many young people have in attempting to unite what may be disparate mobility pieces into a coherent migration trajectory. This idea, of migration in pieces, obviously challenges many of the traditional views we have about our subject and also how we study it. For instance, it is extremely difficult to credibly quantify 'migration' via analysing statistical trends due to the inherent fluidity of the subject matter. Statistics retain some value, as heuristic tool for identifying broad socio-demographic trends over time and the evolution of specific issues of interest, such as gender and class differences (see Vögtle 2021, in this volume), but in relation to piecemeal migration, vague estimates are of limited value.

It seems that migration in pieces must be studied taking an equally fragmented approach. Fortunately, in this book we have accounts of many of these episodes, out of which we can begin to assemble some answers. One classic example in the European context is the undergraduate exchange. The popularity of this form, or forms, of circulation explains why Chap. 15 of this book looks at the Erasmus programme and platforms that follow similar formats in other parts of the world. However, given that Erasmus undergraduate exchanges are already heavily researched, we will concentrate largely on engagement with the more recent Erasmus+ phase, which has expanded its scope to cover areas such as training, volunteering and work placements, as well as postgraduate education and academic staff exchanges.[3]

A good example of a relatively undocumented piece of mobility relates to the Erasmus Mundus programme, which provides opportunities to extend engagement with the programme via a two-year international study programme at master's degree level. Karolina Czerska-Shaw and Ewa Krzaklewska's (2021) account of the 'super-mobile students' participating in this programme notes that for some young people 'one Erasmus mobility phase is simply not enough,' meaning that they will undertake multiple exchanges within the same institutional framework. This explains why the Erasmus Mundus master's degree programme integrates multiple chances for mobility into its structure, moving to universities in as many as four different countries as part of the same course of study, and doing so as part of a cohort of intercultural learners. Also stressed is the importance of the Erasmus Mundus programme network, echoing a view from Nowicka (2012) that highly skilled cosmopolitan migrants move across networks rather than between countries, putting students in (spatial) control of their own learning, something that can be both a privilege and burden.

Outside Erasmus, we can observe the construction of different migration trajectories in other parts of the world. For example, Syed Zwick (2021) looks at recent developments in a range of Central Asian countries (Afghanistan, Kyrgyzstan, Mongolia, Uzbekistan, Tajikistan and Turkmenistan) that have historically been at the periphery of student mobility, while França and Padilla (2021) consider the development of a relatively recently established student exchange programme in Brazil, hosting learners from Portuguese-speaking African countries. These accounts help us appreciate the diversity in mobility practices that exists across the world, providing insight into the costs, benefits and challenges of engagement.

Moving towards Reflexive Mobility

How then might seemingly disparate mobility phases be tied together? In this book, we can observe examples of moving abroad: participating in education programmes, voluntary work placements and vocational training, being an international au pair, and seeking secure employment. These are all widespread practices across a wide range of global regions, and while having value in isolation, there is the potential for this value to be multiplied through becoming successive mobility episodes.

To help explain how this mobility interlocks, young people make deliberate decisions using their own resources and intuition, informed by the knowledge and information available to them, however imperfect. Using their agency, they make the best of whatever options are open to them, whether advancing their education, developing a career or just wishing to become a more interesting person. While they will generally do this alone, they also discuss their options with friends, relatives and other interested parties such as educators, trainers and employers. However, with the responsibility for mobility decisions basically privatized, it is up to the individual to make the right choices and take responsibility for the ensuing consequences of their decisions. In more theoretical terms, what we are moving towards is a nuanced understanding of mobility, recognizing reflexivity in the planning and practising of various forms of youth mobility, and, ultimately, the production of a migration trajectory. Certain paths will be followed with a view to accessing other, perhaps more distant, possibilities. The decision to study abroad for a short period might then be taken with a view to ascertaining the viability of securing employment in a particular place or within a specific occupational field. Reflection about mobility therefore comes to encompass not only the immediate present but also the indistinct future.[4]

Adopting reflexivity extends our ability to think about how mobility choices are made beyond taking into account simple financial considerations. We might even see this as an ontological imperative: how will living in a different place shape one's 'being' in terms of social relationships and professional development? While it is an individual process, fellow travellers also play an important role. The mobility experience may be perceived as positive or negative, or both. It is only through a successful evaluation from one's peers, colleagues and superiors that the episode can be interpreted as having paid off, whether this be the completion of an educational course, integration into a training institution or becoming established in an occupational field. Equally crucial to appreciate is the self-rationalization taking place. Events that are perceived as ostensible failures at the time they take place may be retrospectively re-evaluated as successes, perhaps in terms of lessons being learnt through hardship. From this point of view, the actual value of reflexive mobility may only become clear at a later point in the life course.

Invoking reflexivity also enables us to place youth migration within an existing theoretical tradition. For example, Margaret Archer has published in a series of books and articles illustrating how sociologists can interpret reflexivity (see, e.g., Archer 2003, 2007, 2012). This work recognizes human agency and individual capacities in life planning; that the process of being reflexive about oneself can support, or hinder, personal evolution, and the idea that there is an 'internal conversation' within people's heads that helps them arrive at decisions. That people actively plan their lives and make use of agency is also very important to acknowledge (see also Archer 2000). Furthermore, Archer's work describes many of the basic difficulties people have in overcoming what appear from the outside to be trivial problems but, internally, feel like quite significant barriers, for instance, difficulty in accessing job opportunities or coping with lifestyle issues.

At a more imaginative level, dreams and aspirations also matter: thinking about what one wants to do and where one wishes to go. This involves making an association between mobility and expectations of success, and ultimately a better life. In the next chapter of this book, Mette Ginnerskov-Dahlberg (2021) also recognizes the importance of parents' dreams, particularly when they lacked the capacity to be mobile themselves (see also Wilken and Dahlberg 2017). Reflexive mobility therefore relies upon having a vivid imagination, with a possible intergenerational dimension. And mobility itself can help to stimulate this process, with a short duration visit possibly opening up a degree of mental space for thinking about further travel.[5]

Conclusion: The Costs and Benefits of New Migration

Bringing this discussion to a close, can we now begin to talk about new ways of being a migrant, in the sense of there being large numbers of young people circulating via reflexive mobilization of their own spatial agency? Perhaps not yet given the amount of effort required to sustain a viable migration trajectory, and recent global developments may impede this development even further (see Cairns et al. 2021). That many young people are aware of the difficulties is also evident. To quote one of the interviewees cited in Maria Carmen Pantea's (2021) chapter, they realize that the 'streets are not paved with gold' in foreign countries. This form of circulation is always likely to be a minority rather than a majority experience. Other hidden costs entailed in the reflexive mobility idea also raise concerns. Some of the overheads of short-duration stays are effectively paid by local communities, outlined in the chapter by Daniel Malet Calvo (2021), but the greatest burden is placed upon individual movers. Mobility is expensive, but it can also take a toll on personal well-being. This helps explain why in their chapter Aresi and Marta (2021) look at the mental and physical health of travelling youth, including the tendency to engage in risky and unhealthy behaviour. The winners are of course the institutions who profit from groups such as international students, and societies who get to import migrants without appearing to do so.

The costs and benefits of a new form of migration are therefore coming to light, illustrating that while there are important capacities that can be acquired through spending time abroad, there is quite possibly no such thing as 'free' movement. What remains to be seen is how fragmented and fluid forms of circulation adapt to the changing circumstances of the Covid-19 pandemic. This event has obviously interrupted many incipient migration trajectories, perhaps terminally, with many students, trainees and workers having already curtailed or indefinitely suspected their stays abroad. The severity of this event may eventually signal a move back towards more traditional migration modes (i.e. more or less permanent settlement) due to the need to find stability and security, as well as having access to a reliable national health service, facets that can be somewhat hard to obtain when feeling one has to be constantly on the move.

Notes

1. The idea of mobility and migration decisions being reliant upon sufficient levels, and the right combination, of social and economic capital is another theme explored in prior work on intra-European circulation. See especially Cairns (2014).
2. Mobility capital can also be conceptualized in more abstract terms, relating to the adoption of a particular kind of cosmopolitan predisposition; in fact, Murphy-Lejeune (2002: 51) goes so far as to describe mobility capital as 'a taste for living abroad' possessed by a migratory elite, and less convincingly, seeing this resource as a sub-component of human capital. See also Kaufmann et al. (2004).
3. Exploration of Erasmus includes work by the editor and other contributors to this book (see, e.g., Feyen and Krzaklewska 2013; Cairns 2017; Cairns et al. 2018).
4. To explain this process, we have used terms like 'reflexive mobility,' recognizing a cause and effect relationship within life planning. As the name suggests, reflexivity is a process mediated by personal reflection: a choice is made by an actor, with the validity of that choice contingent upon a positive (societal) reception (Cairns et al. 2017: 19). If the feeling is that taking a specific mobility pathway has been a success, the journey is more likely to continue in this particular direction.
5. These reflections must of course be accompanied by a major caveat concerning the actual numbers of young people willing or able to extend mobility to migration. As Czerska-Shaw and Krzaklewska (2021) remark in their chapter, only a small number of traditional Erasmus students participate in Erasmus Mundus, where there is an extremely limited number of places, which are also restricted by geo-demographic quotas. We cannot therefore say that we have arrived at a point in time were the individual construction of migration trajectories is a general experience for youth, but certain possibilities exist.

References

Archer, M. S. (2000). *Being human: The problem of agency.* Cambridge: Cambridge University Press.

Archer, M. S. (2003). *Structure, agency and the internal conversation.* Cambridge: Cambridge University Press.

Archer, M. S. (2007). *Making our way through the world: Human reflexivity and social mobility.* Cambridge: Cambridge University Press.

Archer, M. S. (2012). *The reflexive imperative in late modernity.* Cambridge: Cambridge University Press.

Aresi, G., & Marta, I. (2021). Youth mobility, mental health and risky behaviours. In D. Cairns (Ed.), *The Palgrave handbook of youth mobility and educational migration.* Basingstoke: Palgrave Macmillan.

Bourdieu, P. (1986). The forms of capital. In J. G. Richardson (Ed.), *Handbook of theory and research for the sociology of education* (pp. 241–260). New York: Greenwood Press.

Cairns, D. (2014). *Youth transitions, international student mobility and spatial reflexivity: Being mobile?* Basingstoke: Palgrave Macmillan.

Cairns, D. (2017). The Erasmus undergraduate exchange programme: A highly qualified success story? *Children's Geographies, 15*(6), 728–740.

Cairns, D. (2021). Mobility becoming migration: Understanding youth spatiality in the twenty-first century. In D. Cairns (Ed.), *The Palgrave handbook of youth mobility and educational migration.* Basingstoke: Palgrave Macmillan.

Cairns, D., Cuzzocrea, V., Briggs, D., & Veloso, L. (2017). *The consequences of mobility: Reflexivity, social inequality and the reproduction of precariousness in highly qualified migration.* Basingstoke: Palgrave Macmillan.

Cairns, D., Krzaklewska, E., Cuzzocrea, V., & Allaste, A.-A. (2018). *Mobility, education and employability in the European Union: Inside Erasmus.* Basingstoke: Palgrave Macmillan.

Cairns, D., França, T., Malet Calvo, D., & Azevedo, L. (2021). Conclusion: Youth migration in the age of pandemic immobility. In D. Cairns (Ed.), *The Palgrave handbook of youth mobility and educational migration.* Basingstoke: Palgrave Macmillan.

Czerska-Shaw, K., & Krzaklewska, E. (2021). The super-mobile student: Global educational trajectories in Erasmus Mundus. In D. Cairns (Ed.), *The Palgrave handbook of youth mobility and educational migration.* Basingstoke: Palgrave Macmillan.

Dahlberg, M. G. (2021). Inherited dreams of 'the West': Eastern European students' paths to Denmark. In D. Cairns (Ed.), *The Palgrave handbook of youth mobility and educational migration.* Basingstoke: Palgrave Macmillan.

Feyen, B., & Krzaklewska, E. (2013). The Erasmus programme and the 'generation Erasmus' – A short overview. In B. Feyen & E. Krzaklewska (Eds.), *The Erasmus phenomenon – Symbol of a new European generation* (pp. 9–20). Frankfurt: Peter Lang.

Fong, V. (2011). *Paradise redefined: Transnational Chinese students and the quest for flexible citizenship in the developed world.* Stanford, CA: Stanford University Press.

França, T., & Padilla, B. (2021). South-South student mobility: International students from Portuguese-speaking Africa in Brazil. In D. Cairns (Ed.), *The Palgrave handbook of youth mobility and educational migration.* Basingstoke: Palgrave Macmillan.

Hu, A., & Cairns, D. (2017). Hai Gui or Hai Dai? Chinese student migrants and the role of Norwegian mobility capital in career success. *Young, 25*(2), 174–189.

Kaufmann, V., Bergman, M. M., & Joye, D. (2004). Motility: Mobility as capital. *International Journal of Urban and Regional Research, 28*(4), 745–756.

Leung, M. W. (2013). 'Read ten thousand books, walk ten thousand miles': Geographical mobility and capital accumulation among Chinese Scholars. *Transactions of the Institute of British Geographers, 38*(2), 311–324.

Li, W., & Lo, L. (2012). New geographies of migration? A Canada-US comparison of highly skilled Chinese and Indian migration. *Journal of Asian American Studies, 15*(1), 1–34.

Lo, L., Lu, Y., Li, W., Tan, Y., & Lu, Z. (2021). Youth educational mobility: The start of intellectual migration. In D. Cairns (Ed.), *The Palgrave handbook of youth mobility and educational migration.* Basingstoke: Palgrave Macmillan.

Malet Calvo, D. (2021). A wonderful but uncertain time: Youth transitions of Erasmus students and Lisbon's housing crisis. In D. Cairns (Ed.), *The Palgrave handbook of youth mobility and educational migration.* Basingstoke: Palgrave Macmillan.

Murphy-Lejeune, E. (2002). *Student mobility and narrative in Europe: The new strangers*. London: Routledge.
Nowicka, M. (2012). Cosmopolitans, spatial mobility and the Alternative geographies. *International Review of Social Research, 2*(3), 1–16.
Pantea, M. (2021). Beyond skills: Facets of mobility in Romania's vocational education and training. In D. Cairns (Ed.), *The Palgrave handbook of youth mobility and educational migration*. Basingstoke: Palgrave Macmillan.
Pustulka, P., & Winogrodzka, D. (2021). Unpacking the mobility capacities and imperatives of the 'global generation'. In D. Cairns (Ed.), *The Palgrave handbook of youth mobility and educational migration*. Basingstoke: Palgrave Macmillan.
Ribeiro, A. (2021). Erasmus at 30: Institutional mobility at higher education in perspective. In D. Cairns (Ed.), *The Palgrave handbook of youth mobility and educational migration*. Basingstoke: Palgrave Macmillan.
Samuk, S., Nienaber, B., Kmiotek-Meier, E., Vysotskaya, V., Skrobanek, J., Ardic, T., Pavlova, I., Marinescu, D. E., & Muresan, L. (2021). Learning in transition: Erasmus+ as an opportunity for internationalization. In D. Cairns (Ed.), *The Palgrave handbook of youth mobility and educational migration*. Basingstoke: Palgrave Macmillan.
Teferra, D. (2005). Brain circulation: Unparalleled opportunities, underlying challenges, and outmoded presumptions. *Journal of Studies in International Education, 9*(3), 229–250.
Vertovec, S. (2001). Transnationalism and identity. *Journal of Ethnic and Migration Studies, 27*(4), 573–582.
Vögtle, E. M. (2021). Mobile and immobile students' characteristics and programme choices. In D. Cairns (Ed.), *The Palgrave handbook of youth mobility and educational migration*. Basingstoke: Palgrave Macmillan.
Wilken, L., & Dahlberg, M. G. (2017). Between international student mobility and work migration: Experiences of students from EU's newer member states in Denmark. *Journal of Ethnic and Migration Studies, 43*, 1347–1361.
Zwick, S. (2021). Intra-regional academic mobility in Central Asia: The OSCE Academy in Bishkek, Kyrgyzstan. In D. Cairns (Ed.), *The Palgrave handbook of youth mobility and educational migration*. Basingstoke: Palgrave Macmillan.

Chapter 5
Inherited Dreams of 'the West': Eastern European Students' Paths to Denmark

Mette Ginnerskov-Dahlberg

This chapter is concerned with factors that can help turn students into geographically mobile subjects. Scholars have long argued that the urge to cross borders is not natural but rather needs to be learned and socialized (see, e.g., Murphy-Lejeune 2002), and when focusing on individuals, a common assumption is that family experience of mobility increases the probability of the next generation pursuing tertiary education abroad, with parents transmitting their mobility capital onto the next generation (Brooks and Waters 2011; Cairns 2014; Carlson 2013; Van Mol and Timmerman 2014). If so, how then can we account for mobility among students whose parents are less experienced travellers, where border crossing was not an integral part of their upbringing?

Exploring this debate, this discussion engages with narratives of students from the European Union's (EU's) central and eastern member states who are pursuing master's degrees at a Danish university. Assisted by the sociologist Margaret Somers' (1992, 1994) narrative framework, the analysis unpacks some of the factors that have turned students into mobile subjects and brought them to Denmark. A characteristic shared by many is belonging to the generation who have grown up with open borders in the former state socialist states (Wilken and Dahlberg 2017). Notably, their freedom to move is in marked contrast to the societal realities that characterized the lives of the previous generations in these countries. Between 1945 and 1989, freedom of movement within the communist block was strictly regulated (Bianchi and Stephenson 2014), with repressive measures put in place by state apparatuses, meaning that most citizens were not allowed to travel freely to 'the West.' More specifically, this chapter will explore narratives pertaining to how the

---

M. Ginnerskov-Dahlberg (✉)
Uppsala University, Uppsala, Sweden
e-mail: mette.ginnerskov@edu.uu.se

© The Author(s), under exclusive license to Springer Nature Switzerland AG 2022
D. Cairns (ed.), *The Palgrave Handbook of Youth Mobility and Educational Migration*, https://doi.org/10.1007/978-3-030-99447-1_5

curtailed desires and restricted travel activities of previous generations have played a role in generating a mobility imperative among the generation who grew up after the fall of the Iron Curtain.

Research Launch Pad

While youth during the communist period were subjected to a restrictive and authoritarian form of paternalism, the post-socialist period has been characterized by the incorporation into societies of global economic and cultural discourses from which previous generations were relatively 'sheltered' (Abbott et al. 2010; Walker and Stephenson 2010). A combination of open-border policies and the subsequent enlargement of the EU have led to successive waves of young people from post-socialist countries circulating around Europe (Lulle and Buzinska 2017). This tendency is noticeable at higher education institutions, where students from EU's newer member states increasingly make use of their spatial liberty to move across borders and pursue tertiary education (Genova 2016).

As part of this process, students from Central and Eastern European countries have become an increasingly normalized component of the Danish educational landscape. According to the Danish Ministry of Higher Education and Science they account for almost 41 per cent of all international students enrolled in Danish higher education (UFM 2018). Out of this cohort in Denmark, the majority come from Romania—approximately one in every five students—followed by Slovakia and Poland. The popularity of Denmark as a study destination relates, among other things, to the fact that students from the EU and European Economic Area (EEA) do not need to pay tuition fees in Denmark, and following a controversial ruling by the European Court of Justice in early 2013, these students have now become eligible to receive the monthly Danish study grant (roughly €800 per month) if they work 10–12 hours a week alongside their studies.

While student mobility has become a key area of study in the migration research field, only a small number of studies look at the flow of students from Central and Eastern European countries, and their motivations for studying abroad. A common theme found in works that do engage with this trajectory is that financial considerations are a key factor in their decision-making. For example, Lulle and Buzinska's (2017) study of Latvian students highlights how the attractiveness of pursuing an education in another European country can be linked to unequal opportunities within higher education at home. Many young people are therefore prevented from attending higher education in their country of origin, as state-funded scholarships do not cover basic needs and loans to cover living costs are hard to obtain. A similar pattern can been found in Marcu's (2015) study of Romanian and Bulgarian students in the UK and Spain. Focusing on 'life-strategy expectations,' her work illustrates how some students regard educational mobility as a future resource to guard against poverty in their home countries and a means for their families to maintain their financial position. [1]

Methodology

While the 'no tuition fees' argument is seductive, this may not be the only consideration in accounting for the mobility of these students. This explains why in this discussion I will follow Carlson (2013), who regards the decision to study abroad not as the result of a rational choice at one point in time but rather as an outcome emerging from a range of long-term biographical and social processes. As such, the narrative approach adopted in this chapter focuses on various factors that have made Central and Eastern European students go abroad, in this case, to Denmark.

The study itself is based on empirical material collected through ethnographic fieldwork among master's degree students at a Danish university. The fieldwork was conducted over a period of two years, in localities inside and outside the institution. In addition to classroom observations, I participated in social events, accompanied students to their homes, workplace and churches. In total, I conducted and recorded 65 narrative interviews with master's degree students of various nationalities; and to obtain a more systematic understanding of how their experiences and perceptions changed over time, they were interviewed repeatedly during their stay in Denmark (see Elliott 2005). During the interviews and conversations with the students, I focused on obtaining a comprehensive understanding of their individual biographies and gaining insight into parents' life stories (as narrated by the students), especially their mobility trajectories. In this chapter, I mainly draw on insights from interviews with 18 of these students, all of whom were from Romania, Hungary, Lithuania, Czech Republic, Bulgaria and Poland, and share the characteristic of a marked contrast between their own and their parents' mobility possibilities.

Narrative as an Ontological Part of Life

In regard to theoretical approach, I have drawn on Somers' (1992, 1994) conceptual toolbox for analysing and ordering the narrative patterns of the informants. Somers advocates a reconfiguration of identity through the concept of narrative. Using the notion of *narrative identity*, she addresses a turn in the social sciences in which narratives are viewed not only as a method or a question of representation, but also as an indicator of the ontological condition of social life (see also Ferber 2000). Narratives, then, are the medium through which individuals come to know, understand and make sense of the world, and it is through narratives that we construct our social identities; essentially, they lay the ground for future action. More specifically, it is through narratives that 'people are guided to act in certain ways, and not others, on the basis of the projections, expectations, and memories derived from a multiplicity but ultimately limited repertoire of available social, public, and cultural narratives' (Somers 1994: 606).

With the notion of narrative identity, Somers accentuates the fluidity of identity by highlighting how narratives are processual and relational. The merging of narrative with identity entails an analytical focus on the aspects of time, space and relationality. In her work, we also find a distinction between four different narrative levels. The first, ontological narratives, refers to stories social actors use to make sense of their lives, defining who we are, not just knowing what to do: 'Locating ourselves in narratives endows us with identities—however multiple, ambiguous, ephemeral or conflicting they may be (hence, the term narrative identity)' (Somers 1994: 18). Ontological narratives are tightly interwoven with both the second and the third narrative dimensions: public narratives and metanarratives, respectively. Public narratives refer to 'those narratives attached to cultural and institutional formations larger than the single individual, to intersubjective networks or institutions, however local or grand' (Somers 1994: 619). They vary in strength and range from the intimate narratives of the family to those emanating from the workplace, the church, governments and the nation. Metanarratives meanwhile are something we relate to and become entangled in as contemporary actors in history, often unconsciously (Somers 1994: 619). They are the grand cultural paradigms of how stories go, a narrative of progress or the Enlightenment for instance. This chapter deals specifically with the metanarratives of Eastern and Western Europe and the way they influence Central and Eastern European students' mobility aspirations. Finally, Somers speaks of a fourth level, conceptual narratives, that is, the ideas used by researchers in the process of making explanations.

Travel during Communism

My analysis begins with an overview of interviewees' accounts of travel restrictions in their home countries during the era of communism. Overall, they presented a very similar picture of their parents' experiences of international travel, or rather, the lack of it. As Paul highlighted when I interviewed him in his hometown in rural Romania: 'My parents were brought up here and they live here and they have lived here all their lives.' Apart from occasional trips to neighbouring Hungary, his parents travel only within Romania. Paul added, 'My sister and I were probably the first [in my family] who went abroad more often.' In sharp contrast to their parents, both Paul and his sister have visited and lived for long periods in various foreign countries. In addition to having a master's degree from a Danish university, Paul is currently studying for a PhD in Ireland and has no plan to return to Romania. He belongs to the first generation for whom international travel is more or less a natural part of life. Like the rest of the interviewees, he can be placed in the category of what Szewczyk (2015: 155) termed 'European searchers,' referring to the people who grew up in a climate marked by widespread sociopolitical change and increased possibilities for mobile lifestyles in an expanding EU.

To understand the previous generations' lack of experience of international travel in Eastern European countries, an appreciation of historical context is essential. As already emphasised, freedom of movement within the communist block was limited for both foreign and local citizens, which kept international migration at very low levels. The 'draconian restrictions' (Bianchi and Stephenson 2014: 4) upheld by the communist regime did not, however, ban all tourist activities. Travel was predominantly organized by state enterprises, trade unions and youth organizations, and aimed at cultivating 'the ideal socialist citizen' (Bianchi and Stephenson 2014: 4), with foreign travel largely restricted to other socialist countries (Horáková 2010). With communist era travel restrictions now belonging to the past, another interviewee, Ada, highlighted how both her well-educated parents remained strangers to border crossings, despite nothing in theory hindering them from exploring the world outside the Czech Republic. She interpreted this pattern as a relic of the past: 'Because the country was closed for many years, so I think that people just generally got used to living and travelling within the country.'

This partly involuntary immobility of previous generations was something the students were eager to discuss during the interviews, and many regarded this as pivotal to inspiring their own wanderlust. They emphasised that it was not an unwillingness to travel that restricted their parents' movement to countries inside the communist bloc but rather that people living under communism were forced to accept a more immobile lifestyle, as underlined by Etel:

> My parents could not travel because we were a member of the Soviet Bloc, but nobody asked them, they did not want to be a member of the Soviet Bloc, we were forced to be and nobody helped us. And in western Europe, you were so much luckier because you did not have that burden on you. (Etel, Hungary)

Even though Etel has lived all of her life after the fall of communism, she became agitated when talking about the east/west division that marked Europe in the latter part of the twentieth century. Thus, despite the fact that the students have no direct personal experience of life during communism, it constitutes an essential part of their collective memory and continues to affect how they experience the present (see also Roberts 2009). Etel clearly resented the restricted environment that characterized her parents' lives and she sees the communist period in an overwhelmingly negative light, a foreign element that was forced upon her native country against the will of many Hungarian citizens. Olga from Poland presented a similar narrative of her parents' mobility, who were young adults during the Soviet era:

> Well, they were born basically when the Soviet Union still existed, so when they were in their twenties, they could not just go abroad because of those restrictions from Russia and from the government in Poland. They could not do this. That was one reason. Another reason was that even if they could, there was always the financial matter because they did not come from wealthy families, they were quite poor. They were farmers, so they were not very wealthy. (Olga, Poland)

Olga's explanation recognizes another important obstacle to travel, namely the lack of sufficient financial means. There were however students whose parents were well-educated and, in a local context, earned a decent salary, but still could not travel due to lack of money. Even after the fall of the Iron Curtain, finance remains an obstacle. For instance, despite Jacob's parents working as a university lecturer and a high school teacher, respectively, he explained that they do not regard countries outside the EU as viable travel destinations because of the amount of money required. While people might enjoy greater freedom when it comes to international border crossing in theory, the marked difference in prices between Eastern and Western Europe is an obdurate obstacle for many who wish to visit the richer countries. However, despite this situation, and in contrast to their parents, many of the students have managed to build an impressive personal travel record, and their parents appear to have played an important role in encouraging them.

Travelling Narratives

While communism and a lack of finance seemingly restricted earlier generations' movement, especially to Western countries, the interviewees emphasised how their parents remained strongly oriented towards a broader world. As highlighted by Salazar (2011), a person's imagination may be in movement—travelling to other destinations that otherwise remain unapproachable—even if not physically moving. One example of this comes from the interview with Ania, who grew up in the Polish countryside as the eldest daughter of two hard-working farmers. Despite her parents' limited experience with international travel, Ania described how her mother idealized France to the point of teaching herself to speak fluent French. Her mother's language acquisition should be put in context, as it was not until fairly recently that she had the opportunity to visit France in person:

> I think my mother, she is very crazy about France and she speaks French fluently, and maybe she could imagine herself living in France, but once she had me, it was the most important thing for her. She finds France very… She thinks that people have very good taste, very good manners. Like everything is so sophisticated for her, like the music, she likes French music. And actually, she went to France for the first time this summer and so I'm very happy for her. It's still incredible that she speaks fluently French even though she has had no direct contact with the language. (Ania, Poland)

Ania presented a narrative of a woman who has remained oriented towards a world outside Poland in spite of her own limited travel experience. As the above quote indicates, France is considered to be a place that offers a superior mode of existence. Thus, from an early age, Ania has been influenced by her mother's narrative of France and the metanarrative of 'the West' as a highly dynamic, developed and progressive entity (Sztompka 2004).

While Ania's mother may have influenced her daughter imaginatively, many of the other students underlined that their parents were actively invested in opening their eyes to the world. Some described how they had been enrolled in international schools from an early age, while others were members of singing or dancing troupes that gave performances in the United Kingdom and France. Hence, from a very early age, they have had an awareness of an alternative mode of life compared to that of their immediate and familiar surroundings. Jacob, for instance, spent two months alone in the United States at a summer camp when he was 14 years old, supported by a scholarship he won in a competition. He explained that it was his mother who initially encouraged him to apply. In a similar fashion, Clara noted that it was her father who directed her attention towards the possibility of pursuing a master's degree outside Romania: 'So having him always telling me that [travelling] is a good thing ... actually he was the first one that came to suggest studying abroad.'

As was the case with Clara's father, some parents have invested substantial financial sums in facilitating their children's pursuit of an education abroad (see also Olwig and Valentin 2015). Etel also highlighted that her parents were '100 percent against' her moving back to Hungary and quitting her job in Denmark, where she has stayed and worked for several years following graduation. Both of her parents strongly believe that Denmark would be able to offer a superior life compared to Hungary, even though it means putting considerable geographical distance between her and her family.[2] Another characteristic of the students in this study is that their parents have urged them to pursue what they themselves were hindered in doing: exploring the world outside their national borders. As highlighted by Liechty (2003: 25), narratives flow through time; they are passed from generation to generation and carry the momentum of the past into the present, and onto dreams for the future. The interviewees described how their parents had passed on a positive narrative of travelling, where the act of travelling symbolizes 'the good life.'

In contrast to older generations, the informants also regard themselves as being fortunate in having grown up as part of a generation released from the restrictions of national borders, being able to choose their geographical coordinates more freely. Adam interpreted his parents' curtailed desires during the years of communism as fundamental to the fact that he was 'always attracted to travelling':

> It was my parents wish to travel when they were young but they couldn't travel a lot because there was communism and all that before 1989. So, they always wanted to travel but they couldn't. And in the 1990s, in the beginning after communism, everything was chaos because that is how countries are after 25 years of communism. [...] They always wanted to travel and they kind of genetically send me the wish also to travel. They always encouraged me to travel, to want to travel, to be interested in travelling to new places. (Adam, Romania)

Adam clearly connected his own desire to live abroad to his parents' high valuation of travelling. It seems that because it was such a rarity under communism, the mere act of travelling attains an intrinsic value—something which appears to have been passed on to the next generation. As Somers reminds us, narratives guide action. Therefore, this positive narrative of travelling and the students' ontological narratives as 'fortunate' provide part of the explanation as to why they are so eager to cross borders.

A Metanarrative of 'the West'

The period of communism strengthened the symbolic boundaries between Eastern and Western Europe, leaving a strong imprint on collective imaginations in post-socialist countries (see Verdery 1996). During a recent trip to Hungary's capital,

Budapest, I passed by a bar with a Scandinavian name and noticed several posters on the walls of the café where I was having lunch, which depicted life in the Scandinavian countries in various attractive ways: joyful bicycle rides in Copenhagen and tourists exploring the beautiful scenery of the Norwegian fjords. The young local waiter even informed me that the coffee beans served at that particular café originated from a small Danish micro roastery, as if this 'Danish touch' indicated superior quality. When asked about his experience of life in Budapest, he immediately drew attention to how the capital—despite its marked transformation since 1989—had a pronounced 'Eastern European vibe.' In an attempt to clarify what this 'Eastern Europeanness' entailed, he gave the example of the metro in Budapest which, due to its lack of ticket automatization, felt far 'less modern' than those typically found in Western Europe. Although our conversation was fairly short, it quickly became clear that he understood Europe as a continent 'divided into different zones of mastery over social, political and economic processes' (Vigh 2009: 94)—with Western Europe at the upper end of the development scale.

As has been touched upon, this way of contrasting Eastern and Western Europe in spatial and temporal dimensions also permeated the narratives provided by the interviewees. Their explanations indicate that they grew up influenced by a dominant metanarrative of 'the West' as more advanced, naturalized to the point where people seldom question it. The student interviewees not only inherited the urge to cross borders from the previous generation but also a firm belief in Western superiority. We observed this in Ania's portrayal of her mother, who viewed France as ultimate symbol of sophistication despite the fact that she had only visited the country for the first time relatively recently. In a similar manner, Paul described how Western Europe had been an object of desire for as long as he could remember. As a boy, he appreciated every step of what he interpreted as Romania's 'Westernization.'

After the revolution, they introduced Western style garbage bins in my town, and I remarked as a kid that Romania is becoming a Western country. For me, it all began with comparing Western and Eastern bins. (Paul, Romania)

Paul's childhood memories indicate how the metanarrative of 'the West,' as something positive and progressive, influenced him from a very early age. Similar to the symbolic status of the 'Danish' coffee beans at the café in Budapest, Paul regarded the garbage bins as 'emblems of Westernness' (Dombos 2008: 132), and he interpreted their arrival in Romania as signifying that the country was 'catching up' and developing into a more progressive country.

There are many stories from the student cohort that resembles Paul's account. Borge, who also grew up in Romania, described how he had dreamt of moving to 'the West' ever since he was a child. At one point, he even tried to escape to France when visiting Paris with a school group. While Borge's attempt to flee did not succeed, he argued that his long-term fascination with Western culture was highly influential to his later decision to pursue a master's degree in Denmark. Thus, in general, Denmark' geo-symbolic location in the metanarrative appears to be instrumental for the students' choice of study destination. The students' conviction that a university degree from a Western university would benefit their future career strengthens this assumption, as illustrated by Etel:

> [If] employers in Hungary see that I went to Western Europe and I did a degree in English [they will know that] I have a good level of English and that I was able to manage my life in Western Europe. And I think it's very positive, like something that I can stand out of the crowd with. (Etel, Hungary)

For Etel, this 'Western quality stamp' won out over other factors such as university rankings or the specific educational programme on offer. Adam, similarly, described how he did not want to study at universities in 'Arabian countries' despite the fact that they also offered free tuition. Paul also noted that he did not want to study in Russia even though the country in his opinion offered high-quality education. In line with Etel's reflections, both Adam and Paul attributed significant value to their university diploma being from a Western European university. Their explanations hence indicate how dominant metanarratives of Eastern and Western Europe, which have been highly salient from an early age, steer their cross border activities in certain geographical directions.

Conclusion

Various scholars have pointed out a positive correlation between experiencing mobility early in life, especially within families, and students having an interest in going abroad. However, little research exists on the drivers behind the mobility of students whose parents are less-experienced travellers, where border crossing has not been an integral part of their upbringing. Central and Eastern European students are an interesting case in the sense that they belong to the first generation to come of age with open borders in an expanding EU. Their level of spatial freedom thus stands in marked contrast to the societal realities that characterized previous generations, whose travel between 1945 and 1989 was strictly regulated by communist regimes.

In this chapter, I have focused on the narratives of incoming students from these countries in Denmark. While I am not denying that free tuition plays a role in the choice of Denmark as a study destination, the analysis seeks to highlight factors that have spurred the students' wanderlust in the first place. Assisted by Somers' narrative framework, I have shown how students often connect their parents' resentment with the travel restrictions prior to 1989 to their own wanderlust. Furthermore, they show how their parents have played an active role in encouraging them to do what they themselves were hindered from doing: to embrace every opportunity to taste life outside national borders. Thus, even though these parents have not been able to cross borders freely, they remained open to the world.

For this reason, I would argue that these parents have 'handed-down' a positive narrative relating to travel to their post-communist-era children, where crossing borders has intrinsic value. Following Somers, I argue that this positive narrative of travelling and the students' ontological narratives of being 'fortunate' not to be confined to the nation state guides their actions and, therefore, provides part of the explanation as to why they have been so eager to lead a mobile life. Beyond direct learning outcomes, educational mobility to Denmark means taking advantage of opportunities that previous generations were denied. Finally, I have highlighted how while growing up the students appear to have been influenced by a dominant metanarrative of 'the West' as more advanced than Eastern Europe. As such, the students have inherited not only the urge to travel from previous generations but also a firm belief in Western superiority, and this metanarrative of 'the West' seems to be pivotal in their mobility decision-making.

Acknowledgements This study was conducted as a part of a broader research project, *Internationalisation and Social Practice within the Field of Danish Higher Education*, funded by the Danish Independent Research Council (FKK).

Notes

1. Guth and Gill (2008) make somewhat similar arguments, stating that socio-economic factors and labour market characteristics in the sending and host countries have an influence on mobility decisions, albeit not in the traditional sense of moving abroad to earn more money. Instead, a key pull factor is the level of expenditure on science at foreign educational institutions.
2. The pivotal role played by parents in encouraging their children's international mobility is also found in an earlier study by Findlay et al. (2017), which suggested that an interest in an international studies and lifestyle is not only motivated by students but also, in some cases, strongly structured by parents.

References

Abbott, P., Wallace, C., Mascauteanu, M., & Sapsford, R. (2010). Concepts of citizenship, social and system integration among young people in post-Soviet Moldova. *Journal of Youth Studies, 13*(5), 581–596.
Bianchi, R. V., & Stephenson, M. L. (2014). *Tourism and citizenship: Rights, freedoms and responsibilities in the global order.* New York: Routledge.
Brooks, R., & Waters, J. (2011). *Student mobilities, migration and the internationalization of higher education.* Basingstoke: Palgrave Macmillan.
Cairns, D. (2014). *Youth transitions, international student mobility and spatial reflexivity: Being mobile?* Basingstoke: Palgrave Macmillan.
Carlson, S. (2013). Becoming a mobile student—A processual perspective on German degree student mobility. *Population, Space and Place, 19*(2), 168–180.
Dombos, T. (2008). 'Longing for the West': The geo-symbolics of the ethical consumption discourse in Hungary. In P. Luetchford, G. D. Neve, & J. Pratt (Eds.), *Hidden hands in the market: Ethnographies of fair trade, ethical consumption and corporate social responsibility* (pp. 123–141). Emerald Group Publishing.

Elliott, J. (2005). *Using narrative in social research: Qualitative and quantitative approaches.* London: Sage.
Ferber, A. L. (2000). A commentary on Aguirre: Taking narrative seriously. *Sociological Perspectives, 43*(2), 341–349.
Findlay, A., Prazeres, L., McCollum, D., & Packwood, H. (2017). 'It was always the plan': International study as 'learning to migrate'. *Area, 49*(2), 192–199.
Genova, E. (2016). To have both roots and wings: Nested identities in the case of Bulgarian students in the UK. *Identities, 23*(4), 392–406.
Guth, J., & Gill, B. (2008). Motivations in East-West doctoral mobility: Revisiting the question of brain drain. *Journal of Ethnic and Migration Studies, 34*(5), 825–841.
Horáková, H. (2010). Post-communist transformation of tourism in Czech rural areas: New dilemmas. *Anthropology Notebook, 16*(1), 59–77.
Liechty, M., (2003). Suitably modern: making middle-class culture in a new consumer society. Princeton University Press, Princeton, N.J.
Lulle, A., & Buzinska, L. (2017). Between a 'student abroad' and 'being from Latvia': Inequalities of access, prestige, and foreign-earned cultural capital. *Journal of Ethnic and Migration Studies, 43*(8), 1362–1378.
Marcu, S. (2015). Uneven mobility experiences: Life-strategy expectations among Eastern European undergraduate students in the UK and Spain. *Geoforum, 58*, 68–75.
Murphy-Lejeune, E. (2002). *Student mobility and narrative in Europe: The new strangers.* London: Routledge.
Olwig, K. F., & Valentin, K. (2015). Mobility, education and life trajectories: New and old migratory pathways. *Identities, 22*(3), 247–257.
Roberts, K. (2009). *Youth in transition: Eastern Europe and the West.* Basingstoke: Palgrave Macmillan.
Salazar, N. B. (2011). The power of imagination in transnational mobilities. *Identities, 18*(6), 576–598.
Somers, M. R. (1992). Narrativity, narrative identity, and social action: Rethinking English working-class formation. *Social Science History, 16*(4), 591–630.
Somers, M. R. (1994). The narrative constitution of identity: A relational and network approach. *Theory and Society, 23*(5), 605–649.
Szewczyk, A. (2015). 'European generation of migration': Change and agency in the post-2004 Polish graduates' migratory experience. *Geoforum, 60*, 153–162.
Sztompka, P. (2004). From East Europeans to Europeans: Shifting collective identities and symbolic boundaries in the New Europe. *European Review, 12*(4), 481–496.
UFM (2018). Offentlige indtægter og udgifter ved internationale studerende.
Van Mol, C., & Timmerman, C. (2014). Should I stay or should I go? An analysis of the determinants of intra-European student mobility. *Population, Space and Place, 20*(5), 465–479.
Verdery, K. (1996). *What was socialism and what comes next.* Princeton, NJ: Princeton University Press.
Vigh, H. (2009). Wayward migration: On imagined futures and technological voids. *Ethnos, 74*(1), 91–109.
Walker, C., & Stephenson, S. (2010). Youth and social change in Eastern Europe and the former Soviet Union. *Journal of Youth Studies, 13*(5), 521–532.
Wilken, L., & Dahlberg, M. G. (2017). Between international student mobility and work migration: Experiences of students from EU's newer member states in Denmark. *Journal of Ethnic and Migration Studies, 43*(8), 1347–1361.

Chapter 6
Unpacking the Mobility Capacities and Imperatives of the 'Global Generation'

Paula Pustulka and Dominika Winogrodzka

This chapter looks at the changing face of Polish young people's mobility. We aim to demonstrate that while people born between 1984 and 1990 might, to some degree, continue the migratory modes of previous generations and older cohorts (see, e.g., Szewczyk 2015; Grabowska and Jastrzębowska 2019), they might also perceive themselves as being 'mobile' rather than being 'migrants' in the classical sense of the term (Pustulka et al. 2019). We will attempt to show that their patterns of border crossings go beyond the typical economic motivations that can be linked to structural conditions and high mobility imperatives (Cairns 2018). On the contrary, the young adults we have interviewed experience 'mobile transitions' (Robertson et al. 2018) and exercise their 'mobility capacity' (Cairns 2018) somewhat independently of negative pressures. As we will attempt to argue, the young Poles who participated in our research, all of whom had tertiary education level qualifications, appear to have quite similar characteristics to mobile young people from other, mostly Western/Northern European sending states (Cairns 2014; Cuzzocrea and Mandich 2016; King et al. 2016), situating them within what can be termed a new 'mobile generation of choice' (Pustulka et al. 2019).

This is not to say that economic migration has disappeared, but rather, we can no longer assume that such motivation has universal pertinence, particularly as this would obscure the importance of the highly variegated mobility capacity many Polish young adults seem to possess. In broader terms, we contend that Poles born in the late 1980s and early 1990s have cosmopolitan dispositions (King and Ruiz-Gelices 2003; Skrbis et al. 2014), and are staking a claim to be part of the 'global generation' (Beck 2008). More specifically, we empirically test the assumptions

---

P. Pustulka (✉) • D. Winogrodzka
SWPS University of Social Sciences and Humanities, Warsaw, Poland
e-mail: ppustulka@swps.edu.pl

made about the relationship between mobility imperatives and capacities. Using aspects of Cairns' (2018) typology, we illustrate how profound social change in Poland during recent decades has transformed our understanding of youth spatiality, focusing on the so-called idea of 'multiple migrants' (Salamońska 2017): young people who engage in various types of educational, career-driven and lifestyle mobilities (see also King et al. 2016).

Mobile Polish Young People Today

The broad conceptual inspirations of this chapter can be related back to 'the mobility turn' in sociology (Urry 2007) and an understanding of young people's lives as being increasingly 'on the move,' typified as transnational and nomadic (Frändberg 2014; Yoon 2014). This position directly relates to looking at youth mobility as a diversified practice in terms of durations, destinations and motivations (Cairns 2014; Cuzzocrea and Mandich 2016; King et al. 2016) rather than migration driven by relatively straightforward economic imperatives (see also Robertson et al. 2018). Taking into account this viewpoint, we seek to distinguish young people from Poland, specifically those who engaged in mobility during early adulthood in the late 2000s and 2010s, from their counterparts who partook in the outgoing migration flows of the 1980s, 1990s and early 2000s (see also Pustulka et al. 2019), representing a break with the sentiment of previous studies that have consistently—and for the most part correctly—positioned Poland as a semi-peripheral 'stockpile' of cheap labour for Western and Northern Europe centres of employment (Ślusarczyk and Pustulka 2016).

In the past, a focus on the structural shortcomings of the home state has meant that Polish migration has been predominantly studied through the prism of economic necessity and earning money (see, e.g., Kaczmarczyk and Okólski 2008). Taking this perspective has been justified by drawing attention to subpar employment conditions and poor prospects in Poland prior to 2004, especially for young graduates, something that has been viewed as a push factor for people searching for a better future elsewhere (Szewczyk 2015); even those born in the 1970s and early 1980s tended to start their migrant journeys by taking on 6D-jobs in the secondary sectors of Western economies (Eade et al. 2007). There has however been a shift in economic prosperity in post-2004 EU accession Poland. Beyond being one of the few countries to avoid major implications associated with the 2008 global financial crisis, mass migration reduced internal competitiveness and altered the prospects for those born roughly a decade later. We also need to consider people with other motivations. Besides family migrants (Ryan 2011), Polish students are recognized as being highly active in international scholarship and degree programmes (Feyen and Krzaklewska 2013), and complementary observations about lifestyle mobility have been put forward. Consequently, migration researchers are now able to focus on Poles who are 'chasing' certain global orientations that relate to paradigms that are defined by transnationalism and an orientation towards multiple mobilities, attesting to the permeability of cosmopolitan ideas about space and belonging.

Theorizing around the traits of the global generation, especially as propounded by Beck (2008), we can acknowledge the new, or at least relatively recent, phenomenon of a cosmopolitan culture of immediacy, typifying the 'common present' of constantly connected youth. Crucially, Beck specifically states:

> The active global generation is definitely not the Western, but the non-Western generation, rising up against inequality across nation state borders, putting down a claim on equality. 'I want in' is the watchword of this worldwide generation standing at the gates of the Western societies and vigorously rattling the bars. (Beck 2008: 208)

This position strengthens the validity of our empirical exploration of Polish youth, often still seen as a mobile semi-periphery (see Ślusarczyk and Pustulka 2016). Beck's focus on the challenges of global risk generation (e.g. precarization and climate change) intersect with migration dreams and aspirations. We can see this framework's connectivity to the idea of 'spatial reflexivity,' defined as a 'recognition of the importance of geographical movement and acting upon this realization' (Cairns 2014: 28). This points towards choosing 'a life' rather than subscribing to a lifestyle (ibid.).[1] This position helps explain why we fully acknowledge that mobility is an unevenly distributed resource (Skrbis et al. 2014), but nevertheless argue that mobility via spatial reflexivity can enhance certain strengths or capacities.

In our argument, we concur with King et al. (2016) in regard to the spatial mobility of young Europeans crisscrossing with momentous transitions. Mobility/migration needs to be seen as a *rite de passage* to adulthood (see Eade et al. 2007), relatively explicitly in the Polish case (Sarnowska 2019). Static or universalizing topologies of movement also need to be revised when we talk about the experiences of young people. As Robertson et al. (2018: 7) advocate, contemporary trajectories of youth destabilize what we know about certain aspects of migration. For instance, the ideal types of youth mobility offered by King et al. (2016: 2), encompassing students and higher and lower skilled graduates seeking work, should become more granular as even temporary transnational experiences assist youth in the process of finding their 'true selves' (Yoon 2014: 1018–1022), as well as in forging 'mobility links' that may have long-lasting effects on the life course (Frändberg 2014), and make an impact upon a distinctly European sense of belonging and subsequent migration behaviour (King and Ruiz-Gelices 2003).

Within the variety of mobility pathways open to youth, it is vital to note the extra-monetary reasoning in mobility narratives often found in education/student mobility, something that has helped propel researchers to speak of the 'generation Erasmus' in relation to 'credit mobility' cohort experiences. Together with 'diploma mobility'—or undergoing an entire degree course abroad—these types of migration are strongly related to the idea of borderless higher education in the EU (Davies 2001). At an individual level, they often signal transnational professionalization pursuits in a world seen as open and global. 'Post-diploma' cross-border movement meanwhile describes the circulation of graduates, who may not be entirely focused on a singular reason for moving, instead looking for work, training or educational opportunities (Cairns 2014), seeking out humanitarian/voluntary engagements (Simpson 2004) or just wanting a change concurrent within broader trends in lifestyle migration (Benson and O'Reilly 2009).[2] What is crucial to note is that rather than being mutually exclusive, these different types of mobility can co-exist and may even be interlaced with one another (Robertson et al. 2018).

When we examine youth mobility and mobile transitions, we need to consider not only the (inner) motivations behind mobility but also the possibilities and barriers within the phenomenon. To capture these factors in youth migration, the concepts of 'mobility capacity' and 'mobility imperative' (Cairns 2018) are especially fitting. These ideas not only go beyond traditional 'push and pull' theories about origin and destination, but also allow an interplay of factors from a macrostructural layer to take place (see also Van Mol and Timmerman 2014), with traits, aspirations and desires that are individualized and form the backbone of the 'mobile generation of choice' (Pustulka et al. 2019).

'Mobility capacities' encompass the usually positive attributes associated with personal situation, such as socio-economic background, as well as family and peer resources. Internationally transferable skills and credentials, fluency in foreign language(s), having financial means and an emotional support system or the presence of family and peers abroad are some of the capacity examples we explore in this paper. In that sense, one of the key capabilities guiding our analysis relates to thinking spatially: 'not only on what to do but also where to do it' (Cairns 2018: 472), also taking a broad strokes approach to an accumulated human, social and spatial capital that can be mobilized beyond borders.

Moving on, 'mobility imperatives' can be ascribed to the often more negative, structurally challenging or 'pushing-out' aspects of present place of residence. This notion accords with recognizing the significance of a macro-economic context of labour market and welfare that individuals encounter, with their mobility imperatives comprised of features such as limited local opportunities, the promise of better-paid work or more security of tenure abroad, and local cultural insularity that limits horizons. Consequently, the more globalized ideas of 'mobile capacity' (individual traits, networks, resources) and a quite localized 'mobile imperative' (societal conditions and pressures) recognize the importance of a broad spectrum of subjective considerations and objective conditions, demonstrating how the personal choices of young people are mediated by circumstances at meso and macro levels.

Data and Methods

The empirical material used for the analysis stems from a project entitled, *Education-to-domestic and foreign labour market transitions of youth: The role of locality, peer group and new media*. This research is a four-year qualitative longitudinal study (QLS) using a format developed by Neale (2019), carried out in three waves of in-depth interviews (IDIs) with international and internal migrants from three mid-sized towns in Poland (see also Pustulka et al. 2017).[3] We adopt a lens of 'walking alongside' the interviewees to observe the shifts in their life transitions and pathways, migration notwithstanding.

While the entire dataset is comprised of close to 200 interviews, in this chapter we use a sub-sample of 20 interviews carried out with ten migrants. This means that we will utilize data from Wave 1 and Wave 2 of the project, conducting a case study–level analysis rooted in an explanatory approach (Stake 2008). At every stage, the project adhered to rigorous ethical standards about anonymity and internal confidentiality characteristic of QLS projects (Pustulka et al. 2017: 55–56). All interviews were meticulously transcribed and coded. For the purpose of the analysis included in this chapter, the original material was subject to open recoding.

The selection covers a broad range of examples representing Poles with various, extra-economic rationales in their international mobility narratives. Our ten case analyses concern two men and eight women born between 1984 and 1990, interviewed in 2016 and 2018, respectively. While they all have university degrees, they come from heterogeneous, small-town backgrounds and currently work in diverse fields. Most importantly, they are all multiple migrants (Salamońska 2017) in the age that enables them to experience 'mobile transitions' (Robertson et al. 2018) during varied international mobility trajectories (Table 6.1).

Table 6.1 Mobility pathways of the selected case study interviewees

Ada 1990	Credit mobility to Hungary; post-diploma mobility to United Arab Emirates; currently transnational commuting between United Arab Emirates and Poland
Anna 1986	Credit mobility to Spain; seasonal migration to the United Kingdom and Greece; international volunteering in Brazil; lifestyle migration to India, Nepal and Balkans; currently in Poland
Beata 1984	Economic migration and credit mobility to Italy; post-diploma mobility to Switzerland and the United Kingdom; currently in the United Kingdom
Daria 1990	Economic migration to Spain; post-diploma mobility to the United Kingdom; currently 'transnational commuting' between the United Kingdom and Poland
Iga 1990	Seasonal economic migration to Italy and the United Kingdom; currently 'lifestyle migration' to Mexico
Kamil 1987	Diploma mobility to France; international internships in Egypt, Spain and the United Kingdom; post-diploma mobility to the United Kingdom; currently in the United Kingdom
Klara 1986	Seasonal migration to Ireland; post-diploma mobility to the United States; currently in Poland
Marek 1988	International internship in Germany; post-diploma mobility to Germany; currently in Germany
Natalia 1989	Credit mobility to France; international volunteering in Honduras, currently in Poland
Olena 1989	Credit mobility to Denmark, post-diploma mobility to the United States, currently in Poland

Lasting Significance of Mobility Imperatives among Polish Youth

In this section, we focus on mobility imperatives, with demonstrable continuity between Millennials and previous cohorts of migrants from Poland. One of the repeatedly expressed convictions shared by the participants involved a vocal contestation of their places of origin: 'It's a very nice place to grow up, but it is not somewhere for one to live in later' (Anna). This indicates that the interviewed Polish migrant young people are drawing interesting boundaries between their home locality/country and the broader, global world. While they were reticent to renounce their roots, they drew attention to the sociopolitical context of Poland as a post-transformation society and alluded to a pronounced elder deferential work culture, often connected to young people's broader perceptions of a widespread corruption (see also Długosz 2016):

> There is no work here. In many places, the 'old guard' work. (…) People who don't have connections, acquaintances … it is harder for them to find a job that would suit them or simply allow for a fairly decent life. (Kamil)

Thus, the interviewees clearly understood that the capital they had accumulated over time no longer fitted with what was required within the socio-spatial contexts in which they grew up. For many of them, forging the boundary-less career paths they aspired to came within the scope of their job searches, which had expanded to encompass offers from abroad, mostly for structural reasons. Illustrating limited local opportunities and insufficient life chances in the place of origins, the participants remarked:

> In (my hometown), the labour market situation is not too bright in the long run. (Olena)

> I had a feeling that I was simply choking there, I didn't want to be there, needed something else. (Iga)

We can see that the 'pushing-out' aspects of the place of origin are just as much about the structural aspects, like low salaries or corruption, as they are a function of individually desirous career aspirations. These realizations, early on, resulted in internal educational mobility decision:

> It is automatically understood that people move out of X to study. (Olena)

> I wanted to study. This possibility doesn't exist in my city, so I had to leave. (Marek)

And the claim about internal mobility being a common stepping stone for international migration (Sarnowska 2019) is connected with local cultural insularity:

> I would like to change the mentality of people in the city a bit, make them more open, a little more tolerant, a little more curious about the world. (Kamil)

Such localism is even more noticeable after a mobility experience, as the perceptions of insularity came to be extended to Poland as a whole:

> Poland has a bit of a climate that there are two political parties and we will argue which is better. People can't go beyond that. They're sitting in this sauce until they go somewhere abroad. (Anna)

This was seen by the young participants as something that limited their horizons and produced a culture of fear. Natalia observed this in the reactions to her decision to take part in the Erasmus programme:

> When I was going to Paris, some said, '(what if) you have no (money)', others said 'you might not find friends' (and) 'are you not afraid that you will not manage at the university?' Everyone had their own idea about why I would fail.

On this note, looking at a gamut of imperatives, it is easy to discern mobility impulses in the shape of success stories from other migrants who operate as important reference points:

> All in all, I never wanted to leave because I felt very well at the university in Krakow. Krakow was my place (…). And, finally, my friend said that she got a job in Berlin, that she found an internship and will leave. (…) For me it was such an impulse. (Marek)

Concurring with the idea of membership of a global generation (Beck 2008), success stories are very often shared between peers. Below an interviewee explicitly talks about generational change, as well as aspirational and experiential components of youth mobility:

> We live in a very globalized world today. Social media (…), everything shows us that some people go abroad and try something (…) I don't want to say that they achieve something but they are experiencing something (…), so I think that Poles (from) my generation (…) think 'I don't want to be worse, I also want to have such an experience. Why can't I live in Paris for a while and eat breakfast overlooking the Eiffel Tower every morning? Why not?' (Kamil)

Our findings suggest that the 'pushing-out' components do not necessarily need to be tangible: it suffices that the Polish Millennials are prompted to seek study or work opportunities abroad because they imagine them to be better paid or, more likely, to have more security of tenure.

Concluding this section on imperatives, these interviewees demonstrate that structural factors and employment-related motivations cannot be disregarded, and in fact remain strong in many cases. In fact, we can see how they work alongside what might be described as the 'new' youth mobilities. Even with the diminishing presence of structural pressures and imperatives to move, youth mobility can still be narrated through a familiar structural prism. But the idea of mobility also functions as a kind of 'mental' escape from perceptions of social control and the 'small world' of certain localities, which stands contraposed to imagined futures associated with the pursuit of high aspirations and global ambitions (Cuzzocrea and Mandich 2016; Moroşanu et al. 2018).

The Emerging 'Mobile Generation of Choice' and Mobility Capacities

As hinted above and based on an in-depth analysis of migration decision-making among interviewees, it seems that the mobility of these young adults stems less from a high mobility imperative, being more firmly rooted in possessing a high mobility capacity. Ada's statement illustrates this well:

> I was hungry, wanted more, had a desire to travel. I generally knew that there's more to life than just Poland, Warsaw. I don't know, it was such a strong conviction inside me that I wanted to see something else, try something abroad. (…) I was hungry for knowledge about different cultures, about people. (…). It was absolutely not caused by financial motivations.

From this account, we see an open discreditation of the idea that mobility can result from dissatisfaction with subpar conditions on the local labour market:

> I left the day after the final exams, so I didn't have this experience of, 'God, it's so hard in Poland, you can't find a job, you have to look for a better life.' I just went to college (abroad), and then I liked it so much (that) I settled, found a job, nice friends. So I stayed. (Daria)

Such an attitude is different from the young graduates in Poland before 2004 who migrated, mainly, to search for better futures elsewhere (Szewczyk 2015), and having even less in common with the escapist and survivalist strategies from the past (see Slany and Małek 2005). The narratives of Anna, Beata, Natalia, Marek and Olena, all of whom experienced educational/student mobility, fit under the umbrella of the 'generation Erasmus' and indicate self-actualizing, extra-monetary rationales for going abroad (see Davies 2001; King and Ruiz-Gelices 2003; Feyen and Krzaklewska 2013). Often, credit and post-diploma mobility are interconnected, as young people's biographies are rooted in subsequent mobilities within peer networks:

> The relationship with Janek (…) was important to me. (…) He studied in two countries and he motivated me to do Erasmus (…). I owe him my motivation to travel. (Natalia)

As representatives of 'diploma' or 'post-diploma' mobility trajectories, Kamil, Klara and Marek all placed emphasis on self-development and transnational professionalization as the main reasons for their moves:

> I was considering moving back to Poland (…) but then got an offer (to continue) in Frankfurt. This was a large design company, very well known in France. This was very enticing for me and I liked it a lot. I was learning a lot of things there. (Marek)

Evidently, thinking in transnational categories about educational and professional paths indicates a cosmopolitan perspective of the 'global generation' (Beck 2008), shaped by the spread of the English language and awareness of continental labour markets, but emanating in non-westerners' drive:

> I like to feel that the world belongs to me and I am everywhere at home and I can go anywhere. (Anna)

> I knew that I felt at home in an international setting. I never had—even for a moment—a realisation when I thought, 'What am I doing here? I totally don't fit', just the opposite! I wanted more and more of this. (Ada)

The findings of our study suggest that one of the strongest capacity components among the Polish 'mobile generation of choice' in fact concerns internationally transferable skills and credentials acquired in Poland, and globally, especially foreign language fluency. Representatives of generation Y start formal and informal language education early, consequently improving their skills during university and work. They understand that being multilingual can be a platform for international success:

> I wanted to speak as many languages as possible. I wanted to focus on languages because this was – for me – a stepping stone for leaping out into the world. Language education – learning English, French, Spanish – completely dominated my degree choices and then contributed – or perhaps could have been the main factor – of my going abroad, migrating. (Kamil, currently learning Portuguese as well)

Foreign language fluency and linguistic boldness has an effect on ease of communication with other people but also denotes the capacity of being able to encounter foreign cultures with different competences:

> I have really improved my language skills. (…) This is also somewhat (related) to a cultural (development). It is a total cultural opening. (Natalia)

> (Learning foreign languages) simply broadens your horizons. (Anna)

These young people realize that living and working in different environments has allowed them to acquire the new capacities needed for 'making it' in the world, along with a global generational sense of personal identity. Additionally, these processes were conducive to self-growth, particularly in the realms of self-efficacy, independence and self-confidence. Through participation in prestigious, and well-paid, international internships, Kamil strengthened his self-assurance, self-worth and conviction, to the extent that he can afford to be picky about opportunities, saying:

> I didn't extend a contract in 2013 because the financial conditions they offered me didn't suit me. I just thought 'I can do better,' despite some fears related to the foreign labour market. I thought it would be harder for me because I'm young and Polish.

Kamil subsequently developed his career abroad successfully. In the same vein, Natalia decided to embark on a 16-month international volunteering placement in Central America and described her mobility experience as a 'spiritual gap year' favourable to personal growth. She believes it has fostered a personal transition for her:

> Thanks to migration, I have developed my personality and I have fought my fears, and have learnt to overcome my limits. (…) I learned there that my professional achievements or how many languages I speak are not necessarily important, but it is just (about) who I am.

Iga, who travelled to North America, also pointed out some of the inner workings of a high mobility capacity and the facet of finding one's 'true self' (Yoon 2014):

> I'm more open to taking risks. It is thanks to going abroad. (…) I no longer care that much about things that I was worried about before. I just know that there are so many options out there, many things that you can do and you really don't need to agree to be put in a situation that you don't enjoy.

The presented stories help account for the link between spatial and social mobility, or 'motility' (Kaufmann et al. 2004), is very much present in Polish young people's capital mobilization, recognition and actualization. Additionally, we see its strong impact on transferable competencies, which are mediated by foreign language fluency. This tends to change aspirations in a temporal perspective. While they rarely recalled societal validation of mobility as a life planning strategy, when it did happen, they felt pride and awe:

> Everyone's jaws just dropped when I managed to get (this offer). They were all so happy (…) because this was the best thing, best contract, that you could get as a young person who wants to go abroad and get international experience. (Kamil)

In the case of the Polish 'mobile generation of choice,' success associated with mobility substantiates the decision to become a migrant, in accordance with what Cairns (2014: 32) describes as the 'impetus for movement (being) sustained and multiplied via a process of reflection, thus creating a mobility capacity for the life course and not just the youth phase.' At the same time, descriptions of societal validation of mobility during youth, such as adventurous experimentation and delaying adulthood, also appeared:

> So I thought, okay, I am young, I have the opportunity to see something before the moment when I will settle down and before I have children. It would be worth using this time. (Ada)

Just like Marek, who needed a 'friend-trigger' to move to Germany, others also talked about initial mobility experiences as 'turning points' (Neale 2019) that opened them up to an alternative array of pathways for the future:

> I was just looking for something, some experience after this Erasmus and I didn't want to go back to Poland, I just wanted to experience something else. (Natalia)

> I think I caught the bug. (…) I was an Erasmus student in Budapest and then wanted more. (Ada)

Quite evidently, credit mobility enhances curiosity and the willingness to travel, stimulating further youth mobility. Besides peer influences discussed above, support from educators is not without significance here:

> I went for the Erasmus because of the people I met during my studies. (…) For example, I had a very nice French language mentor who motivated us from the first year about (Erasmus) being the best experience we can have. She believed in us and she said that I would manage (as opposed to people from my local community who said I wouldn't). (Natalia)

In Natalia's story, a recognized capacity overpowered a localism imperative. Often intangible support from educators might indirectly facilitate generally empowered attitudes and behaviours:

> (Middle-school) was absolutely awesome (…), had a big impact on what steps I have taken. (…) I felt I could actually be myself there more rather than just fit into boxes. (Iga)

> I achieved a lot (in high school): I met a lot of cool people, I decided what I wanted to do (and) what I didn't want to do, which was just as important. (It) directed me towards my current life. (Kamil)

Moving onto other factors, financial and emotional support from parents seems to be equally meaningful in defining mobility pathways. In addition to straightforward encouragement, the parents of the interviewed Polish millennials influenced their decision to leave indirectly by choosing socialization practices conducive to heterogeneous life-views (Sarnowska 2019). This position held even for parents without migration experience:

> Nobody travelled at home but my dad had travel books. (…) As a little girl, I read them and was so excited that you can just let everything go and go hitchhiking without money. (Iga)

Our study participants narrated the emotional and financial support they received from their parents at various stages of their lives, and in the context of mobility:

> (My parents) had no problem (with migration). My dad would like me to be in X, although he realizes that I can't imagine living (there). (…) My mother (…) would like to see me more often, like any mother would, but there was never a problem when I wanted to leave. They supported me in this and really always helped. When my financial situation got difficult, I could always count on them. (Marek)

Simultaneous with parents being the agents of societal endorsement and validation of mobility (capacity), young people treated the parental 'safety cushion' as a bonus:

> I have a family and I know that they will help me if I need it. I'm not in a situation where I'd be without food, without means of subsistence, without a roof over my head. (…) It gives you the feeling that you can take a risk, you can be destitute in the middle of nowhere and somehow it will be (fine). (Anna)

In the last collection of quotations, Polish Millennials display strong similarities with their counterpart Europeans in the global generation, often taking gap years and engaging in nomadic or voluntarism motivated journeys (see Vogt 2018). It needs to be reiterated that—unlike their parents—our interviewees did not connote mobility with instability. Conversely, the persistence of 'living on the move' is not an aberration but is rather a well-founded personal goal and craving (Pustulka et al. 2019).

Contemporary youth mobility breaks away from both economic (Kaczmarczyk and Okólski 2008) and family migration (Ryan 2011) as pillars of border crossing popular among older generations. The interviewees are largely unbounded by families and delay their transitions to adulthood. Nowadays, individualized migration decision-making and behaviours can be spotted as Polish young migrants are largely single and childless, so the presence of family abroad has little significance. Nevertheless, diffuse and 'weak' ties are exemplified by how previous migration experience in the family of origin provoked mobility aspirations of the young people.

> I think my aunt who worked for a very long time in Germany had a big impact on all these travels of mine. (…) She would visit and have various things that we could not get in Poland, sweets and stuff. (…) So she was an influence on my decision to search for a job abroad. (Ada)

Such accounts can be interpreted as a long-term socialization into mobility but are also indicative of a broader turn: although the interviewees are demographically at the stage of transitioning to adulthood, the spatial aspect of their life remains intentionally unresolved:

> Many options are open, I don't lock myself down to a place. (Iga)

> I am just at the exploration stage and I chose this job (requiring mobility) to see (the world), get to know a lot of different cultures and places, and just choose the one place that I will like the most. For now, I can't tell you where I would like to live. (Ada)

Conclusions: A Global Generation with Spatial Reflexivity as a Key Mobility Capacity?

Acknowledging social continuity and change, we can argue that economic migration motivations have not disappeared, but have been diluted by other non-financial factors. The stories shared by our interviewees are spatial and temporal, reminiscent of what usually emerges from Western European youth narratives (King et al. 2016), yet with a clearer indication that researchers must adopt a nuanced perspective towards youth mobility: as heterogeneous, multifaceted and non-linear (see also Robertson et al. 2018). Despite coming from small-in-population localities with some mobility imperatives, educated multiple migrants from Poland downplay these factors in their decision-making, and talk more about their personal mobility capacity (Cairns 2018) and motility (Kaufmann et al. 2004), enabled through 'taking time out' (Eade et al. 2007; Pustulka et al. 2019). It would therefore seem to be the case that unlike the cohorts studied by Szewczyk (2015), Millennials are the first generation to have forged their identities in a borderless Europe, perceiving the EU as a shared and available space.

For our interviewees, the lack of anchoring is not just the result of mobile imperatives but also reflexivity rooted in self-efficacy impelled by an exceptionally strong mobility capacity. For this reason, we argue that Polish young people are much more transnational and mobility oriented, and their journeys represent a form of mobility by choice propelled through spatial reflexivity (Cairns 2018), as well as being connected to cosmopolitan ideas about space and belonging (King and Ruiz-Gelices 2003; Beck 2008). The interviewees did not subjectively internalize the high mobility imperative in Poland, instead claiming its objective obverse: a high mobility capacity that typifies an ideal type of European youth mobility. We also argue that a low mobility imperative can be overpowered by a high mobility capacity, resulting in the high probability of international mobility taking place, even in the absence of major structural considerations. The nature of 'small worlds' not only mobilizes people to leave but also prevents them from returning, especially when they try to resist traditional norms pertaining to employment, family or sexuality (Moroşanu et al., 2018).

The findings discussed previously confirm that contemporary forms of mobility (i.e. 'diploma' and 'post-diploma mobility,' international humanitarian/voluntary engagements or lifestyle migration) intersect with momentous transitions (see King et al. 2016), and also, in the Polish case, we find an illumination of the pervasiveness of the cosmopolitan and global generational aspirations of youth across Europe. Among all the aspects of mobility capacities found in our data, perhaps the most conspicuous one entailed 'spatial reflexivity' and the ability to think geographically about life choices (Cairns 2018). This coincides with aspiring to be part of a 'global generation' (Beck 2008) on several planes. First, it is evident in the socio-spatial contestations of the home localities, and especially vivid for Polish millennials who come from dilapidated European urban peripheries. In line with Beck's arguments, as aspiring Westerners, they seem prone to seeing themselves as outliers wanting much more that is locally available. Secondly, as we have argued elsewhere (Pustulka et al. 2019), international migrants from the Polish 1984–1990 cohort belong to what we call a 'mobile generation of choice': these young adults make their migratory decisions autonomously and in a clearly individualized manner. Through spatial reflexivity, they describe being constantly in motion and moving around the world as something that suits them.

Notes

1. 'Lifestyle' is also a term that is relevant to discussions about 'motility,' which conceptually conjoins spatial and social mobility, and ascribes the capitalization of movement to those who have power over access, competence and appropriation (Kaufmann et al. 2004).
2. In addition, European youth are prone to interspersing their educational milestones with a 'gap year' between secondary and tertiary education, or as a postgraduate intermission preceding other pursuits (Simpson 2004; Vogt 2018).
3. The project *Education-to-domestic and foreign labour market transitions of youth: The role of locality, peer group and new media* is funded by the National Science Centre Poland under the Sonata Bis Project Contract. No. 2015/18/E/HS6/00147.

References

Beck, U. (2008). Global generations in world risk society. *Revista CIDOB d'Afers Internacionals, 82*(83), 203–216.

Benson, M., & O'Reilly, K. (Eds.). (2009). *Lifestyle migration: Expectations, aspirations and experiences*. Aldershot: Ashgate.

Cairns, D. (2014). *Youth transitions, international student mobility and spatial reflexivity: Being mobile?* Basingstoke: Palgrave Macmillan.

Cairns, D. (2018). Mapping the youth mobility field. Youth sociology and student mobility and migration in a European context. In A. Lange, H. Reiter, S. Schutter, & C. Steiner (Eds.), *Handbuch Kindheits- und Jugendsoziologie* (pp. 463–478). Wiesbaden: Springer.

Cuzzocrea, V., & Mandich, G. (2016). Students' narratives of the future: Imagined mobilities as forms of youth agency? *Journal of Youth Studies, 19*(4), 552–567.

Davies, J. L. (2001). Borderless higher education in continental Europe. *Minerva, 39*(1), 27–48.

Długosz, P. (2016). Pokolenie przegranych? Kondycja psychospołeczna młodzieży w Europie Środkowo-Wschodniej. *Zeszyty Pracy Socjalnej, 21*(2), 77–90.

Eade, J., Drinkwater, S., & Garapich, M. (2007). *Class and ethnicity—Polish migrants in London.* Surrey: University of Surrey.

Feyen, B., & Krzaklewska, E. (2013). The Erasmus programme and the 'generation Erasmus'—A short overview. In F. Feyen & E. Krzaklewska (Eds.), *The Erasmus phenomenon—Symbol of a new European generation* (pp. 9–20). Frankfurt: Peter Lang.

Frändberg, L. (2014). Temporary transnational youth migration and its mobility links. *Mobilities, 9*(1), 146–164.

Grabowska, I., & Jastrzębowska, A. (2019). The impact of migration on human capacities of two generations of poles. The interplay of the individual and the social in human capital approaches. *Journal of Ethnic and Migration Studies.* https://doi.org/10.1080/1369183X.2019.1679414.

Kaczmarczyk, P., & Okólski, M. (2008). Demographic and labour-market impacts of migration on Poland. *Oxford Review of Economic Policy, 24*(3), 599–624.

Kaufmann, V., Bergman, M. M., & Joye, D. (2004). Motility: Mobility as capital. *International Journal of Urban and Regional Research, 28*(4), 745–756.

King, R., & Ruiz-Gelices, E. (2003). International student migration and the European 'year abroad': Effects on European identity and subsequent migration behaviour. *International Journal of Population Geography, 9*(3), 229–252.

King, R., Lulle, A., Morosanu, L., & Williams, A. (2016). *International youth mobility and life transitions in Europe: Questions, definitions, typologies and theoretical approaches.* Working Paper No. 86, University of Sussex, Sussex Centre for Migration Research, Sussex.

Moroşanu, L., Bulat, A., Mazzilli, C., & King, R. (2018). Growing up abroad: Italian and Romanian migrants' partial transitions to adulthood. *Ethnic and Racial Studies, 45*(9), 1554–1573.

Neale, B. (2019). *What is qualitative longitudinal research?* London: Bloomsbury.

Pustulka, P., Juchniewicz, N., & Grabowska, I. (2017). Participant recruitment challenges in researching peer groups and migration retrospectively. *Przegląd Socjologii Jakościowej, 13*(4), 48–69.

Pustulka, P., Winogrodzka, D., Buler, M. (2019). Mobilne pokolenie wyboru. Migracje międzynarodowe a płeć i role rodzinne wśród Milenialsek. *Studia Migracyjne—Przegląd Polonijny, 4*(174), 139–164.

Robertson, S., Harris, A., & Baldassar, L. (2018). Mobile transitions: A conceptual framework for researching a generation on the move. *Journal of Youth Studies, 21*(2), 203–217.

Ryan, L. (2011). Transnational relations: Family migration among recent Polish migrants in London. *International Migration, 49*(2), 80–103.

Salamońska, J. (2017). Multiple migration—Researching the multiple temporalities and spatialities of migration. *CMR Working Papers, 102*(160).

Sarnowska, J. (2019). Efekty wąskiej i szerokiej socjalizacji dla trajektorii migracyjnych młodych dorosłych. *Studia Migracyjne—Przegląd Polonijny, 1*(171), 61–83.

Simpson, K. (2004). 'Doing development:' The gap year, volunteer-tourists and a popular practice of development. *Journal of International Development: The Journal of the Development Studies Association, 16*(5), 681–692.

Skrbis, Z., Woodward, I., & Bean, C. (2014). Seeds of cosmopolitan future? Young people and their aspirations for future mobility. *Journal of Youth Studies, 17*(5), 614–625.

Slany, K., & Małek, A. (2005). Female emigration from Poland during the period of the systemic transformation. In K. Slany (Ed.), *International migration. A multidimensional analysis* (pp. 115–154). Kraków: AGH Press.

Ślusarczyk, M., & Pustulka, P. (2016). Mobile peripheries? Contesting and negotiating peripheries in the global era of mobility. In E. Peeren, H. Stuit, & A. van Weyenberg (Eds.), *Peripheral visions in the globalizing present* (pp. 141–163). New York: Brill/Rodopi.

Stake, R. (2008). Qualitative case studies. In N. K. Denzin & Y. S. Lincoln (Eds.), *Strategies of qualitative inquiry* (pp. 119–149). Thousand Oaks: Sage.

Szewczyk, A. (2015). European Generation of Migration: Change and agency in the post-2004 Polish graduates migratory experience. *Geoforum, 60*, 153–162.

Urry, J. (2007). *Mobilities*. Cambridge: Polity.

Van Mol, C., & Timmerman, C. (2014). Should I stay or should I go? An analysis of the determinants of intra-European student mobility. *Population, Space and Place, 20*, 465–479.

Vogt, K. C. (2018). The timing of a time out: The gap year in life course context. *Journal of Education and Work, 31*(1), 47–58.

Yoon, K. (2014). Transnational youth mobility in the neoliberal economy of experience. *Journal of Youth Studies, 17*(8), 1014–1028.

Chapter 7
Why Student Mobility Does Not Automatically Lead to Better Understanding: Reflections on the Concept of Intercultural Learning

Thor-André Skrefsrud

Increased internationalization in tertiary education has drawn attention to student mobility as a means of enhancing students' intercultural understanding. As the speed and scale of migration and globalization changes societies, students need to develop the capacity to analyse and comprehend global issues, and learn how to interact respectfully with one another despite their cultural differences. This helps explain why, across secondary schools and universities, students are encouraged to globalize their experiences through encountering different cultures in international learning contexts, with studying abroad perceived as supporting and complementing students' intercultural competencies. In a similar vein, mobility programmes—such as Erasmus, AFS Intercultural Programmes and others—strongly emphasise that studying in a foreign learning context changes student lives in a positive manner (see Chap. 15 of this book). Through such programmes, students receive the opportunity to improve their cultural and linguistic skills, increase tolerance and broaden perceptions of 'the other.' Studying abroad is believed to make students more open-minded and less afraid of the strange and the stranger. The AFS Intercultural Programmes illustrate this as follows:

> We can agree that much of xenophobia or, more simply, fear of differences arises from stereotypes, gross exaggerations, misrepresentations and dehumanising 'the Other'. These stereotypes typically come from a lack of awareness, a lack of experience or a lack of understanding and empathy about people and ideas different from us. They derive from a lack of appreciation that there is no single way of being; that 'our' own ethnocentric way is not the way for most on this planet. (AFS Intercultural Programmes 2018: 1)

Here, we see how the AFS Intercultural Programme suggests that increasing levels of xenophobia in society are the result of people not respecting other people and having ideas different from the mainstream. Moreover, this lack of understanding

T.-A. Skrefsrud (✉)
Inland Norway University of Applied Sciences, Hamar, Norway
e-mail: thor.skrefsrud@inn.no

and empathy is closely related to a sea change in global politics, giving more weight to ethnocentric and nationalistic orientations in policies across Europe. International migration into and within the European Union has not necessarily enhanced people's cosmopolitan outlook. Instead, it may have led to increased scepticism and sometimes even hostility towards those who are different from what is perceived as 'normal.' Moreover, we are now witnessing a huge comeback from nationalist and right-wing populist parties, which have made significant electoral gains in most countries on the continent. Although these parties may differ fundamentally in terms of ideology and policies, they share some common themes, such as anti-immigrant and anti-Muslim sentiment, as well as a national-oriented—often EU-sceptical—rhetoric that criticizes globalization and cosmopolitanism. Within such a horizon, mobility programmes such as the AFS Intercultural Programmes aim to counteract stereotypes and make the unknown more familiar and thus less frightening:

> Our programmes – in particular our mobility or exchange programmes where young people leave the home they've grown up in to travel to an entirely different part of the world and become part of a new home, community and school – as well as our teacher and classroom trainings, our volunteer programmes and all of our materials, resources and events are designed to help make unknown become the known. They help transform 'the Other' into the sister, the brother, the mother, the father, the student, the friend. (AFS Intercultural Programmes 2018: 2)

The programmes' main idea is that the specific experience of being part of a new context provides several benefits with regard to enhancing multicultural competencies among youth and young adults, making them better equipped for interacting, communicating and engaging with others worldwide (e.g., Holmes et al. 2015). Thus, we can see a parallel to Allport's (1954) classical formulation of the contact hypothesis, suggesting that intergroup interaction and interpersonal contact can effectively reduce prejudice between people from different cultures and contexts. According to Allport, and not unlike Habermas' (1990) procedural ethics, positive contact experiences may arise in situations characterized by certain conditions, including equal status, intergroup cooperation, common goals and support from social and institutional authorities. Thus, by being placed in a completely different reality and everyday life, students who study abroad are assumed to be developing positive attitudes towards diversity and increasing their tolerance of ambiguity. The experience of being a minority and the challenges of adaptation that follow from this then, in theory, allow the students to better develop intercultural understanding. However, the intercultural claims made by international exchange programmes also raise issues in the research field.

Many scholars have in fact raised concerns regarding the transformative potential of student mobility programmes (e.g., Breen 2012; Klein and Wikan 2019; Sharpe 2015). In light of the trend towards shorter stays—for instance, when students live with a host family or on a campus for a few weeks during the school year or summer—one critique has been that students adopt a rather superficial understanding of cultural contexts, accepting student mobility may not always foster broader understanding but rather illustrate 'an ongoing employment of an objectifying tourist gaze,' and that students 'do not truly enter the culture' (Sharpe 2015: 228) and suffer from a lack of attention towards 'how people are bound to other economies, nations and peoples, which thus reinforces an "othering" process between visitor and host community' (Klein and Wikan 2019: 99).

This last point illustrates perhaps the most serious critique from various post-colonial scholars, who have asked whether learning within such programmes paradoxically actually serves to promotes neo-colonial attitudes and strengthen cultural stereotypes that reinforce colonial tendencies from the past. This calls into question the entire endeavour of fostering interculturality via mobility, and that learning within student exchanges and international training programmes does not necessarily enhance participants' understanding of other cultures, but might instead strengthen an imperialist view, thereby reifying the very cultural barriers that education abroad is meant to erase. Thus, being immersed in an unfamiliar culture does not necessarily guarantee enhanced learning and better understanding and may in fact have a confounding effect on fostering tolerance and understanding.

Against this backdrop, we need to discuss the concept of intercultural learning more thoroughly than is often the case. If we still believe that mobility can be a site for transformative and immersive experiences for students, in which they enhance their intercultural competencies, we need to ask questions relating to what students' acquiring knowledge, attitudes and skills for encountering and interacting with people from diverse backgrounds really means. Are there then ways of conceptualizing intercultural learning that paradoxically may lead to less understanding, and like the post-colonial critique argues, actually strengthen cultural stereotypes instead of reducing them? In other words, how can we conceive of intercultural learning in ways that tap the potential for better understanding via student mobility?

A Conventional Approach to Intercultural Learning

Intercultural learning typically refers to the acquisition of knowledge, skills, attitudes and behaviours that support learners' ability to interact with and understand people from cultures different to their own (Horst 2006; Lane 2012). This special category of learning has attracted widespread interest since the Second World War, which, due to an increase in diplomacy, travel and international business, has led to a greater need for cross-cultural communication. Having elicited numerous training programmes on cultural awareness and intercultural communication, the intercultural learning field has been dominated by what might be framed as a functionalistic approach (Dahl 2006: 9). Within such a frame, intercultural learning fulfils an important function by helping people acquire the knowledge, skills, attitudes and behaviours they need to be able to face an increasingly interconnected and globalized world, as well as in practising their professions within this new frame of reference.

This approach to intercultural learning is characterized by an objective to predict, explain and control the intercultural encounter (Nynäs 2006). Intercultural learning is perceived as the process through which the interpreter of another culture makes the stranger more familiar by gradually acquiring cultural knowledge about customs, practices and worldviews within a specific cultural community. For example, in the field of comparative cross-cultural studies, a leading figure has been Hofstede, who, together with his team, developed an enormously influential and widely used framework for clarifying, solving and unlocking cultural differences between people from different countries and cultures (Hofstede 1989; Hofstede et al. 2010). According to Hofstede, most countries share a national character, what he calls 'the collective programming of the mind, which distinguishes the members of one human group from another' (1989: 21). Based on surveys of employees at multinational companies conducted in the 1970s, Hofstede (1989) developed a model in which cultural differences were plotted along four dimensions: power distance; masculinity versus femininity; individualism versus collectivism; and uncertainty avoidance. Later, he added a fifth dimension related to cultural communities' long-term orientation versus short-term thinking (Hofstede 1994), developed further in later publications (Hofstede et al. 2010). For Hofstede, these five dimensions can be quantified and compared across nations, offering anyone who needs to manage or handle cultural differences a tool with which to learn about the cultural stranger.

In a similar vein, Samovar et al. (2007: 35)—leading scholars in the field of intercultural communication—argue that 'how a culture views the world can be found in its *deep structure*.' Moreover, 'it is this deep structure that unifies a culture, makes each culture unique and explains the how and why behind a culture's collective action.' This deep structure's content is described in much the same way as Hofstede's dimensions. With reference to Huntington's reasoning (1993: 25), Samovar and colleagues view the deep structure of culture as consisting of core elements that have been part of cultures for centuries. This includes different views on the relations between God and man, the individual and the group, the citizen and the state, parents and children, husbands and wives, and differing views on the relative importance of rights and responsibilities, liberty and authority, and equality and hierarchy (Samovar et al. 2007: 36). Therefore, learning from others who hold different views requires knowledge of the essence of the specific cultures that communicate with each other. Cultural differences are viewed as measurable, affecting intercultural encounters in a predictable way, and intercultural learning is understood as a means of deciphering cultural codes that make the message in the interaction process understandable. For Hofstede, Huntington, Samovar, Porter and McDaniel, a fundamental difference exists between intra-cultural and intercultural communication settings; the latter are more complicated than the former in the sense that a person's successful cultural communication requires in-depth knowledge of the other cultures (e.g., Skrefsrud 2016: 36–37).

The educational implications of such thinking are that students and teachers, to learn from others, must have the cultural knowledge needed in order to be able to read the scripts or schemes that are believed to characterize various ethnic groups, countries and cultures. For students travelling abroad, new insights and learning imply a need to decipher various receiving communities' cultural codes and an ability to use this information to get to know and relate to the cultural stranger, thereby exploring differences that make communication difficult. From this perspective, intercultural learning is primarily about accessing information about how different cultural backgrounds, traditions and worldviews are structured manifestations of human behaviour in social life. Through this information, 'intercultural learning' helps students overcome cultural barriers to understanding. By identifying core cultural elements or deep structures, travelling students can acquire knowledge about a culture and, thus, understand its people and provide explanations about them and the receiving cultural context.

Limitations of a Conventional Approach

A conventional approach to intercultural learning should be problematized for several reasons. First, an important question is the relationship between the individual and cultural context. Within a conventional paradigm, individuals are primarily viewed as products of their culture; people are, first and foremost, assumed to be representatives of 'their' cultural communities and are interpreted in the context of what is assumed to be this cultural background, with its 'deep structures' (Samovar et al. 2007: 35). The conventional conceptualization therefore runs the risk of trapping people in schematic formulations relating to certain cultural beliefs and practices. When actions, worldviews and behaviours are being traced back to specific cultural communities, differences may in fact be reinforced in ways that shut off other identity options for people (Skrefsrud 2018). As Sen (2006) has emphasised, a person's identity is rarely bound to one particular community, but reflects the range of communities of which the person is a part. Moreover, human beings are self-reflective and self-defining in a unique way, producing and reproducing identity in transformative processes of cultural exchange (Nynäs 2006). This underlines the fact that cultural identity is dynamic and non-categorical, something that the conventional understanding seems to neglect.

Second, due to increased mobility and interactions between people, drawing clear boundaries between cultures is extremely difficult (May and Sleeter 2010). Cultural communities are constantly being renewed and reshaped. People from different cultural backgrounds meet and interact with each other. Thus, cultural encounters can be described as a 'contact zone' (Pratt 1991) in which traditions are being continually interpreted in a transformative process of change. Therefore, the conventional tendency to identify cultures as closed systems is built on the false premise that cultures can be described according to a more or less static essence. Cultural traditions and communities can be much more deeply interrelated, hybrid and constantly evolving, more so than is assumed in a conventional approach.

Third, within this conventional thinking, cultural differences are inevitably constructed as hindrances to meaningful interaction. While the objective is to deconstruct and overcome cultural strangeness, intercultural learning is viewed as a tool for removing strangeness by gradually making the unknown more familiar. In this way, cultural differences are primarily constructed as a problem, an obstacle that prevents intercultural interactions from taking place instead of a possibility for new learning. However, there are reasons for asking to what extent such a conception take differences seriously in the sense that it (paradoxically) misses deeper, more radical perceptions of differences. Instead, the process of intercultural learning seems to be reduced to controlling and predicting cultural encounters, which, according to Nynäs, 'aim at dismantling human interpersonal interactions into a mechanistic set of laws' (Nynäs 2006: 24). However, the eagerness to secure the process of intercultural learning may turn it into a closed process with a limited number of potential outcomes. By removing risks from intercultural interactions, which is the conventional paradigm's objective, a danger exists that one will ignore the potentially creative and unpredictable aspects of the learning process.

Obviously, for students travelling abroad, it is highly important to have nuanced knowledge of the receiving context's history and background. However, by aiming to control, explain and predict the outcome of the learning process, a mechanistic model that is too simplified emerges. Instead, we must try to account for complexity.

Transculturality: An Alternative Approach

Unlike the conventional approach represented, for example, by Hofstede, the German philosopher Welsch (1999, 2017) has developed an alternative understanding that may be helpful when reflecting on intercultural learning. In opposition to an understanding of culture oriented towards essence, Welsch argues for a transcultural shift in understanding culture at both the micro and macro levels. At the micro level, cultural identity is dynamic and embedded in an ongoing process of cultural negotiation and exchange (Welsch 1999: 198). With reference to Berger, he suggests that life in the twenty-first century will be understood as 'a migration through different social worlds and as the successive realisation of a number of possible identities' (Berger et al. 1974: 77). Human beings construct their individual identities in a unique way; therefore, cultural habits, practices and life views do not end at national cultures' borders. Instead, they develop and transform as people from different backgrounds communicate and engage with each other more and more. On this basis, Welsch argues that cultural identities should not be understood as categorically determined, but rather as relational and dynamic; existing, developing and transforming within a changing social context.

This point is well made by Sen (2006), who challenges the idea that people can be uniquely categorized by single and overarching systems. According to Sen, 'the world is increasingly seen, if only implicitly, as a federation of religions or of civilisations, thereby ignoring all the other ways in which people see themselves' (2006: xii). Thus, Sen underlines the argument that cultural identity is dynamic and non-categorical, supporting Welsch's transcultural understanding of identity as dynamic, plastic and hybrid at both the macro and micro levels. Sen writes:

> In our normal lives, we see ourselves as members of a variety of groups—we belong to all of them. The same person can be, without any contradiction, an American citizen, of Caribbean origin, with African ancestry, a Christian, a liberal, a woman, a vegetarian, a long-distance runner, a historian, a schoolteacher, a novelist, a feminist, a heterosexual, a believer in gay and lesbian rights, a theatre lover, an environmental activist, a tennis fan, a jazz musician [...] Each of these collectivities, to all of which this person simultaneously belongs, gives her a particular identity. None of them can be taken to be the person's only identity or singular membership category. (Sen 2006: xii–xiii)

At the macro level, increased migration and global mobility make cultural communities entangled, hybrid and complex (Welsch 2017: 13). Therefore, defining the very essence of cultures is difficult without simultaneously presenting a normative understanding of what, for example, 'Asian' culture *is* as such.

Of course, this will not be a neutral perspective, even when presenting itself as such. According to Welsch (1999, 2017), this view overlooks internal diversities within a community, as well as the interaction and exchange of ideas and materials across the borders of the so-called cultural communities. Therefore, culture, at the macro level, is characterized by dynamic interplay between variables, including cultural, linguistic and religious backgrounds and socio-economic status. Cultural complexity is increasing; more young people of migrant heritage are expressing a strong sense of belonging to their present home, in terms of global popular culture and identification with a distant territory (Dewilde et al. 2021). Products, trends, ideas and worldviews travel and interact with each other, turning cultural communities into hybrids that are intertwined and constantly changing (Vertovec 2009). Therefore, transcultural processes are not restricted to urban areas. They characterize all settings where people meet, so diverse cultural communities are created in urban and rural surroundings worldwide.

A personal experience may illustrate this transcultural aspect of culture. Recently, I was driving through a rural part of Norway surrounded by Alpine mountains. Having dinner at a local restaurant in the small village of Hemsedal, I was struck by a Buddhist altar on the top of the stairs by the entrance. On the altar, a stone-carved statue of Siddhartha Gautama sat, surrounded by vivid flowers, fresh fruit and candles, aesthetically balanced by two massive ivory tusks on each side of the statue. Being challenged to reflect on this experience of 'strangeness,' it was not the beauty, size or colours of the altar that amazed me most, but the way the altar may be said to correspond with local knowledge about safety in the Norwegian mountains, taking care to be prepared for all eventualities. Although located far from the 'traditional home' of Buddhist customs and everyday life, the altar was a reminder that insight comes from experience, application of knowledge and critical reasoning, in line with the teachings of Buddha. It also illustrates how cultural ideas interact, travel and recontextualize in new settings.

However, an important point is that cultural dynamics are not something new. Cultural traditions always have been in a process of formulation and reconstruction in a communicative process of exchange and preservation, making hybridization a basic feature of being a human being (Welsch 2017: 56). In this sense, Welsch helps us see that the concept, or vision, of transculturality is an invitation to human interaction, communication and the exchange of ideas and worldviews. It calls for a continual renewal of tradition, not a rejection of tradition, and reflects a basic openness towards the possibility of identity formation and transformation through learning (e.g., Skrefsrud 2018). From this perspective, intercultural learning as part of student mobility is not primarily about collecting and assessing adequate and sufficient information on the receiving context to better understand it. Rather, a transcultural perspective reminds us that as hybrid cultural human beings, we are in a continuous dialogue with ourselves and others. This may help us challenge our own understandings as part of the learning process, as well as providing a means to avoid embracing negative stereotypes that encapsulate and label 'the other' in a highly problematic way. Instead, from this perspective, intercultural learning involves a curiosity and openness for the host context which does not trap otherness within predefined conceptions and understandings.

A transcultural perspective may help students recognize that traditions are also flexible and in flux. Traditions bind groups of people together in the past, present and future (Hervieu-Léger 2000: 86). However, while some elements remain the same, others are renewed and reconstructed in new ways with new generations. From this perspective, as we acquire more knowledge about a subject or an issue, things often become more complex and nuanced. Knowing the receiving communities and countries' history, practices, beliefs and customs may thus help familiarize the student with the host culture without reducing cultural traditions to an explanation of actions. For students travelling abroad, becoming familiar with a foreign tradition means recognizing its dynamic features.

Enhancing Intercultural Learning through Scaffolding and Preparation

Mobile students are supposed to learn something that goes beyond the body of knowledge and information they are supposed to acquire in a given subject or content area, such as English language, mathematics, arts, sciences or social sciences. Exploring other learning contexts in a foreign country will hopefully lead to less prejudice, increased tolerance, better understanding and peaceful behaviour. However, as I have argued in this chapter, if we really believe that student mobility will enhance intercultural competencies, we need to discuss the concept of intercultural learning more thoroughly than is often discussed.

A growing body of research has shown that students' first-hand experiences with cultural otherness in a foreign context is insufficient to foster intercultural learning (Foster 2016; Holmes et al. 2015; Messelink et al. 2015). Global awareness is unlikely to occur of its own accord. Of course, it is wonderful when this happens, but as Hannam and Biesta (2019: 58) remind us, knowing more about someone's background 'does not automatically translate into empathic action.' On the contrary, in some cases, negative stereotypes and prejudices may even be strengthened as part of students' mobility experiences. Therefore, maximizing the benefits of studying abroad requires preparation and scaffolding among travelling students before, during and after the exchange to a foreign country.

Foster (2016: 362) reminds us that enhancing students' global awareness and understanding of people from other cultural and linguistic settings requires institutions to 'ensure an effective preparation for students involved, including raising students' awareness of their own culture of learning and preparing students for the intercultural encounters prior to engaging in student mobility.' According to Foster, a key to successful student mobility lies in the ability to draw a line between students' mobility experiences and appropriate reflection and analysis. On this basis, one could say that reflecting intercultural learning as part of a mobility programme is a highly important task for educators engaging in mobility for students. How then might this happen?

Upon reflection on intercultural learning, students should be encouraged to relate their thinking to targeted knowledge, skills and attitudes that allow them to interact with other people in an atmosphere of communication and mutual understanding. With regard to knowledge, the theoretical transcultural perspective outlined in this chapter implies a need to move away from essentialist and stereotypical perceptions of the Other and instead embrace a dynamic understanding of culture. Consequently, students' cultural self-awareness and culture specific knowledge should be developed, followed by a sociocultural awareness that acknowledges the hybridity of both individual and collective identities. Because we all easily fall victim to colonizing others' essence and experiences, students' own experiences with intercultural encounters could be a starting point from which to reflect on issues such as othering, negative stereotyping and cultural essentialism.

Intercultural learning is also about having the skills to understand, act and communicate in cultural encounters of various kinds. From a transcultural perspective, this involves the ability to view the world from the perspective of the Other, but without reducing the distance between the self and the Other. The latter would be to follow colonial tendencies from the past, in which the West invented and objectified the Other to better understand itself (see Said 2003). Rather than claiming to have understood the Other's perspective, a transcultural perspective on learning encourages openness and curiosity, recognizing that not everything could be shared or understood through an intercultural encounter.

Finally, as part of intercultural learning preparation and scaffolding, mobility students should be given the opportunity to develop positive attitudes and critical-ethical thinking that may challenge power structures and discrimination in education and society. This includes counteracting a well-established opinion that we often hear from the media, politicians and even educators: that people from cultural minorities are deprived and inferior, both socially and linguistically, and in need of repair. Instead of interpreting differences as a problem, as a barrier that should be removed for communication to succeed, a transcultural perspective on intercultural learning may help students view cultural diversity as an opportunity for interaction and better understanding. Summing up the argument, to achieve the desired objective of student mobility—and to develop interculturally competent students—we need to consider a reflective approach to working with mobility students. This includes developing targeted support for pre- and post-mobility that enhances students' understanding of intercultural learning, while going beyond a mechanistic model. As this chapter has argued, interpreting intercultural learning from a transcultural perspective can be helpful in this regard.

References

AFS Intercultural Programs. (2018). *The power of mobility programs in fighting Xenophobia and promoting diversity*. Étrelles: AFS.
Allport, G. W. (1954). *The nature of prejudice*. Reading, MA: Addison-Wesley.
Berger, P. L., Berger, B., & Kellner, H. (1974). *The homeless mind: Modernisation and consciousness*. New York, NY: Random House.
Breen, M. (2012). Privileged migration: American undergraduates, study abroad, academic tourism. *Critical Arts: A Journal of South-North Cultural and Media Studies, 26*(1), 82–102.
Dahl, Ø. (2006). Bridges of understanding: Perspectives on intercultural communication. In Ø. Dahl, I. Jensen, & P. Nynäs (Eds.), *Bridges of understanding: Perspectives on intercultural communication* (pp. 7–22). Oslo, Norway: Unipub forlag.
Dewilde, J., Kjørven, O. K., & Skrefsrud, T. A. (2021). Multicultural school festival as a creative space for identity construction—From a minority parent perspective. *Intercultural Education*.
Foster, M. (2016). Exploring intercultural awareness: International student mobility in China and the UK through a non-essentialist lens. In D. M. Vellaris & D. Coleman-George (Eds.), *Handbook of research study abroad programmes and outbound mobility* (pp. 349–369). Hershey, PA: IGI Global.
Habermas, J. (1990). *Moral consciousness and communicative action*. Cambridge: Polity Press.
Hannam, P., & Biesta, G. (2019). Religious education, a matter of understanding? Reflections on the final report of the Commission on Religious Education. *Journal of Beliefs & Values, 40*(1), 55–63.
Hervieu-Léger, D. (2000). *Religion as a chain of memory*. New Brunswick, NJ: Rutgers University Press.
Hofstede, G. (1989). *Culture's consequences: International differences in work-related values*. Newbury Park, CA: Sage Publications.
Hofstede, G. (1994). *Cultures and organisations: Software of the mind: Intercultural cooperation and its importance for survival*. London: Harper Collins.
Hofstede, G., Hofstede, G. J., & Minkov, M. (2010). *Cultures and organisations: Software of the mind: Intercultural cooperation and its importance for Survival* (3rd ed.). New York: McGraw-Hill.
Holmes, P., Bavieri, L., & Ganassin, S. (2015). Developing intercultural understanding for study abroad: Students and teachers' perspectives on pre-departure intercultural learning. *Intercultural Education, 26*(1), 16–30.
Horst, C. (2006). *Interkulturel pædagogik*. Vejle: Kroghs forlag.
Huntington, S. P. (1993). The clash of civilisations? *Foreign Affairs, 72*(3), 22–49.
Klein, J., & Wikan, G. (2019). Teacher education and international practice programmes: Reflections on transformative learning and global citizenship. *Teaching and Teacher Education, 79*(1), 93–100.
Lane, H. C. (2012). Intercultural learning. In N. M. Seel (Ed.), *Encyclopaedia of the sciences of learning* (p. 97). Boston: Springer.
May, S., & Sleeter, C. E. (Eds.). (2010). *Critical multiculturalism: Theory and praxis*. New York: Routledge.

Messelink, A., Maele, J. V., & Spencer-Oatey, H. (2015). Intercultural competencies: What students in study and placement mobility should be learning. *Intercultural Education, 26*(1), 62–72.
Nynäs, P. (2006). Interpretative models of estrangement and identification. In Ø. Dahl, I. Jensen, & P. Nynäs (Eds.), *Bridges of understanding. Perspectives on intercultural communication* (pp. 23–37). Oslo, Norway: Unipub forlag.
Pratt, M. L. (1991). Arts of the contact zone. *Profession, 91*(1), 33–40.
Said, E. W. (2003). *Orientalism*. London: Routledge.
Samovar, L. A., Porter, R. E., & McDaniel, E. R. (2007). *Communication between cultures* (6th ed.). Belmont, CA: Thomson Wadsworth.
Sen, A. (2006). *Identity and violence: The illusion of destiny*. New York: Norton.
Sharpe, E. K. (2015). Colonialist tendencies in education abroad. *International Journal of Teaching and Learning in Higher Education, 27*(2), 227–234.
Skrefsrud, T.-A. (2016). *The intercultural dialogue: Preparing teachers for diversity*. Münster: Waxmann.
Skrefsrud, T.-A. (2018). Barriers to intercultural dialogue. *Studies in Interreligious Dialogue, 28*(1), 43–57.
Vertovec, S. (2009). *Transnationalism*. London: Routledge.
Welsch, W. (1999). Transculturality: The puzzling form of cultures today. In M. Featherstone & S. Lash (Eds.), *Spaces of culture. City, nation, world* (pp. 194–213). London: Sage.
Welsch, W. (2017). *Transkulturalität. Realität, Geschichte, Aufgabe*. Wien: New Academic Press.

Part II

Chapter 8
Free Movement in Education

David Cairns and Leonardo Francisco de Azevedo

Chapters 9, 10, 11, 12, 13 and 14 focus on examples of migration taking place within formal education, with emphasis on student mobility at tertiary level. In keeping with some of the ideas already introduced in this book, there is recognition that young people, including students, tend to make their own mobility, using their agency to help them cope with the challenges of living in foreign countries. It is also largely up to these individuals to make value, and make sense, out of this mobility, and to secure the transition from one mobile learning phase to another. Therefore, while the topics discussed in the subsequent chapters are all substantially different, they share recognition of students' role in managing their own mobility. As such, what we have are accounts of free movement in tertiary education; free in the sense of being guided by one's own needs and desires, but not free in terms of emotional and economic costs.

These chapters also recognize the significance of external contexts; the range and quality of mobility chances open to tertiary educated young people and the challenge of moving between the Global North and Global South. Starting point clearly matters a great deal and the liberty people have to make spatial choices is affected by place of residence, alongside limitations relating to personal circumstances and barriers associated with cultural and social norms. As observed during the Covid-19 pandemic, major societal events can also have a devasting impact on the freedom to practice mobility, enforcing a rapid and hard-to-reverse change in circulation patterns. Nevertheless, Chaps. 9, 10, 11, 12, 13 and 14 provide some examples of how young people have used their agency to become mobile for educational purposes,

D. Cairns (✉)
ISCTE – Instituto Universitário de Lisboa (ISCTE-IUL), Centro de Investigação e Estudos de Sociologia, Lisbon, Portugal
e-mail: david.cairns@iscte-iul.pt

L. F. de Azevedo
Universidade Federal de Juiz de Fora, Fora, Brasil

across a range of different global contexts: Greece and the United Kingdom (Chap. 9), Brazil and Germany (Chap. 10), Finland and Sweden (Chap. 11) and Italy (Chap. 12). Also included is a discussion of migrant teachers (Chap. 13) and a case study on the internationalization of science (Chap. 14).

We begin with an exploration of what Lucia Lo and her colleagues term 'intellectual migration.' One of the defining features of the development of internationalized tertiary education is the fact that while there may be a certain amount of cooperation between universities and conviviality among students and staff, these institutions are ultimately in competition with one another, including the enticement of student migrants from whom universities profit in terms of tuition fees and an international presence. This chapter brings together some of the key aspects of intellectual migration; for example, acknowledging the need to integrate internal and international migration, two facets that are frequently presumed to be unrelated. Such a perspective is important for this book, which also, without intending to do so, privileges cross-border mobility. In keeping with another theme in these chapters, there is also acceptance that free movement in educational contexts can have a durable influence on the development of subsequent careers. And while being an educational migrant can be facilitated or limited by individual, institutional and structural factors, the constraints of time, resources, places of origin and destinations all come into play in determining success.

The system itself can also be disrupted by existential threats to tertiary education. Prior to the 2020 pandemic, one of the greatest challenges facing educational mobility was the 2008 economic crisis. This is a topic revisited by Vasiliki Toumanidou, focusing on Greek students' migration to the United Kingdom at the time of the crisis and prior to Brexit. At this time, it was noted that students' decision-making was grounded in two outstanding factors, relating, on the one hand, to using educational mobility as an opportunity for self-discovery and self-growth, representing a path to independence and autonomy, and on the other, as the first step in a broader migration project, in keeping with the idea of migration as incremental, as introduced in Chaps. 1 and 2 of this book (see Cairns 2021a, 2021b). Major world events such as the economic crisis, Brexit and now the pandemic however challenge the ability to follow these highly individualized migration trajectories, putting mobility back on a more instrumental footing (à la classical migration norms), leaving us to ponder if we might soon witness a move back to more rigidly structured forms of student mobility, catering to a small population, and undertaken with a view to settlement as opposed to circulation.

Regional diversity in the practice of educational migration is also explored in Chaps. 9, 10, 11, 12, 13 and 14. Javier A. Carnicer and Sara Fürstenau look at transnational mobility in education as part of a process of 'social positioning' between Brazil and Germany. This topic, of educational migration in Brazil, will be returned to later in this book (see França and Padilla 2021), but outgoing mobility to Europe has been increasing significantly in scale since the 1990s, particularly among specialists and the children of higher and middle class parents, introducing claims of a possible brain drain. Nevertheless, their research shows that international educational opportunities appeal to young people from a diverse range of socio-demographic contexts, enabling us to explore divergences in experience according to issues such as personal and familial wealth. For example, how the children of the rich can afford to attend private schools in Germany, benefit from multilingual education and international credentials and use this mobility as a means of enriching their families' social and economic capital, while young people from disadvantaged backgrounds rely on au pairing and care work to gain access to forms of higher education in Germany from which they are excluded in Brazil. This work also brings to light some of the gender dimensions of inter-continental youth migration, liked with broader societal inequalities linked to the gendering of certain professions, in this case, the undervalued status of women who work in social care. Boutros et al. (2021) meanwhile in their chapter emphasise the gendering of refugee movement, with disproportionate numbers of young women forming part of what they term a 'lost generation.'

Not all student mobility takes place following inter-continental dynamics. In fact, movement between neighbouring countries and regions may be much more prevalent. One example in this book concerns the Nordic countries, with Blanka Henriksson's chapter looking at the migration of Finnish students to Sweden. While often presented, locally, as a form of brain drain, with highly educated young Finns supposedly 'fleeing' to Sweden in search of better opportunities, this situation is nuanced for those who are members of the Swedish-speaking minority in Finland and are seeking education in their own language. Doing so raises a number of important issues, including the impact of language on decision-making, the initial decision to leave Finland and whether or not to remain in Sweden for the foreseeable future. How these moves are perceived by students also differs. Moving to another country might be seen as a migration process for some but more of an expected life change for others. In some cases, spatial choices are pragmatic, linked to seeking a higher quality of education, while others talk about finding themselves and wishing to move away from small communities, as well as being able to study in their mother tongue. This chapter is therefore a reminder that what, from a distance, can appear as a relatively straightforward migration trajectory involves taking into account a range of different factors, some of which we can also observe in other chapters.

One of the most misunderstood areas of the migration field concerns the circulation of young people legally defined as refugees. While not often discussed as active participants in defining their own migration pathways, beyond having chosen to escape from difficult or even dangerous circumstances, refugees have nevertheless made spatial decisions and enact these choices using their agency. Furthermore, they may demonstrate a desire to move out of problematized categories and be recognized as migrants rather than refugees. Tertiary education represents one means of doing so, and the chapter of Marcela Gola Boutros, Dulce Pimentel and Alina Esteve explores this scenario in the Italian context. While there may be a strong aspiration to self-redefine oneself as a migrant, various barriers and restrictions remain, also limiting the ability of these young people to access higher education and, eventually, the labour market in the host country. The agency of these individuals is hence curtailed, locking them, involuntarily, within refugee status.

Two further contributions in this book address different aspects of mobility at tertiary-education level. The first, by Grada Okken and Robert Coelen, takes a look at how internationalization became an essential part of teacher education study programmes. As school classrooms diversified, professionals were required to develop the ability to cope with multicultural learning, with study abroad experience being one means of helping newly qualified teachers become better prepared. Internationalization also applied to scientific disciplines. The chapter of Nicolás José Isola looks at mobility dynamics within Physics at a Brazilian university. This demonstrates how students from other South American countries came to study in Brazil, taking advantage of the ability to undertake entrance exams in their home countries before migrating.

Chapters 9, 10, 11, 12, 13 and 14 of this book confirm the importance of various forms of transnational circulation in education, with students, academic staff and host institutions dependent upon the existence of international systems of exchange and circulation. Significantly, while we can talk about student migration as a system, it is dependent upon the efforts of many individuals. Public and private investment may establish and sustain the institutions but the participation of young people who populate the global centres of learning is essential and neither should we forget to acknowledge the efforts made by staff to support internationalized education. This human dependency produces both dynamism and fragility, flexibility and predictability, not to mention a potential for the reproduction of inequality alongside addressing social exclusion where people seek to profit at the expense of others. It is, in short, a very difficult system to manage in a fair and equitable manner.

In summing up, when we talk about 'free movement' and the once taken-forgranted liberty to globally circulate, we might do well to remember that this was always an incomplete and somewhat inefficiently realized aspiration. Even in global centres of heightened circulation such as the United States and the European Union, unpredictable elements served to confound and limit the spread of student migration as a generalized practice, but occasionally led to successful outcomes in individual cases. While we may now be looking back on the later years of the twentieth century and first two decades of the twenty-first as a golden age of sorts for educational free movement, this does not mean that everything was perfect or that there is nothing more to learn from looking at what happened during this period. For example, students do not necessarily circulate for simple reasons, or for one simple reason. A range of factors are at work—social, cultural, economic and political—that help define mobility choices and migration trajectories in terms of destinations and durations, as well as the likelihood of realizing one's educational dreams abroad. The chapter of Grada Okken and Robert Coelen (2021) also recognized the importance of values in decision-making, introducing what might be interpreted as an ethical dimension into choices about internationalized education. Institutions and teaching professionals also play an important role, with much of their expertise acquired through engaging in mobility.

Also, and in keeping with one of the main themes of this book, we have reminders that educational migration cannot be regarded as a discrete form of migration, disconnected from other forms of circulation, especially in the discussion of

Toumanidou (2021). Inter-dependency exists in many forms and at different levels, linking the work of policymakers at national and supra-national levels to individuals seeking to improve or at least change their lives through a change of location. Unforeseen events, such as the Covid-19 pandemic (see Cairns et al. 2021), drastically alter these scenarios, repositioning mobility protagonists in different ways, with the most impact likely to be felt by those least equipped in terms of social and economic resources. Institutions may survive, but many individual mobility trajectories will not.

References

Boutros, M. G., Pimentel, D., & Esteves, A. (2021). Refugees' access to higher education in Italy: An opportunity lost for the 'lost generation'. In D. Cairns (Ed.), *The Palgrave handbook of youth mobility and educational migration*. Basingstoke: Palgrave Macmillan.

Cairns, D. (2021a). Mobility becoming migration: Understanding youth spatiality in the twenty-first century. In D. Cairns (Ed.), *The Palgrave handbook of youth mobility and educational migration*. Basingstoke: Palgrave Macmillan.

Cairns, D. (2021b). Migration decision-making, mobility capital and reflexive learning. In D. Cairns (Ed.), *The Palgrave handbook of youth mobility and educational migration*. Basingstoke: Palgrave Macmillan.

Cairns, D., França, T., Malet Calvo, D., & Azevedo, L. (2021). Conclusion: Youth migration in the age of pandemic immobility. In D. Cairns (Ed.), *The Palgrave handbook of youth mobility and educational migration*. Basingstoke: Palgrave Macmillan.

França, T., & Padilla, B. (2021). South-South student mobility: International students from Portuguese-speaking Africa in Brazil. In D. Cairns (Ed.), *The Palgrave handbook of youth mobility and educational migration*. Basingstoke: Palgrave Macmillan.

Okken, G., & Coelen, R. (2021). After mobility: The long-term impact of study abroad on professional teacher behaviour. In D. Cairns (Ed.), *The Palgrave handbook of youth mobility and educational migration*. Basingstoke: Palgrave Macmillan.

Toumanidou, V. (2021). Understanding educational migration from Greece to the UK in times of crisis. In D. Cairns (Ed.), *The Palgrave handbook of youth mobility and educational migration*. Basingstoke: Palgrave Macmillan.

Chapter 9
Youth Educational Mobility: The Start of Intellectual Migration

Lucia Lo, Yixi Lu, Wei Li, Yining Tan, and Zheng Lu

Migration is a complex phenomenon, involving different actors and agents moving in multiple directions. As no single theory can explain all types and aspects of migration, our focus here is on laying down 'a middle-range theory (that) would allow analysis of the regularities and variations in specific types of migration that share some important common characteristics' (Castles 2010, 1574–75). Our specific concern is with educational migration and skilled migration, which are highly connected especially in terms of career development. Examining them as a spectrum enhances our knowledge of mobility for purposes beyond immediate economic gain and enriches migration theory. We have therefore proposed a conceptual framework, 'intellectual migration,' to capture such dynamics, connecting internal and international migration, student migrants and highly skilled migrants (Li et al. 2015, 2020), with youth migration in education marking the beginning of an intellectual migration process.

L. Lo (✉)
York University, Toronto, ON, Canada
e-mail: lucialo@yorku.ca

Y. Lu
Southwestern University of Finance and Economics, Chengdu, China

W. Li • Y. Tan
Arizona State University, Tempe, AZ, USA

Z. Lu
Sichuan University, Chengdu, China

© The Author(s), under exclusive license to Springer Nature Switzerland AG 2022
D. Cairns (ed.), *The Palgrave Handbook of Youth Mobility and Educational Migration*, https://doi.org/10.1007/978-3-030-99447-1_9

Intellectual Migration: A Conceptual and Analytical Framework

Literature is full of theories explaining migration motivations and practices. Approaches range from emphasising neoclassical economics and labour migration to proposing network and institutional theories as attempts to identify causality for migration (see Massey et al. 1993). While some theories are applicable to educational and skilled migration, others insufficiently relate to the 'global race for talent'. Our own conceptualization of intellectual migration, as detailed in Li et al. (2020), is grounded in three ideas from migration studies: mobility, transnationalism and brain circulation.

Mobility

Recent research on migration has used mobility as an underpinning concept for examining the forces that produce and are produced by the movement of people, capital, information and networks, as well as their impact on individuals and society (Cresswell 2006; Sheller and Urry 2006). Mobility denotes an ability to move to a specific place at a specific time, by a specific means (Adey 2009), but it is not a resource uniformly shared across populations, space or time. The physical and social components of mobility are bounded and interdependent but do not necessarily fall together (Kaufmann et al. 2004). While physical mobility is multi-scalar, social mobility is relational and contextual, and many different social actors and agencies, represented by national institutions, regional structures, community dynamics, and family and individual characteristics, influence the mobility status of a diverse range of migrants (Conradson and Latham 2005).

Student migrants, especially at higher education level, and highly skilled migrants can be more mobile than others due in part to opportunities for international students and their often greater command of resources (education, money, social networks) to facilitate more flexible and agile movement (Fong 2011; Leung 2013). Their mobility, however, is not absolute, but constrained by the restrictions and fixities produced by time, space, boundaries and contextual environments at point of origin and destination, as well as personal identities and experiences (Li and Lo 2012; Teferra 2005; Vertovec 2001). Student mobility in particular is marked by temporality. As fixed-term migrants, students pursuing international higher education are considered desirable by virtue of their youthfulness, educational credentials and linguistic abilities (Han and Appelbaum 2016). Their mobility is affected by the worldwide expansion of higher education opportunities, individual career considerations (Pherali 2012) and, to a certain extent, the neoliberal demand for flexible labour (Bauder 2012).

Transnationalism

In the current context of international migration, higher education migration and highly skilled migration do not fit well with the ideas of 'unidirectional migration', 'adaptation' and 'assimilation'. Rather than making a single substantial movement, students pursuing higher education and highly skilled professionals often conduct a series of short-term cross-border movements (Portes et al. 1999), which then accumulate into a bespoke form of migration, an idea that fits well with transnationalism theory, which stresses 'in-betweenness in simultaneous nations' (Dutt-Ballerstadt 2010: 10).

Transnationalism stipulates that migrants are engaged with their origin and destination countries at the same time, and, according to Tsuda (2012: 631), it is possible that 'increased engagement in one country leads to increased involvement in the other.' For tertiary education level students, postgraduate students in particular, and highly skilled professionals, their activities often involve knowledge exchange (Mayr and Peri 2008), which often incurs some form of transnational networking (Coe and Bunnell 2003; Ho 2011; Meyer and Wattiaux 2006). Transnational mobility is not unconditional. On the one hand, transnational networking enables the mobility of the highly skilled to happen, especially when the operations of many professions today are transnational in nature (Iredale 2001), and when nation states become active in mobilizing the highly skilled to move across borders through the institutionalization of talent development, recruitment and retention strategies. On the other hand, some nation states make use of power relations and governmentality techniques to restrict the mobility of talent for political and economic aims (Xiang et al. 2013).

Brain Circulation and Return Migration

Highly educated or highly skilled migration, historically more often from less economically advanced to more economically advantaged regions, impacts on source and host regions, particularly in regard to brain drain and brain gain phenomena. Whereas the former denotes a source country's loss of skilled people, the latter refers to the inflow of skilled migrants to a host region or their return to the source region. However, two recent developments have changed the rhetoric. One concerns the global rise of the knowledge economy, which has made highly skilled knowledge workers increasingly mobile (Pherali 2012). The other development relates to rapid economic development in (re)emerging economies such as China and India, which has fueled the outward migration of self-funded degree-seeking students, offering them unprecedented opportunities to return home after their studies abroad have finished (Wadhwa et al. 2011). 'Brain circulation', the circular movement of skilled labour across nations, is a more appropriate term for describing this form of movement among the tertiary educated and highly skilled. It is considered mutually beneficial to both sides of the migration equation as cross-cultural fertilization promotes innovation and improves productivity in both the origin and destination regions (Dutt-Ballerstadt 2010; Saxenian 2005).

The Intellectual Migration Framework

The intellectual migration framework is proposed to remedy fragmentation in understanding tertiary education and highly skilled migration (Li et al. 2015, 2020). Firstly, existing literature generally covers the mobility of different migrant groups such as students, professionals and entrepreneurs separately, as if there is little or no connection between these groups. Secondly, with return migrants, there is an overemphasis on the role of entrepreneur in economic development (Saxenian 2005; Wadhwa 2012). Thirdly, little attention is paid to the relationship between internal and international migration (e.g., circulation within a country and studying abroad), between the temporal (or life course) and geographical aspects, and the impact of cultural, social and human capital on migration decisions. Last but not least, the main focus tends to be upon migration from the periphery to the core, but not the other way around. Understanding that education migration and skilled migration are complex dynamic processes, the intellectual migration framework recognizes the importance of systematically and simultaneously examining different types of migrant under the same set of contextual conditions: students and professionals, young and older professionals, and those moving within a country and between countries.

At the outset, intellectual migration is defined as a means to acquire, upgrade and/or utilize intellectual capital among higher education students and highly skilled professionals for the purpose of career advancement whereas intellectual capital—a concept that goes beyond the notions of transferable academic capital (Badley 2000), transnational identity capital (Kim 2010) and forms of capital (Bourdieu 1986; Lave and Wenger 1991)—is a combination of social, cultural, symbolic capitals à la Bourdieu (1986), and human capital which is a concept widely used in the social sciences today in reference to the knowledge, experience and skills of workers in the economy. Intellectual capital is thus cumulative and transferable.

Castles (2010) was concerned about a lack of cumulative knowledge as to why some people are more mobile than others, and its meaning for societies. The intellectual migration framework addresses these concerns by examining knowledge-related migration, which includes people leaving home for education inside or outside a country (movers), staying where they complete their education and working there (stayers), returning home after completing their education or gaining professional experience where they have studied and stayed (returnees), or moving to a third region (onward migrants). The mobility of these groups is affected by an array of individual, institutional and structural forces that include transnational/translocal activities conducted by migrants and/or their families. These forces enable simultaneous involvement of source and host regions in apprising migration intentions, decisions and actions.

Who are Intellectual Migrants?

Intellectual migrants include (post-secondary) students, academics and other knowledge professionals who live outside their place of origin. They are often temporary migrants to begin with. For example, they may hold temporary residency registration in a host city in China, or student visas or work permits in Australia, Canada or France. When they complete their studies or academic exchange activities, they may stay, go home or move on to a third region. At a later stage, stayers may move back to their former home region or where they previously studied/worked for family reunification, career/professional or retirement purposes (Ley and Kobayashi 2005), and become re-migrants. These varying statuses can happen immediately after graduation or at any time after, thus giving intellectual migration a multi-stage temporal dimension. They can make use of their accumulated intellectual capital to find job opportunities commensurate with their credentials and experiences in their home region, the receiving area or another region (Bauder 2005; Waters 2006; Erel 2010). Whether the post-study step is the end of a unidirectional migration process or the beginning of a new intra-national or transnational migratory cycle depends, in part, on their satisfaction with their career and life in the destination region and perceptions of potential job opportunities elsewhere.

Why Do Intellectual Migrants Move?

Intellectual migrants are assumed to be making migration decisions on the basis of a potentially better future. Most do not have pre-existing family support networks in the destination region as would be the case with family reunification migration, and their primary motivation is not making a living as with labour migration. As 'middling migrants,' they are neither global elites nor poor migrants (Conradson and Latham 2005; Parutis 2014). Their mobility is affected primarily by personal and contextual factors, including life stage (Murphy-Lejeune 2002; Parutis 2014), the intellectual capital they possess, career aspirations, migration regulations and the socio-economic-political conditions in their origin and destination areas.

At a personal level, intellectual capital, determined by academic training, foreign language proficiency, work experience, knowledge-based translocal and transnational connections, sociocultural adaptability and influential leadership, matters most. Migrants further along the international migration continuum possess higher levels of intellectual capital due to having received more advanced training, work experience and larger social networks. Depending on the intensity of their activities, connections and other ways in which they can decide to use, or not use, their intellectual capital, its value can stay the same or decrease. The longer the intellectual migrants stay in a destination region, the more likely it is that they can gain cultural-social capital through the acquisition of local knowledge and professional networks, albeit at the expense of their cultural-social advantage in their place of origin (Leung 2013; Pherali 2012; Yu 2016).

Higher levels of intellectual capital envisage greater adaptability. Hence, people with higher levels of intellectual capital are more mobile. Their own assessment of where best to utilize their intellectual capital is an influencing factor on subsequent migration decisions. Generally speaking, with decision-making influenced by a combination of micro, meso and macro factors, intellectual migration is a multi-scalar process.

Where Do Intellectual Migrants Move To?

Similar to the geography of innovation (Koser and Salt 1997) which identifies a functional (human capital) and a location perspective (Eder 2019), intellectual migration commands a set of nodes, gateways and peripheries on various spatial scales. An academic/research institution or a major employer of highly skilled workers functions as an intellectual node that draws in migrants to study or work there. Intellectual nodes and the knowledge economy are mutually reinforcing of one another, especially when the knowledge economy hires local college graduates. Metropolitan regions that have a larger number of high-quality intellectual nodes serve as intellectual gateways that attract intellectual migrants with their abundant job opportunities and educational/research resources. As examples, Toronto, Montreal and Vancouver, Canada's largest cities, continue to attract the bulk of skilled migrants and international students going to the country. Similarly, 45 per cent of all foreign students with postgraduate Optional Practical Training status work in the same US metropolitan area where they received their academic degree (Ruiz 2014). Intellectual gateways attract and retain intellectual migrants not only because of their infrastructure, but also due to the size of their knowledge-based economy and the sociocultural environment that is able to cultivate intellectual capital and facilitate transnational migration and knowledge circulation. Transnational connections at both personal and institutional levels are often the strongest among top-tier intellectual gateways (Saxenian 2005).

Areas with fewer intellectual nodes are intellectual peripheries, somewhat like Fielding's (1992) 'escalator regions.' Like lower-ranking intellectual gateways, they lose skilled people to more important hubs. For instance, many of their students move to gateways for higher education and stay there after graduation due to the availability of better career opportunities. Intellectual peripheries that put in appropriate policies and complementary infrastructure to attract intellectual migrants may become intellectual gateways in due course. Whether a city is denoted a gateway or not is a scalar question. Often a gateway in a smaller region is considered peripheral to a larger region. Within a region, migration experience may influence people to stay where they can upgrade their human capital, return to their home area, move to a higher-ranking gateway nationally or internationally. At a national level, the more developed a country is, the more proactive the recruitment/retention policies are, and the more conducive the work and living environments are, the more likely they will attract and retain foreign-born professionals. This situation can, of course, change over time due to changing geopolitics and the associated economies.

The intellectual migration framework recapped above structures those involved as mobile subjects who are capable of moving to further their education or career. Specifying migration as a means to achieve intellectual development through heightened social and spatial mobility and via translocal/transnational connections, it stipulates the need to simultaneously consider translocal and transnational practices of migrants at various stages of the intellectual migration spectrum (Fong 2011), and to connect internal and international migration studies (King and Skeldon 2010; Tindal et al. 2015). This multi-stage, multi-scope and multi-scalar framework is analytically useful to understanding the reasons for, and the patterns and trends of migration at various life stages, and the migration trajectories of the highly skilled. It contributes towards a more comprehensive and integrative thinking about the mobility affairs of knowledge-related migration.

Youth Educational Mobility: The Onset of Intellectual Migration

Youth migration and education intersect. Existing literature highlights that educational opportunities motivate youth migration (Boyden 2013; de Brauw and Giles 2017), and that education migration can be conceptualized as intellectual capital investment. In some countries, it has become a common practice for youth to migrate domestically or overseas at secondary or post-secondary levels. The purpose of such migration, often with parental financial support, is to acquire and accumulate intellectual capital for better career opportunities in the future (e.g., Thomas 2017; Wang and Miao 2015). In this regard, youth are situated at the starting point of the intellectual mobility continuum.

Who are the Young Educational Migrants?

Privileged youth have traditionally enjoyed a higher level of educational mobility (Murphy-Lejeune 2002). Now, moving for educational opportunities is no longer the exclusive privilege of the well-off. Increasingly, more youth from disadvantaged backgrounds join such movement. For example, in some African, Asian and South American countries, due to economic growth, social transformation and the expansion of formal education, migration to cities for (higher) education has become the primary mechanism for rural youth to pursue a non-agrarian future and attain upward mobility (e.g., Boyden 2013; Du 2018; Ma and Pan 2014; Ma et al. 2009;

Schewel and Fransen 2018). In fact, a shifting strategy is taking place. Instead of sending their children away for short-term remittance-oriented jobs, disadvantaged families send their children to cities or abroad for long-term educational investment-oriented opportunities. Heckert (2015) has observed this phenomenon in Haiti, where urban-bound rural youth gain access to work opportunities in the new job market where the expanding service sector demands educated workers. Among disadvantaged families, especially in developing countries, educational migration is not only a means to upgrade the intellectual capital of youth, but also a long-term strategy to increase families' future economic capital (e.g., Boyden 2013; Heckert 2015; Smith and Gergan 2015). However, educational migration as such is not necessarily smooth sailing. It has negative impacts on agricultural development and does not guarantee youth access to professional employment due to entrenched social hierarchies and restricted labour market in these countries (Boyden 2013; Schewel and Fransen 2018).

Youth educational migration at times has also become the ultimate reason for parental migration and the creation of transnational families. The phenomena of 'astronaut' and 'wild geese/kirogi' families and 'parachutes kids' have been widely observed among East Asian upper-middle-class families since the 1990s. The term 'astronaut families' emerged from the migration of affluent Hong Kong, Taiwanese and now mainland Chinese immigrants to countries like Australia, Canada and the United States. These families sometimes migrate overseas together initially, but after a while one (most likely the father but sometimes the mother) or both parents return to the home region to work and periodically engage in circular migration between the home and host countries. Their children, known as 'parachutes kids,' are often left living alone or under the supervision of relatives or friends (Bohr and Connie 2009; Ho 2002; Kobayashi and Preston 2007; Orellana et al. 2001; Waters 2003, 2010). 'Wild geese' families, mainly originating from South Korea, tend to send their children to Western countries at a young age for primary or secondary education. Often, the mother will accompany the children and move overseas with them while the father continues working in the home country (Kang and Abelmann 2011; Lee and Koo 2006). Huang and Yeoh (2011) also report a similar phenomenon in Singapore, where many students from China have their mothers with them while their fathers remain in China.

Generally speaking, 'astronauts' and 'wild geese' migrate for the sake of their children's education. Children of these families, 'parachute kids' in particular, face a tremendous challenge in settlement and integration in the host country. However, in addition to academic capital, they subsequently obtain critical cultural capital such as independence, resilience and creativity in navigating different social/cultural environments, and develop their own goals and pathways (Huang and Yeoh 2011; Tse and Waters 2013; Waters 2015).

Why Do Young People Migrate for Education?

Youth migrate for educational purposes, both domestically and internationally. Domestically, youth educational migration has been a trend in developed countries like Canada, the United Kingdom and the United States. Apart from institutional expertise and prestige, many young people move away from their hometown to gain independence if they can afford to do so through family resources, loans or scholarships. Recently, this trend has gained importance in emerging countries like China where tertiary education opportunities are unevenly distributed. Based on an analysis of the 2010 Chinese census, Eberstadt et al. (2019) found that provinces with a higher education overcapacity (more seats available in universities than local people can fill) tend to attract inter-provincial youth migrants.

Internationally, young educational migrants from developed countries/regions often participate in international exchange programmes with financial support from governments, agencies and/or parents (Tiessen 2007; Brooks and Waters 2011; Weichbrodt 2014; Perna et al. 2015; Cairns 2017). These moves can be career-oriented or experience-oriented. Career-oriented students have clear motivations to increase the academic/professional dimensions of intellectual capital, including academic knowledge, foreign languages, intercultural sensitivity and adaptability to change which can be capitalized or future employment. The experience-oriented group focus on the personal development and cultural dimensions of intellectual capital, such as obtaining new experiences, learning about new cultures, improving interpersonal communications and learning to be independent and confident (Collins 2014; Conradson and Latham 2005; King 2013).

Where Do Young People Migrate To?

Some tidal shifts are occurring in the landscape of youth educational migration. Firstly, international education was once thought to be a Global South to Global North phenomenon, but emerging economies such as China and India are now becoming attractive to some international students. For example, in 2018, about 492,185 international students studied in China (MoE 2019). This amounts to 10 per cent of all international students worldwide, making China the third-largest recipient of international students after the United States (24 per cent) and the United Kingdom (11 per cent) (IIE 2018). Studying in Asia, some young people from the Global North are actually converting some academic dimensions of their intellectual capital (e.g., language skills and Western educational qualifications) into economic capital by teaching English (Ansell 2008; Collins 2014; Stanley 2013).

Secondly, some literature notes that career-oriented students are more likely to move to intellectual portals, whereas experience-driven students are less bound by gateways. The latter can find an intellectual node in an intellectual periphery attractive as long as its culture and environment fit their interests in terms of exotic experiences and personal development (Dolga et al. 2015; Lu et al. 2019). However, largely due to the 2008 economic crisis and the growing youth unemployment trend in 'the West,' young people increasingly move to intellectual gateways for education and future job opportunities.

Thirdly, a notable phenomenon has emerged in domestic youth-centred migration in China, a country that administers a very competitive college entrance examination system known as gaokao. Because of fixed quota admission policies, the distribution of higher education resources in the country is uneven (Peng 2005; Wang 2010). Therefore, some high school students seek to move to regions where admission grades are lower because of the less well developed secondary education system or where admission rates are higher due to the presence of more higher education institutions (Li 2015). As local resident registration is a prerequisite for the national college entrance examination, some parents seek help from state and provincial employee transfer programmes. Others may seek local resident registration inappropriately (Jia 2015; Xu and Yan 2010).

Youth Mobility in Intellectual Migration: A Roadmap for Empirical Analysis

The intellectual migration framework puts youth at the onset of the mobility spectrum. An ideal analysis of this process would be a true longitudinal study—following the same group of migrants as they move through the various life stages, documenting how they accumulate and utilize intellectual capital during a professional career, and beyond. Short of such ideal situations, due to time and resource constraints, an alternative advocated by Li et al. (2020) is to simultaneously study different segments of the intellectual migration spectrum, to understand how the same set of factors impact on individual decisions at various life stages. These segments include students studying at home and in host regions, professionals returning home, staying at host countries or moving to a third region at various stages of their professional lives. On an international scale, analysis should go beyond looking at migrants moving from the Global South to the Global North, which is the focus of the bulk of current literature, to include movement from the Global North to the Global South, a new trend signalling a changing landscape of the 'global race for talent'. In sum, we consider youth education migration as the onset of intellectual migration, and that empirical investigations on the facilitators and constraints of youth mobility with a comparative lens would enhance our understanding of highly educated and highly skilled migration in our ever increasing knowledge-based economy, and possibly contribute to overall economic equality and social justice among different stakeholders in this world of migration.

References

Adey, P. (2009). *Mobilities*. New York: Routledge.
Ansell, N. (2008). Third world gap year projects: Youth transitions and the mediation of risk. *Environment and Planning D: Society and Space, 26*(2), 218–240.
Badley, G. (2000). Developing globally-competent university teachers. *Innovations in Education and Training International, 37*(3), 244–253.
Bauder, H. (2005). Habitus, rules of the labour market and employment strategies of immigrants in Vancouver, Canada. *Social and Cultural Geography, 6*(1), 81–97.
Bauder, H. (2012). The international mobility of academics: A labour market perspective. *International Migration, 53*(1), 83–96.
Bohr, Y., & Connie, T. (2009). Satellite babies in transnational families: A study of parents' decision to separate from their infants. *Infant Mental Health Journal, 30*(3), 265–286.
Bourdieu, P. (1986). The forms of capital. In J. G. Richardson (Ed.), *Handbook of theory and research for the sociology of education* (pp. 241–260). New York: Greenwood Press.
Boyden, J. (2013). 'We're not going to suffer like this in the mud:' Educational aspirations, social mobility and independent child migration among populations living in poverty. *Compare: A Journal of Comparative and International Education, 43*(5), 580–600.
Brooks, R., & Waters, J. (2011). *Student mobilities, migration and the internationalization of higher education*. Basingstoke: Palgrave Macmillan.
Cairns, D. (2017). The Erasmus undergraduate exchange programme: A highly qualified success story? *Children's Geographies, 15*(6), 728–740.
Castles, S. (2010). Understanding global migration: A social transformation perspective. *Journal of Ethnicity and Migration, 36*(10), 1565–1586.
Coe, N. M., & Bunnell, T. G. (2003). Spatializing knowledge communities: Towards a conceptualization of transnational innovation networks. *Global Networks, 3*(4), 437–456.
Collins, F. L. (2014). Teaching English in South Korea: Mobility norms and higher education outcomes in youth migration. *Children's Geographies, 12*(1), 40–55.
Conradson, D., & Latham, A. (2005). Friendship, networks and transnationality in a world city: Antipodean transmigrants in London. *Journal of Ethnic and Migration Studies, 31*(2), 287–305.
Cresswell, T. (2006). *On the move: Mobility in the modern western world*. New York: Routledge.
Dutt-Ballerstadt, R. (2010). *The postcolonial citizen: The intellectual migrant. Volume 3*. Bern: Peter Lang.
de Brauw, A., & Giles, J. (2017). Migrant opportunity and the educational attainment of youth in rural China. *The Journal of Human Resources, 52*(1), 272.
Dolga, L., Filipescu, H., Popescu-Mitroi, M. M., & Mazilescu, C. A. (2015). Erasmus mobility impact on professional training and personal development of student beneficiaries. *Procedia – Social and Behavioral Sciences, 191*, 1006–1013.
Du, H. (2018). Rich dad, poor dad: The impact of family background on educated young people's migration from peripheral China. *Journal of Youth Studies, 21*(1), 90–110.
Eder, J. (2019). Innovation in the periphery: A critical survey and research agenda. *International Regional Science Review, 42*(2), 119–146.
Eberstadt, N., Coblin, A., Joy-Pérez, C., & Wang, K. M. (2019). *Urbanization with Chinese Characteristics: Domestic Migration and Urban Growth in Contemporary China*. Washington DC: The American Enterprise Institute.
Erel, U. (2010). Migrating cultural capital: Bourdieu in migration studies. *Sociology, 44*(4), 642–660.
Fielding, A. J. (1992). Migration and social mobility: South East England as an escalator region. *Regional Studies, 26*(1), 1–15.
Fong, V. (2011). *Paradise redefined: Transnational Chinese students and the quest for flexible citizenship in the developed world*. Stanford, CA: Stanford University Press.
Han, X., & Appelbaum, R. (2016). *Will they stay or will they go? International stem students are up for grabs*. Kansas City: Ewing Marion Kauffman Foundation.

Heckert, J. (2015). New perspective on youth migration: motives and family investment patterns. *Demographic Research, 33*, 765–800.

Ho, E. (2011). Migration trajectories of 'highly skilled' middling transnationals: Singaporean transmigrants in London. *Population, Space and Place, 17*(1), 116–129.

Ho, E. (2002). Multi-local residence, transnational networks: Chinese 'astronaut' families in New Zealand. *Asian and Pacific Migration Journal, 11*(1), 145–164.

Iredale, R. (2001). The migration of professionals: Theories and typologies. *International Migration, 39*(5), 7–26.

Huang, S., & Yeoh, B. S. A. (2011). Navigating the terrains of transnational education: Children of Chinese' study mothers' in Singapore. *Geoforum, 42*, 394–403.

Jia, L. (2015). Following 1,500+ Gaokao migrants in Inner Mongolia. *Chinese Youth Daily*, 11 June 2015.

Kang, J., & Abelmann, N. (2011). The domestication of South Korean pre-college study abroad in the first decade of the Millennium. *The Journal of Korean Studies, 16*(1), 89–118.

Kaufmann, V., Bergman, M., & Joye, D. (2004). Motility: Mobility as capital. *International Journal of Urban and Regional Research, 28*(4), 745–756.

Kim, T. (2010). Transnational academic mobility, knowledge, and identity capital. *Discourse: Studies in the Cultural Politics of Education, 31*(5), 577–591.

King, A. (2013). Recognising adulthood? Young adults' accomplishment of their age identities. *Sociology, 47*(1), 109–125.

King, R., & Skeldon, R. (2010). 'Mind the gap!' Integrating approaches to internal and international migration. *Journal of Ethnic and Migration Studies, 36*(10), 1619–1646.

Kobayashi, A., & Preston, V. (2007). Transnationalism through the life course: Hong Kong immigrants in Canada. *Asia Pacific Viewpoint, 48*(2), 151–167.

Koser, K., & Salt, J. (1997). The geography of highly skilled international migration. *International Journal of Population Geography, 3*(4), 285–303.

Lave, J., & Wenger, E. (1991). *Situated learning: Legitimate peripheral participation*. Cambridge: University of Cambridge Press.

Lee, Y.-J., & Koo, H. (2006). 'Wild geese fathers' and a globalised family strategy for education in Korea. *International Development Planning Review, 28*(4), 533–553.

Leung, M. W. (2013). 'Read ten thousand books, walk ten thousand miles:' Geographical mobility and capital accumulation among Chinese scholars. *Transactions of the Institute of British Geographers, 38*(2), 311–324.

Ley, D., & Kobayashi, A. (2005). Back to Hong Kong: Return migration or transnational sojourn? *Global Networks, 5*(2), 111–127.

Li, W., & Lo, L. (2012). New geographies of migration? A Canada-US comparison of highly skilled Chinese and Indian migration. *Journal of Asian American Studies, 15*(1), 1–34.

Li, W., Lo, L., Lu, Y., Tan, Y., & Lu, Z. (2020). Intellectual migration: Considering China. *Journal of Ethnic and Migration Studies* (Forthcoming).

Li, W., Yu, W., Sadowski-Smith, C., & Wang, H. (2015). Intellectual migration and brain circulation: Conceptual framework and empirical evidence. *Journal of Chinese Overseas, 11*(1), 43–58.

Li, Y. (2015). Inner Mongolia takes severe measures against 'Gaokao Migration'. *The China Youth Daily*, May 27, 2015.

Lu, Z., Li, W., Li, M., & Chen, Y. (2019). Destination China: International students in Chengdu. *International Migration, 57*(3), 354–372.

Ma, L., Yue, C., & Min, W. (2009). Regional distribution of colleges and regional flow of college students. *Research in Educational Development, 23*, 31–36.

Ma, L., & Pan, K. (2014). Stay or migrate? An empirical study of the relationship between place of work, place of study and birthplace. *Chinese Education and Society, 47*, 80–95.

Massey, D. S., Arango, J., Hugo, G., Kouaouci, A., Pellegrino, A., & Taylor, J. E. (1993). Theories of international migration: A review and appraisal. *Population and Development Review, 19*, 431–466.

Mayr, K., & Peri, G. (2008). Return migration as a channel of 'Brain Gain.' *NBER Working Paper No.14039*. Cambridge, MA.

Meyer, J.-B., & Wattiaux, J.-P. (2006). Diaspora knowledge networks: Vanishing doubts and increasing evidence. *International Journal on Multicultural Societies, 8*(1), 4–24.

Ministry of Education. (2019). *Statistical report on international students in China for 2018*.

Murphy-Lejeune, E. (2002). *Student mobility and narrative in Europe: The new strangers*. London: Routledge.

Orellana, M., Thorne, B., Chee, A., & Lam, W. S. (2001). Transnational childhoods: The participation of children in processes of family migration. *Social Problems, 48*(4), 572–591.

Parutis, V. (2014). 'Economic migrants' or 'middling transnationals'? East European migrants' experiences of work in the UK. *International Migration, 52*(1), 36–55.

Peng, X. (2005). '*Gaokao* Migration': Causes and solutions. *Modern Education Science, 3*, 24–25.

Perna, L. W., Orosz, K., Jumakulov, Z., Kishkentayeva, M., & Ashirbekov, A. (2015). Understanding the programmatic and contextual forces that influence participation in a government-sponsored international student-mobility program. *Higher Education, 69*(2), 173–188.

Pherali, T. J. (2012). Academic mobility, language, and cultural capital: The experience of transnational academics in British higher education institutions. *Journal of Studies in International Education, 16*(4), 313–333.

Portes, A., Guarnizo, L., & Landolt, P. (1999). The study of transnationalism: Pitfalls and promise of an emergent research field. *Ethnic and Racial Studies, 22*(2), 217–237.

Ruiz, N. G. (2014). *The geography of foreign students in US higher education: Origins and destinations*. Washington: Brookings Institution.

Saxenian, A.-L. (2005). From brain drain to brain circulation: Transnational communities and regional upgrading in India and China. *Studies in Comparative International Development, 40*(2), 35–61.

Schewel, K., & Fransen, S. (2018). Formal education and migration aspirations in Ethiopia. *Population and Development Review, 44*(3), 555–587.

Sheller, M., & Urry, J. (2006). The new mobilities paradigm. *Environment and Planning A, 38*(2), 207–226.

Smith, S., & Gergan, M. (2015). The diaspora within: Himalayan youth, education-driven migration, and future aspirations in India. *Environment and Planning D: Society and Space, 33*(1), 119–135.

Stanley, P. (2013). *A critical ethnography of 'westerners' teaching English in China: Shanghaied in Shanghai*. London and New York: Routledge.

Teferra, D. (2005). Brain circulation: Unparalleled opportunities, underlying challenges, and outmoded presumptions. *Journal of Studies in International Education, 9*(3), 229–250.

Thomas, S. (2017). The precarious path of student migrants: Education, debt, and transnational migration among Indian youth. *Journal of Ethnic and Migration Studies, 43*(11), 1873–1889.

Tiessen, R. (2007). Educating global citizens? Canadian foreign policy and youth study/volunteer abroad programs. *Canadian Foreign Policy Journal, 14*(1), 77–84.

Tindal, S., Packwood, H., Findlay, A., Leahy, S., & McCollum, D. (2015). In what sense 'Distinctive'? The search for distinction amongst cross-border student migrants in the UK. *Geoforum, 64*, 90–99.

Tse, J. K. H., & Waters, J. (2013). Transnational youth transitions: becoming adults between Vancouver and Hong Kong. *Global Network, 13*(4), 535–550.

Tsuda, T. (2012). Whatever happened to simultaneity? Transnational migration theory and dual engagement in sending and receiving countries. *Journal of Ethnic and Migration Studies, 38*(4), 631–649.

Weichbrodt, M. (2014). Learning mobility: High-school exchange programs as a part of transnational mobility. *Children's Geographies, 12*(1), 9–24.

Vertovec, S. (2001). Transnationalism and identity. *Journal of Ethnic and Migration Studies, 27*(4), 573–582.

Wadhwa, V. (2012). *The immigrant exodus: Why America is losing the global race to capture entrepreneurial talent*. Philadelphia: Wharton Digital Press.

Wadhwa, V., Jain, S., Saxenian, A. Gereffi, G., & Wang, H. (2011). *The Grass is Indeed Greener in India and China for Returnee Entrepreneurs: America's New Immigrant Entrepreneurs–Part VI. SSRN 1824670*.

Wang, H. (2010). Research on the influence of college entrance examination policies on the fairness of higher education admissions opportunities in China. *Chinese Education & Society, 43*(6), 15–35.

Wang, H., & Miao, L. (Eds.). (2015). *Annual report on the development of Chinese students studying abroad (2015)*. Beijing, China: Social Sciences Academic Press.

Waters, J. (2003). 'Satellite Kids' in Vancouver: Transnational migration, education and the experiences of lone children. In M. W. Charney, B. S. A. Yeoh, & C. K. Tong (Eds.), *Asian migrants and education* (pp. 165–184). Dordrecht: Kluwer Academic.

Waters, J. (2006). Geographies of cultural capital: Education, international migration and family strategies between Hong Kong and Canada. *Transactions of the Institute of British Geographers, 31*(2), 179–192.

Waters, J. (2010). Becoming a father, missing a wife: Chinese transnational families and the male experience of lone parenting in Canada. *Population, Space and Place, 16*(1), 63–74.

Waters, J. (2015). Education imperatives and the compulsion for credentials: Family migration and children's education in East Asia. *Children's Geographies, 13*(3), 280–293.

Xiang, B., Yeoh, B., & Toyota, M. (2013). *Return: Nationalizing transnational mobility in Asia*. Durham, NC: Duke University Press.

Xu, D., & Yan, X. (2010). The legal thought on the policy of blocking migrants for national college entrance examination. *Journal of Schooling Studies, 7*(5), 12–15.

Yu, W. (2016). To stay or to return? Return intentions and return migrations of Chinese students during the transition period in the United States. *Papers in Applied Geography, 2*(2), 201–215.

Chapter 10
Understanding Educational Migration from Greece to the UK in Times of Crisis

Vasiliki Toumanidou

While educational migration is not a new phenomenon, in recent decades student migration has grown in stature at European and international levels, attracting research attention across various disciplines.[1] English-speaking countries seem to attract the largest numbers of EU and non-EU students, with the UK being the second most popular destination after the US according to the UNESCO 'global flow of tertiary-level students' database. At the same time, Greece has been among the countries with the largest outbound student flows, significantly increasing during the period following the 2008 economic crisis, when youth unemployment increased and opportunities for new graduates severely declined.[2] The rise in intensity of Greek student migration flows seems to have overlapped chronologically with a more general increase in outward migration, especially among the highly educated, presumably due to the lack of employment opportunities and spread of precarious forms of employment at home.[3] Focusing on mobile students originating from Greece, the main aims this chapter will be to examine how educational migration was perceived and used by students at a time of social, political and economic change, a situation now further complicated by the arrival of Brexit.

Methodological Approach

This chapter analyses the findings of 31 semi-structured interviews conducted with students who migrated from Greece to the UK to pursue taught postgraduate degree programmes in the 2017/18 academic year. The fieldwork lasted approximately eight months, from December 2017 to July 2018, with the interviews conducted with students in one city in the north of England and London. The selection of these

V. Toumanidou (✉)
University of Leeds, Leeds, UK

© The Author(s), under exclusive license to Springer Nature Switzerland AG 2022
D. Cairns (ed.), *The Palgrave Handbook of Youth Mobility and Educational Migration*, https://doi.org/10.1007/978-3-030-99447-1_10

locations was made to examine variations in regard to students' migration and educational aspirations, as well as their decision-making processes, perceptions and attitudes towards the labour market and post-study plans.

Regarding sample characteristics, the majority appeared to be of medium/medium-high family cultural and economic capital backgrounds.[4] In the present study, students' family cultural capital was mainly indicated by parental educational level, family economic capital and parental occupation. Pseudonyms have been assigned to all the participants to protect their anonymity and confidentiality. In addition, nine interviews were conducted with key informants, comprised of two education agents based in Greece and seven staff members working at recruitment/international offices in higher education institutions of the UK. These interviews shed more light on the patterns and trends of students' migration to the UK, complementing the analysis of existing data sources.

Exploring Students' Perspectives: Educational Migration and Employability

The findings of the study show that in the case of this national group of students, educational migration cannot be regarded as a discrete form of migration, disconnected from other practices. Students' decisions for educational migration were found to be embedded in lifelong mobility aspirations. Students appear to be engaging in life planning, with their motivations for educational migration associated with subsequent mobility (see also Findlay et al. 2017). Educational migration thus becomes interconnected with migration for work purposes, for almost all the participants, with their educational migration perceived as a means of facilitating a transition to employment abroad; that is, the first stage in a migration strategy.

The socio-economic conditions in Greece, including a lack of employment opportunities and precarious working conditions, were identified as some of the most important drivers. Considering the labour market conditions in Greece, the majority of participants had already decided to move abroad for study and/or work purposes even before completing their undergraduate degree programmes: 15 out of 31 students migrated to the UK after completing their undergraduate degrees, while the rest started their courses one or more years after their graduation. Prior to migration, ten participants had already entered the labour market, most having been employed in short-term low-paid job positions that were often irrelevant to their studies. Some had been unemployed after graduation, highlighting the difficulties they encountered while searching for employment. Their experiences of being unemployed and/or working in precarious types of employment in fact enhanced their desire for migration; migrating for study and then work purposes was seen as the 'natural' path and, in some cases, a 'one-way' option that they would pursue for the rest of their lives:

> Poor working conditions have set migration as a 'one-way option' [...] When you think of the working conditions, the prospects you may have for the next five years or maybe ten years, you can't turn a blind eye. [...] My main goal was to get a job, and getting a Master's degree first was seen as a 'small step' in order to achieve my goal. (Marina, F, 25, Engineering, London)

One strategy that students deployed to enhance their employability during educational migration was the accumulation of social and cultural capital. This finding is consistent with those of previous studies which found that accumulating cultural and social capital was one of the main drivers of students' migration aspirations and decision-making processes (Brooks and Waters 2009a; Waters 2012). More specifically, the accumulation of 'institutionalized cultural capital' (Bourdieu 1986: 243), through the acquisition of 'highly valued' British academic qualifications, was expected to enhance employment prospects and advance a career in the labour market in the home country and in countries other than the UK. The acquisition of such a qualification was perceived, especially by many students pursuing Business and Administrative studies, as a 'passport' that might 'open doors' to better career opportunities:

> British universities have a very good reputation. A British Higher Education degree has a different value to degrees awarded by universities in other countries. They are very highly valued in the labour market even beyond the UK. I believe it may improve my career prospects a lot! (Despoina, F, 26, Business, N. England)

As seen in the following statement, apart from this form of capital, many participants also perceived their educational migration as a way to accumulate valuable social capital through network formation, which might then enhance their career progression and facilitate the transition to employment:

> I wanted to do a Master's course here in order to enter the country and do some networking because I have some friends who came here straight after their bachelor's study and faced some difficulties with networking. (Marina, F, 25, Engineering, London)

When choosing a higher education institution, apart from the university ranking tables, the students also seriously considered the city where the institution was located in terms of living and studying costs, quality of living, employment opportunities, lifestyle, infrastructure and other sociocultural factors. Most of the Business students in London mentioned that they wanted to study there because, apart from the status attached to a degree awarded by a prestigious university, studying and living in one of the biggest financial centres in the world might allow them to build professional networks and stay updated about the latest labour market conditions. Furthermore, a number of participants also appeared to be attempting to enhance their employment prospects by gaining relevant work experience, another highly valued element of cultural capital. Reflecting on the findings of previous studies on graduate employability, the students in this study also seemed to be aware that in order to increase their chances of being employed and advancing their career prospects beyond acquiring a higher education degree, they also need to develop additional skills and attributes (see, e.g. Tymon 2013).

More specifically, aside from pursuing a taught postgraduate degree, a few students expressed their desire to stay in the UK, especially London, for a few more year or to migrate to another country after graduation, not only because of personal and sociocultural aspirations but also as they perceived the UK as an 'escalator region' (Fielding 1992). They hope that the skills and work experience they obtain might help them develop and enhance their social, cultural and economic capital, and advance their career prospects. By doing so, some expect to gain a competitive advantage over their counterparts, not only in the British labour market but also abroad or in their home country. For example:

> I'd like to stay here, but maybe for a while. [...] Mostly because I'd like to return to Greece after having gained some work experience here [...]. In this way, maybe I'd be in a more advantageous position among the thousands of applicants there. (Dimitra, F, 24, Education, London)

In general, this study has revealed that within the context of post-economic crisis labour market conditions and a high level of competitiveness, temporality and various uncertainties, educational migration is identified as a strategy to facilitate the transition from education to the labour market in a range of different countries, thus broadening the field of possibilities.

Educational Migration as a Path to Independence and Autonomy

Another finding of this study was that educational migration is perceived by a significant number of students as a 'route' to independence and autonomy, an opportunity for self-discovery and self-growth. These findings echo previous studies on intra-EU mobility which show that intra-EU migrants often move abroad driven by not only economic and career-related factors but also self-exploration and self-development (Cuzzocrea and Mandich 2016). Leaving the parental home and becoming independent were also identified as strong motivating factors for migration in the first place, especially in the case of interviewees who had never lived outside the family home:

> Definitely my migration was seen as a way of becoming more independent. In Greece I had learnt, you know, to drive my car and then go home straight after. And my parents did anything I wanted. [...] You know, if I got a cold, I was sure that someone would go and get me some medicine from the pharmacy. So, living alone is a much bigger experience than studying. You learn better how to stand on your own feet. (Dimitra, F, 24, Education, London)

> I had studied at a university in my hometown. So, I had never left home. So, I surely wanted to leave. However, I still don't feel autonomous because I get by with my parents' money [...]. I will become autonomous next year once I've started working and this is something I really want to do. (Sofia, F, 24, Engineering, London)

Leaving the parental home and entering the labour market are often considered key moments in the life course, and in the transition to adulthood, associated with attaining a state of independence and autonomy. For many participants, these two types of transitions seemed to have been postponed in their home country due to financial constraints. Migrating to the UK was perceived by many as an opportunity to, belatedly, reach these two goals. And for them, the state of independence is to be achieved not only by leaving the parental home and forming their own household but also becoming financially self-sufficient. In enhancing their employability through the ways described and analysed in the previous section, these students expect educational migration to help them become financially independent, as most are currently fully or partially financially reliant on their families.

Furthermore, apart from professional and career related aspirations, many were also driven by experiential motivations, especially those with a high level of family economic capital to draw upon. More specifically, in line with previous studies, sociocultural and experiential aspirations such as an interest in experiencing foreign countries and cultures were identified as significant motivating factors (see King 2002; King and Ruiz-Gelices 2003; Van Mol and Timmerman 2014). The findings also indicate that experiential aspirations significantly underpin aspirations and decision-making, especially regarding selecting a location of study. Supporting previous literature on youth mobility (Lulle et al. 2018), this study concurs with the idea that London has been a popular destination among students not only for professional and career-related reasons but also for sociocultural and lifestyle factors, such as multiculturalism, social and cultural attractions, and a wide range of sociocultural activities.

Specifically, within the contemporary Greek context, studying, working and living abroad also seems to have become 'normalized' and perceived by many participants as a part of a common mobility pattern which young people, especially of the generation that was hardest hit by the crisis, tend to exhibit as a response to the current difficult socio-economic conditions, reflected in the following quotes:

> My friends are spread out. My best friend has been living permanently in Switzerland over the last three years. My other friend left to go to Switzerland when I also left from Greece. Our generation learns how to cope with different conditions. [...] We learn to adapt. (Marina, F, 25, Engineering, London)

> I see that more and more friends of mine tend to migrate abroad. Others for studies and others for work. [...] Many just want to go and live somewhere for some time, get familiarized with the new environment and find a job. (Anthi, F, 25, Transport Studies, N. England)

Although students follow their own life journeys as individuals, the contexts within which they are situated seem to significantly influence their decision-making. As shown in the above statements, as individuals are situated within a wider society, their mobility practices are inextricably linked with broader social networks, which seem to play a crucial role in 'normalizing' particular mobility patterns (Brooks and Waters 2010: 146; Conradson and Latham 2005: 294). Confirming the findings of previous research, this study has found that students' social networks, mostly comprised of family, friends, peers and former university lecturers/professors, play a crucial role in establishing cultures of mobility and influencing students' migration and educational decisions through offering advice and sharing their travel, study and/or working-abroad experiences (Beech 2015: 335).

Post-Study Migration Scenarios

As mentioned above, almost all of the students perceived their educational migration as a 'path,' opening up post-study migration plans, providing support for the idea of constructing a migration trajectory incrementally, albeit more self-consciously than tacitly. At the time of the interviews, only three students planned to return to Greece immediately after graduation, mostly because of personal and family reasons, and their initial plans were to stay in the UK. twenty-seven students intended to remain in the UK. Although they are uncertain about how long they will actually stay, the vast majority want to enter the labour market and remain there for at least the next few years. The main determinants of their decision are economic and career-related factors, specifically more and better employment opportunities and prospects, and in general the hope of a better future in the UK compared with Greece.

These findings indicate a different trend regarding Greek mobile students' post-study plans compared to previous decades. In the past, one of the main drivers was failure or the fear of failing the university admission exams in Greece (Panhellenic examinations), although in the case of migration for postgraduate study, the main motivating factor was the limited number of places offered by Greek higher education institutions (ADMIT, 2001; Eliou 1988). Students would also migrate to study in order to enhance their career prospects (ADMIT, 2011), and a large proportion returned to Greece after graduation (Eliou 1988). However, in the last decade, a large number seem to have migrated for study with the intention of remaining in the host country after graduation (Pratsinakis et al. 2017), a trend which emerged in the present study.

Moreover, supporting the findings of other UK-based research on graduates' and/or students' post-study intentions and life mobility aspirations (Findlay et al. 2017), this study has shown that students, apart from staying in the host country or returning to their home country, many have additional migration scenarios in mind. In an era characterized by constant change, fluidity and temporariness (Bauman 2000), 'liquid migration' (Engbersen and Snel 2013)—a concept which can conceptualize the openness and flexibility of young people's migration plans and 'spatial trajectories' (King et al. 2018: 5)—seems to be on the rise. In this study, 20 respondents reported that apart from remaining in the UK, they are also 'open' for onward migration in case they find better employment opportunities in another country, within and/or beyond Europe. For example, aside from northern and central European countries, other destinations were identified as particularly popular, mainly due to the availability of employment opportunities in their career fields, higher salaries and their perceptions that the work experience they would gain in such countries might also advance their career, as one of them reported:

> I'd like to go to Middle East because I want to cover some financial issues I have. […] Apart from the economic motives, the experience I could get there may be more valuable. I mean, compared to working in a graduate scheme here for two years. (Rafail, M, 25, Engineering, N. England)

Moreover, the 'open-endedness' of students' future plans seems to have intensified within the uncertain atmosphere surrounding Brexit. Many respondents expressed concerns regarding the potential implications for their rights of residence, employment, study and travel, as well as sociocultural impacts. One of the most widely cited concerns was whether EU nationals might need to apply for a visa to secure their residence and employment. Due to these issues, a number reported that although their initial intention had been to remain in the UK after graduation, they have now started considering other potential destination countries. The following statement was typical:

> I got mostly worried about what will happen in terms of employment, because I knew that if anything happened that would be at least after 2018-2019. So, I had in mind about how difficult it would be finding a job here because the conditions might be very different if you need a visa or something like that to work. […] That made me think about going to other countries. If that happened, I mean the visa thing, I'll search for other places in Europe. (Aris, M, 22, Business, London)

These findings are indicative of the role that surrounding political, economic, labour market and sociocultural environments play not only in mediating migration aspirations and decision-making processes, but also post-study pathways. The fluidity of students' plans seems to have been heightened with the uncertain of Brexit, prompting a response characterized by flexibility and various strategies aimed at securing a better future.

Conclusion

As shown in prior research, educational migration is not only limited to study purposes but is also grounded in students' life course aspirations and lifetime mobility intentions. The current study has found that educational migration cannot be approached and examined as a discrete form of migration, disconnected from other modalities, and is inextricably linked to migration for work purposes. Specifically, the students view and utilize their migration to the UK in two main ways. Firstly, as a response to difficult socio-economic conditions in their home country, using migration to the UK as the first step in a broad migration project in search of better employment and life opportunities abroad. In migrating, they appear to be trying to accumulate social and cultural capital in order to enhance employability and manage the risks and uncertainties surrounding contemporary society and labour markets. Secondly, for many, migration and the decision to stay abroad after graduation is driven not only by career-related factors but also experiential and other personal motivations. More specifically, living abroad is seen as an important opportunity for self-discovery and self-growth, and a 'route' to independence and autonomy associated with the transition to employment and financial self-sufficiency, and leaving the parental home.

Regarding students' future plans, the findings have shown that within the context of economic crisis, austerity and highly competitive neoliberal labour market conditions, and Brexit, mean students have more than one post-study migration scenario in mind. Almost all intend to remain abroad after graduation and a large number are open to onward migration. Within this uncertain context, many students seem to be flexible and are likely to follow job openings wherever they may be, keeping their post-study plans options. Under these conditions, mobility for study and work purposes seems to have been established as a part of youth mobility culture, with students' social networks playing a significant role. This culture does not seem fixed and is associated with experiential and lifestyle mobility aspirations, as often discussed in Anglophone literature, but receives a different meaning across time and space, as young people's perceptions, aspirations, decision-making and mobility practices are in a dynamic relationship with the political, socio-economic and cultural contexts in which they are grounded. The findings of this study indicate that although migration may be perceived and experienced at an individual level, as a path towards personal and professional development, it is not just based on individual expectations and choices but informed and influenced by a number of contextual and structural factors that need to be seriously considered in order to better understand students' migration aspirations, decisions and life planning processes.

Acknowledgements This chapter is part of the doctoral study 'Student migration from Greece to the UK: A life course perspective,' conducted at the School of Sociology and Social Policy, University of Leeds, UK. Some of the material included in the chapter is also developed from the working paper 'Student migration from Greece to the UK: Understanding aspirations, decision-making and future plans,' presented at SEESOX Conference, *Homeland–diaspora relations in flux: Greece and Greeks abroad at times of crisis*, 22-23 June 2018, University of Oxford, Oxford, UK (see Toumanidou, 2018). I am particularly grateful to the University of Leeds for awarding me with the Leeds Anniversary Research Scholarship (LARS) to undertake my doctoral project, my supervisors, Sarah Irwin and Sharon Elley, for their invaluable supervision and help at every stage of my research, and all the respondents for their participation. Also, I want to deeply thank my family for the inspiration and their constant support, motivation and encouragement throughout my research.

Notes

1. See, for example, work by Findlay et al. (2006), Brooks and Waters (2009a, 2009b) and King and Raghuram (2013)
2. According to Eurostat (2019a, 2019b), in 2013 the unemployment rate for 15–24-year-olds in Greece was estimated at 58.3 per cent, whereas the overall unemployment rate attained a peak of 27.5 per cent.
3. For further exploration of this issue, see Triandafyllidou and Gropas (2014), Pratsinakis et al. (2017) and Sakellariou and Koronaiou (2018).

4. Seventeen respondents were female and 14 male. Nine pursued courses in Economics, Business and Administrative Studies, nine in Education and Social Sciences, seven in Engineering and Transport Studies, four in Natural Sciences, and two in Creative Arts and Design. The majority were aged 21–24 and 25–29 years, and four were aged 30 years and over. With regard to the mode of study, 26 pursued full-time degree courses and only five respondents were part-time students.

References

ADMIT. 2001. *Higher Education admissions and student mobility within the EU*. [Online]. London: Centre for Educational Research (LSE). [Accessed 2 September 2018]. Available from: http://www.lse.ac.uk/socialPolicy/Researchcentresandgroups/ERG/pdf/cmp18.pdf

Bauman, Z. (2000). *Liquid modernity*. Cambridge: Polity.

Beech, S. E. (2015). International student mobility: The role of social networks. *Social and Cultural Geography, 16*(3), 332–350.

Bourdieu, P. (1986). The forms of capital. In J. G. Richardson (Ed.), *Handbook of theory and research for the sociology of education* (pp. 241–258). New York: Greenwood Press.

Brooks, R., & Waters, J. (2009a). International higher education and the mobility of UK students. *Journal of Research in International Education, 8*(2), 191–209.

Brooks, R., & Waters, J. (2009b). A second chance at success: UK students and global circuits of higher education. *Sociology, 43*(6), 1085–1102.

Brooks, R., & Waters, J. (2010). Social networks and educational mobility: The experiences of UK students. *Globalisation, Societies and Education, 8*(1), 143–157.

Conradson, D., & Latham, A. (2005). Friendship, networks and transnationality in a world city: Antipodean transmigrants in London. *Journal of Ethnic and Migration Studies, 31*(2), 287–305.

Cuzzocrea, V., & Mandich, G. (2016). Students' narratives of the future: Imagined mobilities as forms of youth agency? *Journal of Youth Studies, 19*(4), 552–567.

Eliou, M. (1988). Mobility or migration? The case of Greek students abroad. *Higher Education in Europe, 13*(3), 60–66.

Engbersen, G., & Snel, E. (2013). Liquid migration: Dynamic and fluid patterns of post-accession migration. In B. Glorius, I. Grabowska-Lusinska, & A. Rindoks (Eds.), *Mobility in Transition: Migration Patterns after EU Enlargement* (pp. 21–40). Amsterdam: Amsterdam University Press.

Eurostat. 2019a. *Unemployment rate, 2008-2018 (%)*. [Online]. [Accessed 30 May 2019]. Available from: https://ec.europa.eu/eurostat/statistics-explained/images/7/7d/Unemployment_rate_2008-2018_%28%25%29_new.png.

Eurostat. 2019b. *Youth Unemployment figures, 2008-2018 (%)*. [Online]. [Accessed 30 May 2019]. Available from: https://ec.europa.eu/eurostat/statistics-explained/index.php?title=File:Youth_unemployment_figures,_2008-2018_(%25)_T1.png.

Fielding, A. J. (1992). Migration and social mobility: South East England as an escalator region. *Regional Studies, 26*(1), 1–15.

Findlay, A., Prazeres, L., McCollum, D., & Packwoo, H. (2017). 'It was always the plan': International study as 'learning to migrate.'. *Area, 49*(2), 192–199.

Findlay, A. M., King, R., Stam, A., & Ruiz- Gelices, E. (2006). Ever reluctant Europeans: The changing geographies of UK students studying and working abroad. *European Urban and Regional Studies, 12*(4), 291–318.

King, R. (2002). Towards a new map of European migration. *International Journal of Population Geography, 8*(2), 89–106.

King, R., & Ruiz-Gelices, E. (2003). International student migration and the European 'year abroad:' Effects on European identity and subsequent migration behaviour. *International Journal of Population Geography, 9*(3), 229–252.

King, R., & Raghuram, P. (2013). International student migration: Mapping the field and new research agendas. *Population, Space and Place, 19*(2), 127–137.

King, R., Lulle, A., Parutis, V., & Saar, M. (2018). From peripheral region to escalator region in Europe: Young Baltic graduates in London. *European Urban and Regional Studies, 25*(3), 284–299.

Lulle, A., Moroşanu, L., & King, R. (2018). And then came Brexit: Experiences and future plans of young EU migrants in the London region. *Population, Space and Place, 24*(1), e2122.

Pratsinakis, M., Hatziprokopiou, P., Grammatikas, D., & Labrianidis, L. (2017). Crisis and the resurgence of emigration from Greece: Trends, representations, and the multiplicity of migrant trajectories. In B. Glorius & J. Domínguez-Mujica (Eds.), *European mobility in times of crisis. The new context of European South-North migration* (pp. 75–102). Bielefeld: J. Transcript Verlag.

Sakellariou, A., & Koronaiou, A. (2018). Young people, transition to adulthood and recession in Greece: In search of a better future. In S. Irwin & A. Nilsen (Eds.), *Transitions to adulthood through recession: Youth and inequality in a European comparative perspective. Youth, young adulthood and society series* (pp. 156–175). London: Routledge.

Triandafyllidou, A., & Gropas, R. (2014). 'Voting with their feet': Highly skilled emigrants from Southern Europe. *American Behavioral Scientist, 58*(12), 1614–1633.

Tymon, A. (2013). The student perspective on employability. *Studies in Higher Education, 38*(6), 841–885.

Van Mol, C., & Timmerman, C. (2014). Should I stay or should I go? An analysis of the determinants of intra-European student mobility. *Population, Space and Place, 20*(5), 465–479.

Waters, J. L. (2012). Geographies of international education: Mobilities and the reproduction of social (dis)advantage. *Geography Compass, 6*(3), 123–136.

Chapter 11
Transnational Mobility, Education and Social Positioning between Brazil and Germany

Javier A. Carnicer and Sara Fürstenau

Transnational youth mobility, education and migration are often looked at through different lenses, depending on social context. Mobility with regard to schooling, study or work is encouraged for high-skilled professionals and their relatives but often thwarted for the low-skilled, giving rise to a division into classes of privileged and disadvantaged migrants (Levitt et al. 2017: 5). This hierarchization is reflected in different public and scientific discourses on education: 'mobility' is positively connoted, and 'migration' is related to poverty and issues of 'integration' (Faist 2013: 1640-1644). This chapter looks at migration, or transnational mobility, as an educational strategy in different social contexts. For the most part, this mobility is funded by students and their families, not governments or philanthropic institutions (Altbach and Knight 2007: 194). It therefore becomes largely the prerogative of the privileged classes in possession of the required social and economic resources, particularly if the move is intercontinental. The research discussed in this chapter reveals, however, that educational aspirations also compel young people from less privileged socio-economic backgrounds to migrate, a process that in itself can reproduce social inequalities within transnational contexts. The discussion that follows investigates the connections between migration and education in different social contexts, including influences on migration decisions and educational aspirations, and the ways in which plans are realized. We focus on social inequalities, compare trajectories in very different socio-economic conditions and ask if, and how, the different social contexts interact, using the example of educational migration from Brazil to Germany.[1]

J. A. Carnicer (✉) • S. Fürstenau
University of Hamburg, Hamburg, Germany
e-mail: javier.carnicer@uni-hamburg.de

Transnational Youth Mobility, Migration and Education

In characterizing youth mobility that crosses international borders as 'transnational,' we draw on a migration research perspective that has attempted to understand 'the processes by which immigrants forge and sustain multi-stranded social relations that link together their societies of origin and settlement' (Basch et al. 1994: 8). This perspective analyses the social practices of migrants and non-mobile persons embedded in broader contexts, like families and social networks, and describes the contributions of individuals and families to processes which elsewhere have been labelled as globalization. In the context of educational mobility, this means that students and their families are not merely reacting to the internationalization of education but also actively contributing to pedagogical transnationalization processes.

Transnational migration research stresses the fact that migration, or international mobility, is rarely accomplished by isolated individuals. Social relations, and in particular family relations, are in fact seen as crucial to the decision to move. The transnational perspective points towards the emergence of novel social realities and emphasises that 'linking together their societies of origin and settlement' (Basch et al. 1994: 8), migrants contribute to the arousing of 'pluri-locally spanned *transnational* social spaces' (Pries 2001: 3). Accordingly, transnational educational spaces 'emerge and consolidate themselves by relations, interactions and perceptions' (Kesper-Biermann 2016: 93), re-enforcing social inequalities between those who do and do not have access to transnational educational markets (van Zanten et al. 2015). At the same time, transnational educational mobility may also facilitate social upward mobility, even if this only occurs in exceptional cases. As stated above, our findings indicate that educational aspirations may be an important reason for migrating among the underprivileged, especially if related to educational upward mobility (Carnicer 2018, Carnicer 2019; Fürstenau 2019). But lacking the resources to access the transnational educational market at the outset, they rely mainly on paid work and informal support to enter this field of opportunities.

To understand transnational educational orientations in different social contexts, we will use the concept of educational resource environment. The concept is derived from research on transnational social protection. It differentiates four sources of social protection: states, markets, third sector organizations (like NGOs, church groups or labour unions) and social relations in families and social networks (Levitt et al. 2017: 6). Access to educational provisions of states, markets and third sector organizations tends to be highly formalized and led by codified rules. In contrast, families and social networks contribute to the education of individuals in informal ways, mostly based on variable reciprocity relations (Faist 2017: 22). Transnational migrants rely on different sources of educational provisions in more than one nation state, and the availability of provisions depends 'upon the nature of the market, the strength and capacity of sending and receiving states, the third sector organizational ecology (…) and the characteristics of individual migrants and their families' (Levitt et al. 2017: 6). Based on this assumption, migration motivated by educational aspirations can be seen as a reaction of certain individuals and families to a 'national' resource environment perceived as inadequate to supporting their educational aspirations (Carnicer 2019; Fürstenau 2019).

Educational Environments in Brazil and Germany

The inequality between rich and poor in Brazil is among the world's greatest, and the poverty rate is high. Social inequality is reinforced by an educational system paradoxically divided between public and the private sectors. Access to high-quality education is very much dependent on economic resources. At primary and secondary levels, the quality of public school varies greatly, but on the whole, according to Programme for International Student Assessment (PISA) and university transition rates, it remains low compared to the quality of private schools. For graduates of public schools, it is very difficult to win a place at one of the public tuition-free universities that, unlike public schools, rank higher than the private ones. Graduates of expensive private schools have clear advantages, as they are better prepared to pass the entrance examinations (Exame Nacional do Ensino Médio—ENEM) (Pfeiffer 2015).[2]

Educational expansion since the end of the twentieth century is noticeable, however, and has driven elites to use new strategies of social closure. One of these strategies is to imbue an educational trajectory with a certain international touch. According to the Brazilian sociologist Ana Maria F. Almeida:

> Internationalization, especially when accompanied by some form of certification, represents an alternative to university experiences that are increasingly becoming less distinctive and maybe too ordinary in the eyes of the elite. (Almeida 2015: 79)

Skills such as fluency in foreign languages and having the corresponding certification constitute a form of cultural capital that helps someone attain or legitimize a privileged position, something that is very difficult to achieve in public schools. Private international schools and degrees from universities abroad have thus gained importance (Aguiar and Nogueira 2012; Almeida 2015; Windle and Nogueira 2015). Different educational strategies depending on social position have been shown. For part of the Brazilian elite, experience abroad and foreign university degrees are crucial in order to maintain social position. But for an economically more powerful elite, the prestige connected with certain certificates and educational institutions would be sufficient to legitimize inherited privileges (Windle and Nogueira 2015). Expensive international schools and universities protect not only the *social* position of the elites, but also their *space*, keeping the striving middle classes literally at a distance.

Compared to Brazil, private schools seem to have played a minor role in Germany and have only gained significance very recently (Deppe et al. 2015). In our study, migrant parents from Brazil in Germany hold that public accountability for equality in education and public funding of good schools and professional training are important reasons for staying in Germany, sending their children to school there, and organizing their families' (re-)migration accordingly (Fürstenau 2015: 82–84). Typically, these parents commend the high quality of state schools in Germany and declare that they could not afford a private school in Brazil of comparable quality. They do not always acknowledge the fact, however, that the German school system has gained notoriety for disadvantaging students from migrant families, as social class and family migration status have been shown to notably influence chances of success (Bildungsbericht 2018).

An important issue in our study is the question of access to German universities for Brazilians. While students already enrolled in Brazilian universities benefit from exchange programmes and grants, for others the German Studienkolleg offers a different kind of opportunity to study in Germany. The Studienkolleg is a one-year course that prepares foreign students and entitles them to study at a university in Germany. In the overall sample of our study, various young migrants from Brazil passed the entrance exam for the Studienkolleg; on average, they needed a period of two years in Germany to prepare for it and learn the German language (Carnicer 2018: 11). As an alternative to university studies, other young migrants try to get into the vocational training as part of the dual system. Whereas professional training in Brazil is rarely free of charge, the German dual system offers free professional training plus a small salary for apprentices who work and attend vocational school at the same time.

Methodological Approach

Following a multi-sited ethnography approach (Marcus 1995), data was collected in different locations in Germany and Brazil, as well as in different social fields. The sample includes migrants who came in search for a 'better life' as well as members of transnational social elites. In line with the ethnographical approach, different methods were used: participant observation, guided and narrative interviews, ego-centred network analysis and the compilation of family trees (Carnicer 2018). The research followed the 'networks of people linked to each other across national boundaries' (Mazzucato 2008: 72), with these networks treated as the unit of analysis.

In our discussion, we will compare the transnational educational trajectories and aspirations of two young people who belong to different networks. The cases of Luciana and Alexandre are analysed not only on the basis of individual narratives but in the contexts of their networks: Luciana belongs to a transnational network of Brazilian care workers (Fürstenau 2019; Carnicer 2019) and Alexandre is a graduate of the German School Abroad in a large city in Brazil, who also belongs to a network of graduates from this school who study at universities all over the world.[3]

Case Studies

Luciana

Luciana grew up in a favela in South-East Brazil that we have called Campo Roxo. Surrounded by affluent urban neighbourhoods and with an estimated population of more than 70,000 inhabitants, Campo Roxo is a city in a city that houses the janitors, domestic servants, clerks and other workers of its rich neighbourhoods.

Luciana's school career is very unusual for a child from the favela. Until the age of 12, she attended a municipal school in one of the richer neighbourhoods. But then, with the help of scholarships, she was able to attend some of the better private schools. Luciana has always been a very good student, and after completing secondary school, she passed the university entrance examinations (ENEM) without problems. She found, however, that she could not afford the studies, or even the transportation costs to the tuition-free, public university in her city; although she wanted to study abroad, the possibilities she had were financially out of reach. Lacking alternatives, she worked for several months as a secretary, gave private lessons to children and attended an English course outside Campo Roxo. There she met a lady whose daughter was living in Germany and looking for a Brazilian au pair. This daughter would provide accommodation and pay for the flight as well as for German lessons. Luciana accepted, insisting that her goal was to study in Germany, and, at the age of 19, travelled there.

As an au pair with the 'host family,' her working conditions turned out to be unregulated and exploitative. With the help of friends from the German course, Luciana found a new 'host family,' where she was content working as au pair. Just before her resident status as au pair expired, she tried the entrance exam for the Studienkolleg, which opens access to German universities for students from abroad after a one year course, but did not pass. She wanted to stay longer to improve her German skills and try the exam again. In the meantime, she had met other young women from Brazil, who were doing care work. Most came as au pairs, also looking for educational opportunities. They advised her to do a voluntary year (Freiwilliges Soziales Jahr, FSJ) in a residential care home for the elderly. Luciana obtained another 12-month visa for the voluntary year and received €380 a month. Then she applied for a three-year apprenticeship as a geriatric nurse at the same nursing home and was accepted. Luciana has now a stay permit for three years.

The vocational training takes place in the German dual system. Luciana earns a small salary working in her field of apprenticeship and attends classes at a vocational school. She says that the final exam of the vocational training in German will be a challenge for her. Although she originally wanted to study International Relations, Luciana finds her work satisfying and admits that she has developed an interest in psychiatry and medicine. She plans to work and earn money after the vocational training, and then study medicine in Germany. In the meantime, she has brought her younger sister Anita to live with her in Germany, to also begin a voluntary year in the residential care home for the elderly.

Alexandre

Luciana's mother continues to live in Campo Roxo and is employed as a nanny by Alexandre's family, who lives in an affluent urban area nearby. This is where two very different social contexts and the networks of Luciana and Alexandre overlap. Alexandre's great-grandparents were German migrants in Brazil. His grandfather, who migrated at a young age, became an engineer and founded his own company, which is now run by Alexandre's father.

Alexandre was 23 years old at the time of the interview, studying engineering at a private catholic university and preparing for a three-month stay in Germany. Having attended the German School Abroad—a prestigious and expensive private school—from nursery until the end of secondary school, he is thinking of pursuing a postgraduate degree or MBA in Germany, and this trip is conceived as preparation. He wants to find out about internships and working opportunities, improve his German language skills and maybe attend some university courses. But first, he wants to meet friends who are studying in Germany and Great Britain, to travel with them and visit some relatives in Germany as well. He already knows places in Europe from family holidays, and his family is going to pay for everything. As he puts it, an important motive for going to Germany is to improve his CV. He says, Germany is the land of engineering, and having work or study experiences there would open many opportunities in Brazil. However, to stay in Germany for work would also be good.

Judging from his account, Alexandre's plans also appear to be a reaction to the economic recession in Brazil. He complains that when he started studying, his degree was much sought after in Brazil but now it would be not so easy to find even an internship there. During the interview, Alexandre seems a bit worried about his German language skills and what he will find in Germany, but generally, perceives his trip as a sure bet, literally one that he 'can only win.' As he seems to imply, even if all fails, he can return to Brazil, continue his studies, work in his father's company and add the stay in Germany to his CV, earning some symbolic capital.

Two Mobilities

Probably most striking when comparing the cases of Luciana and Alexandre are the social differences. The reproduction of social inequality in daily interactions can be traced in the interview with Alexandre. He seems happy to use the interview situation with the German professor to ask all kinds of questions concerning his stay in Germany, but he deftly ignores the interviewer's repeated hints that his family's nanny, Luciana's mother who has two daughters living in Germany, is by now an expert on migration from Brazil to Germany. For Alexandre, to have common issues with the nanny seems unimaginable.

To better understand how differences in social backgrounds affect the educational trajectories and transnational orientations of Luciana and Alexandre, we can compare the resources available in their networks (cf. Levitt et al. 2017), considering that educational provisions derived from states, markets, the third sector and social networks. Luciana's career path in Germany was opened by a network of Brazilian care workers whose members willingly advise each other on questions about residence status, housing, jobs, as well as educational opportunities. This transnational network offers patterns and proven strategies for migrants that are shared among friends and family. During the last few years, it has attracted numerous young people, mostly women, from different places in Brazil, among them Luciana's younger sister Anita. The young women who migrated to work in the care work sector—and to eventually follow their educational aspirations—have attended public schools, mostly schools in the periphery with poor facilities. The case of Luciana, who benefitted from scholarships to attend some of the better private schools, is a great exception. But just as with the other young women of her network, she felt excluded from educational opportunities in Brazil when she could not afford to finance university studies. Luciana developed a transnational orientation because of this experience of exclusion, just like the other people in her network. To prepare herself for her migration, she worked and took expensive English lessons, thus participating in the private education market. But otherwise she did not have access to formal support for a transnational career, such as exchange programmes or international scholarships. Her transnational move depended on informal support which led her, by pure chance, to Germany. Even though Luciana did not speak German, she embraced the offer to work as au pair in Germany as an opportunity.

In Germany, she soon became part of a network of young women from Brazil, which turned out to be an important environment for informal support. It provided career orientation and contacts to a care home for the elderly in Germany that employs women from Brazil. It also provides information about the German dual system for vocational training. The network members know that migrants from non-EU states do not have unrestricted access to this system, but they have discovered the niche of care work, where a (mostly female) migrant workforce is welcome. Young women from Brazil can profit from the German dual system by following vocational training in the area of care work, although their educational trajectories are subject to the gender regimes, care regimes and migration regimes of Germany.

Alexandre's network of graduates from the German School Abroad (GSA) relies on powerful formal resources for transnational educational trajectories. The GSA—like other international or bilingual private schools in Brazil—is known for providing access to high-quality education for those who can pay high school fees and thus participate in the private education market. The GSA is also financed to a small degree by the German state, so Germany is effectively providing public support for elite education in Brazil.

At the GSA, Alexandre and his friends were well prepared for the competitive university entrance examinations in Brazil, and for a transnational educational career. The pupils receive not only intensive teaching in German and English but also advice on study opportunities in Germany, Brazil and other countries. During class trips to Germany, financed by their families, they visited various universities, so are informed about local admission requirements and study programmes. Some graduates go on to study in Germany, many others, like Alexandre, study at prestigious public or private (mostly catholic) universities in Brazil. There they have opportunities to participate in international exchange programmes and can receive scholarships for studying abroad. The German Academic Exchange Service

(DAAD) offers scholarships that are aimed exclusively at graduates of GSA. At the same time, as a consequence of being part of the GSA community, Alexandre and his friends also have informal resources in the form of transnational social networks. The GSA also actively encourages the formation of alumni networks.

The different resource environments of Luciana's and Alexandre's networks have led to differences in the predictability and security of transnational educational mobility. For the graduates of the GSA, it appears obvious to move to Germany to study. The clear regulation of the formal resources that supports their mobility protects individuals from uncertain arrangements with eventually unforeseeable outcomes. In contrast, Luciana was barely able to plan her transnational move and her educational career. She was only ready to seize the opportunity to migrate when it appeared. Luciana's path to an informally arranged stay as au pair in Germany was not completely risk-free at the outset, which is confirmed when she left her first 'host family' because of difficult working conditions. Unlike Alexandre, Luciana has to compensate her lack of economic resources and institutional support through remunerated work and informal support, which implies a deep involvement in social relations. As family members, friends and workers with restricted residency and work permit dependency, Luciana and her fellow care workers have to cope with challenges and conflicts that are absent in the educational careers of Alexandre and other graduates from private international schools.

Conclusion

The analysis presented here shows how social positions influence the educational resource environments of individuals, and how different environments can lead to different transnational orientations and trajectories. We have approached educational youth mobility as a form of migration motivated by educational aspirations. Drawing on the concept of educational resource environment, this can be seen as the reaction of certain individuals and families to perceiving the 'national' resource environment as insufficient to support their educational aspirations, reformulating the general view of migration as a strategy to reduce social risks and threats (Faist 2017).

Based on this realization, we have to ask about the perceived social risks that give rise to transnational educational orientations. For Alexandre, it is a labour market he perceives to be increasingly competitive that seems to justify his trip to Germany, a perception that can be seen as a reflection of the Brazilian economic recession since 2015. In Alexandre's narrative, the social risk seems not very serious but moving to Germany appears as a way to improve his cultural capital and to secure a privileged position. For Luciana, in contrast, transnational mobility constitutes a way to pursue educational opportunities that, in Brazil, seemed out of reach. In fact, Luciana and other young women of her network have experienced that, lacking economic resources, educational success at secondary school far from guarantees access to higher education or even vocational training, which puts them at a permanent risk of social exclusion (cf. Carnicer 2019; Fürstenau 2019).

On the whole, the cases of Luciana and Alexandre illustrate that transnational educational trajectories between Brazil and Germany reflect extremely different socio-demographic conditions. Young people from the social elite and the upper middle classes in Brazil can take part in the transnational educational market, thus benefitting from formal support of public institutions, and in the private market. On the other hand, young people who, feeling excluded from educational opportunities in Brazil and having no access to formal support structures, try to fulfil their high educational aspirations by going transnational. In their moves, they find and create informal support structures to help themselves, but also to help others. In this way, transnational social networks arise that contribute to further migration. These networks channel information and support, and create a setting which makes educational migration a more plausible option. This does not mean, however, that transnationalization, or transnational social networks mitigate social inequalities, at least not in a simple way.

Our research indicates that privileged young migrants benefit more often from formal resources, even in the third sector. Their academic paths and credentials, as well as their symbolic capital and habitus not only help them to access better educational institutions but also to obtain grants and scholarships. Often, these institutions actively promote alumni networks as a source of informal support for their graduates. In contrast, the scarcity of resources and the lower formality in underprivileged contexts determines much longer and more unpredictable trajectories. The effect of such informal resources may be rather ambivalent, as Luciana's case shows. She perceives her vocational training and her life in Germany as significant improvements, but she has still not fulfilled her aspirations to study at university, neither have the other women of her network. Their trajectories are subject not only to interlaced migration regimes and educational regulations but also to labour market precarity and the unpredictability of care regimes. Au pairing and the voluntary social year meet a demand for care workers on the edge between family and volunteering, or work, and this is the way through which migrants like Luciana try to open up educational opportunities. This is also a gendered strategy, as care work is constructed as a female domain, and the social networks that arise in this context are also gendered (cf. Lutz 2010). Transnational educational resource environments (provided by states, markets and the third sector and social networks) depend therefore not only on class, but also on gender.

Much of the research on educational youth mobility has concentrated on the mobility of students in higher education. Cases like Luciana, who aspires to higher education yet takes (first) a vocational path, appear less relevant to research agendas that focus on young people who have succeeded in entering universities outside their countries. The fields beyond universities, as well as informal and non-formal educational settings, thus remain a blind spot (Adick 2018). Luciana's case also shows how clear distinctions between labour migration, marriage migration, educational migration and so on fail to represent the complexities of (educational) youth mobility and, particularly in underprivileged contexts, researchers' focus on specific elements like work or family can blur the educational components of migration to the point of invisibility.

Notes

1. This chapter is based on a study conducted at Universität Hamburg, funded by the German Research Foundation (DFG), on 'Transnational education and social positioning between Brazil and Europe.'
2. Policies intended to facilitate access for black students have contributed to an increase in the number of students from disadvantaged backgrounds studying at public universities, yet extreme educational inequality prevails (Nierotka and Trevisol 2016).
3. The empirical corpus related to Luciana's network included 16 in-depth interviews as well as informal conversations and participant observations in different places in Brazil and Germany, where members of the network live. The main sources for the analysis presented in this chapter are interviews with Luciana, her parents and her two sisters conducted between 2015 and 2017. For Alexandre, his network included 11 in-depth and expert interviews with school staff, parents and graduates between 2014 and 2017, as well as informal conversations and participant observations in the school.

References

Adick, C. (2018). Transnational education in schools, universities, and beyond: Definitions and research areas. *Transnational Social Review, 8*(2), 124–138.
Aguiar, A., & Nogueira, M. A. (2012). Internationalisation strategies of Brazilian private schools. *International Studies in Sociology of Education, 22*(4), 353–368.
Almeida, A. M. F. (2015). The changing strategies of social closure in elite education in Brazil. In A. van Zanten, S. J. Ball, & B. Darchy-Koechlin (Eds.), *World yearbook of education 2015* (pp. 71–81). London: Routledge.
Altbach, P. G., & Knight, J. (2007). The internationalization of higher education: Motivations and realities. *Journal of Studies in International Education, 11*(3-4), 290–305.
Basch, L., Schiller, N., & Szanton Blanc, C. (1994). *Nations unbound. Transnational projects, postcolonial predicaments, and deterritorialized nation-states*. Langhorne, PA: Gordon and Breach.
Bildungsbericht – Autorengruppe Bildungsberichterstattung. (2018). *Bildung in Deutschland 2018: Ein indikatorengestützter Bericht mit einer Analyse zu Wirkungen und Erträgen von Bildung*. Bielefeld: wbv.
Carnicer, J. A. (2018). Transnational family and educational trajectories. *Transnational Social Review, 8*(2), 170–184.
Carnicer, J. A. (2019). Transnational migration and educational opportunities. A case study of migration from Brazil to Germany. *London Review of Education, 17*(1), 14–25.
Deppe, U., Helsper, W., Kreckel, R., Krüger, H.-H., & Stock, M. (2015). Germany's hesitant approach to elite education. In A. van Zanten, S. J. Ball, & B. Darchy-Koechlin (Eds.), *World yearbook of education 2015* (pp. 82–94). London: Routledge.
Faist, T. (2013). The mobility turn: A new paradigm for the social sciences? *Ethnic and Racial Studies, 36*(11), 1637–1646.

Faist, T. (2017). Transnational social protection in Europe: A social inequality perspective. *Oxford Development Studies, 45*(1), 20–32.

Fürstenau, S. (2015). Educação transnacional e posicionamento social entre o Brasil e a Europa. Um estudo qualitativo com famílias migrantes. In J. Bahia & M. Santos (Eds.), *Recortes interdisciplinares sobre a migração entre o Brasil e a Alemanha* (pp. 69–86). Porto Alegre: Letra and Vida.

Fürstenau, S. (2019). Educational aspirations of underprivileged female migrants. An ethnographic case study of a transnational network of care workers between Brazil and Germany. In I. Gogolin & K. Maaz (Eds.), *Migration und Bildungserfolg* (p. 34). Wiesbaden: VS.

Kesper-Biermann, S. (2016). Putting the nation in perspective: Educational spaces – a concept for the historiography of education. *International Journal for the Historiography of Education, 6*(1), 92–95.

Levitt, P., Viterna, J., Mueller, A., & Lloyd, C. (2017). Transnational social protection: Setting the agenda. *Oxford Development Studies, 45*(1), 2–19.

Lutz, H. (2010). Gender in the migratory process. *Journal of Ethnic and Migration Studies, 36*(10), 1647–1663.

Marcus, G. E. (1995). Ethnography in/of the world system: The emergence of multi-sited ethnography. *Annual Review of Anthropology, 24*(1), 95–117.

Mazzucato, V. (2008). Simultaneity and networks in transnational migration: Lessons learned from an sms methodology. In J. DeWind & J. Holdaway (Eds.), *Migration and development within and across borders* (pp. 71–102). Geneva: International Organization for Migration.

Nierotka, R. L., & Trevisol, J. V. (2016). Os jovens das camadas populares na universidade pública: acesso e permanência. *Katálysis, 19*(1), 22–32.

Pfeiffer, D. K. (2015). Das Bildungssystem Brasiliens unter besonderer Berücksichtigung des Hochschulwesens. In V. Oelsner & C. Richter (Eds.), *Bildung in Lateinamerika: Strukturen, Entwicklungen, Herausforderungen, Vol. 15 of Historisch-vergleichende Sozialisations- und Bildungsforschung* (pp. 78–97). Münster: Waxmann.

Pries, L. (Ed.). (2001). *New transnational social spaces: International migration and transnational companies in the early twenty-first century*. London: Routledge.

van Zanten, A., Ball, S. J., & Darchy-Koechlin, B. (Eds.). (2015). *Elites, privilege and excellence: The national and global redefinition of educational advantage. World yearbook of education 2015*. London: Routledge.

Windle, J., & Nogueira, M. A. (2015). The role of internationalisation in the schooling of Brazilian elites: Distinctions between two class fractions. *British Journal of Sociology of Education, 36*(1), 174–192.

Chapter 12
Refugees' Access to Higher Education in Italy: An Opportunity Lost for the 'Lost Generation'

Marcela Gola Boutros, Dulce Pimentel, and Alina Esteves

> As refugees are coming, and there is the so-called 'refugee crisis' in Europe, we are always known as those who create problems, especially in countries like Italy or Eastern Europe. Usually, we are not known for the good things, but for the negative image that the natives have of us. The best way for integration is to let us access education. It would be proof that we are ordinary people who can study, who can be part of the community, who can be useful. Tomorrow we will graduate, and we can work and contribute to society in our own way.
> (Interviewee, personal communication, 23 May 2018)

Tertiary education is a restricted resource, with only 34 per cent of the world's young people estimated to have access to universities (UNHCR 2016). Among refugees, this figure drops to 1 per cent, and many have been interrupted in their academic development. The high visibility of the so-called 'refugee crisis' in Europe has pushed governments to work towards the integration of these people, with Italy the country in the European Union (EU) with the highest numbers of such arrivals (UNHCR 2017). This study identifies a series of measures adopted by Italian academic institutions and government—central and regional—to integrate refugees into the country's higher education system. In this chapter, we will analyse the challenges refugees face in accessing tertiary education, and from this analysis, identify possible areas for improvement to enable students to make the most of their potential.

M. Gola Boutros (✉)
NOVA FCSH, Universidade Nova de Lisboa, Lisbon, Portugal

D. Pimentel
CICS NOVA, Universidade Nova de Lisboa, Lisbon, Portugal

A. Esteves
IGOT, Universidade de Lisboa, Lisbon, Portugal

© The Author(s), under exclusive license to Springer Nature Switzerland AG 2022
D. Cairns (ed.), *The Palgrave Handbook of Youth Mobility and Educational Migration*, https://doi.org/10.1007/978-3-030-99447-1_12

Tertiary education can play an important role in the lives of young refugees, helping them to settle into a new country and re-establish independence (Marcu 2018). Additionally, host countries can benefit from skilled and qualified workers. To explore this issue, and better appreciate how projects developed by universities and government operate, we conducted research with 16 students and seven professors at eight universities across Italy, between April and August 2018.[1]

Methodological Approach

Our methodological approach categorized the students according to four statuses: asylum seekers, refugees, subsidiary protection holders and humanitarian protection holders. Refugees and subsidiary protection holders have similar rights in Italy and are eligible for public and private funded scholarships. Humanitarian protection holders are allowed to be in the country for a shorter period than refugees and subsidiary protection holders. They are also entitled to a limited set of rights in relation to government scholarships, for which they are not eligible. Asylum seekers have not yet received international protection but have submitted an asylum claim and are waiting for a decision from government. By law, they are not admissible to Italian universities, except in a few exceptional situations.

Most of the participating students classified themselves as members of the middle or upper-middle class in their countries of origin. This is an important fact, contradicting the heavily stereotyped view that refugees are poor, destitute and lack social and economic capital. Refugees are also an extremely small population, and constitute only a tiny proportion of the migrant population, explaining why the interchangeable use of the terms 'migrant' and 'refugee' is highly problematic. In reality, the number of refugees who actually reach Europe is miniscule, especially compared to the volume of asylum seekers in Africa, Asia and the Middle East. And only those who have access to information and a reasonable amount of savings are able to flee to European countries.

Research Context and Findings

By investing in effective strategies to accommodate refugees, the EU can help prepare them for the labour market. Prior work on the inclusion of migrants into European society, including economic migrants and international protection holders, has also cited the importance of tertiary education as a means to achieve satisfactory levels of integration (Entzinger and Biezeveld 2003). On the other hand, research in Germany has found that even if migrants improve their educational level, they still face severe integration problems in the labour market (Kogan 2011). When it comes to the more specific cases of asylum seekers and refugees, there are additional difficulties related to the nature of their migratory processes. However, as

Hooper et al. (2017: 1) argue, assisting migrants to access the labour market 'is crucial to their successful integration into these communities, as it reduces their reliance on local welfare systems and strengthens their broader social inclusion.'

Marcu et al. (2018) point towards the fact that active labour market policies, along with improvement of the educational background of migrants in secondary education, results in a decrease in unemployment rates, although Kogan (2011) found in Germany that undertaking tertiary education does not necessarily support the integration of migrants in host countries. This does not mean that enabling access is useless. On the contrary, it reinforces the need for a reconfiguration of labour market policies, governmental support and tertiary education (Marcu et al. 2018).

Legal Impasses

Italian legislation determines that refugees and subsidiary protection beneficiaries have the same right to study as foreigners legally residing in Italy. In contrast, the procedures imposed by the Ministry of Internal Affairs suggest that asylum seekers can only access vocational training courses; that is, they do not have the right to attend long-term courses leading to undergraduate, master's and PhD-level degrees (Consiglio Italiano per i Rifugiati 2012).[2]

Recognition of Skills

Europe has its own guidelines to recognize the university degrees of third country nationals. It is called the Lisbon Recognition Convention (LRC) and suggests useful structures for the recognition of foreign qualifications and periods of study abroad. Unfortunately, 70 per cent of the countries who signed the LRC have not put Article VII into practice (UNESCO 2019). That means that most states do not have regulations at any level to recognize the qualifications of refugees and other displaced persons.

In Italy, these criteria and procedures are regulated directly by universities, and academic institutions have full decision-making authority to set their own rules. The Italian European Network of Information Centres in the European Region (ENIC-NARIC) office, called Information Centre on Academic Mobility and Equivalence (CIMEA), oversees the enforcement of the LRC along with the Conference of Italian Rectors (CRUI). Both entities are responsible for ensuring the LRC's effectiveness through the provision of training on recognition issues.

Italy also has active services to support the recognition of qualifications for refugees and subsidiary protection beneficiaries. Besides recognition services from the universities, the Ministry of Foreign Affairs provides a 'declaration of value' for individuals entitled to international protection, and CIMEA processes 'certificates of comparability of foreign qualifications' both for secondary and tertiary education. The Bologna Process and the European Qualifications Framework determines the European equivalent for qualifications obtained in third-party countries. The certificate does not formally recognize foreign titles in Italy. Instead, it is a tool that Italian institutions use to evaluate these qualifications in the recognition procedure.

In 2016, Erasmus+ launched a project in partnership with ENIC-NARIC offices in six countries. It consisted of a 'Toolkit for recognition of higher education for refugees, displaced persons and persons in a refugee-like situation.' This project was followed by 'REACT—Refugees and Recognition,' which aimed to improve the practices of the toolkit. This time, it included people who lack official documentation concerning their educational background. CIMEA on its own has a recognition programme called Attivazione del Coordinamento Nazionale sulla Valutazione delle Qualifiche dei Rifugiati (CNVQR). This consists of an informal network of experts to share assessment practices, handle problematic cases and provide guidance on relevant methodological strategies for making an accurate evaluation of the qualifications held by refugees, even in the absence of documentation.

Scholarship Offers

Refugees in Italy can access tertiary education through scholarships provided by the Ministero dell'Interno along with the Conferenza dei Rettori delle Università Italiane (CRUI), the Agenzia per il Diritto allo Studio Universitario (ADISU) or directly, from the universities. Some of the scholarships offer only services, while others provide an amount in cash directly to the students. The scholarships programmes from academic institutions are funded either by private initiative or by universities' own reserves.

Scholarships that offer services only usually provide students with housing in shared apartments and credits for meals in university refectories. However, without 'pocket money,' these students lack an ability to buy products in supermarkets and pharmacies, or to pay for services such as mobile phone top-ups. Transportation costs are not covered either, which is a major problem. More often than not, the books needed by the students are not available in public libraries or universities, potentially jeopardizing their academic experience and career prospects. Therefore, refugees who are awarded scholarships that offer only services have no choice but to work and study simultaneously. Universities that create and manage the scholarships themselves, funded by the private sector or out of their own budgets, are more malleable about the needs of the students. Their international offices usually receive students' claims and work on the improvement of services provided, adapting rules to the limitations of the aid.

The Measurement of a Challenge

The students interviewed reported difficulties after they had arrived in Italy, a lack of information being one of the hardest challenges. None of the refugees we interviewed knew how to apply for asylum or how this process would take place before arriving in Europe. NGOs and government reception centres supported some on their arrival and others made friends who helped them during their journeys or upon entry, but the majority had to learn to understand the system on their own. It was also hard to find scholarship opportunities. Many of the webpages relating to this matter are written in Italian, a language no one understood before reaching the country. However, all began to learn Italian as soon as they arrived, eventually achieving full proficiency. Nevertheless, academic vocabulary is a lot more complicated than everyday life idioms. For this reason, language-related difficulties remain in the classroom, particularly considering that advanced-level private language courses are expensive.

Changing Careers

Some students applied for degrees outside the areas in which they had previously studied or worked in their home countries; they thought that by making this choice, they would have fewer difficulties finding jobs in Europe. For example, one interviewee, an engineer, decided to study Linguistics and Intercultural Communication. He said it would be hard to gain recognition for his engineering degree in Italy, while he can use his language skills, speaking eight languages.

Mental Health Support

Psychological support plays a vital role in the integration of the students into academic institutions. Some received this kind of support when they arrived in Italy; others found it only after liaising with the universities, and there are those who never had access to it, either because they could not find it or did not want it. Sometimes, the lack of information within universities is so severe that certain students are provided with psychological support while others are not, even though they would have liked support. The professional in charge of communication and adaptation issues is the cultural mediator, who is fundamental to informing students about available services and assisting them with any difficulties they might have.

How Much of a Welcome?

Students who were attending the same institution had different perceptions about the way they were received. Even some who felt welcome mentioned that their institutions were not fully prepared to assist them. One interviewee, for instance, reported that she needed help to look for a home and to understand other things about the institution. If she had had an orientation session upon arrival, everything would have been easier. Another highlighted that cultural mediators help international students solve these problems. Very few universities have this category of professional to help foreign students with their adaptation. The international offices lack skilled staff to explain to students the evaluation system and the enrolment procedures in their courses. The Italian educational system also differs a lot from non-EU countries. Therefore, students need guidance from qualified professionals to understand it fully.

Due to some universities' planning issues, a few students were only able to begin to attend lectures a month after their courses had started. This situation delayed the learning process in comparison to the Italian students, as they lost a lot of content and had many difficulties in catching up.

When Studies and Work Collide

Most students were looking for a job, if not already working. The Ministero dell'Interno has defended the idea that foreign students should be able to work in the same way as Italian students. Such a comparison is irresponsible. Refugee students endure an arduous adaptation once they arrive in a new country and enter a new academic institution. Moreover, they are usually alone, while the majority of Italians can rely on their families and friends. They also have to face prejudice that often prevents them from being absorbed by the labour market. This situation does not relate to their set of skills or experience.

For foreign students, the first year of studies is the hardest in terms of adaptation. Providing scholarships that would allow them to only study would make it possible to take better advantage of the chance to attend university. Most students were in their own way able to rise to the challenges, both academic and professionally, despite all the difficulties, although improving the conditions to which they are submitted would significantly increase their potential to succeed. Some of the students who enjoy scholarships directly provided by the universities decided not to work because they could report their needs directly to the university staff if they were struggling with specific expenses. On the other hand, those who depended on government scholarships could not rely on easily reachable sources to process their claims. As one interviewee (personal communication, 29 May 2018) explained, the value of the award was quite small but the university was generous enough to pay for her accommodation, even though the standard benefits of her scholarship were not supposed to cover that.

Seven of the 16 students were employed. Four did not have jobs in their area of studies, while the other three were performing their roles as skilled workers. The latter faced difficulties with finding qualified jobs and said it was tough to reconcile work and studies. Those who were not working as qualified personnel found it easier to manage their professional and student lives. This scenario might be due to the pressure that those who were in skilled jobs put on themselves, trying to stand out not only in class but also in their careers. Those who had 'random jobs'—that is, work not related to what they were studying—did not need to make a career out of their occupation. Therefore, they could focus better on their studies.

Aspirations

Finding the opportunity to (re)access university is appreciated by all the students, and pursuing a PhD or using their own experience to help others in similar situations is an aspiration shared by many. Either way, students mentioned that academia is the best path towards the achievement of their goals and restitution of their independence. The previously cited interviewee (personal communication, 29 May 2018) referred to the university as an opportunity to 'change this title of "refugee,"' since as a student, she feels integrated into society. These students also believe that a degree from a European university will raise their chances of being hired in Italy. When asked if they intend to stay in Italy or not, most of them say that this is their goal, unless they do not have a stable job.

Five Steps to Improve the System

In bringing this discussion to a close, we will identify five specific means through which we believe the current system in Italy can be improved, based on ideas emerging out of the preceding analysis:

1. *Access to information and the status barrier*

The students highlighted that university procedures were not clear once they started their studies. They said it would have been less of a struggle to understand the system if they had received proper guidance from a dedicated professional. They did not know where to find basic information such as the schedule of their lectures, the subjects that were available for them in each semester and the structure and dates of the exams. It was also a struggle to find information about scholarships in languages other than Italian. There is also a need to translate websites of the government and universities into different languages so that refugees can find opportunities more quickly. The content could be enabled in English, French and Arabic to improve online searches. The Università degli Studi di Trento and the Università Telematica Uninettuno found ways to provide scholarships for applicants whose asylum applications were still being evaluated by the government. They got around the bylaws of the Italian government in enrolling asylum seekers, since it might take years to complete the international protection granting process. We suggest that other universities try to do the same, according to their possibilities and limitations.

2. *Absence of documentation and application procedures*

Since the universities have the autonomy to handle the application process from beginning to end, the way that the lack of documents will be managed depends exclusively on the institution. Most refugees were not able to take their academic transcripts and diplomas with them when fleeing their countries. Therefore, universities that are keen to accept refugee students must create alternative solutions to evaluate whether the applicants are ready to enrol. We gathered some examples of ideas to overcome this issue are the acceptance of digitalized documents and the application of assessment tests to identify the primary skills of the candidates and the areas of interest to study. The graduate programmes available in the countries of origin of the candidates and Italy differed a lot. For this reason, it is crucial to understand which graduation programmes the knowledge brought by the candidate fit best.

The degrees that require entry tests, such as medicine and nursing, are barely accessible for refugees. Applicants must take specific assessment exams, and while regular international students can perform them in English, refugee students—who are considered EU students—have to do them in Italian. To overcome this issue, we suggest that refugee students are put in the same group as international students. The exams in Italian evaluate knowledge about the country's culture, in which refugees do not usually score highly. Such knowledge is not demanded in English-performed tests for international students.

3. *International mobility programmes*

The need for international mobility programmes in universities was mentioned multiple times by the students. Several European academic institutions are part of the Erasmus programme scheme, in which students can benefit from a semester abroad in a European university other than that where they are enrolled. However, the financial aid in this programme for students is tiny, and hinders the participation of refugees. It is essential to work on solutions to provide refugees with the possibility to participate in academic exchange programmes, especially when they are studying other languages and planning to become intercultural mediators.

4. *Lessons for the future*

We asked the students what should be done differently with new refugees so their academic experience could be better than theirs. Current students explained that refugees do not have time to celebrate when they are granted legal immigration status in Italy. The financial support given by the government expires six months after refugee status is confirmed. From this moment, they start to worry about finding a place to live and a job. The fear of not being able to arrange minimum living conditions prevents them from focusing on applying for universities. Accessing higher education is an excellent chance to secure a stable life in the future (Marcu 2018). If they do not have the time to search for opportunities and apply, those who have a background that matches the higher education system requirements are wasting their best chance to succeed in the hosting country. Furthermore, both Italian society and prospective students would benefit from a screening system once they are granted refugee status. Such a system could be directed towards universities whose refugees have an interest in (re)accessing tertiary education. With this initiative, beneficiaries of international protection would not have to struggle to find accommodation and employment. They would have guidance to enrol in a university and receive proper support for their future.

Once the students are enrolled, it is of utmost importance to provide them with Italian courses focused on the academic language. The university is the right place for them to find the most appropriate professionals to help them with this issue. Higher education institutions (HEIs) could encourage native students to assist the refugees with the language, giving them an extracurricular activity certificate or an acknowledgement for volunteering.

5. *Expanding opportunities*

The interviewed students also suggested that the number of scholarships is too small in comparison to the number of candidates. It is vital to encourage the private sector to engage in this initiative by funding the scholarships. Enterprises could even sign agreements with the universities to employ the students after their graduation with internship or trainee programmes. This sort of agreement would be a way to persuade companies to support migrants not only in the academy, but also to boost their careers. When setting up the terms of the agreement, though, institutions and students should be careful. The agreement should not put students in a position of owing the value spent in their studies to the company. The principles of labour mobility should be respected and the students, who will be professionals by then, should be free to switch jobs as they wish.

As for the incompleteness of the services provided by the scholarships funded by the government and universities—such as transport, pocket money and books—this could also be fixed with more investment from the private sector. With more companies engaged in this cause, it will be possible not only to increase the number of scholarships but also improve the quality of the support given to the students.

Conclusion

The number of available scholarships in Italy is higher than the number of refugees who (re)access tertiary education. 'Immigration status' is the biggest obstacle for applicants who have not yet been granted international protection. Refugee status or subsidiary protection is only granted to a small proportion of migrants who arrive in the country. Hence, the universities have a higher number of vacancies than eligible candidates. It is therefore vital to spread information about scholarships in more efficient ways. It is hard for the candidates to find opportunities and understand the requirements for enrolment, especially when content is written in a language that they do not fully understand. For applicants who meet all the criteria for enrolment in the universities but do not have refugee or subsidiary protection status, institutions could make efforts to sponsor student visas to welcome them either way.

While some Italian universities take 20 refugee students, others have none. Increasing the involvement of (more) HEIs is essential to improve the integration system. Furthermore, students need more flexibility from the universities to adapt. For instance, the Università degli Studi di Pavia does not require a minimum number of credits to be completed by students in each year. They can study at their own pace and even have an additional year if they are not able to complete their studies in the standard period.

We found that those who have the power to encourage the integration of refugees in society are responsible for the success or failure of initiatives. In universities where staff are motivated to help refugees, and projects are worked on with (com) passion, the results tend to be positive. However, when the people involved are not committed or engaged in making the projects work and grow, this fails to boost inclusion within universities. Some institutions are also establishing agreements with non-EU universities. This practice can help, especially in the reconstruction of the students' home countries. The Università Telematica Uninettuno is a partner with universities in the Mediterranean and beyond, to facilitate recognition of the students' qualifications in their countries of origin if they decide to go back.

The opportunity to study was perceived by the students in this research as a turning point in their lives. Through this, they can validate and improve their skills, increasing their chances of being hired by the Italian labour market. When studying, they are not labelled as refugees anymore. They become professionals of high importance for global development. But even though the scenario is favourable, the challenge remains to provide the opportunity to study for more refugees. HEIs and society must expand the network to create ways of regularizing the situation of all suitable candidates so they will be able to enrol. Supporting refugees can be highly profitable for the hosting countries. It allows European countries to expand its young and skilled workforce, and vulnerable migrants can take back their dignity. Refugees tend not to give up: they are resilient either by nature or due to their circumstances. The human capital that comes along with them is the most valuable asset for European society, teaching us how to survive a crisis and keep battling to empower the next generations.

Acknowledgements The material included in this chapter was developed in a project entitled, 'Access to higher education among refugees and migrants in emergency situations in Italy: An opportunity for the so-called "lost generation,"' written by Marcela Gola Boutros under the supervision of Professor Dulce Pimentel and Professor Alina Esteves at Nova University of Lisbon.

Notes

1. There was also a two-month engagement in participant observation, which took place in a state-run school that provides Italian language courses for foreigners, where most refugees encounter the challenge of learning Italian for the first time
2. Only two Italian provinces are not subject to regional power, Trento and Bolzano, and can create and manage their own legislation. For instance, the Università degli Studi di Trento signed an agreement with the Autonomous Province of Trento and the Cinformi (Immigration Information Centre) that allowed asylum seekers to start their tertiary education studies before being granted international protection.

References

Consiglio Italiano per i Rifugiati. (2012). *Il Regolamento Dublino e la procedura di asilo in Italia. Conosci i tuoi diritti? Guida per richiedenti asilo*. Italy: Consiglio Italiano per i Rifugiati.

Entzinger, H., & Biezeveld, R. (2003). *Benchmarking in immigrant integration. Report for the European Commission*. Rotterdam: European Research Centre on Migration and Ethnic Relations.

Hooper, K., Salant, B., & Desiderio, M. V. (2017). *Empowering cities through better use of EU instruments improving the labour market integration of migrants and refugees improving the labour market integration of migrants and refugees*. Brussels: Migration Policy Institute Europe (MPI).

Kogan, I. (2011). New immigrants—Old disadvantage patterns? Labour market integration of recent immigrants into Germany. *International Migration, 49*(1), 91–117.

Marcu, S. (2018). Refugee students in Spain: The role of universities as sustainable actors in institutional integration. *Sustainability (Switzerland), 10*(6), 2082.

Marcu, N., Siminica, M., Noja, G. G., Cristea, M., & Dobrota, C. E. (2018). Migrants' integration on the European labor market: A spatial bootstrap, SEM and network approach. *Sustainability (Switzerland), 10*(12), 4543.

UNESCO & Council of Europe. (2019). *Monitoring the implementation of the Lisbon Recognition Convention*. Paris: UNESCO.

UNHCR. (2016). *Missing out: Refugee education in crisis*. Geneva: UNHCR.

UNHCR. (2017). *Desperate journeys. January 2017–March 2018*. Geneva: UNHCR.

Chapter 13
After Mobility: The Long-Term Impact of Study Abroad on Professional Teacher Behaviour

Grada Okken and Robert Coelen

> My vision changed dramatically. I now realize how many perspectives there are; are you really sure about what you see and observe when you look at a child; is this the real and only truth? (Okken et al. 2019)

This statement was made by a teacher in a reflective interview about her study abroad experience during a Teacher Education (TE) programme. It illustrates not only the transformation of the teacher as an individual but also shows that study abroad experience affected her as a professional. We can be reasonably confident that such a teacher will also be able to maximize opportunities to transfer these insights into teaching practice and ensure that the children in her professional care are provided with opportunities to appreciate multiple perspectives born out of diversity. Given its potential significance, this chapter provides insight into this particular form of internationalization. Since the beginning of this century, research on this topic has mostly focused on the tertiary education domain, leading to various approaches to internationalization in tertiary education being explored. In contrast, this chapter focuses more on the learner, and learning outcomes, recognizing the importance of mobility in sequential levels of education: primary, secondary and tertiary (see Coelen 2016).

The creation of lifelong learning lines, dealing with international awareness and intercultural competence, allows for revisiting the notion that internationalization should be present only within the tertiary education domain. The use of learning outcomes implicitly promotes a transformative learning approach (Biggs and Tang 2011), aligned with a more desired form of internationalization of the curriculum (Mestenhauser 1998). It is important to recognize that the learning outcomes of internationalization can also be viewed as enabling teachers to understand,

---

G. Okken (✉) • R. Coelen
Centre for Internationalisation of Education, University of Groningen,
Groningen, The Netherlands
e-mail: grada.okken@nhlstenden.com

effectively deal with and use diversity on the basis of ethnicity, culture and/or nationality.

Recognizing the opportunity to extend internationalization into secondary and primary education has two potential effects: firstly, the total curricular space for internationalization increases, and, secondly, the level of proficiency in respect to the learning outcomes can be extended provided continuous learning lines are established across various education sectors. Currently, the prevailing experience in higher education is that we barely get through the stage of 'getting used to' various learned forms of diversity (e.g., ethnic, cultural and disciplinary) and more inherent categories such as gender, race and sexual orientation (Hewlett et al. 2013). Indeed, there is ample evidence of reluctance on the part of students to join culturally diverse collaborating groups (Ledwith et al. 1998; Volet and Ang 1998; Montgomery 2009; Kimmel and Volet 2012). We need to go beyond this stage if we are to equip graduates to effectively leverage diversity for solving complex problems, be they societal or professional (Hunt et al. 2018). This would represent a good reason to focus on internationalization or diversity more generally earlier in life (e.g., starting from primary education).

Already at pre-tertiary level therefore we would need to create experiences that show how various kinds of diversity can bring about a cognitive diversity bonus that leads to groups possessing more than an additive advantage (Page 2017). For many students, their tertiary education (even at bachelor level) is the last step before entering the workforce. After graduation, they should be able to work in a diverse team of colleagues, although to dissimilar degrees in various parts of the world. Well-developed skills relevant for these working settings might lead to higher effectiveness of teams. For example, in the Netherlands, the Dutch Education Council (2016) has suggested that internationalization, in the form of activities that ensure being able to interact, to work effectively with and to understand cultural, ethnic, or national diversity, should start at primary education and continue through all levels of education as continuous learning lines.

The Internationalized Classroom

The multicultural classroom, experienced in many nations, becomes a potentially rich learning context for both teachers and pupils. The term 'multicultural classroom' seems overly broad, often intertwined with the notion of intercultural education, which 'emphasizes teaching that accepts and respects that diversity is normal in all areas of life' (Osad'an et al. 2016: 77). And in terms of diversity, intercultural education embraces a wide array of diversity, from multicultural education, to active citizenship, inclusive education, gender and LGBT matters, multilingualism and any other form of education that focuses on acceptance of others (Osad'an et al. 2016). Three aspects of intercultural education show the many opportunities and responsibilities for teachers to implement diversity in their profession: (1) teaching a classroom of diverse students, (2) using intercultural teaching methods, and (3) implementing multicultural content or teaching materials (Osad'an et al. 2016).

Unfortunately, although the international classroom exists in many countries, many TE programmes are not comprehensively preparing student teachers for intercultural education (Dutch Education Council 2017; Delk 2019). Teachers who are not aware that pupils with a migration background may have different approaches to solving problems, or indeed have different knowledge and skills, may not be able to build on the knowledge and experience of these children (OECD 2015). Depending on the country, between about three per cent to 47 per cent of teachers reported the need for professional development for teaching in a multicultural setting (OECD 2015). Other reports show evidence of similar levels of systemic problems in multicultural classrooms with teachers being insufficiently prepared (European Commission 2019). International aspects of teaching thus require more attention in TE curricula to ensure that all children can learn regardless of their cultural background (Gay 2000; Cushner and Mahon 2002). Only teachers who are culturally responsive and internationally oriented can in turn educate pupils in primary school classrooms to broaden their perspectives and to become interculturally competent themselves.

This represents a clear call for TE programmes to prepare their students for an intercultural learning setting. This can be achieved through focusing on Internationalization at Home (IaH) (Billingsley 2016); 'developing intercultural/ international awareness locally for home-based students' (Heffernan et al. 2018: 1). In literature, IaH is viewed from wide-ranging to narrow perspectives, and shows the connection to Internationalization of the Curriculum in Higher Education, described as the purposeful integration of international and intercultural dimensions into the formal and informal curriculum for all students within domestic learning environments (Beelen and Jones 2015: 8). IaH can offer students the opportunity to explore their study content through international lenses, by following internationalized courses and additional study programmes or by having an international team of lecturers, showing different approaches to the subjects. All these international dimensions in home campuses should be embedded in higher education institutions (HEIs) holistically (Knight 2004), with a transformative approach (Mestenhauser 1998), preferably integrated across as much of a degree programme as possible (Böckenhauer 2017).

However, IaH is aiming to achieve international learning outcomes through education at home. This might be too limited to stimulate intercultural learning and behaviour among students, as this type of learning mostly stays within students' own familiar settings and comfort zones. Yet, actual intercultural learning requires genuine and authentic intercultural experiences for student teachers, which is the anchor of effective teaching in multicultural contexts after graduation (Gay and Kirkland 2003). Therefore, instead of IaH, Internationalization Abroad might be more effective for students, as many studies show the achievement of valuable learning outcomes of student mobility (e.g., Shaftel et al. 2007; Braskamp 2009; Walkington 2015), even if the study abroad period is short in duration (Abraham and Von Brömssen 2018). In TE programmes, Internationalization Abroad can take the form of exchange programmes, courses at other universities and/or internships abroad. These forms of mobility help student teachers prepare for the teaching profession and the internationalized classroom, as study abroad programmes can generate a revised perspective on learning and teaching, contributing to professional teacher development (Mesker et al. 2018; Okken et al. 2019).

Motivations for Study Abroad

Motivation for study abroad has received a great deal of research interest, leading to our understanding of a wide array of motivational factors (e.g., Salisbury et al. 2009; Presley 2010; Li et al. 2013; Pope et al. 2014; Janda 2016; Bretag and Van der Veen 2017). Student characteristics, in the form of social, human, financial and cultural capital appear to be crucial factors in the decision to become internationally mobile (Salisbury et al. 2009). These include gender, parental educational level, prior international experience, age and household income (Hackney et al. 2012; Coelen and Nairn 2017). Thus, one could infer that some groups of students might need more support to decide whether or not to study abroad than those whose characteristics predispose them positively towards such activity. National and supra-national support systems have been shown to be effective in enhancing opportunities for students, but unequal participation between different socio-economic groups seems to persist (Wiers-Jenssen 2011).

Personal values are also seen as motives for study abroad. These values drive mobility intentions and actions of students. Based on personal values, students have specific reasons to study abroad and, in turn, choose a certain destination, programme content and learning goals for their international journey. Yet, beliefs and values play a crucial role in the decision-making process. Bargal (1981) states that values arise from socio-economic background, home life and earlier personal experiences. Viewing values as a combination of beliefs, attitudes, aspirations, and perceptions, they 'serve to frame and constrain choices' (Salisbury et al. 2009: 123). In this sense, values can be defined as the deputies of motivations and the associated behavioural component will be translated into codes of ethics, impacting on professional practices (Rokeach 1973). Goel et al. (2010) have also argued that behavioural beliefs are the primary drivers for students to take part in a study abroad programme; thus, personal values are an important motive, alongside more pragmatic considerations relating to the economic value of stays abroad.

Relating to values as motivating actions, in one of our prior studies (Okken et al. 2019) we analysed terminal and instrumental values as motivational factors for respondents who had studied abroad during TE programmes (see also Rokeach 1973). Terminal values—or forms of desirable existence—are divided between social (focused on others) and personal values (self-focused). Instrumental values are behavioural descriptors, identifying the preferred behaviour to reach the terminal values. These values include morality and competence. In our study, respondents were asked to describe their motives for studying abroad during a TE programme. Most teachers referred to personal terminal values (e.g., adventure, becoming independent, interest in education) and instrumental values (e.g., helping others, broadening horizons) instead of social terminal values (e.g., equality, social recognition). Notably, a possible relationship appeared between the values mentioned, motives and destination of study abroad.

The aforementioned instrumental value 'interest in education' appears to be an important motive for student teachers to go abroad. This is in line with Peden (as cited in Presley 2010), who argued that students who consider going abroad for study purposes are especially motivated to increase their professional development, including academic credit, language credit, practical experience and resumé building. At the same time, a more personal motivator as a desire for individual growth like 'becoming independent' could also lead to a stronger intent to study abroad, leading to a combination of professional and personal motivational factors. But while the above describes motivational factors mostly related to individual students, higher education institutes (HEIs) in their own right cannot be excluded from the list of study abroad motivators. Indeed, academics play a significant role, and the institution, and the way it represents study abroad opportunities, are also significant factors (Asaoka and Yano 2009; Engle 2012; Paus and Robinson 2008). Special attention to internationalization in various forms, including study abroad opportunities, could encourage students to broaden their horizon (Bishop 2013).

Study Abroad Learning Outcomes

A growing number of Internationalization of Education studies have examined the wide-ranging and short-term effects of study abroad. These short-term effects concern mainly personal and professional skills, and competencies such as personal development (Shaftel et al. 2007), intercultural competence development and twenty first century skills (Teichler 2004; Deardorff 2006; European Union 2014), as well as global citizenship (Braskamp 2009). Few empirical studies have looked at the long-term impacts, instead focusing on a specific skill or attitude rather than professional development holistically. To illustrate, Browne (2005) and Shimmi et al. (2017, 2018 cited in Ota and Shimmi 2019) have looked at career progress. Other research has investigated career choices influenced by study abroad (Norris and Gillespie 2009).

Effect on Teacher Behaviour

Recent data from the Dutch TE programmes shows that 15 per cent of all full-time students in bachelor programmes for education (primary and secondary) go abroad for a study period. This represents the least mobile group, although participation is growing (Huberts 2016). Findings of the application of study abroad experiences on teacher behaviour include shaping and changing a teaching philosophy, improved cultural consciousness and reflection on teaching and learning (e.g., Shiveley and Misco 2015; Okken et al. 2019). It is worthwhile highlighting the fact that value development can benefit from extra attention during study abroad. Since students are in a foreign country for educational purposes, they have the opportunity to examine their own values, beliefs and world views. This examination might lead to either 'the accentuation of values brought by the students' or 'the acquisition of new structures and combinations of values and world views' (Bargal 1981: 48). The opportunity for, and degree of, examination of values depends on factors such as the study abroad destination (Biraimah and Jotia 2013; Okken et al. 2019). Some educational contexts can lead to an increased appreciation for one's own educational systems or materials, while other destinations tend to incubate a more negative opinion about one's own system and educational strategies. These adaptations of values influence the professional identity and educational philosophy of teachers.

Other studies concerning the application of study abroad experience in the teaching profession (e.g., Cushner and Mahon 2002; Lee 2011; Biraimah and Jotia 2013) describe the impact on teacher's self-efficacy and self-awareness, appreciation for curricular materials, a sustained growth in knowledge of teaching methodologies and making considered choices for curricular content. Another observation was that pre-service teachers were more open and tolerant towards people from another culture after study abroad (Shiveley and Misco 2015; Klein and Wikan 2019). In their study, Klein and Wikan showed that 98 per cent of respondents felt better prepared and more competent as teachers in multicultural classrooms. This could be the result of more empathy through better understanding of various learning styles and language learners (Boynton-Hauerwas et al. 2017). This would be further aided by a greater oral proficiency after study abroad (Freed 1998; Van de Berg 2009). This could help TE students to become culturally responsive by becoming more differentiating, based on cultural and educational needs (Cushner and Mahon 2002; Cushner and Brennan 2007).

The described learning outcomes for the teaching profession can be influenced by several factors. In an earlier unpublished study, we asked teachers with study abroad experience to describe the elements that influenced their perceived study abroad outcomes. In response to this question, a range of enablers as positive influential factors for learning was discussed, of which three seemed to be most influential. First, social contact was described as an important enabler for a positive experience. Besides making new friends with other study abroad students from the same home country, respondents mentioned that they became friends with people from the local community as well, including teachers from the local primary school in which they taught, and local students from national TE programmes or universities. This gave them a feeling of security and led to more confidence in learning.

Whereas contact with peers and mentor-teachers was described as a positive influence on learning outcomes by some teachers, others mentioned the opposite, as less connection with the local community led to emotional situations; for example, one teacher described:

> Well, I didn't feel a total outsider, but they did look at me in a certain way. [...]. I therefore felt different, because I came from The Netherlands. That was also due to our transportation to the school; we actually had a taxi driver and while we were driving to the school in the morning, the children were walking next to the taxi and this almost made me feel like someone else... like a queen or something.

The second important enabler for learning outcomes which was mentioned by respondents was having a contact person in the home and/or host country. This was a lecturer or teacher from a TE programme or local primary school. The possibility to discuss critical issues and study progress helped them to focus on their development. Third, an organized and structured study abroad programme was an appreciated enabler, mostly mentioned by exchange students who studied in another university within a TE programme. Being able to start studying right away with clear guidelines and explanations made the experience very positive for these students.

Aside from the positive elements of study abroad, interviewed teachers also described blockers for study abroad learning. Many were concerned with research in the host country. Teachers mentioned the discrepancy in research standards, the suitability of research topics and time to conduct research; the lack of time, due to many expectations on hosting mentor-teachers in the study abroad destination, led to fewer learning outcomes. This resulted in a lower number of academic outcomes or professional development with regard to research and/or academic skills.

Most participants also indicated that the differences in educational systems and teaching methods were a blocker of academic development, especially during the first weeks of the period abroad. Being exposed to aggression, unfamiliar and physical behaviour, management policies, other communication patterns and solely teacher-centred learning activities led to feelings of frustration and insecurity. However, referring to the theory of transformative learning (Mezirow 2009), one might argue that these situations could result in even more learning outcomes, albeit unexpected. These experiences might also cause students to change their structures of knowledge and their current beliefs, by being exposed to new or unexpected information in another country. Namely, learning will occur through facing challenging situations and disoriented dilemmas (Mezirow 2009), which purposefully leads to questions, moments of reflection, and discussions with peers. In turn, this can create an adjusted view of the world. Nevertheless, students should be completely aware of this learning process and have the skills to critically reflect on situations to translate these moments into effective learning. Otherwise, study abroad would be an experience without meaning.

Reviewing the literature on outcomes of student-teachers' mobility, the relevance of study abroad becomes obvious. Short and long-term effects will influence the teaching profession and the behaviour of a young professional in the classroom. Considering all universal study abroad effects described in literature, the newly qualified teacher with study abroad experience will have essential qualities to work effectively in the current educational setting in primary schools with culturally diverse student populations. Once reflection as essential part of study abroad (Engle and Engle 2003) is included, study abroad learning can move beyond the short-term learning of knowledge and skills and also have a profound influence on the intercultural learning of the next generations.

Concluding Remarks

While the importance of student mobility is becoming obvious for student teachers and curriculum developers in the field of education, we also recognize the fact that it takes years to fully utilize mobility outcomes in their profession. Therefore, more initiatives are needed to internationalize pre-tertiary education. An internationalized world requires intercultural competencies and an international orientation, meaning that children need to be prepared, something that cannot wait until the current generation of student teachers graduate. Therefore, we recognize the importance of training and creating suitable training instruments for employed teachers in primary schools to develop their own intercultural competencies that broaden their international perspective, and which they can hand over to the next generation at once. At the same time, after recognizing positive outcomes and with an increasing awareness of its necessity, HEIs should revise policies for student teachers' mobility. This might start with an overview of the needs of pupils in the primary school classroom. What kind of teacher do they need? And how could teachers with study abroad experiences connect to these needs? What should be essential in mobility programmes? A valuable approach would be for TE programmes to strengthen the connection to the primary education work field. Indicating which challenges are included in the field of primary schools will better prepare student teachers for the actual profession. A mutual transformation agenda is key in achieving these goals (Kumar and Parveen 2013).

Also, although the percentage of TE students going abroad is increasing, there will still be many teachers entering the multicultural classrooms without such international experiences. Given the fact that the majority of TE students in the foreseeable future are not going abroad, more work is required to develop IaH. TE curricula need to be redeveloped to ensure non-mobile TE students also achieve mastery of the requisite skills through other activities and content, although it remains to be seen whether IaH is sufficient to suitably equip teachers. Still, it would be reasonable to assume that these IaH activities could also potentially enhance the effectiveness of a study abroad period. A small glimmer of hope are the observations by Abraham and Von Brömssen (2018), who show that even short periods of study abroad have some learning effects. This, together with the growing diversity in education, shows the importance of internationalization at all levels of education. Because even schools with little or no culturally diverse classrooms have pupils and teachers who are consciously or subconsciously part of the globalized world. We believe it is of extreme significance that their education prepares them for this.

References

Abraham, G. Y., & Von Brömssen, K. (2018). Internationalisation in teacher education: Student teachers' reflections on experiences from a field study in South Africa. *Education Inquiry, 9*(4), 347–362.

Asaoka, T., & Yano, J. (2009). The contributions of 'Study Abroad' programmes to Japanese internationalization. *Journal of Studies in International Education, 13*, 174–188.

Bargal, D. (1981). Social values in social work: A developmental model. *The Journal of Sociology and Social Welfare, 8*(1), 45–61.

Beelen, J., & Jones, E. (2015). Looking Back at 15 Years of Internationalisation at Home. *Forum,* Winter, 6-8.

Biggs, J., & Tang, C. (2011). *Teaching for Quality Learning at University – What the Student Does.* New York: Open University Press.

Billingsley, B. (2016). Ways to prepare future teachers to teach science in multicultural classrooms. *Cultural Studies of Science Education, 11*, 283–291.

Biraimah, K. L., & Jotia, A. L. (2013). The longitudinal effects of study abroad programs on teachers' content knowledge and perspectives: Fulbright-Hays group projects abroad in Botswana and Southeast Asia. *Journal of Studies in International Education, 17*(4), 433–454.

Bishop, S. C. (2013). The rhetoric of study abroad: Perpetuating expectations and results through technological enframing. *Journal of Studies in International Education, 17*(4), 398–413.

Böckenhauer, M. (2017). Developing an intercultural competence intervention. In R. Coelen, K.-W. Van der Hoek, & H. Blom (Eds.), *Valorisation of internationalisation – About internationalisation of higher education* (pp. 208–225). Leeuwarden: Stenden.

Boynton-Hauerwas, L., Skawinski, S. F., & Ryan, L. B. (2017). The longitudinal impact of teaching abroad: An analysis of intercultural development. *Teaching and Teacher Education, 67*, 202–213.

Braskamp, L. A. (2009). Internationalization in higher education: Four issues to consider. *Journal of College and Character, 10*(6), 1–7.

Bretag, T., & Van der Veen, R. (2017). 'Pushing the boundaries:' Participant motivation and self-reported benefits of short-term international study tours. *Innovation in Education and Teaching International, 54*(3), 175–183.

Browne, C. (2005) 2005 HEDS alumni survey: Class of 2000. St. Paul, MN: Institutional Research Office, Macalester College.

Coelen, R. J. (2016). A learner-centred internationalisation of higher education. In E. Jones, R. J. Coelen, R. Beelen, & H. De Wit (Eds.), *Global and Local Internationalization* (pp. 35–42). Rotterdam: Sense Publishers.

Coelen, R. J., & Nairn, P. (2017). Student motivation for non-degree international mobility. In R. J. Coelen, K.-W. Van der Hoek, & H. Blom (Eds.), *Valorisation of internationalisation – About internationalisation of higher education* (pp. 239–259). Leeuwarden: Stenden.

Cushner, K., & Brennan, S. (Eds.). (2007). *Intercultural student teaching: A bridge to global competence*. Lanham, MD: Rowman and Littlefield Education.

Cushner, K., & Mahon, J. (2002). Overseas student teaching: Affecting personal, professional, and global competencies in an age of globalization. *Journal of Studies in International Education, 6*(1), 44–58.

Deardorff, D. K. (2006). Identification and Assessment of Intercultural Competence as a Student Outcome of Internationalization. *Journal of Studies in International Education, 10*(3), 241–266.

Delk, T. D. (2019). Are teacher-credentialing programs providing enough training in multiculturalism for pre-service teachers? *Journal for Multicultural Education, 13*(3), 258–275.

Dutch Education Council (Onderwijsraad). (2016). *Internationaliseren met ambitie*. Den Haag: Onderwijsraad.

Dutch Education Council (Onderwijsraad). (2017). *Vluchtelingen en onderwijs: Naar een efficiëntere organisatie, betere toegankelijkheid en hogere kwaliteit*. Den Haag: Onderwijsraad.

Engle, L. (2012). The rewards of qualitative assessment to study abroad. *Frontiers: The Interdisciplinary Journal of Study Abroad, 9*(1), 1–20.

Engle, L., & Engle, J. (2003). Study abroad levels: Toward a classification of program types. *Frontiers: The Interdisciplinary Journal of Study Abroad, 9*, 1–20.

European Commission/EACEA/Eurydice. (2019). *Integrating students from migrant backgrounds into schools in Europe: National policies and measures*. Eurydice Report. Luxembourg: Publications Office of the European Union.

European Union (2014). The Erasmus Impact Study. Effects of mobility on the skills and the employability of students and the internationalisation of higher education institutions. Luxembourg: Publications Office of the European Union

Freed, B. F. (1998). An overview of issues and research in language learning in a study abroad setting. *Frontiers: The Interdisciplinary Journal of Study Abroad, 4*, 31–60.

Gay,G. Culturally Responsive Teaching (2000) – ik weet even niet welke editie jij hebt gebruikt. De eerste was gepubliceerd in 2000, maar 2nd edition 2010 en laatste editie (3rd) in 2018

Gay, G., & Kirkland, K. (2003). Developing cultural critical consciousness and self-reflection in preservice teacher education. *Theory into Practice, 42*(3), 181–187.

Goel, L., de Jong, P., & Schnusenberg, O. (2010). Toward a Comprehensive Framework of Study Abroad Intentions and Behaviors. *Journal of Teaching in International Business, 21*, 248–265.

Hackney, K., Boggs, D., & Borozan, A. (2012). An Empirical Study of Student Willingness to Study Abroad. *Journal of Teaching in International Business, 23*(2), 123–144.

Heffernan, T., Morrison, D., Magne, P., Payne, S., & Cotton, D. (2018). Internalising internationalisation: Views of internationalisation of the curriculum among non-mobile home students. *Studies in Higher Education, 44*(12), 1–15.

Hewlett, S. A., Marshall, M., & Sherbin, L. (2013). How diversity can drive innovation. *Harvard Business Review, 91*(12), 30–30.

Huberts, D. (2016). *Outgoing student mobility in Dutch higher education, 2015-2016*. The Hague: Nuffic.

Hunt, V., Prince, S., Dixon-Fyle, S., & Yee, L. (2018). *Delivering through diversity*. London: McKinsey and Company.

Janda, S. (2016). Segmenting students based on study abroad motivations, attitudes, and preferences. *Journal of International Education in Business, 9*(2), 111–122.

Kimmel, K., & Volet, S. (2012). University students' perceptions of and attitudes towards culturally diverse group work: Does the context matter? *Journal of Studies in International Education, 16*(2), 157–181.

Klein, J., & Wikan, G. (2019). Teacher education and international practice programmes: Reflections on transformative learning and global citizenship. *Teaching and Teacher Education, 79*, 93–100.

Knight, J. (2004). Internationalization remodelled: Definition, approaches, and rationales. *Journal of Studies in International Education, 8*(1), 5–31.

Kumar, I. A., & Parveen, S. (2013). Teacher education in the age of globalization. *Research Journal of Educational Sciences, 1*(1), 8–12.

Ledwith, S., Lee, A., Manfredi, S., & Wildish, C. (1998). *Multiculturalism, student group work and assessment*. Oxford: Oxford Brookes University.

Lee, J. (2011). International field experience – What do student teachers learn? *Australian Journal of Teacher Education, 36*(10), 1–22.

Li, M., Olson, J. E., & Frieze, I. H. (2013). Students' study abroad plans: The influence of motivational and personality factors. *Frontiers: The Interdisciplinary Journal of Study Abroad, 23*, 72–89.

Mestenhauser, J. (1998). Portraits of an international curriculum. In J. Mestenhauser & B. Ellingboe (Eds.), *Reforming higher education curriculum: Internationalizing the campus*. Phoenix: Orix Press.

Mesker, P., Wassink, H., and Bakker, C. (2018). Experiential continuity: how newly qualified teachers' past international teaching experiences influence their current personal interpretative framework. *Professional Development in Education, 44*(3), 444–459

Mezirow, J. (2009). Transformative learning theory. In J. Mezirow & E. W. Taylor (Eds.), *Transformative learning in practice – Insights from community, workplace, and higher education* (pp. 18–31). San Francisco: Wiley.

Montgomery, C. (2009). A decade of internationalisation: Has it influenced students' views of cross-cultural group work at university? *Journal of Studies in International Education, 13*, 256–270.

Norris, E.M., and Gillespie, J. (2009). How study abroad shapes global careers. *Journal of studies in International Education 13*(3), 382–397

OECD. (2015). *Helping immigrant students succeed at school - and beyond.* Paris: OECD.

Okken, G. J., Jansen, E. P. W., Hofman, W. H. A., & Coelen, R. J. (2019). Beyond the welcome-back party: The enriched repertoire of professional teacher behaviour as a result of study abroad. *Journal of Teaching and Teacher Education, 86*, 102927.

Osad'an, R., Reid, E., & Belešová, M. (2016). Intercultural primary education in the second half of the decade. *Acta Technologic Dubnicae, 6*(2), 77–86.

Ota, H., & Shimmi, Y. (2019). Recent trends in learning abroad in the context of a changing Japanese economy and higher education situation. In R. J. Coelen & C. Gribble (Eds.), *Internationalization and employability in higher education.* Abingdon: Routledge.

Page, S. E. (2017). *The diversity bonus – how great teams pay off in the knowledge economy.* Princeton: Princeton University Press.

Paus, E., & Robinson, M. (2008). Increasing study abroad participation: The faculty makes the difference. *Frontiers: The Interdisciplinary Journal of Study Abroad, 17*, 33–49.

Pope, J. A., Sánchez, C. M., Lehnert, K., & Schmid, A. S. (2014). Why Do Gen Y Students Study Abroad? Individual Growth and the Intent to Study Abroad. *Journal of Teaching in International Business, 25*(2), 97–118.

Presley, A., Damron-Martinez, D., & Zhang, L. (2010). A Study of Business Student Choice to Study Abroad: A Test of the Theory of Planned Behavior. *Journal of Teaching in International Business, 21*(4), 227–247.

Rokeach, M. (1973). The nature of human values. Free Press

Salisbury, M. H., Umbach, P. D., Paulsen, M. B., & Pascarella, E. T. (2009). Going global: Understanding the choice process of the intent to study abroad. *Research in Higher Education, 50*(2), 119–143.

Shaftel, J., Shaftel, T., & Ahluwalia, R. (2007). International educational experience and intercultural competence. *International Journal of Business and Economics, 6*(1), 25–34.

Shimmi, Y., Akiba, H., Ota, H., and Yokota, M. (2017). Long-term impact of undergraduate study abroad experiences on career: Comparative survey results among degree-seeking study abroad, credit-bearing study abroad and non-study abroad groups. Ryugakukoryu 74, 14–26

Shimmi, Y., Yonezawa, A., and Akiba, H. (2018). Effect of study abroad experiences on income and career. In M. Yokota, H. Ota, and Y. Shimmi (Eds.) Impact of study abroad on career development and life (pp. 156 – 178). Tokyo: Gakukubunsha

Shiveley, J., & Misco, T. (2015). Long-term impacts of short-term study abroad: Teacher perceptions of preservice study abroad experiences. *Frontiers: The Interdisciplinary Journal of Study Abroad, 16*, 107–120.

Teichler, U. (2004). The changing debate on internationalisation of higher education. *Higher Education, 48*(1), 5–26.

Van de Berg, M. (2009). Intervening in student learning abroad: A research-based inquiry. *Intercultural Education, 20*(1), 15–27.

Vande Berg, M., Paige, R. M., & Connor-Linton, J. (2009). The Georgetown consortium project: Interventions for student learning abroad. Frontiers: *The Interdisciplinary Journal of Study Abroad,* XVIII(Fall), 1–75.

Volet, S. E., & Ang, G. (1998). Culturally mixed groups on international campuses: An opportunity for intercultural learning. *Higher Education Research and Development, 17*(1), 5–23.

Walkington, J. (2015). Enhancing multicultural perspectives in the formation of preservice teachers through immersion in a culturally different context. *Multicultural Education Review, 7*(3), 140–154.

Wiers-Jenssen, J. (2011). Background and employability of mobile vs. non-mobile students. *Tertiary Education and Management, 17*(2), 79–100.

Chapter 14
Dispositives of Internationalization in Brazilian Science: The Unified Postgraduate Examination in Physics

Nicolás José Isola

International circulation has historically been considered an intrinsic characteristic of science (Bourdieu 1995; Gingras 2002). State policies, the higher education system and technological-scientific organisms have been influenced by and influenced processes of internationalization of knowledge all over the world, for example, exchange through scientific travel, international research projects and international cooperation between schools (Morosini 2006; Siméant 2015). Fluxes of internationalization in science related to the circulation of people are, in general, stimulated by complex geopolitical dynamics which go beyond the logic of knowledge production (Muñoz-Garcia and Chiappa 2016). These dynamics in developing countries can be structured by, at least, two movements. The first refers to the flow of students that leave from developing academic systems to more central, already prestigious, ones (Maiworm and Teichler 1996). The second relates to the opening of certain peripheral countries to foreign students in similar positions, where the asymmetry tends to be smaller. This work focuses on this second dynamic, considering the promotion of South-South circulation: Latin American students in Brazil (Daniel 2014; Nogueira and Ramos 2014).

Brazil is a country that has been establishing itself as a destination for students from other Latin American countries. This is due to the institutionalization of the national system of science and technology, especially the stability of funding, guaranteeing an increasing level of professionalization in Brazilian postgraduate programmes and, no less important, the availability of scholarship grants. To better understand the phenomena of the import-export of high-level human resources (Bourdieu 2002), this study analyses an aspect of this multidimensional process: the international circulation of PhD students in Brazil, focusing on the creation of the Unified Postgraduate Examination in Physics, Exame Unificado de Pós-graduações de Física (EUF). The EUF is an innovative and collaborative strategy initiated and

N. J. Isola (✉)
Campinas State University, Campinas, Brazil

implemented, in the beginning, by the coordinators of some postgraduate programmes in the state of São Paulo, that has rapidly become accepted by many Brazilian postgraduate programmes in Physics. This dispositive of evaluation has been implemented during the last ten years as an important inflection of international openness and regional positioning, allowing students in Brazil and abroad to undertake, in their hometowns, the entrance exam to some postgraduate programmes in Physics. This exam, in a short period of time, has promoted processes of international circulation in a subject strongly structured, professionalized and already internationalized. It is therefore a question of considering how some specific flows in the region are produced, since internationalization does not happen by chance. There are scientific policies, investments, institutional contacts and different dispositives that encourage some fluxes to emerge and hamper the development of others.

This chapter relates to research on the circulation of Latin American students in Brazil (Isola 2018), taking the creation of EUF as a starting point. Previously in the Brazilian case, research has described foreign teachers' circulation in the country during the process of institutionalization of the first universities in Brazil, such as USP and Universidade do Brasil (Costa Ribeiro 1994). Other work has analysed the mobility of Brazilians who studied abroad, especially in France (Muñoz and Garcia 2005). However, few studies have described the dynamics of circulation of foreign students in Brazil (Desidério 2006; Subuhana 2009).

The methodology used in this work is based on document analysis and in-depth interviews with scientific managers, scientists and students. The interviews allow us to understand the history of constructing the EUF and the way professors establish alliances, which allow the deepening of a strategy guided beyond their institutional spaces to take place.[1] In addition, we consulted the internal documents of EUF Organizing Committee, composed of informal notes on internal meetings. These primary sources allowed us to chronologically follow the steps that were taken to build, methodologically and operationally, the EUF, as well as part of the negotiation and consolidation of the institutional cohesion that gave it vigour and efficiency. To make this description, we start by pointing out that the creation of this dispositive took place within a subject with very particular characteristics and that the level of academic exchange and internationalization in Physics were preconditions allowing for the implementation of the Unified Exam and the enrolment of hundreds of Latin American students.

Physics: An Internationalized Subject

Science disciplines are systems of knowledge production that vary in their social and intellectual organization, in part through different institutional dispositives that determine access to resources in the international scientific system and the connection pathways to their specific subject (Whitley 2012). In Physics, this community has an intense global unity, and the manuals and text corpora used in undergraduate and postgraduate programmes tend to be the same around the world. In other words, different subjects or subtopics, the clusters that compartmentalize Physics, are part of an established globally shared cannon.

Physics presents a type of development and linear scientific growth based on previous established knowledge (Becher 2001). Prestige is connected to recognition from peers from other subjects who consider Physics to have common goals vital to the evolution of science in general, as well as a group of highly professionalized interlocutors, relatively small and homogeneous (Whitley 2012). Physics also shows fewer constraints in regard to local conjectures or strictly national discussions compared to other sciences, something that increases and incentivizes its international character (Bourdieu 2002). Institutionally, the establishment of the main international centres with a routine of tasks and formalized control of procedures, as well as a differentiated division of labour, have helped with the hierarchical coordination of these spaces, strengthening the cohesion and interaction of physicists' research agendas (Whitley 2012), and this in turn has stimulated the creation of international interdependent agendas.

Historically, the many disputes among dominant groups in a small number of core countries defined the problems and priorities that became global (Krige 2001). The main research centres, such as the European Organization for Nuclear Research (CERN), the main laboratory of Particle Physics in the world located in Geneva and the Abdus Salam International Centre for Theoretical Physics (ICTP) in Trieste, Italy, have functioned as loci for the circulation of researchers from all over the world to participate in research activities and continue to collaborate with the research agendas of these institutions on returning to their countries. The strong concentration in central spaces has determined a functional (results and standards) and strategic (agenda and funding) interdependence in the articulation of research, and the different national spaces of developing countries were influenced, in different ways, by these historic processes, according to their distinct conditions (social, scientific, political and economic).

The Origin and History of the EUF

How then is an institutional dispositive for internationalization created? Normally, it is a process much less linear and guided than might be supposed, in which the agents, as the central enablers of internationalization dynamics, try to take actions and confront difficulties and limitations that require new actions, until they can reach a certain objective. To demonstrate how this happens, I will present a brief history of the Unified Postgraduate Examination in Physics.

In February 2003, Professor Celso Lima, from IF-USP, criticized the selection criteria for the admission of postgraduate students in his institute. He presented some issues related to the way new students were admitted. At the time, candidates were divided into three groups (A, B and C) according to their grades and the duration of their undergraduate studies, as well as the grades of their original courses in the evaluation of CAPES, one of Brazil's leading funding agencies. Foreign students, in general from Latin America, were classified in group C because of the lack of information about their qualifications. Faced by an admission system which hindered equality of opportunities, Lima suggested that there should be an exam to grant scholarships or entry to postgraduate study. Those who had the highest grades would be eligible. As a side effect, the exam would show the possible weaknesses of the undergraduate programmes in the country. The proposal was to be applied to the exam in the affiliated Physics Institutes and, through the Commission of International Cooperation of USP, make contact with the consulates nearest to the universities of origin of foreign students. However, the idea remained untouched. In a subsequent meeting in 2005, in the city of Santos, the coordinators of USP and UNICAMP proposed a similar idea, but without trying to establish a negotiated consensus with other postgraduate programmes. The smaller programmes meanwhile were apprehensive about a unified exam, considering it a 'São Paulo topic.'

A year later, in May 2006, the XXIX Brazilian Physical Society Meeting was held. During that meeting, Professor Eduardo Miranda, then the coordinator of the programme at IFGW-UNICAMP, talked with some colleagues of the need to implement a unified exam for postgraduate programmes in Physics.[2] The idea was more welcome, and the talks continued at the Meeting of Coordinators of Postgraduate Programmes in Physics that took place in Rio de Janeiro in December of the same year. One of the central motivations for the EUF, according to Professor Miranda, was to offer students who lived far from the participant universities the possibility to sit the exam, as this would lead to a higher volume of candidates and, logically, better selection. About the negotiation process, one professor said:

> Then, immediately, everyone thought it was a great idea. There were many reasons to do that. First one is that you gather the efforts, if you have one entrance exam in USP, another in UNICAMP, another in IFT, you waste a lot of energy to do different exams. And more, if you do many of these exams and the candidate wants to enter in USP, UNICAMP, IFT, etc. the student will sit five or six exams. If you do only one, he will do one exam, has a grade and, with this grade, he can try to enter many programmes and choose whichever he thinks is better. Many other reasons as well: the possibility to apply the exam abroad. At first, we had in mind the possibility to apply this exam abroad and attract people from other countries, initially any country, but we knew the biggest attraction would be here in Latin America. What, in fact, happened.

The professors who created it considered it relevant to increase the possibility of Brazilian students far from participant universities applying for the exam. However, some also had in mind internationalization, which indeed took place once it was implemented.

After this meeting, negotiations on the implementation of the exam started. IFGW from UNICAMP, IF-USP, São Carlos Institute of Physics from USP (IFSC), and the IFT-UNESP held the first EUF on 16 and 17 October 2007 to the candidates for the first semester of 2008. Out of the 366 Brazilian and foreign students who registered, 236 actually took the exam. After this first exam, the numbers would increase. For instance, for the second semester of 2015, a total of 685 candidates registered to take the EUF in Brazil and abroad, slightly less than double the 2007 total. A total of 77 candidates (11 per cent) registered to take the exam outside Brazil, and 72 out of the 77 (10.5 per cent of the total) asked to take the exam in Latin American countries. On the EUF for the first semester 2016, 1035 students registered, of whom 96 (9 per cent) asked to take the exam in Latin American countries. Thus, we can see that the number of Latin American students among the total volume of foreign students is considerable.

The Internal Organization of EUF

The organization of EUF is collaborative and each programme has one task. For example, at the beginning, committee meetings were held in UNICAMP, where they also graded the exams. Photocopying was done at Fundação Universitária para o Vestibular (Fuvest-USP), and the IFSC-USP was in charge of administrative issues. Since the beginning, the EUF has had two annual exams, each one coordinated by a different professor. The committee responsible for the creation and grading of the exam questions is formed by seven professors in the participant postgraduate programmes; five are responsible for the elaboration of the questions and two their revision. The committee has the autonomy to elaborate and grade EUF.

Each of these professors contributes two questions. The exam consists of ten questions that are answered during two days, five questions each day, four hours a day. The questions go through two or three revisors 'to see if they are right and not too easy or too difficult. We really try to have a uniformity on the level of difficult among the questions of different areas,' said one professor. The evaluating professors did not know the names of the students, who were identified, from the start, by numbers. After the evaluation, the grades were presented to students indicating the quintile of their grade, in general as well as in each area. In turn, each coordinator of the participating postgraduate programme receives the total grade of the students and, afterwards, each programme uses its own criteria to admit them. Today, around 800 candidates register for the first semester, and 500 for the second one. Over time, a great number of programmes from different states have joined the exam. The level of growth undergone by EUF and, we can suppose Brazilian Physics, has given it more regional visibility.

EUF Internationalization

The EUF has become an internationalization dispositive that has enabled many Latin American students to pursue a previously non-existent possibility in their countries: high-level postgraduate study with funding. To do so, there was a need for a complex organization on top of the common work done by the participant postgraduate programmes. The first EUF in 2007 was held in the following Latin American countries: Colombia (24 candidates), Chile (2) and Peru (2). Each new

EUF has attracted candidates from other countries who demanded to do it abroad. Therefore, in less than ten years, the exam has been held, at least once, in 19 countries: Germany, Argentina, Armenia, Bolivia, Brazil, Colombia, Costa Rica, Cuba, Spain, the United States, France, Honduras, Mexico, Pakistan, Paraguay, Peru, Russia, Sweden and Venezuela. The candidates can take the exam in Portuguese, English or Spanish.

The process of sitting the EUF outside Brazil aimed to have all exams conducted at the same time around the world. Since 2010, the coordinator of IFT/UNESP has been personally responsible for finding locations for the students to sit the exam abroad. In their registration, the candidates must take the exam in a place close to their address outside Brazil. The exam is sent by mail to the responsible professor in those countries. Later, they send the answer sheets to be graded in Brazil. As they register in the exam, the foreign candidates also have to look for a professor affiliated to a Brazilian programme to advise them in the future. This is for reasons of internal security of the exam and is a crucial factor in having the scholarships. As a student comments: 'The EUF is not the only prerequisite to enter. The other 50 per cent depends on a professor accepting to support you.'

It is worth highlighting that Brazilian and foreign students compete equally for the institutional scholarships, all of them offered by Brazilian funding institutions: Conselho Nacional de Desenvolvimento Científico e Tecnológico (CNPq), the Coordenação de Aperfeiçoamento de Pessoal de Nível Superior (CAPES) and the Fundação de Amparo à Pesquisa do Estado de São Paulo (FAPESP). When considering the candidates enrolled in EUF who did the exam outside Brazil, we can see that in the first semester of 2016, 86 per cent came from Peru or Colombia. Something similar happens when we look at the data from the three main funding agencies offering PhD scholarships, including data relating to programmes which do not participate in EUF. According to data provided by the Coordination of Statistics and Indicators of CNPq, 144 Latin American students in Physics earned their PhD scholarship from CNPq between 2008 and 2015, 120 men and 24 women.

There are a considerable number of Colombians (42 per cent) and Peruvians (30 per cent). More than seven out of ten Latin American scholarship holders were from one of these two countries. According to data from the General Coordination of Activities to Support Postgraduation (CGAP) from CAPES, 168 Latin American Physics students had a PhD scholarship from CAPES during 2008–2016, 134 men 34 women. Almost nine out of ten students come from Colombia (49 per cent) or Peru (39 per cent). Considering the PhD Latin American students that circulate in Brazil with a Fapesp scholarship for Physics, between 2008 and 2014, we only find these two nationalities: 15 Colombians and 5 Peruvians. This trend needs to be further researched to reveal the processes that are incentivizing this specific form of circulation and not others. Finally, we have to mention that, of the three agencies mentioned (CNPq, CAPES and FAPESP), Physics is always one of the two subjects with the highest number of scholarship holders. In CNPq and FAPESP, it is first and since 2008 the total flow of this subject has increased, indicating that EUF may be one of the causes.

The Unified Postgraduate Examination in Physics and Internationalization

EUF has not appeared spontaneously. It was inspired by other evaluation experiences, such as the National Admission Test for prospective Master's students in Economics, held by the Brazilian Association of Graduate Programmes in Economics. Besides this national experience, another exam was used as a reference to the creation of EUF: the Graduate Record Examination (GRE). This exam is used in the United States to enter all postgraduate programmes in Physics and other. In some areas, this type of large-scale international exam, world recognized, operates as a legitimator and global regulator of demanded competencies, as it simultaneously reinforces the institutionalization of professional standards. On the connections between GRE and EUF, a professor explains:

> I did my PhD abroad. When I registered for the doctorate, I did this exam here in Brazil, I got a grade and with this grade I could apply for a candidacy in several programmes in the USA. I was accepted by some, chose, and ended up going. I thought there should be something similar in Brazil.

Thus, the GRE was explicitly used as a model exam. Organizers think it is undeniable that the progress and success of Physics research in Brazil depends on the consolidation of connections abroad.

This professor's comments point to, at least, four further issues. Firstly, another allusion to his own personal trajectory of international circulation as part of an argumentative base to create EUF; the construction of this evaluation tool was not independent of the professional internationalization of its creators. Secondly, the mention of student recruitment in the United States, a central space taken as a reference and a system to be imitated. Thirdly, the need to increase the universe of students to have a broader spectrum and, thus, be able to choose the best. Lastly, we can suppose a reference to the role intended for Brazil as a centre of intermediation for Physics as produced in central countries and the incipient creation of postgraduate programmes in Latin American countries. The exam is much more than a test: it is a positioning (of Brazil) in the geopolitics of the subject.

It is meaningful to analyse the trajectories of the professors who created the EUF. Considering those who participated in the beginning of EUF, three were alumni of state universities in São Paulo and one from Universidade Federal de Minas Gerais, all recognized institutions and among the most eminent universities in the Brazilian higher education system, wherein, possibly, students have a certain familiarity with foreign countries. The international strategy (Dezalay and Garth 2002) of attracting foreign students meanwhile was established by professors with professional and study experience during their postgraduate and/or research activities outside Brazil, that is, people with an international habitus. Their circulations abroad inspired those professors to create a dispositive that promoted the internationalization of their programmes. Some had experienced, as students, evaluation dispositives during their international circulation. In a way, there was, in the genesis of this dispositive, a strategy of scientific internationalization; these professors had circulated abroad, learnt adaptability to displacement and new contexts, and increased their professional disposition towards scientific internationalization (Wagner and Réau 2015).

We could consider this naturalized awareness of internationalization under the notion of migrant habitus (Xavier de Brito 2004), characterized by a greater familiarity with spatial displacement. This can be seen as a system of dispositions that help create a perception, appreciation, and action when faced by international mobility. These dispositions are a product of a specific type of pedagogical action, connected to the disputes of international capital, that make possible the election of objects, the solution of problems and the evaluation of solutions (Bourdieu 1999, 2000). This international habitus (Wagner 1998) gave these professors a familiarity with the international: speaking different languages, a socialization broadened by and extended into international contexts, and access to international academic/professional capital through a network of contacts. It is thus second nature acquired over a series of successive experiences of spatial mobility and academic cooperation that promotes the construction of mental schemes and moral and corporal dispositions.

At the same time, in the field of Physics, there is among researchers an internationalized illusion, that is, an understanding and an awareness that the academic game is being motivated by recognition that goes way beyond the national space itself. The rules of legitimation, respect, classification and collaboration are crossed by this interest in participating in a global conversation and, in Brazil, also connected to the long historical process of the development of the Physics field.

Brazilian Power in Regional Physics

It is necessary to understand the level of internationalization of this subject in Brazil, the importance of sustainable funding and its role in Latin America. Scientific policies in Brazil were not abandoned, even during moments of crisis. In 2010, Brazil answered with more than 60 per cent of all investments in research in Latin America, and Brazilian scientists produced half of the works done in the region (Regalado 2010). In 2014, Brazil was the Latin American country that invested most in Research and Development (R&D), with 1.24 per cent of GDP (Argentina 0.64 per cent, Mexico 0.54 per cent, Colombia 0.25 per cent and Peru 0.14 per cent; see Albornoz 2016).

The comparison of institutional structures and investment in Science and Technology of the two countries with the most candidates in EUF allows us to understand possible motivations behind these flows. In 2013, while Brazil invested $27,779 million in R&D, Colombia invested $1037 million, and Peru $164 million. Considering the number of researchers, in 2010 Brazil had 2.3 researchers for every 1000 people in the economically active population; Colombia 0.77, and Peru 0.03. In Colombia, in 2015, 392 students finished their PhD, while in Brazil, this number reached 17,048. In 2015, Colciencias, Colombia's main scientific agency, granted a total of 650 PhD scholarships and 222 in 2016 (Diario El Tiempo, 13 February 2017). In 2015, Brazil granted 42,779 PhD scholarships.

The most relevant Physics programmes in Peru and Colombia are recent, charge fees, grant only a small number of scholarships and have less accumulated institutional capital and graduates than their Brazilian counterparts. The Universidad Nacional de Colombia in Bogota, for instance, started its doctoral programme in 1986. Today, more than half of the undergraduate professors are not doctors. Also, in Colombia, the Universidad del Atlántico started its undergraduate Physics course in 2002. At the Universidad Nacional de Ingeniería, the most important in Peru in Physics, only 39 out of 188 professors have a PhD; in the last 18 years, eight students finished their PhDs.

Most Latin American Physics students who circulate in Brazil are not from social spaces that have contact with foreign countries, nor do they have an international habitus learnt within the family. For many, their arrival in Brazil was their first contact with a foreign country. The interviews allowed us to see that, according to them, access to a scholarship has changed their professional trajectories as it allowed them to leave their countries for a project seen as conducive to improving their careers, and created a perception of social climb through education. Thus, we can consider that the circulation of Latin American students in Brazil is connected, among other issues, to the extreme difficult conditions that these students have in obtaining funding and dedicating themselves full-time to their research. And in the case of Physics, there is a need for high investment to maintain quality labs.

In the case of the programmes of São Paulo, the IF-USP was created in 1969. Until 2016 it had schooled more than 2000 master's and doctoral students, and the PhD programme of UFSCAR, which started in August 1991, already has 97 doctoral students. Besides the size of the programmes, there is constant contact with foreign countries and institutions. Two examples give us a more precise impression of the level of development and internationalization of Physics in Brazil: (i) more than 100 Brazilian researchers are involved in CERN projects (Duarte 2008); (ii) in 2010, the South American Institute for Fundamental Research (ICTP-SAIFR) was created, a collaboration between ICTP, IFT/Unesp and FAPESP.

The programme of scholarships and research grants abroad, as well as policies to incentivize the internationalization of postgraduate programmes, has contributed to the increased number of collaborations between researchers in Brazil and their peers abroad. The internationalization of scientific production can also be highlighted. Several international exchanges have stimulated collaborative scientific productions with different countries (Sociedade Brasileira de Física 1987). From this perspective, there has been an increase in the proportion of publications from authors affiliated to Brazilian institutions in 'top level' journals, influencing the international visibility of Brazilian research (King 2004). The promotion of partnerships, the constant flux of foreign professors and student scientific mobility in different directions has consolidated the construction of a collective internationalized identity, stimulated by institutional agreements that have incentivized even more of these exchanges (Agência Brasileira de Cooperação 2015), and the same has not happened in other countries in the region.

Final Remarks

The broadening internationalization of the subject and large-scale curricular unification of Physics has allowed foreign students to consider the EUF, proposed by some Brazilian postgraduate programmes. This flow was helped by the granting of scholarships by state agencies to allow students to dedicate themselves full-time to their research: a rare or non-existent resource in their home countries. The process of establishing and implementation of the EUF was negotiated and decided by a group of coordinators of postgraduate programmes with experience of international circulation. It has had considerable expansion, and an increase in internal and external demand, being held in at least 19 Latin American countries. Coming back to the original research questions, EUF seems to dictate part of the internationalization flows of the region. In fact, data shows a sizable increase in the number of candidates enrolled, especially Colombians and Peruvians, as well as a relevant contingent of scholarships to the area.

Pierre Bourdieu pointed towards internal disputes in each national scientific field regarding the struggle to define what is 'national' (Bourdieu 2002). This tendency seems to be overshadowed in the testimonies of the EUF creators, in which the tensions between the national and international spheres are veiled, in a way, by the 'naturality' of Physics internationalization. However, we can consider the EUF as a strategy to showcase their universities and research centres to the central countries of the North.

In this sense, the EUF can also be seen as a way to position Brazilian postgraduate programmes in relation to the subject's geopolitics and the position of Brazil as a 'semi peripheral' country compared to the central nations, that is, a 'secondary centre' of qualified formation for the countries in the region (de Swaan 1998). The analysis of EUF creation history and its process of implementation nevertheless makes us question other possible cases of dispositives and policies that aim to promote international circulation. Studies connected to dynamics of international circulation can increase the volume and depth of an important but still incipient area of research in Latin America.

Acknowledgements This study was financed by the São Paulo Research Foundation (FAPESP) (n. 2017/17826–0).

Notes

1. I interviewed three professors who were coordinators of their postgraduate programmes in 2007, when EUF was created: Eduardo Miranda (Universidade Estadual de Campinas, Unicamp), Celso Lima (Instituto de Física da Universidade de São Paulo, IF-USP) and Roberto Kraenkel (Instituto de Física Teórica da Universidade Estadual Paulista, IFT-UNESP). We also interviewed Professor Eduardo Granado (UNICAMP), EUF coordinator in 2016, and Professor Otavio Thiemann, who was the coordinator of the postgradu-

ate programme in Physics at the Instituto de Física de São Carlos, USP. Twenty Latin American PhD students were also interviewed (15 men and 5 women) in the following universities: IFT, UNICAP, UFABC, USP and UFSCAR. The study was financed by the São Paulo Research Foundation (FAPESP) grant no. 2017/17826-0.

2. Eduardo Miranda, professor of UNICAMP, holds a PhD from Rutgers University and has a postdoc degree from National High Magnetic Field Laboratory, in the United States. He is a project referee at The National Science Foundation. Roberto Kraenkel, professor of IFT-UNESP, holds a postdoc from Institut des Hautes Études Scientifiques, Bures-sur-Yvette (France). He was also an invited researcher at Université de Montpellier II and invited professor at Institut de Recherche sur les Phénomènes Hors Équilibre (IRPHE), both in France. The professor of IFSC-USP, Tito José Bonagamba, holds a postdoc from University of Massachusetts in Amherst, the United States. He was a hired researcher at Ames National Laboratory (US Department of Energy) and, several times, a visiting professor at Université Paris Sud (Institut de Chimie Moléculaire et des Matériaux d'Orsay), in France, and at Martin-Luther University Halle-Wittenberg (Physics Department) in Halle, Germany. Celso Lima, professor of IF-USP, holds a PhD in Physics from Eberhard Karls Universität Tübingen (Germany).

References

Agência Brasileira de Cooperação. (2015). *Acordos vigentes*. Brasília: ABC.
Albornoz, M. (2016). *El Estado de la Ciencia, Principales Indicadores de Ciencia y Tecnología Iberoamericanos / Interamericanos 2016*. Buenos Aires: Organización de Estados Iberoamericanos (OEI), RICYT.
Becher, T. (2001). *Tribus y territorios académicos. La indagación intelectual y las culturas de las disciplinas*. Barcelona: Gedisa.
Bourdieu, P. (1995). La cause de la science. *Actes de la recherche en sciences sociales, 106–107*, 3–10.
Bourdieu, P. (1999). *Intelectuales, política y poder*. Buenos Aires: Eudeba.
Bourdieu, P. (2000). *Los usos sociales de la Ciencia*. Buenos Aires: Nueva Visión.
Bourdieu, P. (2002). Les conditions sociales de la circulation internationale des idées. *Actes de la recherche en sciences sociales, 145*, 3–8.
Costa Ribeiro, J. (1994). A Física no Brasil. In F. Azevedo (Ed.), *As ciências no Brasil*. Rio de Janeiro: Editora da UFRJ.
Daniel, C. (2014). Building a South-South connection through higher education: The case of Peruvian university students in Brazil. *Cahiers de la recherche sur l'éducation et les savoirs, 13*, 19–137.
de Swaan, A. (1998). Pour une sociologie de la société transnationale. *Revue de synthèse, 01–03*, 89–111.
Desidério, E. (2006). *Migração internacional com fins de estudo: o caso dos africanos do Programa Estudante-Convênio de Graduação em três Universidades públicas no Rio de Janeiro*. Master dissertation, Escola Nacional de Ciências Estatísticas, Rio de Janeiro.
Dezalay, Y., & Garth, B. (2002). *La Mondialisation des guerres de palais*. Paris: Seuil.
Diario El Tiempo. (2017). *Profesores inquietos por menos becas doctorales*. February 14.
Duarte, R. (2008). Cooperação Internacional para o Desenvolvimento em Ciência e Tecnologia: a participação brasileira na Organização Europeia para Pesquisa Nuclear (CERN). *Journal of Technology Management and Innovation, 3*(4), 133–151.
Gingras, Y. (2002). Les formes spécifiques de l'internationalité du champ scientifique. *Actes de la recherche en sciences sociales, 141–142*, 31–45.

Isola, N. (2018). Argentinos à brasileira. A circulação de antropólogos argentinos pelo Museu Nacional (PPGAS-MN/UFRJ). *Mana, 24*(2), 68–108.
King, D. (2004). The scientific impact of nations: What different countries get for their research spending. *Nature, 430*, 311–316.
Krige, J. (2001). Distrust and discovery: The case of the heavy bosons at CERN. *ISIS, 92*(3), 517–540.
Maiworm, F., & Teichler, U. (1996). *Study abroad and early career: Experiences of former Erasmus students*. London: Jessica Kingsley Publishers.
Morosini, M. (2006). Estado do conhecimento sobre internacionalização da educação superior. Conceitos e prática. *Educar, 28*, 107–124.
Muñoz, M.-C., & Garcia, A. (2005). Les étudiants brésiliens en France (2000–2001): Parcours intellectual et inscription académique. *Cahiers du Brésil Contemporain, 57–58/59–60*, 107–128.
Muñoz-Garcia, A., & Chiappa, R. (2016). Stretching the academic harness: Knowledge construction in the process of academic mobility in Chile. *Globalisation, Societies and Education, 15*(5), 635–647.
Nogueira, M., & Ramos, V. (2014). Mobilité des étudiants sud- américains: le cas du programme ESCALA. *Cahiers de la recherche sur l'éducation et les savoirs, 13*, 97–118.
Regalado, A. (2010). Brazilian science: Riding a gusher. *Science, 3.330*(6009), 1306–1312.
Siméant, J. (Ed.). (2015). *Guide de l'enquête globale en sciences sociales*. CNRS Editions: Paris.
Sociedade Brasileira de Física. (1987). *A Física no Brasil*. São Paulo: Sociedade Brasileira de Física, Instituto de Física da USP.
Subuhana, C. (2009). A experiência sociocultural de universitários da África Lusófona no Brasil: entremeando histórias. *Pro-Posições, 20*(1), 103–126.
Wagner, A. (1998). *Les nouvelles élites de la mondialisation. Une immigration dorée en France.* Paris: Presses Universitaires de France.
Wagner, A., & Réau, B. (2015). Le capital international: Un outil d'analyse de la reconfiguration des rapports de domination. In J. Siméant (Ed.), *Guide de l'enquête globale en sciences sociales* (pp. 33–46). Paris: CNRS Editions.
Whitley, R. (2012). *La organización intelectual y social de las ciencias*. Bernal: University Nacional de Quilmes.
Xavier De Brito, A. (2004). Habitus de herdeiro, habitus escolar. Os sentidos da internacionalização nas trajetórias dos estudantes brasileiros. In A. M. F. Almeida, L. Canedo, A. Garcia, & A. Bittencourt (Eds.), *Circulação internacional e formação intelectual das elites brasileiras*. Editora Unicamp: Campinas.

Chapter 15
'I had to move somewhere:' Leaving Finland to Study in Sweden

Blanka Henriksson

Sweden has been a long-standing destination for Finnish migration, but recent years have witnessed an increase in youth migration from Finland to Sweden (Kepsu & Henriksson, 2019). Contemporary media discourses talk of 'brain drain' and the young and supposedly well educated people 'fleeing' Finland to find their future elsewhere (e.g. Nyberg, 2016). This chapter is focused on young adults from the Swedish-speaking minority, who left Finland to pursue higher education in Sweden between 2010 and 2017. The aim is to map and analyse causes and motivations for moving in the light of this contemporary media discussion, where the exit of a linguistic minority has become a concern (e.g. Övergaard, 2016). Previously, migration to Sweden mostly contained low qualified people finding employment in industry (Svanberg & Tydén, 1992; Häggström et al., 1990), while those leaving during the 2010s are thought to be highly qualified and working in high status professions (cf. Kepsu, 2016). In this study, migrants have the opportunity to tell their stories of moving from one country to another: their own motives for moving and their experiences of migration. The analysis thus focuses on their own interpretations of mobility, using the theoretical category of young (or emerging) adults as an analytical tool (Arnett, 2004; cf. Zackariasson, 2001).

Young Adults and Finnish Migration to Sweden

Sweden has been one of the main destinations for Finnish migration since the end of World War II. Between 1945 and 2000, over half a million Finns moved to Sweden (Korkiasaari, 2001; Korkiasaari & Tarkiainen, 2000; Björklund, 2012).

B. Henriksson (✉)
Åbo Akademi University, Turku, Finland
e-mail: Blanka.Henriksson@abo.fi

Finland is also a bilingual country with Finnish as one language and Swedish as the other. The Swedish speakers of Finland (5.2 per cent of the population) have the legal right to use their mother tongue, for example, in contacts with authorities, in public service and in education at all levels. Today, around 150,900 persons born in Finland live in Sweden (Statistiska centralbyrån, 2018) and around 25 per cent are believed to belong to the Swedish-speaking minority of Finland (Parkvall, 2009).

While overall Finnish migration to Sweden has decreased, the Swedish speakers of Finland are experiencing an outward migration boom, with a peak in 2016 (Kepsu, 2016; Kepsu & Henriksson, 2019, p. 10), especially among young people (Kepsu & Henriksson, 2019). Two thirds of Swedish-speaking migrants end up in Sweden, while only one in five Finnish-speaking migrant moves there (Kepsu & Henriksson, 2019, pp. 15–16). Currently, most Finns decide to live abroad for the sake of their studies, work and life experiences, and intend to stay only temporarily (Heikkilä & Alivuotila, 2019). Contemporary migration between Finland and Sweden can thus be seen as a form of highly skilled migration (Koikkalainen, 2011), including people who already have tertiary education and students without degrees. The open labour market in the Nordic countries for citizens since the 1950s, and the larger range of interesting positions and study programmes in Sweden, make Sweden an ideal target for Finnish migrants (Kepsu & Henriksson, 2019, p. 22). Of these migrants, young adults from Ostrobothnia (North east coast of Finland) and the Åland Islands mostly leave Finland to study in Sweden, while those leaving the south (Turku and Helsinki regions) go west to find work (Kepsu & Henriksson, 2019, p. 14).

This chapter focuses on what Arnett (2004) calls emerging adults, the period of life between adolescence and adulthood, marked by searching for and experimenting with identity. By focusing on this cohort, we can gain new knowledge, since every generation has its own experiences. Even if life can be seen as a continuing process of change and movement, some periods are characterized by more and deeper change, and for many people the time spent as a young adult is such a phase, filled with reflections about education and future professions, and the consequences of following these choices on the future (Zackariasson, 2001, p. 30).

Migrants' Life Stories

The research material analysed for this chapter is part of a bigger project on young adult migration to Sweden from Finland, called 'Go West! Life is Better There?— young Swedish-speaking Finns in Sweden tell about their migration,' conducted by Blanka Henriksson. For this chapter, 18 interviews out of a larger body of source material have been analysed. The informants were aged between 18 and 30 at the time of interview (2016–2017), and were all Swedish-speaking Finns who moved to Sweden between 2010 and 2017 to pursue higher education. All names used in this text are pseudonyms.

These interviews can be characterized as semi-structured (Fägerborg, 2011), with a focus on the informants' own experiences of being Swedish speaking and moving to Sweden, and identity creating processes wherein language and cultural belonging can be important components. What we have are biographical stories formulated by the migrants themselves, or life stories. Birgitta Svensson (1997) defines life stories as 'a story where you present yourself from a structured self-understanding' (my translation) to illustrate how people create meaning and identity. These stories are produced in dialogue with society and as a comment on society (Nylund Skog, 2005, p. 149). This is especially apparent when the interviewees talk about their move in relation to the prevailing discourses of young people fleeing their home country.

It is important to acknowledge that narratives 'reproduce what has happened, but the stories are not the events that they reproduce' (Palmenfelt, 2017, p. 33). The event and the story of the event are two different phenomena and there is a long process between them. The informants had lived in Sweden for half a year to several years when the interviews took place, which will also affect their life stories. The time passed in Sweden has made them re-evaluate and analyse their decision to move; sometimes the move becomes even more self-evident than it was in the beginning, while in other cases, a decision that felt simple in the past becomes more ambivalent now.

Studying in Sweden

Being an emerging adult means living in a period of instability, with frequent moves within a country or smaller geographical areas. Research show that young adults (20–30 years old) from a general point of view are more inclined to move house than any other age group (Hedberg & Malmberg, 2008, p. 8ff). The reasons for moving are often practical (labour market, education, family) but an international move can also be inspired by the fact that global mobility has become an important part of the identity process for young adults (Hedberg & Malmberg, 2008, p. 9). Young adults in the Nordic countries leave home relatively early compared to the rest of the world. In for example Slovakia and Slovenia, 70 per cent in the age group 18–34 still live with their parents, while only 20 per cent are doing the same in Norway, Sweden and Denmark (Boverket, 2013).

All persons interviewed moved to Sweden in order to pursue higher education. Where study is the main goal for the move, it is often because certain study programmes cannot be found in Finland, or there is high competition in local study programmes. Swedish education becomes enticing with educational programmes believed to be better than corresponding Finnish programmes, or even lacking in Finland. Rosa, for example, moved from a small city in Southern Finland to study something that cannot be found in Finland: 'This subject [I am studying]. There is nothing in Finland. I would really have liked to study in Finland if there was a possibility to do so.' Nevertheless, immediately after that statement was made, she said that living in Sweden had for some time been a dream for her. Even when a very specific educational course is the goal, there can be other factors contributing to the decision to move away.

Different education courses mentioned by the young adults in this material not found in Finland can be everything from musical education and marketing to language technology and nutrition studies. Some Swedish universities, for example, Umeå University, are also actively recruiting students from Finland (Kepsu & Henriksson, 2019, p. 36). For the student the aim is to find the education with most potential to offer in terms of knowledge, skills and employability. This corresponds with the idea of emerging adulthood and the ideal of self-realization, where studies and future career development are important parts (Arnett, 2004).

One particular group of student migrants are those aiming for a specific education, such as medicine, dentistry and law. Some very popular programmes in Sweden have been easier to access with a foreign high school diploma. This quota has been adjusted from 2017 (Universitets- och högskolerådet, 2017, 2018), which might affect the number of Swedish-speaking Finns in Sweden (Söderlund, 2017), a fact mentioned by some interviewees. It is also simpler to apply for higher education in Sweden, especially compared to Finland (cf. Kepsu & Henriksson, 2019, pp. 34–36). Several talk about the lack of an entrance examination in Sweden; you just 'send in your papers' and your application is done. In Finland, some study programmes require thorough preparations in order to pass the entrance examination. This system is now under reform (Rönnberg, 2018), and the results may change the patterns of where students apply.[1]

One of the interviewees applied to several study programmes in Finland after graduating secondary school, but also realized how 'easy it is to apply for Sweden;' so she sent her applications to several Swedish universities as well. As she puts it, 'you don't lose anything by applying to Sweden' (Agnes). Stella had similar thoughts when answering the question of why she ended up in Sweden:

> Because of my studies, and because it has been easier to be accepted to programmes like medicine and dentistry here in Sweden. That is why I applied here. Because it felt a convenient way, when you just send in your [high school] diploma and are spared [laughing] the entrance exam. It felt an easier way to go. I didn't believe I would be accepted to Helsinki [University in Finland]. But I knew I had good enough grades to get in here [in the Swedish university].

Sweden as 'Close'

When choosing to study in Sweden instead of Finland, the migrants often talk about Sweden as something 'close.' Distance is not always about national borders. It is also about what feels near. To many young people, the step to adulthood includes moving away, not just from the childhood home, but from a home district, in search of education or work. What then becomes close or far away varies. To Ellen Sweden was not far away when she moved across the water from Vaasa to Umeå:

I was 19. I had never lived away from home. Umeå was sort of close. It is just, what is it, 8 miles across Kvarken [the narrow region in the Gulf of Bothnia between Finland and Sweden].

It is easy to take an airplane or the ferry, not just for the young adult who moves away, but also for the family still living in Finland. There is a feeling of proximity expressed in the life stories where people move in a space that, for different reasons, is easy to grasp. The different modes of transportation are many, comfortable and economically manageable even for students. Sometimes Sweden is even described as geographically closer than other (Finnish-speaking) parts of Finland, and statistically, Swedish speakers move less within the country. Instead of moving to the bigger cities in southern Finland, they move within a cultural sphere, but abroad, to Sweden (Kepsu, 2016, p. 6). Iris describes her feelings of distance after moving from the Helsinki area to Stockholm for formal education: 'It is still so close [to home] and the fact that it is only a 45 minute flight back home feels safe in some way. You are not that far away.' (Iris)

Sweden is also culturally close because of the knowledge the young adults have before moving. They talk about watching Swedish television, listening to Swedish popular music and even having a knowledge of Swedish politics. There is a perceived cultural similarity based on mutual frames of reference (e.g. Henriksson, 2017; Klinkmann, 2011, pp. 241–242). The conception of Sweden is not only based on personal experience, with school trips and shopping sprees, and popular cultural references. Many times, there is a direct connection via other Swedish-speaking Finns who have lived, or are still living, in Sweden (cf. Hedberg, 2004). Migration feeds migration, and in many cases, we can talk about migrant networks where earlier migrants make way for new migration (Castles et al., 2014). Otto for example was explicitly enticed by his older sister to come to Sweden to study:

> It was partly my sister [that was the reason for moving to Sweden]. My older sister that was studying here to become a doctor of medicine. And she had been studying for five years already. And she was on me all the time about coming here. She said it was so good, and that Finland couldn't offer such a study milieu at all. So I thought I'll try it out then.

Other times the personal connection is not so strong. One young woman stated that she 'didn't really have any contact' with Sweden before she moved there to study, but before that, she talked about friends, acquaintances and relatives from Finland who have migrated there. She tells about watching Swedish TV programmes and 'growing up with this [Swedish] culture' which makes it 'not feeling so different.' The closeness to Sweden is a mixture of cultural knowledge, short vacation trips and having acquaintances or relatives who have settled there.

When they actually move to Sweden, the closeness is not only constructed out of distances measured in kilometres, mentality or language, but through what is often daily contact with friends and family in Finland, especially among the generation that grew up with the internet and different forms of social media (Bolton et al., 2013; Tapscott, 1998). Many interviewees describe how physical distance diminishes through frequent contact through text messaging, phone calls, Skype and social media. It is also common not to feel ties to only one country (cf. Povrzanović

Frykman, 2015). Instead, these young adults move freely between countries to work, study and be together with friends and family; they do not see themselves as nation bound but maintain strong ties, 'transnational networks,' with family and friends through social media wherever they live in the world (Goulbourne, 2010).

The interviews show clear patterns of behaviour about when the migrants travel to Finland. Those studying in Sweden go 'home' during summers, often to work, and celebrate Christmas with the family at home. Agnes, studying in Sweden to become a doctor, says, 'I will go back now for the summer also, and all of last summer I was at home in Finland.' Other students travel back even more often during longer weekends in autumn and spring. Since this era of life is a period of movement, many of the informants point out that they are not the only ones that have moved away. Their friends from childhood have often also migrated somewhere to study or work, even if it is not abroad. Going back to Finland to your childhood area does not automatically mean meeting friends where you left them. Many young adults have several places to call home, as both family and friends may be scattered around the country.

Education in Your Own Language

Agnes answers the question of her relationship to Sweden before the move by describing Sweden as 'a neighbour-country. [...] Maybe a bit more open than Finland, but not that much. A neighbour country, where they speak Swedish.' Her last statement is one of the keys to many young adults' migration stories. Sweden is a well known neighbouring country, but it is also the country where the mother tongue is the main language spoken. The 'pluricentricity' (Soares, 2014) of Swedish becomes a major fact in the migration process.

The construction of Sweden as something well known and safe is of course partly based on a mutual language. Growing up as a Swedish speaker in Finland is mostly growing up as part of a minority meaning that not everything can easily be done in your mother tongue. Sweden is a society where Swedish can be used, and is used, everywhere. The majority of the interviewees cite language as either the sole reason, or at least partly a reason to move to Sweden. Living a life totally in Swedish, studying, maybe working part-time but also having everyday communication in Swedish feels attractive. Several persons in the material express a feeling of relief when Swedish can be used in all situation without being called in question or misunderstood.

It is sometimes stated that migration from Finland to Sweden, when it comes to Swedish speakers, maybe is more of an internal migration than migration abroad, since to many migrants it is easier to move across the national border to Sweden than to cross the linguistic and cultural borders to Finnish-speaking Finland (Hedberg & Kepsu, 2003; Kepsu, 2006; Kepsu & Henriksson, 2019, p. 7). The move to Sweden for some becomes a move *to* Swedish; for others it is more of a move *from* Finnish. Finding higher education in Sweden, rather than studying at the Swedish-speaking Åbo Akademi University in Finland avoids Finnish altogether as the surrounding society demands knowledge in Finnish. Ellen explains her choice to go to a university in Sweden instead of Åbo, Finland:

> But I chose [the subject] partly because I was tired of Finnish I think. I was very bad at Finnish in school, and I felt like I needed a break. To let my head rest from the Finnish language, which wouldn't be possible in Åbo.

Language is closely connected to studies for the young adults examining themselves and their abilities to study in a language other than Swedish, and also the possibilities to reach their full potential when using something else than Swedish. Language is a part of their cultural identity and the migrants often talk about being able to 'be themselves,' for example, living their life in their mother tongue. Studying in Sweden becomes a part of a bigger identity project where the young adults are trying to find their place to be and become who they want to be.

Sweden as 'Something Else'

If Sweden is close and familiar in some respects, it is also exiting and different in others. Being a young adult means searching for identity and ways of fulfilling oneself. One way of doing so is by looking for adventure and personal challenges. Travelling is not only an obvious part of being young, something 'everyone' does, it is also seen as a means to get to know yourself and become an adult (Tolgensbakk, 2014, p. 191). The gap year is an example of this normalized travelling, from the beginning, meant to break free from education and a career focus. The concept of 'abroad' can be seen as something structuring young adults' way of relating to the surrounding world, which makes it interesting to look at national migration compared to international migration (Frändberg, 2015, p. 4). Living abroad for a period of time becomes part of shaping one's own identity and fulfilling oneself, and it might not always be a specific country that pulls, but the idea of exploring the world.

Several of the interviewed young adults express the idea that their move to Sweden was a yearning away in one way or another. They talk both about challenging oneself and about escaping something too safe and secure, and sometimes too small and narrow-minded. Some want to leave a small society or a feeling of living in a Swedish-speaking bubble in Finland, in the same way as Ida Tolgensbakk (2014, p. 188) writes of young Swedes moving to Norway in order to 'get away' from small town life. Iris went to Sweden together with her partner, in order to study, but she also describes other motivations:

> What made us come [to Sweden] was also to escape this small bubble of Finlandswedishness. Where it feels like you know everyone, and everyone knows you, and you have seen it all. It felt like you had seen Finland. It feels different now of course [laughing]. But I think that

was it. Partly a small flight too. To see something new, but still really safe with the same language and the same culture, sort of.

This longing away can be expressed as a longing, 'To travel, to break up from your local connection and go off on the big adventure has become a central part of many contemporary young adults' identity-projects' (Lalander & Johansson, 2002/2006, p. 94). The move to Sweden can then be formulated and experienced as the big adventure. Taking the step to another country can become a way of affirming dreams and plans for the future, irrespective of whether it includes a sought after education or a more existential maturing as a human being.[2]

Moving to Sweden in this material becomes a way of challenging yourself by going out into the world (cf. Tolgensbakk, 2014, p. 192), but still keeping it relatively safe by not going so far away geographically and culturally. Alternatively, as Ellen describes her choice to study in Sweden:

> But I wanted to get away from home. I was looking for adventure. I wanted to see more of the world. And that was of course something that could have led me anywhere [in the world]. At the same time, I was, and am, a bit cautious as a person, otherwise I could have gone to a university in, I don't know, the US for example.

In the life stories analysed, Sweden is presented as being safe and exciting at the same time. By moving to the neighbouring country, you can both expand your horizons and stay close to friends, family and other points of attachment. Otto explains his view:

> So, I thought, well I have to try it [move to Sweden]. At the same time, I felt that I have lived all my life... I mean... [my hometown] felt so, I have been there all my life, and it felt fun to see something new and widen my views. It sounded good to go to Sweden, so I thought 'yeah, why not?' It's close to my family in Finland anyway. It seemed like a natural choice.

Emerging adults are in many ways very aware of being in an identity shaping period of life (Tolgensbakk, 2014, p. 196). A move abroad can be motivated as a way of challenging yourself, with personal development as a goal rather than following surrounding expectations. Even if the expectation of a good education exists, it is also seen as normal to set aside a period of life for exploring and trying out when it comes to work, lifestyle and sexual relations, before you become fully adult, says Tolgensbakk (2014, p. 198). Living abroad becomes a way of doing something different when you do not have fixed plans. 'I didn't really know what to do with my life,' Asta explains her decision to move to Sweden, and to Amanda, it is definitely a search for an alternative lifestyle, not as simple and obvious as staying in Finland, that made her move to Sweden to pursue her Master's degree:

> I think I felt like I wanted to move abroad and to check out some other alternatives. And this [Master's programme] in Gothenburg felt so exciting. And I also wanted to move to Sweden, because it felt less... sort of easy.

Sweden as Something 'Better'

In pursuit of the big adventure abroad, the idea of the country you are choosing to move to plays an important role. Many informants tell of their ideal picture of Sweden before moving there. In these life stories, Sweden is described as a country being ahead, especially when it comes to trends, fashion and popular culture. Linda explains that to her 'Sweden always felt a little bigger, and ahead of Finland. [...] Finland is always a step after.'

On the other hand, there seems to exist a widespread apprehension of 'international Sweden' (e.g. Felicia) or in some cases, 'international Stockholm,' a more open country, with the Swedes as more social and welcoming than Finns. The interviewees speak in terms of mentality, disposition and approach to life. This perceived mentality is not necessary what makes them move to Sweden, but several mention this as something positive and desirable. Even if more self-centred than earlier generations, they are also, at least in Finnish urban contexts, eager to strive for authenticity and to be honest to their true self (Mikkola et al., 2007, p. 24). Some claim to feel more at home in Sweden culturally and mentally. Frida for example says that she fits into the Swedish society better because of being 'very spontaneous and open,' which, according to her, made her a misfit in Finland.

Experiences of mental climate are also named as a pull factor to leave Finland. Many 'global professionals' are not only attracted by well-paid positions but also driven away by a perceived stifling and not encouraging atmosphere in Finland (Kiriakos, 2011). More personal reasons are not always distinctly separate from professional reasons. Emerging adults are also affected by the situation they are in when it comes to experiences and interpretations. A real adventure presupposes some kind of exoticism and differences, and these are often connected to stereotyped ideas and narratives about the country of origin and the country of destination.

Moving Back to Finland?

How does the future look for these young migrants? Are they planning on staying in Sweden, move back to Finland, or maybe even away somewhere else? Just like when it comes to motivations to move to Sweden, there are no easy answers. An eventual 're-move' is dependent on both outer circumstances and the individual's own point of view. It very much has to do with the reasons to move away in the first place as well. For a person in the middle of an adventure, where circumstances dictate the direction, the future often feels abstract and very far away. A decision concerning where to live after graduation is not very urgent—who knows what will happen in life before then? Agnes answers the questions on where she sees herself in the future like this:

> I think that the future will show me. You just have to see. At the moment I could very well move back to Finland [after graduation], but just as well stay here. Because I like it in both places. [Interviewer: What would make you decide, do you think?] It is going to be work, or friends, or family, or something. You will see when that day comes.

Other informants have a clearer view of finishing the big adventure and then moving back home. If the goal, apart from studies, was self-fulfilment, challenging yourself or maybe moving away from a too ingrained life, maybe a couple of years in Sweden are enough. A finished education may force decisions of whether life will continue in Sweden or in Finland. For some the decision is easy—they never meant to stay in Sweden, as Linda also expresses:

> I don't know about the others, but when I moved here it was because of the education. It was—'well now I move there [to Sweden] and then I get my degree and then I move back home.'

If studies have prepared someone for a certain line of work and career, this might hinder a future re-move, even if they would like to move back. In some cases, the language makes it more difficult. Some express feelings of losing their knowledge of the Finnish language, or that they do not know the right terminology in Finnish. Other times they fear not getting the right employment or work they feel deserving of, or even no work at all (cf. Heikkilä, 2011). Only half of the migrant Finns studied by Elli Heikkilä and Maria Pikkarainen (2008) anticipated finding a job in Finland without any problems.

Being educated in Swedish might close some doors in Finland, or make it more difficult at least. Studying law in Sweden means that you have do complementary education to in order to practice in Finland; at the same time, law work demands skill in Finnish. However, moving to Sweden to become a dentist means starting work immediately after moving back according to Stella:

> If you are a dentist, you can communicate in other ways [...] it doesn't matter if you say something in the wrong way, and you don't really talk so much with the patient.

One of the consequences of a life in Swedish also seems to be that people get used to it, which makes it hard to move back. In another study, Finns living in Europe enjoyed themselves partly because of the positive and warm atmosphere, the friendly people and an international living environment in their new home countries (Haanpää & Laine, 2013). In addition, the Swedish-speaking migrants not only feel that their Finnish deteriorates, but they become used to the feeling of 'being oneself' as several informants formulate it. Other things that might have happened in Sweden also affect the decision to move back or stay. Sometimes the equation now holds more than one person, and a new Swedish partner with no knowledge of Finnish can for example be a hindrance for a remove (cf. Heikkilä, 2011; Haanpää & Laine, 2013). Personal reasons like strong home longing, or close family members becoming ill are also motives that come up in the interviews. This complies with similar research on young adults and return migration, showing that relationships and family ties influence young migrants when it comes to moving away to another country, and in moving back again (Krasteva et al., 2019; Yehuda-Sternfeld & Mirsky, 2015).

These young adults have not returned, and at the moment, we don't know if they will do so. Nevertheless, return migration is something they deal with or think of every now and then. None of the interviewees planned to migrate when they moved to Sweden. For some it was clear they wanted to stay a couple of years, while others had no actual time schedule. Most talk about circumstances, some want to move back, for example, if they have children (or in one case when the child starts school), but they admit to themselves that it might not be so easy to uproot again and leave their life in Sweden. The thought of leaving a social life and a feeling of belonging for something unknown once again is scarier than it was several years ago when the first decision to move was taken.

Concluding Discussion

The life stories of these young migrants show how different conceptions of mobility are at work. Moving to another country might be a big step, a migration process for some, but more of a natural life change for others. While some migrants have education as a goal, others talk more about finding themselves, moving away from a small community or being able to study in their mother tongue. These life stories are often easy to fit into conceptions of what it means to be a young adult today. There is often no single factor driving the migration trajectory forward, but rather a feeling that there is the existence of something else somewhere else. One way or another, these young adults stand at a crossroads, with many ways to go and many decisions to make, but it might be hard to even grasp what is waiting in the future. And this period of life, marked by a search for the right place, occupation and identity, can lead to a longer or shorter stay abroad.

Moving to Sweden is in most cases in the analysed interviews not a definitive decision. We are not dealing with classical 'migration' where the old home country is left for good; instead, the informants are in a place in life where circumstances are allowed to define the future. Factors like career and family are something the young adults expect will matter in the future, but not right now (cf. Smith & Snell, 2009). But Sweden might be just be one alternative among others. If you are looking for good education, you might have to move to find what you are really looking for. Agnes, who moved from a small municipality in the archipelago to a big city in southern Sweden to study medicine, says, 'I had to move somewhere. So, if it happened to be Turku or Helsinki or Gothenburg or somewhere else… It didn't really matter.' If you have to move anyway, Sweden might be, as another informant puts it, 'suitably far away.' It is abroad, but not as much abroad as moving south to continental Europe or a country with a totally different language. Moving to Sweden is 'simple.' Simple because others have done it before you, simple because you know the country from earlier visits and its popular culture, simple because you know the language, simple because travelling there is cheap, fast and convenient.

Notes

1. The media in Finland has paid attention to the fact that young people look for education in Sweden in order to escape entrance exams (e.g. Savonius, 2016).
2. Greg Madison introduces the concept existential migration, meaning that migrants rather than being drawn by work, career or a better economic situation, seek bigger opportunities to self-realization, and in order to achieve that, explore foreign cultures (Madison, 2006). Russell King writes about self-fulfilment where the driving force for migration might be more than a dream for a better life economically (King, 2002).

References

Arnett, J. J. (2004). *Emerging adulthood: The winding road from the late teens through the twenties.* Oxford University Press.
Björklund, K. (2012). *Suomalainen, ruotsalainen vai ruotsinsuomalainen? Ruotsissa asivat suomalaiset 2000-luvulla.* Siirtolaisinstituutti.
Bolton, R. N., Parasuraman, A., Hoefnagels, A., Migshels, N., Kabadayi, S., Gruber, T., Komariva Loureiro, Y., & Solnet, D. (2013). Understanding Generation Y and their use of social media: A review and research agenda. *Journal of Service Management, 24*(3), 245–267.
Boverket. (2013). *Ungdomars boende – lägesrapport 2013. Karlskrona: Boverket.* https://www.boverket.se/globalassets/publikationer/dokument/2013/ungdomars-boende-lagesrapport-2013.pdf
Castles, S., de Haas, H., & Miller, M. J. (2014). *The age of migration. International population movements in the modern world* (5th ed.). Palgrave Macmillan.
Fägerborg, E. (2011 [1999]). Intervjuer. In L. Kaijser & M. Öhlander (Red.), *Etnologiskt fältarbete* (pp. 85–112). Studentlitteratur.
Frändberg, L. (2015). *'Året utomlands' och det unga vuxenlivets geografi. En studie av utlandsflyttningar, vuxenblivande och transnationell rörlighet bland unga.* Göteborg: Göteborgs universitet.
Goulbourne, H. (2010). *Transnational families: Ethnicities, identities and social capital.* Routledge.
Haanpää, R., & Laine, T. (2013). Takaisin Suomeen -kysely Euroopan suomalaisille. In O. Tuomi-Nikula, R. Haanpää, & T. Laine (Eds.), *Takaisin Suomeen? Euroopan ulkosuomalaisten ja heidän lastensa ajatuksia Suomesta maahanmuuton kohteena* (Kulttuurituotannon ja maisemantutkimuksen julkaisuja, 42) (pp. 11–56). Turun yliopisto.
Häggström, N., Rosengren, A., & Borgegård, L.-E. (1990). *När finländarna kom—migrationen Finland-Sverige efter andra världskriget.* Statens institut för byggnadsforskning.
Hedberg, C. (2004). *The Finland-Swedish wheel of migration. Identity, networks and integration 1976–2000.* Uppsala universitet.
Hedberg, C., & Kepsu, K. (2003). Migration as a cultural expression? The case of the Finland-Swedish minority's migration to Sweden. *Geografiska Annaler, 85*(B/2), 67–84.
Hedberg, C., & Malmberg, B. (2008). *Den stora utmaningen. Internationell migration i en globaliserad värld.* Underlagsrapport nr 18 till Globaliseringsrådet. Västerås.
Heikkilä, E. (2011). Finns abroad—The profile of emigrants and their thoughts about returning to Finland. In E. Heikkilä & S. Koikkalainen (Eds.), *Finns abroad. New forms of mobility and migration* (Migration Studies, C21). Siirtolaisuusinstituutti.
Heikkilä, E., & Alivuotila, M. (2019). Finn's contemporary emigration abroad, their profile and willingness to return migrate: A special view of their human resources. In *Transnational Finnish mobilities: Proceedings of FinnForum XI* (pp. 185–200). Migration Institute of Finland.

Heikkilä, E., & Pikkarainen, M. (2008). *Väestön ja työvoiman kansainvälistyminen nyt ja tulevaisuudessa*. Siirtolaisuustutkimuksia A 30. Turku: Siirtolaisuusinstituutti. www.migrationinstitute.fi/files/siirtolaisuustutkimuksia_a30_esr_1.pdf

Henriksson, B. (2017). "Snusförbudet är ett hån mot vår finlandssvenska kultur!!!"—framställningar av minoritet, tradition och region i finlandssvensk snusdebatt 2008–2011. In S.-E. Klinkmann, B. Henriksson, & A. Häger (Eds.), *Föreställda finlandssvenskheter. Perspektiv på det svenska i Finland*. Svenska litteratursällskapet.

Kepsu, K. (2006). Finlandssvenska flyttningsmönster och språkgränser. In M. Junila & C. Westin (Eds.), *Svenskt i Finland—finskt i Sverige. Om migration, makt och mening* (pp. 124–148). Svenska litteratursällskapet i Finland/Atlantis.

Kepsu, K. (2016). *Hjärnflykt eller inte? En analys av den svenskspråkiga flyttningen mellan Finland och Sverige 2000–2015*. Magma-pamflett 2. Helsingfors: Magma. http://magma.fi/uploads/media/post/0001/01/a7418a6c7e08be3247c3332e5a735839c9718c13.pdf

Kepsu, K., & Henriksson, B. (2019). *Hjärnflykt eller inte? Del II. Svenskspråkig ungdomsflyttning till Sverige: trender och drivkrafter*. Helsingfors: Tankesmedjan Magma. http://magma.fi/wp-content/uploads/2019/06/118.pdf

King, R. (2002). Towards a new map of European migration. *International Journal of Population Geography, 8*, 89–106.

Kiriakos, C. M. (2011). Finns in Silicon Valley: Motivations and identities in relation to place. In E. Heikkilä & S. Koikkalainen (Eds.), *Finns abroad. New forms of mobility and migration* (Migration Studies, C21). Siirtolaisuusinstituutti.

Klinkmann, S.-E. (2011). *I fänrikarnas, martallarnas och dixietigrarnas land. En resa genom det svenska i Finland*. Svenska litteratursällskapet.

Koikkalainen, S. (2011). Highly skilled Finns in the European labor market: Why do they move abroad? In E. Heikkilä & S. Koikkalainen (Eds.), *Finns abroad. New forms of mobility and migration* (Migration Studies, C21). Siirtolaisuusinstituutti.

Korkiasaari, J. (2001). *Suomalaisten Ruotsiin suuntautuneen siirtolaisuuden yhteiskunnalliset syyt 1900-luvulla*. Siirtolaisinstituutti.

Korkiasaari, J., & Tarkiainen, K. (2000). *Suomalaiset ruotsissa. Suomalaisen siirtolaisuuden historia, osa 3*. Siirtolaisinstituutti.

Krasteva, V., McDonnell, A., & Tolgensbakk, I. (2019). Mobile young individuals: Subjective experiences of migration and return. In B. Hvinden, J. O'Reilly, M. A. Schoyen, & C. Hyggen (Eds.), *Negotiating early job insecurity: Scarring, resilience and well-being of European youth*. Edward Elgar Publishing.

Lalander, P., & Johansson, T. (2002/2006). *Ungdomsgrupper i teori och praktik*. Studentlitteratur.

Madison, G. (2006). Existential migration. *Existential Analysis, 17*(2), 238–260.

Mikkola, T., Niemelä, K., & Petterson, J. (2007). *The questioning mind: Faith and values of the new generation* (Publication, 58). Church Research Institute.

Nyberg, B. (2016, May 12). Positiv grundton låter lockande. *Österbottens tidning*.

Nylund Skog, S. (2005). Hisnande historier och talande tystnader. In C. Hagström & L. Marander-Eklund (Eds.), *Frågelistan som källa och metod*. Studentlitteratur.

Övergaard, L. (2016, May 9). Flyttvåg till Sverige oroar Henriksson. *Vasabladet*.

Palmenfelt, U. (2017). *Berättade gemenskaper. Individuella livshistorier och kollektiva tankefigurer*. Carlsson.

Parkvall, M. (2009). *Sveriges språk—vem talar vad och var?* Rapporter från Institutionen för lingvistik vid Stockholms universitet. Stockholm: Stockholms universitet.

Povrzanović Frykman, M. (2015). Att höra hemma både "här" och "där": transnationella familjer och materiella praktiker. *Laboratorium för folk och kultur*. bragelaboratorium.com/2015/05/27/att-hora-hemma-bade-har-och-dar-transnationella-familjer-och-materiella-praktiker/

Rönnberg, O. (2018, June 28). HBL guidar: Så förändras antagningen till högskolor. *Hufvudstadsbladet*. Retrieved September 30, 2019, from https://www.hbl.fi/artikel/hbl-guidar-sa-forandras-antagningen-till-hogskolor-2/

Savonius, A. (2016, September 15). Tuffa krav får många att välja Sverige—"Inträdesprovet till medi diskuteras nog". *Svenska Yle*. Retrieved January 16, 2019, from https://svenska.yle.fi/artikel/2016/09/15/tuffa-krav-far-manga-att-valja-sverige-intradesprovet-till-medi-diskuteras-nog

Smith, C., & Snell, P. (2009). *Souls in transition: The religious and spiritual lives of emerging adults.* Oxford University Press.

Soares, D. S. A. (Ed.). (2014). *Pluricentricity.* De Gruyter Mouton.

Söderlund, L. (2017, August 17). Sverige blev strängare mot studenter från Finland—Fanny kom på reservplats 653 till juridiklinjen i Lund. *Svenska Yle*. Retrieved January 16, 2019, from https://svenska.yle.fi/artikel/2017/08/17/sverige-blev-strangare-mot-studenter-fran-finland-fanny-kom-pa-reservplats-653

Statistiska centralbyrån. (2018, March 21). *Befolkning efter födelseland och ursprungsland 31 december 2017.* Excel-file. Retrieved January 16, 2018, from https://www.scb.se/hitta-statistik/statistik-efter-amne/befolkning/befolkningens-sammansattning/befolkningsstatistik/

Svanberg, I., & Tydén, M. (1992). *Tusen år av invandring: en svensk kulturhistoria.* Gidlund.

Svensson, B. (1997). Livstid. Metodiska reflektioner över biografiskt särskiljande och modern identitetsformering. In G. Alsmark (Ed.), *Skjorta och själ. Kulturella identiteter i tid och rum.* Studentlitteratur.

Tapscott, D. (1998). *Growing up digital: The rise of the net generation.* McGraw-Hill.

Tolgensbakk, I. (2014). *Partysvensker; GO HARD! En narratologisk studie av unge svenske arbeidsmigranters nærvær i Oslo.* [diss] Institutt for kulturstudier og orientalske språk, Oslo.

Universitets- och högskolerådet. (2017, December 18). Ny bedömning av utländska gymnasiebetyg. www.uhr.se/om-uhr/pressrum/debattartiklar/ny-bedomning-av-ut-landska-gymnasiebetyg/

Universitets- och högskolerådet. (2018, October 18). Ny omräkning ska göra betygen mer likvärdiga i antagningen till högskolan. www.uhr.se/om-uhr/nyheter/2018-nyheter/ny-omrakning-ska-gora-betygen-mer-likvardiga-i-antagningen-till-hogskolan

Yehuda-Sternfeld, S. B., & Mirsky, J. (2015). Return migration of Americans: Personal narratives and psychological perspectives. *International Journal of Intercultural Relations, 42*, 53–64.

Zackariasson, M. (2001). *Maktkamper och korridorfester. En etnologisk studie av kulturella processer och gruppinteraktion i två studentkorridorer.* Etnolore 23. Skrifter från etnologiska avdelningen. Uppsala universitet.

Part III

Chapter 16
Institutionalized Mobility Inside and Outside Erasmus

David Cairns and Thais França

Having looked at various aspects of free movement in tertiary education in the previous section of this book, we now direct our attention towards young people's participation in student mobility programmes, the most prominent example being the European Commission supported Erasmus programme. The popularity of Erasmus as a research topic is equally evident, to the point where the study of student mobility is largely equated with Erasmus, although many other less well documented institutionally hosted platforms can be found throughout the globalized world of tertiary education. Given that Erasmus is so familiar, this section of the book will move beyond describing the programme and consider what other exchange mechanisms contribute to our understanding of youth migration.

Chapters 17, 18, 19, 20 and 21 consider different aspects of Erasmus, beginning with an account of the 30-year history of the programme by Alexandra Ribeiro. This chapter helps contextualize the place of Erasmus within the development of systemic student mobility at tertiary education level and, more questionably, as an instrument of European integration. As various studies have made clear, Erasmus can be seen as a symbolic success for the European institutions, as a sign of an integrating Europe, linked with internationalization processes at tertiary education level, especially in the highly commercialized universities of the Global North. However, this apparent progress is tempered by a failure to integrate socio-demographic and geo-demographic inclusivity into the programme, challenging the idea of Erasmus as an unqualified success story. Ironically, in a programme that is explicitly international, failure to take

---

D. Cairns (✉) • T. França
ISCTE – Instituto Universitário de Lisboa (ISCTE-IUL), Centro de Investigação e Estudos de Sociologia, Lisbon, Portugal
e-mail: david.cairns@iscte-iul.pt; thais.franca@iscte-iul.pt

© The Author(s), under exclusive license to Springer Nature Switzerland AG 2022
D. Cairns (ed.), *The Palgrave Handbook of Youth Mobility and Educational Migration*, https://doi.org/10.1007/978-3-030-99447-1_16

into account differences at national and regional levels undermines aspirations towards equality of access, with the price of entry highest for those in receipt of least support. Taking a 'one size fits all' approach to student participation simply does not work, suggesting that symbolic success was not matched by actual achievement (see, e.g., Feyen and Krzaklewska 2013; Cairns 2017).[1]

Less contentiously, the idea of internationalization via Erasmus is explored by Sahizer Samuk and colleagues in Chap. 18. Using evidence from a European Commission–funded study entitled *MOVE*, they look at how Erasmus has diversified the learning of mobility among young people. Rather than being a migration incubator, the idea seems to be that Erasmus should make a contribution to future employment aspirations, facilitating the adoption of new lifestyles and what these authors term an 'Erasmus-ization' of life experience (Samuk et al. 2021). In practice, this entails enculturation to European values and global citizenship (Deardorff 2006), experiential learning (Kolb 2014), and a broadening of opportunity structures in relation to a future transition to the labour market. This work is a reminder that Erasmus, as well as being a platform that offers mobility experience, is also a programme with an ethos, and that while student participants will want to enhance their present educational and future occupational profiles, they ought to be doing so in a manner that demonstrates some form of loyalty to the European Union.

This 'Erasmus-ization' practice is of significance, particularly since 2014, when the programme was rebranded as Erasmus+, with a €14.7 billion budget to provide a broader range of opportunities for millions of Europeans to study, train, and gain work experience abroad up until the year 2020, also embracing learners outside the EU via initiatives such as Erasmus Mundus. While complex, this expansion basically involved using geographical mobility as a pedagogical tool, especially within the field of youth work, thus integrating initiatives nested under the preceding *Youth in Action* programme, such as interventions aimed at socially disadvantaged youth, centred around not only education and training but also sporting activities. In principle, we might say the idea was that they should accumulate mobility capital to enhance their employability (Cairns 2021b). Mobility also became a project, or perhaps a series of projects, to be hosted by civil society agencies rather than universities, disconnected further from the idea of spatial circulation as permanent migration but consistent with the notion of mobility as fluid and fragmented (Cairns 2021a).

In more concrete terms, an area of interest among authors exploring institutionalized exchanges has been examining the process of diffusing the Erasmus brand, especially this exporting of a mobility-centric programmatic ethos to civil society organizations. In this book, the analysis of Airi-Alina Allaste and Raili Nugin looks at agency-mediated mobility in Estonia, bringing into play another antecedent theoretical framework, namely the new mobilities paradigm of Sheller and Urry (2006). This is a familiar idea within the study of human mobility, especially in Anglophone societies, recognizing the importance of a generalized spatial dimension of life, moving us even further away from the idea of 'mobility as migration' in a definitive sense. Significantly, Allaste and Nugin (2021) contend that mobility is not only about mappable physical movement but also the circulation of ideas and capitals, reflecting the idea that mobility can be seen as a form of capital in itself (Cairns 2021b).

Short-duration exchanges within projects supported by Erasmus+ hence become a means of generating mobility capital, designed presumably to enhance the life chances of the participants, albeit without this approach having taken into account the potential for mobility to alienate and create resentment in host communities.[2]

Erasmus has also gained a foothold in postgraduate level education, which has been previously described as 'post-diploma' mobility (Cairns 2014). A prominent example concerns internationalized Master's degree programmes that provide opportunities for circulation and cooperation among students and between universities from different countries. In Chap. 20, Karolina Czerska-Shaw and Ewa Krzaklewska look at the Erasmus Mundus programme, and how it has attempted to create what they term the 'super-mobile student,' enabling small numbers of learners to study in up to four countries during a period of two years. Significantly, their analysis takes into account the costs and benefits of this form of learning. On the one hand, there is a suggestion of a new form of de-nationalized belonging being sought by the funders of the programme, which students experience as a kind of reflexive, cosmopolitan identity. On the other, for individual participants, there are high levels of stress and anxiety, various logistical and legal hurdles, and a sense of social dis-embeddedness, including a feeling of exclusion from the host universities (Czerska-Shaw and Krzaklewska 2021). This position highlights the ambivalent relationship between institutionalized mobility and belonging, with new forms of conviviality created at the cost of older, most established, identifications. Belonging to an abstract, even idealized, Europe may therefore come at a cost of detachment from national and regional structures that offer a more solidified idea of 'home.' Chapter 20 moves the discussion of Erasmus Mundus outside Europe, looking at students in South Africa. Author Samia Chasi also introduces a socio-demographic dimension into the discussion, highlighting the fact that as most South African young people cannot afford to study in South Africa, let alone abroad, Erasmus scholarships are an important mechanism in enabling them to benefit from educational mobility. The chapter reflects on the conditions for successful mobility partnerships, specifically referring to the high levels of inequality at institutional and individual levels that are a legacy of apartheid South Africa (Chasi 2021).

Even less well documented in prior studies is the experience of student mobility in Kyrgyzstan. The chapter of Hélène Syed Zwick provides a reminder that student mobility outside Erasmus exists, in this case, via the OSCE Academy in Bishkek. While looking towards 'the West' remains popular for Central Asian students, intra-regional exchange has been growing in scale. This discussion looks at some of these experiences and the extent to which they fulfil the aim of promoting regional cooperation, preventing conflict and ensuring good governance of tertiary-education level mobility in Central Asia (Zwick 2021). Thais França and Beatriz Padilla meanwhile focus on recent developments in the Global South, looking at student mobility between Portuguese-speaking Africa and Brazil. This example of South–South exchange further contributes to the debate on the meaning of student mobility, integrating discussions of issues such as colonialism, and the difficult relationships that exist between metropole and colony, as well as challenges that are less evident in the Global North (França and Padilla 2021).

Finally, we have some additional ramifications of institutionalized student mobility to consider. Eva Maria Vögtle looks at participation in mobility across the European context (not only via Erasmus), including consideration of gender disparities, while Louise Kaktiņš looks at some of the pathways for non-English-speaking students in Australia, and the difficulties they experience due to a lack of fluency in the language of the host institution; in this case, English. Both these chapters emphasise the importance of recognizing socio-demographic barriers to participation in institutional mobility and the frequent lack of inclusivity facing many students due to their gender or socio-demographic origins.

One of the key impressions emerging from this work concerns the ramifications of the expansion of institutionalized mobility, particularly in the EU via Erasmus but also in other global regions, where there may have been insufficient foresight as to the viability and sustainability of expanded flows of incoming and outgoing students. Furthermore, there is the quality of the mobile learning experience to consider, for students and institutions, which in itself can be compromised by commercialism and de-intellectualization (see Kaktiņš 2021). These processes can result in a compromised academic culture, focused on processing rather than educating students, with needless pressure put upon staff to sustain an unsustainable level of student circulation. In attempting to appreciate why this has happened, there may have been an element of political fantasy regarding the use of mobility as a social integration mechanism, and a somewhat fanciful belief that the acquisition of mobility capital unlocks employability. Universities may also be focusing on the potential revenue without considering the actual costs required to sustain mobility systems, especially in non-English-speaking learning environments. It may also be that 'mobility' became something of a political fetish, acquiring a perverse value in and of itself for certain politicians, divorced from the economic and emotional consequences for programme participants.

In regard to this distancing of mobility from reality, just the idea of there being a large population of free-floating students, especially in the EU, seems to have been enough for some policymakers to justify putting their faith, and European taxpayers money, into an expanded Erasmus. More cynically, we might argue that institutionalized mobility was a means of, if not exactly controlling, then attaching certain practical and even ideological limits upon spatial circulation, in particular, giving platforms such as Erasmus a (geo)political significance. This obviously relates to the symbolic value of programmes like Erasmus but also to the values which participants were expected to embody as Erasmus students. This, of course, was always highly questionable considering that they may have identified with 'European values' irrespective of their involvement with the programme, making the Erasmus 'effect' a potential false positive (Mitchell 2013). And they may even reject what they are presented with, perhaps due to the non-conformity of youth, suggesting possible overreach in Erasmus+. Furthermore, if project-based mobility is restricted to certain interest groups, such as single-issue civil society organizations, this significantly limits the impact of the programme through focusing on small groups of young people at the margins of society rather than the much larger centre ground. The easy-to-foresee implications of this approach should have been considered at the time of the programme's reformulation and, in not doing so, the European Commission may have driven its own programme into the ditch for no great purpose. Erasmus+ may have been an attempt to give European institutions what *they* wanted, but it was not what many students required at the time. The neoliberal underpinnings of Erasmus are also painfully exposed in Erasmus+, especially the distasteful bun fight for funding to which agencies were subject and the privatization of costs for student participants who effectively suffered a drop in levels of financial support, all of whom nevertheless carry the Erasmus brand regardless of how unhappy they became with the experience.

Even stranger in existing studies of institutional mobility is the lack of representation of what are extremely obvious failings in the governance of student exchange systems. A lack of recognition of the different nature of the problems facing institutions in the Global North and Global South is made clear in various chapters in this section, especially where nasty colonial legacies and deeply embedded sociodemographic inequalities are reproduced rather than eliminated by existing opportunities, especially in regard to gender and social class. Utterly bizarre is the lack of discussion in student mobility literature of the linguistic challenge facing students, including many learners who lack adequate levels of social and economic capital (see Kaktiņš 2021, in this volume). Assuming all students speak perfect English is an absurd notion and the impact of a lack of common language fluency on learning should be taking into account in all internationalized learning environments.

Notes

1. This topic of social inclusivity is also a theme several contributors to this section of the book have collectively explored in Cairns et al. (2018).
2. For further exploration of this theme, see Murphy-Lejeune (2002) and, for a more recent discussion, Cuzzocrea et al. (2021).

References

Allaste, A.-A., & Nugin, R. (2021). Mobility and participation: Intertwined movement of youth and ideas. In D. Cairns (Ed.), *The Palgrave handbook of youth mobility and educational migration*. Basingstoke: Palgrave Macmillan.
Cairns, D. (2014). *Youth transitions, international student mobility and spatial reflexivity: Being mobile?* Basingstoke: Palgrave Macmillan.
Cairns, D. (2017). The Erasmus undergraduate exchange programme: A highly qualified success story? *Children's Geographies, 15*(6), 728–740.
Cairns, D. (2021a). Mobility becoming migration: Understanding youth spatiality in the twenty-first century. In D. Cairns (Ed.), *The Palgrave handbook of youth mobility and educational migration*. Basingstoke: Palgrave Macmillan.

Cairns, D. (2021b). Migration decision-making, mobility capital and reflexive learning. In D. Cairns (Ed.), *The Palgrave handbook of youth mobility and educational migration*. Basingstoke: Palgrave Macmillan.

Cairns, D., Krzaklewska, E., Cuzzocrea, V., & Allaste, A.-A. (2018). *Mobility, education and employability in the European Union: Inside Erasmus*. Basingstoke: Palgrave Macmillan.

Chasi, S. (2021). Educational mobility of South African youth: Insights from Erasmus Mundus Action 2. In D. Cairns (Ed.), *The Palgrave handbook of youth mobility and educational migration*. Basingstoke: Palgrave Macmillan.

Cuzzocrea, V., Krzaklewska, E., & Cairns, D. (2021). 'There is no me, there is only us': the Erasmus bubble as a transient form of transnational collectivity. In V. Cuzzocrea, B. Gook, & B. Schiermer (Eds.), *Forms of collective engagements in youth transition: A global perspective*. Leiden: Brill.

Czerska-Shaw, K., & Krzaklewska, E. (2021). The super-mobile student: Global educational trajectories in Erasmus Mundus. In D. Cairns (Ed.), *The Palgrave handbook of youth mobility and educational migration*. Basingstoke: Palgrave Macmillan.

Deardorff, D. K. (2006). Identification and assessment of intercultural competence as a student outcome of internationalization. *Journal of Studies in International Education, 10*(3), 241–266.

Feyen, B., & Krzaklewska, E. (Eds.). (2013). *The Erasmus phenomenon – Symbol of a new European generation? Frankfurt*. Peter Lang.

França, T., & Padilla, B. (2021). South-South student mobility: International students from Portuguese-Speaking Africa in Brazil. In D. Cairns (Ed.), *The Palgrave handbook of youth mobility and educational migration*. Basingstoke: Palgrave Macmillan.

Kaktiņš, L. (2021). Identity challenges and pedagogical consequences: International students in higher education pathway programmes in Australia. In D. Cairns (Ed.), *The Palgrave handbook of youth mobility and educational migration*. Basingstoke: Palgrave Macmillan.

Kolb, D. A. (2014). *Experiential learning: Experience as the source of learning and development*. FT Press.

Mitchell, K. (2013). Rethinking the 'Erasmus effect' on European identity. *Journal of Common Market Studies, 53*(2), 330–348.

Murphy-Lejeune, E. (2002). *Student mobility and narrative in Europe: The new strangers*. London: Routledge.

Samuk, S., Skrobanek, J., Ardic, T., Pavlova, I., Marinescu, D. E., & Muresan, L. (2021). Learning in transition: Erasmus+ as an opportunity for internationalization. In D. Cairns (Ed.), *The Palgrave handbook of youth mobility and educational migration*. Basingstoke: Palgrave Macmillan.

Sheller, M., & Urry, J. (2006). The new mobilities paradigm. *Environment and Planning A, 38*, 207–226.

Zwick, H. S. (2021). Intra-regional academic mobility in Central Asia: The OSCE Academy in Bishkek, Kyrgyzstan. In D. Cairns (Ed.), *The Palgrave handbook of youth mobility and educational migration*. Basingstoke: Palgrave Macmillan.

Chapter 17
Erasmus at 30: Institutional Mobility at Higher Education in Perspective

Alexandra Ribeiro

The Erasmus programme has been a visibly successful programme for European Union (EU), facilitating mobility among students from different nationalities and cultures. 'Erasmus' was created in 1987 to raise awareness about the countries of the European Community, alongside a greater purpose to consolidate the idea of a 'people's Europe' (European Council 1987). This represented a milestone in the history of education policies at European level, although it took more than 20 years from the Treaty of Rome for the education sector to acquire a formalized supranational dimension, and 17 more years for the flagship Erasmus programme to be born (Klose 2013). More recently, Erasmus has aimed to promote civic participation and raise social capital within European democracies, reduce unemployment and improve skills required in the labour market, especially among young people (European Commission 2017). Higher education institutions also use the programme as a mechanism to promote their internationalization, and prepare their students for the various problems that exist in our societies today (Klose 2013: 40).

The European Commission considers Erasmus to be 'an instrument capable of promoting the inclusion of people with a low social background' (European Commission 2017). However, the participation of such people in the programme is limited. For a better understanding of 'fairness' within Erasmus, I will use John Rawls' Second Principle of Theory of Justice. According to Rawls, justice should be ruled by two principles. The first principle relates to individual liberties, such as freedom of association, thought and religion. These democratic liberties cannot be restricted or violated. In this chapter, this first principle is irrelevant for this analysis because we already know that is accomplished. The second principle however states that social and economic inequality needs to satisfy two conditions: the greatest benefit of the least advantaged (principle of difference) and attached to offices and positions open to all under conditions of fair equality of opportunity (Rawls 1993:

A. Ribeiro (✉)
University of Minho, Braga, Portugal

239). For this reason, I will argue that fairness is related to equality of opportunities, focusing in this analysis this last principle in the context of Erasmus on the occasion of its 30-year anniversary.[1]

Methodological Approach

During the course of conducting this research, mobility within the Erasmus programme was analysed, focusing on the context of higher education, the area that has traditionally supported most participants in Erasmus.[2] In analysing the inclusivity of the programme, I will look at the Portuguese case due to the fact that Portugal was one of the countries that suffered most from the 2008 economic crisis, and during the post-crisis period, suffered a small decline in Erasmus participation (Agência Nacional Erasmus+ 2017a: 42). To examine the post-crisis period in Portugal, and the operation of the current Erasmus+[3] phase of the programme (2014–2020), the analysis covers 2014 until 2018.

To understand students' perceptions about equality in the programme, 25 semi-structured interviews and two focus groups were conducted. The students were from the University of Minho, University of Porto, University of Aveiro and University of Trás-dos-Montes and Alto Douro, from different areas of studies, including social sciences, engineering, law and psychology, all aged between 19 and 25 years. To enable contrasts to be made, the interviewees belonged to two different groups: Erasmus students (participants in the programme) and non-Erasmus students (who did not participate in the programme). To control for the social passivity factor, non-Erasmus students were only considered if they assumed an active role in society (e.g. belonging to different non-government organizations, such as AIESEC, International Amnesty or a student associations).

The interviews allow us to appreciate the importance of competences and soft skills for students' employability and their perceptions about participation in the Erasmus programme, issues already introduced in the preamble to this section of the book. The focus group followed the same principles and kept an equality criterion in mind: two Erasmus students and two non-Erasmus students to create a balanced debate. With this approach, it was possible to compare and discuss these students' perceptions around participation in the programme, with both interviews and the focus groups being anonymous.

The 'Erasmus Effect' and Soft Skills

Students can use mobility to differentiate themselves from their peers and enrich their CVs. They can demonstrate new or better skills, different competencies or proof of individual autonomy that translates into professional competence (Vieira 2015). Prior studies show a positive connection between Erasmus mobility and students' employability due to the competencies gain during the experience (see, e.g.

Prokou 2008; Janson et al. 2009; Deakin 2013; Botas and Huisman 2013; Cairns 2017; Cairns et. al. 2018; Van Mol 2018). If we look at soft skills growth, we can see a difference between the students who joined the Erasmus programme and the other students who did not participate. Due to the confidence gained in the experience, labour market entrance can become easier, and might even help during the employment experience (Jacobone and More 2015). The soft skills associated with this mobility include independence, adaptation, responsibility, open-mindedness and communication (Krzaklewska 2013; Klose 2013). A study by Hermans (2007) also highlighted the importance for students of being multidisciplinary, empathic, creative, adaptable and having leadership skills. For them, an academic degree is not enough; they need to have these different qualities to demonstrate soft skills. Students from Eastern and Southern Europe that participate are also expected to become more entrepreneurial and have a higher chance of growing in the workplace. They can also be more flexible and international, which helps in making labour market entrance, an issue promoted by Erasmus authorities. For example, a study by the Portuguese National Agency for Erasmus+ (2017a) notes that the reason why students apply to this programme is due to the soft skills gained during the experience, enhancing their employability.

Vieira (2015) emphasises an important issue in this regard: due to the higher chance of developing soft skills during Erasmus mobility those who did not participate are effectively being 'punished' for not joining. This means that social background and other important barriers are not being taken into consideration. The impression is that non-participating students do not put in enough effort rather than being inhibited by certain barriers. For Vieira (2015), this issue creates an unjust inequality between students. Furthermore, when compared to students who did not participate in the programme but are pro-active within society, it is perceptible that gaining soft skills and personal growth actually emerge to their general life and professional experience rather than Erasmus itself, making the 'Erasmus effect' a potential false positive (see also Mitchell 2013). Therefore, even if soft skills are emphasised by the European Commission as some of the most likely outcomes of being an Erasmus student, it is not possible to confirm that this is actually taking place due to current participation patterns in the programme being skewed towards those already in possession of these qualities, potentially creating a new form of inequality between students (see also Prokou 2011; Ballatore and Ferede 2013; Ballatore and Stavrou 2017).

The Erasmus Effect in Portugal

Portugal in the Erasmus Programme Context

Portugal was one of the first countries to enter the Erasmus Programme in 1987. Although the negotiations for the Erasmus programme were already well advanced when the country joined, for Rogério Bordalo Pinheiro, the Portuguese delegate at the Education Committee of what was then known as the European Economic Community, it was essential for Portugal to be part of this programme. For him, the expectations were high, as in many other European countries waiting to implement the programme (Cunha and Santos 2017: 19). During its implementation, there were some problems with the agreement. One issue was the insufficient grant funding, considering that in relatively peripheral countries like Portugal, students have higher costs because of issues such as distance from host institutions. This creates a 'natural' barrier to participation, potentially generating inequality between countries. At the beginning, the European Commission was sceptical about changing the rules for the grant and Portugal had only the support of similar countries such as Greece and Ireland. This position changed after support from more countries approved rule changes and decreased the gap between nations (Cunha and Santos 2017).[4]

Soft Skills and Employability

An important motivation to join the Erasmus programme, as we have seen before, relates to the competences and soft skills increase during this experience, improving the capacity to stand out from others when looking for a job (Deakin 2013; Botas and Huisman 2013; Krzaklewska 2013; Klose 2013; Deakin 2014; Jacobone and Moro 2015). This point was referenced by every interviewed student. For example:

> I think Erasmus can improve us when we try to access the labour market. (…). I think that every mobility programme, in general, brings some advantage, but the Erasmus programme is highlighted. And I think more and more everyone talks about it, and more and more it is assumed that everyone participates in this programme. (20-year-old non-Erasmus student)

In this vision, the Erasmus programme has a greater capacity to help students during the entrance in the labour market compared to other mobility programmes, even from the point of view of a non-participant. Another student described how the programme can be seen as an opportunity:

> I wrote 'opportunity' because although I didn't participate in this programme, it is the idea that I have about it. It was a wasted opportunity for me but for the people that participate, it opens a lot of opportunities. It is always the word that came to my mind when I think about Erasmus. (22-year-old non-Erasmus student)

In general, this is the majority opinion but there are some exceptions. Three students didn't participate but felt that it was unnecessary as their academic skills are already well developed, while another Erasmus participating interviewee pointed out that employers 'hire people and not CVs.' Furthermore, the advantage is not transversal in the Erasmus programme itself but relates to where people go to. For some students, the higher education institution of the country has connotations that influence the objective value of the experience, with this choice tied to being able to surpass the socio-economy barrier associated with gaining entry to elite institutions.

I wanted to go to Maastricht or Edinburgh, but I did not go because of the higher living costs. And, Maastricht, that the university is amazing and when you try to enter the labour market with this in your CV, you can go beyond a lot of people. But not if you have other universities—in Poland or from Eastern Europe—where in comparison the living cost are lower, and you can have a better academic life then England or Germany. (22-year-old non-Erasmus student)

Erasmus and Social Networking

Besides the competences and easier entrance to the labour market, there is another indirect point about employability that students mention: the international network they create during the programme. For example, here is an extract from the focus group discussion:

Erasmus student:	I study economics, and every relationship that I have, every network that I have around the world, increases my chances of finding a job in a bank or something else.
Moderator:	Do you think that Erasmus is an advantaged?
Erasmus student:	In economics, yes.
Non-Erasmus student:	I think this is subjective, the Erasmus value. Because, for example, you say that you have a big network but for us [that did not participate in the programme], and don't get me wrong…
Erasmus student:	No, no.
Non-Erasmus student:	This is the easier side that Erasmus creates, you do not have work like in Portugal. In my case, I study IR [International Relations] and I need to have a network to be able to promote myself in the future. So, in Portugal, I need to waste my time looking for something that I can do in institutions or somewhere to create this network. Erasmus is going on and because you are in something new and the people are organized to integrate you, you can integrate contacts that will be given to you easily. Here in Portugal, you need to fight for it a little bit more. I think that Erasmus is an advantage because it gives to you the tools and networking and the soft skills and other knowledge that you do not have in your university, for your life and you can use this in your CV. Here you can get this too, in a different way, but you need more work to have that.

This network construction can help students to gain faster access to the labour market and have more points of reference around Europe or the world. But, besides the easier construction, the problem is the value employers give to this. Some non-Erasmus students do not consider it to be a disadvantage because they already have an active network, and competences and soft skills that are well developed through other activities.

> I'm not inferior to someone that participated in Erasmus. For example, during a job interview… I will not say that I did an Erasmus and I did not participate in another mobility programme, but I got in touch with a lot of people that participate in volunteering here, and things like that. And, if you want, they can have the same equivalence. I think that to do an Erasmus should be personal growth because it is an activity, a life, for six months minimum (…). However, there is a lot of volunteer work that you can be engaged with for one, two, three years that can develop another thing. That is why I think that no one is inferior because they did not do an Erasmus, if you work for it. But yes, it [Erasmus programme] increase, invariably increases something within you. (21-year-old non-Erasmus student)

On the other hand, it was mentioned by another student that even though he does not feel disadvantaged, he feels the pressure from the labour market:

> I want to believe that I am not in a disadvantaged position on a personal level, I want to believe that I am not. I am always up-to-date, I invest in my international education, where I can meet other people, other things. At a labour level the Erasmus is over-valued (…). I have two international experiences in my CV, that is good, but would it be better if I had done an Erasmus? (…). I do not feel in disadvantaged on a personal level, but I feel that the labour market makes the pressure for me to feel this. (21-year-old non-Erasmus student)

Following the same line of thinking, another student highlights this pressure more clearly:

> I was talking with my friend because she went to a conference, and the facilitator was an old guy that wanted to appear modern and 'always on top of things.' One time he was choosing between applicants during the recruitment and he said that discards right away the applicants that did not do an Erasmus during the Bachelor or Master's degree. And I think that is degrading because there are people that did not join the Erasmus but instead were working… working no, without money, volunteering. And, I speak for my own experience, that I already apply to many things and I am not admitted. And I know some people that only have a Bachelor or Master's degree and an Erasmus, without any volunteer work or a part-time job and they did not work on the extra-curriculum activities, but they are chosen because they have an Erasmus. I think that people should have a more holistic vision: ok, did not have an Erasmus but was not stopped. (23-year-old non-Erasmus student)

The Erasmus programme and the value that countries give to this experience is not the same in the students' visions. We can observe this discussion about the different type of experiences during the focus group:

Non-Erasmus student: I already apply to a lot of things, talked with a lot of people from different areas even with a lot of companies. And the value of Erasmus was not the same for everyone. If you want to apply to a thing that will be only in Portugal, it does not have so much importance. For example, I applied to a place in the British Embassy in Lisbon for digital communication and there they valued a lot people who had this mobility experience, but I did not have it. (…). I applied to the Ministry of Foreign Affairs in Portugal to an internal job where the functions where more domestic, more administrative and bureaucratic and, even though we are

	talking about Foreign Affairs, they did not value any outside experience. The job itself did not require this type of experience. So, I think that it will depend a lot of what you want, where do you want to go and the path that you want to build.
Erasmus student:	I want to say that there is different cultural value about the Erasmus programme. Because, for example, in Italy, my friends from the local Erasmus Student Network participated in the programme, not all but a lot. And when I asked for fun why they joined the programme, they said that it was 'to party hard,' they always said that they could stay in Italy for that, but the Italian labour market values a lot the Erasmus programme. I do not know if it is because the programme was born there in a way or because of the Bologna Process but, for example, the domestic market, even to be a secretary, a basic job, even a lawyer's secretary, that takes care of papers and calls, schedules meetings, they value Erasmus programme participation. (…). I think everyone should do it regardless of wanting to work in the EU, it is essential to do an Erasmus—is a symbol that you belong to a generation.

In general, the non-Erasmus students with an active role in society look at this programme as a positive and rich experience. The pressure that they feel is not made by the programme itself but instead the marketing behind the programme, and from the labour market. All the students that join Erasmus feel an advantage because they perceive this programme as a good way to enrich their personal growth, faster, and improve soft skills and other competencies. Whether or not this is objectively true is another matter.

Conclusion: Is Inequality an Unintended Erasmus Effect?

Erasmus is an important programme and is becoming increasingly relevant to a fragile Europe. The number of participants has been growing but the economic barrier is still an important issue, even though the European Commission perceives the programme to be 'an instrument capable of promoting the inclusion of people with a low social background' (European Commission 2017). The different perceptions students have about their competences and soft skills, and employability, are important if we are to understand if the programme is creating unintended forms of inequality between students. The programme itself is fair in one sense because it allows practically every student to apply, including students with low incomes, with basically the same Erasmus grant (plus a national grant) on offer. But the economic barrier is still an issue (Agência Nacional Erasmus+ 2017b).

Even if the majority of students perceive Erasmus as a good programme, it will always create a gap between Erasmus students and non-Erasmus students, not only because of the programme itself but also the fact that non-Erasmus students feel the pressure from the labour market to join, and when they cannot, they feel excluded. The marketing around the programme is strong and helps to build the idea that Erasmus is important to improve soft skills and other competencies, but obviously there are other ways of increasing these competencies: for example, volunteer work (national or international) in other organizations. Even when they have these other experiences that enrich their lives, the majority of students notice that Erasmus gets more recognition, and that is why it is more important regardless of other good experiences.

The Erasmus programme's 'success' has been demonstrated by the preceding discussion of student experiences in Portugal. Participants can be pro-active, more communicative and more independent. When they join, they can raise the level of their competences and soft skills to improve labour market entry chances. In Portugal, participant numbers are still a small percentage of all students, and there are evident concerns about fairness related to their participation. The 'Erasmus effect' may be present, but it is not available to everyone. A relationship between labour market entrance and the Erasmus programme is also there, although some authors (e.g. Vieira 2015; Ballatore and Stavrou 2017) argue that this is creating a new form of inequality between students that participate and those do not.

Notes

1. Although the principle of difference is presented first, because of the lexical order, the equality of opportunities under the principle of difference prevail (Rosas 2013).
2. In the budget from the Erasmus+ Programme (2014–2020), 78 per cent went to education, and from this, 43 per cent to higher education institutions (European Commission 2014).
3. An education mobility programme in Europe has been discussed since the Janne Report in 1974, and the Erasmus programme negotiated since 1985 (Cunha and Santos 2017).
4. In more basic terms, in 2016 the number of participants from Portugal was 11,047, or 3 per cent of students (European Commission 2017 and author calculations according to Pordata).

References

Ballatore, M., & Ferede, M. K. (2013). The Erasmus programme in France, Italy and the United Kingdom: Student mobility as a signal of distinction and privilege. *European Educational Research Journal, 12*(4), 525–533.

Ballatore, M., & Stavrou, S. (2017). Internationalisation policy as a (re)producer of social inequalities. The case of institutionalised student mobility. *Rassegna Italiana di Sociologia, LVIII*(2), 1–23.

Botas, Paulo Charles Pimentel, e Jeroen Huisman (2013). "A Bourdieusian analysis of the participation of Polish students in the ERASMUS programme: Cultural and social capital perspectives." Springer 741–754.

Cairns, D. (2017). The Erasmus undergraduate exchange programme: A highly qualified success story? *Children's Geographies, 15*(6), 728–740.

Cairns, D., Krzaklewska, E., Cuzzocrea, V., & Allaste, A.-A. (2018). *Mobility, education and employability in the European Union: Inside Erasmus.* Basingstoke: Palgrave Macmillan.

Cunha, A., & Santos, Y. (2017). *Erasmus'30. A História do Programa e a Participação dos Estudantes Portugueses* (1st ed.). Silveira: Bookbuilders/Letras Errantes, Lda.

Deakin, H. (2013). How and why we should encourage undergraduate geography students to participate in the Erasmus programme. *Journal of Geography in Higher Education, 37*(3), 466–475.

Deakin, H. (2014). The drivers to Erasmus work placement mobility for UK students. *Children's Geographies, 12*(1), 25–39.

European Commission. (2017). *New figures show record number of participants in Erasmus+.* Retrieved July 30, 2019, from https://ec.europa.eu/programmes/erasmus-plus/anniversary/30th-anniversary-andyou_pt.

European Commission. (2014). Acedido em 13 de 10 de 2017. https://ec.europa.eu/programmes/erasmus-plus/sites/erasmusplus/files/erasmus-plus-in-detail_en.pdf.

European Council. (1987). "7/327/CEE: Decisão do Conselho de 15 de Junho de 1987 que adopta o programa de acção comunitário em matéria de mobilidade dos estudantes (Erasmus)." 15 de 06. Acedido em 15 de 06 de 2017. http://eur-lex.europa.eu/legal- content/PT/TXT/?uri=CELEX:31987D0327.

Formação, A. N. E. E. e. (2017a). *A implementação do PALV em Portugal 2007–2013.* Agência Nacional Erasmus+ Educação e Formação: Lisboa.

Hermans, J. (2007). High potentials: A CEO perspective. *Journal of Studies in International Education, 11*(3–4), 510–521.

Jacobone, V., & Moro, G. (2015). Evaluating the impact of the Erasmus programme: Skills and European identity. *Assessment and Evaluation in Higher Education, 40*(2), 309–328.

Janson, K., Schomburg, H., & Teichler, U. (2009). *The professional value of Erasmus mobility.* Bonn: Lemmens.

Klose, U. (2013). The making of a success story: The creation of the Erasmus programme in the historical context. In B. Feyen & E. Krzaklewska (Eds.), *The Erasmus phenomenon – Symbol of a new European generation?* (pp. 39–50). Frankfurt am Main: Peter Lang.

Krzaklewska, E. (2013). Erasmus students between youth and adulthood: Analysis of the biographical experience. In B. Feyen & E. Krzaklewska (Eds.), *The Erasmus phenomenon – Symbol of a new European generation?* (pp. 79–96). Frankfurt am Main: Peter Lang.

Mitchell, K. (2013). Rethinking the 'Erasmus effect' on European identity. *Journal of Common Market Studies, 53*(2), 330–348.

Mol, Christof Van. (2018). "Becoming Europeans: the relationship between student exchanges in higher education, European citizenship and a sense of European identity." Innovation. *The European Journal of Social Science Research*, 1–15.

Prokou, E. (2008). The emphasis on employability and the changing role of the university in Europe. *Higher Education in Europe, 33*(4), 387–394.

Prokou, E. (2011). The aims of employability and social inclusion/active citizenship in lifelong learning policies in Greece. *The Greek Review of Social Research, 136C*, 203–223.

Rawls, J. C. (1993). *Uma Teoria de Justiça.* Lisboa: Presença.

Rosas, J. C. (2013). Liberalismo Igualitário. In J. Cardoso (Ed.), *Manual de Filosofia Política* (pp. 35–66). Coimbra: Almedina.

Van Mol, C. (2018). Becoming Europeans: The relationship between student exchanges in higher education, European citizenship and a sense of European identity. *Innovation: The European Journal of Social Science Research, 31*(4), 1–15.

Vieira, M. M. (2015). *Das disposições cosmopolitas a mobilidade como competência? Ensino superior, Programa Erasmus e mobilidade estudantil.* Lisboa: Instituto de Ciências Sociais da Universidade de Lisboa.

Chapter 18
Learning in Transition: Erasmus+ as an Opportunity for Internationalization

Sahizer Samuk, Birte Nienaber, Emilia Kmiotek-Meier, Volha Vysotskaya, Jan Skrobanek, Tuba Ardic, Irina Pavlova, Daniela Elena Marinescu, and Laura Muresan

As discussed in the previous chapter, when first established in 1987, the Erasmus programme (rebranded Erasmus+ in 2014) aimed to encourage transnational collaboration between higher education institutions without involving national authorities (Ribeiro 2021). One of its first functions was to enhance cultural integration (González et al. 2011), but within a few years the European Commission started to include topics such as social and economic inclusion, which led to a diversification of its programmes (Cairns 2017), culminating in Erasmus+ encompassing areas such as volunteering, entrepreneurship and training (European Commission 2018: 3). The objective of this chapter is to look at this expanded range of opportunities for internationalized learning, focusing on experiences in Norway, Romania and Luxembourg, and a process we have termed 'Erasmus-ization.' In practice, this can take many forms. For example, the interviews from Romania describe an enculturation to European values and global citizenship (Deardorff 2006), and experiential learning (Kolb 2014). In the case of Norway, a broadening of opportunity structures

---

The *MOVE* project received funding from the European Union Horizon 2020 research and innovation programme under Grant Agreement No. 649263.

S. Samuk (✉)
University of Luxembourg, Luxembourg City, Luxembourg

University of Pisa, Pisa, Italy

B. Nienaber • E. Kmiotek-Meier • V. Vysotskaya
University of Luxembourg, Luxembourg City, Luxembourg

J. Skrobanek • I. Pavlova
Western Norway University of Applied Sciences, Haugesund, Norway

T. Ardic
University of Bergen, Bergen, Norway

D. E. Marinescu • L. Muresan
Academia De Studii Economice Din Bucuresti, Bucharest, Romania

© The Author(s), under exclusive license to Springer Nature Switzerland AG 2022
D. Cairns (ed.), *The Palgrave Handbook of Youth Mobility and Educational Migration*, https://doi.org/10.1007/978-3-030-99447-1_18

and an elongated transition to employment is found, and for young people who move to Luxembourg the future after Erasmus+ and the intrinsic value of exchanges can manifest many years after the experience. We therefore have a diversification of meaning, as well as a broadening of programmatic scope.

The Erasmus-ization process can itself be conceptualized as highly time dependent, with an interlacement of requirements and outcomes from an assemblage of mobility experiences, reflecting the idea of contemporary youth mobility and migration trajectories as incremental or piecemeal in character (see Cairns 2021a, b, in this book). This chapter reveals other influential factors in this process, specifically the importance of socio-economic status, recognizing the role played by the economic and psychological support families provide to their children. Learning that takes place during internationalization is also thought to lead to a more progressive vision of the future. Therefore, the term 'Erasmus-ization' relates not only to the experience of mobility but also to the shift in perspective that emerges from it.

Self-Improvement via Cultural, Economic and International Encounters

Countless prior studies on Erasmus+ have focused on themes such as socio-economic and individual barriers to mobility, and self-development or self-transformation using terms such as 'internationalization' (see, e.g. Feyen and Krzaklewska 2013; Cairns et al. 2018). A small number of studies also raise questions regarding participation, including barriers to taking part in the programme (see Ribeiro 2021, in this book), providing a reminder that not everyone can become mobile despite the availability of funding opportunities from Erasmus+. Even those who have participated note the existence of structural barriers (Kmiotek-Meier et al. 2019). Young people from richer countries tend to participate more, and in poorer countries there are obviously going to be fewer people with the requisite levels of social and economic resources. However, there are other, more generic, impediments that affect young people regardless of geographical point of origin: fear of separation from family, a lack of access to programmes at home and abroad and limited language skills being just some of the most prominent (Kehm 2005; Isserstedt and Schnitzer 2002; Ottesen and Colbjørnsen 2016).

For those who can take part, there is also the potential for developing social skills. For example, a study by Endes (2015) found that students became more confident and risk-taking after the experience; they travelled more, were more open to other cultures and made friends from other cultures, with a positive effect on communication skills in general. Additionally, exposure to a multiplicity of cultures is important in developing intercultural skills, and according to Jacobone and Moro (2015), Erasmus students are more concerned with cultural enhancement, personal development and foreign language proficiency, suggesting that employability might also improve after Erasmus mobility.

These developments might be interpreted as signs of Europeanization, and a personal form of de-nationalization, something that is another popular theme in student mobility literature. For instance, Mitchell (2015) argues that student exchanges might in some circumstances positively influence interest in European news and knowledge. However, Ieracitano (2014) found that while the cultural aspects of being European (humanism and improving intercultural dialogue) are more prominent among Erasmus students, the political idea of European citizenship is not. In his study, Wilson (2011) reveals that Erasmus students were not necessarily more pro-European after their Erasmus experience, while Oborune (2013) claims Erasmus participants are already pro-European, even before their mobility, implying that no change is taking place. This view is strongly supported by other studies, including research by Mutlu (2011), who questions the assumption that Erasmus+ creates a sense of being European, although Jacobone and Moro (2015: 324) conclude that identification with a national identity diminishes as European identity 'escalates,' suggesting that it is not so much a matter of developing a European identity but rather becoming less ethnocentric (see also Deardorff 2006; Skrobanek 2004).

There are obviously challenges as well as opportunities linked to the mobility experience. Erasmus might increase the chances of finding a job (Bryla 2015; Standley 2015; Bracht et al. 2006), or at least a different kind of job. Parey and Waldinger (2010: 219) suggest that 'those who have studied abroad are more likely to indicate that their interest in foreign cultures has led them to seek employment abroad.' On the contrary, Petzold (2017) noted that employers do not look for such experience when hiring university graduates. Young people who do Erasmus might benefit from it as a door-opener but not to the extent of making it a significant career booster as contextual differences continue to hold: for example, employers in Eastern Europe give more importance to studies abroad and foreign language skills (Engel 2010). Dvir and Yemini (2017) also argue that individual mobility schemes rarely address structural problems, and mobility chances are most available to those who already have the resources to become internationalized, specifically highly educated young people and already rich in social and economic capital (see also Cairns 2014; Cairns et al. 2017).

Methodology and Analysis

In this chapter we discuss cases from three countries to contextualize contemporary Erasmus+ experiences: incoming and outgoing mobility in Norway, outgoing mobility from Romania and incoming and outgoing mobility in Luxembourg. The choice of these three countries relates to the different contexts that young people find themselves in these countries. In what follows, we will use a pool of 38 semi-structured interviews conducted between 2015 and 2016, 23 having been involved in Erasmus mobility, with 10 cases used in this chapter, 7 female and 3 males.

These interviewees, all of whom were 18–29 years of age, were encountered in diverse mobility settings: volunteering activities, entrepreneurship and higher education. Three interviews were also conducted with those who had done Erasmus in the past (six- to ten years ago) and were employed at the time of the interview in the highly internationalized labour market of Luxembourg. Whether the mobility was for study, international volunteering or young entrepreneurs, the interviewees proved to be a rich source of material, with detailed questions about mobility, hindering and encouraging factors, and changes of perceptions after the experience in relation to career, lifestyles, skills, cultural understandings, mobility structures and learning.

Self-Development and Experiential Learning

Erasmus can be an eye-opening experience, in line with transformational cultural change taking place via socialization and experiential learning (Kolb 2014). All interviewees mentioned that their mobility had contributed to developing new competences and encouraged them to take risks as they learnt how to overcome difficulties. In the following interview extract, Loredana underlines how new conditions and a new environment motivated her to become more flexible and deal with adversity:

> How has the experience abroad changed you?
> I would say that it has changed me in a very positive manner… because you encounter new situations, new people and new circumstances. You don't have your family around anymore, telling you what is good and what is bad, so you are practically pushed forward into an environment and you have to respond as an adult, you are responsible for your own actions, for the words you say and then you begin to understand what it means to be on your own, but not isolated, and to adapt no matter how difficult the situations might be. (Loredana, Erasmus+ HE from Romania to Italy)

Adapting to difficult situations and gaining new skills in new and often challenging circumstances are integral parts of developing self-confidence during and after the experience. The positivity of mobility was also appreciated by young entrepreneurs and volunteers, as well as by those combining different forms of mobility, as in Mihaela's case:

> How has this mobility experience changed you?
> I thought it was a unique opportunity to meet several nationalities in one place… and I think this had a very big impact because the university itself was very international and placed emphasis on many kinds of cultural events… I became more open, it has changed me very much, it has shaped my personality because I have borrowed a lot from the mentality of other nationalities and, most certainly, it has made me more willing to experience and to get to know the world to know more countries and nationalities not only from a tourist's perspective. (Mihaela, involved in Erasmus+ projects visiting Greece, Luxembourg, Malta, Spain and Turkey)

The learning experience has been accompanied by increased awareness and acceptance of a multitude of perspectives—'the others' views'—and a broadening of cultural horizons. Mihaela underlines the deeper foundations that are created through being with people from different nationalities in the same place ('not only the tourist's perspective') and feels more involved in the experience of living together.

In the case of the respondents who had benefited from an Erasmus+ Grant for Entrepreneurs, their mobility was often targeted at familiarization with different business models. Romanian respondents with this type of experience have confirmed its usefulness for comparative purposes and subsequent integrating new models within their own business environment:

> I have a model for comparison. I've seen how they market their products, what they want to sell, what they target… what they include in their portfolio… and this way my wish for more knowledge has been satisfied. […]
> And would you repeat the experience, if you had the opportunity?
> Yes, definitely… we are the sum of our experiences. Now I have seen this model and consider it very good, but if I went also to another country in Europe […], yes, I would like to see also other aspects. (Victor, Erasmus+ entrepreneurship for agribusiness from Romania to Italy)

Victor conceptualizes new possible ways of learning in different countries, and wishes to have another mobility experience in order to learn more. A recurrent theme in the interviews with Romanian Erasmus+ participants is in fact the desire and determination to continue learning from all possible sources and to explore other parts of the world. Most mobile youth from Romania also reflect on how Erasmus+ helped them to develop an 'international mentality':

> And you get to see several perspectives and this is why I said I'd like to stay more, to learn, to get to know several cultures, to understand what this is all about. […] This [mobility] has made me think very internationally. […]
> And I have become a cosmopolitan citizen, that is, I think I could live anywhere in this world. I have become interested in travelling, and indeed, I have travelled a lot over the last few years; … with each new experience I would like to see and to know more. (Mariana, Erasmus+ HE and entrepreneurship from Romania to Norway)

Mobility stimulates a new dimension of personality. 'World citizens' can live wherever they want in the world, which goes beyond having a 'European identity.' One mobility experience increases the odds for further mobility, with this concatenation varying in form: some return to the same host country again and again, while others head for other destinations through different mobility actions (Roman et al. 2018).

Opportunities for Employment After Erasmus+

All the employees in the sample group that moved to Norway used different Erasmus+ mobility options, but all mentioned how their experiences had played a decisive role in determining future employment mobility. For example, they used experience and knowledge gained during Erasmus+ to search for job opportunities elsewhere in Europe. Susan stayed in Norway for two reasons, linking her mobility as an Erasmus student to employment. She travelled to Norway for study reasons and returned home when the programme finished. This type of mobility experience was perceived as 'amazing':

> I was an Erasmus student before in Norway. It was for a period of time. I knew that I would be there for a while and tried to experience how it is to live in that country. However, it feels very different now. To come to a place where you stay for a longer time is a bit more serious, and this changed my perspective about Norway. First time I was here, I was a student and I thought that everything was amazing, but to come here for work is different, it is more serious. (Susan, Erasmus+ HE from Germany to Norway, finally finds employment in Norway)

Susan illustrates the difference between living in a country for a short period in a structured mobility context and a longer stay as an employee, without the safety net of institutions; the second form of mobility is perceived as 'more serious,' since more autonomy and responsibility are required.

Concerning professional development, Patricia's case below illustrates how Erasmus can help students and young professionals leave 'a bad situation' behind, and to move to a place where they feel as if they are 'winning the lottery.' Patricia first did European Voluntary Service (EVS) in Norway, and after returning to Spain and looking for new possibilities, she returned to Norway, this time for full-time work:

> I was applying to the European Voluntary Service for youth to experience social community work. So, I decided that I wanted to go abroad and I got selected for Norway. In Spain, our situation was very bad, we had quite hard crises. After so many years being unemployed, it was the time for me to do something. The only way to go abroad without spending any money was the EVS, because I did not have money and it was the fastest one […]. It is crazy here. I could not be more grateful. I feel like I won the lottery… I am very glad that we have a crisis (in Spain) and I had no choice and moved. (Patricia, EVS from Spain to Norway, then goes back to Spain and finally finds employment in Norway)

Patricia sees the crisis as a factor that forced her to move. This step created the impetus to escape a bad economic situation in her home country. Furthermore, the escape was not only good in the short term. Using the low-cost opportunity window, she was able to develop a career in the host country; being in Norway (first) for a while, developing a network and getting familiar with the new system prepared her for the second period, providing an illustration of a mobility exercise leading to eventual migration.

The case of Grete illustrates the positive impact of Erasmus in her transition from education to employment:

> I did a course called Erasmus Mundus Master's in journalism, media and globalization, which is one year in Denmark and the second year is in Wales. … That kind of prepared me for jobs later and I also thought that one year in Wales could make it possible for me to look for jobs here and maybe start off with some contacts or something else, I knew that the university helps people with jobs after. They have a pretty high rate of people being employed after the programme. So that was kind of the way into the work experience I have here now. (Grete, Erasmus Mundus MA programme from Norway to Denmark and Wales and now employed in England)

This is yet another example of how to become a migrant via Erasmus+, and Grete's interview points towards the institution's role, with the university in Wales helping people find jobs after the programme.

The Erasmus experience has been materialized into goals of employment especially for those moving to Norway. The interviews conducted there hence demonstrate a very optimistic picture of the opportunity windows that have become available and the contribution being made to employability by Erasmus+. Moreover, mobility 'produces' mobility. Returning to the previous country of residence or simply continuing to live in the new society is easier when the programmes allows young people to adapt to the environment, develop new skills and networks. Moreover, a combination of different schemes under the Erasmus umbrella means mobility can be supported at different points in a career trajectory, and in a number of different places, creating this means of becoming a migrant in a new, non-traditional sense as hypothesized in Chap. 3 of this book (Cairns 2021a).

Memories and Effects of Erasmus+ in Temporality

When we examine the interviews from Luxembourg, we find similarities with the Norwegian cases: young people finding employment opportunities on the internet before arrival, in some cases starting on lower ladders of the job market and receiving training, being content with salaries and internationalization, mobile peers who motivate their friends to do the same, alongside positive support from the family for mobility. The interviews with young people living in Luxembourg were with those who either had Erasmus experience there or had moved on to another EU member state. The interviewees characterize Luxembourg as a destination country with an open labour market, and, in some cases, a temporary stop at which to accumulate experience before moving to the next mobility phase. For those who are temporarily moving out of Luxembourg, the multilingual background of the country (with three official languages French, German and Luxembourgish) makes it easier to study and work abroad.

One such person is Maite, who provided insight about how she travelled to Germany for study and then had her first Erasmus exchange in the Netherlands in the publishing industry:

> I went to [city A in The Netherlands] for my Erasmus semester and met so many different people who were doing different things and after that I thought I could just maybe try it and see what's what, what would happen. That's how I, it started actually. (Maite, Erasmus+ HE from Luxembourg to The Netherlands, then internship and employment in Germany)

In some other cases, the Erasmus experience carries emotional, cultural and professional experience that young people take with them as they move. For instance, Thomas feels nostalgic for his Erasmus environment, which was a multicultural one, and he is striving to reproduce a similar experience in various settings:

> I went to England, to an international language school, I was in [city A in the UK], there I was really studying English 25 hours a week, and I got really in touch with a lot of people from all over the world, there were people from Asia, from South America, Africa, Saudi Arabia. If I can keep on rolling in this kind of environment, I actually really enjoy, so I came back to Belgium after I studied my Bachelor, I also was involved in Erasmus world, so I headed the student association ... it was in charge of welcoming and organizing events for international students who were coming to my university, so these four years, so I was

always involved in multicultural environment. Then I went to do my master in another city in Belgium and I had a chance to do an Erasmus too. (Thomas, from Belgium to Luxembourg—in the context of Erasmus+ student association and Erasmus+ HE and he found a job in Luxembourg)

It can be inferred from Thomas' interview that international experience and being in a multicultural context in Luxembourg collides with the experiences gained during Erasmus. The case of Leonardo, who is an Italian working in Luxembourg, demonstrates that the country, with its ethnically diverse population, provides the same 'wavelength' of Erasmus:

Working in Luxembourg is like Erasmus?
No, it is not like working in Luxembourg, that is, Erasmus, but I mean when you hang out with friends, you meet new people from new countries, and you speak the languages you know. And it, it is like on the same wavelength of the Erasmus thing. It is just a matter of being surrounded by people you do not know, whose cultures you do not know. (Leonardo, employee from Italy to Luxembourg, did Erasmus+ HE in Spain)

On the other hand, the interviewees differentiate between the Erasmus experience and their subsequent working lifestyles, especially when they compare their responsibilities then and now. For those who have done Erasmus, it was a remarkable time in their life, reminding them of a carefree period without many obligations. That is why Erasmus can be referred to with nostalgia, a happy reminiscence for working young people:

I mean, it (Erasmus time) was completely different because I mean I am working, I am responsible for myself. I get my own salary, and I am, I am responsible for the money I earn. For the time, for the time management. Time management, money management, and personal management. Relationship management. All these kinds of things, I am responsible for. I am more alive now than ever. (Leonardo, same as above)

To sum up, the examples from Luxembourg go beyond illustrating pragmatic ends and employability. Erasmus+ sparks the interest of young people in places, spaces and cultures. Moreover, it helps young people in choosing their profession as it did in the case of Maite. It leads to further mobility where the young mobile person can easily feel at home in internationalized environments, becoming almost a habit.

Conclusion: Erasmus+ Beyond Its Initial Aims and Gains

These findings illustrate that most of the interviewees benefited greatly from participating in Erasmus+. More substantially, they have undergone a transformative experience that has not yet ended, as the quest for heightened internationalization continues (Ottesen and Colbjørnsen 2016; Nienaber et al. 2017). The young people interviewed express a desire to know more, and to discover more places in which they can do so, demonstrating how a kind of personalized internationalization is achieved through successive mobility exercises, amounting to a new kind of migration within European space. This continuity of mobility across mobility experiences, a theme elaborated throughout this book, is the defining feature of the education to work transitions of these interviewees, with Erasmus+ a key part of this process, and participation in one programme leading to another (see also Mitchell 2012). The main tendency is thus to combine and utilize diverse Erasmus actions at different stages in the life course. For example, an undergraduate exchange leads to European Voluntary Service, which promotes a work placement or an international internship that may in turn lead to employment abroad.

The implementation of Erasmus illustrated in this chapter is also contextual: Romanian outgoing Erasmus+ participants and their Norwegian incoming Erasmus+ counterparts show similar traits regarding their satisfaction and opportunity windows. It is also an all-engrossing experience, Erasmus becoming a way of life of sorts (see also Feyen and Krzaklewska 2013). A kind of familiarity is generated, or feeling of being at home, despite not being in the home country but rather with 'others' who are in a similar situation: we call this the total experience Erasmus-ization, characterized by a curiosity for other cultures, the urge to be more mobile and a desire to learn and work in international environments, and we believe that the process lasts well beyond the end of the original mobility exercise (see also Messelink et al. 2015; Cuzzocrea et al. 2021).

There are also divergent characteristics according to country and at the micro level: for example, the Romanian interviewees (Loredana, Mihaela, Victor and Mariana) tend to focus on learning based on curiosity and experience. The incoming interviewees to Norway in contrast are from two different contexts; Susan from Germany focuses on the differences between Erasmus and work life; Patricia and Grete on opportunities they had found after EVS and Erasmus Mundus. Finally, the Luxembourgish outgoing interviewee, Maite, tells us that Erasmus gave her the courage to move, leading to a crystallization of her professional position, while Thomas and Leonardo underline the multicultural environment of Erasmus within which they feel at home.

In conclusion, we are arguing that Erasmus+ is a door-opener and a creator of opportunities, offering intercultural socialization, internationalization and a transferrable into the future mobility imperative for European youth. There are different preferences in varying contexts, just as there are different uses of Erasmus according to macro and meso levels, and individual wants. For the incoming cases in Norway and Luxembourg, the accent is on integration into the labour market, while interculturalism is slightly more prominent for the Luxembourgish case. In Romania, the themes of internationalization, integration into the global market (for business purposes) and Europeanization are the dominant themes. The type of mobility makes a difference as well. Romanian business owners (Erasmus Entrepreneurship) want to be mobile to see how others work; the ones who go to Norway for EVS are amazed at the job opportunities that follow training and internships; those who visit Luxembourg and who leave Luxembourg crystallize career choices in diverse countries. However, for almost all the interviewees, Erasmus is the catalyst for surpassing their national, cultural and individual limits, with internationalization, and in specific Erasmus-ization, the defining feature of a spatialized transition from education to the labour market.

References

Bracht, O., Engel, C., Janson, K., Over, A., Schomburg, H., & Teichler, U. (2006). *The professional value of Erasmus mobility. Final report*. Kassel: International Centre for Higher Education Research.

Bryla, P. (2015). Self-reported effects of and satisfaction with international student mobility: A large-scale survey among Polish former Erasmus students. *Procedia-Social and Behavioural Sciences, 191*, 2074–2028.

Cairns, D. (2014). *Youth transitions, international student mobility and spatial reflexivity: Being mobile?* Basingstoke: Palgrave Macmillan.

Cairns, D. (2017). The Erasmus undergraduate exchange programme: A highly qualified success story? *Children's Geographies, 15*(6), 728–740.

Cairns, D. (2021a). Mobility becoming migration: Understanding youth spatiality in the twenty-first century. In D. Cairns (Ed.), *The Palgrave handbook of youth mobility and educational migration*. Basingstoke: Palgrave Macmillan.

Cairns, D. (2021b). Migration decision-making, mobility capital and reflexive learning. In D. Cairns (Ed.), *The Palgrave handbook of youth mobility and educational migration*. Basingstoke: Palgrave Macmillan.

Cairns, D., Cuzzocrea, V., Briggs, D., & Veloso, L. (2017). *The consequences of mobility*. Basingstoke: Palgrave Macmillan.

Cairns, D., Krzaklewska, E., Cuzzocrea, V., & Allaste, A. A. (2018). *Mobility, education and employability in the European Union: Inside Erasmus*. Basingstoke: Palgrave Macmillan.

Cuzzocrea, V., Krzaklewska, E., & Cairns, D. (2021). 'There is no me, there is only us': The Erasmus bubble as a transient form of transnational collectivity. In V. Cuzzocrea, B. Gook, & B. Schiermer (Eds.), *Forms of collective engagements in youth transition: A global perspective*. Brill: Leiden.

Deardorff, D. K. (2006). Identification and assessment of intercultural competence as a student outcome of internationalization. *Journal of Studies in International Education, 10*(3), 241–266.

Dvir, Y., & Yemini, M. (2017). Mobility as a continuum: European Commission mobility policies for schools and higher education. *Journal of Education Policy, 32*(2), 198–210.

Endes, Y. Z. (2015). Overseas education process of outgoing students within the Erasmus Exchange Programme. *Procedia-Social and Behavioural Sciences, 174*, 1408–1414.

Engel, C. (2010). The impact of Erasmus mobility on the professional career: Empirical results of international studies on temporary student and teaching staff mobility. *Belgeo. Revue belge de géographie, 4*, 351–363.

European Commission. (2018). *Erasmus plus programme guide*. Luxembourg: European Commission.

Feyen, B., & Krzaklewska, E. (Eds.). (2013). *The Erasmus phenomenon – Symbol of a new European generation*. Frankfurt: Peter Lang.

González, C. R., Mesanza, R. B., & Mariel, P. (2011). The determinants of international student mobility flows: An empirical study on the Erasmus programme. *Higher Education, 62*(4), 413–430.

Ieracitano, F. (2014). New European citizens? The Erasmus generation between awareness and scepticism. *European Journal of Research on Social Studies, 1*(1), 16–21.

Isserstedt, W., & Schnitzer, K. (2002). *Internationalisierung des Studiums: ausländische Studierende in Deutschland; deutsche Studierende im Ausland*. Bundesministerium für Bildung, Wissenschaft, Forschung und Technologie.

Jacobone, V., & Moro, G. (2015). Evaluating the impact of the Erasmus programme: Skills and European identity. *Assessment and Evaluation in Higher Education, 40*(2), 309–328.

Kehm, B. (2005). The contribution of international student mobility to human development and global understanding. *US-China Education Review, 2*(1), 18–24.

Kmiotek-Meier, E., Skrobanek, J., Nienaber, B., Vysotskaya, V., Samuk, S., Ardic, T., Pavlova, I., Dabasi-Halázs, Z., Diaz, C., Bissinger, J., Schlimbach, T., & Horvath, K. (2019). Why is it so hard? And for whom? Obstacles to intra-European mobility. *Migration Letters, 16*(1), 31–44.

Kolb, D. A. (2014). *Experiential learning: Experience as the source of learning and development.* Upper Saddle River: FT press.

Messelink, H. E., Van Maele, J., & Spencer-Oatey, H. (2015). Intercultural competencies: What students in study and placement mobility should be learning. *Intercultural Education, 26*(1), 62–72.

Mitchell, K. (2012). Student mobility and European identity: Erasmus study as a civic experience? *Journal of Contemporary European Research, 8*(4), 490–518.

Mitchell, K. (2015). Rethinking the 'Erasmus effect' on European identity. *Journal of Common Market Studies, 53*(2), 330–348.

Mutlu, S. (2011). Development of European consciousness in Erasmus students. *The Journal of Education, Culture and Society, 2*, 87–102.

Nienaber, B., Vysotskaya, V., & Kmiotek-Meier, E. (2017). Why do young working people find Luxembourg attractive? Internationalisation and youth mobility in Europe. *English Language, Oct/Nov*, 51–53.

Oborune, K. (2013). Becoming more European after Erasmus? The impact of the Erasmus programme on political and cultural identity. *Epiphany, 6*(1), 182–202.

Ottesen, E., & Colbjørnsen, T. (2016). Internationalisation in leadership education: Opportunities and challenges in an Erasmus Intensive Programme. *Acta Didactica Norge, 10*(4), 166–182.

Parey, M., & Waldinger, F. (2010). Studying abroad and the effect on international labour market mobility: Evidence from the introduction of Erasmus. *The Economic Journal, 121*(551), 194–222.

Petzold, K. (2017). The role of international student mobility in hiring decisions. A vignette experiment among German employers. *Journal of Education and Work, 30*(8), 893–911.

Ribeiro, A. (2021). Erasmus at 30: Institutional mobility at higher education in perspective. In D. Cairns (Ed.), *The Palgrave handbook of youth mobility and educational migration.* Basingstoke: Palgrave Macmillan.

Roman, M., Muresan, L.-M., Manafi, I., & Marinescu, D. (2018). Volunteering as international mobility: Recent evidence from a post-socialist country. *Transnational Social Review – A Social Work Journal, 8*(3), 258–272.

Skrobanek, J. (2004). Soziale Identität und Ausländerfeindlichkeit. Das integrative Moment europäischer Zugehörigkeit. *Berliner Journal für Soziologie, 14*(3), 357–377.

Standley, H. J. (2015). International mobility placements enable students and staff in Higher Education to enhance transversal and employability-related skills. *FEMS Microbiology Letters, 362*(19), 1–5.

Wilson, I. (2011). What should we expect of 'Erasmus generations'? *Journal of Common Market Studies, 49*(5), 1113–1140.

Chapter 19
Mobility and Participation: The Intertwined Movement of Youth and Ideas

Airi-Alina Allaste and Raili Nugin

This chapter looks at young people's short-term mobility and how this intertwines with other aspects of their lives. To fulfil this purpose, we analyse the mobility experience of young people from Estonia who have attended Erasmus+ youth exchange programmes. As noted in the preceding two chapters (Ribeiro 2021; Samuk et al. 2021), Erasmus+, starting in 2014, is the result of the aggregation of several pre-existing non-academic programme elements alongside university exchanges, with a greater emphasis on social inclusion. The designers of the programme emphasise that 'Europe needs more cohesive and inclusive societies which allow citizens to play an active role in democratic life' (European Commission 2017), implying that Erasmus+ was intended to serve the purpose of promoting European citizenship and active participation. We also take account of the idea that mobility is a complex phenomenon, interlinked with other journeys in life, and interrelated with various form of capital, social spaces and identities (see also Sheller and Urry 2006).

In regard to theoretical framework, youth mobility has attracted the attention of researchers from different fields, creating an interdisciplinary understanding of the spatial dimension of youth life. Just as social change led to prolonged and diversified transitions in a previous era (Furlong and Cartmel 1997), more recently, incorporating a geographical dimension into young people's life planning processes has become common in studying the transition to adulthood (Cairns 2014). Mobility, it is argued, becomes an important marker of transitions for youth in and of itself, in many different contexts globally (Robertson et al. 2018), becoming, arguably, the 'central motif' in contemporary transitions (Thomson and Taylor 2005).

This recognition in itself reflects broader trends in sociology. Since the turn of the century, several researchers have criticised the approach of studies which focus on movement in space and time rather than the complex relations between mobility,

---

A.-A. Allaste (✉) • R. Nugin
Tallinn University, Tallinn, Estonia
e-mail: alina67@tlu.ee

different social actors, different capitals and the impact of movement on spaces and society at large (Kaufmann et al. 2004; Sheller and Urry 2006; Cresswell 2010). These authors call for a definition of mobility as socially and culturally produced motion in itself, accounting for not only physical and calculable movement but also the generation of particular meanings, capitals and forms of cultural communication (Cresswell 2010, 2014; Merriman 2015; Farrugia 2016). Youth mobility, or mobilities, can also be understood within the framework of mobile lifestyles being a product of reflexive modernity, implying that their lives are less determined by class and more by individual choices (e.g., Giddens 1991), with lifestyles shaped by different choices including networks, recreational activities and civil participation (see also Allaste and Bennett 2013). Mobility choices can thereby be perceived as attempts at self-realisation, looking for adventure, experience and challenges. This makes mobility decisions stratifying forces in society: it is not only important to move but also to use this movement to help you move up the social ladder.

We can also argue that mobility choices are connected to the accumulation of capital, discussed as 'mobility capital' elsewhere in this book (see Cairns 2021a, b), due to the fact that spatial movement enables entry to a global field of opportunities, especially for highly qualified youth (Cairns et al. 2018). In this respect, the Erasmus programme in its traditional form of undergraduate exchanges could be seen as having promoted a mobility favouring *habitus* for a particular youth milieu (see Bourdieu 1984). In this chapter, rather than seeing such a habitus as having had a determinative role in youth life, we see it as one of a number of co-existing *habitus*, which together have a performative and reflexive function (Lahire 2011). And as already noted, accumulating mobility can become a capital in and of itself (Kaufmann et al. 2004), reliant upon networks as well as shared information and ideas, but allowing access and deployment of differentiated resources (see also Hu and Cairns 2017).

Mobilities and the idea that people are constantly on the move has also led to debate about the centrality and relevance of a fixed sense of place in people's identities (Giddens 1991; Bauman 1998; Power et al. 2014). A multiplicity of mobility practices have the potential to transform the meaning of belonging and place attachments, which in themselves become multi-layered, complex and dynamic (Haartsen and Strjiker 2010), but not irrelevant (Massey 2005; Halfacree 2012; Nugin 2019). The construction of boundaries between locations can also become fluid. Young people stretch the limits of their belongings, constructing identities that sometimes cross national borders, yet at other times, remain local and narrow. At the same time, localism and cosmopolitanism are often just different sides of the same coin rather than being exclusive to one another (Thomson and Taylor 2005). The negotiation of structural inequalities becomes thus both social and spatial, as mobilities affect identities (Cairns 2014) and contribute to heterolocal identities (Halfacree 2012) and elective belonging (Savage et al. 2005; Savage 2010). At the same time, structural inequalities are affected by different flows of mobility, be this the mobility of capitals or other global processes (Farrugia 2016: 838).

Research Context and Methods

Among the former republics of Soviet Union, Estonia (with population 1.3 million) is known for its radical reforms and fast transformation to liberal capitalism (Norkus 2007). This process also had an ethnic dimension. The Russian-speaking minority lost their status compared to Soviet times, as Estonian national sentiments were the basis of restoration of the independence in 1991. This minority became disadvantaged in several ways, and compared to ethnic Estonians, they face relative economic deprivation, spatial segregation and a weaker position in the labour market (see also Allaste and Cairns 2016).

The opinions and dispositions of the ethno-linguistic groups differ greatly, not least in cultural terms; for example, ethnic Estonians tend to follow Estonian media and Russian-speakers, Russian media channels. One-third of the Russian-speaking population live in the north-eastern region that lost its industrial importance after the collapse of the Soviet Union, and has been characterised by high unemployment ever since (see also Allaste et al. 2014). Deprived social conditions have affected even the civic participation of young people, particularly in the north-east. However, it has to be noted that young people in post-socialist countries in general tend to have lower levels of civic engagement compared to their western counterparts, and many citizens appear to have inherited passive attitudes from the socialist regime and the negative effects (especially poverty and corruption) of the post-socialist transformation (Vukelic and Stanojevic 2012).

Due to unbalanced regional development, the incomes in regions other than the Estonian capital (especially the aforementioned north-east) are significantly lower, which keeps the human flow towards Tallinn growing. Many people commute to the capital daily for work or study purposes. Study mobility is already commonplace at secondary-school level (at the age of 15). That means that study decisions even at an early age involve mobility choices, and young people in the smaller or less well-developed regions come to consider moving as an option in the process of coming of age.

Most of them also see that their peers, parents or other notable people within their communities commute or move to the larger regional centres. Many choose to work abroad as well. Estonia is a country where the number of people who have worked abroad or are currently working abroad is among the highest in Europe, and young people are eager to use programmes for studying and training abroad. Through the Erasmus+ tertiary level education programme alone, during 2014–2018, more than 170,500 people were involved in exchanges. It is perhaps significant in the light of this particular finding that 86 per cent of those who participated were ethnic Estonians and only two per cent Russian speakers.

Empirical data for further analysis has been gathered within the framework of the RAY research project on the long-term effects of Erasmus+/Youth in Action on participation and citizenship. We have analysed 24 interviews with eight young people from Estonia who have participated in mobility projects. These interviews were conducted in three separate waves: before the core activities of a project had started, (at least) seven months after participation in the projects had finished, and finally, two to three years after the project's end. In terms of timeframe, the 'before project' interviews were conducted at the end of 2015 and in the first half of 2016, 'immediately after participation' interviews in November and December 2016 and final interviews in October and November 2018. During the first interview, the participants were 14–16 years old, three being Russian speakers from north-eastern Estonia and five ethnic Estonians from the countryside or small towns. The interview material was transcribed and analysed using an open coding method (Charmaz 2006), the interview schedule covering a wide range of topics about citizenship knowledge, values and political practices. For the purposes of this chapter, categories coded under 'social capital', 'European identity' and 'future plans' in the process of open coding are mostly used.

Mobility as Capital

Possible involvement in youth exchange projects was on most occasions connected to young people's networks. In contrast to the assumption discussed previously, that young people are passive in Estonia, these interviewees were civically and socially active prior to their mobility project experience; this has often been the reason they participate in a youth exchange project in the first place. For example, Stanislav, a Russian-speaker from the north-eastern part of Estonia, had been involved for a longer period in different forms of school participation and also participates in drama and dancing. As he had the reputation of being an active person, his youth leader asked him to join the project, or as he puts it himself: 'Anyway, they took me to this project because I'm a member of the parliament. I constantly receive calls somewhere [laughs] And that's good!' (Stanislav, I interview)

This pattern of behaviour is typical of other participants—mostly they developed an interest in a particular youth exchange project through being invited, either by a responsible adult or friends who had told them about the opportunity. Although information about exchange projects is, in theory, available for everybody, in practice young people are more likely to get involved through personal contacts. The motivation to participate in an international project can also be connected to the wish to develop English language skills, have new experiences and get to know more people, but a pre-condition was pre-existing contact. For example, Kersti said that before joining a youth exchange project: 'I definitely want to make new acquaintances and because I have acquaintances there, I felt like going' (Kersti, I interview). Also, after the project experience she still stressed that possible future mobility and participation depends on the people she knows, while she depends on others to make this decision: 'I need to have people who guide and help me. If there are a couple of nice people I know, then I go there' (Kersti, II interview). The project proved to be, for her, the site in which her self-confidence grew, along with friendship and the support of others. In the following statement, she describes her positive feelings: 'There was one girl—a very, very positive girl, /… / who always said, I believe in you—you can handle it' (Kersti, II interview). For her, short-term mobility became a form of capital that was crucial for her further development as that provided a network she could rely on. Common experiences and emotional support have encouraged her to experience more in the future, or as she put it herself, 'It was so great that I got even more involved because I just wanted to experience it. /.../I'm more active so that I can have more of this' (Kersti, II interview).

Somewhat similarly to Kersti, Kristi also received emotional support from the exchange project, which motivated her to strive for better and encouraged her to take on more responsibilities:

> Well, the project really did give me a lot of inspiration to go on because I met a lot of new people, who mostly had the same goals [...]. Now I've been the president of the youth council for three months already. (Kristi, II interview)

Although she was already a very active person, the mobility experience probably raised her self-esteem to such an extent that Kristi felt able to run for the presidency of a youth council. She became even more active than before in multiple ways—she joined the youth section of Social Democrats, and later, the Estonian Union of Student Representatives, and was organising protests as an animal right activist. Through her activities she has become well known in her community and is able to inspire others to follow her. In this sense, it could be interpreted that the youth exchange project boosts self-esteem, in the way that it channels an existing resource rather than creating an entirely new disposition. In Kristi's case, ultimately the potential was already present but (more) mobility influenced her capabilities and opportunities to make more changes at the local level. Becoming the local leader whom others approached with their ideas extended her network locally.

On some occasions, simply including different people in a personal network was an eye-opening experience; for example, Stanislav, who was used to his parents' critical views towards other cultures, changed and became more open towards different people.

> I have Muslim friends—from Turkey and England. Because the English ones actually visited us. They were Pakistanis living in England. And now, I try to avoid using crude words, and try to re-educate my parents. (Stanislav, II interview)

This is an obvious case of new knowledge generated within a mobility project being put to good use. We can also observe the value of mobility; a shift in spatial location during the knowledge-acquisition process. The Eastern European context matters a great deal in this respect, and the interviewee asserted that there was less understanding of different cultures or religions in Estonia compared, for example, to what she terms the 'old European countries.' Especially in some communities, encountering people from a different background is still a new phenomenon, and some people are not accustomed to living with diversity.

Another Russian-speaking person, Maria, who was originally from the northeastern part of Estonia and went to a Russian school, stressed the importance of communication with people from other cultures as a source of facilitating relations within her everyday life. As she compares her attitudes before and after the project: 'if it was an Afro-American, I was afraid, because s/he was somebody different, or something like that. It's not like that anymore. Basically, they're people just like us' (Maria, II interview). Both Stanislav and Maria had especially limited opportunities to meet people from different backgrounds in the undeveloped north-eastern part of Estonia, and project experiences were crucial for facilitating everyday communications with new people. As Maria, who had meanwhile moved to an Estonian-speaking town and school, explained in her third interview:

> Now when I study in Kadrina, there are a lot of exchange students from abroad. We had a guy from France, and I have a classmate from Albania /.../ last year, we had girls from Georgia. I communicate with them very easily /.../ most likely the project has influenced me /.../ all these are people from other countries, and I no longer am afraid, for me it's normal. (Maria, III interview)

It can be argued that this case exemplifies how intercultural communication skills are developed through increased tolerance and open-mindedness towards people of other religions, cultures or races, and that intercultural competence facilitates communication. On the one hand, Maria has kept on-going relations from the projects at an international level, and on the other, mobility experience was useful in communicating with different people in her daily life. As internationalisation has been rapidly increasing in Estonia, even outside the capital through student exchanges and migration, these competences become especially important. For Maria, mobility experience was also connected to her decision to get out of the 'comfort zone' of her hometown and move to a place where she has more of chance of achieving her life goals.

Mobility gave different people different knowledge, and new ideas. Karin, who had moved from the countryside to a small town, had lot of youth exchange experiences, partly because her aunt has been the organiser of these projects. For her, one experience led to another, and she has now participated in seven youth exchange projects/voluntary services. She already felt very confident during the first interview about joining another project, as she knew many others there. She emphasised the importance of learning from others and the relevance of learning about other cultures: 'I think it was most important that we were able to be like within another culture, and just like socializing and being ourselves' (Karin, I interview). She considered these projects as having been an important part of her education, contributing to her personal growth and in a way contrasting with fact-based education at school. For example, she talked about a project that focused on leadership and considered that she had learnt more there in a couple of weeks than in her 12 years in secondary school. As with other informants, she got involved because of close personal contacts, but in her case, knowledge and experiences accumulated over a longer period. Maybe partly because of her mobility experiences, she was considering learning psychology in the future.

Although mobility experience through youth exchange has had a mostly positive impact, it would be an over-simplification to interpret this as a straightforward causal relationship, but it can be interpreted as part of a negotiation between different experiences. In general, increased self-confidence as well as curiosity sparked the informants' interest in projects, travelling and becoming acquainted with other cultures. New contacts from projects extended informants' networks, but also led to them being more open-minded. In many cases young people stayed in touch with others they had encountered from foreign countries after the project had finished, but the same experience also intensified communication locally.

Mobility and Identity

As pointed out earlier, the borders of identity are not necessarily tied to only one geographical location but keep shifting, and the more abstract cultural and local identities can be intertwined rather than conflicting with each other. One example of localism and cosmopolitanism co-existing was Kristiina, who was originally from a small rural area in south-west Estonia. Her mother being one of the municipality leaders, she actively took part in local community events, helped out and attended events whenever she could. But as Kristiina was studying and living in a town nearby, she could not be at home and contribute to the local community as much as she wanted, but she nevertheless had a strong place attachment to her home area. However, in addition to her local identity, her Estonian and European identity were just as strong, and got stronger during the period of the research. During the first interview, she referred to Europe as a place where all the countries should 'care and pay attention' to each other. In the second interview, she said that communicating with others from other European countries had strengthened her sense of belonging to the European community: 'I would say [Europe] is a unified community in a sense ... all the countries are familiar and discuss all political topics together' (Kristiina, II interview).

This attitude was not unique. In fact, besides treating Europe as one community, several informants used other words with connotations referring to values on personal level, such as 'big-big family,' 'friends' and 'helping each other out.' Kadi described the relations between the Estonian state and the European Union using metaphors usually referred to when speaking about individuals: 'we have friends, who share something with each other' (Kadi, II interview). According to Kadi, her attachment to European identity strengthened after the project, when Lithuanian guests came to Estonia and they shared the mutual feeling of being European. Thus, mobility as a culturally constructed motion (see Sheller and Urry 2006) can potentially strengthen a European identity and shape the boundaries of belonging even if one does not move him/herself. Potential mobility, and Europeans who visit Estonia, can broaden such place attachments.

It is noteworthy that European identity is in these cases strongly intertwined with mobilities: either with someone from Europe coming to Estonia, the informants' visits to Europe or just potentially going there. Kristi, described the essence of the EU: ' it creates kind of unity ... a lot of free borders' (Kristi, II interview). Thus, for her, the possibility of free movement was one of the core meanings for her in terms of the EU and democracy in general. Mobility and democracy were sometimes treated as synonyms.

Borders which were broader than one's locality was a common feature among all the interviewed young people; their belonging differed and, in the case of our small case study, was connected to ethnolinguistic identity. For example, Sergei was a citizen of Russia, but lived in a predominantly Russian-speaking town. His home language was Russian and he evaluated his Estonian language skills as rather poor. Sergei had sensed in the local media a sharp tension between Russia and Europe. According to him, the EU used 'double standards' in their foreign policy, diminishing all the 'mistakes' of the US, but depicting the same acts by Russia as major crimes. This clash in values between Europe and Russia meant for him that feeling part of one excludes the other. Being deeply interested in international politics, he has shaped his opinion of the EU along international power lines, being inclined towards the Russian side. Thus, after the events in Maidan and Ukraine, he felt his attitude towards EU changing for the worse. He suggested that although Russia is geographically part of Europe, its value base differs, and that is why he feels Russian rather than European:

> A large part of the inhabitants of Russia also live in Europe, but the traditions and values differ... /.../ every country, every nation has chosen one's own road for development. (Sergei, I interview)

His point of view did not change during the three interviews. Throughout these years, he excluded the possibility of Russian and European identities co-existing together, explaining this position with 'historical reasons'. During the years of this study, he moved to Russia to study law and thus mobility played an important part in his life transitions (and identity of belonging) as well. His belonging was also influenced by his feeling that his ethnolinguistic group was stigmatised in the Estonian (and European) cultural and political fields.

The EU did not evoke emotional attachment or association with words such as 'family' or 'community' for Sergei, but was defined from the viewpoint of pragmatic international politics. Similar to him, another Russian-speaking informant, Stanislav, also treated the EU in economic terms:

> Naturally, a lot changed when the euro was first introduced. Then roads were renovated and built, everything started to change. Then, I remember, at the beginning—everything was financed, everything. Then, all of a sudden, the money ran out and was nowhere to be found. So, of course, Europe affects in a way, but not particularly to people. (Stanislav, I interview)

For both Sergei and Stanislav, the EU was foremostly useful in terms of the economy. Stanislav also brought out the question of travelling and the discomfort of having a Russian passport during his European travels. He admitted that political relations between Russia and Estonia (and Europe) affected his feeling of belonging and his personal attitudes. However, there was also the example of Maria, another Russian-speaking interviewee, whose identity and feelings of belonging changed during the time of the study, possibly because of her mobility practices. When asked about her European identity while she was at a Russian school, she confessed that she feels Russian rather than European. She said she feels displaced in the EU, but not in Russia:

> If you go to Russia, there is no such thing [as in Europe]. Maybe because there is this language, but I don't feel [displaced] there. In Russia, it's like ... Russian. You feel you belong, fit in. But here, there are problems with language. (Maria, I interview)

Thus, both mobility (going to Russia) and language skills have affected her identity and place attachment. After attending the project (and improving her language skills), she felt confident enough to go to study at another school in a different part of Estonia, where the language was Estonian. She admitted that within one country, she appeared to be in midst of a 'completely different culture.' This move seemed to have had an impact on her in terms of identity, as she said during the second interview that she now 'probably' feels European. During the third interview, she admitted that she has become an alien in her hometown, and when going to Russia, she feels like a European there: 'You immediately feel the difference, here it is one way, there, another.' In Maria's case, then, mobility within a country changed her feelings of belonging, while for Sergei, transnational mobility (going to study in Russia) strengthened his existing identity. It seems that place attachment and feelings of belonging are connected to mobility, yet these aspects work in multi-layered ways, being intertwined with language and culture.

Mobility and Future Plans

All the informants were at a stage of their lives when they had to make decisions about the future. Coming mostly from small (and often rural) locations, their decisions concerning their studies almost inevitably entail some kind of spatial mobility. The examples in this section illustrate how mobility has, for them, wider meaning in being an integral part of becoming an adult (see also Cairns 2014; Nugin 2014, 2019).

When speaking about future plans, mobility in itself can be a goal without being specifically tied to any location or destination. Kadi stated: 'I would definitely want to be away as a volunteer,' stressing the concept of being 'away' as signifying new experiences and knowledge, without specifying either the type of voluntary work or the destination. This mobility is, according to her, something which is implicitly part of her youthfulness: 'I am young and want to explore the world.' This disposition of mobility during the transition to adulthood was expressed by many others, as this entailed in itself seeing, experiencing and exploring. Karin, in the future, wanted to 'go everywhere and discover new things.' Thus, the mobility in these accounts is a compulsory part of becoming, knowing and maturing.

Besides gaining knowledge, moving is often depicted also as a lifestyle choice and a way of having fun. Stanislav told the interviewer about his dream of travelling further than just the neighbouring countries, and that he sometimes envies his classmates who have travelled more than he has. Yet, he said that even travelling around Estonia is something to enjoy and look forward to. In fact, one of the reasons he decided to become an actor was connected with mobility:

> I have not regretted once that I have been involved with theatre. It is very… first, it involves the trips, that means also getting to know different people. (Stanislav, II interview)

In order to become an actor, he applied to study at theatre school in Moscow, and although he made it to the last round, he did not succeed in enrolling. Yet, he considered the entire experience to have been highly motivating and this boosted his self-confidence (as he was one of only 34 pupils chosen to go through to the last round). Thus, as was the case with many others, mobility mingled with study plans, integrating 'free time' and a future profession. At the same time, mobilities affected all these plans, as the experiences increased different capitals and urged one to pursue more.

In the case of Kersti, the ambition of mobility was further projected onto her potential future involvement in politics. When asked if she could herself put up a candidacy in elections, she answered that she could run for European Parliament as she likes to travel. Though she was also concerned about the environment, one of the issues she wanted to deal with while in European Parliament would have been to ensure people could travel more:

> We could have the borders within Europe even more free and like … the shipping and air flights could be cheaper because this would mean like unified Europe. People could travel more—to find out more about the world and to see the nature and to know things about politics and, things like that. Many people cannot afford it due to financial costs. I would change this—people could travel more. (Kersti, III interview)

She had as yet no thorough knowledge about the current members of European Parliament or any deeper understanding about the political processes at European level. However, she had studied the laws and regulations of different EU states in order to find out more about the options of going to study in different EU states, and her attitude towards Brexit was also shaped by the potential of limitations of travelling and studying there.

Conclusions

Mobile lifestyles have become increasingly common and mobility is believed to contribute to better life chances, particularly among youth. Several programmes, including Erasmus+ in the EU, have been designed to increase youth mobility. Although there is an extensive body of literature on different aspects of youth migration or long-duration studying (see also Chap. 8 of this book), participation in short-term mobility projects has not been a major focus in research. Our study illustrates that short-term mobility is worth exploring further, as Erasmus+ exchange projects can be inspirational for young people, providing a place in which they can meet people, get new ideas and sometimes start to feel more European.

According to our study, getting involved in projects depends on existing network integration and possession of social capital, but participating in a project extends the network, which then becomes 'a source of support and motivation' (Lin 2001).

Communicating with people from different backgrounds establishes both new contacts and knowledge that has a relevant impact on people's lives. Most importantly, our informants felt that these new experiences and extended networks raised their self-esteem, willingness to participate more actively in society and to have more ambitious plans for the future.

Due to the Eastern European context of the research, the impact of a short-duration project can be interpreted as being more significant for offering encouragement for civic participation, where general passivity is more widespread compared to western Europe. On the other hand, young people getting involved in these projects could be described as belonging to 'small group active people' (see also Allaste et al. 2014), examples of people who have the right preconditions for subsequent mobility experience. That might raise some questions as to the effectiveness of the Erasmus programme's aim to promote 'inclusive societies' and reaching a diverse audience (see also the previous two chapters of this book).

In theoretical terms, participating in the Erasmus programme can contribute to supporting but not creating a mobility favouring habitus (see also Cairns 2014). This might potentially widen the gap between those who have enjoyed prior mobility opportunities and others who have been left aside, as they were passive or badly informed in the first place. It could be said that young people with active lifestyles, for whom mobility experience in projects is 'fun,' have the advantage of turning the spatial movement to their favour in moving up the social ladder. Youth exchange project experience, in turn, favours future choices that include mobility becoming an integral dimension of a lifestyle and part of the process of becoming an adult, as has also been pointed out by previous studies (e.g., Nugin 2014, 2019; Cairns 2014; Farrugia 2016). Our intention here is to draw attention to the importance of short-term mobility practices as potentially strengthening networks and increasing capitals that can shape the future of young people.

Positioning ourselves within the debate about the importance of place in young people's identities on the scales of 'cosmopolitanism-localism' (Thomson and Taylor 2005) and 'belonging-not belonging' (Nì Laoire 2007), we can deduce that Erasmus+ favoured lifestyles do not necessarily induce conflicting identities when more particular local place attachments compete with more abstract identities. On the contrary, in some cases, the (more abstract) European identity strengthened involvement in local communities. For many informants, Europe was not defined through its borders, but rather through a network of 'connections' and 'flows.' Making sense of European identity happened through personal contacts and communications, and European and (in our study) Estonian identities became 'just two sides of the same coin (always in play together)' (Thomson and Taylor 2005).

While we did not find conflicting identities at the level of particular (local) and abstract (European/Russian), we did notice that identities on a more abstract level compete or clash. This was particularly the case with the informants who consumed Russian media channels, which kept political interests to the forefront of national identities. Paradoxically, the shift from Russian to European identity was initiated by mobility on a local level, moving within Estonia to a cultural environment dominated by an Estonian-speaking culture. Thus, mobility can be a powerful influence in shifting or strengthening identities, yet in each case, mobility takes different forms and entails cultural and social motion as much as physical movement. It can also be in the form of someone else coming to visit, or in information flows (Russian media); moving within the same country but ending up in a different cultural environment.

References

Allaste, A.-A., & Bennett, A. (2013). Lifestyles in former socialist society. In A.-A. Allaste (Ed.), *'Back in the West' changing lifestyles in transforming societies* (pp. 9–28). Frankfurt am Mein: Peter Lang.
Allaste, A.-A., & Cairns, D. (2016). Youth political participation in a transition society. *Studies of Transition States and Societies, 8*(2), 3–8.
Allaste, A.-A., Pirk, R., & Taru, M. (2014). *Mapping and typologising youth activism (Tartumaa and Ida-Virumaa). Research report.* European Commission: Luxembourg.
Bauman, Z. (1998). *Globalization. The human consequences.* Cambridge: Polity Press.
Bourdieu, P. (1984). *Distinction: A source critique of the judgement of taste.* London: Routledge.
Cairns, D. (2014). *Youth transitions, international student mobility and spatial reflexivity. Being mobile?* Basingstoke: Palgrave Macmillan.
Cairns, D. (2021a). Mobility becoming migration: Understanding youth spatiality in the twenty-first century. In D. Cairns (Ed.), *The Palgrave handbook of youth mobility and educational migration.* Basingstoke: Palgrave Macmillan.
Cairns, D. (2021b). Migration decision-making, mobility capital and reflexive learning. In D. Cairns (Ed.), *The Palgrave handbook of youth mobility and educational migration.* Basingstoke: Palgrave Macmillan.
Cairns, D., Krzaklewska, E., Cuzzocrea, V., & Allaste, A.-A. (2018). *Mobility, education and employability in the European Union: Inside Erasmus.* Basingstoke: Palgrave Macmillan.
Charmaz, K. (2006). *Constructing grounded theory: A practical guide through qualitative analysis.* London: Sage.
Cresswell, T. (2010). Mobilities I: Catching up. *Progress in Human Geography, 35*(4), 550–558.
Cresswell, T. (2014). Mobilities III: Moving on. *Progress in Human Geography, 38*(5), 712–721.
European Commission. (2017). *Erasmus+ programme guide version 2.* Luxembourg: Publications Office of the European Union.
Farrugia, D. (2016). The mobility imperative for rural youth: The structural, symbolic and non-representational dimensions rural youth mobilities. *Journal of Youth Studies, 19*(6), 836–851.
Furlong, A., & Cartmel, F. (1997). *Young people and social change: Individualization and risk in the age of high modernity.* Buckingham: Open University Press.
Giddens, A. (1991). *Modernity and self-identity: Self and society in the late modern age.* Cambridge: Polity Press.
Haartsen, T., & Strjiker, D. (2010). Rural youth culture: Keten in The Netherlands. *Journal of Rural Studies, 26*, 163–172.
Halfacree, K. (2012). Heterolocal identities? Counter-urbanisation, second homes, and rural consumption in the era of mobilities. *Population, Space and Place, 18*(2), 20–224.
Hu, A., & Cairns, D. (2017). Hai Gui or Hai Dai? Chinese student migrants and the role of Norwegian mobility capital in career success. *Young, 25*(2), 174–189.
Kaufmann, V., Bergman, M. M., & Joye, D. (2004). Motility: Mobility as capital. *International Journal of Urban and Regional Research, 28*(4), 745–756.
Lahire, B. (2011). *The plural actor.* Cambridge: Polity Press.
Lin, N. (2001). *Structural analysis in the social sciences: Social capital: A theory of social structure and action.* Cambridge: Cambridge University Press.

Massey, D. (2005). *For space*. London: Sage.
Merriman, P. (2015). Mobilities I: Departures. *Progress in Human Geography, 39*(1), 87–95.
Nì Laoire, C. (2007). The 'green green grass of home'? Return migration to rural Ireland. *Journal of Rural Studies, 23*(3), 332–344.
Norkus, Z. (2007). Why did Estonia perform best? The North-South gap in the post-socialist economic transitions of the Baltic states. *Journal of Baltic Studies, 38*(1), 21–42.
Nugin, R. (2014). 'I think that they should go. Let them see something.' The context of rural youth's out-migration in post-socialist Estonia. *Journal of Rural Studies, 34*, 51–64.
Nugin, R. (2019). Space, place and capitals in rural youth mobility: Broadening the focus of rural studies. *Sociologia Ruralis, 60*(2), 306–328.
Power, N. G., Norman, M. E., & Dupré, K. (2014). Rural youth and emotional geographies: How photovoice and words-alone methods tell different stories of place. *Journal of Youth Studies, 17*(8), 1114–1129.
Ribeiro, A. (2021). Erasmus at 30: Institutional mobility at higher education in perspective. In D. Cairns (Ed.), *The Palgrave handbook of youth mobility and educational migration*. Basingstoke: Palgrave Macmillan.
Robertson, S., Harris, A., & Baldassar, L. (2018). Mobile transitions: A conceptual framework for researching a generation on the move. *Journal of Youth Studies, 21*(2), 203–217.
Samuk, S., Nienaber, B., Kmiotek-Meier, E., Vysotskaya, V., Skrobanek, J., Ardic, T., Pavlova, I., Marinescu, D. E., & Muresan, L. (2021). Learning in transition: Erasmus+ as an opportunity for internationalization. In D. Cairns (Ed.), *The Palgrave handbook of youth mobility and educational migration*. Basingstoke: Palgrave Macmillan.
Savage, M. (2010). The politics of elective belonging. *Housing, Theory and Society, 27*(2), 115–161.
Savage, M., Bagnall, G., & Longhurst, B. (2005). *Globalisation and belonging*. London: Sage.
Sheller, M., & Urry, J. (2006). The new mobilities paradigm. *Environment and Planning A, 38*, 207–226.
Thomson, R., & Taylor, R. (2005). Between cosmopolitanism and the locals. Mobility as a resource in the transition to adulthood. *Young, 13*(4), 327–342.
Vukelic, J., & Stanojevic, D. (2012). Environmental activism as a new form of political participation of the youth in Serbia. *Sociologija, 54*, 387–399.

Chapter 20
The Super-Mobile Student: Global Educational Trajectories in Erasmus Mundus

Karolina Czerska-Shaw and Ewa Krzaklewska

> First Krakow. Then Olomouc. Yes, but what about the third semester? I'm not sure. An internship in Brussels? Or maybe the research track in Groningen. There is also the Japan option, but I don't know. The fourth semester, yes, back to Krakow with everyone else. After that? Who knows, maybe another traineeship? Probably in Strasbourg, we'll see.

This extraordinary sense of freedom, ease of movement and access to an array of mobility patterns characterizes participants of programmes like the Erasmus Mundus Master's in *Euroculture: Society, Politics and Culture in a Global Context*, whose students, at first glance, seem to be transnationalism personified. They constitute a small yet symbolically significant grouping, the precursors to the so-called 'Eurostars' (Favell 2008), and personification of Europe's ideal type of citizen: cosmopolitan, flexible and 'at home everywhere.'

These Masters students are taking part in a European Union supported Erasmus Mundus Joint Master Degrees (EMJMD), a form of institutionalized mobility involving stays in two, three or even four different destinations during the course of a two-year study programme, ending with a double, multiple or, ideally, joint degree. EMJMDs are supported by the Erasmus+ framework and are meant to attract highly qualified candidates to study in consortium programmes that have a group dynamic ingrained into their structures (see also Cuzzocrea et al. 2021). In the era of *chasing mobility* and 'global experience,' one Erasmus mobility phase is simply not enough for some young people. What we observe is the increasing attraction of higher education programmes that include mobility as a central and institutionalized part of a course of study.

K. Czerska-Shaw (✉) • E. Krzaklewska
Jagiellonian University, Krakow, Poland
e-mail: karolina.czerska@uj.edu.pl

© The Author(s), under exclusive license to Springer Nature Switzerland AG 2022
D. Cairns (ed.), *The Palgrave Handbook of Youth Mobility and Educational Migration*, https://doi.org/10.1007/978-3-030-99447-1_20

In this chapter, we showcase Erasmus Mundus as a reflection of current trends in the European Higher Education Area, in particular the internationalization and institutionalization of inter-university networks. We argue that the slow and steady development of these networks has facilitated the emergence of a new model of what we term 'super-mobile student.' This is someone who is not rooted in one particular institution, or even between two, but is rather to be found circulating inside a network of institutional ties that operate in the spaces between traditional higher education structures. Overlooked within mobility and higher education studies, which concentrate mostly on single stage mobility (e.g., Feyen and Krzaklewska 2013; Cairns et al. 2018), this institutionalized framework of 'super-mobility' carries with it particular social, psychological and educational consequences that we wish to highlight. At first glance, these mobility experiences are evaluated as largely positive, leading to a diversified educational and intercultural experience and enhanced soft skills; an intensive forging of bonds and belonging in the mobile group bubble; and self-development and the conscious construction of one's own reflexive, cosmopolitan identity. Nevertheless, the super-mobility experience also carries with it costs with high levels of stress and anxiety, logistical and legal hurdles to be overcome, and a new kind of social disembeddedness, including the feeling of being excluded from traditional higher education structures.

Our findings conclude that while maintaining these highly internationalized networks is financially taxing and emotionally exhausting for both students and institutions, the outcomes in the form of soft skills and non-formal learning may prove to be the golden ticket to succeed in a fast-changing and diversified labour market and increasingly multicultural societies. What it entails for social and psychological well-being and academic achievement, however, remains ambiguous and depends on the process of socialization into an explicitly transnational habitus, itself dependent upon a myriad of factors, starting with economic and social capital, and what is discussed elsewhere is this book as mobility capital (Cairns 2021a, 2021b), as well as an ability to surmount institutional barriers tied to the ambiguous legal status of the super-mobile individual.

Mobility in European Higher Education: The Erasmus Mundus Framework

Institutionalizing mobility in higher education is not a new phenomenon. As the preceding chapters in this section of the book demonstrate, we have in fact witnessed the normalization of what we might term one-time mobility, most often, an exchange between two partnered institutions, as is the case with much Erasmus mobility, but we are now seeing a growing trend for two or multiple (yet single destination) Erasmus mobility experiences (Cairns and Krzaklewska 2019). Erasmus Mundus Joint Master Degrees, first launched in 2004 under the heading of Erasmus Mundus Masters Courses (EMMC), aims to take the internationalization of European higher education institutions (HEIs) to this next level. Highly integrated networks of organizations offer attractive scholarships to mostly non-EU (partner country) students in order to enhance cooperation between European and non-European HEIs with a view to increasing their competitiveness on the global market, while at the same time, providing students with the chance to develop unique competencies and skills (European Commission 2018). Multiple, sustained mobility throughout the entire duration of a degree programme has thus become the undisputed and unique international selling point.

At the time of writing, Erasmus Mundus Joint Master Degrees (EMJMD) accredited programmes are around 120 in number, across different fields of higher education, and spread between the hard sciences, humanities and social sciences (European Commission 2018: 36). Financial support has steadily risen for EMJMDs, with the number of scholarships supported mushrooming since its inception; altogether, we now count approximately 25,000 scholarships throughout the lifetime of Erasmus Mundus, not including self-funding students. However, the numbers in comparison to traditional Erasmus exchanges remain modest: approximately 223,500 students benefitted from Erasmus+ exchanges in 2017, whereas only 1556 students received scholarships for Erasmus Mundus, less than one per cent of the total number (European Commission 2018: 24).

While this group of 'super-mobile' students is statistically small in size, we argue that it is symbolically important in the context of current transformations in higher education. We define the super-mobile student, firstly, as one whose educational experience is embedded within mobility, where this mobility constitutes the bedrock of the study experience. Secondly, there is an anchoring in the consortium of universities itself: mobility takes place within a network wherein additional short duration study trips or intensive programmes organized for participating students further underscore the unified aspect of the course structure. Finally, the mobility itself is an intensive and routinized group experience in multiple locations within as little as two years. These three dimensions mean that 'super-mobile' students comes to embody the multi-layered and complex entwining of contemporary transnational flows, similar to Vertovec's 'super diversity' concept (Vertovec 2007, 2019), also underscoring the attractiveness of enhanced experiences for young people and the rush that accompanies being constantly on the move.

The structure of this institutionalized mobility varies across programmes, the most basic being a continuation model, wherein all the students within a programme start at the same higher education institution and then move on, as a group, to subsequent universities. We have also observed the fork model, wherein mobility phases are a choice between two or more institutions, and the star model, where students start at different universities and then mix and match mobility according to their needs. The latter model is relevant to our respondents and is also the most complex and institutionally challenging arrangement. As a result, student groups are reconstituted throughout the programme in different institutions—as are their complex social networks—yet mobility remains within one closed consortium structure. While students generally have some choice in defining their mobility pattern, movement in this framework is also a group process, with common orientations and shared experiences in a myriad of destinations.

This model is also interesting in another respect: in practice one may say there is no home university for these schemes. Thus symbolically, that the students are never 'academically at home,' reflected in their statements about feelings of detachment from their actual homes (or countries of origin). This reflects observations within research on youth mobility, wherein 'liquid migration', characterized by temporality, flexibility and open-ended trajectories is normalized , and 'placelessness' and social 'disembeddedness' (Castells 1996) become key struggles. In more practical terms, the locus of responsibility for the educational process shifts from one specific higher education institution and towards the Erasmus Mundus programme network, echoing the view from Nowicka (2012) that highly skilled cosmopolitan migrants move between networks rather than countries, providing choices for the students who are then ultimately put in control of their own learning to a certain extent; something that can be seen as both a privilege and burden.

Taking this highly diverse and intensely mobile framework, it is not surprising that for a majority of Erasmus Mundus graduates, the most important outcomes from their studies are the intercultural competencies they gain, as indicated in the Erasmus Mundus Alumni Impact Survey (Terzieva and Unger 2018: 3). While these students are highly integrated with one another by shared values of openness, intercultural sensitivity and cosmopolitan reflexivity, the group remains differentiated internally: geographically, ethnically, culturally and socially. This is also a reflection of the recruitment process, as EMJMDs stratify participation according to partner country, between EU and non-EU students, roughly 20 per cent the former and 80 per cent the latter (Terzieva and Unger 2018). In this study, we nevertheless chose a programme that hosts a majority of European students, in contrast to the wider trend, with only four out of twelve partner institutions being extra-EU (Mexico, India, USA and Japan). This allows us to focus on the European Higher Education Area and its transnational yet mostly 'Europeanized' framework, and to use the European student as a reference point in relation to how both European and non-European students reflexively construct their expectations.

The Value of Being a Super-Mobile Student

To inquire about the experiences of these students, we conducted seven focus groups during 2018–19 in different cities around Europe (Krakow, Groningen, Uppsala, Bilbao and Olomouc), with first and second year students of the MA in Euroculture programme from multiple countries. These students were both European (Erasmus+ programme country students, including countries outside the EU such as Turkey and Norway) and from outside of the Erasmus+ structure. Altogether 40 people participated in the groups. Our results show that the chance to develop an institutionalized multiple mobility was the most important reason for participating in an Erasmus Mundus programme.

A first impression emerging from the accounts was that mobility being treated not as an added value of the programme, but the raison d'être of the experience. This redefines the education process as being founded not on the content but rather on the medium; that is, mobility structures within international consortia. The mobility structure was appreciated as such, even if some would prefer more or less, or a different organization thereof, which reflects the exercise of a mobility imperative within the space of European higher education assuming benefits from dislocation, while negative consequences and challenges are made tacit. This may explain why, notwithstanding the apparent challenges, the interviewed students agreed that the advantages outweigh the disadvantages of constantly being on the move between institutions, albeit with these challenges being unevenly distributed between programme and partner country students.

> The mobility and being able to live for a significant amount of time in a country. To be able to spend five months and actually get to know it. When I started the programme, I never thought I'd end up in the Czech Republic, but the way it opened my eyes, it's a paradigm shift. The way it makes me look at Europe, it's changed all of my former opinions, it's been very significant. (Female, non-EU citizen, year II)

Secondly, our respondents viewed mobility as an important tool for education in its redefined format—mostly through the non-formal learning experiences of exploring new spaces and investing time in new localities and communities (albeit of a transnational character), and the development of soft skills, such as effective decision-making and arriving at creative solutions within teams. Mobility is thus an instrumental good, which acts as an access point to other social goods like wealth, power and privilege through professional engagement. The building of a transnational habitus is one of the desired outcomes of this type of programme. Socialization into a habitus, meaning a process of internalizing social experiences which then constitute a system of durable dispositions and maintain social reproduction (Bourdieu 1984), is apparent here in its transnational form, in the cosmopolitan social imaginary or de-territorialized social geographies that exist outside of the nation-state container (Nedelcu 2012). Building a transnational habitus is seen as an entry ticket to a certain sector of the labour market: in the case of our study participants, linked to the European/transnational sphere of institutions, politics and civil society.

The making of this transnational habitus is also supported through a strong identification with other mobile students within Erasmus Mundus programmes. Unlike other mobility experiences, Erasmus Mundus takes place within a consolidated group. This is a unique feature and constitutes a very important resource, both within a programme, where students become each other's advisors, but also after the programme has formally ended. Alumni networks constitute both practical and symbolic points of reference; for instance, when searching for work. 'We are like a family,' boasts the welcome video of the Erasmus Mundus Alumni Association. Organized group study trips, intensive programmes or joint teaching sessions across the network also enhance the strength of group identification. The creation of this bond, on the basis of the common experience, is described by a student as follows:

> One of the highlights of mobility is meeting people—this is just what I love to do, that sounds really good, I enjoy meeting people, getting to know them. Euroculture has been great for this, because indeed we have the same base, we are interested in the same things. What I did not expect is what good friends I have met. (...) we worry about the same things, the challenges that come up are similar, you feel understood, how great is that (...). It is hard to open up about being so mobile and what comes with the emotional baggage that comes from it. I never say that to anyone, because someone may say, 'Oh this privileged young girl that can move everywhere as a European citizen' (...). I am not going to talk about this to anyone. And then you find friends that it makes sense to talk about it. That you can count on. (Female, EU citizen, II year)

At the same time, the strength of these bonds means there is a paradoxical disconnect between students' cosmopolitan outlook (conceived as participatory, active and 'glocalized') and their ability to actively participate in their immediate local and national surroundings. As one student ironically termed it, 'we fetishize the local,' without the possibility of anchoring themselves into that reality.

Possibly as a result of this disconnectedness to local social structures, mobility becomes a value and an end goal in itself. It comes to embody a certain type of Europeanness and the concept of open borders, treated as a right but also a privilege of this political space and its citizens. More substantially, it is linked with mostly positive attitudes such as open-mindedness, tolerance, knowledge and an understanding of different cultures, and (at least in the first part of the programme) mostly positive emotions, especially the excitement and anticipation of new adventures and challenges. It is a highly desired autotelic social good, and as such becomes a catalyst for shaping personal and group identities; who people are and who they want to become. This process of 'becoming' (Worth 2009) is very strongly felt, particularly by the students who we encountered in the first year of their Masters course, describing it as a process of 'being sculpted' through self-discovery of social and geographical otherness. The aim of this socialization into transnationalism is to become or to refine one's cosmopolitan characteristics, to be a global citizen on the move for whom mobility has become natural and easy, although they themselves remain critical as to whether or not they have reached this goal:

> I am a person who travels easily, I have no problem in getting involved in new cultures, depending on cultures you have been to (...). I would still say my home base is Berlin. I am not saying I am a very free person, and that my home could be everywhere. (...) I am maybe not as cosmopolitan as I would like to be! (Female, EU citizen, II year)

Super-mobility Self-reflected: A Mitigated Value?

As we have noted, mobility acts as a vector for the learning experience while also constituting an individual cosmopolitan project. Yet the process is fraught with obstacles, particularly in dealing with feelings of anxiety, loneliness and the sheer exhaustion of relocating and maintaining ties in multiple loci, geographically and virtually, as well as dealing with the many institutional and formal barriers to mobility. This Janus-faced nature of 'learning in mobility' did not escape the reflections of our respondents.

One of the most evident challenges highlighted by our respondents were the formal barriers that non-EU students faced. Despite the fact that the 2016 EU Directive on students and researchers has been implemented in the majority of states, which is meant to simplify the legal formalities connected to the mobility of highly skilled non-EU students and researchers within the EU, the reality is far from ideal. These students, a majority of whom receive a generous scholarship from the European Commission, constantly find themselves caught in Catch-22 bureaucratic situations: they need to move to their new study location before they formalize their stay in their first country of residence, but must formalize their next stay before they can move. There is an evident dissonance here between the institutionalized and sanctified transnational structure of the programme, and an uncomfortable stratification of rights and privileges of mobility within it. It brings to the fore the often invisible boundaries which European students had all but forgotten about during their previous Erasmus experiences, but which are showing signs of revival, not least in the aftermath of Brexit.

> The visas, just a nightmare. Every three months I'm thinking, how am I going to figure this out? Will I have time not to overstay my visa? This summer I went to Georgia to get out of Schengen. But you can't go home for extended periods of time because of the insurance. I'm not allowed to go home, but sometimes I'm not allowed to be here, so I don't know where to go. It's a nightmare. I feel sick to my stomach. There's no piece of paper that says 'this is what you need to do.' Everyone is very helpful, but no one can tell me exactly what to do. In order to get my Swedish visa, I had to fly to Germany and prove that I was there by taking a picture of myself with a newspaper. I had to fly back to the US to get my original visa. For non-EU citizens, programmes like this are incredibly difficult. (Female, non-EU citizen, II year)

Even without visa considerations, while mobility appears to be an exciting experience of location-jumping around Europe, each move entailed a bigger-than-expected organizational challenge for our respondents. Notwithstanding the substantial institutional support in managing issues like course registrations, university orientation, accommodation, visa support and safety checks—which our respondents highlighted as a much appreciated and crucial service—students were still surprised how often simple institutional differences created large barriers, stopping the flow of information.

As well as these often difficult institutional challenges, our findings revealed that social and psychological hardships were also at the forefront of students' considerations. Somewhat paradoxically, the experience of fleeting relationships was a very strong trope in their reflections despite the strong group identification we described above. As students move between universities, and each semester, their peer group composition changes, and making new friends becomes an exhausting exercise. Many students expressed that they are 'tired of making new friends,' and that at the cost of personal contact they continue to cherish the already-made friendships through virtual networks. This reveals the complexity of the group experience, which gives the illusion of a modern patchwork family of social ties.

Amid this internal patchwork family unit, our study participants find it difficult to locate themselves externally within differing groups of university students, both local and international, which causes feelings of isolation and separation from mainstream student life. Erasmus Mundus has the unfortunate advantage of being confused with the popularized Erasmus exchange programme, which at once makes it recognizable but at the same time categorizes students according to familiar stereotypes associated with the former. For our super-mobile sample, particularly the European students acquainted with the system, self and group identification was centred on being international but *not Erasmus*; they in fact reject the shaping of oneself through identification with the Erasmus significant other. While in many institutions regular Erasmus students form the nexus of the international community within a university, their Erasmus Mundus counterparts are more ambivalent in their participation in what is popularly termed the 'Erasmus Bubble' (Cuzzocrea et al. 2021). While they are naturally drawn to the transnational communities of those from abroad/on the move, they are cognizant of the (sometimes negative) Erasmus stereotypes and seek to emphasize their more academic and professional aims (Courtois 2018). As one student put it:

> All the Erasmus—this is a year off for them essentially. The academic is not a priority. Whereas me, I'm paying for this myself, I'm more invested in it, thinking about my thesis, my career ... These are all very serious decisions. The environment and state of mind is very different from my fellow (Erasmus) students. Different wavelength. We are Erasmus students, but for us it's so different. When I talk to someone, they think, 'ah you're an Erasmus student, you don't have to do anything.' It's not the same. (Female, EU citizen, year II)

Furthermore, while mobility for these students is seen as a privilege, they also note that this privilege comes at a price—being constantly on the move not only cuts them off physically from their local communities, families or friends (which is often mitigated by connections through social media), but more importantly, they lose the connection in a more symbolic sense. The other social groups with which they identified before their programme may not share the value and experience of mobility, with the result that their choices and engagement become misunderstood, leading to a downplaying of their mobility successes as well as the associated challenges that they had to overcome. In consequence, they find consolation in the patchwork group of other Erasmus Mundus students, or other young people on the move for whom mobility remains a goal in and of itself.

While othering practices are evident within this group, they are mostly inclusive in nature, defining themselves based on what they have in common and whom they aspire to be rather than exclusionary practices. These students are highly aware of the effects of stereotypes and discrimination, particularly because there are those among them that have lived experiences of this. Being a foreigner in a country is a common experience, which is accompanied by feelings of otherness. Among our respondents, however, there was a distinct difference in the experiences and perceptions between EU and non-EU students, particularly those from visible minorities. The latter, often in Europe for the first time, were faced with multiple and persistent harassment and acts of discrimination, ranging from staring and microaggression, to more serious incidents. These were present but not limited to countries with traditionally more homogeneous societies, particularly Poland and Czechia in our study, but also documented in countries with a long experience of diversity in western Europe. These individualized cases of discrimination became a group burden as well, which adds to a sense of group solidarity and rejection of exclusionary identities, further sculpting their otherness in relation to increasingly protectionist identities in the European landscape.

Next, the psychological side-effects of super-mobility have become more commonplace and increasingly vocalized and acted upon, particularly with the rise of the demand for mental health services. Our respondents revealed the psychological cost of intensive mobility: stress, anxiety and depression, alongside the lesser-known physical consequences. One participant declared that she loses her hair with every move, another student suffered from insomnia for a whole semester in a new location, and many others had more common physiological reactions to new food and different climates. These physical reactions to mobility, particularly because of its sustained and intensive nature, were often only evident in retrospect or during periods of lull between semesters, often in the student's home country.

Although the participants stress that super-mobility is worth the costs, they are now more open to acknowledging the psychological challenges they face in constantly being on the move. While many students report the excitement and positive anticipation that comes with the next move, the emotional rollercoaster at the same time causes exhaustion and anxiety, making it even harder to study as pending decisions concerning the next location, organizational issues and social relationships come to the fore. Finally, an overarching yet largely subconscious trigger of psychological hardship is linked to the actual process of self-construction, which may result in the reassessment of one's value system, social networks, prospective professional career path and social positioning. As our analysis shows, this is related not only to mobility but also to the process of transitioning to adulthood and making later life decisions (see Krzaklewska 2019).

Finally, this process puts into question not only the emotional but also the financial investment in mobility. The most important value of this part of the programme becomes questioned—the students who were in the second year noticed while searching for work that this kind of experience had also become an obstacle. For instance, while looking for work, they may be perceived as fickle applicants, always wanting to move or change, and not being rooted in a certain national context. Their mobility deprives them of the process of building-up local connections within an institution, which continues to prove useful, especially in an academic career where PhD applicants need to find a potential supervisor. However, while our respondents acknowledged these fears, statistics tell us otherwise. Among those who were actively looking for a job after graduation, 85 per cent found one within six months, whereas 20 per cent of Erasmus Mundus graduates are currently pursuing other forms of education, including PhD programmes (Terzieva and Unger 2018: 4). As we have seen, a specific process of learning how to capitalize and internalize their mobility experience takes place as students proceed within the programme but is largely dependent on institutional, legal obstacles and processes of self-realization.

Conclusions

Our findings point towards an exclusive yet strangely emblematic microcosm of a new European transnational higher education space, where place is a staging post to the next mobility phase, institutions are safety nets on the road of experience, and belonging, a moving target anchored in transnational social relations. The rush of the experience and movement interweave psychological hardship with high-intensity adrenaline, and the honing of intercultural competencies and soft skills supersedes traditional learning. These become markers of 'adulting': the ability to juggle multiple, complex social realities and a reflexive awareness of the psychological implications that may have.

The experience of this group of super-mobile students constitutes an illustration of the impact of European policies on educational processes within higher education. While higher education remains largely within the competence of each EU member state, the impact of the introduction of programmes placing value on intensive mobility is incontestable. The mobility imperative has entered higher education institutions, which act in a competitive environment, and sustained networked mobility becomes a selling point of study programmes. Succinctly speaking, the Erasmus Mundus model is indicative of particular expectations not only towards institutions but also students—assuming that mobility in itself becomes a source of learning and that they have the capacity to be mobile (e.g., not having families or local duties or formal obstacles). It is also indicative of a new model of cooperation in higher education—institutionalized networks of institutions sharing responsibility for educational outcomes of students who are travelling in-between campuses through an organized learning framework.

Moreover, Erasmus Mundus as a concept brings back the elitist perspective into higher education which recently went through various processes of massification. These processes in effect evoke new ways of delineating distinction within higher education, such as through becoming a super-mobile student (see also Ballatore and Ferede 2013). As our study shows, Erasmus Mundus students see themselves as having a certain privilege and construct their distinction against other mobile groups of students (e.g., 'regular' Erasmus students). But the weight of this privilege affects the educational process by enclosing them in an elitist bubble, providing consolation and a source of identification, but also isolation from the host education institution. Thus ironically, they travel to become a part of new academic milieu but are simultaneously cut off from it or kept at the borderlines. What is undeniable however, is that these challenges have fostered a sense of solidarity and collective identity to a growing group of super-mobile students, who are marked by a high sense of reflexivity, intercultural awareness and possession of mobility capital, which may prove to be indispensable skills needed to navigate the murky waters of fast changing social and political environments as well as globalized labour markets.

References

Ballatore, M., & Ferede, M. (2013). The Erasmus programme in France, Italy and the United Kingdom: Student mobility as a signal of distinction and privilege. *European Educational Research Journal, 12*(4), 525–533.

Bourdieu, P. (1984). *Distinction. A social critique on the judgement of taste*. Harvard University Press.

Cairns, D. (2021a). Mobility becoming migration: Understanding youth spatiality in the twenty-first century. In D. Cairns (Ed.), *The Palgrave handbook of youth mobility and educational migration*. Basingstoke: Palgrave Macmillan.

Cairns, D. (2021b). Migration decision-making, mobility capital and reflexive learning. In D. Cairns (Ed.), *The Palgrave handbook of youth mobility and educational migration*. Basingstoke: Palgrave Macmillan.

Cairns, D., & Krzaklewska, E. (2019). Representing Erasmus: Approaches to Erasmus+ and consequences for researching the programme. In A. Rybińska & Ö. Şenyuva (Eds.), *Evidence-based approach in Erasmus+. Warsaw Seminar 2018*. Warszawa: FRSE.

Cairns, D., Krzaklewska, E., Cuzzocrea, V., & Allaste, A.-A. (2018). *Mobility, education and employability in the European Union: Inside Erasmus*. Basingstoke: Palgrave Macmillan.

Castells, M. (1996). *The rise of the network society*. Oxford: Blackwell.

Courtois, A. (2018). From 'academic concern' to work readiness: Student mobility, employability and the devaluation of academic capital on the year abroad. *British Journal of Sociology of Education, 40*(2), 190–206.

Cuzzocrea, V., Krzaklewska, E., & Cairns, D. (2021). 'There is no me, there is only us:' The Erasmus bubble as a transnational community. In V. Cuzzocrea, B. Gook, & B. Schiermer (Eds.), *Forms of collective engagements in youth transition: A global perspective*. Leiden: Brill.

European Commission. (2018). *Erasmus+ annual report 2017*. Luxembourg: Publications Office of the European Union.

Favell, A. (2008). *Eurostars and eurocities. Free movement and mobility in an integrating Europe*. Oxford: Blackwell.

Feyen, B., & Krzaklewska, E. (Eds.). (2013). *The Erasmus phenomenon – Symbol of a new European generation?* Frankfurt: Peter Lang.

Krzaklewska, E. (2019). Youth, mobility and generations: The meanings and impact of migration and mobility experiences on transitions to adulthood. *Studia Migracyjne – Przegląd Polonijny, 45*(1), 41–59.

Nedelcu, M. (2012). Migrants' new transnational habitus: Rethinking migration through a cosmopolitan lens in the digital age. *Journal of Ethnic and Migration Studies, 38*(9), 1339–1356.

Nowicka, M. (2012). Cosmopolitans, spatial mobility and the alternative geographies. *International Review of Social Research, 2*(3), 1–16.

Terzieva, B., & Unger, M. (2018). *Erasmus Mundus joint master graduate impact survey 2018*. Vienna: Institut für Höhere Studien – Institute for Advanced Studies (IHS).

Vertovec, S. (2007). Super-diversity and its implications. *Ethnic and Racial Studies, 30*(6), 1024–1054.

Vertovec, S. (2019). Talking around super-diversity. *Ethnic and Racial Studies, 42*(1), 125–139.

Worth, N. (2009). Understanding youth transition as 'becoming:' Identity, time and futurity. *Geoforum, 40*(6), 1050–1060.

Chapter 21
Educational Mobility of South African Youth: Insights from Erasmus Mundus Action 2

Samia Chasi

In South Africa, as elsewhere, mobility is an integral part of the internationalization efforts of higher education institutions (HEIs). However, as the majority of South African youth cannot afford to study in South Africa, let alone abroad, scholarships become an important mechanism, enabling them to benefit from opportunities to move abroad for educational purposes. This chapter is concerned with educational mobility opportunities provided through the Erasmus Mundus programme in South Africa. Specifically, it reflects on partnerships between European and South African universities in the framework of Action 2 of the programme (EMA2). These partnerships, implemented between 2011 and 2016, have had a considerable impact not only on individual beneficiaries but also the institutions involved, as well as the higher education (HE) sector in the country.

The chapter considers some of the conditions for successful partnerships, particularly the importance of social inclusion in accessing mobility opportunities and in regard to socio-economic background and gender. As a legacy of apartheid, access and inclusion are pertinent issues in South African HE, which is to this day characterized by high levels of inequality at institutional as well as individual levels. In highlighting these issues, the chapter makes a contribution to debates about how international mobility opportunities can become aligned with local priorities such as national development and societal transformation.

S. Chasi (✉)
International Education Association of South Africa, Pretoria, South Africa

Background

In order to better understand the context in which the EMA2 programme was located, it is useful to provide a brief overview of South African HE. In the sections that follow, the focus is on the public HE sector, as it is predominantly responsible for post-secondary education and skills training in South Africa, as well as universities (Statistics South Africa 2019).

Higher Education in South Africa

The South African public HE sector comprises 26 universities, including eleven general universities, nine comprehensive universities and six universities of technology (DHET 2017). These public institutions have a crucial role to play 'in terms of reaching our national development objectives,' which is particularly relevant with regard to addressing national 'challenges of poverty, unemployment and inequality' (DHET 2013b). As 'Access to quality post-school education is a major driver in fighting poverty and inequality in any society' (DHET 2013b), the main overall objective is to transform the HE system and to redress the inequalities of the past, which came about as a consequence of colonialism and, more recently, apartheid. Apartheid was a system of institutionalized racial segregation that existed in South Africa between 1948 and 1994. It enforced racial segregation and discrimination against non-whites in all spheres of life, including HE. To this day, South Africa's HEIs 'continue to ail under the crippling influence of the legacy of apartheid, with statistics of performance, participation, persistence, dropping out, and quality of educational outcomes still quite traceable along racial lines' (Wits 2014).

In this context, historically advantaged institutions (HAIs) are distinguished from historically disadvantaged institutions (HDIs), depending on the different kinds of status and treatment these universities previously received. HDIs generally 'find themselves trapped in a state of under-development and continued financial difficulties compared to their historically advantaged counterparts,' which has prevented them 'from effectively pursuing their missions and establishing themselves as vibrant academic enterprises' (DHET 2013a). Boshoff et al. (2018) note in this regard that 'The legacy of apartheid was a racially divided higher education sector of uneven quality plagued by duplications and inefficiencies.' The system is therefore at times equated to a 'two nation state,' where five universities have world-class status and the rest are being 'under current rules un-gradable' (Wits 2014).

The top five institutions produce more than 60 per cent of the country's entire research output (DST 2018). Not surprisingly, efforts to transform the South African HE sector focus on the development of previously disadvantaged institutions and individuals and address challenges regarding access, participation, throughput and equity, which are often interlinked. This includes, for example, improving the quality of education, guiding the purposeful differentiation of the university sector, improving access, success and throughput rates of students, improving recruitment and retention of academic staff and increasing research and innovation (DHET 2013b). Such transformation efforts have to be taken into account in activities aiming to internationalize HE in South Africa.

Internationalization of Higher Education in South Africa

Due to colonial linkages, internationalization is not a new phenomenon in South African HE. However, it has become increasingly important since the end of apartheid (Chasi 2019), as a 'reflection of globalisation as well as of South Africa's return to the international community' (DHET 2013b). After 1994, internationalization efforts were largely prompted by an increased influx of international students and challenges in dealing with them due to the under-preparedness of South African HEIs. As a consequence, IEASA was formally launched in 1997 in response to the need of South African HEIs to collectively address the internationalization of the country's HE system after its isolation under apartheid had ended (Jooste 2007).

Two decades later, the first national internationalization policy, published as a draft for public comment in 2017 and adopted in 2020, defines internationalization of HE as 'an intentional or steered process to incorporate intercultural, international and/or global dimensions into higher education in order to advance the goals, functions and delivery of higher education and thus to enhance the quality of education and research' (DHET 2019). This process is understood as encompassing a number of different dimensions including student and staff mobility, research collaboration, joint degrees and mutual recognition of qualifications, establishment of branch campuses abroad as well as internationalization of the curriculum (DHET 2013b).

Transformation concerns permeate government policy on HE internationalization. For example, the internationalization policy framework of the Department of Higher Education and Training (DHET) recognizes that HDIs have generally not been able to establish aspired international linkages and are not benefitting from internationalization as much as they should (DHET 2019). Furthermore, it recommends that the country's HEIs design their internationalization activities in such a way that priority is first given to the needs and interests of South Africa, and 'Thereafter, where possible and relevant, the following order of priority focus should be observed in terms of interests: the SADC states; the rest of the African continent; BRICS; the global South and emerging economies; and the world beyond' (DHET 2019).

Outbound Student Mobility

UNESCO data on international student mobility in tertiary education suggests that there were 7273 outbound internationally mobile tertiary students from South Africa in 2014, rising slightly to 8068 in 2017. For the most part, mobile students captured in such databases are privately financed, with some funding provided through scholarships targeting South African nationals, which are often linked to cooperation between the governments of South Africa and the respective host country. In comparison to other African countries, South Africa's tradition of international academic mobility is relatively limited, particularly when the size of its population is taken into account (Kotzé and Lenssen 2015). Given the country's academic isolation under apartheid, findings like this are not surprising.

In the context of this chapter, educational mobility is primarily understood as an integral part of internationalization efforts of South African HEIs, with mobility opportunities generally created in the framework of bilateral university agreements. However, bilateral exchanges tend to cater for very limited numbers of students. In addition, they are seriously hindered by lack of funding at the level of both South African institutions and individuals, as the 'costs of international study opportunities and academic exchange programmes are generally prohibitive for South African universities, even for the more established and better-resourced universities' (Kotzé and Lenssen 2015). In consequence, traditional semester exchanges are rarely reciprocal and beneficial, and a recent case study on North-South HE partnerships highlighted that exchange programmes tend to be one-sided, mostly due to financial constraints limiting the ability of South Africans to take up available study abroad places (Chasi 2019). In this constrained environment, the EMA2 programme made a valuable contribution to the development and internationalization of HE in South Africa by broadening access to international scholarships and by facilitating university partnerships.

Erasmus Mundus Action 2 in South Africa

The Erasmus Mundus programme was designed by the European Union (EU) as a tool to strengthen HE cooperation and mobility between Europe and third-party countries including South Africa. The programme, which was implemented in three actions, aimed to enhance quality in European HE, promote the EU as an excellence centre in learning around the globe, as well as promoting intercultural understanding through cooperation with third countries and developing HE in those countries (EUD 2016).

With strong support from the DHET, South Africa's participation was notably higher under Action 2 than in other actions (Kotzé and Lenssen 2015). Regarding the development of HE in third countries, EMA2 partnerships between South African and European HEIs were meant to support South Africa's efforts in fostering sustainable development. The objective of the DHET, working closely with the EU delegation, was to use the programme to respond to the country's challenges and transformation agenda, specifically regarding redress, equity and quality within the HE system (EUD 2016). Such transformation objectives formed an integral part of the programme's eligibility criteria. For example, in the guidelines for participating HEIs it was stipulated that at least four South African members of each consortium had to be HDIs (Kotzé and Lenssen 2015).

Erasmus Mundus Action 2 Projects in South Africa

Between 2011 and 2016, EMA2 mobility opportunities were afforded to a total of 827 South African beneficiaries in five rounds. The programme was implemented in the framework of 14 European/South African university partnerships. EMA2 stakeholders generally agree that a key success for the programme has been 'the partnership model and the relatively broad definition of eligibility in terms of beneficiaries and academic disciplines' (Kotzé and Lenssen 2015). Regarding the eligibility of beneficiaries, inclusion was a key concern.

The EMA2 programme in South Africa made provisions for 'equal opportunities and representation in gender, population groups and the various universities' (Kotzé and Lenssen 2015). Out of a total of twelve HDIs, nine were involved in the EMA2 consortia as partners. As far as the distribution of beneficiaries across institutions is concerned, 299 beneficiaries (36%) came from eleven HDIs, whereas 528 beneficiaries came from HAIs. Although HDI participation improved at a steady but increasing rate, there was a clear bias for HAIs over the duration of the programme (EUD 2016). Overall, HDI participation remained poor, despite HDIs making up half of the HEIs participating in the programme. Closer examination of the beneficiary figures also reveals that they were unevenly distributed across the HDIs. Out of a total of 299 beneficiaries coming from HDIs, 168 beneficiaries (56%) were based at only two home institutions, whereas the remaining 131 beneficiaries (44%) came from nine institutions. Furthermore, two HDIs had only one beneficiary each, and one HDI did not have any beneficiaries at all (ibid.).

Apart from the requirement to include HDIs in the consortia, social inclusion in accessing mobility opportunities was an important concern for the EMA2 partnerships in South Africa, particularly with regard to the socio-economic background and gender of beneficiaries. The focus on socio-economic issues was informed by South Africa's policy with respect to designated groups, which is linked to the need to redress past inequalities. Consequently, EMA2 programme guidelines stipulated that projects have 'a clear provision to favour real participation of previously disadvantaged individuals' (EUD 2016). In addition to selecting students based on their less favourable socio-economic status, the projects were expected to 'give preference to the selection of students coming from historically disadvantaged institutions' (ibid.). The programme's gender focus, on the other hand, was mainly designed to support horizontal EU policies, particularly by 'promoting equality between men and women and contributing to combating all forms of discrimination based on gender, racial or ethnic origin, religion or belief, disability, age or sexual orientation' (EUD 2016). It also related to South Africa's policy on designated groups. In focusing on both socio-economic status and gender, the EMA2 programme supported South Africa's government policy to increase and broaden participation in HE as part of the sector's transformation process. This included overcoming a 'historically determined pattern of fragmentation, inequality and inefficiency' by, among other things, increasing 'access for black, women, disabled and mature students' (DoE 1997).

The EMA2 projects in South Africa did well overall in terms of social inclusion in the two categories that are part of this discussion. As far as their socio-economic status is concerned, the majority of beneficiaries represented previously disadvantaged groups. More specifically, the beneficiaries included 442 (53%) previously disadvantaged individuals, 357 not previously disadvantaged individuals and 28 beneficiaries whose status was not specified (EUD 2016). Regarding gender, the majority of beneficiaries were female. More precisely, 467 beneficiaries (56%) were female and 360 beneficiaries were male (ibid.). The programme objective of achieving a gender balance was therefore generally achieved and, in most projects, slightly exceeded. Out of the 14 projects, only two 'had more male than female beneficiaries, and only by a very small margin' (EUD 2016). The total percentage of female beneficiaries mirrors female participation in South African HE, where, on average, women made up 58 per cent of headcount enrolments at the country's HEIs between 2012 and 2017 (CHE 2019).

Age is an inclusion dimension that has so far not been elaborated on, mainly because it was not an explicit concern in the context of the EMA2 programme in South Africa. However, since this chapter is part of a book that focusses on youth, particularly on young people aged between 16 and 29, it is noted in that regard that the application procedures for EMA2 projects in South Africa did not stipulate an age limit, and the age of beneficiaries is neither captured in relevant documents such as final project reports nor in the EMA2 overview complied by the EU delegation.

Despite the lack of clear statistical evidence, it is believed that young South Africans aged 16–29 years benefited from EMA2 opportunities. This belief is based on two main assumptions: Firstly, it seems reasonable to assume that the majority of 16–29 year olds were part of the beneficiaries receiving funding for studies at Masters level. Masters students were in fact the biggest cohort, making up 50 per cent of all beneficiaries. This is supported by findings of the EMA2 tracer and impact study, which noted that 'Most of the respondents over 30 years are enrolled in PhD programmes' (Kotzé and Lenssen 2015). Secondly, it is assumed that the age breakdown of the cohorts included in the tracer and impact study is indicative of the EMA2 beneficiaries overall. Out of the 188 beneficiaries who responded to and completed the survey conducted as part of the study, 183 indicated their age. The majority of respondents (65%) fall into the age group of up to 29 years (Kotzé and Lenssen 2015). It is clear that this figure cannot simply be extrapolated to the total number of beneficiaries. However, given the representation of young people in the tracer and impact study, it indicates that, as a trend, young South Africans are likely to have benefitted significantly from opportunities provided in the context of the EMA2 programme.

Lessons Learnt

This section is a reflection on what can be learnt from the EMA2 programme in South Africa, focusing on aspects of inclusivity related to both institutions and individuals. Regarding the latter, gender and socio-economic background of the beneficiaries, as described earlier, are the main areas of interest. In sharing the lessons learnt, the section draws on relevant findings of the EMA2 tracer and impact study. It also incorporates insights from the final reports of the *Ema2sa* project, which were submitted to the EU's Education, Audiovisual and Culture Executive Agency (EACEA) in 2014, 2015 and 2017, respectively. These are worth being included as 'first-hand' evidence of a project that, coordinated by KU Leuven, participated in three rounds of the EMA2 programme in South Africa and benefitted the second highest number (22%) of beneficiaries of the programme overall.

Inclusion of Institutions

In the broader context of inclusivity, it is worth noting that the inclusion of both HAIs and HDIs in the EMA2 programme brought about an unintended benefit, as participating institutions 'learned a lot through it, especially about each other's institutions. This is a particularly significant outcome in a country with a history of a very diverse, historically divided higher education sector, where universities often lived almost in parallel universes (Kotzé and Lenssen 2015). By learning 'how to [delicately] balance the self-interest of one's own institution with the need to act collectively to ensure the best possible outcome' (Kotzé and Lenssen 2015), the EMA2 institutions have made a contribution to building a more inclusive HE sector in South Africa.

As previously indicated, the inclusion of HDIs was an eligibility criterion for EMA2 consortia, and HDIs made up half of the South African institutions participating in the programme. However, it was also pointed out that HDI participation in terms of the number of beneficiaries was very uneven across the projects. This suggests that while HDIs were given the opportunity to participate in the programme, this did not necessarily translate into the institutions being able to equally share the benefits offered by it. For participation to be beneficial, it needs to be aligned to institutional strategy and backed by institutional capacity and resources for programme implementation.

While it is generally assumed that HAIs are 'better equipped, resourced and experienced to successfully participate in the programme' (EUD 2016), two HDIs, namely the University of the Western Cape (UWC) and the Cape Peninsula

University of Technology (CPUT), were very successful in taking part in EMA2 projects and outperformed some of their previously advantaged counterparts (ibid.). As highlighted by the EU delegation, 'There is a clear need for enhanced efforts to increase the involvement of HDIs in future actions and lessons can be learned from the success of CPUT and UWC' (EUD 2016). The findings presented in the tracer and impact study provide some indication as to why these two institutions participated so successfully in the EMA2 programme, highlighting that they developed targeted approaches to strategically align the programme to meet institutional development needs. CPUT, for example, 'decided to utilise the opportunities offered by EM solely to develop and improve the level of academic qualifications of their staff—both academic and professional support staff' (Kotzé and Lenssen 2015). AT UWC, on the other hand, involvement in the EMA2 programme was aimed at 'strengthening the university's research niche areas as important domains for post graduate education' as well as at advancing previously disadvantaged students (Kotzé and Lenssen 2015). As noted in the final *Ema2sa* project report (KU Leuven 2017, personal communication), both universities gained a lot through their early participation in the *Ema2sa* project. Starting as first-time partners in the first round of the EMA2 programme, their management and implementation capacities were strengthened in such a way that they were able to take on the role of South African co-coordinating institutions in later rounds of the programme.

Inclusion of Individuals

Broadening of access and participation of designated groups is considered a success of the EMA2 programme in South Africa. As far as the equal participation of women is concerned, it was indicated earlier that the majority (56%) of beneficiaries were female, in line with overall female enrolments in HE. In South Africa, it is not uncommon that female students, particularly at postgraduate level, have dependants such as children, siblings and other family members. However, the EMA2 scholarships did not make provision for family support and did not, for example, include allowances for childcare. This was highlighted as a factor negatively affecting the recruitment of more female candidates (KU Leuven 2014, personal communication).

Regarding socio-economic status, more than half (53%) of the beneficiaries were from previously disadvantaged backgrounds. For these individuals, the programme created unique opportunities that were previously unimaginable and often described as 'a dream come true' (Kotzé and Lenssen 2015). Supporting the programme's overall mission of broadening participation by 'guaranteeing vulnerable groups access to the grant system' was considered one of the major results of the *Ema2sa* project, especially in comparison to other international scholarships that were often perceived as elitist and exclusive (KU Leuven 2014, personal communication). While the majority of South African EMA2 beneficiaries were previously disadvantaged, it is important to note that participation overall was still imbalanced, as the percentage of previously disadvantaged beneficiaries did not adequately reflect the percentage of previously disadvantaged individuals in the overall population (EUD 2016). Therefore, the 'objective of a balanced representation of SA population groups has not yet been achieved' (Kotzé and Lenssen 2015).

As noted in the final reports of the *Ema2sa* project, low uptake of scholarship opportunities by candidates from previously disadvantaged backgrounds was a major challenge consistently faced by the consortium (KU Leuven 2014, personal communication). Identifying and supporting candidates from disadvantaged groups therefore required considerable efforts on behalf of the participating institutions, especially those in South Africa. Generally, inadequate applicant numbers were a challenge faced by institutions across all projects. Barriers to mobility, particularly at student level, were reported as findings of the EMA2 tracer and impact study. In the sections that follow, these barriers will be discussed in relation to national, institutional and individual factors.

At the national level, the pool of potential applicants for the EMA2 programme was small due to a low percentage of postgraduate students in South Africa as well as relatively high numbers of international students enrolled at South African HEIs for postgraduate degrees (Kotzé and Lenssen 2015). Furthermore, a reason for the underrepresentation of particularly black students in the programme is that 'In this small pool there are also not that many black South African post graduate students' (Kotzé and Lenssen 2015). Another explanation why the uptake of EMA2 opportunities was low relates to a 'sense of insularity' in so far as 'South Africa's long international isolation during the apartheid era and its location at the southern end of Africa could be another contributing factor to the fear of travel and the unknown' (Kotzé and Lenssen 2015). This is linked to a general lack of broader, global perspectives in many sectors of South African society (ibid.).

As far as the institutional level is concerned, programme coordinators experienced a reluctance to allow postgraduate students to participate in the EMA2 programme. It was noted that South African HEIs only reluctantly '"release" their post graduate students to participate in international mobility programmes, as they are (a) a rather scarce "commodity" and (b) there is a lot of pressure from the national higher education authorities to produce more post graduates' (Kotzé and Lenssen 2015). In addition, studying abroad is not an integral part of institutional culture. Rather, it is at times resisted as a 'foreign concept,' which is not integrated into common study formats and timeframes. Another factor cited for institutional challenges was the lack of clarity around the role of South African and European supervisors and how they collaborated (Kotzé and Lenssen 2015).

At the individual level, lack of confidence was a major challenge, especially among students from previously disadvantaged backgrounds; and especially those attending HDIs. Such lack of confidence is often expressed as a feeling of being inadequate, where individuals and institutions are perceived as not being good enough to participate in programmes such as EMA2. All of this is linked to the socio-economic background of previously disadvantaged candidates, where high levels of poverty result in, among others, under-preparedness for studies due to inadequate primary and secondary education as well as financial constraints such as dependence on financial aid and family pressure to leave academia and earn an income. Furthermore, previously disadvantaged students usually have 'no precedents of international travel or studying abroad in their immediate families and communities' (Kotzé and Lenssen 2015).

While the mobility barriers have been presented in three broad categories, it is understood that the national, institutional and individual factors discussed here are all interlinked. For example, it has been noted that the awareness of study abroad is generally rather low in South Africa. Lack of awareness of international opportunities might manifest itself as a consequence of academic isolation under apartheid. Similarly, awareness levels are particularly low among previously disadvantaged groups. Again, this is most likely the result of persistent and systematic discrimination and exclusion suffered by these groups during apartheid.

To overcome mobility barriers, institutions had to quite literally go the extra mile. Regarding the *Ema2sa* project, they reported that they set up additional promotion events such as road shows. They also noted the need to provide personal, one-on-one information and guidance for disadvantaged students (KU Leuven 2015, personal communication). Motivating and persuading students to apply required at many institutions the 'intense, often personal involvement of the EM coordinators' (Kotzé and Lenssen 2015). Reportedly, the coordinators even went 'to the extent of meeting with parents and grandparents to help persuade them of the tremendous benefits that await their children should they get the opportunity to do post-graduate studies abroad' (ibid.).

Conclusions

In many ways, the EMA2 programme in South Africa can be considered a success. It has shown how social inclusivity in accessing mobility opportunities can be addressed in the context of international HE cooperation. With a particular focus on redress and access for disadvantaged groups, the programme is also a good practice example of how international mobility opportunities can support local priorities such as national development and transformation. Through alignment to South African priorities and needs, EMA2 projects have contributed to strengthening the postgraduate pipeline and increasing the number of doctoral students and staff, thus helping build the country's next generation of academics.

EMA2 in South Africa provided life changing educational mobility opportunities to individuals, particularly disadvantaged students. However, it was not merely a mobility programme. Through the consortium approach, the programme was used strategically to further advance the internationalization and larger transformation agendas of the country's HEIs. It was also leveraged to facilitate and enhance research collaboration between South African HEIs and their European partners. Apart from building and strengthening linkages with European institutions, South African universities got to collaborate with each other, strengthening the South African HE system by building capacity locally and by enhancing social cohesion.

In this sense, EMA2 brought about transformative experiences for South African people, institutions and society at large.

In the tracer and impact study it was suggested that the EMA2 programme model 'will serve as the framework and legacy for sustained collaboration between South Africa and the EU, as well as improved institutionalisation of internationalisation at South African HEIs' (Kotzé and Lenssen 2015). However, there has not been a similar programme with comparable objectives, size and reach, including Erasmus+. This raises the question of whether, once concluded, the EMA2 programme has been summarily ended and seemingly forgotten. Be that as it may, strategic relations between South Africa and the EU continue unabated, and South African HEIs persistently face challenges in their efforts to transform and internationalize the country's HE sector. Under these circumstances, policy makers, practitioners and scholars in South Africa and the EU alike need to develop new initiatives that respond to these priorities and find ways of building on the successes of the EMA2 programme to sustain and grow what it was able to achieve.

References

Boshoff, H., Jooste, N., & Pillay, D. (2018). SA higher education overview. In *International education association of South Africa, study South Africa – The guide to South African higher education* (17th ed., pp. 23–32). Pretoria: IEASA.

Chasi, S. (2019). North-South partnerships in public higher education: A selected South African case study. PhD thesis, University of the Witwatersrand, Johannesburg.

Council on Higher Education [CHE] (2019). *VitalStats – Public Higher Education 2017.*

Department of Education [DoE]. (1997). *Education white paper 3: A programme for the transformation of higher education. Notice 1196 of 1997.* Pretoria.

Department of Higher Education and Training [DHET]. (2013a). *Report of the Ministerial Committee for the Review of the Funding of Universities.*

Department of Higher Education and Training [DHET]. (2013b). *White paper for post-school education and training – Building an expanded, effective and integrated post-school system.*

DHET. (2017). *Annual report 2016/17.*

DHET. (2019, April 28). *Draft policy framework for internationalisation of higher education in South Africa. Government Gazette,* 622 (40815).

Department of Science and Technology [DST]. (2018). *Draft 2018 white paper on science, technology and innovation.*

European Union Delegation [EUD] to the Republic of South Africa. (2016, July). *An overview of Erasmus Mundus in South Africa.*

Jooste, N. (2007). *10 years of IEASA history.* Durban: IEASA.

Kotzé, H., & Lenssen, R. (2015). *Erasmus Mundus South Africa tracer and impact study. Final Report.*

Statistics South Africa [StatsSA]. (2019). *Education Series Volume V: Higher education and Skills in South Africa, 2017.* Pretoria: Stats SA.

University of the Witwatersrand, Johannesburg [Wits]. (2014). *Faculty of humanities – Draft framed guidance for curriculum internationalisation. Scholarship for Afro-Global Excellence (SAGE).*

Chapter 22
Intra-regional Academic Mobility in Central Asia: The OSCE Academy in Bishkek, Kyrgyzstan

Hélène Syed Zwick

Institutionalised mobility programmes at tertiary-education level have received extensive attention in prior literature. As implied in the preamble to this section of the book, many studies have focused on the Erasmus programme, looking at its role in encouraging participation and inclusion (Teichler 1996, 2004; Ballatore and Ferede 2013; Cairns, 2017, 2019), employability (Bracht et al. 2006; Teichler and Janson 2007), supporting the development of higher education institutions (Beerkens and Vossensteyn 2011) and mediating European identities (Sigalas 2010; Wilson 2011; Jacobone and Moro 2015). However, despite becoming increasingly globalized, Erasmus is not the only form of student mobility in existence, and other institutionalized programmes are gaining prominence outside Europe, including a platform established by the Organization for Security and Cooperation in Europe (OSCE) at its academy in Bishkek, Kyrgyzstan in 2002.[1]

Based in the heart of Central Asia, an area that includes Afghanistan, Kazakhstan, Kyrgyzstan, Tajikistan, Turkmenistan and Uzbekistan, the academy has become the OSCE flagship education initiative in the region, used to promote the organization's commitments in terms of regional cooperation, conflict prevention and good governance. In more practical terms, the academy has enabled each year since its launch around 60 young professionals from the region to benefit academically, linguistically, professionally and culturally from one-year post-graduate education with full scholarship in Bishkek. The initiative aims not only to disseminate high standards in education and facilitate the creation of a Central Asian Higher Education Area but also to foster multicultural dialogue and mutual understanding in a region that is a significant melting pot of ethnic and linguistic groups, with complex political relations between countries and their governments.

H. Syed Zwick (✉)
ESLSCA University Egypt, Cairo, Egypt
e-mail: helene.syed@eslsca.edu.eg

Although neglected in existing student mobility literature, the region is nonetheless dynamic in terms of regional academic mobility. According to the few reliable and updated available sources of data, when Central Asian students decide to study in another Central Asian country, they usually apply for direct entry as free movers, and for a long-term period. These indications support the view that student mobility is worthy of study outside its traditional Anglophone and European centres, with this chapter aiming to contribute an original perspective to ongoing debates in the student mobility and migration research field.

The OSCE Academy in Bishkek

We begin this study by providing readers not familiar with the OSCE or Central Asia with some background information. The OSCE Academy in Bishkek is a public foundation, established in 2002 thanks to a fruitful partnership between the OSCE and the government of the Kyrgyz Republic. The OSCE itself is an intergovernmental organization, with origins in the Helsinki Final Act in 1975 during the Détente period which led to the creation of the conference on security and co-operation in Europe (CSCE). The multilateral platform aimed to promote dialogue and negotiation between 'the West' and the communist bloc and to enhance regional co-operation on conflict prevention, crisis management and post-conflict rehabilitation through relying on and sharing norms, commitments and expertise. To better reflect on its structural nature, the Paris Summit held in November 1990, at the end of the Cold War, changed the status of the CSCE to permanent structures, with institutions and a secretariat, on one side and operational capabilities on the other. In 1994, the CSCE officially became the OSCE. The organization consists today of 57 participating and 11 partner states from Europe, Central Asia and North America.

Among the many branches of activities and interests of the OSCE is education. The organization believes that education has a pivotal place in the promotion of mutual trust, breaking down stereotypes and broadening understanding of universal human rights. In parallel, the government of the Kyrgyz Republic has been providing significant efforts to modernize an educational system which has barely evolved since the end of the Soviet Union more than 20 years ago. In the 1990s, with the collapse of the Soviet Union, Central Asian governments addressed issues differently and on a different path, regarding quality of education and accessibility. Concerned by such issues, and by corrupt practices pervasive at many levels in education systems, the OSCE started considering several regional options in order to be able to play an active and crucial role in education in the region. In this context, the establishment of the OSCE Academy in Bishkek reflects a willingness to concretise the OSCE's commitments in the region in the fields of education and culture, in addition to the programme offices based in Dushanbe (Tajikistan), Bishkek (Kyrgyz Republic) and Astana (Kazakhstan) representing the Kyrgyz government's priorities in education.

The mission of the academy is clearly stated in its status: 'to promote regional cooperation, conflict prevention and good governance in Central Asia through offering postgraduate education, professional training and intellectual exchange.' Our study focuses specifically on the mobility programme offered within the two Masters of Arts (MA) programme. The first MA, launched with the creation of the academy in 2002, is dedicated to Politics and Security, while the second, launched a few years later in 2011, focuses on Economic Governance and Development. Every year, the institution welcomes up to 30 students per programme selected according to their academic achievements, work experience and quality of statement of purpose. Priority is given to applicants coming from the five Central Asian countries (Kyrgyzstan, Kazakhstan, Tajikistan, Uzbekistan and Turkmenistan) but remains open to those coming from any other participating or partner states, including Afghanistan and Mongolia. Afghanistan is not a participating state in the OSCE but a partner. For that reason, only since 2008 has the programme allowed Afghan students to apply. In order to avoid over-representation, quotas per country of origin are applied by the academy. The process of selection is accurately respected and students enrolled receive full scholarship associated with a monthly housing allowance.

Progressively, the academy has built up several local, regional and international partnerships, public and private. Among these, we can mention the Norwegian Institute of International Affairs (NUPI) and the Geneva Centre for Security Policy. Since 2013, the academy has also belonged to the OSCE Network of think tanks and academic institutions, thus confirming its leading position in the region. Additionally, the foundation has started to boost its research trajectory by publishing articles, policy briefs and research papers on issues relevant to its mission, and hosting associate research fellows.

Since its launch, the academy has welcomed more than 450 students. Since 2015/16, an average of 1000 applications per year have been received, slightly more for the MA in Economic Governance and Development than in Politics and Security. For the academic year 2018/19, the academy received more than 2100 applications. The number of applications from both the five central Asian countries on one side, and Afghanistan on the other almost doubled. For the Economic Governance and Development MA, for instance, more than 60 per cent of applications in 2018/19 were from Afghanistan. While interesting, this recent data does not allow us draw any conclusions in terms of trends, mainly because they show an erratic pattern over time, providing additional impetus for conducting our own research.

Methodological Approach

In this study, we aim to present an overview of the main features of this academic mobility programme. To do so, we surveyed alumni of the programme about their opinions and perceptions of the programme. This section of the chapter explains our data collection methodology and outlines the main features of the SWOT analysis used to shape the data analysis.

Data Collection

This study relies on a primary micro-dataset of 72 respondents from a total pool of around 430 Alumni in 2018, who voluntary completed an online survey accessible from 9 October to 15 November 2018 (i.e., a response rate of 17%). A pilot test with five students confirmed a lack of issues in the survey. Written in English, it was shared through social media website pages used by the alumni office of the academy. We chose to survey alumni for two main reasons: firstly, to collect data that integrate socio-demographic and socio-economic indicators to help analyse the participation of these students in the programme and their professional and academic path before and afterwards. Secondly, to focus on their opinions and perceptions of the programme itself as a step in their career and life in general. Besides, since they belong to the alumni community, they have already proven willing to remain related to the activities of the academy. The survey was structured into three main sections, following a brief introduction and consent information. Screening questions were not included since only alumni were targeted through the alumni's office network of the academy. Section "The OSCE Academy in Bishkek" consisted of several socio-economic and socio-demographic questions; questions about age, gender, birth country and nationality. Section "Methodological Approach" was dedicated to the academic and professional path of the respondent before and after studying at the academy, while section "SWOT Analysis and Discussion" targeted his/her opinions about experiences at the academy.

Following the survey, we decided to conduct semi-structured interviews with respondents drawn from the sample. In order to not guide their answers, we did not use the words 'weakness', 'strength', 'opportunity' and 'threat' either during the interviews or in the survey. A total of 16 interviews were eventually conducted. We selected alumni from each participating country to have a wide range of perspectives. However, this sample does not intend to be representative of the pool of alumni and the views expressed in this study do not necessarily reflect those of the whole pool. Additionally, due to space considerations, only pertinent information from the interviews is included at appropriate points in the discussion. Anonymity and confidentiality were maintained as ethical good practice.

We decided to analyse the data collected from the survey and the interviews by relying on a SWOT analysis. Such a technique is a strategic planning tool used to assess the strengths (S), weaknesses (W), opportunities (O) and threats (T) of any institution or organisation. Used originally in the 1960s by Humphrey, this participatory method may help provide a simplified but useful picture of the actors, dilemmas and opportunities involved, and on the choices to be made. Furthermore, the rich information given and discussed may help identify good practices and match the resources and capabilities to the competitive environment in which the institution operates.

Strengths and weaknesses are primarily internal factors and attributes; in our case, relating to the OSCE Academy. While strengths involve features and abilities through which the institution gains a competitive advantage over others, weaknesses may have the potential to lead the institution into inefficiency and ineffectiveness. Similarly, opportunities and threats are external factors and attributes of the environment. Opportunities can be exploited by the academy to its advantage, while threats can harm it. When carrying out a SWOT analysis, it should be clarified what the limitations can be. Such are provided by Leiber et al. (2018). The analysis was performed in three phases: first, a content analysis of answers given by our respondents was conducted; second, commonalities were identified across the responses; and third, the analysis was complemented by insights from the interviewees.

SWOT Analysis and Discussion

This section of the chapter analyses and structures the answers provided by the alumni respondents, centred around the four dimensions of the SWOT approach; that is, strengths, weaknesses, opportunities and threats.

High Standards in Education and Social Inclusion

Respondents, in answering the question 'from your point of view, what are the main strengths of the programme?' mainly focused their answers on the traditional factors that pushed them to leave their origin country and study abroad. One Tajik alumnus explains:

> I did not study in Tajikistan because of two main reasons: corruption and weak educational system. I think the education system in origin countries matters, when we look at student mobility. I also believe that I would have stayed in my home country to study if we had similar academic institutions.

This respondent indirectly refers to the constrained-schooling thesis which appeared in 1970s and 1980s in literature to explain motivations for overseas studies. According to this thesis, students study abroad because they lack study and training opportunities in their origin country (Lee and Tan 1984; Cummings 1984). Fees might be too high or the tertiary education supply too low (in quantity or in quality). It therefore assumes that there is a negative relationship between tertiary education supply and student outflows (see Chen 2007).

As readers might assume, this thesis was grounded in the emergence of Africa and Asia as post-colonial and origin countries of mobile students. In our case, the fact that tertiary education supply is limited in the origin country of the alumni was an important to very important factor for more than 70 per cent of Afghan, Tajik and Uzbek respondents. Interestingly, the cost of tertiary education supply appears in their answers as a non-essential factor for most respondents, irrespective of their origin country. On average, up to one-third consider this dimension a secondary reason for studying at the academy. In the same vein, the fact that full scholarship is provided appears a primary factor only for Tajik respondents, while it remains at the margins for the other nationalities.

Associated with the constrained schooling factor is the high reputation in the region that the academy built up over the years. A Tajik Alumna points out: 'I chose to study at the academy mainly because of its standing and the academic standards of some of the professors.' This respondent draws our attention to the academy's reputation. The institution has succeeded in establishing credibility based on the evidence of a corruption-free system of degrees and credentials, even subject to external verification. Such a transformation in the 2000s confirmed the profound rupture with the higher education system under the Soviet Union, which was characterised by tight control by central authorities and low standards in education.

The academy also succeeded in introducing new curricula, textbooks, pedagogies and even a new language of instruction. In terms of curricula, political science and economics, as well as journalism or sociology were not taught, unknown by the population at that time. Teaching officially in English also appears as a deep transformation in a region where Russian was the predominant language of instruction. In that sense, the academy attracts students from all over the region. A Kazakh alumnus confirms this aspect: 'Academic freedom was one of the comparative advantages over many other universities in the region.'

The second strength highlighted by most of alumni respondents relates to multiculturalism. A Kyrgyz alumnus admits, 'I think multicultural environment is the key of success in the Academy,' while an Uzbek alumna explains:

> Studying in a multicultural environment is highly essential as I can meet people with different knowledge, mindset and behaviour. I learnt from them, I studied their culture and I exchanged ideas. Moreover, I got very motivated to study along with them. I was interested in their abilities, their behaviour under different circumstances, their consistency and way of studying. Then, I was able to distinguish which origin country's youth is more determined, more successful and smarter.

The presence of several distinct cultural or ethnic groups within the academy seems to be of particular importance for respondents. The young generations do not know each other particularly well within the region. This is for two main reasons. First, ethnic groups tend to live in communities within each country and across countries within each region; national governments have variously tended to promote aggressive nationalist ideas in an authoritarian context which does not contribute to an opening-up to other cultures. Second, our survey shows that the 'mobility capital' of our respondents enrolled at the academy is on average considerably low. This term, introduced by Murphy-Lejeune (2002), refers to the past mobility experience of an individual (see also Cairns 2021a, 2021b in this book). Two-thirds of Kazakh respondents do not have any experience of living abroad for a period of at least six months in duration, while more than three-quarters of Tajik and Afghan respondents respectively have only stayed in one country for at least six months before studying in Bishkek. Such a low level of experience in overseas mobility before studying in Bishkek does not provide these students with an opportunity to have stayed in a multicultural environment for a prolonged period of time.

This reflection leads us to the third strength identified by the respondents, which is social inclusion. The programme seems to contribute to reducing social inequality in regard to access, something that mobility programmes like Erasmus has struggled to achieve (Cairns 2017). According to the socio-economic information collected in the survey, a significant proportion of alumni respondents come from socio-economically disadvantaged backgrounds, especially Afghan respondents coming from rural areas. Ethnic minorities are also well represented in student cohorts. The use of quotas is an explicit measure that allows for a consistent representation over time of each nationality. In terms of mobility capital, we also notice that the programme succeeds in attracting students who have never gone abroad before, especially if we exclude the forced cross-national migration of Afghan and Turkmen respondents. Such an achievement can be partly explained by the full tuition scholarship and financial aid support provided to all students for the entire duration of the programme. Still, it is worth mentioning that such a selective process 'naturally' rejects students who did not study in English.

Weaknesses: A Western Side Obsession

Respondents answering the question 'what could the academy improve?' focused their attention on one main point: 65 per cent expressed frustration in terms of internships, traineeships or job opportunities in European countries, or more broadly, in Western countries. A Turkmen alumna explains:

> When I enrolled, I thought that I would benefit from the network of the academy to find an internship and then a job in Austria or in Germany. Unfortunately, this did not happen.

Such answers were common, especially among Kyrgyz and Uzbek Alumni. A Kyrgyz alumna noted:

> It was very important for me to have an internship abroad, in Europe or the US, I considered my studies at the OSCE Academy as the first step towards living abroad or migrating to another country after graduation.

This dimension reflects the role of imagining future migration, an element recently highlighted by Koikkalainen and Kyle (2016). These authors explain how cognitive migration, defined as the narrative imagining and visualising of oneself as settled in a foreign destination before migrating, influences migration behaviour. In Central Asian countries, communities are characterized by a historical culture of migration to Russia and to European countries. Migration within the region became a norm and aspirations to migrate are therefore transmitted across generations and between people through social networks (Kandel and Massey 2002). An Afghan alumnus confirms:

> My friends told me that applying to the Masters at the academy would be the royal path to western countries. My parents supported this view and pushed me to apply. Once there, I realized that this would not be the case and that maybe I could be useful in my own country.

The concept of self-efficacy applied to migration (Syed Zwick 2019a; 2019b; 2021) provides us with a holistic explanation of such obsession. Self-efficacy, initially introduced by Bandura (1977), not only consists of imaginative experience, but also of vicarious experience, observed experience, social persuasion through coaching and feedback, and performance experience, which refers to the past experience of the individual. In our case, most of our alumni had a high level of self-efficacy that pushed them to believe that migrating to western countries would meet to all their expectations. Not only this, the expected role of the OSCE Academy was misperceived. The academy offers internships in OSCE countries, but it is not able to send its students abroad elsewhere.

Opportunities: Networking and Partnering

Respondents in answering the question 'what interesting trends are you aware of?' focused their answers on two main dimensions: partnering and networking. While the first dimension was identified by 62 per cent of respondents, the second was mentioned by 38 per cent. We believe that both are closely interrelated and have therefore decided to discuss them in this subsection together. A Kyrgyz alumna stated:

> The academy became a reputable institution in the region. […] I think now that it is well established, it needs to develop and improve its network and cooperate more with the public but also private sectors; potential employers in the region but also in other developed OSCE countries.

It also appears that the OSCE Academy started pursuing new opportunities from 2018 onwards to enlarge its network and build new partnerships. For instance, in June 2018 the academy signed a Memorandum of Cooperation with the Riga Graduate School of Law in Latvia. In 2019, at least four more such agreements were signed. In March, a memorandum of cooperation and an agreement of cooperation in the field of academic internships were signed with a German-Kazakh University based in Almaty, Kazakhstan. Two months later, in May 2019, a memorandum of cooperation was signed with Sulkhan-Saba Orbeliani Teaching University in Georgia. Additionally, in June 2019, a Memorandum of Understanding was signed with the Moscow State Institute of International Relations of the Ministry of Foreign Affairs to Russia (MGIMO), which establishes a framework for future cooperation. A month later, in July 2019, an agreement with the University of Valencia in Spain was signed. The objectives are clearly stated in these agreements and include the promotion and fostering of mobility and exchanges of lecturers and students especially through the use of Erasmus+ funding opportunities. In this respect, the academy welcomed its first exchange student from Romania in August 2019 within the Erasmus + framework.

These developments have not passed unnoticed. Interestingly, another comment from a Tadjik alumna indicated the following:

> I see in the international newspapers that we talk more and more about my country or Kyrgyzstan or even Uzbekistan. Everyone talks about the new investments made in the region by the Chinese government. It creates such an enthusiasm that I strongly believe in the development of my region.

The development of the region and its geostrategic location have naturally sparked the interest of international actors like China, India, Turkey and the United States, especially in recent years, with the Chinese Belt and Road Initiative. Such opportunities may therefore continue to arise even more rapidly in the short and medium terms. The EU also renewed its interest in the region with the presentation in July 2019 of a new European strategy on Central Asian and a joint communication entitled, *New Opportunities for a Stronger Partnership* (European Commission 2019). The strategy especially aims to promote investment in youth, education, innovation and culture. In that sense, it implies the potential use of the Erasmus+ programme to help Central Asian universities to modernise and meet the targets of the Bologna process and Torino principles regarding quality assurance and accreditation. It also encourages EU member states' universities to establish more partnerships and branches with Central Asian universities. Such opportunities may also contribute towards international accreditation by quality-assurance agencies from neighbouring countries, like Kazakhstan, which are part of the European Quality Assurance Register for Higher Education.

Threats: A Limited Absorptive Capacity of Local Labour Markets

While talking about the main trends that could be harmful to the programme, most alumni respondents shed light on their difficulties finding a satisfying position after graduation once back in their origin country. Labour market conditions are in this sense the main threat identified, by 68 per cent of our sample. One Tajik alumna points out:

> After graduation I returned to Tajikistan and started searching for jobs, but there were no adequate jobs for my skill set. The employment market in Tajikistan is underdeveloped; employers only need basic [qualifications]. Salary was another disappointment I had, with the average salary of $60. I should not have expected so much.

Similarly, a Turkmen respondent explained that: 'I was one of the students who was not that lucky or quick to find a suitable job position. First months, I was really struggling.' Such responses reflect the narrow absorption capacity of local labour markets in relation to highly educated youth. And such a situation can either lead to unemployment or to educational or skills mismatches.

These potential mismatches between labour supply and demand in terms of qualifications, skills and study fields are of particular importance in the case of our alumni respondents who specialised in economics or political science, with agriculture and trade remaining the most accessible employment spheres for young people making the transition from school to work in the region. These mismatches are also fed by the tertiary educational approach of the Kyrgyz Republic. 64 universities are based in Kyrgyzstan, with 39 based in Bishkek. This number has doubled since 1993 (National Statistical Committee of the Kyrgyz Republic 2019). Data also shows that 50 per cent of youth decide to study at university and most graduates in the region are economists, lawyers and doctors. Such trends naturally cause structural imbalances—a surplus or a shortage—in local labour markets; in Kyrgyzstan and also in neighbouring countries. Quite alarmingly, in her recent study, Jonbekova (2019) talks about a 'diploma disease' in the region. The oversupply of graduates and limited job opportunities, she explains, has led employers to raise the bar for qualifications in selecting job candidates and, ultimately, to a decline in the influence of university credentials on employability.

Conclusion

The OSCE Academy in Bishkek, Kyrgyzstan, offers a unique opportunity for Central Asian youth and to the professionals, to benefit from a high-level educational graduate programme in a multicultural environment with a full one-year scholarship. Such academic mobility within the region not only contributes to the internationalization of higher education as highlighted by Woodfield (2010), which became a priority of governments in its own right, but is beneficial to students and faculty members as well.

Our reflective analysis of the data collected through a survey and semi-structured interviews of alumni is based on a SWOT conceptualization. Analysis of the opinions and perceptions of 72 respondents led us to identify key strengths and weaknesses of the academy, as well as opportunities and threats to its environment. The main conclusion drawn from the analysis is that the academy has solid and structural strengths that can be reinforced if the foundation takes advantage of a wide range of opportunities. These latter opportunities can be easily reframed into possibilities for the academy. It also appears that the main threat, related to local labour markets' capacity to absorb highly qualified young people can be tackled in the medium and long term through the collaborative intervention of public authorities, private actors and civil society. The objective is to promote economic development in the region that can potentially be supported and fastened by the Belt and Road initiative and the renewed roles of international actors like the European Union. Such findings promise a bright future for the OSCE Academy and its wide programme of academic mobility.

Note

1. The author would like to thank the OSCE Academy in Bishkek, Kyrgyzstan, especially Alexander Wolters, Cholpon Osmonalieva, Jazgul Bolot Kyzy and Victoria Orazova for their continued and valuable support.

References

Ballatore, M., & Ferede, M. K. (2013). The Erasmus programme in France, Italy and the United Kingdom: Student mobility as a signal of distinction and privilege. *European Educational Research Journal, 12*(4), 525–533.
Bandura, A. (1977). Self-efficacy: Toward a unifying theory of behavioural change. *Psychological Review, 84*(2), 191.
Beerkens, M., & Vossensteyn, H. (2011). The effect of the Erasmus programme on European higher education. In J. Enders, H. F. de Boer, & D. F. Westerheijden (Eds.), *Reform of higher education in Europe* (pp. 45–62). Rotterdam: Sense Publishers.
Bracht, O., Engel, C., Janson, K., Over, A., Schomburg, H., & Teichler, U. (2006). *The professional value of Erasmus mobility*. Kassel: INCHER.
Cairns, D. (2017). The Erasmus undergraduate exchange programme: A highly qualified success story? *Children's Geography, 15*(6), 728–740.
Cairns, D. (2019). Researching social inclusion in student mobility: Methodological strategies in studying the Erasmus programme. *International Journal of Research & Method in Education, 42*(2), 137–147.
Cairns, D. (2021a). Mobility becoming migration: Understanding youth spatiality in the twenty-first century. In D. Cairns (Ed.), *The Palgrave handbook of youth mobility and educational migration*. Basingstoke: Palgrave Macmillan.
Cairns, D. (2021b). Migration decision-making, mobility capital and reflexive learning. In D. Cairns (Ed.), *The Palgrave handbook of youth mobility and educational migration*. Basingstoke: Palgrave Macmillan.
Chen, L. H. (2007). East-Asian students' choice of Canadian graduate schools. *International Journal of Education Advancement, 7*(4), 271–306.
Cummings, W. K. (1984). Going overseas for higher education: The Asian experience. In E. G. Barber, P. G. Altbach, & R. G. Myers (Eds.), *Bridges to knowledge: Foreign students in comparative perspective* (pp. 130–146). Chicago: University of Chicago Press.
European Commission. (2019). *The European Union and Central Asia: New opportunities for a stronger partnership*. Luxembourg: European Commission.
Jacobone, V., & Moro, G. (2015). Evaluating the impact of the Erasmus programme: Skills and European identity. *Assessment & Evaluation in Higher Education, 40*(2), 309–328.
Jonbekova, D. (2019). The diploma disease in Central Asia: Students' views about purpose of university education in Kazakhstan and Tajikistan. *Studies in Higher Education, 45*(6), 1183–1196.
Kandel, W., & Massey, D. S. (2002). The culture of Mexican migration: A theoretical and empirical analysis. *Social Forces, 80*(3), 981–1004.
Koikkalainen, S., & Kyle, D. (2016). Imagining mobility: The prospective cognition question in migration research. *Journal of Ethnic and Migration Studies, 42*(5), 759–776.
Lee, K. H., & Tan, J. P. (1984). The international flow of third level lesser developed country students to developed countries: Determinants and implications. *Higher Education, 13*, 687–707.
Leiber, T., Stensaker, B., & Harvey, L. C. (2018). Bridging theory and practice of impact evaluation of quality management in higher education institutions: A SWOT analysis. *European Journal of Higher Education, 8*(3), 351–365.

Murphy-Lejeune, E. (2002). *Student mobility and narrative in Europe: The new strangers*. London: Routledge.
National Statistical Committee of the Kyrgyz Republic. (2019). *Education and culture: Dynamic tables*. Retrieved from https://www.stat.kg/ru/statistics/obrazovanie/.
Sigalas, E. (2010). Cross-border mobility and European identity: The effectiveness of intergroup contact during the Erasmus year abroad. *European Union Politics, 11*(2), 241–265.
Syed Zwick, H. (2019a). *Motivation – Opportunity – Ability Nexus: Application to Regional Central Asian Student Mobility*. MPRA working paper No. 93051.
Syed Zwick, H. (2019b). Le modèle de motivation – opportunité – capacité: Application à la mobilité étudiante régionale en Asie centrale. *Journal of International Mobility: Moving for Education, Training and Research, Agency Europe-Education-Formation France, 1*(7): 45–68. https://doi.org/10.3917/jim.007.0045.
Syed Zwick, H. (2021). Egyptian students' disinterest in overseas academic mobility: A behavioural approach based on the capability-opportunity-motivation approach. *Journal of International Students*, 11(2). https://doi.org/10.32674/jis.v11i2.2081.
Teichler, U. (1996). Student mobility in the framework of Erasmus: Findings of an evaluation study. *European Journal of Education, 31*(2), 153–179.
Teichler, U. (2004). Temporary study abroad: The life of Erasmus students. *European Journal of Education, 39*(4), 395–408.
Teichler, U., & Janson, K. (2007). The professional value of temporary study in another European country: Employment and work of former Erasmus students. *Journal of Studies in International Education, 11*(3–4), 486–495.
Wilson, I. (2011). What should we expect of 'Erasmus generations'? *Journal of Common Market Studies, 49*(5), 1113–1140.
Woodfield, S. (2010). Key trends and emerging issues in international student mobility. In F. Maringe & N. Foskett (Eds.), *Globalization and internationalization in higher education: Theoretical, strategic and management perspectives* (pp. 109–123). London: Continuum International Publishing Group.

Chapter 23
South–South Student Mobility: International Students from Portuguese-Speaking Africa in Brazil

Thais França and Beatriz Padilla

As a complex and multi-faceted phenomenon, student mobility involves diverse actors, interests and rationalities. With the globalization of education, universities and other higher education providers have implemented strategies to recruit and attract international students, not least to increase their revenues and levels of internationalization (Findlay et al. 2017). Likewise, destination countries have acknowledged the advantages of hosting international students: financial benefits, an increase in the skilled worker pool and improvements in diplomatic relations (Riaño et al. 2018). Origin countries meanwhile identify student mobility as a means through which talented individuals can become qualified via moving to countries with well-developed higher education system (Findlay 2010). And students themselves, and their families, recognize the potential impact of an international diploma on employability, making them instrumental in establishing educational mobility imperatives at tertiary level (Alberts and Hazen 2005; Holloway et al. 2012).

The combination of these actors' mobility decision-making, a confluence of discourses about the meaning and value of student mobility and the backdrop of global

---

The fieldwork presented here was conducted as part of the project GovDiv multilevel governance of cultural diversity in a comparative perspective: European Union-Latin America project (PIRSES Proposal International Research Staff Exchange Scheme, Grant Agreement 612617 Marie Curie Action. FP7-SP3-PEOPLE_European Commission/7th Framework Programme for Research, Technological Development and Demonstration. 2014–2017).

T. França (✉)
ISCTE – Instituto Universitário de Lisboa (ISCTE-IUL), Centro de Investigação e Estudos de Sociologia, Lisbon, Portugal
e-mail: thais.franca@iscte-iul.pt

B. Padilla
ISCTE – Instituto Universitário de Lisboa (ISCTE-IUL), Centro de Investigação e Estudos de Sociologia, Lisbon, Portugal

University of South Florida, Tampa, FL, USA

inequalities in the distribution of educational opportunities helps explain why students have often travelled from the Global South to the Global North. This helps account for the high number of studies on movement to Anglophone countries and Europe; in particular, Asian students to Anglophone destinations (Riaño et al. 2018; Waters et al. 2011). And despite recent engagement with a broader range of spatial contexts (see, e.g., Chankseliani 2016; França et al. 2018; Kritz 2015; Wilken and Dahlberg 2017), what we know about South–South student mobility remains limited (Daniel 2014; Eyebiyi and Mazzella 2014; Nogueira and Ramos 2014; Rico and Emilia 2015). To address this oversight, this chapter looks at South–South student flows, focusing on the connections generated through colonial legacies. More specifically, the aim is to look at student mobility in Lusophone space: the political, economic, cultural and symbolic space formed by the Portuguese-speaking countries: Angola, Brazil, Cape Verde, East Timor, Guinea Bissau, Equatorial Guinea, Mozambique, Portugal and San Tomé and Principe (Baganha 2009; França et al. 2018).

The example we shall consider concerns the University for International Integration of the Afro-Brazilian Lusophony (UNILAB), located in a small town in the Brazilian north-east region, Redenção. It is a public and federal university that in addition to serving Brazilian students also promotes an innovative student mobility programme, aimed at students from East Timor and African Portuguese-speaking countries. Hence, it fosters a South–South dynamic, contributing to diversify the student mobility landscape. Our research identifies the main features of the experience these students have at UNILAB, considering the specificity of South–South mobility and colonial ties between the countries involved. More specifically, we look at the motivations of these students to choose UNILAB, the role of social and family networks in the mobility of these students, how social class shapes this flow and students' expectations after finishing their undergraduate courses.

Student Mobility in Lusophone Space

As a particular form of migration, student mobility is shaped by a variety of factors: personal ambitions and interests, networks and family influence (Cairns and Smyth 2011; Van Mol and Timmerman 2014), perceptions of the destination country, cost of living, reported quality of university, career chances and labour market development level (Beine et al. 2014; Perkins and Neumayer 2014). Markers of difference, including gender, race and social class, also come into play (Lee and Rice 2007; Sondhi and King 2017), as does the encompassing macro and meso context, especially official migration policies (Findlay 2010; Riaño et al. 2018). We also need to consider political and cultural issues, such as colonial ties and shared language (Perkins and Neumayer 2014; Boerjesson 2017; França et al. 2018), students' own personal desires and interests (Waters et al. 2011; Carlson 2013; Prazeres 2013; Abuosi and Abor 2015; Cairns 2017) and, as Sondhi and King (2017), have argued, how gender norms, relations of privilege, hierarchies and power inequalities within the family and social context shape women's ability to pursue a degree abroad.

In this discussion, we are also concerned with how asymmetric power relations between former metropole and colonies have an impact on student mobility practices. Higher education institutions in the ex-colonies tend to follow a curriculum that mirrors that of the former metropole; however, those located in the colonized territories tend to enjoy less prestige, have fewer globally recognized professors and less modern infrastructure (Boerjesson 2017). Hence, a diploma obtained in the former metropole is still seen as an advantage in the ex-colonies' local labour markets and valued more by society in general. In addition, higher education in the old metropole tends to offer students from ex-colonies special treatment: relatively open entrance systems, reduced fees and exceptional visa policies to increase attractiveness (França et al. 2018). And more generally, a shared colonial past produces relational ties—common language, cultural proximity, a migration precedent—that contributes towards increasing the old metropole's appeal as a destination for students from former colonies (Perkins and Neumayer 2014).

Although there are factors that are transversal to most mobile students, Eyebiyi and Mazzella (2014) highlight the significant differences that exist in the determinants, logics, rationalities and modalities, as well as socio-demographic profiles, personal motivations and study trajectories, of international students from the Global South. For instance, they stress international relations issues such as visa restrictions that tend to limit destination choices. Prazeres (2013) has shown how students from the Global South tend to practice a form of degree-seeking mobility oriented towards developed countries, looking for qualifications that they cannot obtain in their local educational environment. Furthermore, these students are strongly driven by economic factors and human capital demands from their home country, meaning that they will search for countries where they can find better working opportunities and salaries (Wei 2013; Zheng 2014).

Until recently, student mobility in the Lusophone space has received limited attention; however, interest in the topic is increasing, and in the last decade, its flows have become more intense and visible (Fonseca et al. 2016; França et al. 2018). While still under-discussed in comparison with Anglophone student migration (França and Padilla 2019; Nada and Araújo 2018), as Lusophone countries systematically increase their investment in higher education and student mobility platforms, the imperative to study this phenomenon grows. Brazil and Portugal are most prominent in this respect, having relatively solid higher education systems, with some universities now appearing in international rankings and many institutions investing in internationalization (Laus and Morosini 2005; Horta 2009). Angola, Equatorial Guinea and Mozambique are also improving the organizational structures of their universities, while Cape Verde, Guinea-Bissau, St. Tomé and Principe and East-Timor, with their more recently created university systems, have a longer path ahead (Silva 2012; Sani and Oliveira 2015; França et al. 2018).

Student mobility to Brazil has grown significantly in the last decade, although still limited in scope (Ojima et al. 2014). In 2017/2018, international students represented 0.19 per cent of enrolments at Brazilian higher education institutions; in

Portugal, for the same period, this number was 4.4 per cent (DGEEC 2018; INEP 2018). Initiatives to attract students to Brazil can be traced back to 1965, when the Programme Student-Management Agreement (PEC-G) was created by the Brazilian government (Leal and Moraes 2018). This was the first official programme, which still exists, to sponsor students from developing countries with which Brazil maintains cooperation protocols to complete their undergraduate education in a Brazilian higher education institution. It enforces the mandatory return to the home country after the end of the course to ensure a contribution to the development of the country of origin (Leal and Moraes 2018).

Student mobility to Brazil is also shaped by diplomatic relations with other Latin American countries. For instance, in 2000, as a member of the Association of Universities of the Montevideo Group—a university network formed by 28 public universities from Argentina, Bolivia, Brazil Chile, Paraguay and Uruguay—Brazil joined the ESCALA estudantil mobility programme (Nogueira and Ramos 2014). Its main goal is to foster regional cooperation through student mobility and to promote a high-quality international education for the enrolled students. Furthermore, in 2006, the Southern Common Market, MERCOSUR—an economic and political regional block formed by Argentina, Brazil, Paraguay and Uruguay—launched the Mercosur Regional Academic Mobility Programme (MARCA), a cooperation scheme that fosters student mobility among its member states (Sandoval and Krawczyk 2012).[1] The signing of an increased number of academic and bilateral cooperation agreements between Brazil and Portugal in 2000 also translated into an intensification of the flow of Portuguese students to Brazilian universities (França et al. 2018). In regard to impetus, the economic crises that hit Portugal in 2008, aggravated in the period 2011–2014 with the implementation of austerity measures, contributed in particular to many Portuguese students seeking to leave for different opportunities abroad, including Brazil (Cerdeira et al. 2016).[2]

UNILAB: History and Key Facts

UNILAB was created in 2008 in the context of the Brazilian international relations expansion during the second mandate of President Lula da Silva (UNILAB 2017). For historical, geographical, political and symbolic reasons, the university's main building and first campus are situated in the north-eastern state of Ceará, in Redenção a town 72 kilometers from the state capital, Fortaleza. Two other campuses were opened in 2012 in Acarape, a town next to Redenção, and in 2013, another two campus in São Francisco do Conde, in the state of Bahia (UNILAB 2017).[3]

Like the PEC-G programme, UNILAB is a South–South cooperation experience, following the UNESCO global recommendation of increasing the offer of higher education courses to African countries (UNILAB 2013). The difference between these two initiatives is that the latter is based on the principle of a strong commitment to receiving students from the Portuguese-speaking (or PALOP) countries, while the former is a programme attracting students from the Global South in universities across Brazil. UNILAB's mission is to generate human resources that promote the integration of Brazil and the other CPLP member states, especially those in Africa, through regional development and cultural, scientific and educational exchange (UNILAB 2017). As UNILAB is committed to support development through South–South cooperation, undergraduate and graduate courses are developed taking into account common interests between Brazil and partner countries. Thus, social and economic development are privileged: for example, agriculture, community health, education, public management and sustainable development and technology (UNILAB 2013).

The admission process for CPLP's students is entirely managed by the Brazilian government through selective exams. In doing so, UNILAB reserves 50 per cent of its vacancies for Brazilian students and 50 per cent for students from PALOP countries and East-Timor (UNILAB 2013), although this target has never actually been reached. From its inception until 2017, Brazilians have comprised the majority of enrolled students (77%). The other 23 per cent are distributed unevenly, with students from Guinea-Bissau comprising the second largest group with 14 per cent. After students are selected, and after their arrival in Brazil, UNILAB provides free accommodation while the legal procedures are sorted and a three-month welcoming and integration programme to guide and support students in academic life, accommodation, legal procedures and academic registrations (UNILAB 2013). The welcoming programme starts right after registration is confirmed, when students are still in their home countries, using virtual tools (UNILAB 2013). In addition, the university offers financial aid programmes to CPLP students to pay for housing, food and maintenance.

Methodology

To explore this issue, fieldwork was conducted exclusively in the two campuses of UNILAB-Redenção, over the period of April–May 2018. After initial contact, formal authorizations were requested and granted to conduct research on the premises. The qualitative methodology adopted involved two different techniques carried out simultaneously: participant observation and in-depth interviews with 35 undergraduate international students (12 women, 23 men); 28 Brazilian students (16 women, 12 men) and ten UNILAB staff, including professors, psychologists and a former vice-rector. The students' interview questions focused on their motivations, perceived advantages/disadvantages of studying at UNILAB and return plans. This was an opportunity for students to tell their own stories, highlighting what is important for them at UNILAB, and express their own perceptions about their experiences. Recruitment was carried out using a variety of ways: suggestions by colleagues or staff in UNILAB, snowballing and open invitations during participant observation activities.

Participant observation took place during classes, in discussion groups, cultural events and at social activities; for example, lunch at the university refectory, bus rides between campuses and class breaks, allowing the researchers to grasp how social relations take place in a specific context (see de Pina Cabral 1983; Padilla 2017). Informed verbal consent about the interview procedure—recording and transcription—was requested and identity confidentially was explained before the interview took place, with pseudonyms used in this discussion. For the purpose of this chapter, only the interviews with international students are analysed.

Since gender balance among UNILAB's international students is unequal, males representing 59 per cent (UNILAB 2017), the gender imbalance of the sample (23 males and 12 females) was also uneven. Nationality representation was also sought. However, it was not possible to interview students from East Timor. Since 2013, the Brazilian and East Timorese Ministries of Education have had disagreements on how the exchange programme was being developed, leading to retaliations from both sides that resulted in limitations on the number of East Timorese students. And as Equatorial Guinea only officially joined the CPLP in 2014, UNILAB is still concluding its cooperation and diplomatic agreements, meaning no student from this country has as yet enrolled at the university.

Motivations

The question that opened the interview focused on the reasons to study at UNILAB. Although, some variations on the students' responses were found, motivations were very similar: the opportunity to access better education, the chance to contribute to their home countries development upon return and personal growth. For example, in 2015, Vieira arrived at UNILAB to study sociology:

> The decision to come had to do with my desire to attend the university, getting a degree that would help me to find a good job in the future, in my country. I saw in UNILAB a good opportunity, because I would learn about a different country, I could get to know more about the world. And UNILAB is a Brazilian federal university, which has some prestige in Guinea. I thought it would give me a better qualification than if I stayed in Guinea, for example. (Vieira, male, 24 years old, Guinea-Bissau)

Agualusa's decision to move to Brazil to study nursing in 2014 was driven by similar reasons:

> There were many reasons that brought me to UNILAB, if I have to answer very straightforward. I would say it was the desire to leave the country, the possibility of the scholarship and the common language. I always thought that having a diploma from another country, especially a country like Brazil, would help me to find a job when I return to Angola; with the scholarship I wouldn't have to worry about working to have money to pay for my education and studying in Portuguese would be much easier than if I had to learn English, German or French and in addition still study the subjects for my nurse classes. (Agualusa, male, 26 years old, Angola)

Vieira and Agualusa's main motivations to join UNILAB are similar: the opportunity to study at a Brazilian public university and stand out from stay-at-home co-nationals through having a diploma from a well-renowned country. In both cases, as identified in prior literature (Waters and Brooks 2010; Cairns and Smyth 2011; Findlay et al. 2012), pursuing an overseas degree is identified as an opportunity to gain academic and social capital to boost career opportunities.

Speaking a common language is another consideration that influences students' motivations to choose UNILAB. Language can be a driver of student mobility in two different ways: the possibility to learn or improve a different language from their own, especially English (Waters and Leung 2013), and the convenience of sharing the same language, usually due to a colonial past, helping the adaptation and learning processes (Waters et al. 2011; Perkins and Neumayer 2014; Boerjesson 2017; França et al. 2018). Although, there are differences between spoken and written Portuguese in Brazil and the PALOP countries, communication can normally be accomplished (Fonseca 2013). However, some of the hierarchies between variations of the Portuguese language support discriminatory and racist practices towards students from African countries at UNILAB (Souza and Muniz 2017; França and Padilla, forthcoming).

Existing Networks

Other students explained that their decision to join UNILAB was strongly influenced by the fact that they already had friends and/or family at the university.

> I heard about UNILAB through a friend who was already here; he always said it was a great experience. He was part of one of the first groups who came in 2012 and now he is doing his Masters in Recife. He helped me through the whole process by sending me the links that I needed to find all the information about the dates, exams and the courses to choose. By the time I arrived here, I felt I already knew how things were, because we talked a lot about it (…) when I got here, he also helped me to find a house and solve all the visa issues with the federal police [Brazilian authority responsible for the visa process]. (Lito, male, 21 years old, Mozambique)

> My brother was already here, he came two years ago. Then, my father thought it would be a good idea if I join him in Brazil. And I also wanted to be with him, it is also important having family around. (…) He helped me with everything I needed to know, we talked about the entrance exams, the documents I would need to present, which courses I could take. He even spoke to a professor to gather more information about the course I was interested in… how it would be when I arrived. If it was not for him, I would have left, my first months were awful! (Pauline, female, 20 years old, São Tomé and Príncipe)

The two cases above illustrate how social networks and kinship play a major role in the decision to study in Brazil, in providing crucial information and/or assisting people upon arrival and during the integration process (see also Beech 2015). The presence of social ties encourages other members to move, with the promise of support upon arrival, lowering the risk of migration failure. This helps explain why theories on network and cumulative causes of migrations have argued that the growth of migrant communities in a given destination increases the likelihood other community members will move to that country (Fussel 2010: 162). Hence, the presence of students from the same country of origin contributes to attracting more co-nationals, as the latter can rely on the former for information about the selection process, the quality of the university, housing, visa requirements and familiarization with student life in the new country. This information gives them confidence to go abroad, minimizing fears of the unknown.

A 'second best' Choice?

Another relevant aspect identified in the interviews was that in many cases, an institution of choice was not attainable, with UNILAB seen an alternative.

> I always dreamt of going to the University of Coimbra in Portugal to study law, but it was not possible for me to go as my parents could not afford it. I was accepted at the university, but it was way too expensive. Because of that, I missed a full year. So, a friend of mine who was here told me that UNILAB's selection process was open and explained me that it was a public university and that I could even get some subventions. So, I changed my mind and I decided to come here to study public administration. And now I don't think about going there (Portugal) anymore. (Adelino, male 27 years old, Mozambique)

> I was ready to go to Portugal, but I had a problem with my visa, that was not ready when it was supposed to be. I was going to a university in Lisbon, but I can't remember the name. Because of that (the problem with the visa), I would have to miss a whole year at the university and then I thought it was not worth it. This was when I heard that UNILAB was opening its selection process, as my sister told me. And the bureaucracy was much simpler and I could start my classes very soon, so I decided to come here. Maybe I can go to Portugal for a Masters. But now, I am here. (Djanina, female 23 years old, Angola)

These narratives bring to the forefront the influence and prestige that Portuguese universities have in the eyes of students from the former colonies. Different authors have discussed how colonial ties continue to impact on the directions of international students (Madge et al. 2009; Perkins and Neumayer 2014; Boerjesson 2017; França et al. 2018). In some countries, obtaining a degree from a higher education institution from the former metropole is seen as highly prestigious and an advantage in achieving a better position in the labour market. Furthermore, the ex-metropoles tend to have special entry conditions for students from the former colonies, which together with the influence of existing social and kinship migration network, reinforces postcolonial flows (Perkins and Neumayer 2014; França et al. 2018). Therefore, attending a Brazilian university was not always the first choice, but UNILAB became an alternative when financial or academic constraints surfaced.

Future

When asked about their plans for the future, PALOP students declared their intention to return to their home countries.

I want to go back to St. Tomé and work as an agronomist. St. Tome has the world's most diverse biosphere. We are very rich in natural resources. So, I want to go back there and help to develop my country. There is so much that can be done and we don't do it because we don't know how. And now that I have contacts here in Brazil, it is easier to do things there. (Semedo, male 22 years old, São Tomé and Príncipe)

I still want to take a Masters course so I can learn more about public administration and then go back to my country. My idea is that with all I have learnt here already, and I can still learn, I will be able to do many things for my country. With my qualifications, it will be easier for me to get a job in the public sector. I believe if we have better public administration procedures, things in Mozambique could change. (Santiago, male, 24 years old, Mozambique)

Returning to the home country is a fairly common intention among the students from Africa at UNILAB. In general, the interviewees stated their intention to go back to their home countries; however, some mentioned uncertainty about their plans. The students who were willing to postpone their return justified this by stating their interest in pursuing a masters-level course, with the purpose of acquiring extra qualifications before their return.

Several studies have pointed out that students' desires to go back to their home country have different aspects: personal relationships, especially aging parents or partners who were not able to move; cultural values; better working opportunities at home; unemployment in the host country; low levels of cultural integration (Alberts and Hazen 2005; Geddie 2013; Bijwaard and Wang 2016). Additionally, Waters (2006) and Holloway et al. (2012) discuss how a return plan is driven by the awareness of the difficulty of finding a job in the host country because of the language barrier, bureaucratic issues or a high level of labour market competition. However, in the cases presented here, return intentions seem unrelated to such reasons, which may be more applicable to Anglophone and European contexts. Of greater significance is the chance to use skills to contribute to the development of the home country, constituting a less individualized motivation.

Conclusion

Theorization on student mobility has grown immensely in scale during the last two decades, covering many different features of the phenomenon: macro, meso and micro perspectives, institutions' and states' interests, attraction and retention policies, transition to labour market dynamics, city studentification, students' motivations, aspirations and obstacles, and the role of gender, race/ethnicity and social class in shaping students' experiences. Complementary empirical research on the topic has also made important advances, supported by innovative methodologies, namely biographic narratives, longitudinal approaches, ethnographies and comparative studies. Altogether, this work has contributed to legitimize the importance of student mobility and the internationalization of higher education, and create a better understanding of the diversity of experiences among international students. The majority of studies, however, have focused primarily on mobility dynamics into and within the Global North, especially the Anglophone and European countries. Hence, there is still an enormous gap relating to the Global South that needs to be urgently addressed.

This chapter has attempted to do so through contributing knowledge on this topic, focusing on the experience of PALOP students at UNILAB in Brazil, an example of student mobility following a South-South dynamic. Its significance is multi-faceted. From a macro perspective, UNILAB can be seen as an attempt by the Brazilian state, at the time, to expand its influence over the African continent, especially in Lusophone contexts, competing with the established 'power,' Portugal. At the same time, through analysing the UNILAB experience from students' point of view, our findings are in accordance with mainstream trends emphasizing employability motivations and the value of international experience. Moreover, and also in line with the discussion in prior literature, peer networks also have an important influence in shaping this flow, by encouraging and supporting the decision to move to Brazil.

Despite these similarities, some different features were found, for instance, expectations regarding student mobility as a strategy to foster upward social mobility. In our study, contrary to what the majority of the investigations have argued, the majority of the students were from less privileged backgrounds, in many cases the first in their families to attend university. Moving to Brazil is usually the only or the most suitable option for them to earn a tertiary degree. Students that are well-off tend go to Portugal as they have the means to pay for education in institutions that enjoy higher prestige. Our findings also suggest a different approach regarding return plans. Most African students also declared their intention to return to their home countries in order to contribute to the local and regional development. For this reason, we can argue that South–South mobility experiences might be helping to foster a sense of responsibility towards their home countries.

Notes

1. Venezuela is also a member of MERCUSUR; however, its membership has been suspended since 2017 because of its political situation. Chile, Bolivia, Colombia, Ecuador, Guyana, Peru and Suriname are associated members.
2. The creation of the Community of Portuguese Speaking Countries (CPLP)—a multilateral cooperation forum formed by Portugal, Angola, Brazil, Cape Verde, East Timor, Guinea-Bissau, Equatorial Guinea, Mozambique and S. Tome and Principe—in 1996, created a new international space for further exchange, enriching the possibilities for student mobility between Lusophone countries (França and Padilla 2019).
3. Redenção was the first town in Brazil to abolish slavery in 1883 and Ceará is strategically positioned between Europe and Africa.

References

Abuosi, A. A., & Abor, P. A. (2015). Migration intentions of nursing students in Ghana: Implications for human resource development in the health sector. *Journal of International Migration and Integration, 16*(3), 593–606.

Alberts, H. C., & Hazen, H. D. (2005). 'There are always two voices...': International students' intentions to stay in the United States or return to their home countries. *International Migration, 43*(3), 131–154.

Baganha, M. I. (2009). The Lusophone migratory system: Patterns and trends. *International Migration, 47*(3), 5–20.

Beech, S. E. (2015). International student mobility: The role of social networks. *Social and Cultural Geography, 16*(3), 332–350.

Beine, M., Noël, R., & Ragot, L. (2014). Determinants of the international mobility of students. *Economics of Education Review, 41*, 40–54.

Boerjesson, M. (2017). The global space of international students in 2010. *Journal of Ethnic and Migration Studies, 43*(8), 1256–1275.

Cairns, D. (2017). The Erasmus undergraduate exchange programme: A highly qualified success story? *Children's Geographies, 15*(6), 728–740.

Cairns, D., & Smyth, J. (2011). I wouldn't mind moving actually: Exploring student mobility in Northern Ireland. *International Migration, 49*(2), 135–161.

Cerdeira, L., Cabrito, B., Taylor, M. d. L. M., & Gomes, R. (2016). A fuga de cérebros em Portugal: Hipóteses explicativas. *Revista Brasileira de Política e Administração da Educação – Periódico científico editado pela ANPAE, 31*(2), 409–418.

Chankseliani, M. (2016). Escaping homelands with limited employment and tertiary education opportunities: Outbound student mobility from post-Soviet countries. *Population, Space and Place, 22*(3), 301–316.

Daniel, C. (2014). Construction d'une connexion Sud-Sud à travers l'éducation universitaire: Le cas des étudiants péruviens au Brésil. *Cahiers de La Recherche Sur l'éducation et Les Savoirs, 13*, 119–137.

Eyebiyi, E. P., & Mazzella, S. (2014). Introduction: Observer les mobilités étudiantes Sud-Sud dans l'internationalisation de l'enseignement supérieur. *Cahiers de la recherche sur l'éducation et les savoirs, 13*, 7–24.

Findlay, A. M. (2010). An assessment of supply and demand-side theorizations of international student mobility. *International Migration, 49*, 162–190.

Findlay, A. M., King, R., Smith, F. M., Geddes, A., & Skeldon, R. (2012). World class? An investigation of globalisation, difference and international student mobility. *Transactions of the Institute of British Geographers, 37*(1), 118–131.

Findlay, A., McCollum, D., & Packwood, H. (2017). Marketization, marketing and the production of international student migration. *International Migration, 55*(3), 139–155.

Fonseca, A. M. (2013). Em português nos entendemos? Lusofonia, literatura-mundo e as derivas da escrita. *Configurações. Revista de sociologia, 12*, 105–116.

Fonseca, M. L., Pereira, S., & Iorio, J. (2016). International mobility of Brazilian students to Portugal: The role of the Brazilian government and university strategies in Portugal. In J. Domínguez-Mujica (Ed.), *Global change and human mobility* (pp. 265–284). Cham: Springer.

França, T., & Padilla, B. (2019). Movilidad estudiantil en la CPLP: colonialidad lusófona? In *Geo-estratégia de la internacionalización y espacialidad de las migraciones académicas*. Mexico: UDUAL.

França, T., Alves, E., & Padilla, B. (2018). Portuguese policies fostering international student mobility: A colonial legacy or a new strategy? *Globalisation, Societies and Education, 16*(3), 325–338.

Fussel, E. (2010). The cumulative causation of international migration in Latin America. *The Annals of the American Academy of Political and Social Science, 630*, 162–177.

Holloway, S. L., O'Hara, S. L., & Pimlott-Wilson, H. (2012). Educational mobility and the gendered geography of cultural capital: The case of international student flows between Central Asia and the UK. *Environment and Planning A, 44*(9), 2278–2294.

Horta, H. (2009). Global and national prominent universities: Internationalization, competitiveness and the role of the State. *Higher Education, 58*(3), 387–405.

Kritz, M. M. (2015). International student mobility and tertiary education capacity in Africa. *International Migration, 53*(1), 29–49.

Laus, S., & Morosini, M. C. (2005). Internationalization of higher education in Brazil. In H. de Wit, I. Jaramillo, J. Gacel-Ávila, & J. Knight (Eds.), *Higher education in Latin America. The international dimension* (pp. 118–148). Washington, DC: World Bank.

Leal, F. G., & Moraes, M. C. B. (2018). Brazilian foreign policy, south-south cooperation and higher education. *Educação and Sociedade, 39*(143), 343–359.

Lee, J. J., & Rice, C. (2007). Welcome to America? International student perceptions of discrimination. *Higher Education, 53*(3), 381–409.

Madge, C., Raghuram, P., & Noxolo, P. (2009). Engaged pedagogy and responsibility: A postcolonial analysis of international students. *Geoforum, 40*, 34–45.

Mol, C. V., & Timmerman, C. (2014). Should I stay or should I go? An analysis of the determinants of intra-European student mobility. *Population, Space and Place, 20*(5), 465–479.

Nada, C. I., & Araújo, H. C. (2018). 'When you welcome students without borders, you need a mentality without borders' internationalisation of higher education: Evidence from Portugal. *Studies in Higher Education, 44*(9), 1–14.

Nogueira, M. A., & Ramos, V. (2014). Mobilité des étudiants sud-américains: Le cas du programme ESCALA. *Cahiers de la recherche sur l'éducation et les savoirs, 13*, 97–118.

Ojima, R., Aguirre, M. A. C., da Silva, B. L., & de Lima, W. M. (2014). Migrações internacionais motivadas por estudo: Uma análise sociodemográfica dos estudantes estrangeiros radicados no Brasil. *PerCursos, 15*(28), 166–189.

Perkins, R., & Neumayer, E. (2014). Geographies of educational mobilities: Exploring the uneven flows of international students. *The Geographical Journal, 180*(3), 246–259.

Prazeres, L. (2013). International and intra-national student mobility: Trends, motivations and identity. *Geography Compass, 7*(11), 804–820.

Riaño, Y., van Mol, C., & Raghuram, P. (2018). New directions in studying policies of international student mobility and migration. *Globalisation, Societies and Education, 16*(3), 283–294.

Sani, Q., & Oliveira, M. R. (2015). Educação superior e desenvolvimento na Guiné-Bissau: Contribuições, limites e desafios. *Revista Pedagógica, 16*(33), 127–152.

da Silva, D. B. (2012). As contradições da cooperação técnica em educação Brasil-CPLP: O caso do Timor-Leste. *Carta Internacional, 7*(2), 149–162.

Sondhi, G., & King, R. (2017). Gendering international student migration: An Indian case-study. *Journal of Ethnic and Migration Studies, 43*(8), 1308–1324.

Souza, A. L. S., & Muniz, K. d. S. (2017). Descolonialidade, performance e diáspora africana no interior do Brasil: Sobre transições identitárias e capilares entre estudantes da UNILAB. *Cadernos de Linguagem e Sociedade, 18*(2), 81–101.

UNILAB, U. d. I. I. d. L. A.-B. (2013). *Unilab: Caminhos e Desafios Acadêmicos da Cooperação Sul-Sul*. UNILAB: Redenção.

UNILAB, U. d. I. I. d. L. A.-B. (2017). *Estatuto Universidade da Integração Internacional da Lusofonia Afro Brasileira*. UNILAB: Redenção.

Chapter 24
Mobile and Immobile Students' Characteristics and Programme Choices

Eva Maria Vögtle

A scarcity of centres of learning for young adults has been one of the most prominent reasons for educational mobility in the past. More recently, it is not so much the scarcity of learning opportunities but rather the perceived benefits associated with study-related experiences abroad that have made student mobility desirable, in addition to the acquisition of political significance, particularly within the European Union. Cross-border student mobility has been at the heart of EU educational policies, most visibly, with the Erasmus programme, initiated in 1987, and is an integral part of European Higher Education Area (EHEA) policies, with a target set in 2009 of ensuring 20 per cent of those graduating in the EHEA have had a study or training period abroad (Leuven and Louvain-la-Neuve Communiqué 2009).[1]

The benefits associated with mobility closely relate to graduates' employability (van Mol and Timmerman 2014); opportunities to work in intercultural teams (Di Pietro 2015); a wage premium (Kratz and Netz 2018); and help with pursuing an international career (see, e.g., Parey and Waldinger 2011; Oosterbeek and Webbink 2011). Besides job-related and monetary benefits, study abroad is also believed to benefit personality development (Zimmermann and Neyer 2013) and increase problem-solving skills, flexibility, self-confidence and creativity (Di Pietro 2015). Hence, we can see an engagement with professional development and the emergence of soft skills, closely connected to issues of equity and access to higher education.

Across Europe, attempts have been made to eliminate formal barriers to participation in higher education, regarding gender, as well as for different ethnic and social groups. Education has also been diversified, with higher education institutions following a different model compared to 'traditional' universities. This

---

E. M. Vögtle (✉)
German Centre for Higher Education Research and Science Studies (DZHW),
Hanover, Germany
e-mail: voegtle@dzhw.eu

institutional diversification is often accompanied by an increased degree of stratification within different types of institutions, or individual institutions, with different levels of prestige and, possibly, labour market returns (Arum et al. 2007; Reimer and Jacob 2011; Triventi 2013; Marginson 2016). However, students from disadvantaged backgrounds still tend to disproportionally attend lower prestige higher education institutions (Kwiek 2013; Triventi 2013; Marginson 2016; Brown 2018; IIEP, UNESCO 2017), and due to this stratification, different tracks form, some of which are not accessible to all (Brooks 2008), with negative consequences for social mobility (Smolentseva 2012). One example concerns participation in international mobility, which is highly differentiated according to the type of higher education institution and the field of study within which a study programme is situated (Hauschildt et al. 2018).

Students' educational backgrounds are known to influence the transition to university and decision-making within higher education. Engagement in study-related activities abroad is also influenced by parental higher education background and social selectivity (see Bargel 2006; Lörz and Krawietz 2011; Finger 2013; Middendorff et al. 2013; Lörz et al. 2016; Netz and Finger 2016; Neumeyer and Pietrzyk 2016; Key et al. 2017). Taking this position into account, and using a cross-national comparative approach, this chapter looks at gender disparities, differences according to fields of study, type of higher education institution and parents' educational backgrounds in the analysis to student mobility rates. In addition, an overview of how mobility phases are organised and (primarily) funded is provided.

Data and Methodology

In the following discussion, short-term mobility for educational purposes is analysed using data from the sixth round (2016–2018) of the Eurostudent project, to which 28 countries of the European Higher Education Area (EHEA) have contributed, with students in national study programmes at ISCED levels 5, 6 and 7.[2] In general, the Eurostudent project works with focus groups to allow the identification of certain groups of students based on their socio-demographic characteristics, past and current educational situation and current living situation (Hauschildt et al. 2018: 14). For student mobility, the data takes into account different types of study-related experiences: enrolment abroad/foreign enrolment, internships/work placements, language courses, research stays, summer schools and other study-related experiences abroad, encompassing short-term credit mobility but excluding diploma or degree migration.[3]

The median age (in years) of the student population surveyed ranged from 21 to 26 years old; however, there are cases where respondents were over 29 years of age at the time of survey, but in none of the countries does this constitute the dominant national student population. In addition, the group of students ages 25 and older are known to be the least mobile group (Hauschildt et al. 2018).

Mobility Disparities

To obtain an overall picture of the popularity of mobility during studies within the overall student population in the countries observed, we present an overview of the number of students who, at time of survey, have been abroad for educational purposes compared to those who have not (yet) been abroad. The analyses presented in the following focus on mobility of returning students, that is, students who continued their studies at their home institution after a stay abroad. Figure 24.1 also provides an overview of study-related activities abroad, distinguishing between students who have been enrolled abroad (but might have additionally done an internship and/or other types of study-related activities abroad), students who have at least completed an internship/work placement abroad (but might have also been enrolled abroad or travelled for other types of study-related activities) and students who temporarily went abroad for another educational purpose (e.g., summer school, language course) but do not have an enrolment or internship abroad.

In none of the countries observed did students who had been abroad for any type of study-related activity (including enrolments) constitute a majority of the overall student population. The share of students who have already been abroad during their studies ranges from 10 per cent to around 30 per cent. In slightly more than half of the countries, at least 20 per cent of students currently enrolled in higher education have had some kind of study-related experience abroad, including enrolments and internships. In 60 per cent of the countries, the category of any other type of study-related activity abroad (excluding enrolments and internships) is the most common form of activity. This category contains language courses, research stays, summer schools and other (undefined) study-related experiences abroad.

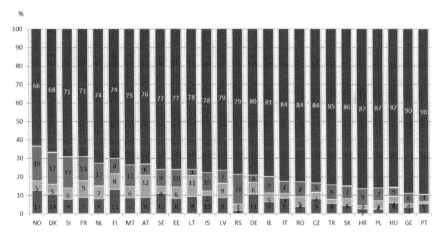

Fig. 24.1 Students' mobility experience (No data for Switzerland (CH)). Share of all students (in %). (Data source: Eurostudent VI)

Age and Gender Differences

Besides the aspects discussed below which impact on the extent to which students participate in international mobility, age is an important predictor for the probability of having been enrolled abroad: the least mobile students are the very young (under 22 years) and those 30 years and over (Hauschildt et al. 2018). Surely related to the latter aspect, student parents are known to be less internationally mobile compared to their peers without children (Vögtle 2019). With regard to gender, we look at students who have been enrolled abroad (binary) by gender in percentage.[4] In only 14 per cent of the countries (Fig. 24.2) did male students form the majority of students who have been enrolled abroad; in the remaining countries, female students tend to enrol abroad to a greater degree than male students. The greatest disparity in this regard is found in Latvia and Slovakia, where over 70 per cent of students enrolled abroad were female.

Variations by Field of Study

The share of students who have been enrolled abroad varies considerably by field of study. Across countries, with some national exceptions, mobility is popular in the arts and humanities, social sciences, journalism and information and business, administration and law fields, where female students also form the majority. The field of study where the smallest shares of students have already been enrolled abroad is Information and Communication Technology Sciences (ICTS). Other than

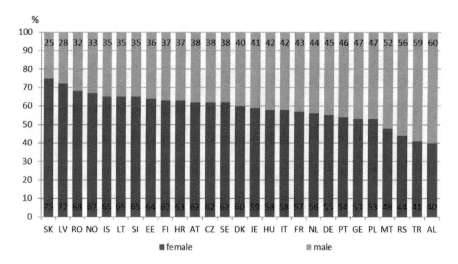

Fig. 24.2 Differences in enrolment abroad by gender. Share of students who have been enrolled abroad (in %). (Data source: Eurostudent VI)

the field of education and teacher training, there seems to be a clear connection between shares of female students and field of study; female students are more likely to enrol abroad compared to their male peers which influences the shares of mobile students in predominantly female fields of study.

Due to the relationship between international mobility experiences and personality development (e.g., Zimmermann and Neyer 2013; Di Pietro 2015), mobility experiences of future educators and teachers are believed to foster skills that they need, since teachers face the challenge to take into account 'the increasing diversity in their classroom' (Gomendio 2017: 13). However, the analysis at hand confirms previous ones that have demonstrated that students of teacher training and education are underrepresented compared to all students when it comes to short-term enrolments abroad (Vögtle 2019), and that largest underrepresentation can be found in countries with a high overall share of students who have been enrolled abroad.

Variations by Type of Higher Education Institution

In Eurostudent, types of higher education institutions are coded binary into universities and non-universities, according to national legislation and understanding. No other type of higher education institutions than university exists in Georgia, Italy, Iceland, Romania, Sweden and Turkey. If a distinction between types of higher education institutions exists within a country, institutions classified as universities are typically allowed to award doctoral degrees. Non-university type of higher education institutions, may, depending on national legislations, include universities of applied sciences, polytechnics and professional higher education institutions.

Across sampled countries, the majority of students are enrolled at universities; the Eurostudent (unweighted) average for enrolment at non-universities is 30 per cent. With regard to enrolment abroad, there are differences in mobility shares between students according to different types of higher education institution. In the vast majority of countries (where different types of higher education institutions exist), university students are more frequently enrolled abroad compared to students at other types of higher education institution. However, this pattern is not apparent in all countries; for example, compared to university students, non-university students have been enrolled abroad to a greater extent in Albania, Austria, France and Malta (Fig. 24.3).[5]

Reasons why we observe this pattern might be related to the fact that the share of part-time students is twice as high among non-university students (30 per cent) compared to university students. Another influential factor for the observed lower mobility rates is that non-university students are dependent on own earnings to a greater extent compared to university students; close to 40 per cent of non-university students are dependent on own earnings in order to afford studying, which constitutes one of the main obstacles to international mobility (Hauschildt et al. 2018).

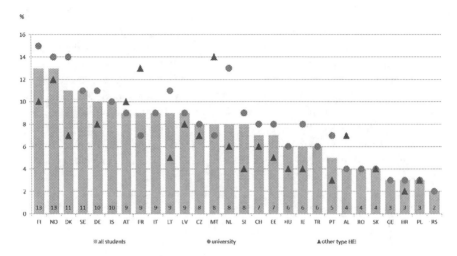

Fig. 24.3 Enrolment abroad by type of higher education institution. Share of students who have been enrolled abroad (in %). (Data source: Eurostudent VI)

Variations by Parents' Educational Background

As the findings of numerous studies have shown (e.g., Bargel 2006; Lörz and Krawietz 2011; Finger 2013; Middendorff et al. 2013; Lörz et al. 2016; Netz and Finger 2016; Neumeyer and Pietrzyk 2016; Key et al. 2017), students' choice of study programmes and formal study status is related to their personal characteristics and background. Previous studies have pointed out that students whose parents are academics perceive themselves to be better prepared for studying abroad due to better schoolgrades, their confidence to succeed in higher education and foreign languageskills. However, causality between higher education background and foreign language proficiency is not straightforward as foreign language proficiency can be both a prerequisite and an outcome of enrolment periods abroad. With regard to language proficiency as an outcome, the benefits of becoming proficient in a foreign language as a result of a studying abroad experience are higher for individuals from low socio-economic backgrounds (Sorrenti 2017).

Another example for the interrelatedness of students' choices and educational background is formal study status. Students without higher education background are more frequently enrolled as part-time students compared to students with higher education background. For Eurostudent countries, the difference in shares between students with and without higher education background is eight percentage points, with larger shares of part-time students within the group of students without higher education background (Hauschildt et al. 2018). Students tend to choose part-time studies when they have to reconcile family and/or professional life with their studies, and having children and/or working are known to be among the main obstacles to international student mobility. Thus, it is not surprising to find a common pattern across countries analysing the educational background of

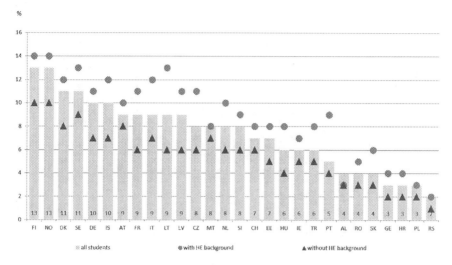

Fig. 24.4 Temporary enrolment abroad by educational background (The binary aggregation of higher education background applied in Eurostudent into 'without higher education background' and 'with higher education background' may obscure the fact that in the different countries, qualifications at the same ISCED level may be regarded to be higher education in one country and vocational training in another. For example, German Master crafts(wo)men vocational qualifications are at ISCED level 6 (professional) in the qualification framework, i.e. equivalent to the level of higher education. However, these types of degrees are not typically regarded to be part of the higher education system in Germany. Austrian Master crafts(wo)men qualifications, in contrast, are at ISCED level 5 (and are nationally not regarded to be higher education either)). Share of students (in %). (Data source: Eurostudent VI)

students who have taken part in a temporary enrolment period abroad: the share of students who have been enrolled abroad is greater for students with higher education background than for students without higher education background in almost all countries (see Fig. 24.4).

Different Uses of Organizational Frameworks for Enrolment Abroad

The organizational framework for students' mobility varies across countries, in particular with regard to funding opportunities. In the majority of countries, students organized their enrolments abroad in the context of EU programmes (see Fig. 24.5). In around a third of all countries, more than three-quarters of students enrolled abroad in the context of an EU programme. In another third of countries other (national, regional, etc.) programmes were used to a greater extent than EU programmes. And in around 18 per cent of countries, relatively high shares of more than a quarter of students organized their enrolment abroad independently.

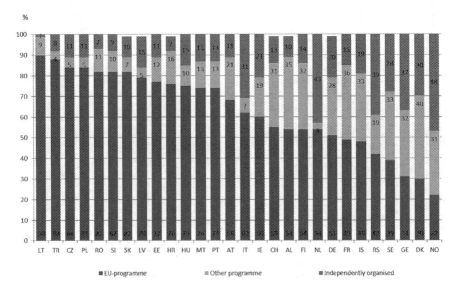

Fig. 24.5 Organisational framework for enrolment abroad. Share of students who have been enrolled abroad (in %). (Data source: Eurostudent VI)

Primary Sources of Funding for Enrolment Abroad

For funding their enrolment abroad, students draw on several different sources: across all countries, the majority of students who have been enrolled abroad used between two and three different sources to finance their enrolment abroad; on average, two-thirds of students receive contributions from parents, family or partner to fund their enrolment abroad (Hauschildt et al. 2018). Looking at the primary source of funding for enrolment abroad (see Fig. 24.6), the biggest primary source of funding are EU study grants in 46 per cent of countries. In a third of countries, at least two-thirds of students drew on public sources to fund their studies abroad and in 18 per cent of countries, more than 50 per cent of students name contributions from parents, family, or partners as their primary source of funding for an enrolment period abroad. More than a quarter of students used their own income from previous jobs or their own savings as primary source of funding for their enrolment period abroad in roughly 15 per cent of countries. Regular study grants/loans from home country constitute the primary source of funding for enrolment abroad in the Scandinavian countries, between 45 to 53 per cent of students state this as their primary source of funding.

Discussion

The mobility patterns of students in Eurostudent countries are quite varied with regard to the extent and types of mobility undertaken. Having been abroad for study-related purposes varies from ten to over 30 per cent between countries, with

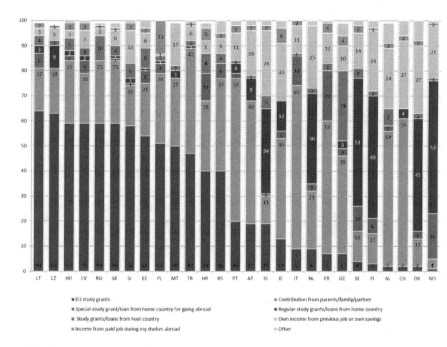

Fig. 24.6 Primary source of funding used for enrolment abroad (No data for Germany (DE). No data for item 'Regular study grants/loans from home country' for Albania, France, Croatia, Italy, Serbia. No data for item 'Special study grant/loan from home country for going abroad' for Austria, Switzerland, the Czech Republic, Malta, Romania, Turkey. No data for item 'Study grants/loans from host country' for Switzerland, Ireland. No data for item 'other' for Italy, Malta, Slovakia). Share of students who have been enrolled abroad (in %). (Data source: Eurostudent VI)

temporary enrolment abroad being the most frequent type of mobility experience. For those students abstaining from study-related activities abroad, financial constraints are the predominant obstacle to mobility, especially for students without parental higher education background or students studying at higher education institutions other than universities. Financial constraints and the need to pursue gainful employment pose one of the main obstacles to mobility (see Middendorff et al. 2013; Hauschildt et al. 2015, 2018; Lörz et al. 2016) currently, almost half of those students who have been enrolled abroad draw on private funds as the main source of funding for enrolments abroad.

In recent years, European Higher Education Area members have started to identify under-represented groups in international student mobility but only some have put in place different measures at the national or institutional level and comprehensive mobility support targeting disadvantaged learners is very rare (European Commission/EACEA/Eurydice 2018). For example, European education ministers have committed to enable the portability of national loans and grants (Berlin Communiqué 2003) and reconfirmed this commitment in the Bergen (2005) and Bucharest (2012) Communiqués, with emphasis on full portability in the latter document. However, the

2018 Bologna Process Implementation Report assessed that there are substantial differences between countries with regard to portability of grants and loans. Unrestricted portability exists only in ten out of fifty[6] higher education systems; in eight higher education systems, all major support schemes are portable for credit as well as degree mobility, but there are various portability restrictions, mainly related to geography (i.e. mobility only towards certain countries). Only in around one-third of all EHEA systems, domestic financial support is portable; countries allowing portability for credit as well as degree mobility are mainly situated in north-western Europe, whereas countries with low or non-existent portability can mainly be found in south-eastern Europe (European Commission/EACEA/Eurydice 2018).

Besides commonalities with regard to parental educational background, cross-country similarities in mobility patterns can also be found with regard to field of study. Mobility rates vary largely across different fields of study and there seems to be a clear connection between shares of female students and field of study. However, the field of education and teacher training is an exemption; previous analyses (Vögtle 2019) have demonstrated that students of teacher training and education are under-represented compared to all students when it comes to short-term enrolment abroad. At first sight, this is surprising considering that female students—who are usually more mobile than their male peers (Hauschildt et al. 2015, 2018)—make up the majority of such students. Taking a closer look at education and teacher training students, in 90 per cent of the observed countries, the share of students' ages 30 years old and older, the shares of student parents, as well as the shares of student whose parents are non-academics is higher for students in the field of education and teacher training compared to the average across the student population (Vögtle 2019). All of these groups are known to be less mobile than their younger/childless peers or those with parents in posession of an academic degree (Hauschildt et al. 2018).

As the example of students in the field of education and teacher training illustrates the socio-economic background of students and the educational choices they make with regard to higher education institutions and study programmes are interrelated. This lends support to the idea that due to increasing stratification within higher education systems, different tracks of higher education foster or block social mobility (Smolentseva 2012), and student mobility remains socially selective in many countries. For the case of students of education and teacher training, mobility experience might enable future teachers to function as a multiplier by positively influencing the attitude of pupils from diverse backgrounds towards international student mobility, thereby also counterbalancing social selectivity patterns of international student mobility. The introduction of mandatory mobility phases into the national curricula of students of teacher training, however, might have unintended consequences for the achievement of policy goals related to equal access opportunities since the shares of 'first generation students' are especially high in the field of education and teacher training. It is a balancing act between opening windows of opportunity for mobility phases and closing doors to groups of students who have just begun to reap the benefits of higher education (Vögtle 2019).

Besides the findings for short-term mobility, students with a higher education background are also more often to be found planning entire degree programmes abroad after the completion of their current Bachelor programme (Hauschildt et al. 2018), pointing towards a process in which degree mobility might come to serve as a new process of distinction. In such processes, students with a higher education background replace practices which have become more common (e.g. temporary enrolment abroad) by more exclusive practices such as degree mobility (Netz and Finger 2016).

Recent developments in European higher education systems are characterised by diversification. A diversified higher education system can offer attractive opportunities for students who may not have otherwise entered higher education at all. However, close attention should be paid to the outcomes of different types of study programmes and higher education institutions to ensure that new inequalities are not created within the higher education systems. For instance, if 'non-traditional' students' access to higher education is more or less restricted to certain types of institutions or degrees, equal access to higher education is clearly only part of the picture. Attention should also be paid to inequalities within the system, for example to social selectivity of student mobility. If funding for mobility periods is not widely available, considering socio-economic criteria in the granting of mobility funds and places might also provide a measure to enhance student mobility for those groups of students who currently benefit from it to a lesser extent.

Notes

1. The 2012 Mobility Strategy adopted in Bucharest specified the 20 per cent quota in that the periods spent abroad shall correspond to at least 15 European Credit Transfer System (ECTS) points or three months within any of the three cycles (credit mobility) as well as stays in which a degree is obtained abroad (degree mobility).
2. Eurostudent is a project that, since a first pilot study in 1994, collates comparable data on the social dimension of European higher education. 28 of the 48 members of the European Higher Education Area participated in the sixth round. The data presented here is based on aggregate data collected from the national contributors; indicators are based on survey responses of more than 320,000 students across Europe. Data was weighted (at least) using population data on sex, age, study programme (BA, MA, etc.), type of higher education institution and field of study. Micro data was not centrally collected, thus differences between countries cannot be tested for statistical significance.
3. Eurostudent data allows the analysis of short-term enrolment from three perspectives: for students who have been mobile, for students planning to go abroad, and for students who do not plan to become cross-nationally mobile.
4. Gender was asked in two ways in the Eurostudent survey, respondents were asked if they are female, male or do not want to assign themselves to one of these categories. Then they were asked with which gender they are registered at their higher education institution and this response was used to assign them to either male or female category used in analyses.
5. In France, the prestigious Grandes Écoles form part of the non-university sector.
6. The Flemish and Walloon higher education system as well as the Scottish are counted separately due to mayor differences at system level.

References

Arum, R., Shavit, Y., & Gamoran, A. (2007). More inclusion than diversion: Expansion, differentiation, and market structure in higher education. In Y. Shavit, R. Arum, & A. Gamoran (Eds.), *Stratification in higher education: A comparative study* (Studies in Social Inequality) (pp. 1–35). Stanford, CA: Stanford University Press.

Bargel, T. (2006). *Soziale Ungleichheit im Hochschulzugang und Studienverlauf*. Konstanz: Universität Konstanz, Geisteswissenschaftliche Sektion, FB Geschichte und Soziologie, Arbeitsgruppe Hochschulforschung. https://nbnresolving.org/urn:nbn:de:0168-ssoar-236632.

Bergen Communiqué. (2005). *The European Higher Education Area—Achieving the goals: Communiqué of the conference of European Ministers responsible for higher education*. Bergen.

Berlin Communiqué. (2003). *Realising the European Higher Education Area: Communiqué of the conference of Ministers responsible for higher education*. Berlin.

Brooks, R. (2008). Accessing higher education: The influence of cultural and social capital on university choice. *Sociology Compass, 2*(4), 1355–1371.

Brown, R. (2018). Higher education and inequality. *Perspectives: Policy and Practice in Higher Education, 22*(2), 37–43.

Bucharest Communiqué. (2012). *Making the most of our potential: Consolidating the European Higher Education Area*. Bucharest.

Di Pietro, G. (2015). Do study abroad programs enhance the employability of graduates? *Education Finance and Policy, 10*(2), 223–243.

European Commission. (2014). *Erasmus impact study*. Luxembourg: Publications Office of the European Union.

European Commission/EACEA/Eurydice. (2018). *The European Higher Education Area in 2018: Bologna Process Implementation Report*. Luxembourg: Publications Office of the European Union.

Finger, C. (2013). Diversität im Ausland? Die soziale Selektivität studentischer Mobilität im Rahmen des Bologna Prozesses. *Qualität in der Wissenschaft, 2*, 37–45.

Gomendio, M. (2017). *Empowering and enabling teachers to improve equity and outcomes for all*. Paris: OECD.

Hauschildt, K., Gwosć, C., Netz, N., & Mishra, S. (2015). *Social and economic conditions of student life in Europe: Synopsis of indicators. EUROSTUDENT V 2012–2015*. Bielefeld, Germany: W. Bertelsmann Verlag.

Hauschildt, K., Vögtle, E. M., & Gwosć, C. (2018). *Social and economic conditions of student life in Europe: Synopsis of indicators. EUROSTUDENT VI 2016–2018*. Bielefeld, Germany: W. Bertelsmann Verlag.

IIEP, UNESCO. (2017). *Six ways to ensure higher education leaves no one behind*.

Key, O., Milatova, P., & Horstmann, N. (2017). *Herkunft macht mobil: Soziale Selektivität bei Auslandsstudium und Auslandspraktikum*. Gütersloh, Germany: CHE Centrum für Hochschulentwicklung.

Kratz, F., & Netz, N. (2018). Which mechanisms explain monetary returns to international student mobility? *Studies in Higher Education, 43*(2), 375–400.

Kwiek, M. (2013). From system expansion to system contraction: Access to higher education in Poland. *Comparative Education Review, 57*(3), 553–576.

Leuven and Louvain-la-Neuve Communiqué. (2009). *The Bologna Process 2020—The European Higher Education Area in the new decade: Communiqué of the conference of European Ministers responsible for higher education*.

Lörz, M., & Krawietz, M. (2011). Internationale Mobilität und soziale Selektivität: Ausmaß, Mechanismen und Entwicklung herkunftsspezifischer Unterschiede zwischen 1990 und 2005. *Kölner Zeitschrift für Soziologie und Sozialpsychologie, 63*(2), 185–205.

Lörz, M., Netz, N., & Quast, H. (2016). Why do students from underprivileged families less often intend to study abroad? *Higher Education, 72*(2), 153–174.

Marginson, S. (2016). The worldwide trend to high participation higher education: Dynamics of social stratification in inclusive systems. *Higher Education, 72*(4), 413–434.

Middendorff, E., Apolinarski, B., Poskowsky, J., Kandulla, M., & Netz, N. (2013). *Die wirtschaftliche und soziale Lage der Studierenden in Deutschland 2012*. Bonn, Berlin: BMBF..

Netz, N., & Finger, C. (2016). New horizontal inequalities in German higher education? Social selectivity of studying abroad between 1991 and 2012. *Sociology of Education, 89*(2), 79–98.

Neumeyer, S., & Pietrzyk, I. (2016). Auslandsmobilität im Masterstudium: Hat die Bildungsherkunft einen Einfluss auf die Dauer und die Art der Auslandsmobilität und falls ja, warum? *Beiträge zur Hochschulforschung, 38*(4), 108–127.

Oosterbeek, H., & Webbink, D. (2011). Does studying abroad induce a brain drain? *Economica, 78*(310), 347–366.

Parey, M., & Waldinger, F. (2011). Studying abroad and the effect on international labour market mobility: Evidence from the introduction of Erasmus. *The Economic Journal, 121*(551), 194–222.

Reimer, D., & Jacob, M. (2011). Differentiation in higher education and its consequences for social inequality: Introduction to a special issue. *Higher Education, 61*(3), 223–227.

Smolentseva, Anna. (2012). Access to Higher Education in the Post-Soviet States: Between Soviet Legacy and Global Challenges. https://doi.org/10.13140/2.1.1431.2646.

Sorrenti, G. (2017). The Spanish or the German apartment? Study abroad and the acquisition of permanent skills. *Economics of Education Review, 60*(S), 142–158.

Triventi, M. (2013). Stratification in higher education and its relationship with social inequality: A comparative study of 11 European countries. *European Sociological Review, 29*(3), 489–502.

Van Mol, C., & Timmerman, C. (2014). Should I stay or should I go? An analysis of the determinants of Intra-European student mobility. *Population, Space and Place, 20*(5), 465–479.

Vögtle, E. M. (2019). *What deters students of education and teacher training from enrolment abroad? (EUROSTUDENT intelligence brief 2)*.

Zimmermann, J., & Neyer, F. J. (2013). Do we become a different person when hitting the road? Personality development of sojourners. *Journal of Personality and Social Psychology, 105*(3), 515–530.

Chapter 25
Identity Challenges and Pedagogical Consequences: International Students in Higher Education Pathway Programmes in Australia

Louise Kaktiņš

In recent decades, the global educational landscape has altered dramatically due to international student mobility, which is occurring on an historically unprecedented scale.[1] Notably, this dynamic trend has been spurred by students from Asia seeking an English language-based university degree, making up 50 per cent of mobile students globally (Trends in International Student Recruitment 2017), especially in the United States, the United Kingdom and Australia (Choudaha 2019). In consequence, Australia's reliance on international students now forms a significant part of its export market, totalling AUS $22 billion in 2016 (an increase of 17% from the previous year), or 28 per cent of all university students in Australia (Maslen 2017), representing Australia's third most lucrative export (Department of Foreign Affairs and Trade 2019). This boost to the tertiary sector comes at a particularly propitious time for Australian universities, which have been battling historic challenges to their financial security due to significantly reduced government funding, hence the transformation of the Australian higher education (HE) sector into one characterized by widespread corporatization (Marginson and Considine 2000) and 'relentless commercialisation' (Connell 2016: 69).

To facilitate international enrolment and satisfy the high demand for university degrees from English language-based universities, a new educational phenomenon has materialised—the pre-university pathway programme (both commercial and non-commercial), particularly for international students who are non-native English speakers and whose qualifications—notably English language standards—require improvement prior to admission into mainstream university degree programmes. For the purpose of this chapter, Andrade's (2006: 134) definition of 'international students' will be utilised as one describing 'individuals enrolled in institutions of

L. Kaktiņš (✉)
Macquarie University, Sydney, NSW, Australia
e-mail: louise.kaktins@mq.edu.au

higher education who are on temporary student visas and are non-native English speakers' and who have crossed national borders for study purposes.

The pre-university pathway programme has become an entrenched part of the contemporary academic landscape to address international demand for HE in Australia. These alternative programmes are based on well-established models of collaborative (symbiotic) relationships between private providers of education and specific universities, operating on the premise that successful pathway students—those who have completed a one year diploma in a private college—can automatically articulate into mainstream second year university to continue their degrees (Shah and Nair 2013). This chapter focuses on one such relationship—an institute (de-identified as a Private Higher Education Provider or PHEP) aligned with a leading university operating in Sydney (de-identified as a Metropolitan University or Met_U). PHEP is one of a number of similar institutions (also affiliated with various Australian universities) owned by a large, for-profit, publicly listed, private higher education conglomerate that is also expanding its operations overseas. It should be noted that while the majority of PHEP students are international, from South-East Asia and between 16 and 29 years of age, there is a minority of domestic students who also pursue a pathway programme as an alternative means of entering tertiary study.

This case study adds another, hitherto under-researched, dimension to the expanding field of student mobility. In this field, Cairns (2014b) differentiates between 'diploma mobility,' which refers to mobility to acquire an initial undergraduate degree, and 'post-diploma mobility,' which refers to the mobility of graduates seeking postgraduate qualifications or advanced study. A further extension of such categories is warranted by the current project which focuses on studying in a pathway programme towards the goal of mainstream Australian tertiary entrance; a category such as 'tertiary pathway programme mobility' or 'pre-university mobility' would aptly describe this scenario. Also, as the students in this category are generally international students who do not have English as their first language, certain other concerns might arise, such as minimal understanding of Western academic culture and potentially limited knowledge of English for Academic Purposes, factors that have specific pedagogical side effects.

Research Context

Cairns' (2014a, b, 2015) work of student mobility suggests that this movement has reached a critical mass and moved from a peripheral (supplementary) concern to becoming an integral feature of young people's way of life, as they seek a social and professional niche in a continuously and rapidly transforming modern world. This work has focused on Portugal (Cairns 2014b, 2015) and Ireland (Cairns 2017); however, fewer studies have been conducted within the Australian HE context, with the notable exceptions of Singh and Doherty (2008), who consider the adaptation of Asian students within a pre-uni preparatory programme, and Brooks and Waters

(2011), who have explored the nexus between education and migration and the heavy reliance of HE on revenue generated from incoming students.

The current study approaches this subject from the perspective of students' identity formation within a pathway programme, and how the identities of international students undergo change and development during this specific period of academic demarcation, as they move into Western-style tertiary education. This educational phase is of a distinct and sophisticated nature (Ballard and Clanchy 1991), emphasising analytical, critical thinking based on questioning existing knowledge and expanding upon it (by original research), and demanding advanced cognitive and attitudinal skills (Brick 2006). Furthermore, they are entering a new educational marketplace. While the marketization of education is the inevitable consequence of an HE sector transformed into a profitable commercial enterprise, attracting significant numbers of students willing to go abroad for study purposes, these consequences have been labelled 'new and disturbing' by Furedi (2011: 2) in recasting 'the relationship between academics and students along the model of a service provider and customer.'

What this situation has created is a compromised academic culture that is focused on mollifying and ingratiating students (in their metamorphosis as 'customers') in preference to offering them a rigorous and disciplined tertiary experience; for example, by putting them under intellectual pressure. Therefore, 'once teaching becomes subordinate to an agenda that is external to itself it will become distracted from maintaining its integrity' (Furedi 2011: 5). In the case of non-English speaking international students, who may have challenges added to those of domestic students, their intellectual development could well be jeopardized, impacting upon the quality and direction of their academic achievements and professional aspirations.

Theoretical Framework

Social identity theory has become influential in a multiplicity of research fields, including education. Tajfel's (1974: 69) definition of social identity is 'the individual's knowledge that he [she] belongs to a certain social group together with some emotional and value significance to him [her] of this group membership.' Hence individuals will classify themselves—or develop a social identity—according to the social categories that apply within that particular group. The significance of groups in human society is encapsulated by Hogg (2003: 462), especially in relation to identity formation as follows:

> The groups we belong to profoundly influence how others know us—they are the lens through which people view us. Groups also profoundly influence how we view ourselves; they influence the type of people we are, the things we do, the attitudes and values we hold, and the way we perceive and react to people around us. Groups furnish us with an identity, a way of locating ourselves in relation to other people. Indeed, our sense of self derives from the groups and categories we belong to, and in many ways individuality may 'merely' be the unique combination of distinct groups and categories that define who we are.

Likewise, members of a group acquire status, within the social identity approach, as a consequence of intergroup comparison on the basis of their taking on positive prototypical preferences of their ingroup, thereby maximizing the ingroup/outgroup contrast (Hogg 2001). One of the critical functions of this process is to facilitate uncertainty reduction, by encouraging a self-concept aligned with prototypical ingroup values, thereby promoting a robust social identity (Hogg and Terry 2000).

This approach is, I argue, of particular relevance in a study focused on international students as they attempt to negotiate a new identity within an alien academic environment, which may contrast markedly to that with which they have been accustomed. Not only are they moving from one educational culture to another, they are also moving from a familiar secondary education situation in their homeland to a much more sophisticated and demanding tertiary one in a foreign land and in a foreign language. It is notable that the academic microcosm in which students have now been re-located is itself located within a macrocosm (the Australian HE sector) undergoing upheavals in focus and purpose.

Methodological Approach

This study adopts a qualitative approach based on focus groups with the international PHEP students and semi-structured in-depth face-to-face interviews with their teachers. Additional data from student surveys is not included in this analysis, but has been published elsewhere (Kaktiņš 2013). There were four student focus groups in total. Of these, the first involved students who had not yet completed their pathway programme. The other groups comprised ex-PHEP students who had successfully transferred to Met_U where they were pursuing their undergraduate degrees. Students are identified according to their focus groups, that is, those in Group 1 are denoted as S1.1, S1.2, S1.3 and so on. A total of 30 teachers (identified as T1, T2 and so on)—12 males and 18 females—were interviewed regarding their perception of the international students in the pathway programme and how the identities of the latter might have changed and developed.

A thematic analysis (after Patton 2002) was generated using the qualitative data from the focus groups and the teacher interviews to illustrate salient points. Key themes were identified via iterative reading of the transcripts. Themes were coded line-by-line and crosschecked for reliability with the research participants. A limitation of the study is that only relatively competent English-language-speakers were recruited for the student focus groups. Based on comments made by one of the student respondents (who was happy to participate as long as he was assured his grade point average was kept confidential), it was possible that weaker students, for example, those with a poor command of English were reluctant to participate. This was regrettable as their input would have been valuable and provided greater insight into the difficulties faced by international students.

Results and Discussion

For international students, the highly corporatized nature of contemporary HE in Australia can foster (by implication and example) identities that are in conflict with the preferred identities teachers seek to develop. The discussion section looks at the variable student identities perceived by teachers, how this relates to social identity theory, especially with a focus on the academic discourse required of students, and what factors impact students' identities and, in turn, lead to engagement/disengagement in their studies. A key pedagogical consideration for this particular cohort of students is the extent to which establishing trust relationships with teachers is crucial for their academic success and how face-to-face teaching achieves this.

Definitions of Students' 'Identity'

From the teachers' standpoint, international students were seen variously as having a *learner* identity (T3/T24/T28/T30), an *academic* identity (T17/T18/T20), a *developmental* one (transitioning from a learner identity to an academic identity—T5/T8/T26/T27), a *consumer* identity ('cash cow'—T6/T5/T17/T21/T24/T28) and a *transactional* identity—to simply acquire a certificate of graduation (T29) or gain permanent residency (PR) (T3). Many of these identities intersect and can affect pedagogy, and ultimately, the learning experience the international students take away from the programme.

Essentially, to integrate some of the teacher responses, one might view the student identities from a starting point of being a 'learner' (T28) and 'intellectual adolescent' (T27), embarking on 'an academic journey in an academy of higher learning' (T26) as a 'student scholar' (T26), and gradually morphing from a 'learner identity' to an 'academic identity' (T8/T17/T18/T20). This progression is supported by the following quotes:

> A 'learner identity'—I never thought the teaching and learning (at PHEP) to be about academic things, just about getting them (the students) to survive and giving them the tools to do that. (T28)

> At the start of their PHEP studies, a learner identity which is being moulded into an academic identity during their pathway programme. (T8)

> The students come to us (at PHEP) as learners, and, hopefully, leave as academics. Or, at least, that is the theory and the aspiration, even if it might be pie in the sky! (T5)

This purported progression may suffer interference or disruption if identities are created on the basis of socio-economics or other factors that impinge on identity formation. Several respondents believed that achieving an academic identity for the international students was compromised by the highly commercialized environment of a for-profit organisation because this facilitated the development of a 'consumer identity' in students (T6) as they were being exploited by the institution that essentially identified them as consumers (T5/T6/T17/T21/T24/T28/). In turn, the international students and their families demanded a return on their (very substantial) investment in education abroad (T8/T28) so the forces of demand and supply were always just below the surface of the PHEP ethos. Students were aware of the commercial context (T8/T28) and exploited it opportunistically for their (often unjustified) academic advancement (T6), especially by pressuring their teachers (and the organisation) to inflate low grades (T2/T6/T8).

By the same token, the programme was used as a means to an end for the students—a stepping stone to their profession or as a shortcut to permanent residency in Australia.

> Accounting and Economics lead to a business degree. The international students are mainly there to learn to make money not for the sake of learning as such. Learning equals money. (T28)

> PHEP was a conduit to permanent residency and their identity as students was a means to an end. (T3)

The choice of degrees and study units was driven by various imperatives. For example, many students reluctantly embarked on business-related degrees based on their parents' decisions (T3/T8/T28) and as a consequence, were not very committed to their studies or engaged in them but were resentful of having to study units they disliked (T1/T8). The commercial imperatives of the programme meanwhile overshadowed the approach to teaching and learning, and especially quality control. There appeared to be only one strategy to reconcile enrolling ill-prepared students who were then unable to cope with the demanding curriculum and, consequently, only managed poor academic results, with PHEP's fundamental goal of generating profits. One respondent put it succinctly: 'It was a production line. Faulty models (i.e. poorly performing students) were approved' (T17).

In summary, the combination of the high demand for conduits to HE from international students and the potential for enormous profits for commercial providers has resulted in casualties: the potential lowering of academic standards and the dilution of academic qualifications. This is alluded to by Choudaha (2017) in a recent report entitled the *Landscape of Third-Party Pathway Partnerships in the United States*, indicating that the major reason for universities not undertaking such an arrangement was fear of a loss of academic standards (65% of respondent universities). Hence, the issue of quality control and sustainability, especially for commercial pathway programme providers, becomes an area of concern (Kaktiņš 2018).

Student Identity Evolving through Academic Discourse

All teacher respondents were convinced that poor English-language skills posed one of the greatest challenges for international students in their efforts to advance academically; a perennial problem for international students (Samuelowicz 1987; Zhang and Mi 2010). The new environment in which students are now located involves complex adjustments as they are often forced into seeking a new social identity based on unfamiliar academic criteria. Acquiring status in this new setting to enable them to become part of the academic in-group, as per social identity theory, means students face the challenge of acquiring competence in 'specialised discourse competencies' (Hyland 2015: 33), including competence in various genres, as an entrée into the scholarly community (the in-group).

As Carbone and Orellana (2010: 295) stress, students in HE are expected to 'enact academic identities' especially by competence in the discursive style valued in academia. It is through this specialized form of discourse that students develop their academic voice and, by extension, voice their identity. As students construct their texts, they construct themselves (Hyland 2015). Naturally, for international students, for whom 'the language barrier is huge' (S4.2), acquiring such an identity poses substantial obstacles. As one teacher comments:

> English is challenging for them [the international students] and it seems to me that some students just can't be bothered so they fight learning and quite often cheat in order to pass. (T16)

One of the most enduring complaints teachers receive from international students is about the challenges of writing essays (T1/T6/T8). S2.3 who had segued from PHEP to Met_U, and was in the final year of his undergraduate degree, still cited essay writing as problematic.

> Hardest part still is doing essays. Really, a huge difference when you use your first language or second language. Sometimes I have to come up with ideas in Chinese and then translate in English. Locals use two days but I have to use a week for 2,500 words. (S2.3).

Certainly, S1.5 indicated his biggest challenge was that his level of English needed to improve, especially as many of his subjects involved extensive written work. It is interesting, that even units that traditionally did not require very advanced levels of literacy (e.g. information technology, computing) now do so (T27/T29). Likewise, interacting with teachers became difficult where language skills were deficient. This certainly posed a challenge for the participants from Group 2 in units such as accounting that specified a participation mark (S2.2). That meant international students felt disadvantaged since they could not answer the lecturer's and/or tutor's questions as quickly as the local students (S2.2) as 'you must quickly answer this (a question) otherwise a local will jump in. We feel we cannot talk much in class …'cos for me there is not enough time to think of an answer. Need time to process,' so often tended to participate less overall (S2.1), which affected their final grades. S2.2 noted that in her accounting unit the participation mark was worth 10 per cent but international students had 'trouble getting this mark.'

This concern manifests itself in other academic activities, notably group work. All student participants noted how much easier it had been to work in groups where the majority of students are international students, mainly from Asia (especially China). This enabled them to achieve a level of comfort in group work that was missing in mainstream university, where groups might be composed of both international and local students (with English as a first language). Naturally, this became particularly worrying where group work was part of an official assignment and attracted a single grade for the group regardless of the contribution of members—S2.1 noted one of his group assignments was worth 20 per cent of the total mark for the unit. S2.3 explained that the stressful nature of group work had meant his grades for group work were lower than those for individually completed assignments and concluded that he much preferred to work independently. In units such as marketing (S2.2), where there is a significant focus on group work, attempts to get marks upgraded were so bureaucratically tedious that this discouraged the international students from complaining even if they felt they were justified. Similar complaints are reflected in the attitudes of international students interviewed by Campbell and Li (2008).

Overall, for these students the cultural adjustment required to adapt to Western academia can be enormous and it may be that during this period of adjustment some teachers feel that the academic identity [of students] is 'more image than substance' and the 'identity of pretence and appearance than reality is rife in this system' (T21).

Student Engagement/Disengagement Nexus

While teachers may aspire that their students be committed to their academic endeavours, the reality may be very different with variable social groups (with their own dynamics) operating in any one classroom. The criteria within which students operate and the characteristics and behaviour they favour may well be at odds with attitudes that foster academic success. One teacher remarked on the environment as follows:

> Everyone is in a sea of struggling mass of people. Lucky to find helpful students. Small percentage of high flyers—they know instinctively what to do—the minority. (T23)

One teacher estimates the percentage of such high flyers as only 30 per cent of each class (T5). Sadly, he also comments that the 'rest are *empty vessels*—they come to PHEP that way and they leave without being changed.' Another (T17) estimated the percentage of students that really wanted to study and learn at a much lower eight per cent (out of a class of 30), while T22 was of the opinion that:

> It is a cataclysmic change for international students, from another country. They are taught to write, argue, challenge theories or beliefs, a move from their comfort zones—so a new identity is inevitable.

How they deal with this change depends on many factors and might lead to the formation of a social identity unsuitable for the complex academic role they are undertaking. Nevertheless, where resistance does appear, the rationale is directly related to social identity theory and its focus on uncertainty reduction:

> Learning for its own good is what they fight against the most. Being without family here may promote the need to cling to others and this could either create an academic identity or in fact increase resistance through the process of groupthink, but resistance is entrenched. (T21)

Thus, the international students' particular circumstances, where they are adrift from their family and friends, often for the first time in their lives, means that support becomes paramount (T1/T8); in some form of in-group even if it is not conducive to the advancement of their studies. Interestingly, being able to move from such a group to a more positive, academically focused one does occur, as noted by one teacher:

> They were a tight knit group who thought they knew their abilities well and believed they were too advanced for my class. They looked to their team leader (the male in a group of five females). He held a prominent position and they would defer to him for encouragement, answering my questions and making smart comments in class ... The male was floundering as his literacy level was poor. The girls were better—one in particular. Fortunately, by week four (in a term of 13 weeks), the girls were moving away from the group—even sitting away from the male. He retaliated by making a formal complaint about me and my teaching. He had lost power over the girls and his ego was crushed. He did manage to pass the course, but his arrogant attitude remained. (T1)

Another key influence on identity formation in the pathway programme is related to the consumer/customer model which in turn affects students' self-perceptions. Furedi (2011: 5–6) commenting on the highly commercialised education industry claims that 'the ideology of choice [being a consumer] has a powerful influence on shaping students' identities and works to distract them from realising the potential of their intellectual engagement.' This is certainly reinforced by teachers' comments:

> I would describe them [the students] as having a consumer identity in that they are buying a degree. (T6)

> The pay-to-pay model works actively against any academic integrity. Plagiarism is the modus operandi. (T21)

> They [the students] have a 'cash cow' identity in terms of the institution and society. (T24)

> I recall several incidents that allowed me insight into the students' self-identity as PHEP students. These were the repeated grade dispute arguments. Virtually immediately, it became apparent that the student was using vocabulary and phrasing choices more consistent with an economic or 'customer' type transaction. (T2)

For T26, the importance of students' ability to adapt appears a key factor: 'from a universal standpoint, humans who fail to learn to navigate the contexts within which they find themselves at risk of failure to survive, develop and thrive.' There is also potential disengagement when students demonstrate little or no commitment because their units of study have been chosen by their families (T1/T3/T8/T20/T25). Additionally, peer group pressure could either cause an acceleration or a deceleration of academic progress (T20). Some teachers directly related the students' difficulties in developing a viable academic identity to the key factors now driving the education industry in Australia.

> International students and their manifest struggles are a tragic reality of the commercialization of tertiary education in Australia and as a major Australian export. (T6)

As part of the commercialisation of HE in Australia, the apparent willingness for HE to accept lower-level students, or as in the case of the pathway programme, international students with a substantially lower level of English literacy, has particularly challenging consequences for the students' struggles in a new academic environment. As many of the teacher respondents suggest, this problem is addressed by a strategy of grade inflation orchestrated by PHEP.

Why Face-to-face Teaching Matters

Face-to-face teaching is wholeheartedly endorsed by all teacher respondents, who in a sense are negotiating the students' identities every time they enter a classroom. At this particular stage of international student education (the pathway programme), bearing in mind that most international students have come from very different educational backgrounds (often involving approaches that may appear anathema to Western forms of higher education), such role models are critical for the students to be competently initiated into Western style academia.

> You cannot have a transformative experience with a computer. You will gain knowledge but you would not be transformed. In class you are experiencing learning on so many levels—the discussion, the debate, mental and cognitive interaction. This cohort would not flourish without face-to-face teaching! (T28)

> Relationship building with students is very important as it is a way of facilitating trust and the flow-on effect is likely to be greater inhibition of students in regard to violation of academic integrity. (T30)

> A positive student-teacher relationship can improve a student's attitude considerably. (T5)

> The more education becomes an anonymous depersonalized exercise the greater the likelihood that contract cheating can occur. Engagement and personal interest and personal investment (by both student and teacher) are crucial. (T25)

In the case of both learning academic discourse and a higher level of engagement in the learning process, all teachers (even those teaching information technology—T27/T29) were adamant that at this vulnerable juncture in the international students' academic careers, face-to-face teaching was absolutely essential and the more it was replaced by online learning, the less successful academically the students would be, and in turn, the greater the possibility of their disengagement.

Implications and Conclusion

To consider the broader trends and their effect on HE, it is not an exaggeration to say that the ease with which student mobility has created an unprecedented international market has also led to the appearance of fault-lines in the HE sector in Australia and, possibly, elsewhere. The convergence of various factors has had unanticipated longer-term side effects from the original scenario when universities first realised the enormous potential of international students as a viable source of sustainable revenue. This financial lifeline has come at a cost. The monetarization of all things educational has permeated the HE sector. It may well be that this is not a period of great upheaval in the sector but an adjustment, should a more manageable and ethical scenario be on the horizon, as many enlightened academics hope.

In the meantime, there are enormous implications for the international students who come to Australia, in terms of their identity development and how this affects (and is affected by) the teachers involved in pathway programmes and institutions that set the current agenda. In the last instance, the teachers who deal with the international students on a daily basis are in a unique position of being able to override some of the negative aspects of this complex scenario and can still operate as ethical and committed scholars who attempt to steer their charges towards genuine and committed academic success.

Acknowledgements The author wishes to thank Dr Agnes Bosanquet for her insights and suggestions, and the students and teachers who participated in this study.

Note

1. The global economic value of student mobility in the year 2016 was estimated at US$300 billion (Choudaha 2019), of which US$19.8 billion was related to Australian education. According to recent reports the number of students pursuing education outside their home countries has tripled since 1990, with approximately five million students now doing so, and a predicted increase to seven million by 2022 (Trends in International Student Recruitment 2017).

References

Andrade, M. S. (2006). International students in English-speaking universities: Adjustment factors. *Journal of Research in International Education, 5*(2), 131–154.

Ballard, B., & Clanchy, J. (1991). *Teaching international students: A brief guide for lecturers and students*. South Melbourne: Longman Cheshire.

Brick, J. (2006). *Academic culture: A student's guide to studying at university*. Sydney: Palgrave Macmillan.

Brooks, R., & Waters, J. (2011). *Student mobilities, migration and the internationalization of higher education*. London: Palgrave Macmillan.

Cairns, D. (2014a). *Youth transitions, international student mobility and spatial reflexivity: Being mobile?* London: Palgrave Macmillan.

Cairns, D. (2014b). Here today, gone tomorrow? Student mobility decision-making in an economic crisis context. *Journal of International Mobility, 14*, 185–198.

Cairns, D. (2015). International student mobility in crisis? Understanding post-diploma mobility decision-making in an economic crisis context. *Sociologia, Problemas e Práticas, 79*, 9–25.

Cairns, D. (2017). Exploring student mobility and graduate migration: Undergraduate mobility propensities in two economic crisis contexts. *Social and Cultural Geography, 18*(3), 336–353.

Campbell, J., & Li, M. (2008). Asian student voices: An empirical study of Asian students' learning experiences at a New Zealand university. *Journal of Studies in International Education, 12*(4), 375–396.

Carbone, P. M., & Orellana, M. F. (2010). Developing academic identities: Persuasive writing as a tool to strengthen emergent academic identities. *Research in the Teaching of English, 44*(3), 292–316.

Choudaha, R. (2017). *Landscape of third-party pathway partnerships in the United States*. National Association for Foreign Student Affairs (NAFSA).

Choudaha, R. (2019). *Beyond $300 billion: The global impact of international students*. Studyportals.

Connell, R. (2016). What are good universities? *Australian Universities' Review, 58*(2), 67–73.

Department of Foreign Affairs and Trade. (2019). *Trade and investment at a glance 2019*. Australian Government.

Furedi, F. (2011). Introduction to the marketisation of higher education and the student as consumer. In M. Molesworth, R. Scullion, & E. Nixon (Eds.), *The marketisation of higher education and the student as consumer* (pp. 1–7). New York: Routledge.

Hogg, M. A. (2001). Social identification, group prototypicality, and emergent leadership. In M. A. Hogg & D. J. Terry (Eds.), *Social identity processes in organizational contexts* (pp. 197–212). Ann Arbor: Sheridan.

Hogg, M. A. (2003). Social identity. In M. R. Leary & J. P. Tangney (Eds.), *Handbook of self and identity* (pp. 462–479). New York: Guildford.

Hogg, M. A., & Terry, D. J. (2000). Social identity and self-categorization processes in organizational contexts. *The Academic of Management Review, 25*(1), 121–140.

Hyland, K. (2015). Genre, discipline and identity. *Journal of English for Academic Purposes, 19*, 32–43.

Kaktiņš, L. (2013). Who do you think you are? Profile of international students in a private HE provider pathway program: Implications for international education. *ACPET Journal for Private Higher Education, 2*(1), 43–51.

Kaktiņš, L. (2018). The impact on academic staff of the collaboration between a pathway provider and its partner university: An Australian case study. *Journal of University Teaching and Learning Practice, 15*(1), 1–19.

Marginson, S., & Considine, M. (2000). *The enterprise university: Power, governance and reinvention in Australia*. New York: Cambridge University Press.

Maslen, G. (2017). Education exports hit record high of nearly US$17 billion. *University World News*, no. 445.

Patton, M. Q. (2002). *Qualitative research and evaluation methods* (3rd ed.). Thousand Oaks, CA: Sage.

Samuelowicz, K. (1987). Learning problems of overseas students: Two sides of a story. *Higher Education Research and Development, 6*(2), 121–131.

Shah, M., & Nair, C. S. (2013). Private for-profit higher education in Australia: Widening access, participation and opportunities for public–private collaboration. *Higher Education Research and Development, 32*(5), 820–832.

Singh, P., & Doherty, C. (2008). Mobile students in liquid modernity: Negotiating the politics of transnational identities. In N. Dolby & F. Rizvi (Eds.), *Youth moves: Identities and education in global perspective* (pp. 115–130). New York: Routledge.

Tajfel, H. (1974). Social identity and intergroup behaviour. *Social Science Information, 13*(2), 65–93.

Trends in International Student Recruitment. (2017). *Study portals*. Retrieved August 1, 2017, from https://www.studyportals.com/intelligence/2017-trends-in-international-student-recruitment/

Zhang, Y., & Mi, Y. (2010). Another look at the language difficulties of international students. *Journal of Studies in International Education, 14*(4), 371–388.

Part IV

Chapter 26
Working towards Mobility

David Cairns

Mobility in training and employment contexts is of high importance for many young people who may wish to use spatial movement as a means of facilitating transitions not only from education to work but also from education to training and training to work, taking advantage of opportunities that may not be available close to home, potentially strengthening intercultural skills and employability at the same time. As with student mobility, much of this movement takes place within institutional structures and involves learning in internationalized groups, using the dynamics such environments offer for exchange and collaboration (see also Cuzzocrea et al. 2021). But while universities do host certain training courses and work placements (as we shall see later in this section), specialist training providers feature more prominently, introducing a new set of protagonists into the mobility equation, along with employment agencies, local and national authorities and entrepreneurial partners (see Nienaber et al. 2021). Therefore, as well as taking into account young people's individual views, and the influence of universities and national and supranational policymakers, these other parties also help hold together migration trajectories through hosting projects and placements, and in this part of the book we wish to represent some contemporary experiences.

More specifically, the chapters in this section acknowledge the significance of vocational training to young people, a durable topic for researchers in different national and regional contexts, especially in Europe. In Chap. 27, Maria-Carmen Pantea looks at Vocational Education and Training (VET) in Romania, the different types of mobility that exist at this level and the meanings young people in VET attach to going abroad. This enables us to look at the development of mobility, and by extension migration, dispositions within the 16–18-year-old age group and its

---

D. Cairns (✉)
ISCTE – Instituto Universitário de Lisboa (ISCTE-IUL), Centro de Investigação e Estudos de Sociologia, Lisbon, Portugal
e-mail: david.cairns@iscte-iul.pt

© The Author(s), under exclusive license to Springer Nature Switzerland AG 2022
D. Cairns (ed.), *The Palgrave Handbook of Youth Mobility and Educational Migration*, https://doi.org/10.1007/978-3-030-99447-1_26

role in stimulating the imagination of learners, in addition to the acquisition of practical skills. In this chapter we also have an opportunity to consider what mobility means in a relatively mainstream context, among those who have only recently exited secondary education, acknowledging both the personal and professional value of geographical circulation at this point in the life course, providing a riposte to the view that mobility in VET is 'just' a default option for those facing harsh socio-economic conditions (Pantea 2021).

Chapter 28 provides further insight into VET in Europe, focusing this time on Luxembourg, Belgium, Germany and France. This discussion, by Birte Nienaber and colleagues, makes many pertinent points regarding the need for cross-border cooperation in VET, considering that opportunities are not evenly distributed within or between countries, and the prospect of international commuting in regions that share borders. Tabea Schlimbach, Karen Hemming and Valentina Cuzzocrea meanwhile consider VET in Germany, a system which has traditionally been seen as a point of reference for other service providers from across Europe. Focusing on mobile German apprentices aged between 18 and 29 years, they explain how their stays abroad are largely short-term group exercises, with institutionally predefined features, often taking advantage of funds from European programmes (Schlimbach et al. 2021).

Chapter 30 by Peter G. Ghazarian meanwhile looks at temporary work schemes in Australia, Canada and New Zealand, and some of the costs and benefits for participants. This includes an elaboration of how temporary worker programmes function, the restrictions on who may participate and the prominence of these programmes in the national discourses of the host countries, alongside discussion of the experiences of individual participants (Ghazarian 2021). While employment, or at least heightened employability, is being actively sought by participants, intercultural skills are another consideration, harking back to a theme discussed previously in this book (see, e.g., Skrefsrud 2021). Sophie Cranston, Emma Bates and Helena Pimlott-Wilson look at the development of intercultural skills in international work placements. One of the benefits of moving abroad for work is believed to be the development of a global mindset: skills and attributes that enable a person to work with individuals from other cultures. These abilities are formed through working and living abroad, and are focused in this chapter on placements situated inside existing undergraduate degree programmes. As Davide Filippi and Sebastiano Benasso also make evident in Chap. 32, the value of these short-term mobility exercises may however be largely symbolic, as markers of distinction on a CV rather than a means of moving towards job security, and even when young people do migrate for work, they continue to face precarious circumstances (Santoro 2021). In these chapters, we therefore have examples of old and new migration narratives intermingling; mobility being used, and abused, by institutional and political interests, a theme that will be expounded upon further in the final section of this book.

An important aspect of these chapters is providing in-depth discussion, most often supported by qualitative evidence from participants in various work and training programmes. The inclusion of these topics reflects the importance of these subjects to the contributors of this book, establishing an appreciation of mobility in some of the most formative aspects of a career. With mobility in VET and work placements generally seen as the poor relation of student mobility in the youth mobility research field, it is therefore hoped that we can move beyond the idea that mobility starts, or ends, in tertiary education, or is confined to relatively elitist contexts. Equally important, some of the participants in these exchanges have representations of their experiences provided here, even though there is still obviously much to be explored. Among the benefits to emerge are intercultural skills, alongside formal learning, emphasising the value of living in other societies (see Cranston et al. 2021).

In keeping with the overall theme of mobility as nested migration introduced elsewhere in this book (Cairns 2021a, 2021b), we can also see that movement for work and training purposes provides more key migration building blocks. This can be imaginative, with an introduction of ideas and a broadening of future parameters taking place, or more literally in cases where involvement in one mobility phase facilitates access to others. We can also see that the temporality of this work is purposeful; for example, in his chapter, Ghazarian (2021) outlines some of the legislative aspects which attempt to keep young people's mobility separate from the migration of 'adults,' including in some cases exclusion from the 'permanent' labour market. This kind of chauvinism, if directed towards certain national or ethnic groups, or towards women for that matter, would invite fierce criticism, but when directed at youth, structural inferiority of the condition and status of migration seems politically acceptable. And, as Ghazarian (2021) also remarks, employers who make use of temporary youth workers abroad have often seen the vulnerability of these workers as an inherent part of their value. We therefore might want to temper our enthusiasm for these mobility practices where exchanges are managed to the benefit of host institutions rather than individual participants.

While the neoliberal underpinnings of student mobility are fairly self-evident, especially the privatization of risks and costs (Cairns et al. 2017, 2018), some of the same issues may also apply to work and training trajectories. From a positive point of view, we can view this is a part of a 'social identity of choice' or 'do-it-yourself biography,' as argued in individualization theory (Beck 1992, 1994), but vulnerability and unsustainability feature so prominently that such thinking needs to be tempered. Multiple factors contribute to this situation. For example, temporary migrant worker programmes create, by design, contractual asymmetry in the hopes of reaping benefits from migrants' labour and economic activity for employers, enabling them to avoid the costs of public services and welfare (Bauböck 2011). Heightened risk and precariousness are not accidental, or incidental, but are rather integral parts of mobility governance, and a reflection of the aforementioned neoliberal values. As further noted by Ghazarian (2021), the temporary status of these workers prevents them from being able to escape these conditions in a way that permanent migrants might have been able to, explaining the need for youth migrants to be codified as such, instead of being marginalized by being labelled as mobile youth.

'Work' itself is no escape, given the endemic precarity that seems to have enveloped young people's employment, even those in skilled and highly qualified professions. Points of labour market entry become semi-permanent liminal spaces rather than temporary staging posts on the path to something better, and for mobile workers, attributes such as interculturality become diluted to a point of meaninglessness (Cranston et al. 2021). Young professionals themselves become complicit in their marginalization through representing themselves as idealized neoliberal archetypes, both in the workplace and in representations of their value, a valuation that is expressed in concrete form on their CVs (Filippi et al. 2021). This extends to tying together the disparate elements of a career into a coherent whole, the post hoc editing of this trajectory aiming to create the impression that there is, and always has been, a trajectory rather than a series of singular and unrelated work experiences. This perspective is of course entirely consistent with the broader conceptualization of migration introduced in Chap. 3 (Cairns 2021a), hypothesizing that a migration trajectory can be comprised of a series of seemingly unrelated mobility episodes via post hoc deduction. Just as failures are obscured by successes in a CV, the discontinuities of piecemeal migration trajectories are glossed over when trying to be recognized as a bona fide migrant.

Why then do so many young people embark on what they must know are exploitative mobility exercises abroad in regard to training and work? We might argue that with the practice becoming normalized as a kind of rite of passage for youth, a stoic acceptance of hardship becomes part of the 'deal.' Pantea (2021) also connects mobility with the celebration of hard work and economic stability for family formation. In more theoretical terms, in Chap. 32, Davide Filippi, Sebastiano Benasso and Luca Guzzetti relate the process of constructing migration trajectories back to ideas related to reflexivity and precarity, acknowledging the symbolic value of including mobility experience on one's CV as a mark of distinction in competitive labour markets. An ability to soak up and surpass mobility-related hardship might even be viewed as a desirable attribute. This just demonstrates how dysfunctional certain forms of youth migration had become in the pre-pandemic years. On the other hand, Monica Santoro's work on young Italian migrants in Manchester, at a slightly later point in the life stage compared to the research discussed in other chapters, provides a more positive perspective on labour market integration. Of particular note is the comparison these professional migrants make with what might have happened in their home country had they stayed; their present situations, they felt, were much more promising than what was on offer in Italy (Santoro 2021). Some places, in this case the United Kingdom, are evidently less precarious than other starting points in life. However, the United Kingdom has now, perhaps irrevocably, changed after Brexit and the pandemic, undermining one of the main advantages that could once be gained there: a relatively high level of job stability.

References

Bauböck, R. (2011). Temporary migrants, partial citizenship and hypermigration. *Critical Review of International Social and Political Philosophy, 14*(5), 666–693.

Beck, U. (1992). *The risk society: Towards a new modernity*. London: SAGE.

Beck, U. (1994). *Reflexive modernization: Politics, tradition and aesthetics in the modern social order*. Cambridge: Polity Press.

Cairns, D. (2021a). Mobility becoming migration: Understanding youth spatiality in the twenty-first century. In D. Cairns (Ed.), *The Palgrave handbook of youth mobility and educational migration*. Basingstoke: Palgrave Macmillan.

Cairns, D. (2021b). Migration decision-making, mobility capital and reflexive learning. In D. Cairns (Ed.), *The Palgrave handbook of youth mobility and educational migration*. Basingstoke: Palgrave Macmillan.

Cairns, D., Cuzzocrea, V., Briggs, D., & Veloso, L. (2017). *The consequences of mobility*. Basingstoke: Palgrave Macmillan.

Cairns, D., Krzaklewska, E., Cuzzocrea, V., & Allaste, A.-A. (2018). *Mobility, education and employability in the European Union: Inside Erasmus*. Basingstoke: Palgrave Macmillan.

Cranston, S., Bates, E., & Pimlott-Wilson, H. (2021). International work placements: Developing intercultural skills? In D. Cairns (Ed.), *The Palgrave handbook of youth mobility and educational migration*. Basingstoke: Palgrave Macmillan.

Cuzzocrea, V., Krzaklewska, E., & Cairns, D. (2021). 'There is no me, there is only us': the Erasmus bubble as a transient form of transnational collectivity. In V. Cuzzocrea, B. Gook, & B. Schiermer (Eds.), *Forms of collective engagements in youth transition: A global perspective*. Leiden: Brill.

Filippi, D., Benasso, S., & Guzzetti, L. (2021). Abroad forever? Embedding spatial mobility in academic work trajectories in Italy. In D. Cairns (Ed.), *The Palgrave handbook of youth mobility and educational migration*. Basingstoke: Palgrave Macmillan.

Ghazarian, P. G. (2021). Youth as temporary workers abroad: The experiences of Australia, Canada and New Zealand. In D. Cairns (Ed.), *The Palgrave handbook of youth mobility and educational migration*. Basingstoke: Palgrave Macmillan.

Nienaber, B., Dörrenbächer, H. P., Funk, I., Pigeron-Piroth, I., Belkacem, R., Helfer, M., Polzin-Haumann, C., & Reissner, C. (2021). Using cross-border mobility in vocational education and training in the Greater Region SaarLorLux region. In D. Cairns (Ed.), *The Palgrave handbook of youth mobility and educational migration*. Basingstoke: Palgrave Macmillan.

Pantea, M.-C. (2021). Facets of mobility in Romania's vocational education and training. In D. Cairns (Ed.), *The Palgrave handbook of youth mobility and educational migration*. Basingstoke: Palgrave Macmillan.

Santoro, M. (2021). Italian youth and the experience of highly qualified migration to the United Kingdom. In D. Cairns (Ed.), *The Palgrave handbook of youth mobility and educational migration*. Basingstoke: Palgrave Macmillan.

Schlimbach, T., Hemming, K., & Cuzzocrea, V. (2021). Vocational learning abroad: The case of German VET mobility. In D. Cairns (Ed.), *The Palgrave handbook of youth mobility and educational migration*. Basingstoke: Palgrave Macmillan.

Skrefsrud, T.-A. (2021). Why student mobility does not automatically lead to better understanding: Reflections on the concept of intercultural learning. In D. Cairns (Ed.), *The Palgrave handbook of youth mobility and educational migration*. Basingstoke: Palgrave Macmillan.

Chapter 27
Beyond Skills: Facets of Mobility in Romania's Vocational Education and Training

Maria-Carmen Pantea

This chapter is based on qualitative research conducted with over 250 young people aged 16–18 years in Romania's initial vocational education and training (VET) system. The fieldwork used a bottom-up approach (see Powell 2013), starting the conversation with what matters to the young people themselves rather than policy imperatives such as employability. Mobility was, inevitably, a cross-cutting theme that mattered to all interviewees, and this chapter will look at the different types of mobility envisaged and, more specifically, the meaning they attach to the idea of 'going abroad.'

In thinking about this issue, it soon becomes apparent that we need to move beyond popular assumptions and consider the evidence. Therefore, even though Romania continues to register record levels of outward migration, interviewees' positions on leaving the country are more nuanced than might be expected. Their accounts are an intricate mix of what might be regarded as conventional aspirations and neoliberal tropes: a normative discourse shaped by expectations of meaningful and stable work, but also the search for novelty, exploration and choice. Part of the conventional narrative (akin to Sennett's notion of 'craftsmanship') is the idea that skills are permanent and that it is possible—'if nothing unexpected happens'—to retire from one's first workplace. However, the aspiration for a stable working life tells only part of the story. At the next level, interviewees unpack the neoliberal belief that their own agency will be enough to help them construct a 'social identity of choice', the 'do-it-yourself biography' as argued in individualization theory (Beck 1992, 1994). This second layer incorporates the prospect of precarious work as part of a rhetoric of choice and experimentation. In addition, the interviewees also incorporate deeply held, and arguably disturbing, expectations that 'things will not work out' regardless of circumstances; that they will navigate uncertainty while

M.-C. Pantea (✉)
Babeș-Bolyai University, Cluj-Napoca, Romania
e-mail: pantea@policy.hu

moving from one form of precarity to another, making temporary forms of migration an expectation rather than a dream. This contention adds a new dimension to the theoretical idea of a precariously constructed piecemeal migration trajectory, as introduced earlier in this book (see Cairns 2021a, b), finding a place for vocational mobility in this conceptual approach.

What this chapter also recognizes is that youth migration, in its recent forms, is in many ways at the intersection of divergent ideological layers: it carries with it the normative grand narrative that celebrates hard work and economic stability for family formation. But migration generates anxieties because of rising concerns about discrimination and nationalism—issues that do not feature prominently in the publicity materials issued by agencies that support mobility programmes or in policies aimed at opening up free movement (see Chaps. 8 to 16 of this book). Migration also serves to coagulate novel aspirations related to consumption and social validation, explaining why this chapter discusses several functions young people in VET attribute to certain assumed-to-be-purely-instrumental forms of mobility: moving away from an overwhelmingly narrow economic focus and towards recognition of consumption-based use of mobility, with stays abroad used as investments in the self, and a period of exploration and even leisure.

The research does not completely refute the idea that for many young people in VET labour migration is often a *default* option because of unattractive economic prospects at home and the presence of networks abroad. We therefore have a potential coexistence of old and new migration rationales, even within the same person's spatial biography. In consequence, the variegated functions of mobility for those in VET call for a more nuanced reading of statistics on migration. We should not exclude the notion that young people in VET *also* have mobility aspirations similar to their socially advantaged peers, and they may see something in going abroad that is much more than an economic project *tout court*. This is an important point of redress that needs to be made in the ongoing debate about the socio-demographic make-up of the mobile youth which took for granted who constituted the 'mobile' cohort. The popular assumption has been—if not since the dawn of time, then at least since the advent of youth mobility research—that mobile young people are largely from the upper and middle classes, and predominantly found in the cosmopolitan centres of European and Anglophone societies. Yet, as this chapter suggests, there are people outside these elite confines who wish to be mobile rather than just migrants in the heavily stereotyped sense of being purely econometric movers. This is mobility as a popular choice that reflects the complex social worlds of many young people, including those in VET.

Ultimately, the research hopes to contribute towards two underrepresented themes: firstly, young people in VET (from rural areas and small towns) as a case in point for interrogating the urban, metropolitan bias that is especially prevalent in youth studies. Secondly, the chapter adds nuance to a policy orthodoxy that invariably links young people in VET with employability discourse. It looks into their social worlds and brings to the fore—besides the blatantly obvious concern with work—deeper aspirations related to mobility, exploration, leisure, consumption, personal growth and social validation. The meanings of mobility that emerge call for research to remain open to the idea that employability is one, but not the only, consideration shaping young people's choices, showing that discourse prioritizing skills at the expense of young people's social worlds is in serious need for revision.

Framing the Context: Romania, Migration and VET

Romania is a European Union country with a special relationship to migration. Its diaspora is the fifth largest in the world and still growing (OECD 2019). Between 2000 and 2015, the country was losing, annually, 7.3 per cent of its total population, and a third of the active population, through migration; this is, worldwide, the fastest-growing number of outward migrants from a country not facing war, the first being Syria (UN 2016).[1] Migration is responsible for more than 75 per cent of a population decline from 22.4 million in 2000 to 19.5 million in 2018 (OECD 2019), and simple calculations circulated by national media show that each hour, Romania's population decreases, because of migration, by nine people. On average, 200 people leave every day, the main destination countries being within the EU: Italy (over one million), Spain, Germany, the United Kingdom and France.

A major push factor for this process is the large discrepancy in incomes within Romania: the richest 20 per cent of the population has an income over eight times higher than that of the poorest 20 per cent (European Commission 2017). Keeping up with a rising cost of living has become a major challenge for the most disadvantaged living in rural areas or small deindustrialized towns, with 46 per cent of those employed working for the minimum gross income of 400 Euros (PIAROM 2018), and despite periodic increases, the minimum wage is still the lowest in the EU (European Commission 2017). In a context shaped by poor investment in infrastructure, corruption, urban/rural divides and regional disparities, working abroad emerges as a solution to poverty, but also as a place for self-realization. One such example is the migration of highly qualified professionals, notably medical doctors and engineers. It goes without saying that the social, economic and political implications are significant: from the 'children left behind' and problems with elder care to 'brain/skills drain' and a skilled labour shortage.

Against this background, initial VET) emerges as a mid-term solution. This is the educational track that is not directly conductive to accessing higher education, although some 'progress routes' into high schools, and later university, are—in principle—present; part of secondary education VET (15–18 years old) leads to tertiary-level qualifications. VET is also high on the policy agenda. After being de facto dissolved between 2009 and 2011, it was recently reintroduced, with annual increases in enrolment levels. Even so, figures from the Romanian National Institute of Statistics published in 2018 state that the proportion of young people in VET is less than 2.5 per cent of the total number of pupils in the entire educational system.

The dual system, which involves close cooperation with industry, is becoming increasingly popular, although the large majority of places remain within the conventional, secondary education system. This does not mean that problems do not exist. Outdated infrastructure and training of mixed quality are major concerns. Furthermore, as many young people in VET come from rural areas or small towns, they end up in VET in a context framed by their severe socio-economic disadvantage, functional illiteracy and an underdeveloped education system in rural areas among others (Pantea 2019a, b). And, as is the case elsewhere, VET in Romania has poor social standing, with the search for a 'parity of esteem' with upper secondary education remaining an unsolved tension.

Across Europe, VET nevertheless has the reputation of being 'the most heterogeneous of the main education and training sectors' (Cedefop 2011: 5). Depending on a country's education system, it can vary on a spectrum that goes from being a separate entity to formal schooling (in which case, it is strongly industry-driven) to being included in formal education, albeit as a strand for students not headed towards university (Billett 2011). In addition, technical university education, some adult learning programmes and many other arrangements may be part of VET (Greinert 2004).

In general, VET is an area where policy interest outstrips the development of research (McGrath 2012). Moreover, a large part of the literature on VET has a utilitarian ethos, with a preoccupation with skills paramount. Young people are hence rarely at the centre of research, which is often structuralist in nature (Powell 2013). Given this situation, the current research aims to contribute to debates on spatial mobility and VET, taking an in-depth look at the Romanian context.

Research Design

This chapter is based on qualitative research with over 250 young people (16–18 years old) in Romania's initial VET system.[2] Data was gathered in 2016–2017 by a team of five researchers who visited over 30 VET schools in five (of the eight) developmental regions of Romania. Interviews and focus groups were carried out on school premises, without the presence of teaching staff and with a deliberate aim of instilling a sense of informality. The interviewees volunteered to take part in the study and the team had a deliberate interest in including young people from different life situations. Research participants were often disadvantaged in various ways: single parental families were close to the norm (in the context of divorce, migration, illness or death) and commuting was frequent, as was a sense of inferiority in relation to peers in high school or from the cities. Over 2500 pages of transcripts were coded in NVivo. In a search for theoretical representativeness, data collection and interpretation were undertaken simultaneously. The research dissociates itself from any claims of statistical representativeness. The fieldwork also included interviews and discussions with nearly 100 teachers, school authorities and employers. However, this chapter will not derive any of its findings from this data.

Migration is not a concept young people generally used, as in Romania it is considered a policymakers' term. Therefore, this chapter will employ a range of terms that emerged during the fieldwork to denote spatial processes that are fluid and contextual, reversible and repetitive. The concept of 'migration' is hence employed in a rather loose manner, although technically 'intra-European mobility' would be a more precise signifier.

The interviewed young people had no experience working abroad themselves, but tried to make sense of this idea through making reference to the accounts of close family members, friends or peers. In doing so, they reinforced existing tropes, built contrasts between 'here' and 'there,' imagined possibilities and questioned choices. Contradictions were inherent in such processes of meaning-making, and in the interviews/focus groups it was noticeable that the most favoured situations were dilemmas that had emerged when young people arrived at a 'dead end in understanding' (Sennett 2004: 10).

Findings and Interpretation

Many interviewees regarded labour migration as the nearest solution on hand for managing poor economic prospects back home and reaching financial independence. Migration was far from being regarded as a 'dream' and almost never seen as a one-way project. Interviewees oscillated between the idea of migration as a silver bullet, ensuring-long term economic security back home and expressing apprehension that such plans may not hold for very long. Contradictory arguments and examples were brought to the fore in an attempt to make sense of this ambivalence, relating to complex working environments amongst which none of those included in research had first-hand experience.

Interviewees' secondary accounts of what work abroad might actually entail generated heated debate. In almost every focus group there was at least one person bringing to the fore powerful counter narratives on migration: 'it is not that easy' and 'streets are not paved with gold.' Often, they came to the realization that their work destinies will be fractured, uncertain and shaped by intermittent migration, or 'arrhythmic mobility' of loss and insecurity (Marcu 2017). Sometimes discussions led to the realization that the choice is between one form of precarity and another: 'You have hard times here; you have hard times there. The difference is that there you have hard times for more money; here, you have hard times for less money. As simple as that.' The notion that work can be dangerous, demeaning or dirty was also implicit:

I: How are the working conditions there?
Irina: Worse.
Ana: If we think a bit, when we go abroad, further away, everyone makes us gypsies.
Elvira: I had a cousin who was in Germany and he worked in the rain with boots and well, he earned money, but the conditions were ... imagine ... in the rain .... overalls.

Elena: You want money, you work. You don't want money, it's free to stay home.
I: Would you go abroad?
Maria: Yes.
Sofia: It depends. … In a way, yeah … you know at least what are you striving for.
I: But would you find a job in your field or not necessarily?
Sofia: No way in this field.
Maria: Whatever I get.

(Focus group, grade 10, VET class in textiles, small town)

The interviewees had grown up watching close friends and relatives 'coming and going.' Moving abroad for work was not considered a remarkable, momentous decision. Their relation to the idea of leaving the country in fact seemed rather fluid, yet not totally free of dilemmas. Many talked with confidence about options and possibilities: a parent working abroad, migrant relatives or friends eager to support them in some way. Favourable stances on working abroad were often a 'default product' of the closed social networks young people are embedded into.

This partially explains their reservations towards the idea of relocating *within* Romania. But typically, young people argued they will join a close friend or relative, yet with the absence of prior arrangements having been made with the already migrated. What is more, the interviewees were very rarely able to name the place this person lived in and work at, and sometimes this applied in the case of their parents as well. Few claimed proficiency in a foreign language or seemed proactive in learning one. Generally, interviewees trusted their 'inner' ability to learn the language rather fast 'once there.' Others rested assured that for the workplace they foresaw, there was not much need to learn the language. For instance, Ana and Matilda attend a VET class in hospitality in a small mountain town with an underdeveloped touristic infrastructure. Faced with poor employment prospects locally, they anticipate going abroad for seasonal work in agriculture, not without an ironic disregard towards such work, since they believe that language would not be a problem. Although when prompted, they consider employment in hospitality abroad appealing, they rule it out because of the language demands. Their account denotes a deep sense of marginality, both here (in rural Romania) and there (abroad). The locally available migration networks capture their imaginary repertoire of options, inhibit the capacity to find alternatives and mobilize change, such as prioritizing learning a foreign language.

The interviews with teaching staff in VET schools, on the other hand, did not seem to suggest that there is a tendency to make the most of young people's willingness to migrate; for instance, through placing a stronger focus on learning a foreign language. Despite high school attendance rates, VET seemed, in many instances, permeated by an ethos of low expectations and low-quality education. In many ways, VET schools are close to a case study for what the World Bank has described as the silent crisis of 'schooling without learning' (World Bank 2018).[3]

It was in fact rare for the young people to envision having a job in the field of VET abroad: because certain domains seemed restrictive to new and foreign entrants (e.g. electrician, auto-mechanic), they felt ill-prepared or did not feel at ease with the VET field altogether. Besides, most research participants ended up in VET without a clear understanding of their future job prospects. Many envisioned working in a different area, with or without a short-term training course later on. Others rested assured that they have the capacity to learn fast once employed, even if this is in an unknown field. To a large extent, the interviews with companies' representatives in Romania confirmed that for getting a job close to the bottom of the occupational pyramid, a broad understanding of the industry helps but is not mandatory, especially where certain soft skills, largely revolving around a 'good work ethic,' are emphasised.

Invariably, discussions on the topic of labour migration opened up a window for the critical examination of work-related issues back home. While the differences in income, home and abroad, were a cross-cutting theme, different modes of employer–employee relations occasionally came to the fore. Interviewees often considered working environments abroad as more respectful and considerate. Many noticed trajectories of resilience among migrants and compared their prospects abroad to what is conventionally available at home. Occasionally, labour migration was imagined as being able to provide the circumstances for one's 'true value' to emerge. For instance, Olivia, a VET student in hospitality in a small town, recalls her hardships as a 'child left behind.' She is judgemental towards her mother for leaving her children back home with an alcoholic father. However, her discourse soon turns into admiration for a neighbour with a troubled history shaped by alcohol, divorce and a bad reputation who, once abroad, underwent an unexpected transformation. According to Olivia, he made a fresh start, without the preconceptions that limited his actions back home. A few years later, he was back in Romania as a respected entrepreneur.

Taking a neoliberal shift, Olivia uses his success story as a model of non-alignment and highly regards the idea of 'sacrificing everything, including the family life for one's dream.' The underlying logic of her (gendered) account is that migration provides a 'moment zero' for someone with a heavy social load back home. Moving abroad provides the necessary circumstances to succeed. However, the locus of the ultimate display of the achievement–revenge nexus is very locally bound:

> And when they see it, they will be surprised that you made it. Even many of our colleagues wonder how many persons became so great. They became this way because they sacrificed their family, they had sleepless nights and now they can inspire others to be the same. (Olivia, 16, VET hospitality, small town)

Work relationships abroad (seen as more democratic) were often counterbalanced by what appeared to be a strong profit-maximization ethos among Romanian entrepreneurs or those managing the Romania production lines of foreign companies. Both young people and teachers offered local examples of where the search for profit had compromised the quality of employer–employee relationships (unpaid extra hours, medical leave replaced for annual leave, inappropriate language and strong pressure on new entrants, etc.). We can infer that the narratives about employment abroad (or the direct experience thereof) offer critical lenses for interpreting a work setting and enable young people to imagine alternative managerial styles.

The interviewees also seem to be aware that the implications of migration extend beyond 'being away for a while.' According to many, 'getting the taste of the money' abroad will influence future choices and one's willingness to work for less back home. Fractured occupational trajectories and circular migration were often framed as consequences of this type of uneasiness.

I: But are you more likely to get a job here if you work abroad first and then return?
Paul: Well ... not really.
I: No?
David: Yes!
I: Paul says 'No' and you, David, say 'Yes' ...
Paul: No, because if you work there for a few years and you come back here ... [f]irst, you won't agree with the salary anymore. So, when you think you were earning thousands of euros and here you get a little over ten thousand Lei [Romanian currency]...
David: That's how it will be.
Paul: And here you work around the clock. And this is work! So, it doesn't suit you anymore. And the employers will think like: 'Why didn't you stay in Romania, why you go abroad.' A bit of discrimination, I mean.
David: But don't you think it's kind of the same? You work here, you get 1400 Lei a month. There, you get 1400 Euros. You come home; you get a low salary. Again, you don't like it and you go back. The same thing over and over.
Paul: But wait a little. So, if you go and come back worse than you left, that's not good. [laughs]
David: Wait a minute.
Paul: So, when you come from there, you have to ... basically you are supposed to get something out of it.
David: If you weren't able to make any savings, you could've as well stayed here, in Romania.
Paul: No?! since you decided to go! It's not that you went and you bought yourself a car and that's it! [laughs]

(Focus group, grade 11, VET class in electrical engineering, large city)

In many ways, for young males, migration becomes a project of self-realization and masculinity, as it involves risk-taking, independence and taking control of one's life (see also Vlase 2018). To the interviewed VET staff, this notion was broader, and youth mobility seemed to incorporate the idea of the 'rite of passage.' For instance, a teacher in a VET class in electrical engineering manifested his disappointment about young people's preference for migration in remote and precarious fields such as constructions and hospitality at the expense of starting low in order to build up their career in their qualification field back home. In his opinion, 'regardless of warnings and advice, young people need to learn the hard way. They go abroad, open their eyes, and after few years, they are back home.' Quality employment is not however open to all. It should also be said that the competences learned in VET rarely bring productivity to employers from day one. Patience, learning on the job and hard work pay off in the long term in certain (masculine) trades, such as welding, locksmithing, plumbing and being a mechanic. These options are heavily used in VET marketing, yet to many young people, a weak habitus in the field, poor job orientation, unreceptive working environments and poor transportation links make going abroad appear more alluring.

To the interviewees, migration is about more than good pay. For those living in rural areas or small towns, it enables transitions towards *independent living and, in some cases*, experimenting life as a couple. Consumption and the alluring image of metropolitan lifestyles also emerged as powerful motivators behind migration projects. Being able to afford a night out matters, as can particular brands of clothes, shoes and expensive gadgets. These are symbolic status markers that carry value for disadvantaged young people:

> I like to have what I need. If I want to buy a pair of shoes, then I buy a pair of bloody shoes. I should not wait for a month, until I've put enough aside. I do not like these things. 'If I want to get a phone, I have to wait until summer.' I don't like those things. You'd better kill yourself and that's it. (George, 17, construction class, major city)

Young people's focus on the social symbols of consumption resonates with the arguments in Winlow and Hall's (2009, 2013) work. Consumerism is viewed as a compelling force that embraces people defined as socially excluded, either as outsiders wishing to gain a place inside the consumer world or marginal insiders, and migration becomes a tool that enables 'consumption for inclusion' back home to happen. As argued in Bauman (1998), in a dystopian realignment of identity markers, consumption replaces work as a source of distinctiveness. Young people who are economically excluded from consumption ('flawed consumers' according to Bauman) are also in a sense deprived of identity due to the emphasis they place on material goods. Young people's readiness to accept work that is dangerous, demeaning or dirty when abroad (and to refuse it in Romania) is part of their attempt to acquire a social life where consumption (and not work, for that matter) is the powerful status indicator. The role of consumption in shaping young people's social worlds, and the instrumentalization of (precarious) migration thereby challenges the mainstream understanding of VET. Ultimately, these interviewees are questioning the potency of work as an identity marker, bringing us closer to the possibility that we need 'to uncouple' social esteem and security from paid employment (Beck 2000: 58).

It is not only the meaning of work that is changing for the young people in VET, but also its mobility. During the focus groups, stories of not (that) successful migration experiences started to be shared. The failure of others' migration projects was often an expression of disenchantment: it became increasingly hard for a migrant to maintain a competitive advantage while being away as prices in Romania were also high, and earning enough to buy a house in Romania becomes a remote aspiration to many, with the situation of migrant friends spending the money they earned in a holiday back home another leitmotiv.

Under these circumstances, young people sometimes arrive at the idea that mobility is valuable for reasons other than economic expediency. To several interviewees, migration is a short-term neoliberal project that combines exploration, self-discovery and personal growth—counterintuitive middle-class aspirations, rarely associated with VET. This research suggests that, while rare, such goals are indicative of the prevailing focus on skills oversimplifying young people's complex social worlds. In simpler terms, those in VET are also interested in 'seeing other places' while avoiding the intricacy of a migration process: 'Being a truck driver! That's cool. It's like being a paid tourist. You see the world; you see interesting places.' Similarly, a young woman in a class on construction (a rare occurrence in itself) envisioned herself doing seasonal work in agriculture in order to allow herself to take exotic vacations, while another, in a forestry class, thinks that some time off for travel would allow more introspection and a clear vision of her *future to emerge*. During this research, indications of this practice also appeared indirectly, as a peer critique of others' poor work ethic, 'starting with a holiday':

> There are many saying 'let's take a one-year vacation, now, that I'm done with school. I stay, I relax and then, I go to work.' But then, if you think again: he throws a good job down the drain and when he comes to his senses, the job is taken. (Victor, 17, VET auto-mechanics, city)

However, for many research participants, the border between safe and precarious migration was rather blurred:

> No, I don't have anyone [abroad]. I simply want a new experience, a new country, to see what civilization is like in other countries, to see what the mentality of people is, to see how they cook out there. Any little thing matters. (Anita, 17, VET in cooking, city)

Anita seemed to turn a blind eye to the risks involved in precarious migration. She was assured by the fact that people who warned her that 'the contract is just for show and she may end up unpaid' were simply wrong: 'maybe they deceived themselves and they picked an unreliable workplace.' By and large, research participants appeared under-equipped for dealing with the risks of precarious migration. The 'management of migration' was an entirely 'personal' issue, without schools paying an awareness-raising role related to its negative implications.

Conclusions

The fieldwork was carried out in a context shaped by alarming data on migration tendencies, notably research claiming that nearly half of 15–24-year-olds in Romania intend to emigrate (OECD 2019: 15). Yet, a survey on a sample larger than 10,000 has suggested that migration intentions among Romanian young people are actually decreasing; about 30 per cent of those aged 14–29 years 'seem to want to leave Romania for a period of at least six months,' compared to 60 per cent in 2014

(Bădescu et al. 2019). The younger migrants come, it is argued, almost exclusively from the most disadvantaged strata, and the young people in VET belong to this group. Our research has aimed to add nuance to these statistics by exploring the meanings young people attach to contemporary migration processes. The findings suggest that we cannot aggregate young people's views on what kind of mobility is worthwhile. In certain ways, 'going abroad' is close to a generic category, filled with ideas that mirror many of the shortcomings young people see in their prospective working lives in Romania. Economic constraints hindering a transition to an independent life in Romania emerged as a major reason for temporary migration, but conventional aspirations and a grand narrative about decent work and family life also came to the fore. This was, in many ways, an expected finding, largely confirmed by mounting statistical evidence.

Besides economic rationales, the idea of migration has brought into focus fundamental questions about young people's social lives, family bonds and economic needs: 'Family and friends are here, money is there.' To the interviewees, those who migrate appeared as tormented by a continuous dilemma about whether or not they have made the 'right choice' and where the limits of mobility lie (see also Marcu 2019), although those who did not migrate were also marked by similar dilemmas. This research further suggests that interviewees' relationship with the idea of mobility includes neoliberal undertones. The potency of consumption helps to explain their readiness to instrumentalize migration (including highly precarious work abroad) in a short-term economic project or for some kind of social validation *back home*. For the young people in VET, 'being able to buy stuff' acted as a powerful status indicator, but the experience abroad can also be exploratory in nature and not seen as just an economic project.

Despite the dominance of work-related policy priorities in VET, an unanticipated finding was that young people's aspirations related to personal growth. For example, there were many instances (especially among young women), where mobility intentions were related to a desire to explore, and to gain a deeper understanding of other cultures. Seeing *other* places, getting to know *other* people and experiencing a world where 'things are done differently' were powerful drivers. However, in such contexts, young people often retained a sense of anguish directed at a system whose benefits are refused to those of 'their kind.' For young males, the possibility of dispatch work (possible, yet unlikely) combined the security of employment in Romania with the competitive advantage of a high salary. The 'in-between-ness' of such options, usually in occupations that meet the Goldthorpe et al. (1969) notion of 'affluent workers,' was favoured to the idea of independent, long-term labour migration.[4]

These findings lead us to identify several policy implications. The research shows that young people in initial vocational education and training have complex social worlds and aspirations. When the conversation starts with what matters to young people, and not from policy priorities (Powell 2013), new facets of their social lives are likely to be revealed. Young people in VET appear as more than just a 'labour force,' although the school and training environments they are exposed to barely cater to their needs that are not directly 'work-related.' Many are interested in experiencing work elsewhere in Europe, yet in more protected environments than the ones likely to be made available through their (precarious) social networks. Several interviewees favoured a 'gap year' that would allow mobility, exploration, discovery and growth. However, these needs are likely to escape the mainstream policy thinking on VET, which has a strong utilitarian bias.

In December 2016, the European Commission launched ErasmusPro, a policy initiative aimed at increasing long-term mobility abroad through work placements for VET learners, apprentices and graduates (European Commission 2019). The initiative does not have the scale and visibility of the other Erasmus+ programme actions, but is timely recognition of the mobility aspirations and needs of the young people in VET. The level of inclusiveness for those at the very bottom remains to be seen, especially given the large heterogeneity of VET (including people from upper secondary, post-secondary and some tertiary education). For those in initial VET included in this research, these types of opportunities seem extremely remote.

This research has implications for youth studies as well, as it maps the complex social worlds of 'non-metropolitan' young people (see also Farrugia and Wood 2017; Cuervo and Wyn 2012). It argues that to a certain extent, their aspirations and sense of belonging are shaped in ways that do not exclude certain middle-class, urban attributes (consumption, travel, exploration, etc.). However, the extent to which their aspirations are actualized and the tensions generated in the context of socio-economic disadvantage resolved call for further investigation.

Finally, the research suggests that debates on the 'changing meanings of work' need to attach fresh insights to the changing meanings of mobility. The implications extend to the social categories for which several mobility facets (e.g. travel, exploration, timeout) have traditionally been ignored. Mobility signals social value in many ways and for (otherwise disadvantaged) young people as well. By looking at the meanings young people in VET attach to mobility, we can get a closer understanding of their social worlds, their aspirations and the constraints that limit their capability to *live* the *life they have reason* to *value* (Sen 1999). It calls for revisiting the politics of mobility that allows for personal growth and exploration for some and demands for work-related value of others.

Acknowledgements This work was supported by a grant of the Romanian National Authority for Scientific Research and Innovation, CNCS—UEFISCDI, project number PN-III-P1-1.1-TE-2016-0368.

Notes

1. In comparison, Poland has lost 21 per cent, the Czech Republic and Slovakia 19 per cent, and Hungary 14 per cent of their active populations in the same period.
2. A simple calculation leads to the finding that this research included at least 0.5 per cent of young people currently in VET (grades 10 and 11).
3. Young people in VET receive a 45 Euros monthly allowance subject to attendance.
4. For Romania, this involves, notably, work as a professional truck driver and, occasionally, welding. Yet, while the idea of having such jobs is alluring, the young people in VET are unlikely to meet the selection criteria.

References

Bădescu, G., Sandu, D., Angi, D., & Greab, C. G. (2019). *Tinerii din Romania: 2018–2019.* Friedrich-Ebert-Stiftung.

Bauman, Z. (1998). *Globalization: The human consequences.* New York: Columbia University Press.

Beck, U. (1992). *The risk society: Towards a new modernity.* London: Sage.

Beck, U. (1994). *Reflexive modernization: Politics, tradition and aesthetics in the modern social order.* Cambridge: Polity Press.

Beck, U. (2000). *The brave new world of work.* Oxford: Polity Press.

Billett, S. (2011). *Vocational education. Purposes, traditions and prospects.* Dordrecht: Springer.

Cairns, D. (2021a). Mobility becoming migration: Understanding youth spatiality in the twenty-first century. In D. Cairns (Ed.), *The Palgrave handbook of youth mobility and educational migration.* Basingstoke: Palgrave Macmillan.

Cairns, D. (2021b). Migration decision-making, mobility capital and reflexive learning. In D. Cairns (Ed.), *The Palgrave handbook of youth mobility and educational migration.* Basingstoke: Palgrave Macmillan.

Cedefop. (2011). *Vocational education and training is good for you the social benefits of VET for individuals* (Research paper No. 17). Luxembourg: Publications Office.

Cuervo, H., & Wyn, J. (2012). *Young people making it work: Continuity and change in rural places.* Melbourne: Melbourne University Press.

European Commission. (2017). *Council recommendation on the 2017 national reform programme of Romania and delivering a council opinion on the 2017 convergence programme of Romania.* Brussels: European Commission.

European Commission. (2019). *Erasmus+ Programme guide.* Luxembourg: Publications Office.

Farrugia, D., & Wood, B. E. (2017). Youth and spatiality: Towards interdisciplinarity. *Youth Studies, 25*(3), 209–218.

Goldthorpe, J. H., Lockwood, D., Bechhofer, F., & Platt, J. (1969). *The affluent worker in the class structure.* Cambridge: Cambridge University Press.

Greinert, W.-D. (2004). European vocational training systems: Some thoughts on the theoretical context of their historical development. *European Journal of Vocational Training, 32,* 18–25.

Marcu, S. (2017). Tears of time: A Lefebvrian rhythm analysis approach to explore the mobility experiences of young Eastern Europeans in Spain. *Transactions of the Institute of British Geographers, 42*(3), 405–416.

Marcu, S. (2019). The limits to mobility: Precarious work experiences among young Eastern Europeans in Spain. *Environment and Planning A: Economy and Space, 51*(4), 913–930.

McGrath, S. (2012). Vocational education and training for development: A policy in need of a theory? *International Journal of Educational Development, 32*(5), 623–631.

OECD. (2019). *Talent abroad: A review of Romanian emigrants.* Paris: OECD Publishing.

Pantea, M. C. (2019a). *Precarity and vocational education and training. Craftsmanship and employability in Romania.* Basingstoke: Palgrave Macmillan.

Pantea, M. C. (2019b). Perceived reasons for pursuing vocational education and training among young people in Romania. *Journal of Vocational Education and Training, 72*(1), 136–156.

PIAROM. (2018). *Studiu privind dinamica pieței muncii la nivelul principalelor industrii angajatoare din România în perioada 2016–2017.* Bucuresti: PIAROM.

Powell, L. (2013). A critical assessment of research on South African FET colleges. *South African Review of Education, 19*(1), 59–81.

Sen, A. (1999). *Development as freedom.* New York: Alfred A. Knopf.

Sennett, R. (2004). *Respect in a world of inequality.* London: Penguin.

United Nations. (2016). *International migration report 2015 highlights.* New York: United Nations.

Vlase, I. (2018). Men's migration, adulthood, and the performance of masculinities. In I. Vlase & B. Voicu (Eds.), *Gender, family, and adaptation of migrants in Europe* (pp. 195–225). Basingstoke: Palgrave Macmillan.

Winlow, S., & Hall, S. (2013). Living for the weekend: Youth identities in northeast England. *Ethnography, 10*(91), 91–113.
Winlow, S., & Hall, S. (2009). 'Living for the Weekend'. Youth Identities in Northeast England. Ethnography, 10(1), 91–113.
World Bank. (2018). *World development report 2018: Learning to realize education's promise*. Washington, DC: World Bank.

Chapter 28
Using Cross-border Mobility in Vocational Education and Training in the Greater Region SaarLorLux

Birte Nienaber, H. Peter Dörrenbächer, Ines Funk, Isabelle Pigeron-Piroth, Rachid Belkacem, Malte Helfer, Claudia Polzin-Haumann, and Christina Reissner

In the course of the neoliberalization of the economy, the mobility of capital and goods along international value chains, and the interregional and international mobility of labour, have played increasingly prominent roles. As part of this trend, vocational education training (VET) mobility has become an important form of youth mobility, particularly considering its imaginative and concrete links to labour mobility. The prevalence of VET mobility between different labour markets and VET regions is, to a major degree, dependent on the distances and different economic profiles of the regions involved, and as discussed in previous chapters, personal dreams and aspirations also create imperatives to move abroad (see also Pantea 2021 in this book). Institutional (cultural and legal) differences also play a decisive role in the intensity of interregional and international VET mobility. But whereas there is a positive relationship between interregional economic and demographic differences in labour market regions and mobility, the relationships between spatial distances, and institutional/cultural differences of labour market regions and mobility are more negative. Therefore, the highest level of interregional VET mobility can be assumed to take place between neighbouring regions whose geographical distances as well as institutional and cultural differences are small, and demographic and economic differences are at the same time large.

In the case of neighbouring regions belonging to different nation states, a high mobility potential, allowing a win-win situation for both regions, is limited only by the institutional differences/distances of respective VET systems. This means that,

---

B. Nienaber (✉) • I. Pigeron-Piroth • M. Helfer
University of Luxembourg, Luxembourg City, Luxembourg
e-mail: birte.nienaber@uni.lu

H. P. Dörrenbächer • I. Funk • C. Polzin-Haumann • C. Reissner
Universität des Saarlandes, Saarbrücken, Germany

R. Belkacem
Université de Lorraine, Nancy, France

especially in border regions, the adaptation and harmonization of different VET systems will lead to increased VET mobility and therefore promises the positive socio-economic effects on both sides of the national borders. That is why this chapter does not address the development of VET mobility in general at the international (i.e., European) level but rather explores the development of approaches and conceptions of transboundary VET mobility, using a particularly exceptional example in the Greater Region SaarLorLux.

European and International Scale of VET Mobility

It is evident that the development of interregional and transboundary cooperation in the field of VET and VET mobility is highly dependent on attempts to harmonize existing national VET systems in Europe. It is therefore not surprising that the Lisbon strategy of the European Union aimed to improve the competitiveness of the European economy by motivating such initiatives, leading to common standards of VET, succeeding the so-called Bruges–Copenhagen process (later on called just Copenhagen process) from 2002 onward. The aims of Europe 2020 strategy (Council of the European Union 2015), together with the Riga Conclusions (Latvian Presidency of the Council of the EU et al. 2015: 4) were, among others,

> to promote work-based learning in all its forms, with special attention to apprenticeships, by involving social partners, companies, chambers and VET providers, as well as by stimulating innovation and entrepreneurship, further [to] develop quality assurance mechanisms in VET in line with the EQAVET recommendation and … [to] enhance access to VET and qualifications for all through more flexible and permeable systems, notably by offering efficient and integrated guidance services and making available validation of non-formal and informal learning.

The permeability of national VET systems and the opening of these systems to new actors allowed by this EU policy were most important and effective in those labour and economic regions bordering the respective regions of neighbouring nation states. The first important framework agreement was signed in the Upper Rhine border region: the cross-border region between France, Germany and Switzerland (RVOR 2013). This agreement can be considered a blueprint for later agreements in other border regions. It has, for the first time, provided young apprentices with a legal framework for performing the theoretical training in their respective home countries and also the practical training in the workplace of the neighbouring country, and can be considered a milestone on the pathway to developing comprehensive and integrated cross-border VET regions.

As has been shown earlier, the highest potential of VET mobility exists between neighbouring regions whose distances from one another are small and whose economic performances (e.g., unemployment rate) and demographic structures diverge. The present article deals with the development of VET youth mobility in the transboundary Greater Region SaarLorLux. It describes and analyses this transboundary VET mobility as the outcome of interregional learning processes (Funk et al. 2020), and in terms of the institutionalization of transboundary VET, initiated and implemented by different actors ranging from regional transboundary politics, economic associations and VET providers (Dörrenbächer 2018).

The Greater Region SaarLorLux: Labour Market and Education Profile

The Greater Region consists of two German Länder (Saarland and Rhineland-Palatinate), the former French region of Lorraine (including the Departments Moselle, Meurthe-et-Moselle, Meuse and Vosges), the Grand Duchy of Luxembourg and the Walloon Region (including the French community in Belgium as well as the German-speaking community in Belgium), with a land surface of 65,401 km^2 and a population of 11.6 million inhabitants, making it the largest transboundary region in Europe. It is not only the largest cross-border region with regard to surface and population but also the region with the highest number of transnational commuters in the EU. Everyday around 240,000 commuters cross the national borders. With almost 200,000 incoming commuters in 2019, the Grand Duchy of Luxembourg is by far the region with the biggest pull. Runner-up is the Saarland, which attracts 16,300 commuters from Lorraine every day (Les offices statistiques de la Grande Région 2018: 17).

Whereas transboundary relations in the Greater Region have a long tradition, the recent dynamic development of transboundary commuter flows is associated with the strong economic and demographic disparities of the regions that make up the Greater Region. While the fast-growing economy (particularly the finance sector) in the Grand Duchy of Luxembourg stimulates a strong commuter influx and the need for a well-trained young workforce, the ageing population of the Saarland necessitates efforts to attract young people for transboundary VET. At the same time, many young people in Lorraine are seeking employment. The Greater Region therefore

> promotes an active labour market policy based on cross-border mobility for all job types and career stages. One of the pillars of professional mobility are cross-border training programmes. The Framework Agreement on Cross-border Vocational Training in the Greater Region signed in 2014 ensures cross-border mobility within initial and continuing vocational training programmes. (Großregion/Grande Région 2019)

History/Institutional Framework of Cross-border VET in the Greater Region

Given the long-standing intensive transboundary interrelations and strong commuter flows in the Greater Region (cf. Dörrenbächer 2015; Belkacem et al. 2018), it is not particularly astonishing that there existed a large number of diverse cross-border VET initiatives, even prior to the Framework Agreement on Cross-border

Vocational Training in the Greater Region in 2014. Cooperation was initiated long before the signing of the Agreement and is well-documented by the Interregional Observatory of the Greater Region's labour market (Netzwerk der Fachinstitute der Interregionalen Arbeitsmarktbeobachtungsstelle 2014: 173) and the Task Force Grenzgänger (2012). Without claiming to be exhaustive, both reports list more than 50 measures and projects related to VET in general, and of these, 20 projects were engaged in VET in a narrower sense. Most of these initiatives and projects have been short-term activities such as transboundary internships. These internships became only feasible, in the context of the Copenhagen process, after France and Germany, in 2005 and 2009, allowed participants to perform portions of their VET abroad.

The development of comprehensive transboundary VET programmes gained momentum with the negotiation and signing of the Framework Agreement on the cooperation in the field of cross-border vocational training and continuing education, which was negotiated and signed by Saarland and Lorraine (RVSL 2014), and also the related Agreement on the implementation of the Framework Agreement (AGBSL 2014). The negotiation and implementation of these agreements can be traced back to the 12th Summit of the Greater Region held in January 2011, which recommended an intensification of cross-border cooperation in the field of VET to strengthen the competitiveness of the Greater Region as well as taking action against high youth unemployment in some member regions. The same summit initiated the setting up of the so-called Task Force Grenzgänger (Task Force Cross-border Commuters) in 2011, which was to provide legal support to cross-border commuters. Apart from this, the Task Force also documented and analysed projects of transboundary VET hitherto initiated.

Most important for the development of the Saar–Lorraine framework agreement was the development of the aforementioned framework agreement in the Upper Rhine border region, signed the year before (RVOR 2013). This agreement can be considered the blueprint for the Saar–Lorraine agreement of 2014, which was itself a blueprint for the Framework Agreement on Cross-border Vocational Training in the Greater Region (RVGR 2014), signed in November 2014. As the denotation 'Framework Agreement' highlights, the purpose of these agreements was to provide a flexible framework for a myriad of cooperations in the field of cross-border VET (see later), allowing for the adoption of so-called experimentation clauses plus the integration of a diverse composition of actors concerned with VET.

Most of the cross-border VET agreements (with different legal statuses) have come into place from 2018 onwards. Very few were fully integrated before this time. However, it is important to add that there is a diversity in cross-border VET mobility that is not institutionalized, but based on individual, actor-based approaches. For example, Iffrig (2019) has analysed cross-border VET taking place on the German–French (Alsace) border, concluding that VET continues to follow very nation-specific approaches (see also Brucy et al. 2013; Goulet and Seidendorf 2017) and cross-border VET remains an exception on a local case-by-case basis, rather than on a national level.

Cross-border VET in the Greater Region

In the context of the Europeanization of employment and training, the implementation of vocational training policies has occurred in each of the territories of the Greater Region through the European Employment Strategy (EES) and the Bologna Process, to meet the needs of the respective cross-border labour markets. Here we have an unprecedented form of development of apprenticeships in the territories of the Greater Region and a turn towards a cross-border labour market. This increasing professionalization of youth education systems is carried out at all levels of education, including universities and specialized vocational schools. For example, in Lorraine, the creation of Bachelor's and Master's degree programmes complies with the growing needs of the cross-border labour market. This development is accompanied by cooperation in the professional world and the world of education in the VET programmes and courses. The industries involved in cross-border VET in the Greater Region are branches that are important for the whole region, as well as areas with overall labour shortages, most explicitly car production, childcare, healthcare, commerce and retail, site managers, construction, industry, carpenters, transport, agriculture and bookbinding.

The types of actors identified in the field of cross-border vocational education and training are broad. Not all actors are actively involved in all types of cross-border VET, but they can be grouped into educational institutions, employment agencies, authorities and entrepreneurial partners and organizations. With regard to the actors engaged in cross-border VET, the whole array of educational institutions, secondary schools, vocational schools and universities takes part in VET initiatives. Vocational schools especially can be seen as the main actors in the field of VET, establishing bilateral agreements and course options that include cross-border mobility. Furthermore, employment agencies like ADEM, FOREM and Bundesagentur für Arbeit are supporting cross-border VET schemes by supervising other actors as well as facilitating this with the authorities. Regional and local authorities are setting the legal and administrative frameworks to enable the fostering of future development. The education sector is not alone in the important development of VET programmes. Companies, enterprise associations (e.g., FagA/CAMT, see later), as well as chambers of commerce, craft trades and employees, are all playing an important role. The needs of these institutions and of regional companies to find young, motivated and often bilingual staff is a leading factor in the framing of the new VET programmes, and enterprises with specific interests in cross-border VET mobility are working closely with the authorities to find straightforward solutions to lower the existing barriers.

The legal as well as the political status of VET programmes also varies. It ranges from conversation, consultation interviews, letters of intent, strategic cooperation agreements and framework agreements, and from regulations, up to the laws that enable cross-border VET mobility for special industries (e.g., bookbinders). Moreover, in some cases there is also funding for cross-border cooperations supported by Erasmus+ as well as by INTERREG. Luxembourg, as a national state, is a distinct case in the Greater Region. In Luxembourgish law, the possibilities of cross-border VET according to the national needs are published and updated each year. The theoretical part of VET is always completed abroad and the training is conducted in Luxembourg. With regard to durations, VET programmes differ. The mobility phase can include vocational education and/or more often training. Depending on the design of the programme, there can be one mobility phase or regular daily mobility between one or more countries. The following mobility durations and types were identified:

- No specified duration period abroad.
- Short stays (from one day up to two weeks).
- Stays of several weeks.
- Internships (up to six months).
- Joint vocational education courses or modules.
- Vocational education in one country and training in another country (e.g., in Luxembourg).
- Double VET degrees with exams wholly in one country.
- Double VET degrees with exams in both countries.

Most of the cross-border VET programmes are bilateral, but there also exists tri and quatro-lateral programmes. In the tri-national VET programme 'Formation professionnelle transfrontalière des éducateurs entre le Luxembourg, la Rhénanie Palatinat et la Sarre/Grenzüberschreitende Berufsausbildung von Erziehern zwischen Lux, RLP und SL' (crossborder VET for educators), the theoretical part of VET is completed abroad. In the bilateral framework between Luxembourg and Lorraine, the theoretical part of the VET is completed in one country whereas the practical part is performed in the neighbouring country. In the programme 'Training without borders' apprentices from Luxembourg complete parts of their practical training in Belgium and France. Another example that shows the wide diversity of existing VET programmes is the French–German car mechanics VET, which consists of obligatory internships in the neighbouring country.

The Plurilingual Dimension of VET

Cross-border VET programmes and VET mobility require, among other skills, language competence. If it is true that all over Europe, and especially in the Greater Region, cross-border formation is an increasingly important issue, we also have to admit the influential role such programmes might play in language learning. However, this has not been developed in parallel with these concepts. Thus, the language question remains an important challenge. Practice and research show that specific concepts that would drive language learning and teaching in these contexts are still lacking. In consequence of the continuous promotion of plurilingualism and cultural diversity, and hence language acquisition, the respective national and regional frameworks have also been transformed since the 1990s. For the Greater

Region, and especially in the Saarland and Lorraine, there is a clear political commitment to support the language of the respective neighbour. On both sides of the border this commitment is reflected in long-term educational policies. In Saarland, there are two core documents regarding language policy:

1. The Sprachenkonzept (Ministerium für Bildung und Kultur Saarland/Universität des Saarlandes 2019, as a continuation of the Sprachenkonzept 2011, cf. Polzin-Haumann and Reissner 2012: 133f.)
2. The Saarland State Government's Frankreichstrategie (France Strategy) (cf. Staatskanzlei Saarland 2014; see also Polzin-Haumann 2017)

On the other side of the border, the 'Stratégie Allemagne', devised by the Académie Nancy for the position of German in the French school context (see Maccarini 2017), aims to foster the learning of German in the Lorraine Region (for details concerning the different political documents and a critical view on the realization of the policies, cf. Polzin-Haumann and Reissner 2018). Most recently, the French–German Treaty of Aix-la-Chapelle (2019), successor to the Élysée-Treaty from 1963, underlines the importance of cross-border cooperation as well as the specific character of border regions. It expresses the intention to overcome any difficulties that might impede cross-border cooperation; furthermore, it refers explicitly to the goal of bilingualism and the commitment of the two signatory states to support the local actors in the development of appropriate strategies in order to achieve this goal. The Convention cadre 'Pour une vision stratégique commune du développement des politiques éducatives en faveur du plurilinguisme et du transfrontalier', signed 16 July 2019 between the Académie Nancy-Metz, the Lorraine University and the départements of the Région Grand Est, is another important political document. Alongside this, the development of German as a language from early ages, and teacher's professionalization, 'un travail spécifique en direction de la voie professionnelle' ('specific work towards the vocational route'), is one of the five axes of this convention. This overview shows that the importance of language learning and teaching in cross-border VET has received recognition.

There are several programmes and projects that have been engaged to deal with VET. One example is the project 'Grenzgänger' set up by the Goethe Institute, which has not only developed substantial material in the area of German–French vocational language training but also organizes seminars in this field, besides other activities. Nevertheless, and despite numerous experiences in the field, a coherent concept for systematically implementing language learning, especially in professional and vocational education, is still missing. A future project at the European Centre for Modern Languages of the Council of Europe (ECML) will attempt to close this gap. By pooling expertise from three different border regions, guidelines and training modules for plurilingual and intercultural teaching and learning will be developed and piloted in the project's border regions. This might be a model for other border regions to innovate in their approaches to VET in border-crossing working environments.

Case Study: Fachstelle für grenzüberschreitende Ausbildung (FagA)/Centre d'aide à la mobilité transfrontalière (CAMT)

The Specialist Centre for Cross-border Training (FagA/CAMT) was established in January 2013 as a non-profit organization. It organizes and promotes internships in neighbouring countries for youth from Lorraine (France), Saarland and Western Palatinate (Germany). The centre was initially financed by the Saarland state government, the Saarland Chamber of Industry and Commerce, the Saarland Metal and Electrical Industry Association and, since July 2014, by the Employment Agency (Dörrenbächer 2018: 292f). Since July 2016, it has continued as a five-year project within the framework of the INTERREG Greater Region programme. The aim of FagA/CAMT is to increase the willingness of young people to gain practical experience in the neighbouring countries through concrete organizational and financial support for internships and training periods in the chosen country, thus promoting their mobility and strengthening their employability in the cross-border labour market.

The target group on the French side are vocational students (Bac Pro level, 22 weeks of training in the form of internships) and other students (BTS/Brevet de technicien supérieur level, 12 weeks of internships). The target groups on the German side are technical secondary school pupils, vocational secondary school pupils, pupils at vocational upper secondary schools and vocational schools, as well as trainees. FagA/CAMT's approach consists of a series of preparatory measures and a package of concrete organizational and financial support for the young people involved (according to information from FagA/CAMT 2019).

In the project year 2018/2019, FagA/CAMT organized and/or financed a total of 109 cross-border internships for 86 Lorraine pupils and students, 22 Saarland technical secondary school pupils, vocational school pupils and trainees, as well as 1 West Palatinate trainee. Within Lorraine, 69 traineeships were in the nearest border department of Moselle and 17 in Meurthe-et-Moselle. Although there are contacts and agreements with the vocational schools of the départements of Meuse and Vosges, which are further away from the border, there have only been company visits to date and no internships abroad (according to information from FagA/CAMT 2019).

With more than 100 organized internships in the project year 2018/2019, more than 3500 young people addressed and contacts to more than 1100 companies on both sides of the Franco–German border, FagA/CAMT is by far the most important player in the field of cross-border vocational training in the Greater Region. The number of organized internships, especially from France to Germany, has risen steadily in recent years. The success of FagA/CAMT is obviously due to the fact that it not only collects and communicates cross-border internship offers and provides financial support, but also actively approaches all relevant actors. In addition to entering into contractual agreements with vocational schools, it is also in contact with the host companies concerned and, last but not least, tries to break down the existing barriers. In particular, young people receive a very hands-on introduction in order to prevent a breakdown in communication due to shyness, to facilitate their journey to the neighbouring country; for example, they are helped to prepare for the interview, and even accompanied to the interview, and FagA/CAMT takes care of (financed) accommodation if necessary. This practical, intensive and individual approach is very costly, but seems to pay off.

According to FagA/CAMT's experience, however, the language barrier continues to play an important role: a large proportion of the young people who completed an internship in a neighbouring country with FagA/CAMT's support had little or no language skills (A1–A2). This meant that FagA/CAMT's internship research usually took longer for them and, according to their own information, young people often found the experience of their first few days in the company extremely difficult. In order to remedy this situation, FagA/CAMT is discussing the use of language assistants in the coming project year and, if necessary, seeks to provide additional support for young people or the host companies concerned (according to information from FagA/CAMT 2019). If the language barrier is already a problem for a large proportion of participants in cross-border internships, it is obvious that the situation concerning non-participants is even more unfavourable.

Conclusion

Cross-border vocational training has not only become an important territorial issue but also one of the most important modes of international exchange for youth mobility. This prominence raises questions about its organization, its contents and its objectives. Expected developments on both sides of the borders in terms of demography, digital development and new ecological constraints will have an effect on the content of occupations, skills and qualifications. Territorial training systems will increasingly require the construction of transferable qualifications from one territory to another. Cross-border VET becomes a crucial subject, common to all the territories on an interregional scale. Indeed, it can be seen as a possible solution for some future challenges of the neighbouring regions (e.g., ageing populations, labour shortages and digitalization).

At the individual level, cross-border regions should be considered a real opportunity for young people to be accommodated in the labour market, by learning from the neighbouring system. Despite a large growth of the variety and supply of cross-border VET in the Greater Region, since the Framework Agreement on Cross-Border Vocational Training in the Greater Region (in 2014), some obstacles can be identified that must be overcome. Most of them are related to the border and its impacts, such as cultural and linguistic differences, national differences of job definition and norms, as well as problems in recognition of degrees.

Acknowledgements We thank Alexandra Schwarz from the Fachstelle für grenzüberschreitende Ausbildung (FagA) at the Verbundausbildung Untere Saar e.V. (VAUS) for her very friendly and comprehensive support.

References

AGBSL. (2014). *Abkommen über grenzüberschreitende Berufsausbildung Saarland- Lothringen/ Accord relatif à l'apprentissage transfrontalier Sarre*. Lorraine: AGBSL.

Belkacem, R., Dörrenbächer H. P., & Pigeron, I. (2018). *Beschäftigung und wirtschaftliche Entwicklung in der Großregion: differenzierte Wirtschaftsentwicklung und Wirkungen der grenzüberschreitenden Beschäftigung/Emploi et développement économique au sein de la Grande Région: développement économique différencié et impacts de l'emploi transfrontalier*. UniGR-CBS Working Paper, Vol. 3 (Territorial Science Echo).

Brucy, G., Maillard, F., & Moreau, G. (2013). Introduction: du CAP à l'Europe. *Cahiers de la recherche sur l'éducation et les savoirs, 4*, 5–15.

Council of the European Union. (2015). *Council Decision (EU) 2015/1848 of 5 October 2015 on guidelines for the employment policies of the Member States for 2015. Official Journal of the European Union, L 268/28, 15.10.2015.*

Dörrenbächer, H. P. (2015). Ein grenzüberschreitender Wirtschaftsraum? Gemeinsame und individuelle Entwicklungen seit der Krise des Montansektors. In C. Wille (Ed.), *Lebenswirklichkeiten und politische Konstruktionen in Grenzregionen. Das Beispiel der Großregion SaarLorLux: Wirtschaft – Politik – Alltag – Kultur* (pp. 21–37). Bielefeld: Transcript.

Dörrenbächer, H. P. (2018). Die Großregion: Ein grenzüberschreitender Berufsbildungsraum? In K. Pallagst, A. Hartz, & B. Caesar (Eds.), *Border futures – Zukunft Grenze – Avenir Frontière. Zukunftsfähigkeit Grenzüberschreitender Zusammenarbeit* (pp. 286–302). Hannover: Akademie für Raumforschung und Landesplanung.

Funk, I., Nienaber, B., & Dörrenbächer, H. P. (2020). La formation professionnelle transfrontalière en tant que processus d'apprentissage et mobilisation du savoir transfrontaliers. In J.-M. Defays & G. Hamez (Eds.), *Réalités, perceptions et représentations des frontières de l'Union européenne – Realitäten, Wahrnehmungen und Repräsentationen von EU-Grenzen*. Louvain-la-Neuve: Editions Modulaires européennes.

Goulet, V., & Seidendorf, S. (2017). *L'Azubi-Bacpro: retour sur une expérience de coopération transfrontalière dans le domaine de formation. dfi compact, Nr. 15*. Ludwigsburg: Deutsch-Französisches Institut (dfi).

Großregion/Grande Région (2019). *The Greater Region at a Glance*. Retrieved from http://www.granderegion.net/en.

Iffrig, A. (2019). L'apprentissage transfrontalier France/Allemagne, à l'une de l'action publique locale alsacienne. *CAIRN INFO, (146)*, 149–168.

Latvian Presidency of the Council of the European Union, Republic of Latvia—Ministry of Education and Science, European Commission. (2015). *Riga conclusions 2015*. Luxembourg: Publications Office.

Les offices statistiques de la Grande Région/Statistische Ämter der Großregion (Ed.). (2018). *Statistiques en bref/Statistische Kurzinformationen*. Koblenz: Les offices statistiques de la Grande Région.

Maccarini, J. (2017). Die Stellung des Deutschen im französischen Schulkontext. Muttersprache, Vierteljahresschrift für deutsche. *Sprache, 1–2*(127), 52–63.

Ministerium für Bildung und Kultur Saarland, Universität des Saarlandes. (2019). *Sprachenkonzept Saarland 2019 – Neue Wege zur Mehrsprachigkeit im Bildungssystem*. Saarland: Ministerium für Bildung und Kultur Saarland.

Netzwerk der Fachinstitute der Interregionalen Arbeitsmarktbeobachtungsstelle (Ed.). (2014). *Bericht zur wirtschaftlichen und sozialen Lage der Großregion 2013/2014 für den Wirtschafts- und Sozialausschuss der Großregion (WSGAR)*. Saarbrücken: Schriftenreihe der Regionalkommission SaarLorLux – Trier/Westpfalz – Wallonien.

Pantea, M.-C. (2021). Facets of mobility in Romania's vocational education and training. In D. Cairns (Ed.), *The Palgrave handbook of youth mobility and educational migration*. Basingstoke: Palgrave Macmillan.

Polzin-Haumann, C. (2017). Frankreichstrategie und Bildungspolitik. Bestandsaufnahme und Perspektiven aus der Sicht der Angewandten Linguistik und der Sprachlehr-/Sprachlernforschung. In H. J. Lüsebrink, C. Polzin-Haumann, & C. Vatter (Eds.), *Alles Frankreich oder was? Die saarländische Frankreichstrategie im europäischen Kontext/ La France à toutes les sauces? La ›Stratégie France‹ de la Sarre dans le contexte européen* (pp. 97–121). Bielefeld: Transcript.

Polzin-Haumann, C., & Reissner, C. (2012). Perspectives du français en Sarre: politiques et réalités. In P. Cichon, S. Ehrhart, & M. Stegu (Eds.), *Synergies Pays germanophones n°5: Les politiques linguistiques explicites et implicites en domaine francophone* (pp. 129–143). Berlin: Avinus.

Polzin-Haumann, C., & Reissner, C. (2018). Language and language policies in Saarland and Lorraine: Towards the creation of a transnational space? In B. A. Jańczak (Ed.), *Language contact and language policies across borders: Construction and deconstruction of transnational and transcultural spaces* (pp. 45–55). Berlin: Logos.

RVGR. (2014). *Rahmenvereinbarung über grenzüberschreitende Berufsbildung in der Großregion/ Accord-cadre relatif à la formation professionnelle transfrontalière dans la Grande Région.*

RVOR. (2013). *Rahmenvereinbarung über die grenzüberschreitende Berufsausbildung am Oberrhein/Accord cadre relatif à l'apprentissage transfrontalier dans le Rhin supérieur.* Oberrhein: RVOR.

RVSL. (2014). *Rahmenvereinbarung für die Kooperation in der grenzüberschreitenden beruflichen Aus- und Weiterbildung. Saarland-Lothringen. Strategische Ziele/Accord-cadre pour la coopération transfrontalière en formation professionnelle initiale et continue Sarre-Lorraine of 20 June 2014.* Sarre-Lorraine: RVSL.

Staatskanzlei Saarland. (2014). *Eckpunkte einer Frankreichstrategie für das Saarland.* Saarland: Staatskanzlei.

Task Force Grenzgänger/Frontaliers (Ed.). (2012). *Grenzüberschreitende Berufsausbildung in der Großregion.* Saarbrücken: Bestandaufnahme.

Chapter 29
Vocational Learning Abroad: The Case of German VET Mobility

Tabea Schlimbach, Karen Hemming, and Valentina Cuzzocrea

In this chapter, we engage with apprentices' experiences of mobility. We shed light, in particular, on how German vocational educational training (VET) appears as a frame for mobility from the perspective of young people, and how they deal with institutional actors. The discussion is based on empirical data collected for the European Commission–funded research project MOVE, which examined various aspects of European youth mobility. A subsample of 16 qualitative interviews with mobile German apprentices aged 18–29 years is analysed and critically discussed against a wider comparative picture from 152 interviews with mobile youth in six countries.

Putting this discussion into a broader context, across the European Union, mobility exchanges within educational pathways have gained importance as tools to promote both learning and labour market integration. This responds to a logic of employability which has governed labour market policies in recent years. However, while relatively commonplace in other fields of education (such as school exchanges), mobility in VET contexts remains exceptional, resulting in limited research engagement. In order to fill this gap, this chapter aims to develop an empirical perspective on German VET mobility, continuing the exploration of a theme initiated in the previous chapter (Nienaber et al. 2021).

The long-established German VET system, part of a broader system famously characterized as the dual system (school and work-based learning) (Ebner and Uhly 2016), is internationally recognized for its capacity to integrate young people into the labour market. In addition, there are systematic efforts to establish VET within mobility systems. Matching the rigid VET structures, German apprentices'

T. Schlimbach (✉) • K. Hemming
German Youth Institute, Munich, Germany
e-mail: schlimbach@dji.de

V. Cuzzocrea
University of Cagliari, Cagliari, Italy

© The Author(s), under exclusive license to Springer Nature Switzerland AG 2022
D. Cairns (ed.), *The Palgrave Handbook of Youth Mobility and Educational Migration*, https://doi.org/10.1007/978-3-030-99447-1_29

stays abroad are largely organized as short-term group mobility with institutionally predefined features (e.g., destination country, length of stay, accommodation), using funds from European mobility programmes, and the implementation of these programmes is fostered through a nationwide network of professional mobility coaches. As a result, German VET mobility has a strong institutionalized character, providing a unique setting for young people's mobility-related actions and decisions (Schlimbach et al. 2019).

European Youth Mobility as a Political (and Individual) Strategy

Youth mobility in Europe is at the centre of sociopolitical debates, especially in regard to its potential to enhance individual transitions and advance national labour markets in Europe, and to balance different skilled labour needs (Scott 2000; Robertson et al. 2017). Seen from an individual perspective, mobility can be understood as a 'move towards better transitions outcomes, thus linking spatial movement with socio-economic self-advancement' (Cairns 2014). For VET mobility, which takes place during a period of life that is a designated part of the transition to work, a strong link to labour market integration seems consequential. However, in recent work on developments in VET, a link to VET mobility is often missing (see for example Guile and Unwin 2019; McGrath et al. 2019), although internationalization and intercultural competences are badly needed in contemporary vocational education (Pylväs and Nokelainen 2019).

The main instruments of political steerage of youth mobility in Europe are programmes such as the Erasmus+ and its predecessors. At a national level, diverse support structures have been established in order to put these programmes into practice, some aspects of which are discussed in other chapters of this book (see especially Chaps. 17–25). And as addressed in the preceding chapters of this section, other institutional arrangements exist to support VET mobility, especially between neighbouring countries and regions.

The German VET System

In contrast to other European countries, where higher education is the dominant site for labour market preparation, VET in Germany is on an equal footing with university studying: in 2018, 514,000 young people took up tertiary level studies, while 722,700 started a dual or school-based vocational training (Statistisches Bundesamt 2019). Learning on the job is a key element embedded in the VET system in different forms. Most prominent is the 'dual VET,' which combines work-based learning in companies and learning in vocational schools. Aside from dual VET, young people can also enter school-based training as well as pre-vocational activities in the so-called transition system (Ebner and Uhly 2016; Schultheis and Sell 2014).

Corporate regulation of training contents and standards secures uniformity and comparability, as well as proximity to labour market requirements. The success of graduate apprentices in the labour market has contributed to what is currently the lowest youth unemployment rate in Europe (5.6 per cent compared to a 14.3 per cent EU average as of July 2019, according to Eurostat 2019), which is why the German system, in particular 'dual VET,' is widely recognized as a model for labour market integration across Europe (Bosch 2010; Hippach-Schneider and Huismann 2019). Despite this situation, the rising trend towards university education affects the readiness of young people in countries with long VET traditions to choose vocational training (Maurer 2019). Promoting stays abroad during an apprenticeship is part of a national strategy to raise the attractiveness of VET and contribute to enhancing its quality in order to keep up in a globalized economy (Bundesministerium für Bildung und Forschung 2019; Frommberger 2013).

Putting this development into a broader context, compared to other fields such as higher education or volunteering, VET is a relatively new corner of the mobility field, with lower participation rates. However, Germany has witnessed consistent increases in participation, and relatively high numbers, with an estimated 6.3 per cent of all apprentices being mobile in 2018 (NABIBB 2019), and the country has set the ambitious aim of reaching 10 per cent in 2020 (Deutscher Bundestag), surpassing the respective European benchmark of six per cent (European Council and European Commission 2012).

Cross-border experiences during an apprenticeship are expected to enhance intercultural competencies and language skills, as well as key vocational qualifications, while at a macro level, VET mobility contributes to further developing and enhancing national VET systems. These stays are largely assessed as positive and beneficial by apprentices as well as by companies and schools (NABIBB 2018). One in every two mobility exercises are co-funded by public money (one in three exclusively) which comes predominantly from Erasmus+ and other specific programmes such as IdA (for low-qualified youth) or MobiPro (for the training of foreign apprentices in Germany). One third of VET mobility is funded by training companies, while others use (often alongside other resources) private capital (NABIBB 2018). In order to promote the use of mobility programmes, the application procedure has been converted into institutional support (one application per organization instead of one application per travelling person), with more flexibility allowed in its implementation. From this brief overview, we can see that investment in VET mobility is substantial, including public funds, on a scale not matched in most other European countries.

Implementation Strategies and Support Structures in Germany

The harmonization of different learning settings in Germany as well as the maintenance of high standards throughout is a challenge. It requires the cooperation of federal, communal, private and economic institutions, as well as strong regulation of the time frame and content of vocational training. Opportunities to go abroad during a traineeship are regulated via the 'Vocational Training Act' (Berufsbildungsgesetz; BBiG). Accordingly, mobility counts as an integral part of the training which, under certain conditions, does not connote an interruption of a training or need an official recognition procedure (in contrast to a vocational measure outside the training company). However, if the mobility is planned to extend for longer than four weeks, a separate training plan usually has to be set up in cooperation with the chambers (e.g., of craft or commerce) to guarantee the elementary training content. The duration should not exceed one quarter of the duration of the training itself. As the training is not interrupted, contractual obligations (such as apprenticeship pay in the dual VET system) remain valid during the stay abroad (BBiG). The National Agency at the Federal Agency for Vocational Education and Training (Nationale Agentur beim Bundesinstitut für Berufsbildung; NABIBB) coordinates the national implementation of Erasmus+ mobility in the areas of job training and adult education in cooperation with the European Commission.

In order to fit in with the rather tight framing of VET in Germany, mobility exercises are largely organized as short-term, cost-effective group actions, where young people travel with their fellow VET students for less than four weeks at a time. These excursions are facilitated by professional mobility coaches who are part of a nationwide coaching network—an advanced support structure (government-funded within the programme 'Training without borders') that stands out in comparison with the rest of Europe. The mobility coaches inform trainees about mobility opportunities, predefine the main parameters, such as duration, timing, accommodation and placements, establish the necessary contacts and relieve the youth from administrative tasks.

The German VET mobility arrangements (short length of stay, embeddedness in a group and work of mobility advisers) are designed to enable experiences abroad for apprentices to function successfully. However, there are downsides. The (limited) literature on barriers to VET mobility points out the difficulty of finding 'mobility windows' within tight training schedules (European Commission 2017) and a lack of active support from school authorities (Werner et al. 2010), and recently there have been suggestions for the reduction of structural barriers to enable mobility experiences for *all* youth (Becker and Thimmel 2019).

Data and Methods

This chapter draws from the EU-funded MOVE project, which used a multi-method design to analyse various aspects of European youth mobility, including quantitative micro and macro level analyses as well as qualitative analyses based on 152 interviews with mobile youth in six European countries: Germany, Hungary, Luxembourg, Norway, Romania and Spain (for an overview, see Samuk et al. 2018). Interviews were conducted in 2015/16. This text is based on a qualitative case study based on 15 'problem-centred' interviews (Witzel and Reiter 2012) with German apprentices aged 18–29 years. All interviewees experienced cross-country mobility for at least two weeks within Europe in the context of their VET, which was the focus of the interview. The sampling strategy considered variables such as gender (9x female; 6x male), age (12x 18–24/3x 25–29), form of VET (11x dual VET/4x school-based VET) and length of mobility (11x 3–4 weeks/3x 5–8 weeks). For the qualitative analyses, computer-assisted thematic coding and the analysis of 'core themes' (Bernard et al. 2017) was used in a first stage. For the purposes of this paper, cross-case comparisons (Cruzes et al. 2015; Miles and Huberman 1984) were conducted, considering codes related to structural frames and institutional actors.

Results

Our analysis was driven by the idea of reflecting on institutional VET mobility framings in Germany through the eyes of the travelling apprentices. As described, these framings are characteristic of the German VET system: mobility programmes as well as national implementation strategies and support structures. These main aspects will be further explored and explained alongside young people's accounts.

German VET Encounters Mobility

As explained earlier, German VET is strongly regulated, which results in limited and short time slots for mobility without consequence for the training programme. The interviewees reflect upon the embeddedness of mobility into a training setting in different ways. A major concern is to harmonize mobility opportunities so that training is as little affected as possible. This means avoiding missing subject matter or having to make up for missed sessions or practical lessons at work. The dual nature of the German VET also requires that the mobility takes place during school and/or training. An integration of mobility (mainly) into the practical period often seems most desirable, as curricula and exam times are not affected: 'It was obligatory not to do [the mobility] during school time […] we have these block weeks […] in this time we take lots of tests and […] many topics are dealt with, so it would have been difficult to pick up on. [...] School is very strict there [laughs]. They do not release you easily' (y16: 185).The trainees' accounts imply that it is easier to compensate for missed time at the company, especially since the mobility itself is mostly practice-oriented, and, in a best-case scenario, officially recognized as a compulsory practical period, which compensates for a potential loss of regular training time. However, going abroad during the school period can be advantageous if the school itself organizes mobility for entire classes. Thus, school procedures and timelines can be considered, and standardized classes can be taken during mobility as compensation for missed regular schooling at home. Sometimes, mobility is established as an integral part of the training, secured by a contract between the company and the vocational school.

Our empirical material suggests that the harmonization of a stay abroad with the narrow and complicated legal framings of German VET exceeds young people's knowledge and capacities. Moreover, VET mobility requires cooperation between various institutions at home (training companies, schools, chambers) and abroad (host companies and supporting organizations in situ). In order to comply with these demanding conditions and the requisite support needs of apprentices (considering that the average age of German apprentices at the start of their training is about 20 years), and their lack of prior mobility experience, mobility is largely organized by institutionally affiliated mobility coaches, as was the case with most of our interviewees. An important success factor of VET mobility is to find a host institution that fits with the training field and the level of knowledge of the trainee. Therefore, centralized management through the coaches is effective as they can refer to networks that have already been established. However, reports by youth about mismatched placements suggest that their increased involvement in the choice of a traineeship would allow them to better exploit their practical experiences abroad.

Working abroad, albeit for such a short time, allows the trainees to draw comparisons between the quality of the German VET system and that of others. This is perceived as one of the purposes of the stay abroad: 'It was in the frame of the training, we visited a vocational school there [...] and could get a whiff [of] how they learn over there and how the training is done there' (y04: 3). The experience of different VET systems prompts critical reflections on their own system, be it on facilities, schooling procedures, on the quality of the training or the value and recognition of training courses: 'Of course, the difference is that we have a three-year vocational training here [in Germany], and in Finland it is more like [university] studies. The job is considered at a higher level than here' (y03: 17). Moreover, while abroad, some become aware of the high appreciation of German VET in general and the value of their job education in particular. However, as the interviewees rarely have contact with local apprentices, young people lack authentic reports of daily VET routines, as is found in other types of mobility (Cuzzocrea et al. 2021).

In the German dual VET, permission from the training body (employers/vocational schools) is a prerequisite for participating in a mobility programme. These institutions, therefore, assume a central gatekeeping function, adding to the power imbalance already existent in employer–employee relationships (Behrens and Rabe-Kleberg 1992):

Well, it was the biggest, or potentially the biggest hurdle, uh, for me, to take part in it, because [my boss] could also have just thrown something in the way and said 'No, won't work out at all.' [T]hen it just would have been over [...] because we really needed his approval to do it. (y07: 186)

Apprentices hence have to manage negotiations with employers mostly by themselves. This is a challenge for many, especially the younger, less-experienced apprentices, as, being trainees, they feel that they are in a dependent position. Most of the interviewed apprentices in dual VETs talk about supportive, encouraging employers who considered mobility as a plus for their company. In cases of their refusal to grant leave to an apprentice (either because they do not see the benefit, or because they could not afford to lose the manpower, a problem particularly for small and medium sized companies), apprentices tried to find alternative solutions, such as taking holidays for the mobility period. However, as the study accounts exclusively for mobile apprentices, our description of the employers' role might be biased.

Experiencing the Programme

The young people in our sample (except for one case) travelled using a mobility programme, predominantly Erasmus+. However, the programmatic frame of the stay abroad is only marginally reflected in the interviews. The apprentices appear as inexperienced when it comes to travelling abroad (apart from holidays) and have no previous knowledge of organized opportunities within the training context. They become aware of mobility programmes via mobility coaches, informative events or former mobile apprentices rather than via their own initiative.

Especially where mobility coaches are involved, young people have only peripheral contact with programmatic regulations and proceedings. They experience programmes predominantly as low-level funding opportunities for short-duration mobility within Europe. While programmes are designed with the clear political aim of enhancing employability, those aspects which would be most related to the core work experience (e.g., training company/traineeship/work tasks) emerge as rather marginal in the interviewees' narrations. In fact, numerous accounts emphasize leisure time during the mobility period (e.g., weekend trips), suggesting their core motives are to gain intercultural experiences and explore a new country. Targets related to vocational improvement (e.g., experiencing alternative ways of training and working; gaining work experience), as was found prominent in other European countries with different economic situations (Hemming et al. 2019), are rather subordinate. In contrast to other mobility fields and countries, apprentices rated the funding allotted as sufficient:

I just thought it was great, that it was so simple for four weeks, that you could just go there so easily, [...] that you can just say 'I don't have to rent a hotel here [...] there are arrangements for it,' that's superb. [...] You always have a point of contact, yes, it is all organized for you [...] and to get there for so little money. (vy12: 203)

In conclusion, mobility programmes, in the way they are implemented in Germany, are appreciated as uncomplicated and low-cost opportunities for stays abroad. However, Erasmus+ evaluations show that lack of money is also a barrier to German VET mobility, dependent, among other considerations, on apprentices' pay and living costs in destination countries (European Commission 2017).

National Implementation Strategies and Support Structures

The ways in which mobility programmes are put into action differ widely, depending on national features related to education systems and economic situations (Samuk et al. 2018). There are two more salient characteristics that make the German VET mobility system interesting. Firstly, an effective means for realizing short-term VET mobility within the restrictive training curricula and schedules is group mobility, characterized by apprentices going abroad together (often from one field of education or school), an effective handling of accommodation, support in situ, practical/school periods abroad and a duration of usually less than four weeks.

Travelling in a group is a central feature of mobility programmes in the perceptions of the interviewed apprentices, albeit ambivalently. The accompanying peers are appreciated as a safety zone in which mobility tasks and risks are shared: 'I mean alone, I would not have done it at all. That would have been too unsure for me. Because like this you can still support each other, or at least encourage each other, when you're feeling insecure somehow' (Y2: 120). For some, travelling together with others was even a precondition to taking part. However, the group, and the institutional facilitators, are experienced as a barrier to encounters with the people and culture once there. Travelling peers share accommodation, schedules and often even the workplace abroad with their co-apprentices, being more or less constantly supervised by mobility coaches. We find empirical confirmation of the 'compatriot peer effect' (Ardic et al. 2018) as the group of co-apprentices prevents the individuals from intercultural learning and relationship-building. Moreover, groups limit individual space and privacy:

> [W]hen you spend the whole day around each other, then again in the evening, and from early until late, and that for four weeks, it does get annoying after a while, because you want to have your free time or at least your privacy. (y08: 63)

However, going abroad individually proves considerably more complicated and demanding for apprentices: 'I had to [...] obtain permission from the school and the company [...] one needed to take care of the travel organization, say, flights, or how to get to the [airport]' (y11: 31). Individual mobility requires more investment of time and of money. Young people have to take care of travel modalities, need individual solutions for insurance and have to negotiate with the host company/vocational school abroad. They fall behind their fellow apprentices' learning in school and/or company and have to catch up, especially when they go for a longer period. Individual arrangements of travel and accommodation are less cost-effective than group arrangements and expenditure is only refunded upon return to the home country. These findings are in line with results from a recent study showing that German participants in group mobility do not complain about complicated application procedures or financial shortfalls as is the case for Spanish apprentices, whose mobility is, in contrast, highly individualized (Kmiotek-Meier et al. 2019). To summarize, while it seems that groups facilitate mobility, travelling alone is expected to have better long-term advantages as the youth have to fend for themselves and can immerse themselves deeper into the language and culture.

Secondly, young people's ways into the world of work are not isolated processes; they are decisively co-shaped by actors from private and institutional settings. This also applies to VET mobility. Among these 'accompanying actors' (Schlimbach 2015; Walther and Weinhardt 2013), most prominently mentioned in the context of our survey are mobility coaches. Most are organized via the coaching network 'training without borders.' Some practise their advisory role in addition to their usual role as teachers or other institutional staff, while others are employed for this purpose. For youth, the service is mostly free of charge, with the exception of the advisory services of private companies.

Mobility coaches are regarded by young people as omni-competent and omniscient in the different phases of the mobility process:

> Ms. R. organized everything. And she really was available 24 hours a day if we had problems or questions; we could call her or send her a message, she always helped us. That was, that was really a large source of support. (y09: 85)

The mobility coaches often initiate the mobility by promoting VET mobility and by actively approaching youth. Thus, they enable low-threshold entrance to the programme, but at the same time (often through a performance-based selection of participants) reinforce meritocratic principles and linked inequalities. A major task of mobility professionals is to deal with the 'bureaucratic burden' connected with programme participation, something that greatly impairs the mobility of individual movers (see Cairns et al. 2017). There are vivid accounts on how mobility coaches support the application process and the handling of paperwork, mediating the comprehensive formal requirements: 'Well there was sometimes a little stress with bureaucracy, for example with this change of the company, but we apprentices did not see much of it really' (y07: 15), and narrowing tasks down: 'on this day you have to do this and that, or you have to fulfil this or that task' (y02: 151). Mobility advisers define mobility parameters (date, duration, host company) and organize the travel (transport, accommodation). Not least, in most cases they accompany the apprentices abroad or organize support in situ, thus decisively contributing to positive mobility experiences.

In all these steps, the coaches act as 'joints' in the mobility-surrounding network consisting of the young people, the EU/Erasmus programme as well as institutional actors in the home and host country (companies, schools, other supporters). The comprehensive support of the coaches is highly appreciated by all youth in our sample and seems to correspond to the needs of young people regarding safety and 'convenience' in their transitional proceedings (Reiter and Schlimbach 2015). Thus, mobility advisers are a key prerequisite for VET mobility in Germany.

Conclusions

In this chapter, we have explored the functioning of mobility within the German VET system, emphasising three aspects which make the discussion valuable. The first is the ambivalent role of the restrictive German VET system. At first glance, it may appear as an overly rigid framework with regard to mobility, due to the fact that it sets a number of limits (e.g., to the date and duration of the mobility), and that it requires the approval of the training institutions. Apprentices reflect upon the strict training plan as a decisive defining context, and want to fit mobility in without getting off track. However, through the institutionally secured implementation of mobility programmes in Germany, designed not to interfere with the system, participation becomes convenient. The German case exemplifies that estimating VET mobility always demands national contextualization. The German system might be rigorous, yet provides a clearly defined frame for mobility. In many other European countries with less formal and standardized forms of VET, corresponding mobility frames are much more diffuse, and participation in this form of education is scarce (Chankseliani et al. 2017). Rising mobility numbers in this field must respond with a stronger establishment of VET systems and an increased participation of young people and employers in VET in general.

The second aspect is the way mobility programmes are used and understood by travelling youth. They are seen as favourable opportunities which enable them to broaden their life experiences by exploring a new country, but are not essential for their vocational advancement. Therefore, while VET mobility is politically intended to be an instrument to promote individual labour market integration and thus contribute to youth employment rates across European economies, for German apprentices, this aspect is not prominent. One might ask, against this background, why German apprentices should be interested in taking part in the first place.

This reflection leads to the third aspect, namely the specific features that make programme participation easy and attractive for young people. One is group mobility as the most common way of realizing stays abroad for German apprentices. This is an original feature as European mobility is largely individual-based. Group mobility not only appears as age-appropriate, personalized and convenient, it is also a (vocational) system-appropriate, cost-effective way of travelling. However, our comparisons between individual and group travellers confirm that the latter approach offers fewer opportunities for learning and developing (European Commission 2017). Another feature is the sound professional assistance by several institutional actors, among whom mobility coaches are most prominent—a feature which is latent, absent or poorly institutionalized in other EU countries.

Our data suggest that mobility coaches play a key role in all phases of a mobility exercise by offering step-by-step support and guidance. They act as gatekeepers who largely promote, but also control, apprentices' access to mobility, and cushion the challenges young people face throughout the mobility experience. Their support seems appropriate to the extended support needs and the vagueness of the young people's plans, and significantly contributes to the growth of VET mobility numbers. Findings also show that apprentices are only tangentially aware of mobility opportunities in VET and that they often come across support and funding opportunities only through advisers. However, by taking over mobility tasks and by smoothing out challenges, mobility coaches might diminish the learning potential of the experience.

Our research has provided insight into how mobility is adapted to a strongly structured, highly formalized education system, which is prized for its permeance in a (relatively) prosperous youth labour market. The German implementation strategies of mobility programmes gain international interest as they generate above-average participation numbers. One obvious question is that of transferability. Against this background, further research should allow for a comparison of the experiences of German VET apprentices with those in other countries and mobility fields. Hereby, it would make sense to dive deeper into questions of how young people move within these structures and how they see their own role within that process, using an agency-oriented approach. Finally, going abroad during the vocational training remains uncommon in comparison to other mobility fields. More information and awareness-raising is needed for decision-makers, apprentices and training institutions, which also implies a demand for more scholarly attention to the field.

Acknowledgements This publication is based on data produced in the context of the European project MOVE. MOVE has received funding from the European Union's Horizon 2020 research and innovation programme under grant agreement No 649263. In order to collaborate with the MOVE project from which this chapter is drawn, Valentina Cuzzocrea was financially supported by the Marie Skłodowska-Curie grant agreement No 665958 at the Max Weber Centre for Advanced Cultural and Social Studies in Erfurt.

References

Ardic, T., Pavlova, I., & Skrobanek, J. (2018). Being international and not being international at the same time: The challenges of peer relations under mobility. In H. Hogset, D. M. Berge, & K. Y. Dale (Eds.), *Fjordantologien 2018: Universitetsforlaget* (pp. 206–222). Oslo: Universitetsforlaget.

Becker, H., & Thimmel, A. (Eds.). (2019). *Die Zugangsstudie zum internationalen Jugendaustausch. Zugänge und Barrieren*. Frankfurt: Wochenschau Verlag.

Behrens, J., & Rabe-Kleberg, U. (1992). Gatekeeping in the life course: A pragmatic typology. In R. H. Walter (Ed.), *Institutions and gatekeeping in the life course* (pp. 237–260). Weinheim: Deutscher Studien Verlag.

Bernard, H. R., Wutich, A., & Ryan, G. W. (2017). *Analyzing qualitative data: Systematic approaches* (2nd ed.). London: Sage.

Bosch, G. (2010). The revitalisation of the dual system of vocational training. In G. Bosch & J. Charest (Eds.), *Vocational training: International perspectives* (pp. 136–161). New York: Routledge.

Bundesministerium für Bildung und Forschung (BMBF). (2019). *Berufsbildungsbericht 2019*. Bonn.

Cairns, D. (2014). *Youth transitions, international student mobility and spatial reflexivity: Being mobile?* Basingstoke: Palgrave Macmillan.

Cairns, D., Cuzzocrea, V., Briggs, D., & Veloso, L. (2017). *The consequences of mobility: Reflexivity, social inequality and the reproduction of precariousness in highly qualified migration*. Basingstoke: Palgrave Macmillan.

Chankseliani, M., Keep, E., & Wilde, S. (2017). *People and policy: A comparative study of apprenticeship across eight national contexts*. Doha: University of Oxford.

Cruzes, D., Dybå, T., Runeson, P., & Höst, M. (2015). Case studies synthesis: A thematic, cross-case, and narrative synthesis worked example. *Empirical Software Engineering, 20*(6), 1634–1665.

Cuzzocrea, V., Krzaklewska, E., & Cairns, D. (2021). 'There is no me, there is only us:' The Erasmus bubble as a transient form of transnational collectivity. In V. Cuzzocrea, B. Gook, & B. Schiermer (Eds.), *Forms of collective engagements in youth transition*. New York: Brill.

Ebner, C., & Uhly, A. (2016). *Entstehung und Merkmale des dualen Ausbildungssytems*. Bonn: BpB.

European Commission. (2017). Nationaler Bericht zur Halbzeitevaluation von Erasmus+ in Deutschland.

European Council and European Commission. (2012). Joint report of the Council and the Commission on the implementation of the Strategic Framework for European cooperation in education and training (ET 2020)—'Education and training in a smart, sustainable and inclusive Europe' (2012/C 70/05).

Eurostat. (2019). Unemployment statistics. Youth unemployment rates (Statistics explained).

Frommberger, D. (2013). *Qualität und Qualitätsentwicklung in der dualen Berufsausbildung in Deutschland: Wichtige Positionen und Interessen sowie ausgesuchte Befunde der Berufsbildungsforschung*. Bottrop: GIB.

Guile, D., & Unwin, L. (Eds.). (2019). *The Wiley handbook of vocational education and training*. Hoboken, NJ: Wiley.

Hemming, K., Schlimbach, T., Tillmann, F., Nienaber, B., Roman, M., & Skrobanek, J. (2019). Structural framework conditions and individual motivations for youth-mobility: A macro-micro level approach for different European country-types. *Migration Letters, 11*(2), 45–59.

Hippach-Schneider, U., & Huismann, A. (2019). *Vocational education and training in Europe. Germany: Ed. Cedefop ReferNet* (VET in Europe reports, 2018).

Kmiotek-Meier, E., Skrobanek, J., Nienaber, B., Vysotskaya, V., Samuk, S., & Ardic, T. (2019). Why is it so hard? And for whom? Obstacles to intra-European mobility. *Migration Letters, 16*(1), 31–44.

Maurer, M. (2019). Integrating work-based learning into formal VET: Towards a global diffusion of apprenticeship training and the dual model? In S. McGrath, M. Mulder, J. Papier, & R. Suart (Eds.), *Handbook of vocational education and training* (pp. 551–567). Cham: Springer.

McGrath, S., Mulder, M., Papier, J., & Suart, R. (2019). *Handbook of vocational education and training*. Cham: Springer.

Miles, M. B., & Huberman, A. M. (1984). *Qualitative data analysis: A sourcebook of new methods*. Beverly Hills: Sage.

NABIBB (Ed.). (2018). *Study on mobility: Transnational mobility in initial vocational education and training in 2017*. Bonn: Ed. NABIBB.

NABIBB (Ed.). (2019). *Jahresbericht 2018*. Bonn: Ed. NABIBB.

Nienaber, B., Dörrenbächer, H. P., Funk, I., Pigeron-Piroth, I., Belkacem, R., Helfer, M., Polzin-Haumann, C., & Reissner, C. (2021). Using cross-border mobility in vocational education and training in the Greater Region SaarLorLux region. In D. Cairns (Ed.), *The Palgrave handbook of youth mobility and educational migration*. Basingstoke: Palgrave Macmillan.

Pylväs, L., & Nokelainen, P. (2019). Intercultural competence: Toward global understanding. In S. McGrath, M. Mulder, J. Papier, & R. Suart (Eds.), *Handbook of vocational education and training: Developments in the changing world of work* (Vol. V. 37, pp. 1–13). Cham: Springer.

Reiter, H., & Schlimbach, T. (2015). NEET in disguise? Rival narratives in troubled youth transitions. *Educational Research, 57*(2), 133–150.

Robertson, S., Harris, A., & Baldassar, L. (2017). Mobile transitions: A conceptual framework for researching a generation on the move. *Journal of Youth Studies, 21*(2), 203–217.

Samuk, S., Nienaber, B., Bissinger, J., & Vysotskaya, V. (2018). *MOVE deliverable No. 6.7. Final public project report*. Luxemburg: European Commission.

Schlimbach, T. (2015). Begleitende Akteure im Spiegel von Agency. In T. Schlimbach, F. Mahl, & B. Reißig (Eds.), *Handlungsstrategien von Migrantinnen und Migranten auf dem Weg in die berufliche Ausbildung: Ein qualitativer Längsschnitt* (pp. 21–48). München: DJI.

Schlimbach, T., Skrobanek, J., Kmiotek-Meier, E., & Vysotskaya, V. (2019). Capturing agency in different educational settings: A comparative study on youth perceptions of mobility-framing structures. *Migration Letters, 16*(1), 15–29.

Schultheis, K., & Sell, S. (2014). Die drei Sektoren.

Scott, J. (2000). *Social network analysis: A handbook*. London: Sage.

Statistisches Bundesamt. (2019). *Schnellmeldung Integrierte Ausbildungsberichterstattung—Anfänger im Ausbildungsgeschehen nach Sektoren/Konten und Ländern—2018*.

Walther, A., & Weinhardt, M. (Eds.). (2013). *Beratung im Übergang: Zur sozialpädagogischen Herstellung von biographischer Reflexivität*. Weinheim, Basel: Beltz Juventa.

Werner, F., Körbel, M., & Müller, K. (2010). *Study on the impact of the Leonardo da Vinci programme on the quality of vocational education and training systems. Final report*. Kerpen: European Commission.

Witzel, A., & Reiter, H. (2012). *The problem-centred interview: Principles and practice*. London: Sage.

Chapter 30
Youth as Temporary Workers Abroad: The Experiences of Australia, Canada and New Zealand

Peter G. Ghazarian

As globalization reshapes labour markets, young people increasingly look abroad for opportunities to pursue work and training, develop their careers and find the best way forward for their future. Government schemes in place in Australia, Canada and New Zealand cater to these young people by providing visas that often blend work, study and travel. These temporary migration programmes address labour shortages in the regional and sectoral economies of Australia, Canada and New Zealand, and have led to dramatic growth in temporary labour migration (Hugo 2006; Lovelock and Leopold 2008; Spoonley and Bedford 2012; Gross and Schmitt 2012). Youth seeking temporary work abroad can hence pursue a variety of entry points, including working holiday visas, temporary graduate visas, post-graduation work permits and student visas with lax regulations on participation in the labour market.

This growing population of temporary youth workers challenges the traditional understanding of migration in cutting across old categories of migrancy. Robertson (2016) notes the blurriness of new migration flows, and points out how working holidaymakers, international students, former international students on work permits and illegal or 'semi-compliant' (Ruhs and Anderson 2010) migrants can be included in the diverse 'student-workers' and 'tourist-workers' categories, together making up a temporary youth migration field. Though there is a longer history of participation in European and Anglophone countries, temporary work abroad is increasingly common among youth in East Asia (Wattanacharoensil and Talawanich 2018). These young people come from a wide variety of national, cultural and socio-economic backgrounds, and the routes they take to pursue work and training abroad are influenced by their diverse backgrounds and motivations.

P. G. Ghazarian (✉)
Ashland University, Ashland, OH, USA
e-mail: pghazari@ashland.edu

© The Author(s), under exclusive license to Springer Nature Switzerland AG 2022
D. Cairns (ed.), *The Palgrave Handbook of Youth Mobility and Educational Migration*, https://doi.org/10.1007/978-3-030-99447-1_30

De Facto Temporary Worker Schemes

The chapter begins with consideration of how temporary worker programmes function and their role in the national discourses of the host countries. Schemes that facilitate temporary work abroad for young people can be traced back to the working holiday programmes that emerged in the 1960s, with British university students going to summer camps in North America through work and volunteer exchange programmes (Wilson et al. 2010). Working holiday programmes were formalized in the 1970s to allow young people from the Commonwealth nations of Canada, New Zealand and Australia to gain temporary access to Britain before starting a formal career or getting married (Cohen 1973; Wilson et al. 2010). Interestingly, a working holiday scheme in Canada predates the system's spread to other Commonwealth nations, with the first working holiday programme introduced in Canada in 1951 (Immigration, Refugees and Citizenship Canada 2019). Australia and New Zealand both adopted a working holiday scheme soon after the system spread to the United Kingdom. Australia introduced working holidays in 1975 to allow young people to live and work in Australia temporarily (Robertson 2014). Ten years later, New Zealand implemented a working holiday programme with a 1985 bilateral reciprocal agreement with Japan to allow young people to travel for work up to 12 months, and training or studying for up to 6 months (Opara 2018). These schemes marked the beginning of a shift in migration policy towards an emphasis on non-permanent migration and creating a supply of temporary, informal labour.

The conditions for working holiday schemes are set out in reciprocal agreements between countries. Participants are able to take on temporary work but are not allowed to assume a permanent position. Typically, visas are available to people aged 18–30 years, unaccompanied by dependent children and who meet health, character and financial requirements that include sufficient funds for a return ticket (or an actual return ticket) to their country of origin (Kawashima 2010; Robertson 2014; Anderson 2018). These conditions vary, with more stringent requirements on minimum education level and English-language proficiency for particular destinations and participants from certain territories/countries (Opara 2018).

Despite being officially presented as cultural exchange programmes, working holiday visas are however increasingly used for the purpose of work. These programmes allow historically 'settler' nations such as Australia, Canada and New Zealand to 'temporarize' migration and replace roles once filled by permanent migrants with the temporary (Robertson 2016). As a part of this shift, other visa statuses have been introduced or reformed to emphasize service through work, at times targeting particular regions or industries (Howe et al. 2018). In framing these programmes as working holiday schemes, temporary graduate visas or even student visas, governments think that they can attract young people with dynamic migration goals focused around work, education, language acquisition, leisure and even permanent settlement (Robertson 2014). Initially, participation in these programmes was predominantly from Western countries, but they have grown in popularity amongst youth in East Asia (Wattanacharoensil and Talawanich 2018).

As a group, there are very little hard data on young workers undertaking temporary migration. This population is spread across multiple visa categories and may or may not be operating within the legal confines of the visa status (if any) that they hold. This includes illegal and 'semi-compliant' migrants (Ruhs and Anderson 2010), who may have violated the terms of tourist, student or other visas in pursuit of employment. The line between student-workers and tourist-workers is blurred by the fact that working holidaymakers can study during their stays, and international students can work and move between statuses (Robertson 2016). As a result, temporary youth workers are not accurately measured or described in current government statistical instruments.

Statistics on working holidaymakers provide limited insight into the composition of this group. The top five countries/territories of origin for working holiday participants in Australia were the United Kingdom, France, Germany, South Korea and Taiwan (Department of Home Affairs 2018); for International Experience Canada, France, Australia, Japan, Ireland and Germany (Immigration, Refugees, and Citizenship Canada 2019); and for New Zealand, Germany, the United Kingdom, France, the United States and South Korea (Ministry of Business, Innovation and Employment 2018). The relatively greater participation for youth from European and North American backgrounds in these programmes is likely due to the lack of quotas in agreements governing the participant of young people from those countries. Due to limitations on who may participate in working holidaymaker schemes, aspirant youth from other backgrounds often seek alternative ways to gain access to work and training abroad through alternative visa programmes, leading to illegal or semi-compliant statuses that may not be reflected in official statistics. Certainly, temporary youth workers in Australia, Canada and New Zealand no longer come overwhelmingly from English-speaking countries, meaning there is diverse participation of young people from all over the world (Reilly 2014).

Youth Migration in the National Discourse of Host Countries

Governments have a tendency to frame schemes for young migrants to serve as temporary workers through cultural exchange or education visa programmes, and in many host and origin countries, the practice has been normalized as a kind of rite of passage for youth (Ho et al. 2014). As a result of this portrayal of young temporary workers as tourists or students, they are often overlooked as workers or migrants in policy discourse and government statistics; official presentation of these programmes emphasizes the opportunity for youth to have a cultural experience abroad with limited opportunities to work (Reilly 2014). This position contrasts with the reality that temporary workers often make significant contributions to host economies by boosting GDP and expenditure on goods and services (Tan and Lester 2012; Tan et al. 2009). The stereotypes associated with young migrants thus contribute to obscuring their roles as workers. In being associated with international students and backpackers (Dauvergne and Marsden 2014), temporary youth workers are also misaligned with the lens of international education and tourism rather than labour migration (Opara 2018; Robertson 2014), even where there is explicit encouragement to undertake work as a part of these stays (Reilly 2014).

This conflicted view of temporary youth migrants impacts on how they are treated in policy and protected in law, meaning the blurring of categories tends to work to the detriment of youth. As a result of their unclear status, young migrant workers do not feature in policy discussions on migration or labour, despite the fact that they are often a test group for policies related to granting permanent residence or citizenship (Opara 2018; Rajkumar et al. 2012). In being formally undetected in government data, they are rendered 'invisible' (Yuan et al. 2014) and hence do not receive the same protections as other migrants and labourers. In recent years, the exposure of abuses and exploitation of temporary youth workers has led to criticism of these programmes. Critics argue that these visa schemes primarily serve as a de facto low-skilled visa programme (Boucher 2016; Howe and Reilly 2015), with preferential treatment of certain industries to meet their labour shortages. This reality contrasts with government branding that emphasizes cultural exchange and tourism (Berg and Farbenblum 2017; Australian Senate Education and Employment References Committee 2016), although conflicts and abuses within programmes have led to heated debate about government migration policy favouring temporary migration (Opara 2018).

Motivations to Work Abroad

Young temporary workers have diverse motivations that vary dramatically on an individual basis. Some may have specific objectives or end states in mind, while others may be looking to access experiences that are self-transformative (Ho et al. 2014). Common motivations for seeking temporary work abroad include a desire to achieve permanent residency in the host country, gain work experience, pay debts related to costs of studies, experience life in another culture or escape from a mundane life in a home culture (see, e.g., Birrell and Healy 2012; Kawashima 2010; Robertson 2014, 2016). These motivations will vary, but can be found among young people regardless of socio-demographic background.

Some studies nevertheless seek to contrast the motivations of youth by origin, especially from East and West. This work suggests fundamentally different reasoning behind the motivation to pursue temporary work abroad. Yoon (2014) points out that intra-Western studies tend to focus on personal development more than interculturality. The emphasis is often on exploring the world, with work portrayed as a means of facilitating a holiday-like experience (Inkson and Myers 2003; Wilson et al. 2010; Wattanacharoensil and Talawanich 2018). Although case studies on Asian participants also acknowledge a desire for exploration and self-development, the issue of prestige associated with fluency in English and overseas experiences also emerges, 'imply[ing] that young Asians' mobility to the West is motivated by and resonant with the dominant social order and imagination of the West' (Yoon

2014: 589). This perspective sees the motivations of youth from the East seeking to go abroad for temporary work as caught up within Wallerstein's (1989) world-systems perspective, with those from the periphery or semi-periphery drawn to the core.

In studies that examine the experiences of youth from specific countries or territories, a common theme which emerges is the desire to escape. They can feel trapped in what they perceive as a predictable, underwhelming life. Clarke (2004) notes that the purpose of many British temporary youth workers is to escape the stresses of their daily lives, while Kawashima (2010) emphasizes a perceived lack of opportunities for upward career mobility among Japanese youth. Yoon's (2014) work on South Korean and Ho et al.'s (2014) on Taiwanese youth also see escapism as a common motivation. Yet there are also differences. Clarke (2005) found that English, Irish and Dutch youth wished to escape for non-economic reasons, while Kawashima's (2010: 272) found that 'job insecurity, a lack of professional rewards, an increasing sense of job mismatch, and a culture of overwork' contributed to the desire to escape among Japanese youth. Another common theme in the motivations of young temporary workers abroad is the desire to experience life in a new culture, which can take on different meanings. For some, it is a challenge to prove oneself. For others, it is the chance to build understanding and make new connections. In either case, the experience abroad is an opportunity for self-improvement and growth. Likewise, Wattanacharoensil and Talawanich (2018) see a strong desire among Thai youth to learn and live in different cultures and strengthen their cultural connections to the host countries.

Identity and Personal Growth

Young migrant workers come from diverse backgrounds, but universally experience entering into new contexts and assuming new roles that they hope will serve as opportunities for growth and change. Internally, filling these new roles can expand self-understanding and develop one's self-concept. Given the transient nature of much of this work, they may find their identities shifting in ways that undermine past ideas about migration (Robertson 2016), although all this change can also lead to vulnerability stemming from a sense of exclusion (Anderson 2018), or even negative stereotypes and racial biases, as well as homesickness.

These stereotypes vary depending on an individual's personal characteristics and background. For example, Clarke (2005) finds that English, Irish and Dutch youth migrant workers must deal with stereotypes about partying all the time, living in squalid conditions and disrupting the local flow of life—views that can create barriers to finding accommodation or seeking employment. Robertson (2016) and Yoon (2014) argue that Korean youth migrants also deal with stigmas associated with 'student' and 'backpacker' identities, and face additional racial expectations and an association with unskilled labour. For those in a new culture or spending time away from home for the first time, being confronted with these types of stereotypes can be upsetting or disturbing.

Racism in particular has an important impact on the social experience of these workers. Robertson (2016) describes how young workers from particular backgrounds are hired for their cheapness, flexibility and ability to 'pass' as particular ethnicities that appeal to local consumers in ethnic restaurants or businesses: for instance, Koreans as Japanese, or Indians and Nepalese as Turkish. These types of experiences can cause confusion and anxiety for youth, leading to vulnerability and self-doubt. A connection to one's home culture can however provide stability. Diaspora communities in particular can provide familiarity that helps support people at a vulnerable time (Jung 2013).

Exploitation

Vulnerability for youth temporarily working abroad is not limited to personal and psychological issues, but extends to the workplace. Multiple factors contribute to exploitation. Temporary migrant worker programmes create, by design, contractual asymmetry in the hope of reaping the benefits of migrants' labour and economic activity while avoiding the costs of public services and welfare (Bauböck 2011). Furthermore, certain schemes place participating youth in a position of social vulnerability by making them even more dependent upon their, often highly precarious, work (see, e.g., Cuzzocrea and Cairns 2020). As a result, young temporary workers abroad come to possess many of the characteristics of vulnerable workers and end up in positions that are risky and undesirable, for which they are not adequately trained, that often require hard manual labour and have safety requirements and employment protections they may not understand (Reilly 2014). Without knowledge of local living conditions or employer reputations, temporary youth workers abroad can also find themselves confronted with substandard accommodation, underpayment and workplace exploitation (Anderson 2018). The temporary status of these workers prevents them from being able to push back against these conditions in a way that permanent migrants of the past could have.

Employers that make use of temporary youth workers abroad often see the vulnerability of these workers as an inherent part of their value. They are able to avoid costly oversight and indirectly encourage them to enter into a vulnerable state through their hiring practices. In the interest of maximizing profits, employers will hire irregular and minimally regulated migrants over their peers, leading to greater demand for poorly regulated visas that give individuals a perceived edge in securing a position (Toh and Quinlan 2009). They may even prefer undocumented workers (Castles 2006), encouraging temporary youth workers abroad to become uncompliant or semi-compliant in their status. Young temporary workers abroad are also funnelled towards certain types of jobs that often conflict with their original motivations for going abroad: casual, informal, low-skilled positions with atypical temporal rhythms such as horticulture, taxi driving, late-night retail, hospitality and even sex work (Lantz 2005; Neilson 2009; Tan and Lester 2012). Research and government investigations have revealed that young temporary workers are often underpaid or overworked, or both, and face gender and racial discrimination (Procházková 2012). They may have outstanding wages and holiday pay withheld (Stringer 2016), or receive food and accommodation instead of actual pay (Caritas Aotearoa New Zealand 2016).

An individual's origin and motivations for seeking to work abroad interact to influence their degree of vulnerability in the labour market. Those with particular outlooks or from certain backgrounds may react differently when confronted with unfair working conditions. Young people from wealthy, Organization for Economic Cooperation and Development (OECD) member states might temporarily accept abuses in the workplace because they will soon leave for other pursuits; they do not foresee any major long-term harm to themselves, and may even feel they can report unfair treatment or exploitation after leaving the position, while those from lower-income backgrounds may accept unfair working conditions in seeing this as better than what they might experience in their home country (Procházková 2012; Opara 2018).

The Return Home

The return home is covered tangentially in some studies examining the experience of these young people, but the majority focus on their views prior to departure and experiences while taking part within the programmes. In his work on British youth working temporarily abroad in Australia, Clarke (2004: 499) asserts that they 'return home with strong narratives, confident in their ability to tolerate difference and cope with change, re-skilled for a world of episodes and fragments, [and] prepared for the stresses of modern life.' From this perspective, British youth returning from work abroad tend to feel as though they have achieved what they intended to do and experienced forms of personal growth as a result of their experience. This finding contrasts with work on the return of Japanese youth to their home country. In one of the rare works focusing specifically on the experiences of youth after they have returned from temporary work abroad, Kawashima (2010, 2014) found that Japanese youth are largely disappointed with their experience. She points to two major factors: first, the sense that during their time abroad, they did not personally grow or develop as much as they should have, and second, the realities of the labour market in their home country. The imagined benefits of time abroad often do not manifest in the reality of a job on return.

Weighing the Costs and Benefits

Government schemes in Australia, Canada and New Zealand to facilitate youth mobility through temporary work programmes and visas offer the potential for great personal and professional benefits, and new opportunities that could help to subvert the barriers and obstacles present in home societies. Spending time in a new context offers opportunities for self-exploration and a deeper understanding of the world beyond their homes. These benefits however come at a cost, stemming from realities of these programmes contrasting sharply with stated goals, the limited time to pursue potential benefits and negative psychological experiences associated with isolation, racialization and the stigma of transience. The marketing and presentation of schemes for temporary work abroad can also be misleading. While presented as an opportunity for cultural exchange or professional growth, they instead seem to create a guaranteed source of unskilled labour (Anderson 2018). For youth seeking professional growth, there may be disappointment, and the temporal nature of these programmes can become an obstacle to realizing the benefits of their experience abroad.

These young people have a short time to achieve what they seek abroad. Those who want 'sojourner' experiences may find the sense of temporariness experience desirable while others seeking training or professional growth may feel desperate to make the most of their limited time. But restrictions on movement can be direct, in the form of specified regional work requirements within the programmes, or indirect, in the form of high cost of living that drives youth into low-skilled, demanding work as a means of survival. As a result, few are able to access professional jobs or positions in high-demand sectors that provide real opportunities for professional growth. For those seeking adventure, self-discovery and greater exposure to the world, or a competitive advantage in the labour market at home and significant economic returns, disappointment awaits.

References

Anderson, E. (2018). Belonging, temporariness and seasonal labour: Working holidaymakers' experiences in regional Australia. In S. Werth & C. Brownlow (Eds.), *Work and identity* (pp. 117–131). Basingstoke: Palgrave Macmillan.

Bauböck, R. (2011). Temporary migrants, partial citizenship and hypermigration. *Critical Review of International Social and Political Philosophy, 14*(5), 666–693.

Berg, L., & Farbenblum, B. (2017). *Wage theft in Australia: Findings of the national temporary migrant work survey*. Migrant Worker Justice Initiative.

Birrell, B., & Healy, E. (2012). *Immigration overshoot: CPUR research report*. Melbourne: Centre for Population and Urban Research, Monash University.

Boucher, A. (2016). *Australia's de facto low skilled labour immigration program*. Melbourne: Committee for Economic Development of Australia.

Caritas Aotearoa New Zealand. (2016). *Stand up for what's right: Supporting migrant workers*. Wellington: Aotearoa New Zealand.

Castles, S. (2006). Guestworkers in Europe: A resurrection? *International Migration Review, 40*(4), 741–766.
Clarke, N. (2004). Free independent travellers? British working holidaymakers in Australia. *Transactions of the Institute of British Geographers, 29*(4), 499–509.
Clarke, N. (2005). Detailing transnational lives of the middle: British working holidaymakers in Australia. *Journal of Ethnic and Migration Studies, 31*(2), 307–322.
Cohen, E. (1973). Nomads from affluence: Notes on the phenomenon of drifter tourism. *International Journal of Comparative Sociology, 14*, 89–103.
Cuzzocrea, V., & Cairns, D. (2020). Mobile moratorium? The case of young people undertaking international internships. *Mobilities, 16*(3), 416–430.
Dauvergne, C., & Marsden, S. (2014). The ideology of temporary labour migration in the post-global era. *Citizenship Studies, 18*(2), 224–242.
Department of Home Affairs. (2018). *Working holiday maker visa program report*. Canberra: Department of Home Affairs.
Education and Employment References Committee. (2016). *A national disgrace: The exploitation of temporary work visa holders*. Canberra: Commonwealth of Australia.
Gross, D. M., & Schmitt, N. (2012). Temporary foreign workers and regional labour market disparities in Canada. *Canadian Public Policy, 38*(2), 233–263.
Ho, C.-I., Lin, P.-Y., & Huang, S.-C. (2014). Exploring Taiwanese working holiday-makers' motivations: An analysis of means-end hierarchies. *Journal of Hospitality and Tourism Research, 38*(4), 463–486.
Howe, J., & Reilly, A. (2015). Meeting Australia's labour needs: The case for a new low-skill work visa. *Federal Law Review, 43*(2), 259–287.
Howe, J., Stewart, A., & Owens, R. (2018). Temporary migrant labour and unpaid work in Australia. *Sydney Law Review, 40*(2), 183–211.
Hugo, G. (2006). Temporary migration and the labour market in Australia. *Australian Geographer, 37*(2), 211–231.
Immigration, Refugees and Citizenship Canada. (2019). *Evaluation of the international experience Canada Program*. Ottawa: Immigration, Refugees and Citizenship Canada.
Inkson, K., & Myers, B. A. (2003). 'The big OE': Self-directed travel and career development. *Career Development International, 8*(4), 170–181.
Jung, S. (2013). Ambivalent cosmopolitan desires: Newly arrived Koreans in Australia and community websites. *Continuum, 27*(2), 193–213.
Kawashima, K. (2010). Japanese working holiday makers in Australia and their relationship to the Japanese labour market: Before and after. *Asian Studies Review, 34*, 267–286.
Kawashima, K. (2014). Uneven cosmopolitanism: Japanese working holiday makers in Australia and the 'lost decade'. In J. Breaden, S. Steele, & C. S. Stevens (Eds.), *Internationalising Japan: Discourse and practice* (pp. 106–124). New York: Routledge.
Lantz, S. (2005). Students working in the Melbourne sex industry: Education, human capital and the changing pattern of the youth labour market. *Journal of Youth Studies, 8*(4), 385–401.
Lovelock, K., & Leopold, T. (2008). Labour force shortages in rural New Zealand: Temporary migration and the Recognised Seasonal Employer (RSE) work policy. *New Zealand Population Review, 33*(34), 213–234.
Ministry of Business, Innovation & Employment. (2018). *Migration trends 2016/2017*. Auckland: Ministry of Business, Innovation and Employment.
Neilson, B. (2009). The world seen from a taxi: Students-migrants-workers in the global multiplication of labour. *Subjectivity, 29*(1), 425–444.
Opara, O. (2018). From settler society to working holiday heaven? Patterns and issues of temporary labour migration to New Zealand. *New Zealand Sociology, 33*(1), 29–52.
Procházková, J. (2012). *Foreign seasonal workers in New Zealand horticulture: An ethnographic account of the Nexus of labour and immigration policies and employment practices*. PhD dissertation. University of Otago, Dunedin, New Zealand.

Rajkumar, D., Berkowitz, L., Vosko, L. F., Preston, V., & Latham, R. (2012). At the temporary-permanent divide: How Canada produces temporariness and makes citizens through its security, work, and settlement policies. *Citizenship Studies, 16*(3–4), 483–510.

Reilly, A. (2014). Low-cost labour or cultural exchange? Reforming the Working Holiday visa programme. *The Economic and Labour Relations Review, 26*(3), 474–489.

Robertson, S. (2014). Time and temporary migration: The case of temporary graduate workers and working holiday makers in Australia. *Journal of Ethnic and Migration Studies, 40*(12), 1915–1933.

Robertson, S. (2016). Student-workers and tourist-workers as urban labour: Temporalities and identities in the Australian cosmopolitan city. *Journal of Ethnic and Migration Studies, 42*(14), 2263–2279.

Ruhs, M., & Anderson, B. (2010). Semi-compliance and illegality in migrant labour markets: An analysis of migrants, employers, and the state in the UK. *Population, Space, and Place, 16*(3), 195–211.

Spoonley, P., & Bedford, R. (2012). *Welcome to our world? Immigration and the reshaping of New Zealand*. Auckland: Dunmore Publishing.

Stringer, C. (2016). *Worker exploitation in New Zealand: A troubling landscape*. Human Trafficking Research Coalition.

Tan, Y., & Lester, L. H. (2012). Labour market and economic impacts of international working holiday temporary migrants to Australia. *Population, Space and Place, 18*(3), 359–383.

Tan, Y., Richardson, S., Lester, L., & Sun, L. (2009). *National evaluation of Australia's working holiday maker program*. Adelaide: National Institute of Labour Studies.

Toh, S., & Quinlan, M. (2009). Safeguarding the global contingent workforce: Guestworkers in Australia. *International Journal of Manpower, 30*(6), 1024–1053.

Wallerstein, I. (1989). The rise and future demise of the world-capitalist system: Concepts for comparative analysis. *Comparative Studies in Society and History, 16*(4), 387–415.

Wattanacharoensil, W., & Talawanich, S. (2018). An insight into the motivation of Thai working and holiday makers (WHMs). In C. Khoo-Lattimore & E. C. L. Yang (Eds.), *Asian youth travelers* (pp. 15–37). Singapore: Springer.

Wilson, J., Fisher, D., & Moore, K. (2010). The OE goes 'home': Cultural aspects of a working holiday experiences. *Tourist Studies, 9*, 3–21.

Yoon, K. (2014). The racialised mobility of transnational working holidays. *Identities: Global Studies in Culture and Power, 21*(5), 586–603.

Yuan, S., Cain, T., & Spoonley, P. (2014). *Temporary migrants as vulnerable workers: A literature review*. Wellington: Ministry of Business, Innovation and Employment.

Chapter 31
International Work Placements: Developing Intercultural Skills?

Sophie Cranston, Emma Bates, and Helena Pimlott-Wilson

Intercultural skills are generally regarded as a positive and respectful emotional response to cultural difference. However, what this actually means is difficult to define (Deardorff 2006; Griffith et al. 2016), and, consequently, they take various guises: intercultural literacy, global citizenship, international mindedness, to name but a few. And in the critical social sciences, intercultural skills are often conceptualized, either explicitly or implicitly, through the lens of cosmopolitanism and transnationalism (see, e.g., Caruana 2014).

Despite a lack of clarity, we can identify two common aspects that are subject to description and critique in this literature. The first is an association of the development of skills linked with interculturalism through encounters with difference, often facilitated through global mobility. The second relates to how intercultural skills are highly valued within a neoliberal globalized world economy. For example, the global mindset, a term derived from Bartlett and Ghoshal (1992), is used within international human resource management and transnational organizations to refer to a set of skills or competencies that enable an individual or an organization to work internationally. For individuals, this refers to skills enabling them to reflect on how their culture influences their behaviour and attitudes, how culture influences others, and how to use this to adapt and produce the best possible outcomes. Having a global mindset is hence linked to the success of business leaders and transnational organizations as a whole (Cohen 2010; Suutari 2002). This chapter questions whether young people undertaking international work placements (IWPs) are actually developing what can be described as intercultural skills. In neoliberal education-to-work transitions, an onus is placed on young people to become attractive to employers by demonstrating that they are 'work ready' upon graduation (Tymon

---

S. Cranston (✉) • E. Bates • H. Pimlott-Wilson
Loughborough University, Loughborough, UK
e-mail: s.cranston@lboro.ac.uk

2013). Intercultural skills are seen as valuable in relation to being able to physically work overseas and to work within international teams (Jones 2011).

This question is pertinent in the current educational landscape. Universities in the United Kingdom, the geographical focus of this chapter, actively promote the need to develop students' intercultural skills through mobility: 'it's important that our graduates are globally-engaged citizens with the skills our economy needs: attributes which are fostered by outward mobility' (UUK 2018: 44). Therefore, having skills like a 'global mindset' is increasingly seen to be a key attribute of graduates (Minocha et al. 2018). However, despite the value placed on these skills by employers, intercultural skills do not always receive attention within degree courses (Escudeiro and Escudeiro 2012). Pressure is therefore placed on students to distinguish themselves in the graduate talent pool by taking part in activities to demonstrate this beyond their formal learning programmes (Holdsworth and Brewis 2014).

One method through which young people can demonstrate that they have the intercultural skills sought by employers is through mobility, such as undertaking IWPs. In this form of international mobility, young people undertake a period of work experience abroad as a built-in part of their degree programme, typically before their final year of undergraduate study. However, questions have been raised as to whether participating in such mobility exercises actually results in the formation of intercultural skills. In prior studies, mobility is often linked to self-transformation. For example, Prazeres (2017: 908) highlights that '[y]oung people commonly use international mobility to move away from a place, feeling or situation of comfort with the aim to discover themselves and grow as individuals.' On youth volunteering, Jones (2011) explores whether young people on volunteering placements as part of a gap year develop cultural sensitivities as part of a global worker identity, concluding that through engaging with other cultures, volunteers display a global consciousness. Lough and McBride (2014) examine whether volunteers display global citizenship. They illustrate a complicated relationship between mobility and international experience, with respondents, while illustrating 'a greater compassion for, and obligation towards, global humanity,' also reinforcing greater attachments to a national context (Lough and McBride 2014: 465). This demonstrates that although global mobility may lead to a change in personal values, it is difficult to interpret how this translates into intercultural skills.

In transnational migration, similar questions about the response to cultural difference are raised (Ley 2004; Conradson and Latham 2005b). Here, attention is focused less on whether intercultural skills are achieved and more on everyday responses to difference. Dunn (2010: 6) argues that examining migration from the perspective of the body enables a focus on 'encounters between different bodies which lead to all kinds of intimacies and emotions, some that generate sharing and exchange and others which lead to tension, friction.' This research therefore looks at the changes in migrants' identities and practices in response to cultural difference that can be read as a proxy for the positive emotional response to difference we associate with intercultural skills.

Encounters and Friendships

'Encounter' is a key theoretical framework through which transnational migrant lives abroad are theorized (Wilson 2017), and which looks at what happens when people encounter those who are different to them, and enter places which are unfamiliar. Butcher (2011: 7) highlights how this produces liminality: 'a condition of ambiguity brought on by being outside the bounds of cultural frames of reference,' the realization that you are no longer in your comfort zone. The feeling of liminality manifests itself in emotional terms, for example, through discomfort or frustration (Cranston 2016a).

As research on emotional geographies highlights, emotions can shape how we understand and negotiate the world (Davidson and Milligan 2004). For example, Walsh (2012) in her research on British migrants in Dubai illustrates how the frustration with Emirati bureaucracy becomes a way in which a difference between 'us' and 'them' is made. It shows a need to understand not only the emotional response to difference, but also how this becomes manifest in practice. Butcher (2011) suggests three interlinking responses. Firstly, we see adaptation, the changing of practices to address liminal feelings. Secondly, there is resistance to encounter. This takes on two forms: one where people actively avoid difference by looking for familiarity, often taking a spatial form, such as the recreation of their home culture abroad; and the other, a social form, in looking for people who are similar to them for an 'ease of understanding' (Butcher 2011): for example, international students socializing with students who share the same nationality, cooking shared national dishes and speaking the same language (Brown 2009a). This means that through the emotional response to cultural difference, there are differing levels of engagement with difference, which often varies between different spaces of people's everyday lives.

Thinking about the embodied response to difference tends to be viewed from an individual perspective, even though the practices associated with it tend not to be. Walsh (2018) demonstrates that intimacies with others are a way through which migrant encounters are both experienced and shaped, which are deeply implicated in emotional lives. As Beech (2018), drawing upon Rawlins (2009: 18–19), highlights, friendships are a shared project or narrative which evolves over time, with our friends acting as co-actors, co-authors and co-tellers in our own unique life stories. That is, friendships play a role in how belonging is felt and understood (Conradson and Latham 2005a; Bunnell et al. 2012). In this chapter, we highlight the importance of friendships to the everyday negotiation of difference for our respondents, arguing that friendship acts as a strategy in response to liminality. Friendships are a central aspect that emerges from young people's narratives, particularly at university, and are seen to be key in enabling young people to develop skills through interactions with others. For example, forming ties with students of multiple nationalities enables students to learn new languages and cultural practices (Brown 2009b). However, despite this literature highlighting the importance of friendships, it has been noted that considering this issue beyond social networks is surprisingly absent in research on youth mobility (Beech 2018; Robertson 2018).

The few studies that do exist show the role that friendships play in the negotiation of life away from home. For example, Robertson (2018) examines encounters with friends, looking at different ways this constitutes the self in student migration. Beech (2018) highlights that homophilious friendship groups act as a way for international students to feel at home, with co-nationals actively sought out to experience familiarity. Thus, friendships can both act as an encounter with difference, providing an opportunity for students to develop intercultural skills, and as a sense of security against difference, whereby existing cultural practices can be maintained. This chapter therefore examines the emotional response to difference as a means to question whether young people undertaking an IWP develop intercultural skills. It is through the adaptation to cultural difference, and positive framings of encounter, that we can surmise intercultural capabilities. However, the chapter demonstrates that there are two axes of difference that young people discuss in relation to encounter: culture and age. For many students undertaking an IWP, it is their first experience of professional-level employment and the workplace. This puts them spatially in a context which may be unfamiliar to them in terms of national culture, but also in relation to their life course.

Methodological Note

The chapter draws on twenty semi-structured interviews carried out with graduates who had undertaken an IWP as part of their degree at a university in the United Kingdom. Our respondents were all British nationals, 60 per cent male and 40 per cent female graduates, from a variety of degree subjects. All respondents had undertaken at least six months of an IWP as part of a sandwich year integrated into their degree. The majority of respondents undertook their IWP in European countries, and the others in Asia, South America or Africa. Throughout the chapter, to protect the anonymity of our respondents, we provide only a pseudonym and the country of placement.

Analysis focuses on how the respondents discussed their experiences abroad. This includes their thinking about whether their placement challenged their comfort zone, which was often framed in terms of 'I.' However, in their discussions of what their lives were like abroad, they often utilised 'we,' including their friends. The respondents were also asked direct questions about whether they felt they had developed intercultural skills as part of doing their placement. In general, they found this a difficult question to answer. This is something not uncommon in relation to soft skills, which tend to be under-realized and hard to articulate by people regardless of life stage. Rather, their everyday lives were an easier way through which skills and experiences could be framed.

Encountering Cultural Difference

Encounters with difference through global mobility are seen to challenge the comfort zone, testing existing frames of understanding and potentially leading to the development of 'new' selves (Prazeres 2017). When asked about whether their placement challenged their comfort zone, our respondents interpreted this in different ways, which we identify as adaptation, similarity and familiarity.

Some respondents discussed ideas surrounding encountering different cultures as being a central part of their IWP. Mia, for example, highlighted how much she enjoyed being out of her comfort zone, which she framed as 'new experiences': 'I quite like, you know, travelling on my own and just putting myself in new experiences. Like I'm very good at, if I … if I don't know anyone there, I will go and make friends.' She explained how much she liked interacting and learning from others and therefore discussed encountering her multicultural workplace in Denmark in positive terms:

> I worked with people from all over the world, it wasn't just you know European people or Danish people, it was literally, everyone was from all over, which was really, really good.

However, Mia's workplace and social life were blurred, as she 'mostly went with the other interns, so we were kind of, made our own friendship group.' When asked about how her placement changed her, Mia demonstrated adaptation: 'being a bit more open-minded and … because not just open-minded about other people but open-minded about how you work.' Mia's account of her social experience on her IWP exemplifies how her confidence to make friends framed both her work and social experiences. It was important that these friends were tied to her by a similar experience of being interns, even though nationality was not as important.

Others discussed their workplace encounters in less positive terms. Noah felt that he had a different sense of humour to his colleagues in his multinational company in Lichtenstein:

> So, in the UK we like certain types of jokes. […] So, one thing I found in the UK is my social influence is much higher, so here in like, Switzerland, Austria, Germany area, their sense of humour is different.

Noah described how in the United Kingdom he used humour as a means to make friends. The change in cultural understanding reference for him, therefore, was a liminal moment where his terms of reference were challenged: 'you realise that many things that you could have done in the UK to make friends will not necessarily happen here in erm, in a different country.' Noah then looked for friends who were similar to him, in age and nationality, and therefore shared existing cultural references: 'I also had some friends from—not friends, but other people from the UK who I met who were other interns, so I mainly stuck with them.' However, this was an initial strategy. Noah discussed how through his placement he adapted his sense of humour within the workplace. He felt that doing an IWP would highlight to employers that people are 'more open minded, maybe; be able to deal with more stressful situations; places that they are not so familiar with.' Noah's response highlights the value that he placed on forming shared understandings with people through humour, and changing his own approach to humour as a strategy. This adaptation was a method through which a wider social circle could be created.

Others felt that they did not fit into their workplace culture and highlighted practices of similarity. While familiarity suggests looking for practices which remind you of home, similarity works to find people who are like you. For our respondents, these practices worked together. For Tommy, his feelings of frustration at different work cultures led to resistance as opposed to adaptation. Working in a Swiss workplace, he quickly realised the differences between Swiss working cultures and British working cultures:

> I became very aware quite quickly that the people I was working with weren't really my sort of people. Erm ... I think the Swiss in general are very ... you know, it's a difficult thing to explain, but let's say if I finish work and I'd say 'anyone want to go for beer?' erm ... nine times out of ten they'd say 'ah we've got work tomorrow, we can't.' (Tommy, Switzerland)

Tommy used 'going out for a drink after work with his colleagues' as a way to articulate and reaffirm a cultural difference between himself and others; he blamed them for not wanting to interact with him, as opposed to himself for not understanding the difference in work and social practices between the United Kingdom and Switzerland. This blaming of the locals for not wanting to interact is commonly found in accounts of transnational British migration (Cranston 2016b; Walsh 2012). Conflating Swiss people with his colleagues as 'not his type of people,' he sought social practices with people from a similar background. This was, however, not the seeking of co-nationals:

> I mean anywhere you go in the world you play rugby and the mentality and the people that do it are always the same. And there's a good mix of international—you know, there's expats. There's always expats. So, there were a lot of Irish, Welsh, Australian, Italian ... Erm ... you know ... Scottish. (Tommy, Switzerland)

Rather, Tommy, in highlighting a preference for the familiar, used rugby as a way in which to find 'people [who] are always the same' as him. Nielson (1999, cited in Walsh 2018) highlights that leisure activities create a relational context to be part of, producing knowledge of who we are by doing the activity. In this respect, Tommy was looking for a space through which he could find friends who shared the same sports culture, one that he was already familiar with. Finding a feeling of familiarity through sport was a means to find those who were similar to him in terms of social practices.

Encountering the Life Course

While encounters with different cultures are often discussed in literature on transnational mobility and student mobility, age and life stage are rarely referenced, particularly in terms of having children (Walsh 2018). In student mobility, the majority of people encountered by students in their everyday lives will likely be students. In this respect, IWPs are different due to the exposure that young people have to people of different age groups through the workplace. The search for similarity among our respondents as a response to liminality was hence most commonly discussed in reference to age and life stage. For example, Isla undertook two work placements, the second of which was at an organization in Germany which hires hundreds of interns every six months. This created an environment with people of similar ages and experiences. However, Isla did not highlight the presence of people with other nationalities, but rather the person she knew from university and other 'English' people:

> And there was actually another girl on my course who did go at the same time, so we were really good friends as well. [...] We were in the same group straight away. There was about—there was about a dozen of us from England, so that was really nice. Definitely. We all stuck together! (Isla, Germany)

Van Mol and Michielsen (2015), looking at Erasmus students, have suggested that they initially interact with other international students in a similar position to them, but if there is a sizeable group of co-nationals present, it increases interaction with co-nationals. Isla initially seemed to be looking for other people in the same position as her in terms of the life course—the similar, and because there were so many people similar to her, she went one step further by seeking out co-nationals, with the articulation of this as being 'nice,' suggesting a sense of comfort in experiencing familiarity. This was important as it influenced Isla's wider social practices:

> The fact that everyone else is your own age and they are in the same situation as you ... I think that's the thing—everyone is in the same boat erm ... so, it was a lot easier just to merge straight together and go on day trips and do activities.

Therefore, for Isla, even though she undertook a work placement in Germany, in a multinational company where she found a mixture of nationalities, the presence of a large group from England meant that even outside work she remained with people in a similar position as herself. This resulted, as she suggested, in a lack of engagement with other nationalities.

Others directly contrasted the spaces of their everyday lives in regard to how difference was encountered. For Ava, her home space acted in many respects as a refuge from work in Germany. She discussed feeling isolated at work, primarily due to her age and temporary status, which meant that she felt her colleagues did not bother trying to get to know her:

> There was a lot of people in the sort of age band sort of 30-45. And they did seem segregated from the interns, even though we weren't that much younger. But I think the problem [...] at that firm is that there are always two interns every six months.

Friendships often follow the mapping of life course and life stage processes (Bunnell et al. 2012), meaning that as she was differentiated from her work colleagues by her age, Ava was out of her comfort zone when it came to making friends at work. Thus, through her interactions in her IWP, Ava's life stage and youth were reinforced and marked her out as different. Ava, however, lived in shared accommodation with other students, relationships that she describes as 'really the only ones who made me have fun.' She discussed how day-to-day practices such as cooking and having drinks together provided her with a sense of belonging and the opportunity to meet different people:

> That was one of my favourite things—was like, living with really cool housemates. 'Cause I don't know, that was—even if I had a crappy day at work I'd sort of come back and then we'd chat, like have a beer or something. And that was some of the most valuable times of the year, was just meeting new people. But then also like, from … yeah … from different backgrounds. It was really good.

Ava utilised the space of the home as a means to interact with others. With age as a barrier to adaptation in the workplace, Ava's flatmates from different backgrounds, but of a similar age to her, provided the means through which this was enacted. Thus, for Ava, the friendships that she was able to form with those in a similar life stage to her provided an important grounding for her IWP, in which she received reassurance and peer support. The value placed on these friendships by Ava is however unsurprising, as friendship networks can be a central aspect of adjusting to unknown environments and spaces (Maunder 2018). Other respondents actively sought out people in a similar position to themselves in order to overcome loneliness. Freya discussed the challenges of making friends in relation to being out of her comfort zone:

> All my life I had been really put in situations where it was possible to meet people and make friends, just by the way that, you know, when you join uni and you go to fresher's week you just … you meet people and that's it—then you have friends.

She then was challenged by being in an environment where she was not surrounded by people in the same life stage as hers. As a response, Freya used the internet to make friends. It was in this way that she found others who were in a similar position, in The Netherlands for a temporary period of time. Freya then actively sought similarity, in terms of position in life, even though her friends were from different national cultures:

> I found some expat societies [and] clubs. … And it was Friday after-work drinks and that kind of thing. … I think it is more of a mentality thing—because there were a reasonable amount of English people, but also erm, Indians and Ukrainian.

Previous research has highlighted the influence of feeling transient in migration, resulting in people trying to make the most of their time abroad (Cranston 2018). It is these ideas that Freya echoes in her thinking, about people with the same mentality. She was looking for people who wished to have similar experiences to her as a means to combat feelings of liminality within a new spatial environment. Having a group of people with the desire to share experiences, in turn, helped her learn about other cultures: 'about learning how other people do things all of the time. … I guess learning how to be a bit more subtle - a bit more tactful!'

Encountering Difference: Intercultural Skills?

Butcher (2011) suggests that relocation to a different place generates feelings of liminality as the frames of cultural reference are challenged. As the previous sections of this chapter illustrate, by looking at the everyday practices of young people undertaking IWP we see two frames of reference: one of culture and one of life stage. Our respondents were challenged by different national cultures, but many were also challenged by being in an environment with people not in the same stage of life as them. It is due to this change in their spatial perceptions that friendships became increasingly important in grounding people in their new circumstances and aiding them in their negotiation of this new course in their lives.

As highlighted earlier, intercultural skills are difficult to define and measure. This ambiguity is reflected in our study, in which the lack of discussion around intercultural skills and the difficulty of pinning these down in interviews may be a symptom of the lack of understanding about what this term means in practice. However, some respondents did discuss the formation of traits that we associate with intercultural skills. Mia and Noah both discussed becoming more 'open-minded' in relation to how other cultures work, and Freya learnt how to interact with other cultures. However, these changes were formed in relation to friendships. Mia's open-mindedness was a result of a multinational friendship group who were also undertaking placements. Freya's adaptation was a result of finding an international group of people who were in a similar temporal position to hers.

In research in the critical social sciences, the embodied and emotional responses to difference are often used as a proxy to understand changes that can be labelled intercultural skills. Our respondents used discussions of their everyday lives as a means to highlight how they learnt about other cultures and how they operate. However, learning about this difference was enacted through friendships and the activities friendships enabled. As Ava and Mia illustrate, the everyday encounters with people of a similar age, but different nationalities, were ways through which they could learn about different cultures.

Freya and Tommy met different cultures as part of 'expat' activities and societies. Isla and her friends travelled around Europe together enjoying new experiences. Being predominantly friends with similar people can be criticized as a barrier to the formation of intercultural skills (Andersson et al. 2012; Van Mol and Michielsen 2015; Beech 2018). However, this research has illustrated that for students undertaking an IWP, the search for similarity in terms of friendships was not necessarily made utilizing co-nationals. Rather, our respondents were looking for people who were in a similar position in life: young people living abroad for a temporary period of time. This was a search for similarity as opposed to familiarity in most cases. For most respondents, we did not see a retrenchment of national values or the rejection of difference. Rather, the majority of respondents learnt about other cultures to a greater depth than they had experienced previously.

In this sense, international activities beyond the degree course, such as IWPs, assist students' awareness of different cultural contexts at both local and global levels (Le et al. 2018), and friendships were the key way in which this was facilitated. Therefore, for the majority of our respondents the emphasis was on making friends as opposed to directly seeking a cultural experience. Forming friendships appeared to be a priority for young people once abroad, which in turn facilitated further encounters and opportunities to develop intercultural skills. All respondents were looking for people of a similar age to hang out with, finding them in different spaces: work, home and society.

Where there was the presence of multiple nationalities, we saw evidence of what could be read as intercultural skills. Others fell back to hanging out with other British people, potentially as simply the easiest option to make friends. This highlights the importance of IWPs not just for the development of intercultural skills, as is predominantly assumed, but also acting as a key marker in young people's youth–adulthood and education–work transitions. This is demonstrated by how young people's discussions about being out of their comfort zone were often centred around age. This is not to say that intercultural skills were not treated as important in young people's narratives. On the contrary, intercultural skills were heralded as a motivation for, and key benefit of, IWPs. However, in practice, the everyday negotiations of belonging seemed more important in how their IWPs were framed.

Consequently, trying to frame IWPs from the perspective of intercultural skills as part of a global neoliberal economy misses an understanding of what young people seek to get out of their experiences of global mobility. The young people in our study framed IWPs as a benefit in terms of work-based skills, but also referenced the importance of this for them 'growing up' while undertaking their placement. In this sense, IWPs represented much more than heightening their 'employability.' They were also an opportunity for young people to learn more about themselves and make the transition to adulthood. It is therefore clear from our research that IWPs represented a significant transformation for young people. While a large amount of pressure is placed on young people to pursue strategies such as IWPs to prepare them for the workplace, care needs to be taken to consider the emotional responses and experiences of young people during these strategies. Although young people are active agents in their own futures, there must not be the illusion that these pursuits are simply part of a personal 'project of the self' (Holdsworth and Brewis 2014). Rather, they must be put into context with the demands placed on them to pursue a university-level degree, incorporating work-based experience, and acquiring intercultural competency through everyday lived experiences.

References

Andersson, J., Sadgrove, J., & Valentine, G. (2012). Consuming campus: Geographies of encounter at a British university. *Social and Cultural Geography, 13*(5), 501–515.

Bartlett, C. A., & Ghoshal, S. (1992). What is a global manager? *Harvard Business Review, September–October, 1992*, 124–132.

Beech, S. E. (2018). Negotiating the complex geographies of friendships overseas: Becoming, being and sharing in student mobility. *Geoforum, 92*, 18–25.

Brown, L. (2009a). An ethnographic study of the friendship patterns of international students in England: An attempt to recreate home through conational interaction. *International Journal of Educational Research, 48*(3), 184–193.

Brown, L. (2009b). A failure of communication on the cross-cultural campus. *Journal of Studies in International Education, 13*(4), 439–454.

Bunnell, T., Yea, S., Peake, L., Skelton, T., & Smith, M. (2012). Geographies of friendships. *Progress in Human Geography, 36*(4), 490–507.

Butcher, M. (2011). *Managing cultural change: Reclaiming synchronicity in a Mobile world.* Farnham: Ashgate.

Caruana, V. (2014). Re-thinking global citizenship in higher education: From cosmopolitanism and international mobility to cosmopolitanisation, resilience and resilient thinking. *Higher Education Quarterly, 68*(1), 85–104.

Cohen, S. L. (2010). Effective global leadership requires a global mindset. *Industrial and Commercial Training, 42*(1), 3–10.

Conradson, D., & Latham, A. (2005a). Friendship, networks and transnationality in a world city: Antipodean transmigrants in London. *Journal of Ethnic and Migration Studies, 31*(2), 287–305.

Conradson, D., & Latham, A. (2005b). Transnational urbanism: Attending to everyday practices and mobilities. *Journal of Ethnic and Migration Studies, 31*(2), 227–233.

Cranston, S. (2016a). Producing migrant encounter: Learning to be a British expatriate in Singapore through the global mobility industry. *Environment and Planning D: Society and Space, 34*(4), 655–671.

Cranston, S. (2016b). Imagining global work: Producing understandings of difference in 'easy Asia'. *Geoforum, 70*, 60–68.

Cranston, S. (2018). Negotiating expatriate identities: British migrant orientations in Singapore. In P. Leonard & K. Walsh (Eds.), *British migration: Privilege, diversity, vulnerability.* London: Routledge.

Davidson, J., & Milligan, C. (2004). Embodying emotion sensing space: Introducing emotional geographies. *Social and Cultural Geography, 5*(4), 523–532.

Deardorff, D. K. (2006). Identification and assessment of intercultural competence as a student outcome of internationalization. *Journal of Studies in International Education, 10*(3), 241–266.

Dunn, K. (2010). Doing' qualitative research in human geography. In I. Hay (Ed.), *Qualitative research methods in geography* (3rd ed.). Toronto: Oxford University Press.

Escudeiro, N. F., & Escudeiro, P. M. (2012). The multinational undergraduate teamwork project: An effective way to improve students' soft skills. *Industry and Higher Education, 26*(4), 279–290.

Griffith, R. L., Wolfeld, L., Armon, B. K., Rios, J., & Liu, O. L. (2016). *Assessing intercultural competence in higher education: Existing research and future directions.* ETS Research Report Series, Report No. RR-16-25, 1–46.

Holdsworth, C., & Brewis, G. (2014). Volunteering, choice and control: A case study of higher education student volunteering. *Journal of Youth Studies, 17*(2), 204–219.

Jones, A. (2011). Theorising international youth volunteering: Training for global (corporate) work? *Transactions of the Institute of British Geographers, 36*(4), 530–544.

Le, Q., Ling, T., & Yau, J. (2018). Do international cocurricular activities have an impact on cultivating a global mindset in business school students? *Journal of Teaching in International Business, 29*(1), 62–75.

Ley, D. (2004). Transnational spaces and everyday lives. *Transactions of the Institute of British Geographers, 29*(2), 151–164.

Lough, B. J., & McBride, A. M. (2014). Navigating the boundaries of active global citizenship. *Transactions of the Institute of British Geographers, 39*(3), 457–469.

Maunder, R. E. (2018). Students' peer relationships and their contribution to university adjustment: The need to belong in the university community. *Journal of Further and Higher Education, 42*(6), 756–768.

Minocha, S., Hristov, D., & Leahy-Harland, S. (2018). Developing a future-ready global workforce: A case study from leading UK university. *The International Journal of Management Education, 16*, 245–255.

Prazeres, L. (2017). Challenging the comfort zone: Self-discovery, everyday practices and international student mobility to the global south. *Mobilities, 12*(6), 908–923.

Robertson, S. (2018). Friendship networks and encounters in student-migrants' negotiations of translocal subjectivity. *Urban Studies, 55*(3), 538–553.

Suutari, V. (2002). Global leader development: An emerging research agenda. *Career Development International, 7*(4), 218–233.

Tymon, A. (2013). The student perspective on employability. *Studies in Higher Education, 38*(6), 841–856.

Universities UK International (2018). Gone International: expanding opportunities. Report on the 2015–16 graduating cohort. Available at https://www.universitiesuk.ac.uk/International/Documents/Gone%20International_expanding%20opportunities_digital.pdf.

Van Mol, C., & Michielsen, J. (2015). The reconstruction of a social network abroad. An analysis of the interaction patterns of Erasmus students. *Mobilities, 10*(3), 423–444.

Walsh, K. (2012). Emotion and migration: British transnationals in Dubai. *Environment and Planning D: Society and Space, 30*(1), 43–59.

Walsh, K. (2018). *Transnational geographies of the heart: Intimate subjectivities in a Globalising City*. London: Wiley.

Wilson, H. F. (2017). On geography and encounter: Bodies, borders, and difference. *Progress in Human Geography, 41*(4), 451–471.

Chapter 32
Abroad Forever? Embedding Spatial Mobility in Academic Work Trajectories in Italy

Davide Filippi, Sebastiano Benasso, and Luca Guzzetti

Within the framework of the knowledge-based economy, spatial mobility seems to have gained increasing relevance for many people, especially those working in the field of scientific research, where such mobility represents what has been described as a 'moral imperative' (Raffini 2017), functionally fitting into the economic and social neoliberal paradigm that has been explored in many of the accompanying chapters of this book. For academics, the mobility imperative leaves a permanent record of the processes that evaluate scholars' performance at university. Therefore, due to its integration within the broader discourse about human capital, mobility is often represented as the paramount strategy for succeeding in academia. However, through the biographical narratives of 24 Italian precarious academic researchers (aged 27–32 years) and analysis of their CVs, we find more ambivalence. Indeed, as potential 'marketability' rarely appears to compensate for its symbolical and material cost at a subjective level (see also Cairns et al. 2017), we will examine our empirical material to explore the strategies applied by these interviewees in managing their mobility and the different meanings they attach to these experiences.

The Knowledge Economy, Globalization and the Neoliberal University

At the end of the twentieth century, the final crisis of the Fordist production model induced a series of complex economic and social transformations. The appearance of new forms of work organization, the precarization of work relations and the new centrality of financial markets are the main characteristics assumed by the post-Fordist production model (Fumagalli and Bologna 1997; Gorz 1998; see also Beck

---

D. Filippi (✉) • S. Benasso • L. Guzzetti
University of Genoa, Genoa, Italy

1992). This new context informs scientific discussion defining the knowledge economy (Rullani 2004; Jenkins 2008) and 'cognitive capitalism' (Hardt and Negri 2017; Fumagalli 2017; Vercellone 2009), an issue that concerns us in the chapter.

Parallel to the transformation of organizational forms of production, and with the neoliberal turn, globalization processes have transformed the role of the nation state, which no longer regulates the market but operates as a function of the market itself (Boltanski and Chiapello 2005). Furthermore, from a governance perspective, the widespread notion of 'human capital' resonates with the 'new way of the world' (Dardot and Laval 2014), creating a society structured by the market, wherein individuals must be able to compete by self-managing themselves and, above all, improving the marketability of their own human capital. These developments have changed the role and relevance of many academic and research institutions in contemporary forms of production. On the one hand, they can continue to play a crucial role in the production of knowledge and technologies, but on the other, they might also become collective spaces deeply influenced by the pervasiveness of business-oriented organizational models, informed by the New Public Management (NPM) paradigm (Waldby and Cooper 2014).

Several studies have begun to show how the financial crisis in universities, the hiring freeze and the development of a highly segmented labour market are shared phenomena across the advanced capitalist countries, albeit with local differences (Roggero 2009). These dynamics have induced globalized academic institutions to reproduce the organizational forms of the private sector, with the aim of maximizing their productivity in the context of a neoliberal cognitive economy. In academia, this has fostered growing emphasis on evaluation, which results in a permanent evaluation regime where the symbolic and material relevance of the internationalization processes is crucial. Against the backdrop of the broader process of the emergent 'evaluative state' (Neave 1988), the topic of internationalization in academia clearly appears in the European integration process with the publication of the White Paper by the Delors Commission in 1993 (Pinto 2012). This document suggested that to face the new challenges of globalized cognitive capitalism, it was necessary to adopt deep structural reforms in national educational systems, and one of these reforms was the development of a transnational system of evaluation (Pinto 2012).

Since that time, the so-called Lisbon Agreement in 1997 and the Sorbonne Declaration in 1998 have shaped the development of an integrated system of higher education at the European level, known as the 'Bologna Process.' This process was initiated in 1999, in Bologna, when 29 EU and extra-EU countries agreed to develop a set of coordinated national policies aimed at homogenizing their higher education systems, creating the European Space for Higher Education. Since then, in Italy, a multiplicity of structural reforms in academia have been adopted. Recently, some evaluation mechanisms were introduced, consistent with this ideology: for example, the Evaluation of the Quality of Research (VQR), University Self-evaluation Exercise (AVA) and hiring procedures based on a National Scientific Qualification (ASN).

After 30 years of integrating these changes into the European university system, we can argue that evaluation mechanisms have become an important agent and an aim in itself in the restructuring of academia. In turn, internationalization is an instrument and an objective of evaluation processes, influencing governance at a local level and reproducing at the same time the globalizing push towards the market economy. While the culture of evaluation fosters internationalization by incentives at all levels, the adoption of evaluative systems at a transnational level has created a global homogenization of organizational models in universities. In this context, the mobility of researchers assumes a special relevance, becoming one of the main indicators for measuring the level of internationalization of universities, specific departments and researchers themselves. This might explain why

> [t]he drive to assess the performance of workers and to measure forms of labour which, by their nature, are resistant to quantification, has inevitably required additional layers of management and bureaucracy. What we have is not a direct comparison of workers' performance or output, but a comparison between the audited representation of that performance and output. Inevitably, a short-circuiting occurs, and work becomes geared towards the generation and massaging of representations rather than to the official goals of the work itself. (Fisher 2009: 42)

In the globalized market economy, the mobility of workers is also considered to be a constitutive element of the liquid society of knowledge and networks (Bauman and Mazzeo 2013; Castells 1996). Within the global system's permanent flow of goods and capitals, workers must flow within the globalized space in order to show their competence and skills in the labour market (Beltrame 2008). It is in this sense that, for the production and diffusion of scientific research, mobility 'represents today a true moral imperative, functional to the neoliberal economic and social model' (Raffini 2017: 76). The individual attempts to adjust to such an imperative, giving rise to new and diverse forms of mobility, and his/her CV becomes an instrument for analysing the meaning university researchers attach to their own experiences.

Importance of the Curriculum Vitae and Academic Mobility

Researchers respond to the 'moral' imperative of internationalization by incorporating it into their work trajectories, represented through the 'confessional' device (Foucault 1977) of the CV. In general terms, the writing of a CV may be defined as an autobiographical practice, wherein the subject reconstructs a story about himself/herself, offering a strategically oriented image in the context of the relationship between the labour market and the individual (Jedlowski 2000). Such practices are implemented each time an individual is requested to give account of his/her 'presentation of self' (Goffman 1959). When applied to the CV as autobiographical practice, an interactionist perspective suggests that the self exists only as the product of multiple relational frames, where particular representations of the self are strategically selected to fit a situation. The act of presenting oneself is requested in an indirect but highly formalized manner, with the CV seen as a field wherein the tensions between external requests and subjective responses develop, giving rise to a specific form of self-presentation. Therefore, this is a form of objectification of individual human capital, constructed according to variable opportunities and demands present on the market.

Through analysis of the CV it is possible to understand how disciplinary practices operate (Foucault 1977, 2010). Neoliberal governmentality fosters the creation of a form of subjectivity, its action not focused on repression and discipline, but rather directly on subjectivity and its strategies. Within the paradigm of the subject as 'self-entrepreneur,' mechanisms of social atomization and individual accountability transform discipline from being an external element—regulating and legitimizing specific forms of subjectivity—to an incorporated component of the individual self (Dardot and Laval 2014). From this point of view, in post-disciplinary societies the market in cognitive capitalism is characterized by a social dynamic, wherein the subject disciplines himself/herself as human capital (Deleuze 2000; Foucault 1977; Chicchi and Simone 2017).

The development of a global market for scientific research has had a strong impact on shaping new forms for academic professions and, perhaps more subtly, determining specific models of governance for academic mobility. In this framework, researchers take on the mobility imperative, using a process of 'spatial reflexivity' to add another dimension to their career trajectories (Cairns 2014). But because of the shrinking and de-structuring of the European research market following the 2008 economic crisis, the mobility of scientific researchers has become determined more by the imperative to find any job in the field in which they have chosen to structure their life project rather than the hoped-for improvement in levels of human capital (Cairns et al. 2017).

Looking at the spatially reflexive dimension of CV production, before being a 'good academic' it is necessary to demonstrate an ability to face challenging mobility—processes characterized by what feels like a perpetual searching, forcing the researcher to never abandon the mobility imperative. In the frame of the neoliberal university, and its consequences in terms of work precariousness and flexibility, researchers' mobility takes the form of 'Brownian motion,' appearing to be governed by mobility itself (Tazzioli 2017). In other words, in accordance with the theory of the 'autonomy of migrations', mobility becomes a social action to be controlled, steered and governed through a process of differential inclusion (Mezzadra and Neilson 2013). In the case of academic mobility, this is particularly evident: it is valued and invoked as being synonymous with internationalization, with governmental devices in place to orientate researchers' trajectories, sometimes with success, on other occasions clashing with the strategic agency of people on the move.

Methodological Approach

In order to analyse the strategies adopted to represent mobility through CVs, we have conducted 24 interviews with Italian researchers, all of whom have obtained a PhD in Humanities and Social Sciences, who had a current research contract or were looking for one at the end of a preceding contract with an Italian or foreign university. At the time of the interview, three of the interviewees had just signed a permanent contract after several years of precariousness; four were unemployed and looking for a job in the academic field (while continuing to publish and prepare research projects); one was about to enter the second year of a second PhD; and the remaining researchers were employed on temporary contracts or remunerated via scholarships. As far as gender is concerned, we interviewed exactly 50 per cent men and 50 per cent women, aged between 27 and 32 years. Concerning research methods, we carried out biographical interviews, during which the subjects were invited to freely articulate and reconstruct the meaning of their own experience (Cardano 2003).

The Main Axes Organizing a CV

The CV can be considered a specific empirical object defined by a series of tensions, which result from the mediation between the need for standardization and homologation—tied to the objectification required by the rhetoric of evaluation—and the self-representation strategies of workers. In a context where evaluation rhetoric and procedures impose the use of measurable criteria, the structuring of a document that is able to reconstruct the life course of the subject in 'objective' terms becomes an absolute necessity. From this point of view, the 'autobiographies' presented through the CV tend to be structured along predetermined axes. One way to analyse this device is to imagine it as a three-dimensional field with three axes: y would represent time, x space (on which this paper mainly focuses) and z the volume of the productivity of the subject. Using this scheme, our hypothesis describes how a CV should be in order to respect the implicit norms governing the working relations in academia, with the 'marketability' of the CV dependent on the meeting point of these three axes.

The y-Axis: Time

The first element to emerge when exploring the approach to the time dimension of the collected CVs is the inherent precariousness of professional trajectories within Italian academia. For example, in the 'professional experience' section of all the analysed CVs, we found references to contracts lasting no longer than two years. From this point of view, the main requirement—for having an adequate CV that meets the prescriptions of the neoliberal economy—seems to be the ability to show forms of continuity regardless of the actual precariousness experienced. A 'good CV' should not have 'blank spots' since it is expected that the human capital of a worker should be evaluated not only on the basis of the skills listed in the CV but overall, on the basis of the devotion shown towards the labour market itself. In fact, some of the researchers involved in our study strategically attempted to represent their careers as a continuum rather than a fragmentation of experiences so that potential evaluators might perceive this as the result of an overall investment strategy rather than the sum of a series of singular working experiences.

The z-Axis: Productivity

The z-axis represents the volume of scientific productivity developed by the researcher. The CV sections most involved in this dimension are scientific papers, research projects and participation in conferences and workshops. Looking at the empirical material studied, the first option to emerge for the researchers is whether or not to report the totality of their activities or only the parts considered most relevant to the aspired employment. Such a choice is determined by two main factors: the quantity of the researcher's output and the quality and relevance of the production on the basis of the criteria adopted by the potential evaluators.

It is important to note that the researchers who have more experience in the academic labour market may decide to selectively list their products, while younger researchers tend to present the totality of their activities and production, since the volume is much smaller. It is also interesting to explore the differences in the CVs of researchers who have had long working experiences in the Anglophone academic world. On these CVs there are sections where the researchers declare how many external funding grants they have won, and presumably how much money was gained, demonstrating their willingness to participate in national and international calls and competitions for projects, and an aptitude in preparing submissions.

If a researcher has demonstrated the ability to obtain funds from public or private institutions, this also means they are a subject who has already received positive evaluations and public acknowledgement of the value of their CV, increasing its marketability in the eyes of evaluators. As a matter of fact, this phenomenon has already been investigated in a more general context by Merton (1968) in the seminal 'The Matthew Effect in Science,' where he related the Gospel passage—'For unto every one that hath shall be given, and he shall have abundance; but from him that hath not shall be taken away even that which he hath'—to the allocation of scientific resources, with a principle of 'cumulative advantage' prevailing, and a disproportional amount of rewards and economic resources to those who already have them.

The x-Axis: Space

Although in public discourse the internationalization of universities is mostly connected to the international mobility of academics, if we look at their CVs, we find reference to internationalization in all the sections of the document. For researchers whose professional profile is characterized by important mobility experiences—even short stays—the spatial dimension has the appearance of a continuum, cutting through all sections, although most mention their international vocation in the part of the CV regarding professional experiences, usually in a specific section called 'Visiting Period.'

About this topic, an interviewee who has enjoyed long periods of mobility—and is still working abroad—developed an interesting opinion. In his view, the short visiting periods experienced by most researchers do not actually enrich their scientific competence but rather are used to give a good professional image of the researcher's profile.

> And then people do it because universities like to have foreign researchers: it's good for their CVs as well. Since it's good for the researchers, universities don't worry too much and they say to themselves: 'Ok, if this guy comes over, he will take care of himself.' That's it. And people go abroad—and they keep doing it—because they say to themselves: 'Ok, even if I don't learn shit, even if actually it's not useful to me, I'll be able to mention it in the CV,' because everybody is in favour of this fucking internationalization, you see? (Interview with Emilio)

In any case, even for researchers who have decided to structure their career within the Italian labour market, it appears that it is necessary to show an international dimension, although by different means than mobility. Thus, for these people, the sections of the CV regarding publications in international journals, collaboration in international projects and participation in conferences abroad acquire further relevance, as a way to demonstrate their embrace of internationalization.

Meaning and Costs of Mobility

In considering reflexive mobility in Italian academia, we need to start from a critical interpretation of the 'brain drain' discourse, which is still oddly hegemonic in the national political debates about the international mobility of highly qualified workers (Beltrame 2008; Krings et al. 2013). In this discourse, the irresistible attractiveness of foreign labour markets for highly skilled professionals is taken for granted: in terms of better wages, general working conditions and/or chances for professional growth. Alternatively, the proponents of reflexive mobility argue that scholars who focus only on the accumulation of human capital to compete on the global market—thus improving their level of employability—have no connection with the reality of professional and living conditions that are experienced by the majority of peripatetic scientific workers as precarious to the point of lacking the opportunity to accumulate social and economic capital while abroad (Cairns et al. 2017). There are costs and benefits from mobility, but the former tend to outweigh the latter.

There is also the matter of motivation, and the voluntary nature of mobility decision. Researchers' mobility might be prompted by a lack of jobs and the radical precariousness of the labour market at home, but the idea that this constitutes a 'push' factor is counterbalanced by the existence of what may be even higher levels of precarity in foreign labour markets. It is more credible to argue that people move abroad for a chance of success rather than certain outcomes. In this sense, strategies come to be devised on the basis of a 'logic of opportunity,' thinking not only about the present situation but keeping in mind the idea that at some indistinct point in the future, professional chances might arrive when enough mobility capital has been accumulated, although of course this may never happen (Cairns 2014; Benasso 2013). This explains why this logic is somewhat blind, and people tend to only retrospectively realize that one of the most important aspects of the migration experience for academic researchers is that decisions made on the basis of the opportunity logic lead to more of the same or even more severe forms of precariousness than those experienced at home. But as a kind of face-saving exercise, they may seek to interpret their 'misfortune' not only as temporary but also as instrumental to eventual success, even if this means accepting radical forms of exploitation in the present, which are understandably under-reported on a CV in an effort not to spoil the impression that the professional and existential project is proceeding exactly as planned.

To Leave or Not to Leave, That Is the Question…

As we have seen, international mobility is rhetorically represented as one of the possible options a precarious researcher can take to improve the competitiveness of a professional profile in the academic labour market. But, if we look at the biographies of our interviewees, we find out that such a choice often does not *really* improve their careers. In fact, mainly on the basis of this awareness, some of the interviewees have strategically decided not to move, thus avoiding the 'trap' outlined in the previous paragraph.

Various factors intervene in the decision to remain at home. First of all, the material conditions of the subject. In the narratives, we see that paramount in deciding who can leave (and who cannot) are gender and class issues. From this point of view, it does not look like a free choice but rather a consequence of the intersectional positioning of the individual researcher. Another argument presented to explain the decision to remain in Italy is that in many cases the precarious researcher has been working in a specific department for several years, creating a strong network of professional relationships, being involved in various research projects: all this works against the decision to leave. In this regard, a researcher used the expression 'If you go away, everything falls down,' stressing the idea that, although most researchers are in highly precarious conditions, they nevertheless have a major role to play in the functioning of the Italian academic system.

Among the researchers who have chosen to invest in a career within their national borders, a few presented the potential choice of mobility as a 'last resort,' to experiment with only in cases where they face problems in assuring continuity in their career or a capacity to earn enough money. However, in their narratives—and in their CVs as well—these researchers declared that such a situation had never materialized since they were always able to gain a salary from research in Italy.

Another element emerging from the choice for immobility is the belief that today precariousness pervades the entire global academic market. Thus, to follow the mobility imperative would mean making a bet that does not assure more certainty about one's working future. Moreover, the current criteria used in the evaluation of the internationalization level of researchers in the Italian academia are not regarded as coherent in regard to mobility, with a confused understanding of what an international research product is:

> The evaluation criteria of internationalization make me laugh. If you want to do international research, what you write must be read by your colleagues everywhere. If you write a paper in Italian, maybe those in Rome will read it, maybe ... but you can be sure that those in Berlin won't. Internationalization thus means that your work is international when it can freely circulate, and it has an international appeal. Writing in English is not enough. (Interview with Stefania)

Reflexive Strategies

The mobility projects of precarious researchers take different forms depending on the individual's professional strategies. The narratives concerning their mobility experiences implicitly assume that the productive space of research is necessarily globalized. It is thus obvious for them to perceive this international dimension—and to act in it—as it is their 'natural' professional context. As suggested by an interviewed subject, these mobile researchers seem to be the real 'winners of globalization' (Favell 2003).

One group of researchers explained how the decision to leave was connected to a specific foreign country, where they could try to achieve some kind of work stabilization before returning to Italy. Normally such a strategy fails, for two main reasons. The first is that when they live and work in a new country, it becomes difficult to go back home for 'biographical reasons.' One researcher who worked in a foreign country found it difficult to leave behind the networking she had there, and not only for academic reasons. This is not unlike those researchers who decided not to leave Italy and lose their investment in networks there. Staying in one place for a long time implies the creation of networks, relationships and skills that may not necessarily be useful elsewhere. It is also noteworthy that the precarious researchers in Italian academia have an average age that coincides with the one at which people usually decide to have children. This can pose profound questions about the individual decision to privilege professional life, at the (possible) expense of different life choices.

A second group of researchers told us about mobility paths characterized by a fixed point, Italy, and a variable one chosen on the basis of the opportunities present at the time. We might define this as a form of 'spring mobility.' To adopt such a strategy, several researchers explained how they had to negotiate with their professors in Italy and/or abroad. For instance, Michele told us that when he was abroad preparing a new research project in the context of the European Union's Horizon 2020 initiative, he made it clear that he would have accepted a new contract there if and only if he would be permitted to work for ten days each month in Italy. Similarly, another precarious researcher told us of his contract with his professor in Italy: he would have accepted a postdoc grant abroad for some months if the professor would guarantee a yearly contract on his return.

Other researchers took a different approach to mobility. Some were ready to go nearly anywhere to continue to be included in the academic labour market. For these people, who consider the globalized research market as their sphere of action, international mobility appears to be totally 'natural.' They are the subjects who rigorously accept the mobility imperative, and are willing to put at stake their whole professional and personal future to be able to compete in the research global market on the basis of the opportunity ratio.

> So, let's say that every time that I moved from home, and this starting already from the time of the PhD, I've done it because elsewhere there were opportunities to do something. Better opportunities to do things, to grow professionally, to do interesting things, etc. Therefore, sometimes with a great desire to move, sometimes not so much, I have always taken my opportunities, the best for me. (Interview with Carla)

Mobility Costs

As far as mobility costs are concerned, the first issue emerging from an analysis of the narratives of those who have a 'peripatetic' form of life and career (Cairns et al. 2017) is the management of extra-professional relations. In several cases, the complexity of managing their (familial and friendly) relationships also arises from the weak synchronization they feel they have with the traditional calendar of the adulthood markers (Benasso 2013). From this point of view, therefore, age makes mobility more difficult, and is evoked as one of the elements that deepen the sense of uncertainty, generated in the subjects by the combination of precariousness with being pushed towards mobility.

The difficulties encountered by mobile researchers derive as well from the need to reorganize one's life after each move. To find a house in a new place, get to know a new town and confront the institutions in a different country are all activities that require strong material and mental investment. To this, they have to add the problems derived from the effort to understand the working dynamics they find in the new workplace. Finally, some of the researchers who have had prior experience of international mobility suggests that being always on the move entails high levels of mental stress (Fisher 2009), and this—together with the normal stress arising from precarious working conditions—makes it impossible for them to respond positively to the mobility imperative forever.

A common perception among the interviewees was that during their first mobility experiences they felt enthusiastic as they discovered and got to know new places, sometimes very different from where they were coming from. Later, though, when the same experiences lasted for years and the destinations multiplied, the enthusiasm became weariness, and a strong desire for a stabilization in both their professional and personal lives prevailed. In this sense, if we connect the mobility imperative to the existential uncertainty that permeates the precarious forms of life, the costs paid to see oneself as the 'winner' of the academic competition start to appear very high, sometimes much too high.

> So, one person sees my CV, and says: 'Ah, you had two post-doc grants and two visiting experiences.' And the same person tells you: 'Ah, it's very good, isn't it?' Instead, you know that behind those things there is a high level of suffering, a high level of disillusion, a high level of frustration. You have lost a lot of important relationships because it's clear that you have not cultivated them. Then, if you work in research and you take it seriously, you completely lose any sense of the relative relevance of the different aspects of your life. It's hard because clearly, I had to sacrifice some relationships, at least in the medium period, some relationships and affective relations. In any case, I had to go away from some persons, and my relations with my family have become more complicated as well. In the end, this thing is very complex and it makes me suffer, even if it's clear that I cannot write about it in my CV. (Interview to Giuseppe)

Conclusions

By examining the CVs of precarious researchers as confessional devices, we have shown how the CV works as an objectification of the human capital of a subject and, more importantly, the product of a scenic fiction created to respond to the demands of the labour market in the framework of neoliberal universities. Such a fiction does not end with the compilation of the document called a CV, but contributes to defining and steering the everyday activities and life choices of the subjects involved. We hence argue that the CV is an instrument through which the rhetoric of the neoliberal control society orientates the reflexive actions of the subject: in relation to oneself and the world around her/him.

As we described, one of the most important criteria to show in order to work in scientific research is to comply with the internationalization imperative. Although the concept of internationalization may have different meanings, in the debate about the criteria for evaluating scientific research, the geographical mobility of researchers has clearly assumed a central role. However, in this chapter we have tried to show that regardless of the homologation and standardization favoured by the disciplinary device known as the CV, Italian researchers have tried to impose their own autonomous agency to conquer self-determined spaces. This also happens because they are conscious of the contradiction existing between the precariousness inherent in this specific segment of the labour market and the cultural pressure to implement and promote their human capital on the global stage. It is in this sense that the researchers we interviewed criticized the evaluation culture, the crucial importance assigned to the CV and the representation of mobility as a necessary prerequisite to becoming more competitive.

To conclude, we would like to point out a clear aporia existing in the process of Europe's integration and the homologation of its academic systems. On the one hand, public discourse has been focusing on promoting the mobility of academic workers within the EU, while on the other, the EU has disregarded the necessity of creating a system of rights that is able to sustain this mobility process. In policy terms, a debate should start about the offering of housing, welfare, basic income and a minimum salary at a European level to these 'knowledge' workers. We are sure that the implementation of a European plan to support the mobility of researchers would be very important for the success of the European integration project. We would also like to stress that what we have written in this chapter may be true for a large variety of workers in different fields who like scientific researchers live their professional experiences in a completely globalized productive space. It is at this level that we see the real challenges, as we imagine new and more sustainable profiles for European citizenship—new profiles that have to emerge from public debate among, first of all, the researchers themselves.

References

Bauman, Z., & Mazzeo, R. (2013). *On education: Conversations with Riccardo Mazzeo*. Hoboken: Wiley.
Beck, U. (1992). *Risk society: Towards a new modernity*. Thousand Oaks: Sage.
Beltrame, L. (2008). *Realtà e retorica del brain drain in Italia. Stime statistiche, definizioni pubbliche e interventi politici (Vol. 35)*. Trento: Università degli Studi di Trento: Dipartimento di Sociologia e Ricerca Sociale.
Benasso, S. (2013). *Generazione Shuffle. Traiettorie biografiche tra reversibilità e progetto*. Roma: Aracne.
Boltanski, L., & Chiapello, E. (2005). *The new spirit of capitalism*. New York City: Verso Books.
Cairns, D. (2014). *Youth transitions, international student mobility and spatial reflexivity: Being mobile?* Basingstoke: Palgrave Macmillan.
Cairns, D., Cuzzocrea, V., Briggs, D., & Veloso, L. (2017). *The consequences of mobility*. Basingstoke: Palgrave Macmillan.
Cardano, M. (2003). *Tecniche di ricerca qualitativa. Percorsi di ricerca nelle scienze sociali*. Roma: Carocci.
Castells, M. (1996). *The rise of the network society: The information age: Economy, society and culture, Vol. I*. Cambridge: Blackwell.
Chicchi, F., & Simone, A. (2017). *La Società Della Prestazione*. Roma: Ediesse.
Dardot, P., & Laval, C. (2014). *The new way of the world: On neoliberal society*. New York City: Verso Books.
Deleuze, G. (2000). *Pourparler*. Macerata: Quodlibet.
Favell, A. (2003). *Eurostars and Eurocities: Towards a sociology of free moving professionals in Western Europe*. Working Paper 71. The Center for Comparative Immigration Studies. San Diego: University of California.
Fisher, M. (2009). *Capitalist realism: Is there no alternative?* London: John Hunt Publishing.
Foucault, M. (1977). *Discipline and punish: The birth of the prison*. New York: Random.
Foucault, M. (2010). *The birth of biopolitics: Lectures at the College de France, 1978–1979*. New York City: St. Martin's Press.
Fumagalli, A. (2017). *L'Economia Politica del Comune. Sfruttamento e Sussunzione nel Capitalismo Bio-Cognitivo*. Roma: DeriveApprodi.
Fumagalli, A., & Bologna, S. (1997). *Il Lavoro Autonomo di Seconda Generazione. Scenari del Postfordismo in Italia*. Milano: Feltrinelli.
Goffman, E. (1959). *The presentation of self in everyday life*. New York: Anchor Books.
Gorz, A. (1998). *Miseria del presente, ricchezza del possibile*. Roma: Manifestolibri.
Hardt, M., & Negri, A. (2017). *Assembly*. Oxford: Oxford University Press.
Jedlowski, P. (2000). *Storie Comuni: La Narrazione nella Vita Quotidiana*. Milano: Mondadori.

Jenkins, H. (2008). *Fan, bloggers e videogamers*. Milano: FrancoAngeli.
Krings, T., Bobek, A., Moriarty, E., Salamonska, J., & Wickham, J. (2013). Polish migration to Ireland: 'Free movers' in the new European mobility space. *Journal of Ethnic and Migration Studies, 39*(1), 87–103.
Merton, R. K. (1968). The Matthew effect in science. *Science, 199*, 55–63.
Mezzadra, S., & Neilson, B. (2013). *Border as method, or, the multiplication of labor*. Durham: Duke University Press.
Neave, G. (1988). On the cultivation of quality, efficiency and enterprise: An overview of recent trends in higher education in Western Europe, 1986–1988. *European Journal of Education, 23*(1/2), 7–23.
Pinto, V. (2012). *Valutare e Punire. Una Critica della Cultura della Valutazione*. Napoli: Cronopio.
Raffini, L. (2017). Cosmopoliti dispersi. La mobilità dei ricercatori precari tra retoriche e pratiche. In F. Coin, A. Giorgi, & A. Murgia (Eds.), *In/disciplinate: Soggettività Precarie Nell'università Italiana* (pp. 75–90). Venezia: Edizioni Ca' Foscari.
Roggero, G. (2009). *La Produzione del Sapere Vivo. Crisi Dell'Università e Trasformazione del Lavoro tra le due Sponde Sell'Atlantico*. Verona: Ombre Corte.
Rullani, E. (2004). *La Fabbrica Dell'Immateriale, Produrre Valore con la Conoscenza*. Roma: Carocci.
Tazzioli, M. (2017). Governing migrant mobility through mobility: Containment and dispersal at the internal frontiers of Europe. *Environment and Planning C: Politics and Space, 38*(1), 3–19.
Vercellone, C. (2009). Lavoro, distribuzione del reddito e valore nel capitalismo cognitivo. Una prospettiva storica e teorica. *Sociologia del Lavoro, 115*, 31–54.
Waldby, C., & Cooper, M. (2014). *Clinical labor: Tissue donors and research subjects in the global bioeconomy*. Durham: Duke University Press.

Chapter 33
Italian Youth and the Experience of Highly Qualified Migration to the United Kingdom

Monica Santoro

In the last six years, data on migration in Italy has shown a constant increase in the number of Italians leaving their home country. In 2010, approximately 40,000 Italians migrated and since 2011, this figure has steadily increased. According to the most recent figures, 114,000 Italians moved in 2017, compared with 82,000 in 2013 (Istat 2016). A number of factors have facilitated moving and relocating within Europe, including European education and training projects promoting young people's mobility within the European Union. In the past few years, however, the mobility of one particular section of the European population seems to have been influenced by the economic crisis that severely affected Southern Europe.

In Italy, levels of youth unemployment rose considerably: in the EU15 in 2008, the unemployment rate among young people aged between 20 and 29 years was 10.9 per cent, and 15.6 per cent in 2015. In Italy, unemployment levels in this age bracket were far higher than the EU15 average: increasing from 13.8 per cent to 28.1 per cent (Eurostat 2016). The purpose of this chapter is to explore the dynamics of the migration experience among one particular group of young Italians at this time of high unemployment at home: those who moved to the United Kingdom after 2008.

Data on Italians Abroad: The Problem with Quantification

There are two statistical sources for calculating the number of Italians who move abroad every year: the AIRE (Anagrafe degli Italiani Residenti all'Estero—Register of Italians Resident Abroad) and the number of cancellations from the civil registry

---

M. Santoro (✉)
University of Milan, Milan, Italy
e-mail: monica.santoro@unimi.it

of the place of residence to move abroad, periodically quantified by the Italian Central Institute of Statistics (ISTAT). However, the AIRE register underestimates the number of Italians resident abroad, especially those who have moved recently, as migrants often prefer to wait a few years before reporting their new residence. The ISTAT data suffer from the same limitations. Not everyone who goes to live in a foreign country immediately cancels their registration. Usually, these people wait until they assess the possibility of establishing definitive residence in the new country. In fact, according to the Dossier Statistico Immigrazione 2017 (IDOS 2017), cancellations from the registry recorded in Italy represent only one third of Italians who have actually left the country. Consequently, the only way to obtain a more precise picture of the number of migrants in recent years is to refer to both Italian statistics and those of the host country.[1]

According to the ISTAT (2016) data, 102,000 Italians established their residence abroad in the course of 2015, 15 per cent more than in 2014. The main destination countries were the UK and Germany (both with over 17,000 migrants), followed by Switzerland and France (with approximately 11,000 migrants). The majority of those leaving were university graduates aged over 25 years (almost 23,000 in 2015, +13 per cent compared with 2014), although outward migration is also growing among Italians with a medium–low level of education (52,000 Italians in 2015, +9 per cent). As such, we have an opportunity to learn about post-education migration trajectories, building on the work presented on education and training in the preceding chapters.

Italians in the United Kingdom

The UK is one of the European countries most heavily involved in migration from Southern European countries. Until 2012, European migrants in search of employment came mainly from Bulgaria and Romania, after which the migratory flow extended to countries of the EU15, especially the South. Between March 2014 and March 2015, applications for a National Insurance number by European citizens increased by 43 per cent and it has been calculated that approximately half of the migrants from the EU15 area were hired with an employment contract before they arrived in the UK, while the others arrived in search of a job (Office for National Statistics 2015).

In regard to this measure, Italy ranks third among European countries, with 62,000 NI registrations in the period between March 2016 and March 2017 (in 2014–2015 there were 59,000, and in 2016, 63,000), preceded by Romania (182,000 registrations) and Poland (84,000), followed by Spain (44,000) (Office for National Statistics 2017). The increase in European migration to the UK in the past two years has extended to the cities of the north of England as the cost of living is lower than in London (McKay 2015). In 2011, Manchester was the city in the North-West with the largest migrant community (127,000 migrants, an estimated 25 per cent of the migrant population of the North-West) (Krausova and Vargas-Silva 2013). In particular, it has become one of the most desirable destinations for Spaniards and Italians since 2010. In the space of only a few years, the presence of these two nationalities has increased progressively, and they have become the most prominent Europeans, together with Poles. In 2014, 686 Italians and over 1300 Spaniards moving to the city applied for an NI number (Manchester City Council 2015). According to data from the Italian Consulate, there has been a 20 per cent annual increase in the number of Italian workers in the city since 2008 (COM.IT.ES 2014).

The Research in Manchester

This research is based on thirty interviews carried out in Manchester between October 2014 and December 2016 with Italians who had been living in the English city for at least six months and up to a maximum of five years. The time span coincides with the period during which the economic crisis in Italy appeared to have deepened and the data on migration recorded a marked increase in the number of Italians of working age leaving the country to move abroad. The interviewees were mostly aged between 21 and 34 years, with the older ones able to relate stories of their more extensive experience of working abroad while young. This is a broad age bracket that represents the dynamics of Italian migration to the UK, which has increasingly involved young adults with medium-to-high educational qualifications (Istat 2014). Almost all the interviewees had a degree or a high school diploma, and three had PhDs. They came mostly from Italian cities in the Centre-North, with the exception of four residents in the South who had had educational or employment experience in Northern Italian cities prior to moving abroad.

The interviewees were found through an advertisement on the Facebook page of the 'Italians in Manchester' group and on the 'Italian Meetup' website. The former is a place where Italians who have moved—or who intend to move—to Manchester to exchange information, seek advice on how to find jobs or accommodation, and share their migration experiences. The latter is a website on which a series of social events (dinners, pub and cinema evenings, cookery courses, etc.) are offered with the aim of putting Italians resident in the city in contact with each other. There were numerous responses to the advertisement, although some people (five cases) who had initially agreed to be interviewed later refused. As regards employment, all the interviewees had steady jobs. The majority, especially those who had been living in England for fewer than two years, were working in the restaurant sector, and two in a call centre; while two engineers, two nurses and two croupiers had arrived in the city after being hired in Italy.

The interviews sought to elicit accounts of the interviewees' migratory projects and work conditions in Manchester. Specifically, they were asked to retrace the stages of their decision to move abroad, the organization of their journeys and their new lives, and their search for employment. Also explored were certain biographical factors that might have been decisive when the decision to leave Italy was taken, such as previous training, education and employment. Finally, the interviewees were asked to describe how they organized their domestic and working lives in Manchester and what their future plans were, the purpose being to investigate whether they were oriented towards a stable or temporary migratory experience (Santoro 2015a).

Leaving Italy to Work in Manchester

The interviewees' migration stories revolved around their work experiences in Italy and the UK. They had mainly left Italy for work reasons, and in three cases, to accompany their partners. The first distinction that emerges in their migratory paths concerns recruitment practices. Some had migrated after being hired from Italy: this was the case of two nurses, two engineers and two croupiers. The advantage enjoyed by these interviewees was not only that they had jobs matching their professional training, but also that they had obtained employment conditions decidedly better than those they would have been able to find in Italy.

The case of the nurses interviewed, who had graduated less than a year before, is emblematic. Nursing staff are very much in demand in the UK, especially in public healthcare facilities. The two interviewees reported that they had been employed after various selection procedures, and that they had found a stimulating work environment, an initial salary higher than in Italy and promising career opportunities:

> In Italy, it is unthinkable to find a job with a basic wage of €1400 four months after graduation; 'basic' because you can earn more according to the shifts that you do.

The predictability of career paths in the British labour market was appreciated—and not only by these two interviewees. In the case of hospital nursing staff, it is possible to move up a level every three years, and staff are able to provide them with the necessary training:

> In England, they follow a certain protocol: that is, to get here you have to do this. It's a classic situation where here to get to a certain point the path is straight, while in Italy there are roundabouts, crossroads, and so on.

A 33-year-old engineer had worked steadily in Italy, but not in his field of specialization, which was sound engineering. He answered a job advertisement found by chance on the internet, but did not think he would be contacted. An interview was conducted a few days later, however, and a job offer was made immediately thereafter:

> I couldn't believe it; in Italy a job like this doesn't exist, working in the field in which you studied for your PhD; it didn't seem possible. I discussed it with my wife, and we decided to accept and move. In the space of one year, I've become the manager of a project and they have increased my salary.

The employment trajectories of the other interviewees were very different. Moving abroad was a decision made to escape unemployment or feel work conditions deemed unacceptable. In general, several years had passed between obtaining educational qualifications and the decision to leave, during which the interviewees had tried to find a job that satisfied their expectations or, as some stated, enabled them to secure a minimum level of independence.

The years 2011 and 2012 were identified as turning points in the deterioration of employment opportunities, when hopes of being able to find a job were lost (Santoro 2017). One of the interviewees, who had a job in a call centre and had previously worked in the tourist sector in Italy, recalled:

> In 2012, I found myself without a job for the first time in my life. My last job had been in April, in a holiday village, and after that I didn't find anything else, they didn't even answer. ... I found a course to train as a receptionist in London and decided to do it, and then from London I came here.

In the same year, a 34-year-old interviewee had been dismissed after working for the same company for fifteen years:

> 2012 was the beginning of the end, because I had been fired. In fact, the company had already begun to cut its staff two years earlier, but you always think it won't happen to you, and then...

After arriving in England to improve her English, she decided to stay. For the time being, she had found temporary work as a shop assistant, but staying at home in Italy with no prospects would have been much worse.

The younger interviewees retraced their working careers in Italy by listing prolonged experiences of precarious work, unpaid internships and low-paid temporary jobs with no prospect of being hired. One interviewee, a 29-year-old from Rome with a university degree in Communications Sciences in 2011, recounted how since obtaining her degree at the beginning of 2014 she had done two unpaid internships and spent a year employed as maternity cover, all in the communications field. After her last work experience, however, she had not been able to find another job. She therefore decided to move to Manchester. She succeeded in finding jobs in the space of three weeks, first at the call centre. This was not the 'right' job, the one she aspired to after receiving her degree. But she appreciated the opportunity to work and be economically independent without the fear of further long periods of unemployment:

> In Italy, I constantly looked for jobs, but nobody wanted me. From 2011, I looked for work all the time, nothing. ... Here, I finally feel free, more relaxed; here I'm not afraid that if I lose my job I won't know when I will start to work again, like in Italy. I found a job in three weeks, and if I lose it, I'll find another one quickly.

There were also those who saw their work conditions change in a short period of time after obtaining a professional qualification, and found themselves performing tasks not compatible with their training. This was the case of a young psychologist who had won a European scholarship thanks to which she had worked for a year on a project in a rest home for the elderly:

> During my scholarship year, I worked as a psychologist as laid down in the project, and then found myself doing everything: I worked as a fill-in, a teacher, an assistant; I did everything. I helped the old people go to the bathroom, to eat. ... Then money became scarce, and I was not even earning a thousand euros a month.

Disappointed by her employment situation, she decided to leave for England in 2011. To pay her bills, she first worked in a fast food restaurant and then as a waitress in an Italian restaurant, which she was still doing for three days a week at the time of the interview, because, as she explained,

[t]he great thing about England is that you can work full-time two days a week, and you don't pay taxes if you don't reach a certain income level, and so you can keep yourself.

Her intention to return to Italy evaporated in the space of a few months because she began to attend a psychological help centre in Manchester—first as a volunteer and then as a psychologist—an opportunity that had been denied her in Italy.

A Category of Interviewees

In order to fully understand the decision to leave Italy, it is helpful to look closely at two aspects. The first relates to work situation, in particular the motives that induce young people with a high education level to accept low-skilled jobs that they would in all likelihood refuse in Italy. The second is associated with the idea of a migration project: specifically, whether it is a transitory experience, an experimental phase in their lives destined to come to an end when they return to their home countries, or a stable, long-term choice.

If we consider these two aspects, an analysis of the interviews reveals a category that includes three different types of young migrates. The first are 'the expatriates' (two nurses, two engineers and two croupiers). These young people have used their professional skills to find a job in the UK while they were living in Italy. It has not always been a voluntary choice, because the two nurses would have preferred to work in Italy if they had more opportunities in their home country. What distinguishes them is their excellent knowledge of English, often associated to the participation in an Erasmus programme during their university education. Therefore, these young people are used to travelling and living abroad, and are strongly oriented to accepting a job abroad even if temporary. It is very likely that they will end up living permanently in the UK because they appreciate the working conditions, the salary, career opportunities as well as the quality of the professional environment they find in this country. They have generally more advantages there than in Italy.

The second group are those 'in suspense,' waiting to improve their occupational status. Despite their high educational level (university degree), in Manchester they do low-skilled and poorly paid jobs. Most worked in the restaurant sector as waiters and cooks, in large retail stores as sales staff, or for helplines. Unlike those who left with a job in their pocket, those who migrated in search of employment were fleeing the lack of opportunities in Italy, but they did not find optimal working conditions in Britain either. Nonetheless, these conditions were welcomed (and appreciated) compared with the static nature of the Italian labour market and the mortifying experiences they had had in their home country. A limited knowledge of English and the need to find a job quickly so that they could be economically independent were factors that induced the interviewees to look for low-skilled jobs.

At the beginning of their working lives in the UK, the interviewees felt that they had regained control over their futures, and that they could finally make plans. As one interviewee who had moved with his partner declared,

> [y]ou can have a child here, even immediately. Here if you work as a waiter you can have a child, if you work three days a week you can get a home, you can live and pay your bills. If we stay here, I can see a life.

The decision to remain in the UK is reinforced by their time spent in the country. When they left Italy, they did not know very much about how their lives would be organized, and it was difficult to predict if they would manage to become economically independent and have a decent standard of living. Once these objectives had been fulfilled, returning to Italy was seen as a reversal compared with what had been achieved abroad. It would mean returning to a situation of uncertainty and dependence on the family: that is, the same situations that had motivated the migratory project in the first place. One interviewee said:

> I would like to go back to Italy, but I wouldn't have any opportunities. It would be like returning to the same situation as when I left—project work if I'm lucky, otherwise staying at home, waiting, unemployed, with no wages, at home with my parents. At least here I work and I manage to keep myself; then we'll see—maybe I'll manage to find something better, here at least I can hope.

Then there are 'the satisfied' respondents, those who have been successful and achieved a prominent position in their profession. As a matter of fact, only six interviewees achieved such a goal. Usually they began by accepting a low-skilled job for a few years, which allowed them to become fluent in the language and then they tried to change jobs. The strength of these respondents is their specialized education. For instance, a respondent in Italy who was a sound engineer had quite a good level of experience in this field. After working as a waiter for one year in Manchester, thanks to his skills, he managed to work in the concert field. Two young women managed to teach in crèches while another woman, with great tenacity, succeeded in working as a psychologist. These satisfied respondents, who are happy with their working condition abroad are unlikely to go back to Italy. After waiting a long time and making many sacrifices they have succeeded in obtaining their professional recognition, which had been denied to them in Italy.

Finally, there are the 'resigned' ones. They went abroad hoping to change their life and find a job that allows them to be independent. In reality, they are not happy with their low-skilled job and have little hope of improving their working condition. They are aware their qualifications are unattractive on the British job market, which is extremely competitive, especially for foreigners. An interviewee working in an airline call centre stressed that increasing migration into the UK had penalized new arrivals in regard to work: 'A lot of Italians are coming here, but it's late; there were a lot of opportunities before. I arrived late too; it was different in the 1990s.'

Despite their dissatisfaction with their job condition, some Italians want to remain in the UK because they think that they will not find a better job in Italy.

Returning is seen as a reversal compared with what has been achieved abroad. One interviewee said:

> I would like to go back to Italy, but I wouldn't have any opportunities. It would be like returning to the same situation as when I left—project work if I'm lucky, otherwise staying at home, waiting, unemployed, with no wages, at home with my parents. At least here I work and I manage to keep myself; then we'll see—maybe I'll manage to find something better, here at least I can hope.

Conclusions

Giving voice to the narratives of those who have left Italy makes it possible to understand that the reality for young migrants is more composite and complex than a reading of secondary data tells us. The proliferation of studies on the recent migration of young Italians (Bonifazi and Livi Bacci 2014; Cucchiarato 2011; Gjergji 2015; Pugliese 2018; Tirabassi and del Pra 2014) shows that the phenomenon is acquiring numerical weight. In the space of just a few years, the decision to migrate has become a compulsory path for numerous young people to find a place in the world of work.

It would be a mistake, however, not to take account of the different living and working conditions of young people who move abroad. On the one hand, there are those who decide to leave with a highly skilled employment contract and working and economic conditions that are better than those they are leaving behind in Italy; on the other hand, there are those who leave in search of employment without being able to predict the outcome of their migratory project. In the case of the interviewees, the decision was taken after various attempts to find a professional position in Italy and a series of negative experiences in the workplace. Once they had lost their faith in the opportunity to make a change, they decided to leave, often facing non-optimal employment conditions paradoxically better than those that they had left behind in Italy.

It remains to be seen how far it will be possible for these young people to succeed in accessing more highly skilled job sectors, especially in light of the new policy established by the British government to tighten the requirements for access by foreign citizens to certain professions. A further factor is uncertainty concerning the outcome of the Brexit agreements between the UK and the EU, especially on managing migration and the introduction of restrictions on the free circulation of European citizens. The first signs are already apparent in a downturn—albeit a modest one—in migration from European countries. It is also unclear as to whether or not migration will actually result in stability. A decision to remain in Manchester may waver in the face of continuing unsatisfactory work conditions. How long after receiving a university degree is it possible to remain satisfied with working in low-skilled, low-paid jobs? A great deal depends on initial expectations and, judging from the accounts given by the interviewees, these are quite limited. The ease of finding work, changing jobs and not having to cope with long periods of unemployment are the elements of the English labour market that are most valued, and that in part make it possible to accept certain working conditions willingly. However, this assessment seems to be strengthened by the belief (or the hope) that it will be possible to improve the work situation.

Another aspect to consider is how much the new wave of migration costs Italy in terms of lost human capital transferred to other countries at zero cost (Santoro 2015b). The loss of young people in whom the country has invested by supporting their education is not being offset by the arrival of equally skilled young people. Italy's problem is not only that it is unable to set value on young people with high cultural capital, but also that it is unable to attract skilled workers from abroad. The balance between graduates who have left and graduates who choose Italy as a place of work is therefore decidedly negative. Since the 1990s, when the process began (Becker et al. 2003), Italy has continued to lose skilled young people.

Note

1. According to AIRE data, the number of Italians resident abroad progressively increased between 2008 and 2016: the number of registrations rose from +20.2 per cent in 2008 to +54.9 per cent in 2016 (Fondazione Migrantes 2016). There were 243,000 registrations at AIRE in the whole of 2017, of which 52.8 per cent were due to outward migration. To be more precise, 128,193 Italians moved abroad (4117 more departures than in 2016), almost 70 per cent choosing a European destination (Fondazione Migrantes 2017).

References

Becker, S. O., Ichino, A., & Peri, G. (2003). *How large is the 'Brain Drain' from Italy?* CESifo Working paper no. 839.
Bonifazi, C., & Livi Bacci, M. (eds.) (2014). *Le migrazioni internazionali ai tempi della crisi.* Associazione Neodemos.
COM.IT.ES. (2014). Documento di analisi dell'attuale e futuro valore dello sportello consolare di Manchester, COM.IT.ES per la circoscrizione consolare di Manchester.
Cucchiarato, C. (2011). Guerra di Cifre: Perché è Così Difficile Capire Chi e Quanti Sono Gli Italiani All'Estero. *AltreItalie, 43*, 64–72.
Eurostat. (2016). *Eurostat regional yearbook 2016.* Luxembourg: Publications Office of the European Union.
Fondazione Migrantes. (2016). *Rapporto Italiani nel Mondo 2016.* Summary. Todi: Tau Editrice.
Fondazione Migrantes. (2017). *Rapporto Italiani nel Mondo 2017.* Summary. Todi: Tau Editrice.
Gjergji, I. (Ed.). (2015). *La Nuova Emigrazione Italiana: Cause, Mete e Figure Sociali.* Venice: Edizioni Ca' Foscari—Digital Publishing.
IDOS. (2017). *Dossier Statistico Immigrazione 2017.* Rome: Edizioni IDOS.
Istat. (2014). *Anno 2012: Migrazioni Internazionali e Interne della Popolazione Residente.* Rome: Istat.
Istat. (2016). *Anno 2015: Migrazioni Internazionali e Interne della Popolazione Residente.* Rome: Istat.

Krausova, A., & Vargas-Silva, C. (2013). *Briefing. North West: Census profile*. Oxford: The Migration Observatory at the University of Oxford.

Manchester City Council. (2015). *Manchester migration: A profile of Manchester's migration patterns*.

McKay, S. (2015). Young Italians in London and in the UK. In I. Gjergji (Ed.), *La Nuova Emigrazione Italiana: Cause, Mete e Figure Sociali* (pp. 71–81). Venice: Edizioni Ca' Foscari.

Office for National Statistics. (2015). *Migration statistics quarterly report: November 2015*. Immigration to the UK and emigration from the UK, including net migration (the difference between immigration and emigration).

Office for National Statistics. (2017). *Migration statistics quarterly report:* Feb. 2017.

Pugliese, E. (2018). *Quelli che se ne Canno*. Bologna: il Mulino.

Santoro, M. (2015a). *Vivere e Lavorare All'Estero: La 'Nuova' Emigrazione dei Giovani Italiani in Gran Bretagna*. Working paper of the Department of Social and Political Sciences, Università degli Studi di Milano.

Santoro, M. (2015b). Formare giovani e regalarli all'estero. *il Mulino, 3*, 479–486.

Santoro, M. (2017). Trasferirsi all'estero ai tempi della crisi: l'emigrazione dei giovani italiani a Manchester. In P. Rebughini, E. Colombo, & L. Leonini (Eds.), *Giovani Dentro la Crisi* (pp. 141–162). Milan: Guerini.

Tirabassi, M., & del Pra, A. (2014). *La Meglio Italia. Le Mobilità Italiane nel XXI secolo*. Turin: Accademia University Press.

Part V

Chapter 34
Mobility at the Margins

David Cairns, Daniel Malet Calvo, and Mara Clemente

The final part of this book looks at several undercurrents within youth mobility research, many of which have not featured prominently in mainstream studies in this field. In terming this section 'mobility at the margins,' there is also acknowledgement that while moving for education, work or training has been a relatively normative expectation for many young people for many years, there are still forms of youth circulation that are relatively undocumented or misunderstood, perhaps due to a certain level of discomfort in coming to terms with certain situations. Academic research has tended to emphasise the wide variety of individual lifestyle benefits and further professional possibilities available open to young people who move, leaving the task of documenting the negative aspects to journalists, with policymakers perhaps preferring to finance interventions via civil society organizations (with limited budgets for conducting research) or focusing on issues that reflect politicians' own beliefs rather than the voices of migrants. As such, we lack critical engagement with the consequences of exploitation within youth mobility, with a failure to recognize the unsustainability of the hegemonic neoliberal view of young people's circulation as a means of generating economic capital for external parties such as universities. This extends to repercussions emerging from the rapid expansion of both the modes of travel and heightened levels of circulation, in addition to what are often quite obvious vulnerabilities within fragmented migration trajectories (see also Cairns 2021a, 2021b).

Another important point to consider is the somewhat limited view of marginality within the study of youth mobility, especially the approach taken to subjects

D. Cairns (✉) • D. Malet Calvo • M. Clemente
ISCTE – Instituto Universitário de Lisboa (ISCTE-IUL), Centro de Investigação e Estudos de Sociologia, Lisbon, Portugal
e-mail: david.cairns@iscte-iul.pt

© The Author(s), under exclusive license to Springer Nature Switzerland AG 2022
D. Cairns (ed.), *The Palgrave Handbook of Youth Mobility and Educational Migration*, https://doi.org/10.1007/978-3-030-99447-1_34

categorized as 'vulnerable.' A massive amount of scholarship, albeit much of it grey area literature and outside academia, has focused on young people categorized as refugees or having been trafficked—themes on which several of the following chapters focus. But as we have seen in this book, mobility researchers tend to focus on much larger populations, including students and trainees, with a tendency to gravitate towards the movement of groups rather than of individuals. We therefore know relatively little about what may be outlying experiences that nevertheless have importance due to the humanitarian consequences this mobility has for societies and individuals.

Part of the difficulty we have with studying these topics relates to the positioning of these experiences outside the youth mobility research field. There is also the practical issue of the funding of interventions with 'vulnerable migrants' being directed towards agencies rather than academics, leading to a lack of documentation in regard to what is taking place, complicated by the methodological difficulties of working with small, hard-to-find populations. This may explain why a distorted imagining has arisen of various forms of non-mainstream mobility, with media or policy discourse imposing frameworks that revolve around stereotypes and biases. We therefore see these migrants presented as 'victims' of criminality, wars or political, religious and racial persecution rather than youth engaging in mobility using their own agency. As a result, the study of their migratory experiences remains secluded in criminal and human rights studies, where the emphasis tends to be upon political rather than personal impacts. Policies and interventions, despite the frequent use of humanitarian language, hence enforce a top-down pejorative discourse on these forms of circulation, with negative experiences used to justify the control of migration and the fight against criminal networks, often limiting the mobility possibilities for those seeking asylum or 'trafficked' in the process.

Returning to what might be assumed to be less contentious forms of exchange, during the heyday of free movement, especially in the European Union, it was fairly self-evident that a potential to if not exactly marginalize then problematize young people via mobility existed, whether due to a kind of contemporary colonialism wherein mobile youth acted as 'ambassadors' for agencies like the European Commission (Cairns 2014: 94) or being an alienating presence within an unwelcoming local community (see especially Murphy-Lejeune 2002; França and Padilla 2021). We also know, not least from some of the following chapters, that student migrants were seen as ripe for exploitation due to their (artificially) liminal position within society. Even within the EU, the global region thought to have the most porous of internal borders and the least number of serious impediments to circulation, certain mobility-related 'crimes' of exploitation continued to escape censure since students were considered fair game by local interests or, even worse, the systematic divestment of their economic resources was encouraged to the point where they constituted a significant revenue stream for neoliberally governed universities.

'Mainstream' mobile youth have therefore been agents and victims of marginalization: two facets that need to be taken into account when evaluating the meaning and value of their mobility practices. This problem is most visible but not exclusive to international students due to the professionalization of the student mobility 'industry,' especially in regard to the provision of accommodation, generating a high expectation of profits for owners and investors in private property. This will obviously inflate costs for incoming students, but other collateral effects include the exclusion of local students from accessing housing close to their universities and the displacement of the local (non-student) population, whose houses have been converted into apartments with rooms to let for students. International students are also highly vulnerable to fraud and outright abuse from landlords due to their inadequate language competence in a foreign country and lack of knowledge about local and national laws and rights of residence. This is not to mention the targeting of international students by the tourism industry, and the impact of large numbers of incomers on local nightlife, which may lose its traditional flavour and become homogenized in pursuit of profit from foreigners, as well as the organization of 'international nights' that preclude local participation, creating exclusion and segregation (see Malet Calvo 2021).

There is also the question of what young people's geographical circulation means in the twenty-first century beyond the stated objectives of work, training or education; for individuals and institutions. One example concerns the use of youth migration by the European institutions as a form of soft power. While the dominant view of mobility in academic studies remains fairly positive, and very positive in public and policy discourse, the circulation of students and other groups is not always seen as beneficial to society, or even benign, at ground level. We might then want to consider how, for instance, the EU has used its mobility programmes as a means to interact politically with neighbouring countries and regions. In this book, Marine Sargsyan looks at this issue in the context of Armenia, and the role played by youth mobility in mediating between the EU and Russia at a geopolitical level. She argues that following the dissolution of the Soviet Union, Europe has been reconstructing itself politically and economically by interacting with its neighbours intellectually and professionally (Sargsyan 2021). This includes offering scholarships to non-EU citizens to study in the EU via programmes such as Erasmus, which also provide a platform for non-formal education. Through this means the EU can spread its values in a relatively gentle manner, and in using fixed-duration mobility formats, it can ensure mobility stops short of permanent settlement, neatly side-stepping any potential 'brain drain' allegations.

Socio-demographic differentials in mobility take-up also contribute to marginalization among youth. Student mobility may be traditionally associated with the comfortable middle classes frittering away taxpayers' money, but various chapters of this book show how movement outside institutional structures, while ostensibly democratic in terms of access, can come at a high personal cost (see, e.g., Toumanidou 2021), as well as illustrating marked contrasts according to social class within a society through differential consumption of mobility (Carnicer and Fürstenau 2021). Other dimensions of marginality emerge out of refugee experiences. In Chap. 36, Sahizer Samuk Carignani and colleagues look at refugees' narratives, using evidence from Syria, Iraq, Afghanistan, Iran and the Congo to illustrate how competing notions of the idea of 'home' can make refugees feel marginal in their new societies. Equally important is the relationship between socio-economic marginality and 'trafficking'. In Chap. 37, Mara Clemente emphasises that, even today, migration is an unequally distributed privilege: having fewer socio-economic resources, rather than being part of an alleged transnational crime networks traditionally associated with trafficking, can contribute to exploitation during the experience of mobility. This is quite a vivid reminder that despite the positive associations attached to much mobility, extreme situations can arise in regard to youth exchanges leading us to reconsider some of our simplistic, static and binary understandings of mobility, including the relationship between social exclusion and working abroad (Clemente 2021). This (re)definition of trafficking is also evoked by Jeanine van Halteren in Chap. 38, whose study calls attention to one of the challenges which research on trafficking has yet to overcome: the presence of reductive and simplifying images of trafficked young people, with the failure to recognize trafficking as a complex phenomenon, the understanding of which is compromised by dysfunctional hegemonic discourse.

The impression created by these chapters implies that looking at issues such as trafficking is problematic for youth mobility scholars; 'we' don't like addressing subjects that make us personally uncomfortable, and find our access to research subjects limited by the presence of gatekeeping agencies and policies that effectively reproduce victimization. The chapters that follow may therefore directly or indirectly challenge perceived views about various categories of migration—including human trafficking and asylum-seeking, which characterize, or rather polarize, recent public and policy debates.[1] The case studies in some of these chapters challenge these distinctions, agreeing that they can contribute to the current vogue for 'categorical fetishism' (Crawley and Skleparis 2018), also showing how hegemonic approaches fail to capture the complex lived experiences of young people on the move, inhibiting both our understanding of youth migration and obscuring the actual intentions of policy interventions which often seem, on closer inspection, to restrict movement rather than democratize access to circulation.

Less dramatic but no less important is acknowledgement of the negative health consequences for many young people of engaging in migratory behaviour. In their chapter, Giovanni Aresi, lena Marta and Simon C. Moore discuss the connections between mobility and health risks, especially mental health issues. While its social and economic benefits are often extolled, mobility also brings many dangers related to unpredictable societal circumstances, linguistic and cultural barriers, and basic difficulties in accessing healthcare (Aresi et al. 2021). Other risks are perhaps more philosophical or related to the governance of mobility, or lack of effective governance, that creates a potential for economic marginality. The ramifications of short-term mobility for youth are considered by Emrullah Yasin Çiftçia and A. Cendel Karaman in Chap. 40, including the prospects for becoming aware of the 'dangers' of neoliberalism emerging out of participation in mobility programmes.

A further neglected issue is the impact of elevated levels of youth circulation on the urban environment. Student mobility, in particular, cannot be regarded as sustainable in its recent forms, with the interpolation of tourism into programmes like Erasmus being particularly harmful to local communities. As Daniel Malet Calvo discusses in Chap. 41, certain cities become attractive to students due to their tourist image, a factor that also has an influence on urban change and the pace of gentrification, processes linked to the neoliberal managerialism of cities and problems in local housing markets. In consequence, the anxiety of searching for a place to live in is now an integral part of the Erasmus experience, emblematic of wider housing uncertainty in touristified learning hubs (Malet Calvo 2021).

In evaluating these developments, especially our interactions with policymaking, we do need to inject a certain amount of realism into our appreciation of youth mobility practices. While we can critique student mobility in particular for its high cost and uncertain returns, these opportunities would not exist if they lacked economic value for societies and political significance for agencies such as the European Commission. Neither would young migrants be welcome in host societies if they failed to behave like good consumers. In this sense, the freedom of young people to circulate is tied to their ability to act as creators of value, carriers of specific values and depositors of economic capital in host societies. While they may be able to supplement their personal stocks of mobility capital, the expectation is that they will leave something substantial behind. On the other hand, categories such as 'trafficked' and 'refugee' youth, and 'forced' rather than 'voluntary' migrant, rob young people of their agency, putting them into positions of vulnerability. In conjoining different forms of marginality, we are accepting that the traditional views on these topics resolutely fail to account for the complex and ambivalent experiences and expectations of those who lose something important through mobility.

We can therefore argue that these marginal forms of youth mobility, like student exchanges, have become subject to a kind of neoliberal entrepreneurial logic. It is obvious that the problematized categories of youth mobility have become heavy mobilizers of substantial economic resources, used by national and international, governmental and non-governmental organizations, as well as culture industries and, admittedly to much a lesser extent, academia (see also Agustín 2007; Plambech 2017), with 'trafficking' and 'asylum-seeking' seen as particularly value-creating categories which only exceptionally produce a benefit for those to whom they refer (Andrijasevic 2010). What then is to stop us from codifying the work of agencies purporting to address mobility-related marginalization as de facto traffickers of people and capital?

In putting together the disparate pieces of twenty-first century youth migration, neoliberalism seems to be both the reason for the fracturing of migration into mobility episodes and the means of putting these pieces back together again; and this may also be the driving force behind allegedly humanitarian interventions with highly marginalized young migrants. How then could this have happened, and on such a vast scale? Falling back on the older idea of what might be termed 'structuring structures' (Bourdieu 1977: 72), during the last few decades, neoliberal governance of mobility has gained a common sense respectability and, therefore, has become a constant contributor to the (re)production of social inequalities (Çiftçi and Karaman 2021). To a certain extent, mobility programmes in particular were getting away with this due to the promotion of a fantasy version of what was on offer, extolling the potential for individualized success and downplaying the personal and societal costs. This philosophy was also reliant upon relatively favourable external circumstances: everything from the availability of cheap flights to the integration of a tourism dimension into educational mobility. What seems to have been the case is that much, if not most, mobility was being practised without a safety net, something that became particularly evident during the sudden Covid-19 pandemic lockdown. We will observe in the chapters that follow a number of instances in which young people fell to the ground without this net at a time prior to the pandemic, barely surviving in some cases, and at the present time of uncertainty, we will no doubt be discovering many more cases of mobility-related damage emerging out of the immobility pandemic.

Note

1. These categories are currently strengthened by the two recently adopted United Nations (UN) Global Compacts—one on Safe, Orderly and Regular Migration (GCM) and one on Refugees (GCR)—aiming at reinforcing the global governance of migration and asylum through separate legal frameworks.

References

Agustín, L. (2007). *Sex at the margins, labour, markets and the rescue industry*. London: Zed Book.
Andrijasevic, R. (2010). *Migration, agency and citizenship in sex trafficking*. New York: Palgrave Macmillan.
Aresi, G., Marta, I., & Moore, S. C. (2021). Youth mobility, mental health and risky behaviours. In D. Cairns (Ed.), *The Palgrave handbook of youth mobility and educational migration*. Basingstoke: Palgrave Macmillan.
Bourdieu, P. (1977). Outline of a Theory of Practice. Cambridge: Cambridge University Press.
Cairns, D. (2014). *Youth transitions, international student mobility and spatial reflexivity: Being mobile?* Basingstoke: Palgrave Macmillan.
Cairns, D. (2021a). Mobility becoming migration: Understanding youth spatiality in the twenty-first century. In D. Cairns (Ed.), *The Palgrave handbook of youth mobility and educational migration*. Basingstoke: Palgrave Macmillan.
Cairns, D. (2021b). Migration decision-making, mobility capital and reflexive learning. In D. Cairns (Ed.), *The Palgrave handbook of youth mobility and educational migration*. Basingstoke: Palgrave Macmillan.
Carnicer, J. A., & Fürstenau, S. (2021). Transnational mobility, education and social positioning between Brazil and Germany. In D. Cairns (Ed.), *The Palgrave handbook of youth mobility and educational migration*. Basingstoke: Palgrave Macmillan.
Çiftçi, E. Y., & Karaman, A. C. (2021). Rethinking the value(s) of short-term youth mobility: Neoliberal ideals and counterhegemonic possibilities. In D. Cairns (Ed.), *The Palgrave handbook of youth mobility and educational migration*. Basingstoke: Palgrave Macmillan.
Clemente, M. (2021). 'I was not prepared to go to Spain:' Work mobility of young people at the margins in Portugal. In D. Cairns (Ed.), *The Palgrave handbook of youth mobility and educational migration*. Basingstoke: Palgrave Macmillan.
Crawley, H., & Skleparis, D. (2018). Refugees, migrants, neither, both: Categorical fetishism and the politics of bounding in Europe's 'migration crisis. *Journal of Ethnic and Migration Studies, 44*(1), 48–64.

França, T., & Padilla, B. (2021). South-South student mobility: International students from Portuguese-speaking Africa in Brazil. In D. Cairns (Ed.), *The Palgrave handbook of youth mobility and educational migration*. Basingstoke: Palgrave Macmillan.

Malet Calvo, M. (2021). A wonderful but uncertain time: Youth transitions of Erasmus students and Lisbon's housing crisis. In D. Cairns (Ed.), *The Palgrave handbook of youth mobility and educational migration*. Basingstoke: Palgrave Macmillan.

Murphy-Lejeune, E. (2002). *Student mobility and narrative in Europe: The new strangers*. London: Routledge.

Plambech, S. (2017). Sex, deportation and rescue: Economies of migration among Nigerian sex workers. *Feminist Economics, 23*(3), 134–159.

Sargsyan, M. (2021). The soft power of youth mobility: The EU in its shared neighbourhood with Russia. In D. Cairns (Ed.), *The Palgrave handbook of youth mobility and educational migration*. Basingstoke: Palgrave Macmillan.

Toumanidou, V. (2021). Understanding educational migration in times of crisis: Greek student migration to the UK. In D. Cairns (Ed.), *The Palgrave handbook of youth mobility and educational migration*. Basingstoke: Palgrave Macmillan.

Chapter 35
Mobility Choices in Post-Soviet States: How the EU Attracts Youth in Its Shared Neighbourhood with Russia

Marine Sargsyan

The last decade of the twentieth century was marked with tremendous change in world politics, reshaping international, economic, political, social and cultural systems. With the reunification of Germany in 1990, the Soviet collapse of 1991, the formation of the European Union in 1993 and the more recent economic rise of China, a multi-polar world order replaced the bi-partisan system that had been led by the United States and the Soviet Union. In particular, the EU, an alliance of small and medium-size European states, became an important player in Eurasian and global affairs, with the Russian Federation its main rival in the countries of their shared neighbourhood.

Suffice to say, in the immediate aftermath of the fall of the Soviet Union, Russia went through a period of dramatic domestic affairs such as political economic and ideological change, along with uncertainty in the foreign policy arena. A country that was once a superpower began to doubt its place in the international pecking order, and not without good reason. The Soviet collapse left Russia in a state of economic, political and social turmoil, marked by declining economic output and increasing inflation, as well as foreign debt and budget deficits. Meanwhile, Europe was entering a decade defined by two treaties: the Maastricht Treaty (formally known as the Treaty on European Union) in 1993 and the Treaty of Amsterdam in 1999, and its fourth enlargement, which integrated a number of Eastern European countries. It also launched the European Neighbourhood Policy (ENP) in 2003, aimed at building and strengthening bilateral and multilateral relations with its eastern neighbours. Therefore, what had begun as a economic union had by now evolved into a multi-national organization spanning a range of policy areas: from environment and health concerns to external relations and security, as well as justice and

M. Sargsyan (✉)
Roma Tre University, Rome, Italy

© The Author(s), under exclusive license to Springer Nature Switzerland AG 2022
D. Cairns (ed.), *The Palgrave Handbook of Youth Mobility and Educational Migration*, https://doi.org/10.1007/978-3-030-99447-1_35

migration. In fact, the rebranding of the European Economic Community (EEC) to the European Union in 1993 in itself reflected this development.

While the main focus of EU relations with its neighbouring countries within the ENP was on promotion and cooperation in the fields of human rights, democracy, peace and economic development, the EU also focused on youth policy through different projects. This included the aim of increasing mobility and people-to-people contact across borders, via successive Erasmus programmes and *Youth in Action*.[1] Launched in 1987 and 2007 respectively, these projects were, and continue to be, successful in many ways, as formal and non-formal education and training platforms. And as various chapters in this book have pointed out (see, e.g., Allaste and Nugin 2021; Samuk et al. 2021), the EU's use of youth to address political and humanitarian concerns in a non-invasive manner culminated with Erasmus+, an initiative that had a very visible focus on supporting mobility not only among students but also among various politically prioritized youth sub-populations, such as young migrants arriving in Europe following the 2015 refugee crisis.

Even before this time, but particularly since the fall of the Berlin Wall, the EU and its antecedent EEC demonstrated a clear strategic interest in Eastern enlargement at a time when the political situation in Russia was markedly different to what it later became in the twenty-first century. The Soviet Union had collapsed, Russia was weakened internally and internationally, and there was no clear vision on how to deal with its domestic issues, but the idea that Russia is a superpower nevertheless persisted. Relations with most of its former satellite states hence became strained, especially in the Baltic region and in Georgia; there was also uncertainty with Azerbaijan, relative reliability with Belarus, perhaps more predictably solid relations with Armenia and Ukraine and loyalty within Central Asia.

Being mostly focused on the place of Russia in Eurasian geopolitics, its domestic policy was seen as less important. The population in fact declined from 148.7 million people at the start of 1992 to an estimated 142.9 million according to preliminary results of the 2010 census. The decline would have been even more pronounced if not for large-scale migration from the other post-Soviet republics, initially by ethnic Russians who now found themselves in foreign countries after the USSR collapsed but also, increasingly, by non-Russian labour migrants from the Caucasus and Central Asia. Russia, as a destination, was targeted mainly by seasonal workers, although there were 2,960,000 incoming students in 2015/2016 according to Project Atlas' data, mainly from former Soviet Republics and China (Puchkov et al. 2018: 89). At the same time, the EU was also attracting students and highly skilled migrants, particularly to its more prestigious centres of learning. This was an area in which Russia could not compete. Despite having around 900 higher education level institutions, only one per cent can be found in the international rating QS World University Rankings 2017/2018 (Puchkov et al. 2018: 106). Therefore, while the Russian job market was relatively accessible, and there were no complicated bureaucracy barriers for the citizens of most post-Soviet countries, its universities and living standards were considered to be lagging behind the EU.

Migration and Mobility to Russia and the EU

Migration to Russia during the period 1992–1994 acted as a kind of 'objective correlative' to empire-saving sentiments expressed in public opinion polls. Prominent factors associated with the decision to leave the Central Asian and the South Caucasian republics were inter-ethnic violence, national conflicts and the war in Georgia, as well as conflict between Armenia and Azerbaijan over the disputed region of Nagorno-Karabakh. While the Russian population was moving inwards on the eve of the breakup of the USSR in 1991, Russians did not manifest a high rate of hostility towards the former Soviet republics' ethnic minorities, yet they would still distinguish and dislike Caucasians: Armenians, Azerbaijanis, Georgians and Chechens, mostly because these groups had a strong sense of ethnic solidarity and were seen as being more successful in running small and medium-size business. These groups were also visibly different: darker in complexion than many Russians and thus came to be racially denigrated as 'black' [*chernie*] (Dunlop 1997: 60) or seen as the face of a Caucasian nationality [*litso Kavkazskoy nacionalnosti*], 'putting everyone in the same basket' at a grass-roots level, because the political elite and Russian intelligentsia were differentiating these nationalities by history, culture, religion and status, most specifically Armenians and Georgians who had been integrated into the political, cultural and academic life of Russia since the nineteenth century.

The highest level of inward migration to Russia was recorded in 1994, yet the number of migrants from former Soviet republics in Russia during 1991–2000 dropped compared to the 1981–1990 period, and since then departures from Russia to these states has declined even more in real terms. Nevertheless, for its former satellite countries Russia was still the most prominent destination for some migrants.[2] Not all young people from the former republics were moving to Russia. What seems to be emerging is divergence between the 'old' migration mode of economic migration to Russia (for 'adults') and a more diversified set of mobility predispositions for young people, especially the highly qualified. This was evident in research conducted in Armenia by the author in 2018 that confirmed Europe as a popular choice for Armenian students and graduates, using evidence from a qualitative study of 51 young Armenians, some of whom also expressed an interest in moving to the United States and, much less frequently, Russia (see Cairns and Sargsyan 2019; Sargsyan and Cairns 2019).

This study also found that the appeal of Europe, and especially the EU, was multi-faceted. Moving to Europe is in some respects less of a pragmatic choice, or at least less of a choice orientated around economic concerns, and more an attempt to become a different kind of person, attuned to a form of Europeanism associated with social freedom and political openness (see also Cairns et al. 2018), themes that also featured in Chap. 27 of this book in regard to young Romanians' migration orientations (Pantea 2021). Furthermore, while language learning could be a challenge in choosing the EU as a study or work destination, English, the de facto lingua franca of the EU, has been growing in popularity among highly qualified young people in post-Soviet Armenia. This development can also be characterized as a national feature: one of the most popular sayings among Armenians is 'the more languages you speak the more human you are.'

The appeal of the EU should not come as a complete surprise to human mobility scholars or students of international relations. One of the cornerstones of social policy in the EU is upholding the principle of free movement between its member states, and as well as being important for EU citizens, the promise of a high level of spatial freedom is also part of the appeal for incoming migrants. The EU has created a, perhaps unprecedented, politically and economic open space in which not just capital, goods and services but also people can move around relatively unencumbered by bureaucratic concerns. Furthermore, this freedom has to be visible, and in its fun-loving and easy-living Erasmus students, the EU has the perfect image of free-moving Europeans for Erasmus promotional materials.

The European Choice

Having outlined some general ideas that have a bearing upon prospective youth mobility to the EU, and to Russia, from third-party countries like Armenia, the remainder of this chapter will take a more in-depth look at the mechanisms the European institutions use to engage with young people in external regions, also providing some first-hand accounts of how students and graduates make decisions about mobility and migration. This involves re-visiting evidence gathered in Armenia during the summer and autumn of 2018, with emphasis on understanding the EU's attractiveness.

The findings of this study suggest that the overall picture in regard to mobility preferences among the highly skilled and advanced young professionals preference was given to moving west, mostly to the EU and US, rather than to Russia. This is a choice conditioned by long and short-term professional and academic development prospects, a perceived better quality of tertiary education, higher living standards and, especially in relation to everyday life in Europe, the feeling of being appreciated as an equal in regard to personal respect and professional stimulation. These interviews also provide insight on the circular and incremental nature of youth migration in the twenty-first century and how migration trajectories are constructed sequentially and with circularity in mind (see Cairns 2021a, b in this book). From the other side, seasonal for seasonal workers Russian job market was more accessible and easy to reach for both short and long-term temporary jobs due to a visa free regime and knowledge of language, geographical vicinity and the presence of aquantances whether friends or relatives.

One interviewee who has already moved to the EU is Armine, a Cambridge University graduate who, after obtaining a master's degree in development studies, returned to Armenia for work but after a year returned to Europe having been offered a trainee position at the European Commission in Brussels. Another case is Mariam, a researcher at an NGO in Armenia and a former graduate of Yerevan State University's Department of Political Science and Erasmus Exchange student at Masaryk University in Prague, Czech Republic. Speaking about the semester spent at Masaryk University, she described it as being very important, as she 'learnt in one semester more than during those three years at Yerevan State University,' also explaining 'that's the aim of these exchanges: to study abroad, gain experience and bring it home for the development and change within the country, system and society.'

Armenia itself is also something of a regional hub for student mobility in south east Eurasia. Although Mariam is extremely critical of education in Armenia, we have other accounts from incoming students from neighbouring countries, Georgia, Iran and even India, that illustrate positive developments. During 2015–2016, a total of 3798 foreign students from around 35 countries (4.5% of the total enrolment) studied at Armenian universities. The majority came from Russia (31%), Georgia (22%), India (20%) and Iran (10%), and several centres of international excellence focusing on IT and STEM education have been created there (Gharibyan 2017). Furthermore, through having an undergraduate degree from the Armenian universities, many of the interviewees were able to continue their graduate and postgraduate education at some of the world's most renowned universities such as Oxford, Cambridge, Harvard and Duke, thanks in part to the existence of scholarships and student mobility programmes.

The previously cited example of Armine also demonstrates how the EU recruits highly skilled migrants in a fairly tacit manner: attracting professionals and academics through its platforms for mobility in education and training such as, most obviously, Erasmus. The explicit intention is to encourage short duration exchanges, typically of less than a year, with a return to the sending society guaranteed to avoid any possibility of creating a politically unpopular brain drain in the sending society, at least in theory. In reality, such forms of mobility inevitably form part of the wider migration lexicon, encouraging movers to live outside their national and regional comfort zones and fostering the development of intercultural skills associated with living in other countries and working with people from different societies. For this reason, education and training mobility cannot be entirely divorced from the wider field of migration within, and into, the EU, although that no definitive pathway exists to conjoin EU-supported mobility and free movement type migration in the EU means that a high degree of precarity will be experienced, especially given the limited support on offer to those who wish to settle there.

Erasmus Outside Europe

Erasmus, alongside the previously mentioned *Youth in Action* programme (since 2014 interpolated into Erasmus+), is perhaps the highest profile example of this approach of 'enticing' extra-EU youth. Launched in 1987, as Chaps. 9, 10, 11, 12, 13 and 14 of this book detailed, the programme has facilitated millions of youth exchanges between EU member states and supported thousands of projects that support mobility, including cooperation with the EU's neighbouring countries. *Youth in Action* and Erasmus+, in addition to promoting mobility, non-formal learning, intercultural dialogue and inclusion, primarily among people aged 13–30 years, support youth workers and civil society organizations through training and networking activities. That it has a strong extra-EU international dimension, targeting and cooperating with Africa, Asia, Asia-Pacific, the Eastern Partnership, Latin America, North America, the Mediterranean and the Western Balkans, adds geopolitical significance to Erasmus mobility, with the platform being a means through which the EU makes connections with these regions and spreads its values. We might even argue that these exchanges act as a soft power instrument for the EU, making student and other forms of mobility part of tacit foreign policy, using education, work and training as relatively novel political instruments.

The extent to which the EU is able to expand its reach, not through recruiting more countries into its political community but by 'colonizing' the spatial dimension of education, work and training, is debatable, particularly considering that there is little evidence to support the idea that platforms such as Erasmus are effective at strengthening 'Europeanization' inside Europe, never mind in neighbouring regions (see, e.g., Sigalas 2010; Oborune 2013). What is clearer is that the EU has the clear aspiration of transforming the lives of young people through mobility, although many barriers remain towards the realization of this goal, both inside and outside Europe. In regard to what this actually means, Erasmus+ supports employability and the development of interculturality, the creation of conditions and opportunities for all citizens, supporting disadvantaged people to start a new life away from home and highly skilled movers to further develop personally and professionally. But Erasmus is a path, or part of a path, towards the realization of these aims, not necessarily the end destination. The European Commission is not, for instance, a major creator of employment opportunities for skilled and qualified migrants, nor indeed for talented young Europeans. What work it creates for youth tends to be ephemeral and lacking job security, leading to the creation of a small sub-strata of peripatetic Europeans and non-Europeans rather than a new mobile class of Europeanized citizens.

There have been other important developments in this field that might improve matters, such as the EU-wide work permit, the so-called EU Blue Card, introduced in 2009. The card allows highly skilled non-EU citizens to work and live in any country within the EU (except Denmark, the Republic of Ireland and the United Kingdom). According to data from the European Political Strategy Centre, in 2016 EU Member States jointly granted just under 21,000 Blue Cards, up from the 3664 granted in 2012, a 'drop in the ocean' in the ongoing competition for international talent. Furthermore, the overwhelming majority of these Blue Cards were granted by a single Member State, Germany, with restrictive admission conditions and the existence of parallel national schemes being the main barriers to wider use of the card.

All these developments are important, and relatively high profile, in the discussion of intra and extra-EU mobility, but one other dimension of the EU's attractiveness is its perceived egalitarianism. The promotion of European values forms an important part of the EU's appeal, something that is relatively underappreciated in accounts of understanding what attracts young people to Europe—an issue, it has to be said, that is also seriously underplayed throughout the various chapters of this book. This strategy also helps explain the expansion of Erasmus, especially the funding of mobility projects through civil society non-profit organizations, helping to define the EU in terms of its European values.

While a number of chapters in this book have looked at Erasmus in tertiary education, NGOs have become the key instruments for supporting extra-EU youth exchanges, emphasising non-formal education, vocational training and development grants. Through this means, they become essential actors in the implementation of EU initiatives and policies inside and outside the EU, constituting an essential instrument in a new form of twenty-first-century spatialized governmentality and the exercise of a subtle form of soft political power, using 'youth' as a medium. This development may explain why in 2012 a new law 'On Amendments to Legislative Acts of the Russian Federation Regarding the Regulation of the Activities of Non-profit Organisations Performing the Functions of a Foreign Agent' was adopted in Russia, restricting NGO activities and labelling Western-funded non-profit organizations as 'foreign agents.'

Mobility Choices Outside the EU

Western youth sociologists have traditionally viewed moving from full-time education to the labour market as part of the broader process of making a transition to adulthood: a process, among other things, undertaken alongside leaving the parental home and starting a family (see, e.g., Furlong and Cartmel 1997). For the highly qualified, there are many additional challenges in making this transition, not least finding positions equal to their education and skill level. The research conducted in Armenia shows the attraction the interviewees have for opportunities abroad that enable them to enhance their education and skills profiles and to gain work experience.

While the EU as a destination to study and work is preferred due to its relatively close geographical location and assumed-to-be-good conditions for academic development and professional growth, the United States and Canada are also popular, especially where young people are able to access scholarships provided by Armenian philanthropists and foundations. However, education in the United States is more expensive, the system is markedly different to that in Armenia and scholarships do not cover all expenses related to living and studying.[3]

One example is Sona, a graduate of Duke University, whose university and country choice was conditioned by the Armenian Scholarship for Duke University students and the presence of family and friends in the United States. Although for people like Sona finding a job after completing studies can be challenging, opportunities for professional developments abroad tend to be considered more promising than those in Armenia or Russia. Nevertheless, we had a few cases of return migration, from Russia and the United States. Also interviewed was Hanin, an Armenian volunteer at an Armenian NGO from Jordan. Her decision to settle in Armenia was influenced by multiple factors, such as recent political developments in Armenia. Another reason was the connection with roots and identity, people and culture. Although while in Jordan, her family still preserve their Armenian traditions, and her mother converted to Islam after marriage to a Syrian man, though Hanin is engaged to an Armenian man, and for her, Armenian culture is more prominent.

There is also the case of Russian repatriate, Marine, another NGO volunteer from Russia, a graduate of Saratov State University and lawyer by profession, who has been living inside and outside Armenia. Her family has always been connected to homeland. Although based in Saratov, then St Petersburg, they kept their bonds strong which apparently influenced Marine's decision to move to Armenia, first as a volunteer and then with the hope of finding a job and settling in Armenia. She acknowledges Armenia as her country, rather than Russia, having citizenship of the latter and, more recently, the former. There are also practical reasons for Marine becoming an Armenian citizen. She faced difficulties on wanting to study and travel in the EU with her Russian passport, an important consideration as in the future she wishes to study in France.

Looking beyond this empirical evidence, there are other signs that demonstrate the importance of connections with regions other than the EU. There are, for instance, new developments in Armenian-Chinese relations that influence mobility between the two countries. The most recent demonstration was the opening of the Chinese-Armenian Friendship school in Yerevan in 2018. Educational cooperation is being boosted in both directions and China is becoming more interesting to Armenian students, and vice-versa. For example, Armenian is now an optional course at Beijing Foreign Studies University. Over 80 Armenian students are now studying in China, and there are several cases of Chinese students studying and working in Armenia. The most famous Chinese student, who learnt the language and spent a summer internship at the Central Bank of Armenia, is Michael He, a Harvard graduate. While Michael's choice is personal, the president of China motivates students to reach out to all parts of the world, as a part of his Belt and Road Initiative, to enrich minds and the economy at the same time (Liu 2017).

Furthermore, early in the new millennium, the Chinese government started to introduce a series of policies to attract both Chinese professionals working overseas and foreign skilled talents. These policies included pilot schemes like the 'Thousand Talent Programme' and a policy trial of the Green Card system in Beijing and Shanghai. Therefore, mobility and international migration have a global dimension: people are moving from East to West, between Asia and China, and the United States and Europe. This can be seen as a positive development, connecting more societies, reducing regionally grounded inequalities, creating new opportunities for personal and professional development, and empowering economic growth and the exchange of ideas, as well as academic development and scientific discovery. But there can also be negative consequences relating to difficulties with assimilation, a loss of national identity and the weakening of the connection with the homeland and roots, arising out of the personal choice to engage with a global field of migration and mobility.

Conclusion

Geopolitical developments after the 1990s have significantly influenced migration and mobility trends inside and outside Europe. The fall of the Iron Curtain not only united Europe but also opened doors for incoming migrants outside the EU. In 2017, migrant workers accounted for approximately 59 per cent of the world's international migrant population. Opportunities for personal, professional and academic development have also been promoted by the EU as a means of building political, economic, cultural and academic bridges in its neighbourhood. Meanwhile, the situation in Russia was different at this time, as the country was going through economic and political turmoil, reconstructing its status regionally and globally, focusing on the place of the Russian Federation in world politics first and its influence on its former satellite countries later. Nevertheless, Russia is resourceful, and its labour market was and is attracting migrants from former Soviet republics, and elsewhere. Russia's significance as a destination has nevertheless declined due to many factors, especially the recent coming to power of a de-facto authoritarian regime. This became more vivid after the start of the Ukrainian crisis in November 2013, straining Russia's relations with the EU, affecting its economy and influencing migration decision-making.

While Europe is attractive, this does not mean that everyone can go there, and even fewer can settle. As we have learnt elsewhere in this book, migration to and within the EU is characterized by impermanence. Among the interviewees, there were relatively few cases of people actually remaining in the EU; stays tended to be relatively short and entailed a return to Armenia or moving on to somewhere else once an educational course or work placement had been completed. Therefore, while the 'dream' of Europe as a mobility paradise is strong, the actual experience of Europe is superficial, especially in relation to employment.

Notes

1. Launched in 2007, the *Youth in Action* programme was a platform for non-formal learning and exchange between the EU and ENP countries. Additionally, as part of the European Commission's Training Strategy, Salto-Youth also provides non-formal learning resources for youth workers and youth leaders and organizes training and contact-making activities to support organizations and National Agencies within the frame of the European Commission's Erasmus+ Youth programme and beyond. According to online data, in August 2019 it had 12,459 registered organizations and informal groups, with the total number of 7497 international projects (Salto-Youth).

2. For example, the UNESCO Global Flow of Tertiary-Level Students dataset estimated that in 2016 the total number of Armenian students abroad was just under 8000, with the Russian Federation by far the most popular destination.
3. According to Open Doors, there are around 300 Armenian students studying in the United States, with another 400 in Russia and 446 students studying abroad under Erasmus+ (Gharibyan 2017). The number of Armenian students studying in the United States is therefore very high, and along with university funding and scholarships, there may be family that endorse the United States as a destination.

References

Allaste, A.-A., & Nugin, R. (2021). Mobility and participation: Intertwined movement of youth and ideas. In D. Cairns (Ed.), *The Palgrave handbook of youth mobility and educational migration*. Basingstoke: Palgrave Macmillan.

Cairns, D. (2021a). Old migration, new mobility? Sociology and spatiality in the twenty-first century. In D. Cairns (Ed.), *The Palgrave handbook of youth mobility and educational migration*. Basingstoke: Palgrave Macmillan.

Cairns, D. (2021b). Reflections on migration decision-making and reflexive learning. In D. Cairns (Ed.), *The Palgrave handbook of youth mobility and educational migration*. Basingstoke: Palgrave Macmillan.

Cairns, D., Krzaklewska, E., Cuzzocrea, V., & Allaste, A.-A. (2018). *Mobility, education and employability in the European Union: Inside Erasmus*. Basingstoke: Palgrave Macmillan.

Cairns, D., & Sargsyan, M. (2019). *Student and graduate mobility in Armenia*. Basingstoke: Palgrave Macmillan.

Dunlop, J. (1997). Russia: In search of an identity? In I. Bremmer & R. Taras (Eds.), *New states, new politics: Building the post-Soviet nations* (pp. 29–95). Cambridge: Cambridge University Press.

Furlong, A., & Cartmel, F. (1997). *Young people and social change: Individualisation and risk in late modernity*. Buckingham: Open University Press.

Gharibyan, T. (2017). *Armenian Higher Education in the European Higher Education Area*. Inside Higher ED, The World View.

Liu, C. (2017). Why students in Beijing are learning Armenian. *South China Morning Post*. This Week in Asia.

Oborune, K. (2013). Becoming more European after Erasmus? The impact of the Erasmus programme on political and cultural identity. *Epiphany, 6*(1), 182–202.

Pantea, M.-C. (2021). Facets of mobility in Romania's vocational education and training. In D. Cairns (Ed.), *The Palgrave handbook of youth mobility and educational migration*. Basingstoke: Palgrave Macmillan.

Puchkov, Y., Balzhinim, V., & Engurazova, S. (2018). International student mobility: European and Russian practices. *Białostockie Studia Prawnicze, 23*(2), 89–110.

Samuk, S., Skrobanek, J., Ardic, T., Pavlova, I., Marinescu, D. E., & Muresan, L. (2021). Learning in transition: Erasmus+ as an opportunity for internationalization. In D. Cairns (Ed.), *The Palgrave handbook of youth mobility and educational migration*. Basingstoke: Palgrave Macmillan.

Sargsyan, M., & Cairns, D. (2019). Home or away? Pathways to employment for the highly qualified in Armenia after the Velvet revolution. *Young, 28*(3), 259–274.

Sigalas, E. (2010). Cross-border mobility and European identity: The effectiveness of intergroup contact during the Erasmus year abroad. *European Union Politics, 11*(2), 241–265.

Chapter 36
From Forced Migration to Mobility: Dreaming of Home Within 'Rooted Mobilities'

Sahizer Samuk, Derya Acuner, and Yesim Tonga Uriarte

> *Home is the place, where, when you have to go there, they have to take you in.*
> —Robert Frost

'Face Forward ... into my home' is the theme and the name of the project that inspired this chapter: an interactive cultural heritage focused initiative wherein refugees from different countries (including Iran, Iraq, Congo, Syria and Afghanistan) were actively involved in art interpretations of their life stories, group discussions and photography. The project had three phases: interpretation of artworks and storytelling via group discussions, photo-shooting and exhibition of photos and, finally, personal stories. In this discussion, we explore the conceptualizations of home made by the refugees engaged in this project as depicted in their representations. This encompasses both their former home countries and their new home, Greece, examining how they depict their journey from what is sometimes described in their accounts as forced migration towards other imaginings of mobility. Using this line of thought, the participants are able to show us that their home will always be 'there' even though other forms of mobility are now part of their dreams of the future.

Bureaucrats and technocrats, and from time to time, social scientists as well, would like to think of migration and refugees in terms of numbers, in order to quantify and demonstrate the scale of migration flows and to help manage these population shifts. Unfortunately, this also means that governments can easily neglect protection, despite their welcoming and humanitarian language: faces behind the numbers are not always visible and neither are the individual stories, especially

---

S. Samuk (✉)
University of Luxembourg, Luxembourg City, Luxembourg

University of Pisa, Pisa, Italy

D. Acuner • Y. Tonga Uriarte
IMT Institute for Advanced Studies Lucca, Lucca, Italy

when people are moving outside regular channels. Furthermore, a sense of belonging to a culture is not visible in numbers. Emanating from these reasons, quantitative bordering practices are heavily, and justifiably, criticized (see also de Genova 2017).[1]

Nâzım Hikmet, a Turkish poet, asked many years ago: 'what do the numbers indicate?' For sure, they suggest 'something.' They signpost which phenomena might be crucial, as they postulate a framework with a helicopter view, but at the same time, focusing on numbers primarily can blur researchers' views about migrants and populations who are in vulnerable situations. Moreover, numbers can obscure universal understanding of humanity, common and intercultural elements, and personhood (Soysal 1994). When numerical and nationality-based approaches are considered, it is probable that we will be drawn into methodological nationalism and it is also likely that we will start to categorize people as 'us' and 'them.' As a matter of fact, looking at the categorization of refugees, in the news they are represented 'as either deserving of sympathy and refuge or as a threat to (different parts of) Europe' (Goodman et al. 2017: 112). Researchers are however aware of the problems with this classification, which creates an insider and outsider discursive split and lacks scientific validity and empathy.

Methodological and Theoretical Approaches

Before starting this discussion, it is necessary to define some of the central concepts, the most important being the official definition of refugee. According to the (1949) Geneva Convention, a 'refugee' is defined as someone unable or unwilling to return to their country of origin due to well-founded fear of being persecuted for reasons of race, religion, nationality, membership of a particular social group or political opinion. Regarding the concept of home, we have benefited from Boccagni's (2017: 7) book *Migration and the Search for Home*, where he states that 'home' has three predominant qualities: familiarity, security and control. In the same book, he underlines the need to be aware of the immaterial and material qualities of home, and contradictory meanings (of home) that might not seem very obvious at first are also inferred from life stories (see also Allen 2008).

The project 'Face Forward … into my home' meanwhile has provided the possibility to enhance communication between refugees and clarify the human side of what we call 'faces behind the numbers' (Samuk et al. 2019). We have benefited from 26 online storytelling texts available at the webpage of the project. The deductive part of the research focused on home, family, mobility, migration and future plans. Together with the idea of forced migration, there is also the thought of return, although it might be vague and ill-defined in the accounts of the young refugees. Not knowing what has happened to their homes and some of their loved ones, the participants of this project imagine and connect with the past and disclose their attempts to recover from war and a dangerous journey.

Regarding the inductive part of the study, we asked the following questions when examining the data: how is 'home' positioned in regard to past events and future dreams and to what extent do the ideas of new and old 'home' converge/diverge in the forced migration and future mobility nexus? The answers to these questions, and a thematic analysis, paved the way for an inductive analysis and grounded theory-making: rooted migration is one of the main results.

In our theoretical background, we are primarily benefiting from the idea that home is a broader and more complex notion than simply being a dwelling place. This notion has been described as 'slippery and elusive' despite its inherent obviousness, with ambiguity present through being an everyday life category and an analytical tool (Boccagni 2017: 2). There are many different theoretical conceptualizations of 'home,' none hegemonic. Ahmed (1999: 340) demonstrates that not all homes are loved or have the same meaning. She proposes a simple categorization before explaining what home means for those who have transnational lives: 'home is where one usually lives, home is where one's family lives or home is one's "native country."' Kinefuchi (2010) notes that home may be physically or territorially marked (e.g., a neighbourhood, town, region or nation), but what constitutes its salience is more symbolic: that is, emotional, relational, cultural and political significance—in other words, its non-material connotations. These remarks seem curious when we think of refugees whose homes might not be there any more or communities who refuse to take them back or that lack emotional, relational, cultural and political attachment after having been forced to leave. Hence, for refugees, the existence of home creates a dilemma that migrants who can return home do not face to the same extent.

Home is not a pure category; it has to be explored in all its complexity. As noted above, we take the contradictory meanings of home into account. Allen (2008: 94) suggests that 'home can mean many different things simultaneously, and often, these meanings are in tension with each other.' Home, therefore, is very much an emotional place (Rubenstein 2001), wherein one can have mixed feelings: a feeling of belonging but not total obedience to the cultural and social rules imposed by cultural and social elements of 'home.' Moreover, there is this idea of belonging, and if the belonging is not there, the place of residence will not be perceived as home but rather as a place that hosts you for a temporary period or a place of estrangement where you have to wait until you find home or return home (see also Smith 2016).

In the case of refugees who stay in temporary shelters or in houses that are in poor condition, or dwellings they share with many families, the idea of a home as a place of familiarity, control and security can be lost. Still, it can be a place of refuge and the action of homemaking can persist. Furthermore, for refugees, returning home is more problematic. Kinefuchi (2010: 244) says: 'Particularly in the cases of refugees, the need to maintain diasporic identity may be intense and enduring due to their forced resettlement and difficulty, if not impossibility, of returning to their homeland.' Therefore, diaspora can give a sense of 'home' and replace the connections that have been lost.

The estrangement of refugees from home emanates from diverse causes: (1) war and trauma; (2) the idea of not being able to return home due to long years of refuge and further dreams of mobility and (3) the idea of returning home but not considering their old home as their home anymore, since the person has endured enormous personal and social change in these years abroad (as well as those who did not leave). This fact does not stop them from dreaming of further mobility or the idea of return; in some cases, this can let them serve their home country and/or return home proudly.

Finally, we would like to introduce a second analytical and theoretical theme, which focuses on 'rooted mobilities' (Cuzzocrea 2018: 1106), defined as 'strong mobility orientation, which can occur through the unfolding of an imagined continuous "lived" relationship with (a place).' In other words, young people may want to be mobile in Europe or in the world and have their future dreams, but these dreams are entangled with coming back to their 'homes' or related to 'doing something for their homes.' There is a similar phenomenon to 'rooted mobilities' which is also prominent among refugee youth who participated in 'Face Forward ... into my home.' They are involved in past, present and future homemaking. Their past involves forced migration, their present is learning and coping with their new homes, while their future reminds us of rooted mobilities, where they feel that they will travel and see many countries; some will not even stay in Greece and become mobile for any kind of reason (study, curiosity, work, etc.). In some cases, imagined mobilities can last for an undefined period. They may prefer to settle in Greece, learn the language and find a job there. However, in the context of these refugees, mobility is oriented towards an uncertain future. Hence, the hope to set up a new life despite forced migration culminates in an imagination of further mobility, where they consider this transition, in the end, as still serving their home (country).

Home as a Complicated Material and Non-Material Entity

We have found that the refugees who participated in 'Face Forward ... into my home' see home from many different perspectives and attribute very diverse meanings to it. First of all, 'country' was the word used the most in their individual stories, meaning in some cases the home country and in others Greece. The wish to do something about their home country—to contribute to it in the future, after completing education or finding work after the peace process is guaranteed—was among the wishes of the younger interviewees. Hence, regarding age in early age group, imagining doing something meaningful for 'home' was shaped in parallel to their imagined futures that consist of hope and uncertainty. Secondly, references to places back home were made (links between the old and the new home); for instance, some places in Greece reminded them of the calmness of life they had back home. These references were mostly cited if these places evoked similar feelings of calmness and if the new places exhibited similarities to previous homes in social, cultural, geographical or emotional terms.

Thirdly, not all participants had peaceful coexistence and high hopes about families left behind: thinking about returning home was not always a rosy picture, except for a few. Return could have meant conflicting and challenging relations with family members and coping with a changed identity after the migration experience. Family, in this sense, was also a major part of what they define as home, and in cases where the families were left behind and it was not easy to reunite with them for various reasons, the sense of home seemed incomplete and uncertainty blurred the idea of a 'home.' Moreover, this was one of the areas in which gender issues become more prominent. For instance, one woman who was scared to change as a person after her migration experience thought that her mother would not be able to recognize her when she returned. Hence, her return was imagined as related more to not being able to re-integrate again into her family, or exclusion from family or self-exclusion, because of the inevitability of changes in her character and life. There are more gendered aspects regarding the contextualization, considering the subject of family, which will be detailed further in the analysis sections.

Research Findings

Home as a Country and Country as Belonging

This theme involves ideas such as recovery, transformation and return. If we contextualize 'country,' which is among the most utilized words, the participants of this projects are referring to their home countries, namely the destruction brought by the war, the problems that their society faces and a nostalgia for home. They also refer to 'country' in contexts in which they distinguish between nations who received more refugees than others.

Despite the fact that some of the refugees went through difficult journeys and conflicts, the war and destruction could not obliterate the idea of a 'home,' and even though the material part is destroyed, home will be always be home in inspirational and non-material terms. Aboud (26, Syria), who is one of the participants in this project, describes Aleppo realistically and portrays the resistance of the people who stayed:

> The city is unrecognisable because of the massive destruction it has undergone. You see pictures from today's Aleppo and you cannot believe that there can be such a place on earth: a destroyed window here, a pot thrown there… However, some people have remained there in the hope that the city will be rebuilt, convinced that all problems are challenges which drive people to work hard and succeed.

A few still have the urge to return despite the destruction that has taken place and they emphasise the routines that make home a 'home,' which is Nowruz in Amin's (student, Iran) case, a source of joy and an important event to share with others for him: 'Last year I did not celebrate Nowruz. I promise you, though, that when I get a residence permit, I will take you all to Iran, set up a tent out in nature and celebrate.'

Then there is the idealism that is aligned with mobility and dreams about their future occupations, which in the long run reflect the fact that they will be serving home (country). The younger participants who are still studying are especially idealist, as they want to do something for their 'country.' This transition might also be related to the life course (Elder 1994) and how they perceive their future. As Bibiche (33, Congo) says: 'I also have a dream like that: I hope one day to work in the European Union as my country's ambassador and work for peace.' Finally, he unites these two ideas: his future aims and what we can do for his country with the opportunities provided to him with geographical and social mobility.

Old Home and New Home: Links that Calm Thought Processes and Emotional Lives

Calmness (being calm or keeping calm) is a recurrent theme. After the war and destruction one of the most important qualities in life they are searching is to feel calm and to stay calm. The idea of calmness was also directly or indirectly connected with the idea of home. For instance, Farida was looking for security and thinking about her children's future within this peaceful picture she foresaw: 'I am thinking that my children will grow up in a peaceful environment; they will be able to study and build their future. This thought calms me' (Farida, 28, Afghanistan). As observed here, in the life course, when families are built, ideas for the future are focused more on children than themselves and their individualistic ideals.

Sometimes objects can imply great power as memories and remembrances. Something that is made at home, something that is of great value with its authenticity all over the world, such as Iranian carpets, acquires a homely and local meaning:

> In Turkey there is a factory that makes carpets like these and exports them to other countries. Most of the workers there are Iranians. These carpets have motifs from nature, flowers and various plants. When you sit on them, you feel calm and peaceful. (Amin, student, Iran)[2]

In this example, the idea of calmness is ingrained into this handmade object: the carpet. In other cases, the sea and the new dwelling are not good enough to offer a sense of calmness, as one misses 'her balcony' in the calm hours of the evening:

> Before leaving Syria, I liked to sit on the balcony at home, because it was quiet. It brought me peace. Here I haven't found such a place yet. I would love to be in the mountains, but I haven't been to any mountain in Crete yet. The sea close to us does not really impress me. (Reem, 23, Syria)

On the other hand, it is not only geography or geographical qualities but also routines that one misses and wants to repeat to create the sense of a home-like environment. Routines that one used to do at home are replaced by routines one does in the new home. This kind of homemaking gives the possibility to take more control over situations where uncertainty governs. Those who say that home is not necessarily what or who was left behind draw attention to the fact that home can be abstract and can be carried as a non-material entity: '"home" for me doesn't mean the building. A home is what the members of a family create. "Home" means family, memories and feelings, which you can carry with you wherever you go' (Kourosh, 34, Iran).

Home and Family: A Complicated Matter

Home and family when used together prove difficult to conceptualize. It is difficult because some who are beloved are left behind, and family reunification has not been realized yet. It is challenging since there is a possibility of return and a fear of not finding what and who are left behind as well as possible irreversible changes to the young person's character that might affect relations back home. Moreover, there is a strong gender aspect we need to underline: feminization of home and 'motherization' of home. Considering these aspects, the online data on personal stories is quite dispersed under the name of that complex concept: 'family.' Here, we provide space to a couple of examples, as representing the whole theme would be beyond the scope of this chapter.

As underlined above, the idea of home is very much connected with motherhood; for instance, Reem (26, Syria) claims that nowhere can be considered home without her mother, although there are the aspects of control and security in her new dwelling:

> Now I live in a building in the centre of Athens. I asked to be alone in the room, without a roommate, to feel more comfortable. So, I have my personal space, where I can relax and feel safe. Even if I don't feel this place is like home—for me home is only where my mother is …

Here, it is seen that the 'personal space' is related to the theme control in Boccagni's definition of home. A feminization of home is also related to the socio-cultural realities back home. Therefore, it is not only associated with the idea of motherhood but is also connected with identifying home emotionally with the presence of mothers who make a home 'home.' In addition to this emotional approach to home and mothers, as a part of the main gendered socio-economic activity back home, it is observed that women's occupations are realized in the domestic sphere, which offers economic safety to women in Afghanistan. This theme finds resonance again with the 'carpets':

> As far as I know, these rugs are very expensive and most of them are sent to other countries abroad. It's mostly women and not men who work the loom, because women know more about colours and designs and they can draw better. Besides, because of the culture, women don't often leave the house. So, every home has a loom so that the woman of the house can have something to do that will also help her family financially. (Zainab, 16, Afghanistan)

Hence, these memories back home deliver many clues about how the home is feminized and how the women making carpets in their homes possess this specific knowledge of colours and designs.

New families and new ties mean that family is not only biological to some of the participants. Bibiche (33, Congo) feels this way:

> And I want to say to all my brothers and sisters here, to the refugees, compatriots and friends—call them what you will, I think of them as family—that we have the chance here to light up the darker places in our mind, the dark memories of the terrible things we've experienced, and to feel human again.

The family here is not solely biological; it can be reconstructed from the common difficulties a group of strangers experience while they develop a common understanding of humanity. Another example of building a safer idea of a home and having a new family is from Yaser (27, Syria):

> In the house I'm living in Athens today, I feel as comfortable as I did in my house back home. Of course, here I live with another family, but I don't find that a problem. We respect each other and so we can live well under the same roof. The important thing is that I feel safe in the house and there are no bombs falling outside.

Yaser's notion of home is hence united primarily with safety but there is also the presence of the idea of familiarity in the form of a respect between different people under the same roof.

To Deconstruct, Reconstruct and Reimagine Home

Setting up home (in the present and to reconstruct the one from the past) after deconstructing home via mobility and migration (what actual situations and the near future might bring to their lives) is very common in the cited examples. The participants' minds drift from forced migration to rooted mobilities creating a synthesis of their migration pattern, the rootedness of their thoughts and feelings, and the possibility to create new families and homes and to rebuild themselves via calmness and imagination.

Mobility is in their thoughts, and once they become mobile the idea of return becomes less plausible. This is more so especially after what happened in the war-ridden countries; mobility as a predominant theme comes to the fore in some of the participants' words. Reem is talking about what the possible future holds for her from a story that her mother used to tell her since she was a child: '…she decided to leave again and travel forever' (Reem, 23, Syria). She is scared of change but also thinks that this transformation in her life and her character is inevitable.

Mo-sabi meanwhile wants to travel and discover so many new cultures, again being inspired by a famous story of Sinbad and he is excited and anxious to have this mobile future:

> We youngsters play together without any problems. And I want to travel all around the world, that's why I had a second tattoo, which shows the map of the world. Just like Sinbad in the fairy tale, who set off from Baghdad, travelled a great deal and discovered many different cultures. (Mo-sabi, 19, Iraq)

Therefore, this new world they became acquainted with perpetuates more possibilities and ideas to travel, almost as if they are curious about how it feels to move by free will rather than being forced to move. And some of them plan to stay as finding a job in this current place, Greece, sounds like a good option. Dabbas says that he does not feel like a stranger, meaning that he has managed to develop a sense of home in Greece:

> That's why I've come to love Greece. I don't feel like a stranger. The air, the faces, the people, everything seems very familiar to me. Others want to leave and go to another country where it is easier to find a job. I want to stay here. (Dabbas, 24, Syria)

In the face of these three but similar examples, one can say that homemaking is an endless reconstruction for refugees and they are all aware that once home is lost, mobility or more migration or settling are the options left, and they are revealing their own choices: stay, be mobile for a while or be mobile forever. Some still preserve the idea of return, yet not knowing when.

Concluding Thoughts

The data has many dimensions but we have focused on a few that attracted our attention in regard to rooted mobilities and home, combining the two into what might be termed a form of 'rooted migration.' Feminization of home, motherization of home, returning home, not returning home, disappointment in the face of return, acting in order to be beneficial for home (for the country and the family), feeling at home, homemaking, staying, becoming mobile, missing home, missing family members, being calm and 'not feeling like a stranger' were all themes that were present amongst the online stories of the young refugees who participated in 'Face Forward … into my home.' As a result, it is possible to say that home in young refugees' minds encapsulates ideas of security (away from war, with peace and imagination of what the future might bring), familiarity (calmness, similarity of places) and control (having one's own space) (Boccagni 2017).

Home is something that connects and separates, something that entails control and security leading dialectically to conflicting feelings and thoughts. As they define the home country as their home, they underline the idea of lack of 'security' due to the war in the old place versus peace in the new one. As they define new places that remind them of their homes or cities, they emphasise the aspect of 'familiarity.' Additionally, as they talk about family, they mention 'control,' an area where they can have privacy while they are also controlled by other family members, which can have its side effects depending on the power dynamics in the family. A feminization of home also becomes predominant within the gendered categorization of 'home and family': for example, mothers' roles in homemaking and women's role in weaving carpets to contribute to the house economy. This way, carpets become objects of materiality as well as non-materiality, like the magic carpet of Sinbad.

The concept of rooted mobilities realigned with the individual stories proposes a few concluding remarks. These young people leave or are forced to leave with an idea of return and they still want to contribute to their home country (Cuzzocrea 2018). The imagined return is affected by many circumstances apart from macro-level conditions such as the end of the war: changes in the life course including building families, leaving their jobs, travelling from Greece to another country to find work, to be mobile forever, and more. The younger they are, the more prominent the idea of 'returning with glory' is. The idea of returning one day is present in almost all of their thoughts (Botterill 2014). In the end, the sense of a new family that is not the biological one is also ever-present: As Ahmed (1999) would claim, home is abstract and there can be multiplicities of 'home'; in other words, home is not always where one is born.

Combining rooted mobilities, homemaking, homing and the actual return or the idea of return, there is a dialectic process within moving (both when typified as forced migration and more voluntary mobility) that we need to comprehend more in depth: materiality of the home might be what is left behind but moving does not mean leaving literally 'everything' (related to home) behind. This is more striking in the cases described as forced migration. Moreover, non-materiality of home as an ever-changing form continues to haunt the young refugees who participated in 'Face Forward … into my home.' Therefore, their migration is rooted, and their mobilities are rooted, which can be credited to the fact that home means (new and old) country, (new and old) relations and (new and old) family, however horrendous or beautiful that might be.

Notes

1. In Europe, the question of whether or not the European Union is still a beacon for human rights after the March 2016 Readmission deal with Turkey also needs to be raised (see Barbulescu 2017).
2. In the website of the project, not all participants are indicated with their ages. That is why some of the participants do not have the ages indicated.

References

Ahmed, S. (1999). Home and away: Narratives of migration and estrangement. *International Journal of Cultural Studies, 2*(3), 329–347.

Allen, S. (2008). Finding home: Challenges faced by geographically mobile families. *Family Relations, 57*(1), 84–99.

Barbulescu, R. (2017). Still a beacon of human rights? Considerations on the EU response to the refugee crisis in the Mediterranean. *Mediterranean Politics, 22*(2), 301–308.

Boccagni, P. (2017). *Migration and the search for home: Mapping domestic space in migrants' everyday lives* (Mobility and Politics Series). New York: Palgrave Macmillan.

Botterill, K. (2014). Family and mobility in second modernity: Polish migrant narratives of individualization and family life. *Sociology, 48*(2), 233–250.

Cuzzocrea, V. (2018). 'Rooted mobilities' in young people's narratives of the future: A peripheral case. *Current Sociology, 66*(7), 1106–1123.

de Genova, N. (Ed.). (2017). *The borders of 'Europe': Autonomy of migration, tactics of bordering*. Durham: Duke University Press.

Elder, G. H., Jr. (1994). Time, human agency, and social change: Perspectives on the life course. *Social Psychology Quarterly, 57*(1), 4–15.

Goodman, S., Sirriyeh, A., & McMahon, S. (2017). The evolving (re)categorisations of refugees throughout the 'refugee/migrant crisis'. *Journal of Community & Applied Social Psychology, 27*(2), 105–114.

Kinefuchi, E. (2010). Finding home in migration: Montagnard refugees and post-migration identity. *Journal of International and Intercultural Communication, 3*(3), 228–248.

Rubenstein, R. (2001). *Home matters: Longing and belonging, nostalgia and mourning in women's fiction*. New York: Palgrave Macmillan.

Samuk, S., Acuner, D., & Tonga-Uriarte, Y. (2019–2020). *Cultural policy yearbook*. Istanbul: Bilgi University Press.

Smith, E. P. (2016). To build a home: The material cultural practices of Karen refugees across borders. *Area, 48*(3), 278–284.

Soysal, Y. N. (1994). *Limits of citizenship. Migrants and postnational membership in Europe*. Chicago: Chicago University Press.

Chapter 37
'I was not prepared to go to Spain': Work Mobility of Young People at the Margins in Portugal

Mara Clemente

This chapter takes a close look at an important and under-represented example of young people's mobility, cases of what is frequently referred to as 'human trafficking,' focusing on the example of Portugal. In regard to policy context, following the signing and ratification of the most relevant international instruments to fight human trafficking, in 2007, important legislative changes were introduced into immigration law and Penal Code in Portugal, contributing to a definition in line with international law. And in the same year, the First National Action Plan Against Trafficking in Human Beings (2007–2010) was adopted. The progressive consolidation of this institutional focus was accompanied by increased research interest on the topic at the national level. However, in keeping with the approach of legislation, a narrow range of issues tend to be addressed. In particular, from the first exploratory studies and for a long period after, research in this field has focused primarily on the sex trafficking of migrant women, "only occasionally challenging stereotyped images of trafficking and its recurrent identification with prostitution (see, e.g., Silva et al. 2013; Alvim 2018).

In more recent times, other forms of trafficking have started to enter the research lexicon, as well as national and international policy debates. However, most research continues to focus on Portugal as a 'destination country' of trafficked persons and rarely considers the experiences of outgoing trafficked persons (Pereira and Vasconcelos 2007; Clemente 2017a). At the same time, widespread conceptualization of trafficking as a crime seems to contribute to a low level of academic interest in studies of migration and mobility in Portugal but creates visibility in the media, meaning most of our representations emanate from the latter as opposed to the former. This chapter aims to address this imbalance through focusing on the trafficking of Portuguese youth. Based on ethnographic research with a young man trafficked

---

M. Clemente (✉)
ISCTE – Instituto Universitário de Lisboa (ISCTE-IUL), Centro de Investigação e Estudos de Sociologia, Lisbon, Portugal

to Spain, the chapter also aims to challenge the 'deafening silence' (Clemente 2017b) surrounding trafficked persons in Portuguese research through contributing an empirically grounded study.

The study also challenges other stereotypes about Portuguese migration. Since the second half of the nineteenth century, migration has been a structural constant and a symbolic feature of Portuguese society. However, in a context of profound inequalities, it can also constitute an unequally distributed privilege. This study suggests that a lower level of human, financial and social capital continues to affect the mobility of Portuguese young people. In some cases, their experiences of mobility and exploitation could be labelled as 'trafficking' but are not due to the predominant focus on criminal networks of traffickers that fails to adequately capture a more inclusive range of forms and causes of exploitation, as found among the subjects of this study. In providing an empirical account of the trafficking-migration nexus, the chapter aims to contribute to an alternative framing of the problem, as well as providing case study evidence.

In more strategic terms, the chapter challenges current approaches to trafficking and draws attention to opportunities for interventions that actually meet the needs of young people on the move. In the last few decades, a number of European policies and programmes have promoted learning, training and work mobility of young people across countries, inside and outside of Europe. However, mobility, as well as being an integral part of human life, continues to constitute an unearned and unequally distributed 'good' (O'Connell Davidson and Howard 2015). This study confirms the need to reinforce access to resources and support the mobility capacities of young people with fewer opportunities and/or from disadvantaged backgrounds to address societal inequality and social exclusion (Cairns 2017) and ultimately reduce vulnerability to exploitation, starting with a reconsideration of hegemonic views of what constitutes being trafficked.

The Problematic Conceptualization of the Problem

In December 2000, after over two years of negotiation, over 80 countries signed the United Nations Trafficking Protocol, supplementing the UN Convention Against Transnational Organized Crime. Since this time, the definition of trafficking has expanded to include other forms of exploitation in addition to the trafficking of women and girls for purposes of prostitution, something that has motivated the fight against trafficking since late nineteenth century.[1] While multi-faceted, a key characteristic of the definition of trafficking proposed by the now-called Palermo Protocol is the emphasis upon associating trafficking and crime committed by organized criminal networks, meaning that trafficking is to be addressed through law enforcement strategies. This development is highly important, not only for our understanding of what gets defined as trafficking but also for those involved in being trafficked, some of whom have come to be regarded as higher priorities than others (at least according to law-on-the-books).

Despite the popularity of the master narratives on trafficking, they have created many challenges related to the fact that despite the apparent simplicity, trafficking is complex and diverse. In fact, during the last 20 years, there has been a progressive increase in the amount of multi-disciplinary, interventionist, if rarely evidence-based, literature on trafficking being produced. This work, and political debate surrounding trafficking, has in fact been characterized by competing understandings of the nature and causes of trafficking and different ways to address it. For example, Kelly and Regan (2000) identified a number of pre-existing representations of trafficking: as moral, criminal, migration, human rights, public order or labour related, as well as being a gender issue. Aradau (2008) meanwhile pointed towards four main 'problematizations' of trafficking, relating to migration, organized crime, prostitution and human rights abuse. Lee (2011) on the other hand described six major conceptual approaches: trafficking as a modern form of slavery, an exemplar of the globalization of crime, a practice synonymous with prostitution, a problem of transnational organized crime, related to migration and a challenge to human rights. Despite this heterogeneity, the definition of the problem by the main anti-trafficking international instrument, the aforementioned Palermo Protocol, has contributed to a dominant conceptualization of trafficking as a form of organized crime, inseparable from ('illegal') migration (Lee 2011).

The same weakness can be said of claims that trafficking needs to be seen in terms of financial profit and its dimensions—the second or the third largest criminal enterprise in the world, after drugs and illegal arms (Weitzer 2014). Practitioners and critical scholars have also argued that the dominant conceptualization of trafficking as a crime that threatens national and international security ignores the structural causes of the problem and produces a depoliticization of debate, in addition to harming both the 'victims' and those who are not labelled as 'trafficked' through taking a crime and punishment approach (Kempadoo et al. 2005; GAATW 2007; Andrijasevic 2010; Blanchette and da Silva 2014; O'Connell Davidson and Howard 2015; ICRSE 2019). Nevertheless, in the last 20 years, the primary concerns of different states have remained interception, persecution and punishment of traffickers' networks and the control of migration through interventions such as interstate cooperation, increasing border surveillance, restrictive migration policies, raid and rescue operations, and migrant detention and deportation, as well as forced rehabilitation and the limiting of protection for trafficked persons to those who cooperate in criminal investigations.

Since the UN Protocol negotiations, different interventions that move away from a conceptualization of trafficking as a human rights abuse problem have been claimed (Chuang 2014). However, this approach, progressively embraced by various scholars, as well as organizations and states, has also been seen as controversial. According to Aradau (2008), mobilizing one-dimensional personal stories of suffering individuals sees them as passive subjects of violence, while the humanitarian approach implies a distribution of rights that can be (potentially) enjoyed only by certain subjects (i.e., the 'victims') to the exclusion and the detriment of others (such as sex workers and economic migrants). The normalization of new hierarchies and inequalities in accessing mobility, labour rights and citizenship has encouraged criticism in light of the wider conceptual framework of trafficking, emphasising the need to exclude the terms 'trafficking' and 'victims of trafficking' from being characterized as one and the same and, among other things, subjected to a discursive logic of criminality and victimization (Andrijasevic 2010).

Following ratification of the Palermo Protocol, even in Portugal, and despite the use of human rights language, institutional mobilization on the issue of trafficking takes its lead from the hegemonic conceptualization as a criminal issue (Clemente 2017c). Starting with a definition of trafficking as a problem linked to criminal networks, and through partnerships between governmental institutions, law enforcement agencies and NGOs, an anti-trafficking system has been built with the main aim of prosecuting traffickers. Extending the analysis to the Portuguese case, this chapter mobilizes the contributions of migration studies and critical trafficking studies to highlight the limitations of conceptualizing trafficking as a criminal problem, while also recognizing problems with categories such as 'voluntary' migrants and 'trafficked' migrants, all of which are based on simplistic, static and binary views of mobility.

Research Context

Located on the south-western edge of continental Europe, Portugal is a country that is characterized by decades of under-development and structural socio-economic inequalities that have contributed to its peripheral position in the international context and reduced the possibility of social mobility for much of its population (Carmo and Cantante 2015; Ribeiro 2017). The Estado Novo [New State] authoritarian regime (1933–1974), with its rural and anti-modernist politics and ideology, contributed to the poor industrial and techno-scientific development of the country (Silva 2013), and from the end of the 1960s, the repressive and corporative practices of the Salazar-Caetano dictatorship encouraged large-scale emigration, often of *operários-camponeses* [worker-peasants] with low wages and poor social protection.

A first cycle of Portuguese migration had already taken place between 1850 and 1930, when the unequal distribution of resources motivated many male rural laborers to move abroad, initially to the former Brazilian colony (Pires 2011). After the end of World War II, between 1950 and the fall of the Portuguese dictatorship in 1974, there was a spike in the migration rate for men but also migrant women (Baganha 2003). The main destinations for what were increasingly temporary duration forms of migration were the Americas and the African colonies and, after the mid-1960s, the rest of Europe (especially France, the then West Germany and Luxembourg). The end of the dictatorship and the removal of political obstacles to emigration inaugurated a third cycle of Portuguese migration, between 1974 and 2000. In this era, with Portugal's integration into the European Union, there was also an increase in incoming migration, an issue that became central in more recent research and public discourse (Peixoto et al. 2016).

A fourth wave of Portuguese emigration started in 2001 (Pereira and Azevedo 2019). This is described by Pires (2019) as a 'European phenomenon' as it was now almost entirely directed towards traditional and new destination European countries (such as the United Kingdom and Spain), with these countries now hosting over two thirds of Portuguese migrants, many of whom have started or continued their careers there. Portuguese migration of the twenty-first century can hence be seen as closely related to the labour market and the rise in unemployment, especially of young people, due to stagnation in economic growth and the adoption of punitive austerity policies by Portugal. Despite the process of economic recovery from 2014, during its fourth wave, Portuguese outgoing migration witnessed the highest rates of growth since the 1960s. And it is the experiences of 'trafficking' of Portuguese youth within this fourth wave that this research addresses, a time during which both mobility and its inherent precariousness have intensified (see Cairns 2021a, b in this book), with precarity becoming a generalized structural feature of the Portuguese society affecting both the practice of incoming and outgoing mobility (Cairns et al. 2016; Pires 2019).

Methodological Approach

This chapter takes an in-depth biographical look at trafficking in Portugal via the story of a young man from the northern region of the country (see Ferrarotti 1983) who was 'trafficked' to Spain and then labelled as a 'victim' of labour exploitation by Portuguese law enforcement agencies. To protect his identity, I will refer to him as Pedro, obviously not his real name. He was interviewed as part of a qualitative study of Portuguese assistance and reintegration of trafficked persons.

A recent analysis of Portuguese trafficking data indicates that between 2008 and 2014 about a quarter of the 1070 'presumed victims,' whose origin is known and not protected by statistical confidentiality, are Portuguese citizens (Clemente 2017a).[2] There are 269 Portuguese men and women, presumed to be exploited both in Portugal (109) and abroad (160), in particular, in Spain. More recently published data has confirmed this trend. According to the most recent Portuguese report on human trafficking, in 2018, 37 of the 92 'presumed victims' are of Portuguese origin, constituting 86 per cent of trafficked persons of community origin (OTSH/MAI 2019).

Contact details for Pedro were provided by the authorities who participated in his formal identification in the recent past. The first meeting took place in a venue he nominated. Pedro's long interview included pauses to respond to his emotional needs. The interview meeting also marked the beginning of a broader research relationship characterized by subsequent meetings at public events, meaning prolonged contact over time. Despite his formal identification as a 'victim,' at the time of the interview, Pedro was far from being in a state of concrete socio-economic (re)integration. These circumstances prompted the need for constant reflection and ethical practice that involved sharing the researcher positioning and expectations of Pedro in the research, going well beyond ethical guidelines with regard to informed consent, providing opportunities to withdraw from participation in the interview if required. Being formally labelled as a 'victim' also shaped the interviews, that is, Pedro's language and narrative structure. His participation in other interviews, for national media and a write-up of his experience published in a blog, has further contributed to this positioning. In order to respond to the impact made by these different circumstances in shaping data, the interview was constructed without directly asking the participant about his exploitation but asking him to talk about his past and present and expectations for the future in more general terms.

Pedro's Narrative

Life Before Trafficking

Pedro was trafficked to Spain in 2009, during the time of a full-scale European financial crisis in both Spain and Portugal, at a time when he was barely of legal age. During this experience, which lasted a few months, he was exploited in different activities—from small construction tasks to the collection of paper and wood. Pedro's narrative begins with the suicide attempt with which he tried to end his exploitation but quickly shifts back to his past life of poverty, marginalization and violence.

Pedro grew up in a family he describes as 'very poor but very humble.' During his childhood he was entrusted, together with one of his sisters, to his maternal grandparents. He lived for a few years in a rural province in the north-east of Portugal, known for its historical migration traditions. Upon returning to his mother's city of residence in the north, family conditions led to the institutionalization of Pedro at a facility that already hosted his other brothers. The institution for disadvantaged young people that hosted Pedro was not a space of security, but he emphasises the protection provided by his older brother:

> Everyone looked at me sideways, but my brother didn't like to see others look at me that way and always did everything to make me feel good. He always did his best to make sure nothing bad happened to me.

Pedro left school around the age of 16 following an episode of violence that resulted in the murder of a transsexual by a group of young college friends. The event occupied the media for a long time and led to the closure of the institution, contributing to Pedro having to leave school. In his own words:

> It all fell on me too. There were great friends there. There was also the director-general of the school, who was also my friend, and then he committed suicide himself because of everything he was going through. The school after that changed a lot, it changed… Every day was just… during those weeks, it was just journalists wanting to know everything and us… looking away. I went back home, I was studying at the time, and I went back home. I left school.

Pedro also narrates a precarious experience about a food truck on which he took short trips around the country. At the food truck kiosk, he met a customer, who will be identified as his 'trafficker': 'Then [Miguel] immediately started sending words. There began a friendship, between quotes, joking, on both sides. This friendship started to be born like this.'

Miguel offers Pedro a few weeks' work in Spain, during harvest time, at the end of the summer fairs. Both Pedro and his family consider the offer as 'unrefusable':

> He offered twenty-five euros for each work day. My mum thought it was good and I thought, 'It's a great opportunity!' The proposal was good, it was undeniable. I had never been, had never been to Spain before, it was also a chance for me to know Spain.

Life in Trafficking

Pedro drives to Spain with his 'trafficker.' Despite not being seen as such at the time, the experience that he narrates contains numerous 'indicators' that are traditionally associated with 'trafficking.' For example, during the trip, he is deprived of his identity documents and telephone, which are kept by Miguel:

> I got into the van, he asked for the cell phone and wallet—I think that's all I had then, in his hands. He said it was for security… so as not to lose the documents. He said it was for insurance… that kind of stuff.

Contacts with both Pedro's family and with other people in his immediate environment became limited:

> When we arrived in [city name] he warned us that we could not leave the house. He warned us that he would be away for a few days and that he did not want us to talk to the other employees, the other employees that the other house had.

Pedro is forced to live in poor and degraded accommodation, receiving only leftovers to eat:

> And I don't want to talk about the food, because the food, the food was… animal wash, you know?! Many times I was having dinner, he was next to me spitting on my plate, spitting on the floor, making junk food for my plate. Many times there were bones, already gnawed by him, on my plate. I had a lot of hunger over it. When I got to dinner, I didn't even want to eat, I wasn't hungry.

During his stay in Spain, Pedro is exploited in various ways, through hard 'services,' receiving little or no payment for working long hours:

> But sleeping… it was something that was not in that house. There was no way because we leave the house, for example, at six in the morning, come back for lunch at noon, go out at two, and then be on the streets of [city name] until six in the afternoon, back to the house again at seven, dinner at eight and then go around all night to collect cardboard. Sleeping was very rare.

Although employed in arduous activities, different from those originally envisaged, Pedro did not have the possibility to negotiate his working and living conditions and is controlled through insults, abuse and violence:

> Since I was getting fed up with... with the beating that he, the beating that was not well beating, it was ...bludgeoning! I was getting fed up with his behaviour and I ended up... asking questions: 'When are we going to [city name]?', 'When do we go to the harvest and when do I go home?' He said: 'Now, harvest is still a long time from now. Now I want you to work. I want you to get everything to work. Work and, when there is dinner, we have dinner.'

Both Pedro's experience and some of his characteristics, starting from a young age, contribute to his formal identification as a 'victim.' However, his narrative, similar to that of other participants in this research, seems to remain very distant from the presence of transnational organized crime networks. Pedro's recruitment, transportation, transfer, receipt and exploitation see Miguel as the only protagonist. He moves Pedro from Portugal to several Spanish towns where he or his family resides and where Pedro is then exploited, especially for small-scale construction or other jobs as well as family activities. As Pedro explains:

> Early in the trip he said he was no longer going to [city name], but was going to stop in [city name] because his parents were making a small carousel garage, because it was all a family of carnies... In [city name], we were also helping his wife's parents in jobs like chopping wood.

The family of the 'trafficker' certainly benefitted from the exploitation of Pedro but he nevertheless describes them as 'impeccable' people. They, among other things, intervened in defence against the violence inflicted on him by Miguel, with whom moments of tension were created:

> His father made me take off my pants, show him the wound and he was upset with me that I lied to him... I had more beating from [Miguel] because I showed my leg to his father. For this and other reasons, we stopped going to his parents.

Reframing Trafficking

The consideration of the causes and the modalities which favour mobility but also the exploitation of Pedro leads us further away from a static and binary categorization of people as 'migrants' or 'victims.' Trafficking, especially when it involves children and young people, is recurrently seen as a violent isolated event within the 'victim' biography. But Pedro's narrative encourages us to see trafficking as a broader 'process' (Hynes 2010), within which life before trafficking, with its structural marginalities and inequalities, is inextricably intertwined with the mobility and exploitation trajectories that ensued.

Despite the evocation of informal support and the surveillance from his family network, Pedro's life was marked by a context of profound social exclusion and, at times, violence. Within this context, Pedro was basically a young man with a low level of educational attainment and unregulated low-skilled work experience in informal sectors. In his own words, he 'had nothing else to do.' The possibility of temporary work mobility to neighbouring Spain proposed by his 'trafficker' was appealing due to the lack of opportunities for this young man and his family, in a similar way to what has happened to many young Portuguese who, from the beginning of the 2000s, became migration protagonists. In recent decades, despite the decrease in levels of outward migration from Portugal since the 2008 financial crisis, Spain has remained one of the most significant destinations for thousands of unemployed and low-paid precious workers: those without professional and social mobility prospects, mainly from the north-west of Portugal (see also Queirós 2019; Pires 2019). As emphasized by Queirós (2019: 161), the interactions between Portuguese migrants' socio-economic history and the repeated and long-lasting periods of structural constraints help gestate the (re)production of migratory acts 'that are plausible because they are probable.'

Actually, in Pedro's experience of mobility, the need to answer to a labour demand is intertwined with other expectations that are often left behind at the edge of debate and reflection. His work mobility also relates to more worldly ambitions, starting from a desire to travel, discover new places and meet new people, echoing a point made by Pantea (2021) elsewhere in this book regarding vocational work trainees and the personal fulfilment dimension of their mobility aspirations. As Pedro's words suggest, Portuguese migration history also contributes to the desire of those Mai (2011) would describe as having 'individualized and hedonistic' lifestyles and mobility experiences:

> I had to know everything, and there was always a huge desire in me to visit another country. I speak of this desire because I have a lot of family around the world, from France to Spain, and I was always curious to know other lands, new people. So, in the city of [city name], I walked from street to street, until I got tired, and sitting on the sidewalks of each of the streets.

Meanwhile, structural exclusion and inequality encourage but also limit the labour mobility of Pedro. When he was originally offered work for a few months during the harvest, he 'was not prepared to go to Spain,' meaning he went unprepared for the cultural shift of living in another country. In addition to being of a young age and with limited work and mobility experience, Pedro and his family did not have the economic conditions to finance the outward migration as well as the return of Pedro. As he says, when he managed to escape from the situation of exploitation in which he found himself, contacting his family in order to return to Portugal, his mother was faced with the impossibility of supporting the return: '"My son"—she said, "I have no way to get you, I have no money to go there!"' Although migration constitutes a structural feature of Portuguese society, neither Pedro's departure nor his return to Portugal involved the possibility of mobilizing family members and/or close members of his personal network. His poverty can therefore be conceptualized as a lack of social and economic capital. The importance of 'making friends' is in fact constantly evoked in Pedro's narrative. However, the only controversial reference within his mobility experience is represented by the family members of the person identified as his trafficker.

The mobility of Pedro, a Portuguese citizen who moved within EU boundaries, is not subjected—or is not immediately subjected—to the strict migration laws and restrictive border controls that characterize 'fortress Europe,' which render many migrants vulnerable to exploitation (see Aradau 2008; O'Connell Davidson 2015; ICRSE 2019). His trafficker, although distant from how we might imagine the great organized crime networks, takes advantage of Pedro's lack of human, financial and social capital to compel his migration, taking advantage of his need to find a means of survival in a context of profound inequalities and lack of opportunities. All of this makes Pedro's experience a 'labor migration gone horribly wrong' (Chuang 2014: 639).

There is one aspect of Pedro's narrative that cannot be left behind by referring to the internalization and naturalization of domination and exploitation reported by Queirós (2019) in his study of Portuguese construction workers in Spain. According to Queirós, the exceptional and transitory character of contemporary work mobility recurrently contributes to the internalization of social inequalities and the naturalization of moral and physical violence suffered daily in the workplace. These costs of migration are usually justified with the financial compensation involved and are reinterpreted using a logic of male stoicism and professional virtuosity; they are also ways of thinking, and acting, that seem to have been reproduced by Pedro, who thereby normalizes the conditions of labour exploitation to which he is subjected by the family of his trafficker. Despite the completely symbolic value of his salary and the precarious conditions of his life and work, he describes his interlocutors as 'five-star' people:

> Seriously. They always showed up… I speak for myself. They always respected me, always did me good, always offered me everything. A five star person, both he and his wife. He was impeccable. They gave us everything. Every day we were given five euros each, if we wanted to go out, have a cup of coffee, buy a pack of tobacco, we would go. We had a house, we had food, we had a bath…

Before that, when his 'trafficker' communicated that the work in the harvest will only be after some construction work for his family, Pedro reinterpreted the change of work programme as an opportunity to gain experience:

> Then he said to me: 'Let's stay in [city name], let's stay for two, three weeks and a few, to finish this work of my father.' Me there: 'So what about the harvests?' There will be no more harvests, it was a lie on his part. Alright… I liked construction, I didn't like construction, of course not, but I wanted to know more about these parts.

Overall, Pedro's narrative seems to reproduce the feelings of inadequacy and inferiority and the naturalization of exploitation reported by Queirós. Meanwhile, Pedro, unlike other young people with whom he shares his exploitation experience, also seems to oppose these schemes of thought and action. What makes his experience particularly violent, but also contributes to his emergence, is the fact of rebelling. Arturo, a young man who is in the same situation as Pedro, did not do the same thing but sought individualized solutions to his condition:

[Arturo] was basically a saint: he did nothing. If I did something, [Arturo] would tell [Miguel]. [Miguel] also beat [Arturo] a lot. I saw it. But [Arturo] was like his dear little son. Everything I did, [Arturo] told him.

Notes for the Future

When I met Pedro, it had been seven years after his 'trafficking' experience. During these years, Pedro learned that the abuse and violence he had experienced during his stay in Spain could be labelled as 'trafficking.' Pedro was never hosted in any one of the many shelters that in recent years have engaged an increasing number of psychologists and social workers. He had a house. Although he had decided to cooperate in criminal investigations against his trafficker, the trial was still ongoing. Pedro reported the informal support of an organization that, in some occasions, invited him to participate in interviews for the national media. Despite the continuous repetition of his history of violence and abuse, Pedro has never had access to rights entitled to 'trafficking victims,' like compensation.

Pedro had learned to talk about his life during trafficking and to refer to himself a 'victim' and/or 'slave.' However, both his present and the future remained precarious and uncertain. He had returned to a context of profound inequalities and structural marginality, which had motivated his mobility to begin with, but he has remained distant from socio-economic inclusion, still waiting for a 'good chance' to arrive. This study suggests that, if migration is the only 'chance' for many young people with fewer opportunities and disadvantaged backgrounds, the mobility capacities of these young people should be strengthened to reduce their vulnerability to exploitation. Are the needs of young people at the margins sufficiently considered by current European policies and programmes promoting learning, training and work mobility of young people? The experience of Pedro suggests not.

Notes

1. The United Nations Protocol to Prevent, Suppress and Punish Trafficking in Persons, Especially Women and Children, Supplementing the United Nations Convention Against Transnational Organized Crime (also known as the Palermo Protocol), defines 'trafficking in persons' as 'the recruitment, transportation, transfer, harbouring or receipt of persons, by means of the threat or use of force or other forms of coercion, of abduction, of fraud, of deception, of the abuse of power or of a position of vulnerability or of the giving or receiving of payments or benefits to achieve the consent of a person having control over another person, for the purpose of exploitation. Exploitation shall include, at a minimum, the exploitation of the prostitution of others or other forms of sexual exploitation, forced labour or services, slavery or practices similar to slavery, servitude or the removal of organs.'
2. As a component of the Portuguese trafficking monitoring system, the expression 'presumed victim' is used with reference to a person about whom there exist strong indications of a trafficking experience. The 'confirmed victim' classification is designated by law enforcement agencies (Judiciary Police or Immigration and Borders Service) to a person as a result of a police investigation.

References

Alvim, F. (2018). *Só Muda a Moeda: Representações sobre Tráfico de Seres Humanos e Trabalho Sexual em Portugal*. Novas Edições Acadêmicas.
Andrijasevic, R. (2010). *Migration, agency and citizenship in sex trafficking*. New York: Palgrave Macmillan.
Aradau, C. (2008). *Rethinking trafficking in women*. Basingstoke: Palgrave Macmillan.
Baganha, M. I. (2003). Portuguese emigration after World War II. In A. C. Pinto (Ed.), *Contemporary Portugal. Politics, society and culture* (pp. 139–157). Boulder: Social Sciences Monographs.
Blanchette, T. G., & da Silva, A. P. (2014). Bad girls and vulnerable women: An anthropological analysis of narratives regarding prostitution and human trafficking in Brazil. In C. Showden & S. Majic (Eds.), *Negotiating sex work: Unintended consequences of policy and activism* (pp. 121–144). Minnesota: University of Minnesota Press.
Cairns, D. (2017). Analytical paper: Learning mobility and social inclusion. In M. Devlin, S. Kristensen, E. Krzaklewska, & M. Nico (Eds.), *Learning mobility, social inclusion and non-formal education. Access, processes and outcomes* (pp. 23–29). Strasbourg: Council of Europe.
Cairns, D. (2021a). Mobility becoming migration: Understanding youth spatiality in the twenty-first century. In D. Cairns (Ed.), *The Palgrave handbook of youth mobility and educational migration*. Basingstoke: Palgrave Macmillan.
Cairns, D. (2021b). Migration decision-making, mobility capital and reflexive learning. In D. Cairns (Ed.), *The Palgrave handbook of youth mobility and educational migration*. Basingstoke: Palgrave Macmillan.
Cairns, D., Alves, N. A., Alexandre, A., & Correia, A. (2016). *Youth unemployment and job precariousness: Political participation in the austerity era*. Basingstoke: Palgrave Macmillan.
Carmo, R. M. de, & Cantante, F. (2015). Desigualdades, redistribuição e o impacto do desemprego: tendências recentes e efeitos da crise económico-financeira. *Sociologia, Problema e Práticas, 77*, 33–51.
Chuang, J. A. (2014). Exploitation creep and the unmaking of human trafficking law. *The American Journal of International Law, 108*(4), 609–649.
Clemente, M. (2017a). *Cidadãos portugueses traficados, OEm Fact Sheets. 5*. Lisboa: Observatório da Emigração, CIES-IUL, ISCTE-IUL.
Clemente, M. (2017b). Human trafficking in Portugal: An ethnography of research and data. *Studi Emigrazione. International Journal of Migration Studies, LIV*(208), 663–686.
Clemente, M. (2017c). Reservado o direito de admissão. Discursos antitráfico, controlo das migrações e assistência a mulheres. *Bagoas – Estudos Gays: Gêneros e Sexualidades, 17*, 154–200.
Ferrarotti, F. (1983). Biography and the social sciences. *Social Research, 50*(1), 57–80.
GAATW. (2007). *Collateral damage. The impact of anti-trafficking measures on human rights around the world*. Bangkok: GAATW.
Hynes, P. (2010). Global points of 'vulnerability': Understanding processes of the trafficking of children and young people into, within and out of the UK. *International Journal of Human Rights, 14*(6), 952–970.
ICRSE. (2019). *A brief guide on collateral damages of anti-trafficking laws and measures on sex workers*. Amsterdam: ICRSE.
Kelly, L., & Regan, L. (2000). *Stopping traffic: Exploring the extent of, and responses to, trafficking in women for sexual exploitation in the UK*. London: Home Office, Policing and Reducing Crime Unit.
Kempadoo, K., Sanghera, J., & Pattnaik, B. (Eds.). (2005). *Trafficking and prostitution reconsidered: New perspectives on migration, sex work, and human rights*. Boulder, CO: Paradigm.
Lee, M. (2011). *Trafficking and global crime control*. London: Sage.
Mai, N. (2011). Tampering with the sex of 'angels': Migrant male minors and young adults selling sex in the EU. *Journal of Ethnic and Migration Studies, 37*(8), 1237–1252.
O'Connell Davidson, J. (2015). *Modern slavery: The margins of freedom*. New York: Palgrave Macmillan.

O'Connell Davidson, J., & Howard, N. (2015). On freedom and (im)mobility: How states create vulnerability by controlling human movement. In J. O'Connell Davidson & N. Howard (Eds.), *Migration and mobility. Beyond trafficking and slavery short course volume 5* (pp. 10–13). London: Open Democracy.

OTSH/MAI. (2019). *Tráfico de Seres Humanos. Relatório de 2018.* Lisboa: OTSH/MAI.

Pantea, M.-C. (2021). Facets of mobility in Romania's vocational education and training. In D. Cairns (Ed.), *The Palgrave handbook of youth mobility and educational migration.* Basingstoke: Palgrave Macmillan.

Peixoto, J., Tiago de Oliveira, I., Azevedo, J., Marques, J. C., Góis, P., Malheiros, J., & Madeira, P. M. (2016). *Regresso ao Futuro: A Nova Emigração e a Sociedade Portuguesa.* Lisboa: Gradiva.

Pereira, C., & Azevedo, J. (Eds.). (2019). *New and old routes of Portuguese emigration. Uncertain futures at the periphery of Europe.* Heidelberg: Springer Verlag.

Pereira, S., & Vasconcelos, J. (2007). *Combate ao Tráfico de Seres Humanos e Trabalho Forçado: Estudo de Casos e Respostas de Portugal.* Lisboa: OIT.

Pires, R. P. (ed.) (2011). *Portugal: An atlas of international migration.* Lisboa: Tinta da China.

Pires, R. P. (2019). Portuguese emigration today. In C. Pereira & J. Azevedo (Eds.), *New and old routes of Portuguese emigration. Uncertain futures at the periphery of Europe* (pp. 29–48). Heidelberg: Springer Verlag.

Queirós, J. (2019). Working class condition and migrant experience: The case of Portuguese construction workers. In C. Pereira & J. Azevedo (Eds.), *New and old routes of Portuguese emigration. uncertain futures at the periphery of Europe* (pp. 155–170). Heidelberg: Springer Verlag.

Ribeiro, F. B. (2017). *Uma Sociologia do Desenvolvimento.* Ribeirão – Vila Nova de Famalicão: Húmus.

Silva, M. C. (2013). Crise, democracia e desenvolvimento: o lugar semiperiférico de Portugal. *Revista Española de Sociología, 19*, 153–168.

Silva, M. C., Ribeiro, F. B., & Granja, R. (2013). *Prostituição e Tráfico de Mulheres para fins de Exploração Sexual.* Prior Velho: Letras Paralelas.

Weitzer, R. (2014). New directions in research on human trafficking. *The ANNALS of the American Academy of Political and Social Science, 653*, 6–24.

Chapter 38
Crossing the Line: Current and Future Challenges in Youth Mobility

Jeanine B. van Halteren

This chapter discusses challenges in youth mobility, focusing on the story of Jane, a young Nigerian woman who migrated to Europe. As it will be explained in the chapter, the youth mobility she experienced can be framed as human trafficking for the presence of various elements such as false job promises Jane received.

I came to this story as a researcher with a background in career counselling. Traditionally, career counselling about youth mobility focuses on individual linear trajectories, participants' subjective conditions and institutional requirements (Kovacheva 2014). Recently, a more holistic approach has emerged, considering societal structures, sustainable development and social justice in career counselling (Yates and Hooley 2018; Hooley et al. 2018, 2019; van Halteren 2018) and mobility research (Cairns 2019; Cairns et al. 2017; van Geel and Mazzucato 2018). From this work we learn that terms such as 'youth mobility' and related practices such as 'learning mobility' that describe the geographical circulation of young people moving abroad for training, education or work are accompanied by hidden biases, which underplay certain risks and dangers.

These processes are traditionally understood as relatively unproblematic pathways to personal and professional development, self-realization and a demonstration of the power to influence one's own destiny (Kovacheva 2014). However, in reality, there are complex motivations and unpredictable outcomes involved, and young people from backgrounds characterized by social deprivation and poverty, and relative powerlessness, may experience spatialized transitions in a manner different to that of their more privileged counterparts. In particular, they may not have the social and economic resources, or the necessary knowledge, to successfully assemble a migration trajectory. Nevertheless, that these young people feel a strong mobility imperative, follow other family members abroad or rely on significant

---

J. B. van Halteren (✉)
OsloMet - Oslo Metropolitan University, Oslo, Norway
e-mail: jeavan@oslomet.no

others means they move regardless of their relative poverty, with a view to escaping what may feel like impossible to survive circumstances at home.

In this chapter, I consider the situation of Jane, arguing that her case encapsulates many of these tensions and also contributes to our understanding of youth mobility from the Global South to the Global North. This narrative also emphasises the importance of family and gender in making migration decisions and the importance of helping young people who experience problematic spatial transitions to find a sense of security in a new society.

The Life Before Migrating

On a cold winter's day in Oslo, the capital of Norway. Jane, a black woman in her twenties, shares her life story, taking me back to her childhood in a poor neighbourhood of Lagos, at that time the capital of Nigeria. Nigeria, for many years a British colony but independent since 1960, had an educational system quite similar to the British system, with nursery, primary and secondary school levels, followed by college and university. Pupils learned English from the age of three and received mother tongue education on the side. In Nigeria, education was voluntary but parents had to pay for books, uniforms, school fees and transportation. Today, this idea seems to upset the adult Jane: 'In Africa you see, there are some people that can't write. Can't write their names because they didn't go to school. Because their parents didn't have money.' These people need to learn a practical trade, for example, be a hairdresser or tailor, in order to survive. But Jane did not want to be like them. She wanted to study.

Jane grew up with her auntie, a close family friend, from the age of six. She had to work, care for children and do domestic work in order to receive an education. When Jane was twelve, her auntie moved to another part of the country. Jane had to follow along and continue her education at a new school. She was determined to finish and then start studying at university but dropped out after two years. The adult Jane explains this to be a result of several factors. For instance, her auntie did not pay wages, something Jane perceived as unfair. 'No, she wasn't treating me good and I was not getting what I wanted.' Her auntie's chores had to be finished before school, resulting in Jane often being late or not finishing homework since she did not have enough time. The school counsellor gave her a choice: attend school or stay at home. Jane wanted to go to school but felt she had to prioritize work: 'I had to sell, sell yeah. I lived with her to sell. Instead of going to school, I had to start selling.' One year later, at the age of fifteen, Jane decided to go back to school: 'I decided NO, I will not, I need to go to school!' Her stepfather helped with registrations, so Jane could take the exams needed to apply for university. She passed the exams but could not apply for university due to lack of money. In addition, her father became ill and died. 'There's no money, it's very expensive. So, the money stopped all. I didn't have any hope again to go to school.'

Jane explains that she dreamt of university studies, was eager to become a businessperson and wanted to start her own business but was lacking money. At the age of seventeen, a female family friend offered to sponsor a trip to Greece, where Jane had connections. Jane gladly accepted, but the trip did not turn out as expected. 'I travelled from Nigeria to Greece, hmm (sighs)… it was really…. It was a VERY difficult life.' Upon arrival, Jane's sponsor immediately demanded reimbursement of travel expenses plus high interest. 'When I came to Greece, she asked me to pay back. But a BIG, BIG amount, she wanted more money. It got crazy, because it was too much.' As Jane reports:

> But it wasn't the right agreement. Before I came, she said something different and when I came to Greece, she said something different. But then, I was like NO! This was not our agreement! We had fights and quarrels and (hits the palm of her hand hard with her fist) many times.

This was the start of a very difficult period in Jane's life. At the age of seventeen, she wanted to study and thrive but was forced needed to sell sex and experienced threats, violence and police interrogation. Jane's retrospective description is very emotional, manifest in her body language: arched back, head down, hands laying limb on her lap, speaking very slowly, with a soft voice and many pauses, avoiding eye contact.

Studying Human Trafficking

Across the world, young people are encouraged to travel abroad for work, education or training purposes, the incentives being increased international experience, expanded horizons, networks and capital. Due to the unequal distribution of mobility opportunities, related to socio-economic background, age and/or gender, some young people are particularly unable to travel in safe condition (see also Clemente 2021, in this book). This is the case with Jane. She wanted to travel. Jane was not abducted but trusted the female sponsor and accepted her offer to travel in Europe where the conditions established changed by configuring what can be described as trafficking.

Norway, where I conducted fieldwork, is not a member of the European Union but is described as both a 'destination' and 'transit' country for victims, mostly from Eastern Europe and Nigeria. Norway has ratified the so-called Palermo Protocol and the Council of Europe's Convention on action against trafficking in human beings. In 2015 Norway was also one of the countries that adopted the 2030 Agenda for Sustainable Development and its seventeen goals (SDGs). In short, this means that the Norwegian government has promised to mobilize efforts to fight and prevent human trafficking, to fight inequalities and end all forms of poverty.

I contacted Norwegian public services and NGOs, hoping to find gatekeepers that would lead me to potential participants. I interviewed several professionals and volunteers in NGOs and public services about their representations of human trafficking while searching for the 'invisible' survivors. Wanting to be respectful and cautious, I planned to use as little of their time as possible. The gatekeepers expressed interest in my project but did not grant me access: 'they are too traumatized to talk to you. We can handle this. The last thing they need is career counselling.'

This project received no funding, and after several months without success I was about to give up but revised my information letters and decided to make one last effort, sending two emails to Kirkens Bymisjon and Marita Stiftelsen, both Christian NGOs providing shelter for victims of human trafficking. Kirkens Bymisjon asked, 'What's in it for them?' and suggested I should meet former drug addicts, in need for work inclusion, instead. This resulted in a trial project where I could test my career conversations inspired by Savickas' (2011, 2013) Life Design and the use of visual conversation starters, for example, the SØT-model by Kversøy and Hartviksen (2018).

Marita Stiftelsen invited me to visit their women's group, allowing me to only observe until the women would deem me safe enough to approach. This affected my research design in a dramatic way: I had to do non-participatory observation, producing written and visual field notes, for a long time, until the women invited me to participate in meals and conversations on personal and religious topics. I had to invest time in building relationships and prove myself worthy. I visited this group weekly and had individual conversations with group members over a period of several months. When they heard I was a professional career counsellor they asked, almost offended, 'What took you so long? We need your help!' This was in direct contrast to what the gatekeepers had told me. The women's trust enabled me to have personal, in-depth conversations about life and career development, followed by 'member check,' resulting in narratives of vocational mobility, careers and life course development. The fieldwork ended with a creative group workshop, using collage techniques and 'author check,' resulting in participants' 'self-wish-images.' The collected and produced data was transcribed. Visual images were analysed with techniques inspired by Mannay (2016) and Stickley (2012) and the text analysed with Carol Gilligan's listening guide (Gilligan et al. 2003, Gilligan and Eddy 2017) containing four phases:

1. Listen for the plot. Read several times and find the action (what happens where, when, why and with whom), metaphors, themes, contradictions and silence. Find the socio-cultural context for the story (then and now) and be aware of your own responses (relationship, emotions and understanding).
2. Create I-poems. Read several times, listen to the rhythm and 'hear' how the storyteller (sub)consciously talks about herself, to capture what is not directly mentioned but in fact is the core of the message told. Underline sentences starting with 'I' (connected to a verb and relevant words) to find 'phrases.' Place these (in same order as in the story told) under each other, like phrases in a poem (I-poems). Compare these to reveal themes, (dis)harmony or shifts.
3. Listen for contrapuntal voices. Read several times, listen for distinct voices, one at a time and marked with one colour, to discover if one expression is marked

several times. To find and choose two different, unique 'voices,' connected and heard simultaneously. Find out if they (dis)harmonize, oppose or contradict each other. Identify and sort several 'threads' which are related to your research question(s).
4. Compose analysis. The previous three phases create a 'chain of evidence.' Material is gathered, presented and discussed in light of the research questions.

Childhood Memories with Pippi and Troll

These unusual methods gave me access to other hidden mobility stories: one from Jane's childhood and one from her more recent life in Oslo. They illustrate challenges in youth mobility related to the Sustainable Development Goals, the fight against poverty and inequality in particular. Jane's story holds many contrapuntal voices but I chose two, naming them (associated with Scandinavia) Pippi (Longstocking) saying, 'I want to be myself, to realize my own dreams' (spoken with high volume, pitch and pace, laughter and lively body language. Markers: I will, shall, dream, wish, like, want to), and Troll saying, 'I need to do my duty, to meet others' needs' (spoken slowly, with low volume, almost whispered, long pauses and passive body language. Markers: shall, need, should (not), duty, responsibility, punishment).

Jane grew up without her biological (Greek) father, but with her mother, who remarried and had more children. The home soon became too small for the family of ten, all hungry and in need of food, shelter and education. At age six, Jane was sent to live with her 'auntie,' who she explained was not an actual blood relative.

> I still lived with my mother and stepfather
> I left, after some years
> I left, it is not
> I wouldn't say, it's not like a house-help
> I had to move from my family to live with my auntie
> I was about 6–7 years
> No, I was 6 years
> I was 6 years old
> I was but,
> I was like, needed to have my mother
> I had to move out, go to school, could benefit from my auntie
> I-poem #1

This I-poem reflects a particular part of Jane's story that left a deep impression on me. She talked slowly, with low volume, many sighs and pauses. I could almost feel the little girl's pain. We can hear Pippi reminding us 'I needed to have my mother,' but also Troll demanding to be heard 'I had to move out,' almost defending her parents' decision to send her away. This was, to my knowledge, the first time Jane prioritized other people's needs, but the adult storyteller Jane adds quickly (interpreted as self-efficacy) 'I could benefit from my auntie.' We may assume little Jane was looking forward to living with auntie (who had less children and probably more food than her parents did) and to attend school (which she liked very much). The adult Jane retrospectively knows it was not going to be a happy family visit but rather a life where her needs were seldom met. But Jane's mother was in a precarious situation, and in many cultures, collective family needs may trump individual personal needs. Little Jane did not make a mobility choice, her parents did. She could have refused and run away, but I interpreted the situation as such that she wanted to be loyal and obey. I have no substantial evidence to claim Jane was sold, but her story gives evidence of poverty, hunger and child labour. These are past, current and future global challenges for youth mobility and addressed in the UN Sustainable Development Goals.

Jane was allowed to go to school, but before she could start walking the long road, she had to take care of auntie's two (later four) children and help in the house and the bakery. Auntie baked and Jane sold bread, cakes and something called Poof Poof. 'When you put it in the frying oil it goes POOF, it gets BIG, and that's why they call it Poof Poof.' Sometimes Jane felt lucky when allowed to eat leftovers. From an early age, she dreamt of being a businessperson:

> My mother would say: 'I hope you succeed in your business, because when you were a kid, you would pick up some things and would look… hmmm, who could buy that from me?' I loved to sell things. She says I was like 1-2-3 years and I did that. I don't even remember, but business has always been me!

And despite working long hours for auntie, the long walking distance to school and the homework, Jane always looked impeccable and excelled at school. She liked to compete with her best friend to be the best in all subjects.

This episode portrays both the ambitious, individualist Jane who likes to excel and the responsible, conscientious child who performs triple labour: shop-keeping, homework and domestic work. Despite her young age, Jane apparently mastered her complicated life, but it must have been exhausting for her to juggle so many roles. I assume her mother's words (positive feedback from a significant other) and positive experiences from the bakery strengthened Jane's self-efficacy to master selling, which led her to identify with the business world.

The young Jane dreamt of work and well-being. Her story illustrates the challenges many children and young people face today, based upon cultural and contextual (gender) inequalities. They do not have the luxury to make 'career choices.' Instead, they experience happenstance (Krumboltz and Levin 2010; Krumboltz et al. 2013) and are forced by circumstances, fate or faith to undertake mobility in order to survive (van Halteren 2018). Middle and lower class youth interpret 'decent work' and 'well-being' differently. Work, in this case job/occupation, and well-being pose challenges for those promoting mobility programmes and scholarships as a means of reducing inequality.

Love, Lies and the Longing to Belong

As previously described, Jane's ambitions led her to Greece, where she experienced life as a struggle. She proclaims herself one of the lucky ones who managed to flee and meet a man in church who wanted to marry her. After a traditional wedding in Nigeria they returned to Greece, and at age twenty Jane gave birth to a little baby girl. She believed her dream had come true. Two years later, her husband left her a single mom, unemployed and with a toddler, and no money for food or diapers. People around said Jane needed to find a new man but she believed God could fix her marriage. This part of her life is full of contrasts and strong emotions, ranging from euphoria to desperation, freedom and belonging to loneliness. From being cared for, to the need to care for others. Jane wondered how she could survive in a strange country with high unemployment rates. 'It was a difficult time for me; I did have no choice but to send her to Africa. Continue my life.' The only solution, according to Jane, was to send her little girl away, to her big sister, who had children of her own, so both could survive.

> I did not have a house
> I did not have money to feed
> I was in Greece, and Greece is not like Norway
> I tried…
> I sent her to Africa
> When I lived in Greece
> I separated from the father
> I could not take care of her
> I had to stand on my own feet
> I sent her back
> I remember
> I sent my daughter home, Oh my God
> I could not even afford money for her pampers
> I-poem #2

This episode made a deep impression on me. Not caused by the words, but by her low, almost whispering and sighing voice, hands on her lap, head bent down. This I-poem illustrates how happenstance, unexpected life experiences and circumstances lead to mobility. Jane longed to succeed as mother, spouse and businessperson but hit unexpected systemic obstacles beyond her control. Greece was in an economic crisis with high unemployment rates and no social security, as in Norway. This poem relates to poem #1, where we can hear Pippi and Troll, but here they are barely heard.

According to Jane's childhood experiences and cultural thought pattern, she had no choice but to send her beloved child to her beloved family. In my opinion, Jane's choice was not a selfish act based on a need for self-realization but an act of care based on the urge to show compassion, to nurture relationships. In the face of adversity Jane chooses to prioritize others' needs. It must have been extremely painful to do so, but it might be understood as such that she was willing to sacrifice everything for 'The Other,' to suffer in solitude to save her daughter. 'The wisdom of love. A skin turned inside out' (Lévinas 2003: xxxiv).

The 'Destination' Country

'And then life begins. Hard life. It was tough... it got worse, yes it got worse.' Jane had no home, no money and no food. In Greece, nobody was handing out free food or sanitary products. 'It was really tough. When I say tough, I mean really, really tough!' She still had hopes and dreams to succeed and was, according to Jane, saved by her network. Her older sister, taking care of Jane's daughter, sent money, food and products for Jane to sell, and she was given some odd jobs. In 2012, Jane met a new Nigerian, who felt sorry for her and suggested she join him on his trip to Norway. He had never been there but had heard it was the world's best country and was 'selling' her his dream.

> I said GO! If you go there and it is nice, come to pick me up! (Laughs). I did not want to go and start to suffer again... because, oh my God... Sometimes... Really ... oh my God... This is really ...Good to give God thanks! I know... there were problems, even now, but when I look back, I know now that I am more, better now, than before. Really!

Jane told him to leave, but he insisted. She was frustrated, did not know what to do, felt useless and unable to take a decision. This episode shows her strength and resilience but also vulnerability and uncertainty; her self-efficacy having been battered we can still see glimpses of her intentional dream to be a businessperson. Jane loved to sell, showed a willingness to take risks, see and seize opportunities to earn money, to master challenging transitions and to take decisions. These are important career competences, but it is unclear if she was aware of them at that time. Something that becomes very clear during our conversation is that Jane, in describing retrospectively, discovers the personal inner and external outer factors that have influenced her life and career development and complex mobility patterns.

This is the first time Jane mentions God. Her story reveals several important relationships, a network with significant others that helped her to survive, and others, who pretended to be friendly helpers but turned out to be selfish conmen and traffickers. Jane was uncertain. She did not want to go to Norway but did not want to suffer in Greece either. She gives in when the man turns up once more. 'He bought a ticket. And I followed him. To Norway.' He told her he had friends in Norway, but no one came to meet them. They were in Oslo. Homeless, unemployed and poor, they ended up sleeping in the streets and the railway station.

> At the train station
> I was sleeping on a chair and security came and told me to go
> I knew him through my girlfriend
> I went fighting him in Oslo city
> I came to Norway
> I fought a lot

I had to fight a lot
I was afraid
I was scared of men
I-poem #3

Life in Norway was not as expected. Jane had been lured again. The first time, a female 'sponsor' promised her opportunities in Europe. This time it was a male 'friend of a friend.' Life in Greece was hard. Jane expected life in Norway to be better. She saw and seized the opportunity to have an improved life. This poem describes her loneliness and fear, walking the streets in a foreign country, with a strange language and unknown culture, far away from the safety of her own loved ones. One night, Jane met some girls who took her to the shelter in Marita Stiftelsen, where she received food and clean clothes. Little did she know that this place would become her new family. Walking the streets of Oslo, she met a man who promised her the world and she moved in with him. Considering Jane's experiences with lies, abuse, trafficking and betrayal, one would expect her not to. Coincidences and circumstances disturbed and challenged her to act. Jane had found another opportunity for a 'good life,' interpreted as 'heaven sent.' We tend to frown upon the spiritual dimension and assume our rational thoughts and communication style to be universal but forget that millions of people use horoscopes, tarot cards, Holy Scriptures, prayer or god(s) as career counsellors and youth mobility advisors. In Jane's case, God was both a significant other and 'The Other' (Lévinas 2003).

Shortly after Jane moved in with him, her sister and brother-in-law died, and she had to provide not only for her own daughter but her sister's children as well, seven in total. The Norwegian man had a job and supported Jane and the Nigerian children for several years. Jane was cared for and did not have to work, but she got bored sitting at home doing nothing. At Marita Stiftelsen she was allowed to volunteer in the thrift shop and café, learn Norwegian and receive help to understand the Norwegian welfare system. After a while, Jane started earning her own money and regained her independence. Today, she admits it is painful to look back and describe retrospectively but also inspiring to see how far she has come. 'I do tell people stories, my story, to say in this life: be patient. We need to trust God, have the faith, this too must pass. Believe that and move, yeah, move. If I was in the bottom ground, God is lifting me up. Gradually.' Her faith is a beacon for her and might explain why she chose the title of her life story to be 'With God, all things are possible!'

At the end of our career conversations, when asked what she would have changed in life if possible, Jane was quick to answer. She would have gone back to school and studied, which she could not do due to lack of funding. Money is still important to her, but freedom of choice, being allowed to work and do something she likes, is even more important. Today she is thrilled about her small position in a local café. 'I love it! I love it so much! I love selling, I attend to customers, I love it so much!' Ten years have passed in search of a 'good life,' but Jane believes she will succeed as a businessperson, even if it might take ten more years of education, training and work.

Conclusion: Crossing the Lines

Jane crossed lines in many ways, geographically, mentally, morally and spiritually, creating complex mobility patterns (as opposed to the conventional, linear trajectories). Despite a life in poverty, child labour, rejection, abuse and betrayal, losing everything but her life, she proclaims God has kept her safe. In doing so, she emphasises the importance of affect, in contrast to the traditional academic emphasis on reason. As an academic researcher, I was challenged to cross lines as well, to leave my comfort zone in their environment. I had to question academic discourse, the traditional definition of youth mobility, career counselling and research, and take a physical and hermeneutic journey, in order to be able to humanize the numbers and describe Jane's story in 'The sound of silence' (van Halteren 2018).

Based on Jane's story I argue that current and future challenges in youth mobility relate to systemic and individual elements: societal and cultural beliefs, time, personal conditions, ambitions and self-efficacy. We tend to forget other crucial elements: the emotional and spiritual dimensions (affect) and the power of words and relationships (interaction), which are significant influencers on life and career development and youth mobility. In order to reach the UN Sustainable Development Goals, policymakers, stakeholders and professionals need to cross lines. Inclusivity cannot be passive. We need to leave the office and go out to find the people who are marginalized. We need to leave comfort zones and be willing to cooperate interdisciplinarily. We need to move beyond conventional categories and expand our definitions of youth mobility and social inclusion.

In arguing this, I draw on Kovacheva (2014) and Cairns et al. (2017) describing the dilemma in the use of the concepts 'social inclusion' and 'social exclusion' in policy decision-making (Cairns et al. 2017: 169–170). Social inclusion (relating to everyone, creating social cohesion) is challenging but of great quantitative importance, while social exclusion (relating to small groups of people, politically designated as constituting societal concern) has a deep qualitative impact. In order to cross the line and expand definitions, we need to be clear on these dual aspirations within the policy framework. 'Addressing social exclusion needs to take into account nuances in policy decision-making, requiring evidence and intelligent decisions rather than emotions as a rationale for action' (Cairns et al. 2017: 170).

Jane's story gives evidence of a kind of youth mobility that can be framed as trafficking, calling for action on several levels: micro, meso, exo and macro (Bronfenbrenner 2005). Young people need caring peers, parents and teachers and should know where to get professional help. Institutions and organizations need to secure quality and safety control of advertised mobility trajectories and provide adequate information to potential applicants about fake recruitment and the danger of trafficking. More research is needed but career counselling and youth mobility can be used to reach certain societal goals, provided mobility funding, safe environments and training opportunities are made accessible to all (regardless of gender, sexual orientation and religious, political or socio- economic background).

Acknowledgements I wish to acknowledge the staff and volunteers at Marita Stiftelsen and Kirkens Bymisjon (non-profit NGOs) who, with little or no funding, reach out to people in need. They introduced me to (former) substance abusers, sex-workers and victims of modern slavery, one of them being 'Jane.' I am very grateful to her and the others who allowed me to hear, listen to and share their 'voices,' which are seldom heard in scholarly literature. Indeed, their contribution was essential to this chapter.

References

Bronfenbrenner, U. (2005). *Making human beings human: Bioecological perspectives on human development*. Thousand Oaks, CA: Sage Publications.
Cairns, D. (2019). Researching social inclusion in student mobility: Methodological strategies in studying the Erasmus programme. *International Journal of Research and Method in Education, 42*(2), 137–147.
Cairns, D., Cuzzocrea, V., Briggs, D., & Veloso, L. (2017). *The consequences of mobility: Reflexivity, social inequality and the reproduction of precariousness in highly qualified migration*. Basingstoke: Palgrave Macmillan.
Clemente, M. (2021). 'I was not prepared to go to Spain': Work mobility of young people at the margins in Portugal. In D. Cairns (Ed.), *The Palgrave handbook of youth mobility and educational migration*. Basingstoke: Palgrave Macmillan.
Gilligan, C., & Eddy, J. (2017). Listening as a path to psychological discovery: An introduction to the Listening Guide. *Perspectives on Medical Education, 6*(2), 76–81. https://doi.org/10.1007/s40037-017-0335-3.
Gilligan, C., Spencer, R., Weinberg, M.K., & Bertsch, T. (2003). On the listening guide: A voice-centered relational method. In J. R. P.M. Camic, & L. Yardley (Eds.) (Ed.), Qualitative research in psychology: Expanding perspectives in methodology and design (pp. 157–172). American Psychological Association Press.
Hooley, T., Sultana, R. G., & Thomsen, R. (2018). *Career guidance for social justice: Contesting neoliberalism: Volume 1: Context, theory and research*. London: Routledge.
Hooley, T., Sultana, R. G., & Thomsen, R. (2019). *Career guidance for emancipation: Reclaiming justice for the multitude*. New York: Routledge.
Kovacheva, S. (2014). *EU-CoE youth partnership policy sheet*. I.
Krumboltz, J. D., Foley, P. F., & Cotter, E. W. (2013). Applying the happenstance learning theory to involuntary career transitions. *Career Development Quarterly, 61*(1), 15–26.
Krumboltz, J. D., & Levin, A. S. (2010). *Luck is no accident: Making the most of happenstance in your life and career*. Atascadero, CA: Impact Publishers.
Kversøy, K. S., & Hartviksen, M. (2018). *Samarbeid og Konflikt: To Sider av Samme Sak: SØT-Modellen*. Bergen: Fagbokforl.
Lévinas, E. (2003). *Humanism of the other*. Urbana, IL: University of Illinois Press.
Mannay, D. (2016). *Visual, narrative and creative research methods: Application, reflection and ethics*. London: Routledge.
Savickas, M. L. (2011). *Career counseling*. Washington, DC: American Psychological Association.
Savickas, M. L. (2013). The 2012 Leona Tyler award address: Constructing careers—Actors, agents, and authors. *The Counseling Psychologist, 41*(4), 648–662.
Stickley, T. (2012). *Qualitative research in arts and mental health: Context, meanings and evidence*. Ross-on-Wye, UK: PCCS Books.
van Geel, J., & Mazzucato, V. (2018). Conceptualising youth mobility trajectories: Thinking beyond conventional categories. *Journal of Ethnic and Migration Studies, 44*(13), 2144–2162.
van Halteren, J. (2018). *Karriereveiledning for Inkludering: Utforskning av Karriereutviklingen hos Jane, som Overlevde Moderne Slaveri* [The sound of silence. Career counseling for inclusion: An exploration of career development in Jane, who survived modern slavery]. Kongsberg: Universitetet i Sørøst Norge.
Yates, J., & Hooley, T. (2018). Advising on career image: Perspectives, practice and politics. *British Journal of Guidance and Counselling, 46*(1), 27–38.

Chapter 39
Youth Mobility, Mental Health and Risky Behaviours

Giovanni Aresi, Elena Marta, and Simon C. Moore

Travelling abroad can bring many benefits for young people, including academic success, self-esteem, opportunities for international careers, intercultural competence and acquiring a more global perspective (Stone and Petrick 2013). However, the de-contextualization and re-contextualization into a different environment and culture that accompanies spatial mobility brings with it additional challenges during what might already be a turbulent time in the life course (Arnett 2005). Unpredictable social circumstances, language and cultural barriers, coupled with difficulties accessing healthcare and coping resources such as family and friends, have implications for a young person's mental health and may lead to engaging in problematic alcohol and drug use.

There is a robust relationship between poor mental health and other health concerns among young people, including substance abuse and sexual health (Whiteford et al. 2013). Epidemiological studies suggest that one out of every four to five young people in the general population will experience a common mental disorder episode at least once during their youth; five of the ten leading causes of disability-adjusted life years (DALY) in people aged 15 to 44 years are related to mental health (Patel et al. 2007). Young people are also exposed to alcohol-related harm: 25 per cent of 15–29-year-old male (and 10% of young female) mortality is attributable to alcohol (Anderson and Baumberg 2006). High volume alcohol consumption and drug abuse are further associated with academic failure, unintended pregnancy and sexually transmitted diseases (EMCDDA 2015), and when intoxicated by alcohol or other substances, young people, women in particular, face increased risk of sexual victimization (Abbey 2002; Krebs et al. 2009). This chapter discusses prominent theories

G. Aresi (✉) • E. Marta
Università Cattolica del Sacro Cuore, Milan, Italy
e-mail: giovanni.aresi@unicatt.it

S. C. Moore
Cardiff University, Wales, UK

© The Author(s), under exclusive license to Springer Nature Switzerland AG 2022
D. Cairns (ed.), *The Palgrave Handbook of Youth Mobility and Educational Migration*, https://doi.org/10.1007/978-3-030-99447-1_39

of and research into the connections between mobility, mental health and health behaviours among young people. The focus is on students in higher education, although research on international volunteers, expatriate workers and humanitarian aid workers will also be discussed.

Mental Health and Health Behaviours among Mobile Youth

Students in Higher Education

Being an international student compounds the stresses and strains associated with student life (Presbitero 2016); they may have lower satisfaction levels as well as lower positive affect and higher negative affect compared to the general student population (Hyun et al. 2007; Tidwell and Hanassab 2007; Hunley 2010). While many international students acculturate successfully, some struggle in adapting to the host country culture and language and may suffer social isolation, become frustrated by different academic systems and even experience racism and discrimination (Sawir et al. 2007; Iwamoto and Liu 2010; McKenna et al. 2017), as well as maladaptive psychological reactions and mental disorders that occur in response to transitioning from one culture to another (Presbitero 2016).

A recent literature review suggests different behavioural patterns between credit and degree mobility in regard to alcohol use (Aresi et al., 2016a). As the former may be academically motivated and many originate from countries (e.g., China, India) where alcohol and drug use is less prevalent compared to Western host countries (e.g., the United States and Europe), they are less likely to engage in excessive alcohol intake. Moreover, there is evidence that heavy drinking students may self-select into study abroad programmes (Pedersen et al. 2010a) because these programmes provide opportunities for increased socializing (Aresi et al. 2018). Once abroad, exchange students drink heavily, consuming up to twice as much alcohol during their study abroad experience compared to pre-departure levels (Aresi et al., 2016b; Aresi et al. 2019). In consequence, they experience health-related outcomes including injury, assaults, unprotected casual sex and sexual victimization (Hummer et al., 2010; Pedersen et al. 2014). However, this increase in alcohol use is time limited and typically returns to pre-departure levels when students return home (Pedersen et al. 2010b; Aresi et al. 2019).

The only study that has examined drug use longitudinally among study abroad students found no statistically meaningful change in illicit drug use (Aresi et al. 2019). Other studies have however identified sexual health issues in this population. For example, Australian and North American students from overseas have poor sexual health knowledge compared to local students (Burchard et al. 2011) and are at greater risk of sexual victimization (Flack Jr. et al. 2014). When students perceive the study abroad period more as a holiday and drink heavily, they are more prone to display greater disinhibition and engage in casual sex (Brown and Stephan 2013).

Volunteer, Migrant and Humanitarian Aid Workers

Young people can travel abroad as volunteers or seek training and employment opportunities. Although precise figures are missing, the international voluntary service has grown in significance (Sherraden et al. 2006). Opportunities include trips to join workcamps in other countries for a few weeks, young professionals spending one to two years sharing their knowledge and skills in less well-developed countries or students taking a year out from their studies to volunteer. There is no research on young volunteers' mental health and health behaviour, but studies have examined these issues among those who travel because of their occupation.

Traditionally, expatriate workers have been defined as individuals who move abroad on extended work assignments (Adams and van de Vijver 2015). A study in the United States found that these workers are at greater risk of mental health and substance use disorders (Truman et al. 2011). Similar to students who study abroad, they may face adjustment and acculturation difficulties, and studies have examined the role of the receiving cultural and organizational environment (Haslberger et al. 2013). The experience of early career self-initiated migrant workers has received less attention (Yijälä et al. 2012), and little is known on the specificities of the issues they may face.

One type of migrant worker is the international humanitarian aid worker, a relatively high proportion of whom are under 30 years of age (Cardozo et al. 2012). In addition to personal and professional challenges faced by all international travellers, they face a range of additional work-related stressors that include exposure to traumatic and life-threatening events that may adversely affect their mental health and well-being (Cardozo et al. 2012). For this reason, research has often examined mental health issues from a trauma perspective, demonstrating that direct and indirect exposure to traumatic events on the humanitarian field was associated with negative mental health outcomes, including symptoms of depression and posttraumatic stress disorder (see, e.g., Shah et al. 2007). Resilience, greater socio-cultural adaptation and social and organizational support have been identified as protective factors contributing to their psychological well-being (Eriksson et al. 2013; De Paul and Bikos 2015). Few studies in the literature have examined alcohol consumption (Jachens et al. 2016). Results are mixed and it is unclear whether there is an increase in alcohol consumption during missions.

Theories on the Connection Between Mobility, Mental Health and Health Behaviour

Major theories on the connection between cross-border mobility, mental health and health behaviour among youth touch on key elements of the travelling experience, such as acculturation and cross-cultural adaptation, situational disinhibition in a new environment and the effect of perceived social norms, offering opportunities for intervention development.

Acculturation Theories and Mental Health

Acculturation broadly refers to 'all the changes that arise following contact between individuals and groups of different cultural background' (Sam 2006: 11). These changes affect an individual's psychological well-being and social functioning. Psychological adaptation to the host culture refers to the more practical and behavioural aspects of adapting to a different lifestyle, traditions, values and norms, whereas socio-cultural adaptation refers to the emotional and psychological well-being aspects of adaptation, such as feeling out of place and culture shock—that is, maladaptive psychological reactions and mental disorders that occur in response to the transition from one cultural setting to another (Presbitero 2016). Acculturation has been conceptualized as a process influenced by specific cultural orientations, including attitudes and behaviour towards the host and country of origin cultures, and it requires the individual to cope with cultural challenges, including acculturative stressors (Ward and Geeraert 2016).

In terms of cultural orientation, there is evidence that integration or biculturalism, the capacity to integrate one's heritage culture with that of the host country, is positively associated with psychological and socio-cultural adaptation (Nguyen and Benet-Martínez 2013), whereas an increase in the dissimilarity between cultures has been linked to increased acculturative stress and lower psychological and social adaptation (Taušová et al. 2019). Protective factors include greater self-determined motivations to study abroad (Yang et al. 2018), appropriate coping responses (Demes and Geeraert 2015) and social support. For example, affiliation and stronger ties with other international students contribute to psychological adjustment because of the social and instrumental support they provide (Kashima and Loh 2006; Sobré-Denton 2011).

Acculturation and Alcohol and Drug Use

Two theoretical frameworks help conceptualize the connections between intercultural mobility, mental health and alcohol and drug use. According to the first, Social Stress Theory (Madsen 1964; Graves 1967), difficulties with the process of adaptation may result in the use of alcohol and drugs as a maladaptive coping strategy for mental health issues. This premise has received support from research on adolescents and young adult migrants (Ehlers et al. 2009) and study abroad students (Aresi et al., 2016a). For example, Russell et al. (2010) found that a minority of degree mobility students in Australia who were psychologically distressed were also involved in risk-taking behaviours that included alcohol and drug use. Because expatriate workers, and humanitarian aid workers in particular, are at greater risk for mental health and substance use disorders than their US counterparts (Truman et al. 2011; Jachens et al. 2016), this theory is likely to be applicable to this population, although there is no empirical evidence to support it.

A second theory concerns socio-cultural models of acculturation, having been used to describe alcohol use among Latino and Asian migrant populations in the United States (see Zemore 2007). The primary hypothesis is that migrants travel from countries were alcohol use is less prevalent compared to countries to which they travel. As they acculturate, they adopt the customs and habits of the host country. Research findings are mixed, however, suggesting that the relationship between adjustment abroad and drinking depends more on gender and migrants' culture of origin (Zemore 2007; Hendershot et al. 2008; Mills and Caetano 2012). When applying socio-cultural models to students who study abroad, a distinction between degree and credit mobility students is necessary. The former spend a considerable amount of time in host countries, have greater motivation to study, have more opportunities to interact with local people and are exposed to the host country and its traditions. This makes socio-cultural models more easily applicable to their situation than to that of short stayers.

An issue with this approach, however, is that it implies visitors are influenced by the drinking habits of local people through direct contact and exposure. This is problematic because many students remain segregated from the local student population and instead socialize in international student only groups (Sigalas 2010; McKenzie and Baldassar 2017). There are three social networks, each one with its own drinking norms, that students might join: compatriots, other students who study abroad and host nationals (Bochner et al. 1977; Rienties and Nolan 2014). It is unclear which network is most influential. For example, students' acculturation orientation has been found to interact with perceived drinking norms. In a study on US students, those who made little attempt to interact with local residents were influenced by their perceptions of how much their study abroad peers drank, and drank the most (Pedersen et al. 2011). This is consistent with results of other studies in Europe suggesting that engagement with local people and culture may be protective, because they were not adhering to the heavy drinking lifestyle of the typical study abroad student (Ferrari et al. 2017; Aresi et al. 2019).

Theories on Situational Disinhibition

As there are similarities between the behaviour of tourists when on holiday and short-term exchange students (Brown and Stephan 2013), theories drawn from travel and tourism literature contribute to our understanding of the changes in health behaviour among youth who travel. On holiday, tourists enjoy a degree of anonymity and may feel they are in a liminal state that makes acceptable behaviour that would otherwise be considered unacceptable in the home environment (Carr 2002; Bauer and McKercher 2003; Pearce 2005). Situational disinhibition fuels heavier drinking and drug use, which in turn perpetuates disinhibition and encourages extreme behaviour (Josiam et al. 1998; Bellis et al. 2007; Bellis et al. 2009). There is evidence that when young people perceive their time overseas as a holiday, and they have very little academic interest and a short amount of time abroad, they are more likely to display greater disinhibition, drink heavily and engage in casual sex (Brown and Stephan 2013; Aresi et al. 2017). Results of studies on European and American credit mobility students suggest that alcohol use levels tend to return to pre-departure levels when students return home, some even drink less (Pedersen et al. 2010b; Aresi et al. 2019), thus providing further support for the situational disinhibition hypothesis.

Social Norms Theories

According to Social Norms Theory (Borsari and Carey 2003), perceptions about relevant peer groups' drinking predict alcohol use. Beliefs about what constitutes 'normal' alcohol use for similar people and what is acceptable behaviour to others are both influential. The more an individual has close contact and identifies with a reference group, the more he or she is affected by these perceived group norms. However, young people typically misperceive norms, over-estimating the amount of alcohol others consume. Greater levels of misperception have been consistently shown to be associated with heavier alcohol use (McAlaney and McMahon 2007).

The popular social representation of study abroad experiences as a 'party' period (Aresi et al. 2018) may contribute to students' misperceptions of peers' normative alcohol use, encouraging heavy drinking students to self-select into study abroad exchange programmes (Pedersen et al. 2010a). The effect of normative beliefs of study abroad peers has further been associated with an increase in alcohol use as students transition into the host country (Pedersen et al. 2009; Pedersen et al. 2011), although these results have not been confirmed in European samples (Aresi et al. 2019).

Interventions for International Mobile Youth

While interventions have been delivered with the intention of preserving the health and well-being of travelling youth, evaluation research is limited, particularly for non-student populations. Interventions can be broadly grouped into the provision of mental health services, psycho-educational and social interventions to promote acculturation, and work specifically focused on reducing alcohol use. Each group addresses risk and protective factors as indicated by the theories we have described above.

Mental Health Services

Many universities have free at point of delivery or relatively low-cost mental health and counselling services for their students. Utilization rates are however thought to be low in the general student population, with under-utilization particularly acute among international students (Raunic and Xenos 2008). For example, an Australian study showed that 80 per cent of international students who perceived the need for counselling did not engage with a service (Russell et al. 2008). Language and cultural barriers including students' perceived stigma for mental health issues and preferences for seeking help from family or friends over outside sources may explain this (Raunic and Xenos 2008). Moreover, counselling services may not be equipped to respond to the needs of international students (Tidwell and Hanassab 2007). There is a lack of research evaluating counselling interventions for international students (Yakunina et al. 2010).

Psycho-educational and Social Interventions to Promote Acculturation

Adjusting to the host culture and academic system is key to students' well-being. Interventions that enhance international students' adjustment have been designed. These can be grouped into psycho-educational and social interventions. The former aim to enhance students' social skills through classroom activities; for example, the Excellence in Experiential Learning and Leadership (EXCELL) programme is a group programme that is effective in promoting intercultural social competencies, such as group participation, social self-efficacy when communicating and working with those from other cultures, and increasing time spent with people from other cultures (Mak and Buckingham 2007). Results of the pilot evaluation of the Strengths, Transitions, Adjustments, and Resilience (STAR) programme, a brief group psychological intervention to enhance positive coping strategies in international students, showed that participants' psychological adaptation and coping self-efficacy significantly increased following the intervention (Smith and Khawaja 2014). Other examples of effective interventions are Elemo and Türküm (2019) eight-session cognitive behavioural psycho-educational programme and Brunsting et al.'s (2018) semester-long academic and cultural transition curriculum.

Other interventions include peer pairing programmes in which international students are paired with trained local students and encouraged to meet regularly. There is some evidence that these programmes foster the establishment of relationships between native and international students and improve adjustment, including psychological adaptation, and lessen acculturative stress (Abe et al. 1998; Jon 2013; Tolman 2017; Thomson and Esses 2016). Lastly, Sakurai et al.'s (2010) 'Bus Excursion' recreational programme strengthens students' social ties with locals and increases their positive orientation towards the host culture but does not improve students' psychological well-being and adjustment.

Alcohol-specific Interventions

There is only one published evaluation of an intervention aimed at reducing alcohol misuse among study abroad students (Pedersen et al. 2017). There are two components: brief online Personalized Feedback to correct misperceptions of country-specific native adult drinking norms and personalized Sojourner Adjustment Feedback that provides students with tips, strategies and resources to foster positive adjustment to and engagement with the host culture. Both intervention components are administered to students before they depart to the host country. Results show that only the former component is effective, and among lighter drinkers only. This may reflect the intervention's limited intensity, sending feedback and tips by email, and the difficulty of social norms interventions to correct young peoples' alcohol misperceptions generally (Foxcroft et al. 2015).

Conclusions

In this chapter we have provided an overview of the research on the connection between youth mobility, mental health and health behaviours. It has been emphasized that, despite its many benefits, travelling abroad has implications for mental health, alcohol and drug use and sexual behaviour. However, the literature on study abroad students, migrant and international aid work and volunteers is both limited and fragmented, bringing difficulties in identifying cross-cutting features in these populations. In addition, while there are a number of studies on students who study abroad, little is known on the realities of volunteers and workers.

The theories and interventions we have described look at the connection between health and spatial mobility from different perspectives and suggest practical strategies on how to preserve the health and well-being of travelling youth. While there is a relatively robust literature on mental health services for international students, the evaluative research on acculturation and alcohol-related psycho-educational and social interventions remains limited. Acculturation theories focus on the difficulties of the intercultural experience of travelling to a different country and culture and the consequences for the individual's health and psychological well-being. We have offered examples of how these theories have informed the development of interventions for young travellers spending extended periods overseas. The theories on situational disinhibitions, instead, appear to be better suited in explaining the behaviour of those who plan to spend a relatively short amount of time abroad. The feeling of being on holiday accentuates disinhibition, resulting in heavy drinking and casual sex. Social norms theories underscore the importance of misbeliefs for 'normal' behaviour and the risks that are involved when study abroad programmes are perceived as an opportunity for partying and heavy drinking.

In sum, the connection between spatial mobility and health is a growing challenge. It questions the assumption that international youth mobility is positive for young people and their receiving communities and countries. At the European and national level, this relates to return on investments towards the achievement of aims of EU learning mobility programmes. At a global level, it has implications for any kind of spatial mobility, including that of young migrants. These issues need to be addressed by policymakers and the international higher education system to safeguard young people's health, reduce costs for healthcare systems, and achieve the best potential of the experience abroad.

References

Abbey, A. (2002). Alcohol-related sexual assault: A common problem among college students. *Journal of Studies on Alcohol, s14*, 118–128.

Abe, J., Talbot, D. M., & Geelhoed, R. J. (1998). Effects of a peer program on international student adjustment. *Journal of College Student Development, 39*(6), 539–547.

Adams, B. G., & van de Vijver, F. J. R. (2015). The many faces of expatriate identity. *International Journal of Intercultural Relations, 49*, 322–331.

Anderson, P., & Baumberg, B. (2006). *Alcohol in Europe: A public health perspective*. London: Institute of Alcohol Studies.

Aresi, G., Moore, S. & Marta, E. (2016a). Drinking, drug use and related consequences among university students completing study abroad experiences: A systematic review. *Substance Use & Misuse, 51*(14), pp 1888–904.

Aresi, G., Moore, S., & Marta, E. (2016b). Italian credit mobility students significantly increase their alcohol intake, risky drinking and related consequences during the study abroad experience. *Alcohol and Alcoholism, 51*(6), 723–726.

Aresi, G., Alfieri, S., Lanz, M., Marta, E., & Moore, S. (2017). Development and validation of a Multidimensional Motivations to Study Abroad Scale (MMSAS) among European Credit Mobility Students. *International Journal of Intercultural Relations, 63*, 128–134.

Aresi, G., Fattori, F., Pozzi, M., & Moore, S. C. (2018). I am going to make the most out of it! Italian university credit mobility students' social representations of alcohol use during study abroad experiences. *Journal of Health Psychology, 23*(13), 1649–1658.

Aresi, G., Moore, S. C., Berridge, D. M., & Marta, E. (2019). A longitudinal study of European Students' alcohol use and related behaviors as they travel abroad to study. *Substance Use and Misuse, 54*(7), 1167–1177.

Arnett, J. J. (2005). The developmental context of substance use in emerging adulthood. *Journal of Drug Issues, 35*(2), 235–254.

Bauer, T. G., & McKercher, B. (2003). *Sex and tourism: Journeys of romance, love and lust*. Binghamton, NY: The Haworth Press.

Bellis, M. A., Hughes, K. E., Calafat, A., Juan, M., & Schnitzer, S. (2009). Relative contributions of holiday location and nationality to changes in recreational drug taking behaviour: a natural experiment in the Balearic Islands. *European Addiction Research, 15*(2), 78–86.

Bellis, M. A., Hughes, K. E., Dillon, P., Copeland, J., & Gates, P. (2007). Effects of backpacking holidays in Australia on alcohol, tobacco and drug use of UK residents. *BMC Public Health, 7*, 1.

Bochner, S., McLeod, B., & Lin, A. (1977). Friendship patterns of overseas students: A functional model. *International Journal of Psychology, 12*, 277–297.

Borsari, B., & Carey, K. B. (2003). Descriptive and injunctive norms in college drinking: A meta-analytic integration. *Journal of Studies on Alcohol, 64*, 331–341.

Brown, L., & Stephan, Y. S. (2013). Anonymous and uninhibited: Sexual encounters during the international sojourn. *Journal of Tourism and Cultural Change, 11*(1-2), 35–47.

Brunsting, N. C., Smith, A. C., & Zachry, C. E. (2018). An academic and cultural transition course for international students: Efficacy and socio-emotional outcomes. *Journal of International Students, 8*(4), 1497–1521.

Burchard, A., Laurence, C., & Stocks, N. (2011). Female international students and sexual health: A qualitative study into knowledge. *beliefs and attitudes. Australian Family Physician, 40*(10), 817.

Cardozo, B. L., Crawford, C. G., Eriksson, C., Zhu, J., Sabin, M., Ager, A., Foy, D., Snider, L., Scholte, W., & Kaiser, R. (2012). Psychological distress, depression, anxiety, and burnout among international humanitarian aid workers: a longitudinal study. *PloS one, 7*(9), e44948.

Carr, N. (2002). A comparative analysis of the behaviour of domestic and international young tourists. *Tourism Management, 23*, 321–325.

De Paul, N. F., & Bikos, L. H. (2015). Perceived organizational support: A meaningful contributor to expatriate development professionals' psychological well-being. *International Journal of Intercultural Relations, 49*, 25–32.

Demes, K. A., & Geeraert, N. (2015). The highs and lows of a cultural transition: A longitudinal analysis of sojourner stress and adaptation across 50 countries. *Journal of Person Social Psychology, 109*(2), 316–337.

Ehlers, C. L., Gilder, D. A., Criado, J. R., & Caetano, R. (2009). Acculturation stress, anxiety disorders, and alcohol dependence in a select population of young adult Mexican Americans. *Journal of Addiction Medicine, 3*(4), 227–233.

Elemo, A. S., & Türküm, A. S. (2019). The effects of psychoeducational intervention on the adjustment, coping self-efficacy and psychological distress levels of international students in Turkey. *International Journal of Intercultural Relations, 70*, 7–18.

EMCDDA. (2015). *European drug report 2015: trends and developments*. Lisbon: EMCDDA.

Eriksson, C. B., Lopes Cardozo, B., Foy, D. W., Sabin, M., Ager, A., Snider, L., Scholte, W. F., Kaiser, R., Olff, M., Rijnen, B., Gotway Crawford, C., Zhu, J., & Simon, W. (2013). Predeployment mental health and trauma exposure of expatriate humanitarian aid workers: Risk and resilience factors. *Traumatology, 19*(1), 41–48.

Ferrari, V., Aresi, G., & Marta, E. (2017). Acculturazione e consumo di alcolici negli studenti italiani in mobilità internazionale. Uno studio mixed methods. *Psicologia della Salute, 3*, 25–51.

Flack, W. F., Jr., Kimble, M. O., Campbell, B. E., Hopper, A. B., Peterca, O., & Heller, E. J. (2014). Sexual assault victimization among female undergraduates during study abroad: A single campus survey study. *Journal of Interpersonal Violence, 30*(20), 3453–3566.

Foxcroft, D. R., Moreira, M. T., Almeida Santimano, N. M., & Smith, L. A. (2015). Social norms information for alcohol misuse in university and college students. *The Cochrane Database of Systematic Reviews, 12*, Cd006748.

Graves, T. D. (1967). Acculturation, access, and alcohol in a tri-ethnic community. *American Anthropologist, 69*(3-4), 306–321.

Haslberger, A., Brewster, C., & Hippler, T. (2013). The dimensions of expatriate adjustment. *Human Resource Management, 52*(3), 333–351.

Hendershot, C. S., Dillworth, T. M., Neighbors, C., & George, W. H. (2008). Differential effects of acculturation on drinking behavior in Chinese- and Korean-American college students. *Journal of Studies on Alcohol and Drugs, 69*(1), 121–128.

Hummer, J. F., Pedersen, E. R., Mirza, T., & Labrie, J. W. (2010). Factors Associated With General and Sexual Alcohol-Related Consequences: An Examination of College Students Studying Abroad. *Journal of Student Affairs Research and Practice, 47*(4), 421–438.

Hunley, H. A. (2010). Students' functioning while studying abroad: The impact of psychological distress and loneliness. *International Journal of Intercultural Relations, 34*(4), 386–392.

Hyun, J., Quinn, B., Madon, T., & Lustig, S. (2007). Mental health need, awareness, and use of counseling services among international graduate students. *Journal of American College Health, 56*(2), 109–118.

Iwamoto, D. K., & Liu, W. M. (2010). The impact of racial identity, ethnic identity, Asian values and race-related stress on Asian Americans and Asian international college students' psychological well-being. *Journal of Counseling Psychology, 57*(1), 79–91.

Jachens, L., Houdmont, J., & Thomas, R. (2016). Effort–reward imbalance and heavy alcohol consumption among humanitarian aid workers. *Journal of Studies on Alcohol and Drugs, 77*(6), 904–913.

Jon, J.-E. (2013). Realizing internationalization at home in Korean higher education: Promoting domestic students' interaction with international students and intercultural competence. *Journal of Studies in International Education, 17*(4), 455–470.

Josiam, B. M., Hobson, J. S. P., Dietrich, U. C., & Smeaton, G. (1998). An analysis of the sexual, alcohol and drug related behavioural patterns of students on spring break. *Tourism Management, 19*(6), 501–513.

Kashima, E. S., & Loh, E. (2006). International students' acculturation: Effects of international, conational, and local ties and need for closure. *International Journal of Intercultural Relations, 30*(4), 471–485.

Krebs, C. P., Lindquist, C. H., Warner, T. D., Fisher, B. S., & Martin, S. L. (2009). The differential risk factors of physically forced and alcohol- or other drug-enabled sexual assault among university women. *Violence Vict, 24*(3), 302–321.

Madsen, W. (1964). The alcoholic agringado. *American Anthropologist, 66*(2), 355–361.

Mak, A. S., & Buckingham, K. (2007). Beyond communication courses: Are there benefits in adding skills-based ExcelL™ sociocultural training? *International Journal of Intercultural Relations, 31*(3), 277–291.

McAlaney, J., & McMahon, J. (2007). Normative beliefs, misperceptions, and heavy episodic drinking in a British student sample. *Journal of Studies on Alcohol and Drugs, 68*(3), 385–392.

McKenna, L., Robinson, E., Penman, J., & Hills, D. (2017). Factors impacting on psychological wellbeing of international students in the health professions: A scoping review. *International Journal of Nursing Studies, 74*, 85–94.

McKenzie, L., & Baldassar, L. (2017). Missing friendships: Understanding the absent relationships of local and international students at an Australian university. *Higher Education, 74*(4), 701–715.

Mills, B. A., & Caetano, R. (2012). Decomposing associations between acculturation and drinking in Mexican Americans. *Alcoholism, Clinical and Experimental Research, 36*(7), 1205–1211.

Nguyen, A.-M. D., & Benet-Martínez, V. (2013). Biculturalism and adjustment: A meta-analysis. *Journal of Cross-Cultural Psychology, 44*(1), 122–159.

Patel, V., Flisher, A. J., Hetrick, S., & McGorry, P. (2007). Mental health of young people: A global public-health challenge. *The Lancet, 369*(9569), 1302–1313.

Pearce, P. L. (2005). *Tourist behaviour: Themes and conceptual schemes*. Clevedon: Multilingual Matters.

Pedersen, E. R., Cruz, R. A., LaBrie, J. W., & Hummer, J. F. (2011). Examining the relationships between acculturation orientations, perceived and actual norms, and drinking behaviors of short-term American sojourners in foreign environments. *Prevention Science, 12*(4), 401–410.

Pedersen, E. R., LaBrie, J. W., & Hummer, J. E. (2009). Perceived behavioral alcohol norms predict drinking for college students while studying abroad. *Journal of Studies on Alcohol and Drugs, 70*(6), 924–928.

Pedersen, E. R., LaBrie, J. W., Hummer, J. F., Larimer, M. E., & Lee, C. M. (2010a). Heavier drinking American college students may self-select into study abroad programs: An examination of sex and ethnic differences within a high-risk group. *Addictive Behaviors, 35*(9), 844–847.

Pedersen, E. R., Larimer, M. E., & Lee, C. M. (2010b). When in Rome: Factors associated with changes in drinking behavior among American college students studying abroad. *Psychology of Addictive Behaviors, 24*(3), 535–540.

Pedersen, E. R., Neighbors, C., Atkins, D. C., Lee, C. M., & Larimer, M. E. (2017). Brief online interventions targeting risk and protective factors for increased and problematic alcohol use among American college students studying abroad. *Psychology of Addictive Behaviors, 31*(2), 220–230.

Pedersen, E. R., Skidmore, J. R., & Aresi, G. (2014). Demographic and predeparture factors associated with drinking and alcohol-related consequences for college students completing study abroad experiences. *Journal of American College Health, 62*(4), 244–254.

Presbitero, A. (2016). Culture shock and reverse culture shock: The moderating role of cultural intelligence in international students' adaptation. *International Journal of Intercultural Relations, 53*, 28–38.

Raunic, A., & Xenos, S. (2008). University counselling service utilisation by local and international students and user characteristics: A review. *International Journal for the Advancement of Counselling, 30*(4), 262–267.

Rienties, B., & Nolan, E.-M. (2014). Understanding friendship and learning networks of international and host students using longitudinal Social Network Analysis. *International Journal of Intercultural Relations, 41*, 165–180.

Russell, J., Rosenthal, D., & Thomson, G. (2010). The international student experience: Three styles of adaptation. *Higher Education, 60*(2), 235–249.

Russell, J., Thomson, G., & Rosenthal, D. (2008). International student use of university health and counselling services. *Higher Education, 56*(1), 59–75.

Sakurai, T., McCall-Wolf, F., & Kashima, E. S. (2010). Building intercultural links: The impact of a multicultural intervention programme on social ties of international students in Australia. *International Journal of Intercultural Relations, 34*(2), 176–185.

Sam, D. L. (2006). Acculturation: conceptual background and core components. In D. Sam & J. W. Berry (Eds.), *The Cambridge handbook of acculturation psychology*. Cambridge: Cambridge University Press.

Sawir, E., Marginson, S., Deumert, A., Nyland, C., & Ramia, G. (2007). Loneliness and international students: An Australian study. *Journal of Studies in International Education, 12*(2), 148–180.

Shah, S. A., Garland, E., & Katz, C. (2007). Secondary traumatic stress: Prevalence in humanitarian aid workers in India. *Traumatology, 13*(1), 59–70.

Sherraden, M. S., Stringham, J., Sow, S. C., & McBride, A. M. (2006). The forms and structure of international voluntary service. *Voluntas: International Journal of Voluntary and Nonprofit Organizations, 17*(2), 156–173.

Sigalas, E. (2010). Cross-border mobility and European identity: The effectiveness of intergroup contact during the ERASMUS year abroad. *European Union Politics, 11*(2), 241–265.

Smith, R. A., & Khawaja, N. G. (2014). A group psychological intervention to enhance the coping and acculturation of international students. *Advances in Mental Health, 12*(2), 110–124.

Sobré-Denton, M. (2011). The emergence of cosmopolitan group cultures and its implications for cultural transition: A case study of an international student support group. *International Journal of Intercultural Relations, 35*(1), 79–91.

Stone, M. J., & Petrick, J. F. (2013). The educational benefits of travel experiences: A literature review. *Journal of Travel Research, 52*(5), 731–744.

Taušová, J., Bender, M., Dimitrova, R., & van de Vijver, F. (2019). The role of perceived cultural distance, personal growth initiative, language proficiencies, and tridimensional acculturation orientations for psychological adjustment among international students. *International Journal of Intercultural Relations, 69*, 11–23.

Thomson, C., & Esses, V. M. (2016). Helping the transition: Mentorship to support international students in Canada. *Journal of International Students, 6*(4), 873–886.

Tidwell, R., & Hanassab, S. (2007). New challenges for professional counsellors: The higher education international student population. *Counselling Psychology Quarterly, 20*(4), 313–324.

Tolman, S. (2017). The effects of a roommate-pairing program on international student satisfaction and academic success. *Journal of International Students, 7*(3), 522–541.

Truman, S. D., Sharar, D. A., & Pompe, J. C. (2011). The mental health status of expatriate versus U.S. domestic workers. *International Journal of Mental Health, 40*(4), 3–18.

Ward, C., & Geeraert, N. (2016). Advancing acculturation theory and research: the acculturation process in its ecological context. *Current Opinion in Psychology, 8*, 98–104.

Whiteford, H. A., Degenhardt, L., Rehm, J., Baxter, A. J., Ferrari, A. J., Erskine, H. E., Charlson, F. J., Norman, R. E., Flaxman, A. D., Johns, N., Burstein, R., Murray, C. J. L., & Vos, T. (2013). Global burden of disease attributable to mental and substance use disorders: Findings from the Global Burden of Disease Study 2010. *The Lancet, 382*(9904), 1575–1586.

Yakunina, E. S., Weigold, I. K., & McCarthy, A. S. (2010). Group counseling with international students: Practical, ethical, and cultural considerations. *Journal of College Student Psychotherapy, 25*(1), 67–78.

Yang, Y., Zhang, Y., & Sheldon, K. M. (2018). Self-determined motivation for studying abroad predicts lower culture shock and greater well-being among international students: The mediating role of basic psychological needs satisfaction. *International Journal of Intercultural Relations, 63*, 95–104.

Yijälä, A., Jasinskaja-Lahti, I., Likki, T., & Stein, D. (2012). Pre-migration adaptation of highly skilled self-initiated foreign employees: The case of an EU agency. *The International Journal of Human Resource Management, 23*(4), 759–778.

Zemore, S. E. (2007). Acculturation and alcohol among Latino adults in the United States: A comprehensive review. *Alcoholism, Clinical and Experimental Research, 31*(12), 1968–1990.

Chapter 40
Rethinking the Value(s) of Short-Term Youth Mobility: Neoliberal Ideals and Counterhegemonic Possibilities

Emrullah Yasin Çiftçi and A. Cendel Karaman

Within an economic and political climate characterized by variegated forms of neoliberalism and idealized ideas about individual autonomy, entrepreneurship, competition, investment and innovation, young people are often assumed to be benefitting from higher education and international mobility opportunities without suffering adverse consequences in relation to their social and economic development. Individuals who can afford to engage in mobility may consider short-term stays abroad a particularly effective means of enriching their CVs, developing global awareness and acquiring work-related skills such as foreign language fluency and adaptation. However, since they are in an unfamiliar environment and society during their stays, they may also experience otherness and develop a critical consciousness in regard to the meaning, or meanings, of their mobility. They may even start to, or continue to, question the idealized neoliberal conditions that might be causing many others to struggle. Therefore, and as has been observed throughout this book, short-term youth mobility has its positive aspects alongside other, more disagreeable, dimensions, thus making student mobility in particular a field for competing ideologies and interests.

This chapter is based on research conducted for a doctoral dissertation to be submitted to the Graduate School of Social Sciences at Middle East Technical University, Ankara, Turkey.

E. Y. Çiftçi (✉) • A. C. Karaman
Department of Foreign Language Education, Middle East Technical University, Ankara, Turkey
e-mail: yciftci@metu.edu.tr

© The Author(s), under exclusive license to Springer Nature Switzerland AG 2022
D. Cairns (ed.), *The Palgrave Handbook of Youth Mobility and Educational Migration*, https://doi.org/10.1007/978-3-030-99447-1_40

Background: Neoliberalism

A central element of international student and more generic forms of youth mobility is neoliberalism, strongly linked to the globalization of tertiary education (Olssen and Peters 2005). At the heart of neoliberalism, there is the philosophy and practice of free market economics and, by association, a certain spirit of free trade and resulting inequalities. The theoretical roots of current neoliberalism go back to Friedrich von Hayek's programmatic writings. Von Hayek ([1944] 2001) raised a critique of totalitarian regimes that, he believed, were responsible for world wars and the innumerable tragedies associated with these wars. He in turn influenced the Chicago School scholars in terms of considering 'conditions favourable to progress rather than to "plan progress"' (Steger and Roy 2010: 240). Inspired by von Hayek's ideas that focused largely on laissez-faire entrepreneurialism, Milton Friedman and his colleagues at the Chicago School of Economics during the 1950s and 1960s became the leading scholarly figures behind the promotion of neoliberalism as an economic theory.

The work of Friedman and his colleagues became particularly influential in the late 1970s, during which the United States had entered an economic swamp known as stagflation. The causes for stagflation were mainly associated with the Keynesian economics that encouraged state intervention in the market, sometimes in the form of funnelling taxes into social assistance, for example, welfare programmes, healthcare and education. As a solution to stagflation, Friedman and his colleagues insisted on a market free of institutional interventions and eventually they became highly successful in convincing key economists and politicians, at a global level, of the value of neoliberal economic programmes that focused heavily on the supremacy of the market, free trade and entrepreneurialism (Steger and Roy 2010).

Following the theoretical success of the Chicago School, the late 1970s and the early 1980s witnessed several structural changes and reforms in terms of the implementation of the free market economy worldwide. Ronald Reagan in the United States and Margaret Thatcher in the United Kingdom were the leading political names who influenced the adjustment period in the 'developed' countries (Steger and Roy 2010), and through a concerted effort with several think tanks, the International Monetary Fund and the World Bank introduced structural adjustment packages into the economies of different 'developing' countries. Since this time, the free market and trade have remained indispensable to political and economic elites worldwide within the processes of 'accelerated globalization' (Steger and Roy 2010), with continued emphasis on less state intervention, more deregulation and widespread privatization.

Definitions and Theories of Neoliberalism

As regards a definition of neoliberalism, one of the most widely cited scholars is David Harvey (2005) who describes neoliberalism as a theory of political economic practices that prioritizes individual entrepreneurial freedoms and skills within an institutional framework of strong private property rights, free markets and free trade. The role of the state is hence to create and preserve an institutional framework appropriate to such practices (Harvey 2005: 2). This definition, however, reflects largely a Marxian perspective on global political economy and is not the only interpretation available.

Neoliberal theorization tends to fall into two broad camps: Marxian political economy and Foucauldian governmentality (Springer 2012; Wacquant 2012). From the Marxist perspective, neoliberalism restores the economic power of capitalist elites and contributes to the unequal growth of power and capital by offering competitive advantages to those in positions of power, often depicted as 'the one per cent' (Harvey 2005; Holborow 2015). According to this view, the elite gained their advantage through means such as the privatization of public wealth, austerity measures, decreased budgets for public institutions and tax cuts to their own advantage (Chun 2017). Neoliberalism then comes to be seen as essentially a class restoration project, set mainly in opposition to Keynesian economics, even if 'class' has been rhetorically marginalized and the virtues of individualism have been extolled. Such a position helps explain why this camp argues that collective action and the social foundations of solidarity have been strategically devalued and the supremacy of the market, competition and the individual has been valued (Davies and Bansel 2007; Harvey 2005; Holborow 2015).

The Foucauldian perspective avoids interpreting neoliberalism as purely a top-down ideology or a political economic theory. Michel Foucault, through his lectures on biopolitics, attempted to demonstrate how the modern state and the modern individual 'co-determine each other's emergence' (Lemke 2001: 191). The Foucauldian camp posits that modern day neoliberalism 'is concerned with a highly vigilant and intrusive form of government which above all seeks to shape society according to market dictates' (Holborow 2015: 85). This market development requires a new form of rule, which Foucault called 'governmentality.' By imaginatively linking government and mentality, Foucault developed an understanding of merging governance with the rationality through which neoliberal subjects tend to believe that their choices are made through their own 'rational calculations' (Davies and Bansel 2007: 251). In this respect, neoliberal governmentality contributes to the formation of subjects who, ideally, regulate their own conduct, which is to say, mainly engaging in entrepreneurialism (Courtois 2020; Foucault 2008; Holborow 2015; Lemke 2001; Peters 2016; Read 2009). Individuals, therefore, are positioned as free, 'rational' subjects who can compete with others and succeed through mobilizing their own agency. From this perspective, the focus of power has shifted from ruling from top-down to the micro levels of apparent individual self-regulation, with these neoliberal subjects, who act commonly as 'mini-replicas of corporations' (Holborow 2015: 77), seen as being 'eminently governable' (Foucault 2008: 270).

Although the Marxian political economy and Foucauldian governmentality perspectives capture some of the essential aspects of neoliberalism as a political economic doctrine and as a form of governmentality respectively, neoliberalism as a practice transcends both approaches. As some of the work presented in this book has already demonstrated, it is a variegated phenomenon: 'a rascal concept - promiscuously pervasive, yet inconsistently defined, empirically imprecise and frequently contested' (Brenner et al. 2010: 184). Through its complex interactions with individuals and situated elements within diverse political, economic and cultural contexts, neoliberalism becomes hybridized, with many local variations. Therefore, what we have are neoliberalisms (Gray et al. 2018; Ong 2007; Springer 2012; Wacquant 2012) that become extremely difficult to define in strict terms (Bamberger et al. 2019; Brenner et al. 2010; Connell and Dados 2014; Gray et al. 2018; Springer 2012). Nevertheless, neoliberalism retains a 'common genus,' which 'consists of an articulation of state, market, and citizenship that harnesses the first to impose the stamp of the second onto the third' (Wacquant 2012: 71).

Considering its 'protean' and situated nature, as well as its core tenets, Springer (2012: 133) urges us to develop 'more flexible and circuitous understandings of neoliberalism.' Neoliberal discourses merge the political economy and poststructuralist (Foucauldian) approaches 'without privileging either' (Springer 2012: 134). Such a theoretically balanced, flexible approach has the potential to move 'our theorizations forward through an understanding that neoliberalism is neither built from the "top-down", as in Marxian understandings of ideology, nor from the "bottom-up", as in poststructuralist notions of governmentality' (Springer 2012: 135). Both approaches, in fact, fundamentally share the same understanding: capitalism as the central problem. And as the current dominant form of capitalism, neoliberalism constructs material forms through policy and programmes, while at a micro level, individuals are constructed and positioned as rational creatures and entrepreneurs of their own lives (Courtois 2020; Türken et al. 2016).

In this chapter, we refer to both Foucauldian and Marxian approaches 'without privileging either' (Springer 2012: 134). We therefore acknowledge that neoliberal practices and discourses strive to reproduce a neoliberal subject who is the entrepreneur of oneself or 'homo economicus' (Foucault 2008: 226). We also acknowledge that neoliberalism contributes to elite power and the 'structuring structures' (Bourdieu 1977: 72) that influence significantly the acts of agents, especially those from lower socio-economic classes. In short, neoliberal ideology, from this perspective, has gained a common sense status and, therefore, becomes a contributor to the individualization of societies and (re)production of social inequalities.

The Selling of Neoliberal Ideology as 'Common Sense'

Neoliberalism as a concept and practice is complex and multi-faceted. Its complexity increases particularly when there is a significant gap 'between what it proclaims and what its promoters actually do' (Holborow 2012: 14). For example, neoliberal policies have increased the state's influence on corporate enterprises and elites despite an ideology that proclaims to be inherently against state intervention in the market, instead celebrating 'the supreme worth of the individual' (Harvey 2005: 25). In a neoliberal project, unemployment rates and economic inequality also tend to rise (Connell and Dados 2014); in fact, 15 major economic crises have occurred worldwide in the last 30 years (Chun 2017), enabling 'the one percent' to accumulate wealth and property at an unprecedented rate (Duménil and Lévy 2011; Harvey 2014; Piketty 2014).

Despite these massive, and quite obvious, contradictions, neoliberalism has gained a hegemonic currency and become 'the new common sense' (Hall and O'Shea 2013; Harvey 2005). The concept of common sense is associated with Antonio Gramsci, for whom common sense is 'the incoherent set of generally held assumptions and beliefs common to any given society' (Gramsci 1971: 323). This Gramscian understanding posits that common sense is an everyday way of thinking that assists us in interpreting the world, however incorrectly. In other words, 'it is a form of popular, easily-available knowledge which contains no complicated ideas, requires no sophisticated argument and does not depend on deep thought or wide reading' (Hall and O'Shea 2013: 9). Therefore, people who align with common sense notions tend to develop uncritical conceptions of the world and view power, domination and inequality as part of a natural order rather than the outcome of complex historical processes (Block 2018; Chun 2017; Gramsci 1971; Hall and O'Shea 2013; Holborow 2015), and neoliberal ideology certainly seems to have achieved a common sense status.

That neoliberal ideology contradicts itself makes it vulnerable to critique. Long ago, Gramsci (1971: 328) asserted that good sense emerges, which is 'the healthy nucleus that exists in "common sense."' Since Gramsci was mainly concerned with social change, he gave prominence to the growth of good sense discourses for the possibility of social transformation. Through careful observation and identification of contradictions and incoherence, it is possible to develop good sense or counterhegemonic discourses and make common sense beliefs senseless and even discard them (Chun 2017). This leads us to put forward the proposition that the young neoliberal subject, who tends to be an entrepreneur of oneself and seeker of 'better' life opportunities through mobility, can be beholden to the discourses of neoliberal common sense but with the possibility of counterhegemonic good sense emerging.

Neoliberalism and Education

The neoliberal restructuring or adjustment processes that were initiated by various institutions and think tanks during the 1970s and 1980s necessitated the training of a flexible workforce, who would be able to compete in the (global) unstable market as self-interested and lifelong learners. Educators, accordingly, established strong connections to 'knowledge capitalism,' or to the 'knowledge economy,' which is characterized 'in terms of the economics of abundance, the annihilation of distance, the de-territorialization of the state, and, investment in human capital' (Olssen and Peters 2005: 331). Therefore, there is now a strong link between (global) markets and education and the neoliberal notion of human capital. Becker (2002: 3) has argued that the success of both individuals and economies depends largely on 'how extensively and effectively people invest in themselves,' implying that individuals are to be held responsible for the acquisition of marketable knowledge, skills and information through an elongated learning orientation (Block 2018; Peters 2016). In this respect, the homo economicus anticipates the future demands of the job market, self-regulates to meet market demands, pursues endless self-development and persistently feels insecure. If the homo economicus can continue to develop market-related skills and capabilities, their human capital and therefore competition power will be expanded (Holborow 2015). Educational domains, in this regard, are seen as important mediums for the acquisition of knowledge and skills that may return benefits for the homo economicus in terms of competition within the (global) market. However, the neoliberal education that is built upon this notion of human capital also contributes to corporate profits, growing social and economic inequalities, and rising anxiety and depression in societies (Hall and O'Shea 2013). At the same time, it remains a significant factor, contributing to 'highly skilled but lower waged economies' (Holborow 2018: 527).

Neoliberal Higher Education and Short-term Student Mobility

Before the wide, or wild, implementation of neoliberalism, state-funded university education was an important public good under the Keynesian welfare state. However, with the neoliberal transformation, higher education institutions started to align themselves with ideals such as dissemination of the ideology of the ruling elite and raising skilled and flexible labour for industry. Wedded to the notion of human capital, universities now give prominence to internationalization, global university ranking tables, competition for research funding, campus attractions, increased fees, sponsors and external stakeholders (Collins 2018; Holborow 2015; Piller and Cho 2013). Within these institutions, academic activities including teaching are reduced to a few quantifiable outputs, and students are usually fast tracked through courses that deliver limited vocational knowledge and skills. However, young adults face increasing unemployment problems accompanied by debilitating psychological dimensions (Holborow 2015). Nevertheless, they still seek opportunities to expand their human capital during and after their university education, one of which is spatial mobility.

Young adults who study at tertiary education institutions feel pressure to gain international experience and therefore to expand their marketability/employability within the (global) knowledge economy (Courtois 2020; Yoon 2014). Due to this 'rational, economic, human capital framing of mobility' (Bamberger et al. 2019: 207), in addition to diploma/degree mobility, short-term international mobility programmes and resulting employability narratives/discourses have become commonplace. This latter form of mobility is believed to offer 'investment' opportunities for young adults, who are considered as rational actors in terms of being at a point in the life course where they need to discover how to multiply their human capital. In this regard, moving into global education and labour markets becomes the apparent means (Cairns 2019; Cairns et al. 2017, 2018; Dvir and Yemini 2017; Krzaklewska 2013; Paige et al. 2009; Yoon 2014).

To align with discourses of employability, entrepreneurialism and flexibility, the young need to be 'constantly in motion, both figuratively and literally' (Courtois 2020: 240). Therefore, the discourse of student mobility converges with neoliberalism through the formation of hypermobile young subjects who are 'voluntarily mobile geographically in response to the needs of global capitalism (in addition to being flexible, entrepreneurial and "agile")' (Courtois 2020: 238). Therefore, having a study abroad experience on their CV, young adults may gain a feeling of distinction and trust in the power of the CV to support their access to career opportunities, thereby contributing to the construction of short-term mobility as a social norm, even if what it seems to promise may not be achieved (Petzold and Peter 2015; Tran 2016). Furthermore, short-term international programmes borrow significant elements from neoliberal consumerist discourses (Michelson and Alvarez Valencia 2016); the highly visible 'fun' dimension and career-related expectations purposely coexist within the ethos of study abroad (Krzaklewska 2008). Therefore, 'competition for the global labour market' and 'having fun' can be seen as two major motivational aspects for mobile students, with their synergy demonstrating how neoliberalism and associated consumerist discourses strongly influence the discourses of mobility programmes and the conditions facing participants.

At the same time, student mobility is one possible way to help young adults cope with unjust socio-political and economic structures and develop further interests in issues related to social justice (Cairns et al. 2018; Krzaklewska 2013; Tochon and Karaman 2009). Short-term exchanges may help young adults experience otherness and an associated questioning process within an ecology that is largely unfamiliar to them, becoming a possible trigger to question worldviews and identity dimensions. As a result, they may develop social justice sensitivity or good sense discourses despite the dominance of neoliberal common sense within the higher education and international student mobility (Cairns et al. 2018; Krzaklewska 2013; Tochon and Karaman 2009). Therefore, mobility experiences can help young adults develop critical consciousness (Freire 1974 [2005]; Gramsci 1971).

Suggestions for Further Research and Practice

Our rethinking of student mobility opens up several research and practice dimensions, mainly due to the dominant and contested nature of neoliberalism. As scholars who are critical of the current neoliberal age, we place strong emphasis on 'the contested nature of neoliberalism' and therefore aim to reveal and challenge neoliberal discourses of marketability, employability and even 'fun,' which are associated with mobility programmes. Therefore, we acknowledge the need for counterhegemonic discourses that can enlarge the fissures within this dominant ideology and help young adults develop critical consciousness and good sense discourses through their participation in spatial mobility.

With this inquiry, as the multiple theoretical lenses have also underscored, we acknowledge that we cannot formulate and discuss every possible research and practice possibilities but we nevertheless aim to stimulate rethinking and further research in this domain. In this regard, we suggest that studies, firstly, focus on empirical evidence that emanates from discourses and narratives related to short-term student mobility. Such evidence may help us identify the ways neoliberalism, as the dominant form of capitalist ideology and the new common sense, manifests itself within the discourses and narratives of, for example, policymakers, policy and institutional texts, programme implementers and evaluators, participants, and so on. In addition to tracing possible influences of neoliberal ideology, empirical evidence may also help us identify counterhegemonic possibilities within the discourses of these people and texts that influence the evolution of such programmes. One approach might be critical discourse studies (CDS) which posits that power relations, dominance and ideologies are constituted and reproduced through discourse at different scales (Wodak and Meyer 2016). CDS can help us investigate the existence, emergence, or absence of neoliberal ideology and critical consciousness within the discourses of the people who shape and benefit from short-term international student mobility. Since CDS is not a static approach to research, but rather an eclectic way to instigate investigations into the social problems, research can integrate (longitudinal) qualitative and quantitative methodologies and methods such as ethnography, narrative research and corpus linguistics into CDS (Wodak and Meyer 2016).

On the other hand, there is no guarantee that student mobility will offer powerful experiences and help young adults develop critical consciousness, transform and act (Dockrill et al. 2016). Even in the cases of powerful experiences, young adults may not evaluate them in that regard and continue to reproduce neoliberal discourses of human capital and consumerism. Therefore, there might be a need to help participants prepare for the mobility period and reflect on their experiences during their re-entry periods (Çiftçi and Karaman 2018; Dockrill et al. 2016; Härkönen and Dervin 2016; IEREST 2015; Jackson 2015; Vande Berg et al. 2012). It is, thus, important to consider careful design, preparation and debriefing. Such preparation and debriefing components may focus on macro and micro level factors that shape youth mobility and may create opportunities for young adults to consider their motivations and reflect upon their mobility experiences.

Considering our rethinking in this chapter, we posit that criticality is a desirable trait for mobile youth. In this regard, preparation and debriefing components can benefit from the critical interculturality framework as a theoretical backdrop and may offer experiential opportunities during preparation and re-entry periods (IEREST 2015). Such a framework invites us to develop a reflexive awareness of the self and the other and to appreciate the multiplicity and complexity of individuals instead of reducing them to few identity categories. Furthermore, it constantly reminds us of the unequal power relations, conflicts and structural inequalities existing among groups of people, particularly within the neoliberal regime (Dasli and Díaz 2017; Dervin 2016; Halualani 2011; Holliday 2011).

References

Bamberger, A., Morris, P., & Yemini, M. (2019). Neoliberalism, internationalisation and higher education: Connections, contradictions and alternatives. *Discourse: Studies in the Cultural Politics of Education, 40*(2), 203–216.

Becker, G. S. (2002). The age of human capital. In E. P. Lazear (Ed.), *Education in the twenty-first century* (pp. 3–8). Palo Alto, CA: Hoover Institution Press.

Block, D. (2018). Some thoughts on education and the discourse of global neoliberalism. *Language and Intercultural Communication, 18*(5), 576–584.

Bourdieu, P. (1977). *Outline of a theory of practice*. Cambridge: Cambridge University Press.

Brenner, N., Peck, J., & Theodore, N. (2010). Variegated neoliberalization: Geographies, modalities, pathways. *Global Networks, 10*(2), 182–222.

Cairns, D. (2019). Researching social inclusion in student mobility: Methodological strategies in studying the Erasmus programme. *International Journal of Research and Method in Education, 42*(2), 137–147.

Cairns, D., Cuzzocrea, V., Briggs, D., & Veloso, L. (2017). *The consequences of mobility: Reflexivity, social inequality and the reproduction of precariousness in highly qualified migration*. Basingstoke: Palgrave Macmillan.

Cairns, D., Krzaklewska, E., Cuzzocrea, V., & Allaste, A.-A. (2018). *Mobility, education and employability in the European union: Inside erasmus*. Basingstoke: Palgrave Macmillan.

Chun, C. W. (2017). *The discourses of capitalism: Everyday economists and the production of common sense*. London: Routledge.

Collins, H. (2018). Interculturality from above and below: Navigating uneven discourses in a neoliberal university system. *Language and Intercultural Communication, 18*(2), 167–183.

Connell, R., & Dados, N. (2014). Where in the world does neoliberalism come from? *Theory and Society, 43*(2), 117–138.

Courtois, A. (2020). Study abroad as governmentality: The construction of hypermobile subjectivities in higher education. *Journal of Education Policy, 35*(2), 237–257.

Çiftçi, E. Y., & Karaman, A. C. (2018). 'I do not have to love them, I'm just interested in their language': Preparation for a study abroad period and the negotiation (s) of intercultural competence. *Language and Intercultural Communication, 18*(6), 595–612.

Dasli, M., & Díaz, A. R. (Eds.). (2017). *The critical turn in language and intercultural communication pedagogy: Theory, research and practice*. New York: Routledge.

Davies, B., & Bansel, P. (2007). Neoliberalism and education. *International Journal of Qualitative Studies in Education, 20*(3), 247–259.

Dervin, F. (2016). *Interculturality in education: A theoretical and methodological toolbox.* Basingstoke: Palgrave.

Dockrill, H., Rahatzad, J., & Phillion, J. (2016). The benefits and challenges of study abroad in teacher education in a neoliberal context. In J. A. Rhodes & T. M. Milby (Eds.), *Advancing teacher education and curriculum development through study abroad programs* (pp. 290–305). Hershey, PA: IGI Global.

Duménil, G., & Lévy, D. (2011). *The crisis of neoliberalism.* Cambridge, MA: Harvard University Press.

Dvir, Y., & Yemini, M. (2017). Mobility as a continuum: European Commission mobility policies for schools and higher education. *Journal of Education Policy, 32*(2), 198–210.

Foucault, M. (2008). *The birth of biopolitics: Lectures at the Collège de France 1978-1979.* New York: Palgrave Macmillan.

Freire, P. (1974 [2005]). *Education for critical consciousness.* New York: Continuum Press.

Gramsci, A. (1971). *Selections from the prison notebooks.* London: Lawrence and Wishart.

Gray, J., O'Regan, J. P., & Wallace, C. (2018). Education and the discourse of global neoliberalism. *Language and Intercultural Communication, 18*(5), 471–589.

Hall, S., & O'Shea, A. (2013). Common-sense neoliberalism. *Soundings: A Journal of Politics and Culture, 55*, 8–24.

Halualani, R. T. (2011). In/visible dimensions: Framing the intercultural communication course through a critical intercultural communication framework. *Intercultural Education, 22*(1), 43–54.

Härkönen, A., & Dervin, F. (2016). Study abroad beyond the usual 'imagineering'? The benefits of a pedagogy of imaginaries. *East Asia, 33*(1), 41–58.

Harvey, D. (2005). *A brief history of neoliberalism.* Oxford: Oxford University Press.

Harvey, D. (2014). *Seventeen contradictions and the end of capitalism.* London: Profile Books.

Holborow, M. (2012). What is neoliberalism? Discourse, ideology and the real world. In D. Block, J. Gray, & M. Holborow (Eds.), *Neoliberalism and applied linguistics* (pp. 14–32). London: Routledge.

Holborow, M. (2015). *Language and neoliberalism.* London: Routledge.

Holborow, M. (2018). Language skills as human capital? Challenging the neoliberal frame. *Language and Intercultural Communication, 18*(5), 520–532.

Holliday, A. (2011). *Intercultural communication and ideology.* London: Sage.

IEREST. (2015). *Intercultural education resources for erasmus students and their teachers.* Koper: Annales University Press.

Jackson, J. (2015). Becoming interculturally competent: Theory to practice in international education. *International Journal of Intercultural Relations, 48*, 91–107.

Krzaklewska, E. (2008). Why study abroad? An analysis of erasmus students' motivations. In M. Byram & F. Dervin (Eds.), *Students, staff and academic mobility in higher education* (pp. 82–98). Newcastle: Cambridge Scholars Publishing.

Krzaklewska, E. (2013). ERASMUS students between youth and adulthood: Analysis of the biographical experience. In B. Feyen & E. Krzaklewska (Eds.), *The ERASMUS phenomenon – symbol of a new European generation* (pp. 79–96). Frankfurt: Peter Lang.

Lemke, T. (2001). The birth of bio-politics: Michel Foucault's lecture at the Collège de France on neo-liberal governmentality. *Economy and Society, 30*(2), 190–207.

Michelson, K., & Alvarez Valencia, J. A. (2016). Study abroad: Tourism or education? A multimodal social semiotic analysis of institutional discourses of a promotional website. *Discourse and Communication, 10*(3), 235–256.

Peters, M. A. (2016). Education, neoliberalism and human capital: Homo economicus as 'entrepreneur of himself'. In S. Springer, K. Birch, & J. MacLeavy (Eds.), *Handbook of neoliberalism* (pp. 297–307). New York: Routledge.

Petzold, K., & Peter, T. (2015). The social norm to study abroad: Determinants and effects. *Higher Education, 69*(6), 885–900.

Piketty, T. (2014). *Capital in the twenty-first century.* Cambridge, MA: Harvard University Press.

Piller, I., & Cho, J. (2013). Neoliberalism as language policy. *Language in Society, 42*(1), 23–44.

Olssen, M., & Peters, M. A. (2005). Neoliberalism, higher education and the knowledge economy: From the free market to knowledge capitalism. *Journal of Education Policy, 20*(3), 313–345.

Ong, A. (2007). Neoliberalism as a mobile technology. *Transactions of the Institute of British Geographers, 32*(1), 3–8.

Paige, R. M., Fry, G. W., Stallman, E. M., Josic, J., & Jon, J. E. (2009). Study abroad for global engagement: The long-term impact of mobility experiences. *Intercultural Education, 20,* 29–44.

Read, J. (2009). A genealogy of homo economicus: Neoliberalism and the production of subjectivity. *Foucault Studies, 6,* 25–36.

Springer, S. (2012). Neoliberalism as discourse: Between Foucauldian political economy and Marxian poststructuralism. *Critical Discourse Studies, 9*(2), 133–147.

Steger, M. B., & Roy, R. K. (2010). *Neoliberalism: A very short introduction.* New York: Oxford University Press.

Tochon, F. V., & Karaman, A. C. (2009). Critical reasoning for social justice: Moral encounters with the paradoxes of intercultural education. *Intercultural Education, 20*(2), 135–149.

Tran, L. T. (2016). Mobility as 'becoming': A Bourdieuian analysis of the factors shaping international student mobility. *British Journal of Sociology of Education, 37*(8), 1268–1289.

Türken, S., Nafstad, H. E., Blakar, R. M., & Roen, K. (2016). Making sense of neoliberal subjectivity: A discourse analysis of media language on self-development. *Globalizations, 13*(1), 32–46.

Vande Berg, M., Paige, R. M., & Lou, K. (2012). *Student learning abroad: What our students are learning, what they're not, and what we can do about it.* Sterling, VA: Stylus.

von Hayek, F. A. (2001 [1944]). *The road to serfdom.* London: Routledge.

Wacquant, L. (2012). Three steps to a historical anthropology of actually existing neoliberalism. *Social Anthropology, 20*(1), 66–79.

Wodak, R., & Meyer, M. (Eds.). (2016). *Methods of critical discourse studies* (3rd ed.). London: Sage.

Yoon, K. (2014). Transnational youth mobility in the neoliberal economy of experience. *Journal of Youth Studies, 17*(8), 1014–1028.

Chapter 41
A Wonderful But Uncertain Time: Youth Transitions of Erasmus Students and Lisbon's Housing Crisis

Daniel Malet Calvo

The city of Lisbon, with a population of around 500,000 inhabitants (2,800,000 including the surrounding metropolitan region), has recently been attracting the attention of real estate investors, international students, tourists and lifestyle migrants. However, the city's success as an international learning hub and its capacity to attract visitors, and capital, from abroad are far from being random outcomes. In fact, the organization and publicity generated by hosting certain major events reflects a repositioning of Lisbon as one of the most visited, and most touristified, cities in the European Union.

This process arguably began with the entry of Portugal into the European Community in 1986. The rise of Lisbon in the global urban destinations market subsequently stemmed, primarily, from three specific events: its designation as the European Capital of Culture in 1994, the organization of the World Exposition in 1998 and the hosting of the 2004 UEFA European Football Championship (Malet Calvo and Ramos 2018). This trilogy of events served to stimulate the development of a local service industry devoted to visitors, from luxury hotels to souvenir sellers, also providing new infrastructure that made the city more accessible, especially to foreigners. However, first and foremost, these events achieved the founding of a brand: Lisbon was reimagined, represented and finally launched onto the global mass tourism market and was now able to attract lifestyle migrants and international students in large numbers (Santos 2000).

Another turning point arose out of the solution to the 2008 economic crisis, which took advantage of this urban relevance with a neoliberal agenda based on attracting tourism and putting into place policies to attract the interest of global capital investments. Together, tax benefits for investment funds and foreign residents, the liberalization of housing prices and programmes designed to stimulate the rehabilitation of old buildings facilitated evictions and the reduction of tenant rights,

---

D. Malet Calvo (✉)
ISCTE – Instituto Universitário de Lisboa (ISCTE-IUL), Centro de Investigação e Estudos de Sociologia, Lisbon, Portugal

© The Author(s), under exclusive license to Springer Nature Switzerland AG 2022
D. Cairns (ed.), *The Palgrave Handbook of Youth Mobility and Educational Migration*, https://doi.org/10.1007/978-3-030-99447-1_41

soon not only creating a housing crisis (and rampant increases in rents) but also attracting financial resources to the Portuguese capital (Mendes 2018). Taking advantage of the new Lisbon brand, tourism was also boosted by this agenda, especially after the 2011 crisis in Mediterranean North African markets that diverted many traditional sunny-cheap destination routes back towards Europe. In consequence, many residential properties entered the housing market as short-term rental apartments, with their owners (whether private landlords or investment funds) earning much more than they would have from the traditional rental market (Cocola-Gant and Gago 2019).

The global visibility of Lisbon also attracted other middle and upper class international visitors, including lifestyle migrants and international students, who have played central roles in the transformation of the city's urban economy. In fact, due to growing numbers of international students, many owners and investors are now transferring their apartments from Airbnb to Uniplaces, a web-based platform for student housing rentals. However, even for the transnational European middle classes enrolled in university degrees, the current housing situation in Lisbon is exclusive and difficult. Considering that arranging a place in state-run student residences borders on the impossible, the vast majority have to enter the private sector, whether in expensive residences or private apartments found through platforms such as Uniplaces.

Currently, the average monthly cost of a private room (including bills) in a Lisbon apartment shared with other students is €607, with variations above or below depending on the location and the building and room conditions (JLL 2019). In some areas, student accommodation rental prices have in fact rocketed over the last three years. For example, the São Sebastião area, close to many university campuses, experienced rent increases of 61 per cent on average between 2016 and 2017. The high demand for apartments due to the growing size of the international tertiary education market and owner expectations around hosting incoming students (some of whom have significant levels of purchasing power) have generated a process of segregation between Portuguese students arriving in the city from other parts of the country, alongside international students unable to afford the rents in Lisbon (including some Erasmus programme students), and their better-off counterparts.

The Development of the Erasmus Student Housing Market

The highest profile form of human mobility in many European cities is the circulation of university students under the Erasmus framework—arguably, the most successful and renowned programme ever launched by the European Commission. More than three million Erasmus students have circulated across 33 countries since 1987, and from 2014 onwards, the programme has been extended to embrace a broader range of training and learning actions in Erasmus+ (see Chaps. 17–25 of this book). Exchange students generally undertake medium-term stays of between three and twelve months (with an average of six months) within the 27 EU member states in addition to several associate countries. The sojourns of these students are based on bilateral learning agreements between university faculties which have, as their backdrop, a programme of equivalences and grants funded by the European Commission. However, the social lives of Erasmus students have been hidden for decades behind an institutional perspective on the programme that stresses certain pedagogical outcomes of the EU's 'flagship programme' (see, e.g., Maiworm 2001; Teichler and Janson 2007). Thus, the subjective experiences of Erasmus students remain buried under statistical analysis of levels of foreign language proficiency, employability and interculturality, overlooking the importance of students' agency in practising Erasmus and the impact their stays abroad have upon the transition to adulthood.

Outside EU-funded evaluation studies, 'student migration' literature has now begun to view international students as social agents, with often complex relationships in relation to other societal processes (see, e.g., Carlson 2013; King and Raghuram 2013). The work of Murphy-Lejeune (2002) also highlights the condition of students as 'strangers' (following a characterization made by the German philosopher Georg Simmel), drawing on their cross-cultural transitional processes of arrival, adaptation and negotiation in a new, foreign environment as defining their identities; their position as young, middle-class temporary strangers in a university city makes them some sort of a new class of transnational urban consumers (Malet Calvo 2018), willing and able to participate in different urban processes and transformations. This view is supported by Collins (2010), whose study of South Korean international students in Auckland (New Zealand) revealed that student-related identities and economies overlap with that broader urban transformations. It is also important to stress that their presence simultaneously attracts tourist flows (visiting families and friends) and that they often return to the city or country they have visited in subsequent years, having now been transformed into pure tourists.

Some authors go further and consider the international student experience itself as a form of 'academic tourism' (Rodríguez et al. 2012), using the label 'educational travel' (Van't Klooster et al. 2008), since destination choice often involves evaluating the attractions and global image of the urban destination rather than the quality of the respective university (see also Van Mol and Ekamper 2016). In addition to the leisure and night-time economies stimulated by their presence (Chatterton 1999, 2010), the most obvious processes in capitalizing student lives stems from the emergence of a housing market targeting international students, opening up opportunity for powerful economic actors, homeowners and low-capital investors to earn money from the stays of these foreign students. However, in spite of their potential vulnerability as young foreigners, international students have proven capable of organizing their own individual and collective housing strategies, as social actors thereby affirming their subjectivity and lifestyles in a transition to adulthood process that takes place abroad.

Methodological Approach

This issue was explored during the course of interviews with 37 Erasmus students, conducted between 2015 and 2017 as part of fieldwork during a research project on Erasmus students and their relationship to the city of Lisbon.[1] The means of contact with these students ranged from those approached on social network sites including Facebook, where students had posted complaints about housing-related problems, to face-to-face contact at student events, such as parties and reunions. Country of origin, gender and youth lifestyles were considered in order to represent the characteristics of the universe under study. Additionally, every interview included the students talking about the housing experiences of friends in similar situations, which contributed to reinforcing arguments. The study additionally applied the Holton and Riley (2014) methodology to some students, consisting of walking with them through different urban areas to elicit their feelings and understandings of liveability in the buildings we passed along our way.

The majority of the interviews (22) took place individually, with the remainder stemming from focus groups on housing problems (15), always adopting the theoretical framework of interviewing, which was just one facet of ethnographic inquiry in anthropology. In this sense, the interviews represented the culmination of relationships established between the researcher and the students, with the majority held in student homes with the researcher correspondingly able to observe and inquire about household conditions and the problems of liveability, as well as meet some of their flatmates. The selection of excerpts of these 37 interviews in the following analysis aims to present the voices of these foreign students on the housing conditions that prevail in an irregular and uneven housing market.

Looking for a Home: Online and Offline Individual Anxiety

The journey for Erasmus students frequently begins at home, online, several months before departure: checking-up on accommodation prices, watching videos and pictures about the destination city and joining specific foreign student groups on social networks. Within these groups, they may start building a network of friends with future foreign students in Lisbon, simultaneously framing their imaginaries about the city (Beech 2014). This is how Paula, for example, got to know Javier and why, based on their common youth lifestyle affinities (musical tastes, political ideologies), they decided to start searching for a home in Lisbon together even before meeting personally.

> We found a flat in Benfica and we did everything via the internet: we made the reservation, we paid the deposit, and we signed a contract and scanned it because the owner told us that she had problems with the former tenant. It was the cheapest place we found. In spite of being far from the city centre, there were good public transport links to the faculty. Of course, afterwards, we had tons of problems in the flat. (Paula, Spain, 22)

There are two main strategies deployed by Erasmus students to find accommodation in Lisbon: booking a room before travelling (through online platforms and social networks) or personally visiting several rooms to find an appropriate place to live. Booking online represents the first option among students: holding a reservation endows them with a sense of safety, seeing off any potential further problems that they think might appear in the process of searching alone in a city where you are unable to understand the language:

> Ten days prior to my arrival, I was so worried that I just booked a place on the internet. It was my first time living on my own and I wanted a final place where I could arrive at straight from the airport. Even with my parents going with me I changed the plans, which were visiting places while staying in a hostel. However, the problems started right at the beginning: the girl who was supposed to open the house did not appear. (Erika, Germany, 21)

The second option is accomplished by going to Lisbon either in the summer or at the beginning of the semester, usually a few days before starting classes, and staying in a hostel while searching for a room. In this case, students may be accompanied by family or friends to support them even though this is still conveyed as an unsettling experience. The case of Aneta is paradigmatic of those visiting places from a hostel. She arrived in Lisbon with a friend from her faculty with whom she planned to share a room, and they stayed at a hostel while looking for a flat.

> It was a horrible experience. Everything was so expensive or in ruins… and when we refused a room, we felt like maybe we could run out of rooms in the city. After three days, I don't know how many flats we visited, the hostel guy told us that we had two more days and then we should leave because they had other reservations. So, we just picked the next flat we visited. (Aneta, Czech Republic, 23)

The very first source of the anxiety that leads to poor housing decisions being made is the physical structure of the property. A housing supply scarcity and the laissez-faire policy implemented by local and national authorities, against the backdrop of Lisbon's growing success as a tourist and student destination, create an incentive for property owners to maintain poor conditions in their houses and for incoming students to accept these conditions due to the lack of better alternatives.

The structure of the property market itself institutionalizes these problems, with scarcity ensuring that poor quality and high prices are maintained for the benefit of owners and to the detriment of tenants. According to JLL (2019), the student housing market in Lisbon can be divided into three main models: (1) private landlords who advertise around 6000 rooms on specialized booking platforms such as Uniplaces and through digital and traditional methods such as adverts on Facebook, notices in college lobbies and word of mouth; (2) public and private universities offering their own student accommodation in large purpose-built buildings with around 1800 rooms and (3) professional apartment and housing operators offering renovated or purpose-built rooms, studios and apartments (some of them sited in high quality and luxury facilities) that have around 2200 rooms. Therefore, there are only around 10,000 rooms publicly available for students, which represents a huge shortfall considering that 59,000 students are enrolled in Lisbon's universities with home addresses outside of the city (with 17,900 international students).

This situation becomes slightly more understandable when we consider that, traditionally, the majority of incoming students to the city (from elsewhere in the country and Brazilians, Chinese or Cape Verdean students) are accommodated by friends and family members already living in Lisbon. However, Erasmus students arriving from other European countries generally lack the option of relying on such networks and hence have to access the housing market at a time when they experience urgency over finding a home:

> At the beginning, you go wherever you can because you are overwhelmed and you pick the first secure option to have a place to stay. You know how it is: you arrive here in a house and after some months you change to another, better house because you realise that you are paying too much and other people are living in cheaper flats. (José Luis, Spain, 22)

Feeling such housing uncertainty may be exacerbated for Erasmus students due to their young ages and the fact that they are travelling to an unknown, foreign country for six to twelve months, far from their families, often for the first time. Studying abroad is often considered a project of personal and family investment in education aimed at maintaining or improving future working opportunities and the cultural capital of children, in particular from middle and upper-class families (Windle and Nogueira 2015). However, from the students' own perspectives, it is often seen as an emotional adventure characterized by intense and meaningful processes of adult self-affirmation and personal individuation, experiences that are not only full of wonder and but also anguish and sorrow. Thus, it is no coincidence that the current situation of housing uncertainty in southern Europe (characterized by forced evictions, gentrification, high rental prices and exclusivity) is encountered and embodied by these students, contributing to broadening their sense of affliction during the transition to adulthood.

Making a Liveable Home: Power and Sociability in Erasmus Households

According to student narratives, there are three sources of housing anguish during their stays in Lisbon: (1) the liveability of their accommodation, (2) problems with power, control and abuse from landlords and (3) the (lack of) sociability and a sense of belonging in the housing environment. Due to the recent growth in the number of affluent students in Lisbon, some small companies and private landlords have begun housing students in old downtown flats, sometimes without contracts or even the most basic of amenities. In consequence, the most prominent problems centre on the condition of the house itself: no heating, bad insulation, water leaks and damp, issues which become particularly problematic during winter. In the course of the interviews, 18 out of 37 students stated that they had endured significant liveability problems in their houses.

> The house had a central heating system but the landlord said, 'You don't switch this on because otherwise you have to pay a lot more.' So, we bought electric heaters for each room

and we used them secretly every day. At the end of January, the owner came in and said 'Oh my God! The bill is three times bigger than usual!' and we said, 'This is because we were fucking freezing!' Finally, he accepted the situation and we didn't pay a thing. (Martina, Italy, 23)

Various students made specific complaints about such situations, including insulation problems and water infiltration that made it impossible to establish liveable conditions and made them susceptible to health problems, as was the case with two of the interviewees. Some landlords even sought to profit from this situation by charging an extra daily fee to students for using heaters, which was the case for ten interviewees. However, the cold and damp were not the only problems students face in terms of liveability:

As you've just seen, the stairway to access the flat is shit, eaten away by damp. And so it is with the entire house. If you go to the bathroom, you'll see. Also, at the beginning, the beds were supported by a pallet and they were full of bugs. You could even see them running! One of my flatmates told the owner that there were fleas in the beds and he replied: 'Maybe you brought them. Think about the places you went because there were no fleas before in this house.' After complaining a lot, he went to IKEA to buy new beds. (Larissa, Greece, 22)

Erasmus students are always negotiating their precarious situations and the rules imposed by the owner's authority. We have just described how some landlords require special payments during winter even when the rent agreement already includes bills. Moreover, some students suffer further economic abuse from their landlords with requirements for additional security deposit payments (equal to two months' rent in advance) in order to repair any damage or cover the non-payment of rent should the student leave unexpectedly. In some houses, the organized struggle of flatmates to get conditions essential to liveability, including proper beds, usable chairs and proper kitchenware, represents the only way to ensure a decent life in material terms. However, the most significant conflicts confronting owners and students relate to guests spending the night in the house, which in some places is forbidden or incurs an additional charge.

In our house, we have to inform about visitors and pay ten euros for an extra bed (that they bring out from a closed, dirty room) and ten euros per person per night. We always pay because we have a housekeeper and it is impossible to avoid, but in our owner's other house there are no controls and a Spanish guy was evicted because he was caught hosting five friends who spent four days in the house. Finally, the owner allowed him to stay but after paying for all this. Imagine the amount he had to pay! (Giuseppe, Italy, 22)

This control over visitors is maintained either by cleaning ladies, housekeepers or unexpected landlord visits, which creates an atmosphere of continuous distrust. Consequently, they feel controlled and dispossessed in their own environments, a situation involving a lack of intimacy impossible to imagine in the case of adult tenants.

Our owner went to the house to receive the rent in person. If you claimed to be out, he said, 'No problem, leave the money in your room and I'll pick it up' and we said, 'No, no.' But, anyway, he showed up all the time without telling us, to control the situation and stuff. The house had no life at all. A month later, a friend of mine moved to another house, just with Portuguese students and I finally decided to go with her. There's no comparison! In this

> house people are always spending the night or leaving their luggage or coming to have lunch, without the owner controlling what we do all the time. We finally feel like we have a house with life. (Hélène, France, 22)

This leads us to the third concern pointed out by students, relating to sociability in the apartment. The lack of a common space (usually because the landlord has converted it into another bedroom) is mentioned as a central issue in preventing (or complicating) the formation of a community of friends among flatmates that they often refer to as 'family.'

> The owner has two flats in the same building, that's 12 or 13 students altogether. When I arrived, they already knew each other and used to spend some time together. I'm lucky about my flatmates: they accepted me immediately into their family. There is also an older Italian couple living with us and we call them our 'mom' and 'dad.' (Lukas, Germany, 21)

This emphasis on recognizing their flatmates as particular members of a household is repeated continuously in student narratives but there are other patterns of social household organization. Among the many other examples of how students organize their ways of living, there is a house with an absent owner which students took control of, converting it into some sort of commune for alternative Erasmus students (Casa Dona Clara). The sense of belonging to the community, the events organized in the house, and the sharing and circulation of everyday objects and goods substantiate the existence and the attraction of this place, where Erasmus students stay year after year on the recommendation of former inhabitants.

Strategies of Resistance and Adaptation to Student Housing

In order to (re)produce their desires, as in the case of Casa Dona Clara, students engage in some forms of resistance while living and learning. It should be recalled that Erasmus students are relatively defenceless compared to their local peers: they lack networks and the support of family and friends, they are generally unaware of local practices and legal regulations on housing and their Portuguese language competence may be limited. However, this alleged position of high vulnerability is often contested creatively through the ways they inhabit their homes and build solid friendships and support structures, as well as making recourse to new technology and social networks to denounce problem landlords and housing scams. The ability to book a room through platforms and social networks before arriving might be perceived as dangerous for students, who could easily be deceived due to the distance, but this also enables students to disseminate complaints, bad reviews and warnings about housing fraud and bad places for students coming to Lisbon in the next semester. This has been the case for several private residencies installed in old buildings without appropriate conditions for liveability, leading many to warn incoming students by posting warnings on Facebook Erasmus groups:

> DO NOT RENT WITH LISBON MANSION!!!. Hi everyone, I'm writing this because I want to warn you about a problem I faced during my Erasmus. I decided to rent a room with

> the very infamous lisbonmansion... I already knew that some people had trouble with them but decided to do it anyway because I was in a hurry to find a place to live (...) (Alexandre, 27 July 2015)

> Thank you, buddy, it's always good to hear this kind of stuff as early as possible. I have heard some similar problems that people had with LisbonResidences (unfriendly staff, charging €25 for overnight visitors, etc.). So probably it's best to just rent a flat with other students and don't throw money at those organizations that only make problems... Anyway, everybody enjoy your stay and see you around. (Clara, 27 July 2015)

In addition to warning peers, Erasmus students are able to organize individual and collective strategies for housing in a complex and multifaceted process of resistance and mutual support. For instance, another common circumstance which is often turned against them stems from their unregulated status in some houses (with neither real contracts nor bills in their own names), leaving them in a defenceless and exposed position. However, students often make the most of these non-formal, written and verbal agreements (systematically disrespected by the owner), abandoning the house mid-semester or challenging the landlord's authority without there being any major consequences.

> Other students tell us that the landlord never returned the deposit we made at the beginning, using excuses such as we damaged the furniture or we broke some dishes, taking advantage of the fact that we have no time to argue, because usually we take a plane the day after leaving the house. So, since we have one of these fake contracts, we decided that we will not pay the last month to compensate for this scam and the many problems we had in the house. If we are evicted, we can spend the last month at a friend's house. (Marc, Spain, 22)

As foreign students in an unknown country, Erasmus students will in all likelihood fall victim to all kinds of deceptions and misunderstandings. However, their social networks in the new context prove to be strong and reliable sources of information, resources and mutual support, which enables them to be adaptable and strike back when facing conditions of abuse abroad (Smith et al. 2014). Switching to other houses in the middle of their stays or for the second semester constitutes a very common practice among these students and is feared by landlords who then need to find another student quickly to keep receiving their monthly rental payments. These situations however arise out of the consequences of Erasmus and poor student housing conditions in Lisbon, and students' organized responses are leveraged by making recourse to the strong ties developed with other students in the same situation:

> After two months of disrespecting the contract (we were supposed to pay for a weekly cleaning service that never appeared) the final straw was the landlord's violent reaction when he discovered we had a night visitor. He even threatened us by saying he'd call his rough, crazy friend to get rid of us. We kept on living in the house for a few weeks and promised to pay for that visitor and, when it was the time to pay, we all just disappeared from the house at the same time (four students) and we are currently accommodated in friends' houses while looking for a new place. (Camila, Spain, 23)

Following the lessons learned from the previous examples, there emerges a need to refute three interlinked prejudices about the capacities of international students to deal with the housing market even while considering their disadvantaged starting point: students as uninformed consumers, students as unaware strangers and students as reckless youth. Furthermore, this victimization often derives from an 'adultist' perspective (Bell 2018) that disregards student agency and the many ways deployed by young people to contest the student housing market structure in Lisbon. Ultimately, the current housing situation in southern Europe seems to be at least as equally unfair and problematic for informed, responsible local adults as for foreign, inexperienced young students.

Concluding Remarks

The aim of this chapter has been to expound on the strategies and adaptations of a particular group of international students participating in Erasmus when confronting troubling housing conditions in the city of Lisbon, taking into account their relatively defenceless position as young, foreign, non-Portuguese speakers. However, as pointed out by Smith et al. (2014), young migrants such as students have manifold competences in resisting the overwhelming power of institutions and markets in urban contexts, beginning with their ability to build their own social worlds while abroad. Following this line of thought, we can observe their strategies for resisting and fighting back against the deceptions of some landlords, for example, the sudden switching of accommodation mid-stay and the building of supportive groups of flatmates and friends.

Lisbon has increasingly become an exclusive destination, not only for local and international students, such as those on the Erasmus programme, but also for local inhabitants. The close relationship between the pressures of real estate capital over rental prices, the taxation policies enacted by the government to attract investment and the city's success as a tourist destination help explain the current situation. In the city, Erasmus students participate in several overlapping urban economies: the travel and tourist economy (as temporary international visitors), the leisure and nightlife economy (as young people) and the knowledge and education economy (as university students). However, the most relevant economy in which they participate is housing and real estate, a very profitable sector that also causes the most anguish from the beginning to the end of their stays.

In this sense, this chapter adopted the form of a sequential journey through the lives of Erasmus students, from their first contacts with the student housing market to the strategies and resistance they apply to landlord abuses and scams, which are themselves indirectly caused by the lack of regulation and the centrality of real estate capitalism in contemporary urban development, including the student housing market. In February 2019, the Portuguese government approved the Student Housing National Plan under which 4720 new beds will be provided for the next four years in Lisbon (plus 2097 including the metropolitan area). However, it remains dubious whether the introduction of this still insufficient supply at controlled prices will contribute to improving the conditions experienced by the bulk of students. A bolder measure accompanying this provision of public accommodation would involve some sort of rent control over student housing, which represents a central sector targeted by owners and investors when speculating and establishing their market expectations and thereby contributing to the general rise in Lisbon rental prices.

Whatever the case may be, the housing uncertainties of Erasmus students represent the embodiment by the young transnational middle classes of these contemporary features of housing, contributing to a normalizing of a situation of great vulnerability coupled with an overall lack of rights. More specifically, their experiences as international students might be considered within the scope of a deep, unexpected, non-formal education process consisting of learning about the uncertain conditions of contemporary housing during their transitions to adulthood. In this sense, accessing and maintaining a rented home in southern Europe has gradually become an experience packed with uncertainty, in which the temporary ties (whether formal or informal) between the landlord and the tenant are increasingly characterized by mutual distrust. The experiences lived out by these mobile students during their transition to adulthood may thus be considered a non-formal process, recognizing newly prevalent conditions facing their generation within the context of renewed, gentrified and exclusive European cities.

Note

1. This work received support from the Portuguese Foundation for Science and Technology (FCT) under Grant no. SFRH/BPD/85169/2012. The names of students and housing companies are changed to pseudonyms.

References

Beech, S. E. (2014). Why place matters: Imaginative geography and international student mobility. *Area, 46*(2), 170–177.
Bell, J. (2018). Adultism. In B. B. Frey (Ed.), *The Sage Encyclopaedia of educational research, measurement and evaluation*. London: Sage.
Carlson, S. (2013). Becoming a mobile student – a processual perspective on German degree student mobility. *Population, Space and Place, 19*(2), 168–180.
Cocola-Gant, A., & Gago, A. (2019). Airbnb, buy-to-let investment and tourism-driven displacement. A case study in Lisbon. *Environment and Planning A: Economy and Space,* https://doi.org/10.1177/0308518X19869012.
Collins, F. L. (2010). International students as urban agents: International education and urban transformation in Auckland, New Zealand. *Geoforum, 41*(6), 940–950.
Chatterton, P. (1999). University students and city centres – The formation of exclusive geographies. The case of Bristol, UK. *Geoforum, 30,* 117–133.
Chatterton, P. (2010). The student city: An ongoing story of neoliberalism, gentrification, and commodification. *Environment and Planning A, 42*(3), 509–514.

Holton, M., & Riley, M. (2014). Talking on the move: Place-based interviewing with undergraduate students. *Area, 46*, 59–65.
JLL Consultants. (2019). *Portugal Student Housing. 2019 Report*. Lisbon: JLL.
King, R., & Raghuram, P. (2013). International student migration: Mapping the field and new research agendas. *Population, Space and Place, 19*, 127–137.
Maiworm, F. (2001). Erasmus: Continuity and change in the 1990s. *European Journal of Education, 36*(4), 459–472.
Malet Calvo, D., & Ramos, M. J. (2018). Suddenly last summer: How the tourist tsunami hit Lisbon. *Revista Andaluza de Antropología, 15*, 47–73.
Malet Calvo, D. (2018). Understanding international students beyond studentification: A new class of transnational urban consumers. The example of Erasmus students in Lisbon (Portugal). *Urban Studies, 55*(10), 2142–2158.
Mendes, L. (2018). Tourism gentrification in Lisbon: Neoliberal turn and financialisation of real estate in a scenario of austerity urbanism. In I. David (Ed.), *Crisis, austerity and transformation: How disciplining neoliberalism is changing Portugal* (pp. 479–512). London: Lexington Books.
Murphy-Lejeune, E. (2002). *Student mobility and narrative in Europe. The New strangers*. London: Routledge.
Rodríguez, X. A., Martínez-Roget, F., & Pawlowska, E. (2012). Academic tourism demand in Galicia, Spain. *Tourism Management, 33*, 1583–1590.
Santos, M. G. M. P. (2000). Da Expo'98 ao Euro 2004: notas para o estudo do impacto de grandes eventos no turismo regional. *Educação and Comunicação, 4*, 22–47.
Smith, D. P., Rérat, P., & Sage, J. (2014). Youth migration and spaces of education. *Children's Geographies, 12*(1), 1–8.
Teichler, U., & Janson, K. (2007). The professional value of temporary study in another European country: Employment and work of former Erasmus students. *Journal of Studies in International Education, 11*(3-4), 486–495.
Van't Klooster, E., Van Wijk, J., & Go, F. (2008). Educational travel: The overseas internship. *Annals of Tourism Research, 35*(3), 690–711.
Van Mol, C., & Ekamper, P. (2016). Destination cities of European exchange students. *Geografisk Tidsskrift-Danish Journal of Geography, 116*(1), 85–91.
Windle, J., & Nogueira, M. A. (2015). The role of internationalisation in the schooling of Brazilian elites: Distinctions between two class fractions. *British Journal of Sociology of Education, 36*(1), 174–192.

Chapter 42
Conclusion: Youth Migration in the Age of Pandemic Immobility

David Cairns, Thais França, Daniel Malet Calvo, and Leonardo Francisco de Azevedo

This concluding chapter should have been very different, and in fact it was very different before being re-written to take account of recent developments in the field of public health. Had it not been for the global spread of Covid-19 in 2020, youth mobility might well have continued along its decades long course of global expansion and diversification, spreading into different forms of education, work and training, with the dividing line between mobility for these purposes and tourism continuing to blur. These concerns are no longer as pressing as they once were, and may not return to being high priorities for a very long time. Right now, writing in the middle of what has come to feel like an open-ended pandemic, all we can do is look at what has happened in the last few months and attempt to grasp some of the main consequences for young people who still wish or need to be mobile, in addition to engaging with the pressing problem of how to re-orient mobility practices that have stalled or never got off the ground, literally and figuratively. Additional concerns are evident in regard to how to maintain mobility systems at a time when institutions have closed their doors, again literally and figuratively, and are struggling to re-open in any meaningful sense of the word.

D. Cairns (✉) • T. França • D. Malet Calvo
ISCTE – Instituto Universitário de Lisboa (ISCTE-IUL), Centro de Investigação e Estudos de Sociologia, Lisbon, Portugal
e-mail: david.cairns@iscte-iul.pt; thais.franca@iscte-iul.pt

L. F. de Azevedo
Universidade Federal de Juiz de Fora, Juiz de Fora, Brazil

© The Author(s), under exclusive license to Springer Nature Switzerland AG 2022
D. Cairns (ed.), *The Palgrave Handbook of Youth Mobility and Educational Migration*, https://doi.org/10.1007/978-3-030-99447-1_42

The Immobility Pandemic

What then has happened to the mobility field since the arrival of Covid-19? The most obvious change without doubt relates to the quantity of movement that is now taking place, with circulation levels having rapidly shrunk to levels not seen since the last century, obviously a scenario that applies not only to young people, although the impact of the virus on collecting statistics means we do not have accurate indications of the precise scale of the change. What is obvious is that during the pandemic there is a very limited capacity to engage in mobility, within and between countries, accompanied by a change of perception in how we view non-essential travel. Mobility feels different—something to be practised only out of necessity rather than in expectation of pleasure or personal satisfaction. And in places once inundated with foreign visitors, it is not 'immigrant' hating racists and sleep-deprived local residents who are saying that migrants and tourists are not welcome. Virologists and government ministers have become the new gatekeepers, along with citizens concerned about the welfare of their families and future sustainability of local communities.

Reflecting on what this development means for this book, as opposed to assessing the impact of the pandemic on society, which is really too much to think about right now, we have a certain reversal of fortune to integrate into our interpretations of how young people have been engaging in mobility in the recent past. Many of the chapters illustrate how various forms of mobility grew rapidly in scale and acquired a certain familiarity in the first two decades of the twenty-first century, with student exchanges in particular becoming diffused throughout the world as a socially and politically acceptable form of spatial circulation. This dynamic, of expansion and anticipated continuation of this expansion, will now end and may not ever return on the same scale. Outside academia, programmes such as Erasmus+ that sought to integrate circulation into areas ranging from vocational training to postgraduate studies (see, e.g., Pantea 2021) now need to be refocused on what can be practiced safely at home, creating a major political headache for European Union policymakers and education and training institutions across the world.

A move back towards sedentary learning is certainly unfortunate for the proponents of large-scale youth migration, especially when mobility is so reliant upon group activities (see Cuzzocrea et al. 2021), but we should not lament this loss too hard. There were already signs of strain arising from rapid expansion, manifest in the difficulty many young people had in sustaining mobility due to the high emotional and economic costs involved (Cairns et al. 2017), with many host cities simply not equipped to cope with the mass proliferation of incoming mobility (Malet Calvo 2018). In this book, this extends to documenting health consequences and heightened precariousness arising out of mis-managed mobility (Aresi et al. 2021; Çiftçi and Karaman 2021). These concerns will now be replaced with more basic questions about how to re-start a large number of stalled mobility trajectories in a manner that is safe for individuals and society.

We are now looking at a situation, which is likely to continue for a substantial period of time, of restricted freedom of movement. Equally important to consider is the limited value emerging from what is now possible. Even when and where students and trainees are able to travel, they will be locked out of many classrooms by social distancing, meaning little or no opportunity to engage in intercultural learning since this is dependent on physical interaction with peers and conviviality in host communities (Cuzzocrea et al. 2021). The sudden shift towards virtual learning systems may have ensured a certain degree of operational capacity in regard to the delivery of teaching, but this cannot replicate delicate social dynamics. Virtual platforms also have serious downsides through heightening the fatigue of teaching and training, not to mention alienating learners who lack the necessary domestic conditions to engage in remote learning. Putting everything online is obviously not the answer. The challenge then is not just to get young people circulating again, corporeally, but to work out new ways of learning and working during the time that can be spent abroad that conform with the new normal. Otherwise, everyone might as well stay at home.

Moving Out of Immobility

What we do have is an opportunity to use this pause as a moment of reappraisal in which to consider ways forward for mobility, taking into account the concerns that have been discussed in this book, including the preceding paragraphs concerning the immediate impact of the pandemic. There are obvious negative aspects for youth in regard to what is spatially possible and for youth mobility researchers, given the sudden—if totally understandable—shift in research agendas towards Covid-19 topics and public health, opportunities to work in this field are also now limited. Mobility feels like a luxury concern, and given its problematized position, it may also lose its symbolic value. Having attained a totemic position, particularly in the EU (Feyen and Krzaklewska 2013; Cairns et al. 2018), mobility will now undergo a repositioning in regard to changing views of togetherness, the reality of closed borders and reduced capacity to engage in bilateral circulation.

In looking for effective ways of moving beyond this sudden onset of immobility, the most obvious solution is to focus on what is still possible within local communities, thus avoiding what might now be looked upon as 'mobility for mobility's sake' during a time when risks of needlessly spreading contagion remain. Taking into account this position, in what remains of this concluding chapter, we will consider what this immobility position means for individuals, institutions and societies, looking first at some of the vulnerabilities that have been generated by mobility as practised by youth and the attendant fragility of migration, moving on to consider some of immediate consequences for those affected by pandemic immobility.

Vulnerable Migration

We are now in some respects looking at the breaking down of a system that was broken down, in a literal sense and on purpose. Migration devolved into mobility to make it manageable and montarizable: more profitable, less politically contentious and perhaps somewhat more democratic than in previous eras (see Cairns 2021a, b). But converting a migration trajectory into an episodic fixed-term format cultivated vulnerability as a means of deterring young people from 'permanently' settling abroad. While political expedient for governments concerned about alleged 'brain drain,' the devolution of migration left mobile youth to fend for themselves if they got sick, went broke or, heaven forbid, tried to own a home or start a family (Howie et al. 2019). Meanwhile, for institutional movers, certain universities were arguably the main beneficiaries of the wave of youth mobility expansion, gaining an internationalization dividend from hosting exchange platforms, with the presence of international students used to define institutions as globalized learning hubs. Academic institutions were also able to import international staff, students and trainees at bargain prices and in large numbers, with scientific institutions particularly adept at cherry-picking low-cost talent for their requisite centres of excellence.[1]

In retrospect, this expansion looks rather naïve and very hard to sustain given the need for a constant flow of incoming talent, centred upon a relatively small number of internationalized learning centres, meaning that the global circulation of talent may well have 'naturally' reached its limits without the intervention of Covid-19. Within the EU, it was in fact quite obvious that the 'mobility without migration' approach had been stretched to a point where it could easily break due to the huge effort required on the part of individual young people to maintain their mobility, engaging in one phase after another in the hope that this might lead to permanent settlement rather than another 'moratorium' period (Cuzzocrea and Cairns 2020).

Young Europeans in particular were exposed to a narrative strongly implying that spatial circulation would provide a means through which they could all access personalized success and career development, with this belief also providing a raison d'être for the free movement orientation of the European institutions (King and Williams 2018; see also Recchi 2015). 'Mobility' might even be said to have become subject to a kind of boosterism, especially within the European Commission, which seemed to take great pleasure out of the annual increase in numbers circulating via Erasmus, however precariously, regarding rising participation rates and expenditure levels as indicators of growing European integration. This approach, too celebratory and excessively 'self-referential' (King 2018, 2), was never sustainable. Grounding mobility policies in a neoliberal logic was also corrosive, with institutions and agencies ending up fighting one other for funding and exchange students provided with a stipend barely capable of covering their drinks bill, never mind accommodation and living costs. A competitive approach to mobility inevitably meant that not everyone could succeed, bringing with it a potential squandering of social and economic capital and needless delay in entering the labour market.

Despite these harsh words, mobility will continue during the pandemic, whether through virtual platforms, in cut down formats or, in an odd twist, a manner closer to the norms of classical migration: long duration stays without a circulatory or pendular dimension, oriented around economic gain and eventual social integration into the host society. Rather than the piecemeal approach to migration introduced in Chap. 1 of this book (Cairns 2021a), it becomes logical to make a singular decision about where to go and orient stays around settlement, rather than indulging in a succession of peripatetic education, training or work phases. The spatial dimension of the transition to adulthood thereby might become regularized and relatively linear, and perhaps less susceptible to the neoliberal 'migrant as consumer' philosophy (see Çiftçi and Karaman 2021). Mobility chances may however become concentrated in the hands of few dedicated individuals, considering the high level of personal resources required to maintain long duration stays abroad. In this regard, the imaginaries that surround certain mobility destinations and social practices while abroad may change drastically as young people seek safety, security and guaranteed returns rather than adventure, acculturation to new experiences and an expansion of spatial horizons, thus creating new patterns in flows of incoming and outgoing mobility.

Pandemic Immobility

For several years at least, we will be facing the challenge of coping with pandemic-related immobility, challenging the way we live and work, especially our willingness and ability to circulate. Anyone taking a flight during the period of confinement will already have encountered some of the milder difficulties: a limited number of often very expensive flights, invalid health insurance, social distancing and temperature screening at airports, wearing facemasks during transit and, equally as important, the anxiety of not knowing with whom one is going to be sharing an enclosed atmosphere for prolonged periods, with the risk of quarantine, or worse, should a positive test be registered after the flight. The stress, anxiety and depression of the pandemic will take a very long time to recover from, continuing long after we are told by the authorities that it is now safe to travel for non-essential purposes.

For young people still seeking to pursue education and training abroad, plans will need to be put on hold for an indefinite period or entirely re-evaluated. For young workers, there are obviously fewer opportunities, considering the inevitability of recruitment freezes and reductions in the workforce, first in sectors such as hospitality and tourism and later elsewhere as the economic downturn becomes a prolonged recession. This is certainly not a good time to be seeking employment abroad. While many who had previously planned or intended to move may have already changed their minds, there are a substantial number of young people whose mobility was in course when the lockdown began or who had already travelled to their destinations during the early stages of the pandemic, before the scale of the problem was officially acknowledged. What they found on arrival was certainly not what they were expecting.

In our own university, classes were cancelled, without warning, on 11 March, a gloriously sunny Wednesday afternoon. The next day, the university was deserted. To prevent the spread of the virus, institutions suspended face-to-face teaching, switching to online platforms, a change that required a great deal of effort from students and staff, as learning routines were disrupted, examinations put into different formats and extra-curricular activities indefinitely postponed. For members of staff with children, the closure of schools and kindergartens, confinement at home and teaching online has been a particular burden. For researchers, most of whom are on fixed-term contracts, their jobs have become more precarious. Unlike teachers, much of their work cannot be shunted online, with vulnerability enhanced by the refusal of institutions to refuse to re-negotiate contracts or suspend evaluation procedures, then carry on with the sanction of dismissal should (pre-pandemic) targets not be met, even when work cannot be conducted without breaking health and safety regulations. For some students and staff, the issue of internet access at 'home' was also an immediate problem, as was maintaining social distancing and finding appropriate places to work in family houses and shared accommodation, where conditions could be over-crowded, cramped and noisy.[2]

While the main priority for universities was moving teaching online, another visible issue concerned the continued viability of hosting international students. As we have tried to establish in this book, not all international students conform to the affluent Westerner stereotype. Major disparities exist, not least in terms of the capacity to respond to the shutdown of classrooms, including differences between the Global North and the Global South (see França and Padilla 2021) and among those with already precarious financial situations. Some had the means and the opportunity to return home rapidly. Others lacked flight options or preferred to stay in their host city as they feared being infected on the return journey or being repatriated to a country with a high infection rate. We were therefore left with many students living in isolation, apart from their families and outside regular social networks, experiencing high levels of stress and anxiety, facing the prospect of online tuition in a foreign language. Others had to cope with administrative uncertainties regarding the viability of continuing their studies and doubts about the payment and repayment of loans and scholarships. The economic impacts included not only transportation costs related to emergency travel but also family members losing their jobs and not being reimbursed for now uninhabitable accommodation. At the extremes, some experienced racism and xenophobia, especially Chinese students being held accountable for spreading the virus.

How then did these individuals respond to this challenging situation? As might be expected, the strategies developed by international students to cope with the pandemic during their stays abroad were not homogenous. Prior literature (e.g., Murphy-Lejeune 2002) has long argued that socio-economic background shapes student mobility experience, something we would not expect to change during the greatest public health crisis in over a century. To explore this issue, we conducted interviews with approximately 30 international students in Portugal, all of whom were studying at the country's universities when the pandemic began in March 2020. Some returned home almost immediately, while others stayed, despite often difficult circumstances, providing us with an opportunity to look at both these scenarios.

Bearing in mind the discussion in this book of student housing (Malet Calvo 2021), we found that domestic conditions played a central role in determining well-being during the period of confinement, something frequently linked to the decision to stay or leave the city. Having a 'nice house' clearly matters a great deal during a global pandemic. The quality, and the availability, of the parental home was also a consideration. Many students who had moved out when they started university claimed that the houses in which they currently resided were the only places in which they could stay as they no longer had a room in their parents' house. A few also found their student accommodation to be superior to the family home, with more space, large windows, terraces and balconies. Others, however, were confined to small, cramped rooms, particularly in university dormitories, creating an extra stress factor. These interviews hence revealed some vital information about the structural inequalities facing international students in a global learning hub like Lisbon.

Financial situation also had a major bearing upon the ability to cope with the pandemic. The interviews revealed that rather than being dependent upon one form of income, such as an Erasmus grant, students in fact relied upon multiple sources: money from parents, government scholarships, part-time jobs and personal savings. The cessation of one or more of these revenue streams thus created problems. This is another interesting discovery and an aspect of mobility-related precarity, and vulnerability, under-represented in prior studies (including our own work). In some cases, lack of funds prevented people from returning home even though they were desperate to do so. Notwithstanding the disparities that exist in Erasmus grant funding, in general, students travelling via this platform fared better than others who were self-financing or from countries experiencing severe economic difficulties. For example, several students from the Global South relied on home governments, who had now ceased to send money, or parents who were enduring their own hardships.[3] A relatively common situation was however working to help cover learning and living costs. With much of this work taking place in restaurants, bars and the tourist sector (e.g., as guides or 'tuk tuk' drivers), these students lost their jobs due to the lockdown and hence a major part of their income. Given that this situation is unlikely to improve in the near future, especially due to the unviability of tourism, some students have had to find other jobs in sectors in which they are put in potentially risky situations: delivery drivers, working in hospitals and in supermarkets.

In some cases, host universities and student accommodation providers were sensitive to students' needs, leading to the creation of funds for emergency financial aid and free meals, but this was the exception, not the norm. Both host and home universities were an important source of emotional support to students, offering psychological care, motivational sessions and online physical fitness activities, especially yoga. It was, however, more common for international students to make recourse to their flatmates and the friends with whom they shared their accommodation. Indeed, in many cases the decision to stay was made following a friend's decision, with these students feeling safe and confident through staying together. Many in fact reported having a number of pleasant moments at home, cooking together, watching movies or simply going for walks, activities they might not have undertaken with their parents or siblings if they had gone back home.

The preoccupation with families in their home country nevertheless remained constant, particularly among those whose home countries were more seriously affected by the pandemic than Portugal. In response, they tried to mitigate their separation with video calls and messages on a more frequent basis than they would have done otherwise. While some deeply regretted not being able to go back home and stay with their parents, others reasoned that during the return trip there was a possibility of them becoming infected and spreading Covid-19 to their families, thus deciding against making the journey.

Mobility Goes Local

Having looked at the immediate impacts of the pandemic on student mobility, how then are parties such as universities, training agencies and employers to respond in regard to maintaining the integrity of their organizations? A moratorium of sorts on 'non-essential' mobility (i.e., short duration and/or circulatory movement) might be expedient after what has been a *force majeure* event—in other words, a necessary move away from the one-piece-at-a-time Bauman-esque idea of 'liquid migration' (Engbersen and Snel 2013). Temporary and circular mobility replaced by more exceptional but substantial migration is one approach but given this may only be viable for small numbers of young people, it is probably not the answer. The alternative is to apply what has already been learnt from several decades of managing mobility to young people 'at home,' directing the focus of mobility systems inward rather than outward.

The idea of mobility 'going local' is actually consistent with recent developments in the youth field at European level, such as the *Europe Goes Local* initiative, which has engaged in strategic partnerships between municipalities in different countries in the field of Youth Work.[4] It would obviously be a case of following the principle of shared activities simultaneously taking place at municipal levels rather than the actual practices of this programme, which would not be possible with social distancing, and changing from a focus on youth workers to young people. But localizing mobility might be particularly valuable in maintaining some form of activity within institutional programmes such as Erasmus, albeit with a change of emphasis towards supporting youth in local communities as opposed to creating internationalized learning spaces.

Though there is the obvious loss of internationalization and opportunities to engage in intercultural activities, this idea has many possible benefits. Firstly, there is a preservation of expertise, and perhaps of jobs, for people who work in the institutional mobility sector. These professionals will be able to continue their work, albeit in a different context, and justify maintaining mobility infrastructure until such times that it is safe and viable to recommence incoming and outgoing exchanges on a larger scale. This will also make re-starting mobility platforms much easier when the time comes, reducing unnecessary prolongment of pandemic immobility. Secondly, a knowledge transfer of sorts can take place between those who have returned from abroad and those who still wish to move, helping to maintain their levels of interest. While there is little or no opportunity for new forms of interculturality to emerge, it is still viable for those with large stocks of mobility capital to help prepare others who are, hopefully only temporarily, grounded. Thirdly, in regard to institutional activities, local 'exchanges' cost substantially less and involve a lower intensity of bureaucracy, meaning there is no need to request huge levels of external grant funding. There is no travel involved, no accommodation to book and no visas to arrange. Everyone presumably will be speaking the same language, unless they choose not to. Fourthly, in focusing upon physical activities, we have a means of avoiding the digital overload that has accompanied remote working and online teaching and training.

These ideas are speculative and feel somewhat idealistic, but a lack of mobility does not mean the end of mobility. There is certainly a great deal of loss—of life chances and of life—for which it is appropriate to lament, but in moving forward from this position of pandemic immobility, more mature forms of mobility can, eventually, offer a more stable and less precarious means of improving personal and professional positions. Young people will certainly not lose their desire to travel but will want to do so in a safe and meaningful manner rather than in the somewhat reckless fashion which seems to have characterized much pre-pandemic circulation.

Final Remarks

In bringing this book to a close, looking at migration in the new age of immobility has led us to look back and re-evaluate developments in our research field that preceded the pandemic. This includes an unstable globalization of mobility—in the Global North and Global South, and all points in between—and problems relating to a lack of socio-demographic inclusivity. This is not so much a case of mobility creating exclusivity. Rather, a reliance upon institutions that 'naturally' reproduce inequality, and on individuals' social and economic resources (including family inheritances), provides an unfair starting point in the global race for talent. Mobility in itself cannot overcome inequality given such conditions, albeit acknowledging that at a more personal level, decision-making regarding destinations and durations also plays a part in mediating success. But the idea of mobility as an easy and unproblematic path to individualized success for everyone is absurd. Furthermore, while much progress was made in education and training, the internationalization of highly qualified labour markets never really happened in any meaningful way due to the high level of costs involved, creating difficulties in extending migration trajectories beyond education and training and into employment.

A confused notion of what constitutes being a migrant, especially in policymaking and media narratives, hardly helped matters. The idea that to be codified as a migrant should involve undergoing some kind of exceptional experience, centring upon life-threatening events such as war, famine and political persecution, followed by intervention from Western saviours, stigmatizes those put into such narrow categories of experience, excluding numerous others whose life experiences may be different but no less problematic. As this book has shown, young people can be problematized by mobility without having been refugees or asylum-seekers, and problems can be general as well as specific to outlying situations, including issues arising from the high emotional and economic costs of sustaining successive mobility episodes in the same or different destinations. The idea of 'circulation' may have been popular among policymakers and host institutions, but this is be because they realized that they do not have to cover most of the expenses, which are essentially privatized onto individual movers. The greatest lesson to be learnt regarding pre-pandemic youth mobility hence relates to the unsustainability of fragmentated and commodified migration, with negative impacts starting to be felt in host societies as well as among individuals.

To conclude, the diffusion and differentiation of mobility created tensions for youth and for societies. Mobility could be seen as a symbol of internationality but also a reflection of social inequality, while 'migration' for youth was simultaneously enticing and expensive, exciting and dangerous, educational and recreational. That these properties were antonymic made the in-built tensions hard to reconcile, while certain cities struggled to accommodate ever-growing numbers of incoming students alongside bloated tourist populations. After the pandemic, there should be no return to unbalanced flows of incoming and outgoing students or the tiresome over-priced stays abroad that kept many young people in prolonged liminality. The best way forward is therefore to integrate the local with the global, recognizing that mobility ultimately relies upon partnership and co-operation between individuals and societies rather than mutual exploitation.

Notes

1. This is a reference to the editor's current research project, *Circulation of Science: Mobility, Precarity and Economic Growth in Research and Development*, which looks at the development of careers in science in Portugal, funded by the national Foundation for Science and Technology (FCT).
2. One of the more bizarre aspects of the lockdown was the fact that construction work continued unabated. In fact, numerous new public works were initiated, at a time when remote working was legally mandated. For many people, the sound of pneumatic drills will forever be associated with the Covid-19 pandemic.
3. Associations for international students from Angola (AEAP) and Cabo Verde (UECL) in Portugal have been very supportive for those in severe hardship among their communities, providing money for rent or food and personal computers to participate in online teaching.
4. *Europe Goes Local* is an Erasmus+ linked initiative, started in 2016, involving cooperation between local-level stakeholders in European Youth Work.

References

Aresi, G., Marta, I., & Moore, S. C. (2021). Youth mobility, mental health and risky behaviours. In D. Cairns (Ed.), *The Palgrave handbook of youth mobility and educational migration*. Basingstoke: Palgrave Macmillan.

Cairns, D. (2021a). Mobility becoming migration: Understanding youth spatiality in the twenty-first century. In D. Cairns (Ed.), *The Palgrave handbook of youth mobility and educational migration*. Basingstoke: Palgrave Macmillan.

Cairns, D. (2021b). Migration decision-making, mobility capital and reflexive learning. In D. Cairns (Ed.), *The Palgrave handbook of youth mobility and educational migration*. Basingstoke: Palgrave Macmillan.

Cairns, D., Cuzzocrea, V., Briggs, D., & Veloso, L. (2017). *The consequences of mobility*. Basingstoke: Palgrave Macmillan.

Cairns, D., Krzaklewska, E., Cuzzocrea, V., & Allaste, A.-A. (2018). *Mobility, education and employability in the European Union: Inside Erasmus*. Basingstoke: Palgrave Macmillan.

Çiftçi, E. Y., & Karaman, A. C. (2021). Rethinking the value(s) of short-term youth mobility: Neoliberal ideals and counterhegemonic possibilities. In D. Cairns (Ed.), *The Palgrave handbook of youth mobility and educational migration*. Basingstoke: Palgrave Macmillan.

Cuzzocrea, V., & Cairns, D. (2020). Mobile moratorium? The case of young people undertaking international internships. *Mobilities, 16*(3), 416–430.

Cuzzocrea, V., Krzaklewska, E., & Cairns, D. (2021). 'There is no me, there is only us': The Erasmus bubble as a transient form of transnational collectivity. In V. Cuzzocrea, B. Gook, & B. Schiermer (Eds.), *Forms of collective engagements in youth transition: A global perspective*. Leiden: Brill.

Engbersen, G., & Snel, E. (2013). Liquid migration. Dynamic and fluid patterns of post-accession migration flows. In B. Glorius, I. Grabowska-Lusinka, & A. Kuvik (Eds.), *Migration patterns after EU enlargement* (pp. 21–40). Amsterdam: Amsterdam University Press.

Feyen, B., & Krzaklewska, E. (Eds.). (2013). *The Erasmus phenomenon—Symbol of a new European generation?* Frankfurt: Peter Lang.

França, T., & Padilla, B. (2021). South-South student mobility: International students from Portuguese-speaking Africa in Brazil. In D. Cairns (Ed.), *The Palgrave handbook of youth mobility and educational migration*. Basingstoke: Palgrave Macmillan.

Howie, L., Campbell, P., & Kelly, P. (2019). Young people's resilience and post-financial crisis television: Allegories of economic and social survival. *Journal of Youth Studies, 23*(2), 189–204.

King, R. (2018). Theorising new European youth mobilities. *Population, Space and Place, 24*(1), e2117.

King, R., & Williams, A. M. (2018). Editorial introduction: New European mobilities. *Population, Space and Place, 24*, e2121.

Malet Calvo, D. (2018). Understanding international students beyond studentification: A new class of transnational urban consumers. The example of Erasmus students in Lisbon (Portugal). *Urban Studies, 55*(10), 2142–2158.

Malet Calvo, M. (2021). A wonderful but uncertain time: Youth transitions of Erasmus students and Lisbon's housing crisis. In D. Cairns (Ed.), *The Palgrave handbook of youth mobility and educational migration*. Basingstoke: Palgrave Macmillan.

Murphy-Lejeune, E. (2002). *Student mobility and narrative in Europe. The new strangers*. London: Routledge.

Pantea, M.-C. (2021). Facets of mobility in Romania's vocational education and training. In D. Cairns (Ed.), *The Palgrave handbook of youth mobility and educational migration*. Basingstoke: Palgrave Macmillan.

Recchi, E. (2015). *Mobile Europe. The theory and practice of free movement in the EU*. Basingstoke: Palgrave Macmillan.

Index[1]

A

AFS Intercultural Programmes, 63, 64
Agency, 3, 6, 8, 14, 18, 22n1, 25, 30, 31, 77, 79, 84, 91, 146, 148, 150, 152, 172, 175, 245, 291, 297, 298, 315, 318, 362, 369, 386, 388, 389, 418, 419, 425n2, 457, 469, 476, 482, 486
Apprenticeship, 111, 312, 315, 325, 326
Argentina, 148
Armenia, 387, 394–397, 399–401
Asia, Central, 20, 173, 237–246, 394
Astronaut families, 90
Asylum, 120, 121, 123, 126, 129n2, 386, 390n1, 488
Au pairing, 30, 79, 111, 113–115
Australia, 19, 20, 87, 90, 174, 275–285, 292, 337–344, 444

B

Belgium, 193, 194, 292, 313, 316
Bologna Process, 121, 183, 245, 270, 315, 360
Brain circulation, 84–86
Brain drain, 78, 79, 85, 155, 365, 387, 397, 482
Brazil, 29, 78–80, 107–116, 143, 144, 146–152, 173, 249–258
Brexit, 78, 97, 103, 104, 208, 219, 294, 380

C

Canada, 19, 87, 88, 90, 91, 292, 337–344, 399
Capital, cultural
  economic, 2, 8, 26, 32n1, 36, 79, 90, 91, 98, 100, 101, 120, 175, 188–189, 214, 250, 365, 385, 389, 401, 423, 458
  mobility, 14, 20, 25–32, 35, 172–174, 200, 214, 222, 242, 243, 365, 389
  social, 86–88, 99, 177, 202, 208, 214, 255, 416, 424
Categorical fetishism, 388
Chicago School, 456
Citizenship, 132, 135, 172, 187, 189, 199, 201, 202, 338–340, 347, 348, 370, 400, 417, 458
Cosmopolitanism, 15, 20, 64, 200, 205, 347
Covid-19 pandemic, 4, 5, 9, 32, 77, 81, 390, 479–488, 488n2

D

Decade, 393
De-intellectualization, 174
Denmark, 14, 35–44, 157, 192, 351, 398
Depression, *see* Mental health

---

[1] Note: Page numbers followed by 'n' refer to notes.

E

Economic crisis, The 2008, 78, 92, 97, 178, 362, 467
Educational resource environment, 108, 114, 115
Education, teacher, 80, 131
  tertiary, 5, 6, 8, 15, 21, 22, 35, 36, 47, 59n2, 63–72, 77–80, 85, 86, 91, 119–122, 127, 129n2, 131, 132, 171, 173, 201, 228, 237, 241, 242, 246, 249, 258, 276, 277, 284, 293, 299, 308, 324, 396, 399, 402n2, 456, 461, 468
Education-to-work transitions, 347
Employability, 23n3, 98–101, 103, 158, 172, 174, 178–181, 183, 188, 193, 194, 237, 246, 249, 258, 261, 291, 297–299, 318, 323, 329, 356, 365, 398, 461, 462
Entrepreneurship, 187, 189, 191, 195, 312, 455
Erasmus, exchange programme, 199, 220
  Mundus, 29, 32n5, 172, 173, 192, 195, 213–222, 225–235
Erasmus-ization, 172, 187, 188, 195
Estonia, 172, 199, 201–207, 209
European Commission, 18, 133, 171, 172, 175, 177, 179, 180, 183, 184n2, 184n4, 187, 199, 215, 219, 245, 269, 299, 308, 323, 325, 326, 330, 332, 386, 389, 396, 398, 401n1, 468, 469, 482
Europeanization, 188, 195, 315, 398
European Union (EU), 3, 8, 15, 16n3, 35, 36, 38, 40, 43, 48, 49, 58, 64, 80, 97, 103, 119, 120, 126, 135, 172, 174, 177, 183, 193, 205, 206, 208, 213, 216, 218–220, 222, 228–230, 232, 235, 245, 246, 261, 267, 268, 299, 312, 313, 323, 325, 331, 332, 360, 367, 369, 373, 380, 386, 387, 393–401, 408, 412n1, 418, 431, 449, 455, 467, 468, 480, 481
European Voluntary Service, 192, 195
Eurostars, 23n4, 213
Eurostudent, 262, 265, 266, 268, 271n2, 271n3, 271n4

F

Finland, 78, 79, 155–165, 328
France, 87, 144, 148, 153n2, 204, 271n5, 292, 299, 312, 314, 316–318, 339, 374, 418, 423, 474

Free movement, 6–7, 32, 77–81, 171, 205, 298, 386, 396, 397, 482

G

Gap year, *see* Mobile moratorium
Gender disparities, 174, 262
Germany, 56, 58, 78, 79, 107–116, 120, 121, 148, 153n2, 181, 192, 193, 195, 219, 243, 292, 299, 301, 312, 318, 324–327, 330, 332, 339, 351, 353, 374, 393, 398, 471, 474
Global North, 4–6, 9, 17, 19, 21, 22, 77, 91, 92, 171, 173, 175, 250, 258, 430, 484, 487
Global South, 4–6, 9, 17–19, 21, 22, 77, 91, 92, 173, 250, 251, 258, 430, 484, 485, 487
Greece, 431, 435–437, 473

H

Habitus, 14, 16n4, 115, 149–151, 200, 209, 214, 217, 305
Health, mental, 123, 221, 388, 441–449
Housing, 112, 122, 239, 253, 256, 370, 387, 389, 467–477, 485
Hyper-mobile global citizen, 21

I

Immobility, 13, 39, 366, 390, 479–488
Inclusivity, social, 15, 121, 175n1, 199, 225, 229, 230, 234, 241–243, 438
Individualization, 293, 297, 458
Inequality, social, 21, 107, 109, 112, 243, 389, 424, 488
Integration, European, 171, 360, 370, 482
  cultural, 206
Interculturality, 15, 20, 65, 294, 340, 398, 463, 469, 487
Internationalization, 3, 6, 15, 19, 63, 78, 80, 108, 109, 131–133, 135, 138, 143–152, 171, 172, 177, 187–195, 204, 214, 225, 227, 228, 249, 251, 257, 324, 360–362, 364, 365, 367, 369, 460, 482, 486, 487
Internship, international, 10n7, 17, 55, 195
Italy, 78, 119–128, 145, 183, 190, 191, 194, 294, 299, 359–370, 373–381, 473

K

Kyrgyzstan, 29, 237–246

Index

L
Leisure mobility, 298, 340, 387–389, 445, 467–469, 479, 483, 485
Logic of opportunities, 365
Luxembourg, 18, 188–190, 193–195, 292, 313, 315, 316, 327, 418

M
Matthew effect, 364
Mental health, 123, 221, 388, 441–449, 460, 483
Migration, decision-making
  economic, 47, 58, 395
  educational, 4, 78, 80, 83, 90, 91, 97–104, 107, 115
  forced, 2, 403–412
  fragmented, 385
  incremental, 26, 78, 102, 188
  intellectual, 28, 78, 83–92
  involuntary, 2, 9
  labour, 84, 87, 115, 301, 303, 307, 337, 340
  lifestyle, 50, 59
  liquid, 20, 102, 216
  trajectories, 2, 3, 6, 15, 26, 29, 32, 32n5, 78, 80, 89, 165, 188, 291, 294, 374, 385, 396
  for work, 52, 98, 103, 160, 165, 166n2
Mobile moratorium, 21, 57, 59n2, 161, 308, 348
Mobility, as consumption
  barriers to, 188, 219, 233, 326
  capacity, 14, 26, 27, 47–59, 416
  credit, 10n6, 49, 56, 262, 271n1, 445, 446
  decision-making, 14, 15n2, 25–32, 44, 99, 104, 249
  diploma, 49, 276
  imperative, 3–5, 14, 15, 20, 36, 47–59, 195, 217, 222, 249, 359, 362, 366, 368, 429
  leisure, 298, 329
  post-diploma, 54, 59, 173
  student, 7, 8, 15, 18, 19, 29, 36, 49, 54, 63–72, 77–79, 84, 133, 138, 171, 173–175, 189, 228, 237, 238, 241, 249–258, 261, 262, 266, 269–271, 276, 285, 291, 293, 352, 386–389, 397, 455, 460–462
  turn, 48
Motility, 56, 58, 59n1

N
Neoliberalism, 388, 389, 456–462
New Zealand, 19, 337–344, 469

Norway, 18, 27, 69, 157, 161, 187, 189, 191, 192, 195, 216, 327, 430, 431, 435–437

O
OSCE Academy, 173, 237–246

P
Palermo protocol, 416–418, 425n1, 431
Pandemic, *see* Covid-19 pandemic
Parachute kids, 90
Participation, 7, 55, 80, 126, 134, 135, 171, 172, 174, 177–180, 183, 184, 188, 195, 199–210, 216, 220, 226, 228–232, 237, 240, 261, 262, 281, 325, 331–333, 337–339, 364, 365, 378, 387, 388, 420, 447, 462, 482
Pathway programmes, 275–285
Poland, 36, 37, 39, 40, 48, 51–56, 58, 59n3, 181, 221, 308n1, 374
Portugal, 484, 486, 488n1, 488n3
Precarity, 6, 9, 14, 25, 115, 293, 298, 301, 365, 397, 419, 485

R
Racism, 342, 442, 484
Reflexivity, 14, 30, 31, 32n4, 49, 58–59, 216, 222, 294, 362
Refugees, 3, 8, 22, 79, 121–122, 386, 387, 389, 394, 403–407, 410–412, 488
Romania, 18, 36–38, 41, 42, 187, 189–191, 195, 245, 291, 297–308, 327, 374, 395
Rooted mobilities, 403–412
Russia, 39, 43, 148, 206, 207, 243, 387, 393–401

S
SaarLorLux, 311–319
Scholarships, 3, 36, 40, 48, 91, 111, 113–115, 120, 122–128, 143, 146, 148, 151, 152, 173, 215, 219, 225, 228, 232, 233, 237, 239, 242, 243, 246, 254, 363, 377, 386, 387, 397, 399, 402n3, 434, 484, 485
Self-efficacy, 55, 58, 136, 244, 433, 434, 436, 438, 447
Skills, communication
  intercultural, 204
  language, 27, 55, 112, 123, 188, 189, 202, 206, 207, 266, 281, 319, 325
  social, 188, 447
  soft, 178–184, 214, 217, 222, 261, 303, 350

South Africa, 173, 225–235
Soviet Union, 39, 201, 238, 242, 387, 393, 394
Student exchanges, *see* Student mobility
Student mobility, 2, 5, 7, 8, 15, 17–19, 26, 29, 36, 49, 54, 65, 77–79, 84, 133, 138, 171, 173–175, 188–189, 237, 238, 241, 249–258, 261, 262, 266, 269, 271, 275, 276, 285, 285n1, 291, 293, 352, 386–389, 397, 455, 460–462, 480, 482, 484, 486
Super diversity, 215
Sweden, 78, 79, 155–165

T
Temporary worker programmes, 292, 338
Tourism, *see* Leisure mobility
Trafficking, 2, 8, 9, 22, 387–389, 415–425, 425n1, 425n2, 429, 431–433, 437, 438
Training, vocational, 480
Transition, education-to-work, 8, 291, 347
Transnationalism, 49, 84, 85, 213, 218, 347

U
United Kingdom (UK), 20, 36, 40, 78, 91, 97–104, 193, 275, 294, 299, 338, 339, 348, 350–352, 373–381, 398, 419, 456

United States (US), 40, 80, 88, 90, 91, 97, 148, 149, 153n2, 219, 243, 245, 275, 339, 393, 395, 396, 399, 400, 402n3, 442, 443, 445, 456
University for International Integration of the Afro-Brazilian Lusophony (UNILAB), 18, 250, 252–258

V
VET, *see* Vocational training
Vocational training, 8, 30, 110, 111, 113, 115, 121, 291, 292, 297–300, 302–308, 308n2, 308n3, 308n4, 311–319, 323–333, 399
Volunteering, 29, 55, 64, 115, 127, 182, 184, 187, 189, 190, 207, 325, 338, 348, 378, 400, 431, 437, 442, 443, 448

W
The 'West,' 20, 35–44, 71, 92, 173, 238, 340
Work placements, 2, 10n7, 17, 26, 29, 30, 195, 262, 263, 291–293, 308, 347–356, 401

Y
Youth in Action programme, 172, 397, 401n1
Youth, spatiality, 17–22, 48
  transitions (*see* Education-to-work transitions)